RHETORIC
A Text-Reader
on Language
and Its Uses

✵

RHETORIC

A Text-Reader
on Language
and Its Uses

JIM W. CORDER

Texas Christian University

Random House   New York

FIRST PRINTING

© Copyright, 1965, by Random House, Inc.

All rights reserved under International and Pan-American Copyright
Conventions. Published in New York by Random House, Inc. and
simultaneously in Toronto, Canada, by Random House of Canada, Limited.

Library of Congress Catalog Card Number: 65–13759

Manufactured in the United States of America by

American Book–Stratford Press

DESIGN BY TERE LOPRETE

Preface

The rationale and the design of this book are, I believe, adequately stated in the Introduction to Part I and the Introduction to Part II. Forecasting those fuller statements, I should like to say here only that the book is founded upon three primary beliefs: along with his study and exercise of prose method, the student must necessarily study the development and quality of his language; for the student's study and exercise of method, the best examples are to be found in the work of widely recognized and long-established masters of English prose style; and these examples can be arranged in a sequence that will help the student assimilate a body of methods he may use in any situation.

I should like to express my gratitude to Professor Lyle H. Kendall for countless suggestions and ideas, especially in the sections on Planning the Complete Essay and Exposition, and for assorted shouts and grimaces. Fit testimony of my respect I cannot offer.

I should also like to thank some of my students for their kind permission to use their work. I am indebted to Mr. David Parsons, Mr. Steven Neville, and Miss Ruth Ann Starnes.

My wife typed the manuscript, admonished, encouraged, and cherished me. I have already thanked her, and will again.

J. C.

December 1964

Contents

Part I: On the Qualities of Language

On Style and the Uses of the Language 158

Part II: On the Uses of Language

A *Writing Program*   243

The *Right Sentence*   244

Subordination   244

Coordination, Balance, and Parallelism   250

† A dagger preceding an entry indicates that a Commentary by the editor follows the selection.

A Writing Program 292

Planning the Complete Essay 293

A Writing Program 344

Exposition 345

Part One

✵

ON THE
QUALITIES
OF
LANGUAGE

Introduction

The essays in this section, while their method and manner may illustrate and encourage good prose style, were chosen primarily for their material, to foster and enliven knowledge of the language. If they serve other purposes as well, it should arouse no surprise, only delight; but they were selected, and they are offered to the student, for their subject matter. This recommendation of essays for their *content* in a book later preoccupied with *method* requires some explanation.

Style, it may be presumed, should be paramount in a book designed for use in a college course in composition and rhetoric. The many reasons that such a book addresses itself to the procedures and principles of good prose style will be mentioned in Part II. These essays are variously pleasant, effective, and lively; some, of course, are more striking in their procedure than others. Yet they are recommended first for their subject matter.

To understand the relationship of the two parts of this book and the function of the subject matter of the following essays, consider the structure of the first sentence of this Introduction. The complex sentence, with a major and a minor statement, names two things that are important, but by its construction designates style as subordinate to content for this section. The book, an enlargement of the sentence, names two things, but insists that for this text at least, style is more important. Thus these essays, recommended for their ideas and information, have approximately the same relationship to the book as the dependent clause early in the first sentence has to the whole sentence.

These essays will help a student to understand that the study of English language and composition is more than the study of grammar, punctuation, and spelling. They will help him to know that his language is alive and controversial, and that attitudes toward language may be manifestations of philosophical and moral positions. But while their intrinsic worth is great, it is assumed here that their ultimate function is to serve the rest of the book in its primary concern with style. Knowledge of the history, structure, and character of the language cannot but be helpful in developing good prose style, and some of the essays, stylishly written themselves, in turn have style itself as their subject. An educated man should know the nature of his language, and he should be able to write a literate essay. There are few statements so incontrovertible. Part I of this book is designed to help with the first of these duties in such a way that knowledge of the language will help the student fulfill the second.

The essays are arranged thematically in three groups. Those in the first describe, in approximately chronological order, significant stages in the history of the language. Those in the second, devoted to standards of language, are in their several ways given to current issues and controversies arising from the study of language, its usage, and the standards for determining usage. The essays in the third group have style as their subject. They thus serve two functions: to inform the student of various aims and procedures in good style, and to bridge the distance between this first part, given to subject matter, and the larger second part, given to method. The Recommended Readings that conclude Part I are for the student's use. This list of valuable and pertinent essays, articles, and books is given to provide guidance for the student who wants to know more about the history and the character of his language. And it is in the nature of the good student that he wants to know more.

On the Development of the Language

FAMILY RELATIONSHIPS AMONG

LANGUAGES*

Margaret Schlauch

▸ *Families of Languages*

In happier times, it was possible to cross the length and breadth of
Europe by train in so few days that the journey could still be conveniently measured by hours. Paris to Berlin, fifteen hours; Berlin
to Moscow, forty hours; Berlin to Milan, twenty hours. In certain
parts of that complex and explosive continent, it was necessary to
change one's official language three or four times in the course of a
pilgrimage which in the United States would appear to be, in
length, a mere uneventful hop. You could cross the English Channel and find yourself greeted within a couple of hours by the slow
even courtesy of a Dutch immigration officer; a few more hours
and a Belgian would appear at the door of your compartment and,
in French idiom sounding somehow un-French, make the same
routine demands with a courtesy of a different tang. Then eastwards, you could encounter the clipped precision of German of-
ficialdom, followed by softer accents emanating from the speakers
of a series of Western Slavonic national languages. And to the

south there lay, also easily accessible, the varied music of Mediterranean Romance languages, maintaining a certain insidious charm
even as spoken by the stampers of passports and openers of trunks.
The landscape might not change perceptibly at the political borders, but there would be a stir in your compartment, a coming and
going of people, new phrases to be caught on the wing as travelers
passed by in the corridor; and as you sat in your corner eagerly
experiencing the linguistic kaleidoscope of the continent, you
would strain to catch the first sounds of the new idiom as fresh
companions settled themselves about you. The Dutch commercial
travelers condoling or congratulating with one another in measured
tones on the current market would give place to a group of French
permissionaires exchanging rapid chaff on the exploits of their
leave, in an esoteric professional jargon of considerable gayety;
their still-warm places might be occupied by a domestic group on
the German border, *Vati*, and *Mutti* complete with *Brüderlein* and
Schwesterlein who were sure to be the silent, well-behaved recipients of a series of solicitous imperatives. Cries from the station
platforms might echo in your mind in rich polyglot confusion at
the end of such a long journey eastwards: *"Cigarren! Cigaretten!"*
— *"Paris-Soir! Figaro!"* — *"Abfahrt!"* — *"Het is al tien uur."* — *"A la
aduana . . ."* *"Aqua mineral, chocolade . . ."* *"Prüdjóte, Pozháluista!"*

Certainly these differences in tongue would be bewildering in
the extreme to any traveler, until instruction and experience could
bring order out of the chaos of aural impressions. But an enthusiast
who set out to acquire some smattering of the languages in a series
of countries to be so traversed would soon begin to observe some
curious parallelisms in the words learnt to designate the same
object. For two or even more languages he would find repeated
similarities, remote but still perceptible, not only in individual
words but in the manner in which these words were put together
in sentences. Naïve observers explain these similarities by talking
of a vague "mixture" or "corruption." When they come across a
sentence in Dutch like *"Ik heb het gekoopt voor mijnen zoon"*
they are pleased and surprised to observe how much it resembles
English "I have bought it for my son" or German *"Ich habe es
für meinen Sohn gekauft."* And so they inform you gleefully, with
all the assurance of a non-linguist: "Dutch is a funny language;
it's a mixture of English and corrupt German."

A Hollander would of course protest vehemently that Dutch is no more corrupt, funny, or mixed than any other national speech in Europe, and he would be quite right. There is another way of explaining its gratifying resemblance to things we already know.

Let us take a single sentence and follow its land-changes, its mutations, over a fairly wide territory—as territories are reckoned in Europe.

Suppose you begin a trip in Sweden, and you find yourself seated with a mother who is anxiously supervising the box lunch of several small children. She turns solicitously to one of them and says, "Did you get any cookies (or apples, or candies)?" And the child replies: "Yes, Mother, I have three." In Swedish that would be, "*Ja, moder, jag har tre.*" In Norway, to the west, or Denmark, to the south, it would be almost the same: "*Jà, mor, jeg har tre.*"

The slight differences in vowel sound and in sentence melody do not disguise the fact that we are listening to the same words. A moment's reflection will suggest the right explanation. We are not confronted by a borrowing or "mixture" in any case. The three Scandinavian languages mentioned are equally ancient. At one time they were identical, for all practical purposes. A traveler in olden times (let us say the ninth century) could traverse the whole length of Norway or Sweden and pass to the southern extremity of Denmark without any change in his speech. Everywhere he would hear children say: "*Ja, móðir, ek hefi þrja.*" (The last word was pronounced [θrja:].) The changes and differences developed during centuries, rather rapidly in Denmark, more slowly in Sweden. As a result, we now have diversity where once there was unity. Three national languages, equally venerable, have replaced Old Scandinavian. They are extremely close relatives, but none could claim parental precedence over the others. If any branch of Scandinavian could exact respect on the grounds of conservatism (that is, fidelity to the parent, the Old Scandinavian) it would be modern Icelandic, spoken in the distant island which Norwegians settled in the ninth century. Here children still say: "*Já, móðir, ek hefi þrjá.*" The values of the vowels have changed slightly; that is all.

When the train crosses from Denmark into Germany, a greater change becomes apparent. Here the maternal inquiry elicits the answer, "*Ja, Mutter, ich habe drei.*" In Holland or the Flemish-speaking parts of Belgium, tow-headed lads murmur, "*Ja, moeder* (or *moer*), *ik heb drie*." The cleavage is greater, but the separate words still look distinctly familiar. We can even group the versions of our little sentence to show where two or more languages show particular likeness:

ICELANDIC:	*Já, móđir, ek hefi þrjá.*
SWEDISH:	*Ja, moder, jag har tre.*
DANISH:	*Jà, mor, jeg har tre.*
NORWEGIAN:	*Jà, mor, jeg har tre.*
GERMAN:	*Ja, Mutter, ich habe drei.*
DUTCH:	*Ja, moeder, ik heb drie.*
FLEMISH:	*Ja, moeder, ik heb drie.*
ENGLISH:	Yes, mother, I have three.

German stands somewhat apart because its consonants show certain peculiarities: it alone has a [t] between vowels (that is, intervocalic) in the word for mother. Still, it is clear that we are still dealing with variations on the same theme.

Just as the Scandinavian examples revealed close kinship among themselves, so all of those in the extended list show some degree of relationship with one another. Sentences betraying the close linguistic ties within this same group could be multiplied indefinitely. Such being the case, we are justified in speaking of a "family" of languages, borrowing a metaphor from the realm of human relations.

▶ *Parent Germanic*

Detailed comparisons of this sort indicate that all the members of this Germanic group go back to a single parent language, now lost, spoken as a unity somewhere between the first century B.C. and the first A.D. We call this lost parent language Primitive Germanic. Its modern descendants are grouped into what is known as the Germanic family of European languages. English is one of them. The precise geographical location of Primitive Germanic is not known. We can surmise the nature of its sounds (phonology) and inflections (morphology) with what is probably fair accuracy, however, because of some early literature and inscriptions dating back to a time when the separate descendants had as yet separated very little from one another[. . . .]

By comparative study it has been established which sounds in the quoted words are most faithful to the original language. We know that English has preserved the initial consonant of the word "three" [θ] as spoken in Primitive Germanic; but that Icelandic, Flemish, and Dutch have kept the consonant at the end of the first person pronoun singular (*ik*), which has been lost in English and transformed in the others. Back of the multiplicity of extant forms we can feel our way to the existence of the single speech called parent Germanic.

▶ *Romance Languages*

But now let us continue the journey south. In Belgium our anxious Flemish mother may be replaced by a fellow-countrywoman who speaks French. Her child will say something strikingly different from anything heard so far. "*Oui, mère* (or *maman*), *j'en ai trois.*" As the train goes southwards towards that fertile cradle of cultures, the Mediterranean basin, it may be routed towards the Pyrenees, or across the Alps into Italy. If it should cross the Iberian penin-sula you would hear in Spain: "*Sí, madre, (yo) tengo tres*"; and in Portugal: "*Sim, mãe, tenho tres.*" But if it should take you across the barrier which Hannibal—even Hannibal—found all but im-passible, down the steep slopes to the smiling Lombard plains, you would hear: "*Si, madre, ce n'ho tre.*" And even across the Adriatic, on the far side of the Balkan peninsula, hardy descendants of the Roman army and Roman colonists will be saying in Rumanian: "*Da, mama mea, eu am trei.*"

The similarities are apparent:

FRENCH: *Oui, mère, j'en ai trois.*
SPANISH: *Sí, madre, (yo) tengo tres.*
PORTUGUESE: *Sim, mãe, tenho tres.*
ITALIAN: *Si, madre, ce n'ho tre.*
RUMANIAN: *Da, mama mea, eu am trei.*

The situation is comparable to the one which diverted and pos-sibly mystified you in Germanic territory. You have been travers-ing lands where the people communicate with one another in tongues clearly descended from a single parent. This time the parent language was a form of Latin: not the solemn speech, stilted and formal, which was reserved for polite literature and speeches in the forum, but the popular or "vulgar" Latin spoken by common people throughout the length and breadth of the Roman Territory. Plain soldiers, tavern keepers, itinerant merchants, freedmen, small traders, naturalized citizens of all the polyglot Roman provinces, must have used this form of discourse as an international *lingua franca*. In this idiom they bought and sold, exchanged jokes, flirted, lamented, and consoled with one another. We know from late written documents and inscriptions (especially those on the humbler tombstones of poor folk) just how ungrammatical, rapid, informal, and even slangy this Latin was, compared with the intricate and highly mannered periods of a Cicero. People had become impatient with the many case endings required in classical Latin, and were reducing them to two or three. Even these were treated with playful carelessness. The verb was handled in a different way—a more vivid one—to show changes in tense; and the word order was simplified. Moreover, slang words triumphed completely over traditional ones in some provinces. Ordinary people in Gaul (perhaps emulating the jargon of the army) stopped referring to the human head as *caput*, and substituted *testa* or "pot," from which comes modern French *tête*. It is as if all persons speaking English should have fallen into the way of saying "my bean" for the same object, so that it became the accepted word, while "head" was lost entirely.

The popular Roman speech differed from one province to another because popular locutions do tend always to be regional, and because the Romans came in contact with widely differing types of native speech. Thus the pronunciation and even the grammar were affected by the underlying populations. In one place the Latin word *habēre* continued to be used for "to have"; in the Spanish peninsula, however, it so happened that *tenēre*, meaning "to hold," came to be used in its place in the more general sense of "to have." That is why our imaginary Spanish child says *tengo* instead of any form of the classical *habēre*. The number "three," on the other hand, varies only slightly in the series of Romance sentences quoted. The numbers have remained fairly stable in the various daughter languages perpetuated from vulgar Latin. One of the factors tending to preserve a similarity in them throughout the ages has been their similar experience in developing a strong stress accent during the transition to the Middle Ages. This new accentuation caused similar losses in unaccented syllables in a given word in all Mediterranean areas. There were differences, of course, in the forms that emerged; but certainly not enough to make the results unrecognizably alien to one another.

The neo-Latin languages (if the expression may be permitted) give us another example, therefore, of a family which bears its signs of consanguinity very legibly on the external aspect of each of its members. In Roman times, Latin itself could claim cousins (in the ancient *Italic* group) which have since been lost.

▶ The Slavic Family

And here is one further example of language relationship which may metaphorically be called close consanguinity. In eastern Europe a sharp-eared traveler on an international train will also have an opportunity to detect fundamental similarity behind the changing visages of national speech. A far-flung territory is occupied by peoples speaking *Slavic* languages and dialects. It would be possible to pursue the transformation of our key sentence addressed to an imaginary Slavic mother to the east as follows:

CZECHISH:	*Ano, matko, mam tři.*
POLISH:	*Tak, matko, mam trzy.*
RUSSIAN:	*Da, matʲ, u menʲá tri.*

When our international train crosses into the Soviet Union, it will pass through various sections of Russia showing distinct dialect colorings. Ukrainian, for instance, shows enough differentiation to be dignified as a national language, with an official spelling of its own. Even an untutored eye, however, can see how close it is to the official language of Great Russia, the classical medium of literature known to the world as "Russian." In the Balkan states, South Slavic languages show these perceptible nuances of our chosen theme. For instance, the Bulgarian version of it would be: "*Da, maika, imom tri.*"

Once again, we are justified in assuming that centuries ago there was a single language from which these cousins descended. About the seventh century it was probably still fairly unified. In the ninth century a southern dialect of this early Slavic (Old Bulgarian) was written down in a translation of the Bible made by Saints Cyril and Methodius. The text helps us to get quite a clear picture of parent Slavic, just as runic inscriptions bring us close to Primitive Germanic, and unofficial documents of the Roman Empire tell us much about Vulgar Latin.

▶ *Indo-European, Parent of Parents*

Slavic, Romance, and Germanic represent three families of languages spoken in Europe today. But surely it must be clear that similarities link these families to one another besides linking the smaller subdivisions within each given family. In *all* the national languages surveyed so far, it will be noticed, the word for "mother" began with the labial nasal [m]; in a considerable number a dental [t], [đ], or [d] appeared in the middle of the word after the first vowel. Likewise in *all* of the languages listed, "three" began with a dental [t], [d], or [θ], followed by an [r]. Why is this?

Clearly, at a still earlier period than the days of early (prehistoric) Germanic and Slavonic, and of Vulgar Latin, there must have been a more ancient and inclusive unity which embraced all three.

The same procedure, if pursued farther, would have revealed to us other major families belonging to the same larger embracing unity in Europe and parts of Asia. These are:

Celtic, including Irish, Highland Scottish, Welsh, and Breton. (In modern Irish, "mother" is *mathair* and "three" is *tri.*)

Baltic, including Lettish, Lithuanian, and an extinct dialect once spoken in the territory of modern Prussia (Old Prussian). The word for "mother" is *motina,* not closely related to the cognates already cited. *Tris* for "three" is, on the other hand, an obvious cognate.

Hellenic, including modern Greek dialects, some of which go back to very ancient times. (An ancient Greek dialect, Attic, spoken in the city of Athens, produced a body of literature of enduring splendor. Its word for "mother" was *matềr* and for "three," *treis.* This is the classical language studied in school.)

Albanian, the national language of Albania, with no close relatives outside its own borders. Here "three" is *tre;* but the word for "mother" is not related to the forms in the above languages. A new form, *nona,* has replaced the Indo-European term preserved elsewhere.

Armenian, spoken in Armenia (between Europe and Asia Minor), is, like Albanian, a language with many diverse elements borrowed from outside, but it has an independent history traceable back to the fifth or sixth century A.D. Its word for "mother," *mair*, is easily recognizable as a cognate of the others given; not so, however, is *erek* for "three."

Even in Asia there are languages with venerable histories and rich literary heritage which can be recognized as members of the same linguistic clan:

Indian, including Hindustani, Bengali, Marathi, and Hindi. These dialects are descended from Old Indian, preserved to us in a classical literary form (Sanskrit) which dates back to the fifteenth century B.C. or even several hundred years earlier. Sanskrit, despite its great antiquity, still shows close generic resemblance to its modern European cousins. Its word for "mother" was *mātṛ* and for "three," *tri*.

Iranian, very closely related to Sanskrit, was spoken in the Persian highlands while Indian was spreading over the interior of India. It produced an early literature in the form of Zoroastrian hymns. Since those ancient times Persian has been subjected to large foreign infiltration, notably Arabic, but its structure still reveals its kinship with the other groups listed.

Hittite, a language spoken by people frequently mentioned in the Bible, is now extinct. Cuneiform inscriptions give us enough material to reveal its fundamental character. Some sort of relationship it surely must have had with the members of the broad family of families now being surveyed, but the precise nature of that relationship is still under discussion.

Tocharian, now extinct, is represented by some fragmentary texts (probably antedating the tenth century), which were discovered in eastern Turkestan in a Buddhist monastery. The material is too scanty to permit of definitive analysis, but it shows relationship to the above subsidiary groups.

Our railroad trip beginning with Germanic territory has taken us far afield, even to the shores of the Indus River in Asia. Even so, and despite the most baffling diversities, skilled comparison of key words has been able to establish that the miniature families surveyed do undoubtedly belong to the same large, inclusive family already postulated to account for likenesses observed among Germanic, Slavonic, and Romance (from Old Italic).

Back of the smaller families lay a single family; attached to this single family it is almost certain there must have been a single language. We call the whole family by the name "Indo-European," a term generally preferred today to "Indo-Germanic" or "Aryan," both of which could easily be misunderstood. That is to say, every language mentioned so far is an Indo-European language, no matter what smaller group it may belong to.

▶ Homeland of Indo-European

But if they are all related thus, we must assume that a single definite language, parent Indo-European, gave rise to all of them. This is probably true. Some time before 2000 B.C., in some part of the world, a group which was essentially a single community spoke this single parent language. Later, dialect forms of this tribal language were carried into many different countries, from Iceland to India—by emigration, by conquest, by peaceful transfer. We do not know how this occurred in every case, but the expansion had already begun in earliest historical times.

Where the parent language was spoken, and by whom, is something of a mystery. By studying words that are common to a number of the family groups listed above we can, to be sure, get some idea of the culture these people had before their language was spread over a wide area and differentiated by the divisions, migrations, or conquests of a half-dozen millennia ago. We can surmise that they probably lived in a temperate climate because a number of the descended languages have similar words for spring, summer, autumn, and winter. There are common words indicating a developed (though still simple) agriculture: terms having to do with the plow, spade, sickle, and mill; with carting, sowing, and mowing. For instance, the word for plow is *arðr* in Icelandic, *áratron* in Greek, *arātrum* in Latin, *arathar* in Irish, *árklas* in Lithuanian, *araur* in Armenian. The names of certain plants and animals are supposed to offer some guidance. Parent Indo-European had terms for dogs, cows, sheep, bulls, goats, pigs, and horses; also for wild animals such as the bear, the wolf, and the fox. Hermann Hirt, author of an elaborate discussion of the subject, considers the common words for "eel" in several languages as very important. If the original speakers of Indo-European knew this fish, they could not have lived originally near the Black Sea, where it is not found. Another important word is the old term for the beech tree in the various languages. The words *Buche* in German, *fagus* in Latin, *Bachenis* Forest in a Celtic place-name, and *Phegós* (φηγός) in Greek (where it had been transferred, however, to the oak tree), indicate that the beech was a tree known at the time of the parent language. The forms just quoted could all have come from a single root. Now the eastern boundary for the presence of this European tree is a line drawn roughly from Königsberg to the Crimea. Therefore Hirt argues that the parent language must have developed to the west of such a line.

North central Germany, Lithuania, the Danube Valley, and Southern Russia (near the Black Sea) have been suggested in turn as the original homeland of the parent language. India, once regarded as the cradle of our general Indo-European speech, has been relinquished in favor of European territories answering to the geographical clues of the joint vocabularies. Of these it may be said that probability favors those districts in which there are many physical traces of early mankind, such as burial mounds, skeletons, fragments of pottery, signs of human habitation. The Danube Valley is particularly rich in these, and also Germany and Southern Russia. Lithuania can boast an extraordinarily archaic language, similar in many ways to ancient Sanskrit, but its territory is poor in archaeological remains, those mute witnesses to the daily living of people like ourselves who "flourished" (if that is the proper word) in prehistoric times. Lithuania may have been settled early in the age that saw the spread of Indo-European, but it is less likely than other districts to have seen its first development.

No matter where Indo-European developed out of still earlier linguistic stages now hopelessly lost, it is important to remember that we know absolutely nothing about the physical appearance of its first speakers. They have long since been leveled with the dust; we cannot say whether their skin was light or dark, their vanished hair shadowy or bright. Among the broad-skulled and long-skulled and medium-skulled remains of prehistoric man, we cannot tell which—if any—moved their bony jaws in olden times to the sounds and rhythms of the Indo-European parent language. Although most of the contemporary peoples of Europe may be descendants, in part, of members of our postulated Indo-European community, still it is not safe to assume that this community was itself racially homogeneous.

In any event we cannot be sure about what happened in those early ages. It is instructive to think of the mutations of history in the era since writing began. Whole peoples have suffered extinction as nations in past centuries, yet they may perpetuate and hand on the language of the conquerors when the latter in their turn are destroyed or absorbed. A West Indian Negro today can often be found speaking with the faultless accents and intonation of choice classical English; if you closed your eyes you would think he had been nurtured on the playing fields of Eton or by the Cam. He speaks standard English *as his native tongue;* he is aware of nothing alien about it as it leaves his lips; there is no psychological strain involved in employing this particular instrument merely because his ancestors in Africa used a very different one long ago. No doubt flawless Latin was spoken in the streets of Rome by naturalized provincials of many races, showing wide variety in the hues of their epidermises. In somewhat the same way all of us, for that matter, may be using variations of a borrowed instrument. So completely separate are the questions of language and race.

Most scholars would, to be sure, look to one or another of the contemporary people of Europe or India or even Persia to find lineal descendants of those who first spoke Indo-European. Yet two well-known authorities, Sigmund Feist (a German) and Vendryès (a Frenchman), have argued that even the Germans of today— who usually claim that honor—do not have the blood of the parent tribe in their veins even though they speak an Indo-European language (which they now choose to call "Aryan"). Feist and Vendryès point out that German (like Dutch, English, and Scandinavian) shows a very great change from the parent speech which lies back of the other Indo-European offshoots. The Germanic family has changed many of the supposed original sounds. Where Latin had *piscis,* Germanic substituted a form like *fisk* (English "fish"); where Latin and Greek had *patēr,* Germanic showed something like English "father." Thus this one particular group looks quite different from its Romance, Slavonic, Hellenic, and other cousins because of an unusually complete shift of consonants. According to Feist and Vendryès, the reason is that the Primitive Germanic tribesmen were an alien race trying to learn to pronounce an Indo-European or "Aryan" language. They had trouble with sounds like [p] and [t], and so distorted them to [f] and [θ]. If this theory is sound, the Germans of today would be a non-"Aryan" race (granting that the phrase means anything), speaking an "Aryan" language imposed upon them by conquerors in prehistoric times! The whole question is very speculative. It may be pointed out that if Germanic tribesmen had trouble with [p] and [t] in primitive times, at least their descendants soon made good the loss by developing new [p] and [t] sounds out of Indo-European [b] and [d].

At the moment, however, what interests us most is the evidence of underlying unity, not of divergence, in the Indo-European family. As we shall see, the divergences turn out to be fairly regular when they are closely examined. Because they are more or less predictable by an advanced student, they do not disturb seriously his impressions of the underlying unity which justifies him in regarding the whole majestic array of tongues as a close-knit family. The more acutely one observes the principles of correspondence and divergence, the easier it becomes to learn a new member within the widely scattered group.

Cursory as this review has been, it has probably indicated the approach and even something of the methods used in the study of comparative linguistics.

Comparisons of a similar sort have established family relationships for the rest of the world. For the languages less familiar to us speakers of English a briefer survey will suffice.

▶ *The Finno-Ugric Family*

Within Europe itself there are several languages which are completely alien to those of the Indo-European confraternity. A visitor in Finland, for instance, will look at posters and newspapers and remark with a puzzled air: "How strange! Not a word looks or sounds familiar! Why, in most countries you can guess something here and there, at least phrases—but not this; it's *outlandish*." The same remark will be heard from tourists in Hungary, Estonia, and (on rare occasions, I suppose) from visitors among the Laplanders in the far north of western Russia and Scandinavia. The term "outlandish" is here justified in its literal sense. The languages here spoken did come from an "outer land" centuries ago. They reached Europe by migration from the Volga and the slopes of the Ural Mountains, both from the Asiatic and the hither side. The Magyar (Hungarian) speech was transferred in a series of incursions lasting down into the Middle Ages, which were fraught with considerable terror for the turbulent inhabitants already more or less established on the fringes of the Roman Empire.

Finnish, Estonian, Lappish, and Magyar are members of the *Finno-Ugric family*. It also includes minor languages and dialects spoken in restricted areas, such as Carelian, Mordvian, Cheremiss, and the Permian languages (Zyrian and Votiak) which were carried to the northern Urals from the Volga region. Mordvian and Cheremiss are still spoken in scattered communities of the Volga basin.

It is thought that Lappish is a Finno-Ugric language imposed by conquest on a people who originally spoke a quite different tongue. The Lapps, indeed, may be the physical survivors of one of the primeval races inhabiting Europe long before history began.

▶ Finno-Ugric, Nenets, and Parent Uralic

In north central Siberia a number of small scattered tribes speak variations of a language referred to in most textbooks as Samoyedic. The term is an unflattering one, and did not originate with the tribesmen themselves. It is a Russian word used in Tsarist times and seems to mean "self-eaters" or cannibals. (It comes apparently from two common Indo-European roots: *samo*, cognate with English "same," and *ʲed*, cognate with English "edible," from Latin *edere*, meaning "to eat.") According to the *Soviet Encyclopedia* these people refer to their own nation and language as Nenets—a term preferable, therefore, to the contemptuous epithet hitherto current.

Finno-Ugric and Nenets ("Samoyed") together form a supergroup showing remote but still perceptible similarities among themselves. There is one trait of sound patterns common to almost all, which in particular impresses even a beginner in Finno-Ugric linguistics. It is known by the pretty term "vowel harmony." To Finno-Ugric ears, the vowels of single words are like notes in a musical chord. To combine front, back, and mid-tongue vowels in the same word indiscriminately is as bad as striking a group of notes on the piano by bringing down the flat of your hand forcefully on the white keys. In constructing a word, when the first syllable happens to contain a front vowel (*e, i, ä, ö, ü*),[1] then all following syllables must also contain front ones; and if the first syllable contains a back vowel (*a, o, u*), then all suffixed syllables must likewise contain one. You can have words like *äpä, küsöb, vesi, mato,* and *muna,* but not *veso.* Vowel harmony existed, apparently, in early Finno-Ugric, but Magyar shows exceptions and the Permian group and Lappish no longer observe it. A very practical result of this craving for vocalic similarity is the necessity to vary vowels in regular suffixes (inflectional endings). There must be two forms to choose from, according to the root vowel of the word. In Magyar, for instance, *marad-unk* means "we remain," but

---

[1] ä = [ε]; ö = [ε′], a sound formed by rounding the lips while pronouncing [ε]; ü = [y]. Ö and ü are familiar to students of German.

el-ünk means "we live." The vowel of the suffix alternates between [u] (after a back vowel) and [y], written *ü* (after a front one).

Here again we are justified in assuming a single parent language, a common ancestor of Nenets and Finno-Ugric, which we may call parent Uralic. This broad term may be used for all the ramified descendants, just as Indo-European was applied to all the languages descended from it. The geographical location of this lost ancestral Uralic speech is not known. Some of its characteristics can be deduced by reasoning back from extant dialects, as in the case of Indo-European. It has been claimed that a still more ancient kinship existed between Uralic and Altaic (a group centered in the region of the Altai Mountains in Central Asia) and even Japanese, but most specialists regard these speculations as unconvincing.

▶ *Basque*

One more language of an "outlandish" character remains in Europe: Basque, which is spoken by a small but closely knit group in the French and Spanish Pyrenees. The vocabulary and grammatical structure are as alien to Indo-European as can be imagined. Hence the legends (current about Finnish too, by the way) to the effect that the devil himself was foiled in an attempt to learn this language, and his tutor (unlike Faust) emerged safe from the bargain to teach it, with his soul still his own. According to some writers, it is possible that Basque represents the sole surviving fragment of a common speech spoken by Neolithic tribesmen scattered over Europe, long before Indo-European or Finno-Ugric had entered the continent by migration or conquest. Possibly the same type of speech extended into the British Isles and across the Spanish peninsula into Northern Africa in these prehistoric times. The arguments in support of this possibility have to do with similarities in culture and physique among the prehistoric peoples concerned. They are not based primarily on linguistic evidence.

▶ *Semitic Languages*

This brings us to another linguistic family which has had cultural contacts with Indo-European at various points in its history: namely, the Semitic group. The name for it is taken from Genesis 5:32, in which the names of the three sons of Noah are given as

Sem (or Shem), Cham (or Ham), and Japheth. It was believed
that the numerous folk speaking Semitic languages owed their
physical existence to the first son, to whom descendants of remarkable fecundity would appear to have been attributed. In ancient
historical times, branches of Semitic were spoken in the city-
states of Babylonia and Assyria in Mesopotamia. (An earlier language, Sumerian, was superseded by this spread of East Semitic.)
To the West, Phoenician and Hebrew and Aramaic (including
Syriac) occupied territory in Asia Minor which extended to the
eastern shores of the Mediterranean. Hebrew was destined to play
a memorable part, long after the end of political independence for
Palestine, because of the incalculable influence of its Biblical
literature. South of Palestine, and extending far west across the
north of Africa, at one time even including Spain, there lay an
imposing concatenation of peoples using Arabic, which with the
rise of Islam became a world language of prime importance. It is
still one of the first claimants for the attention of students desiring
to broaden their studies beyond the more proximate Indo-European
subgroups. Finally, the dialects of Ethiopian in Abyssinia, though
close to Arabic in many features, constitute a separate division in
the group of southwest Semitic languages.

One striking feature in grammatical structure is common to all
the Semitic languages, and that is a marked preference for verbal
roots using three consonant sounds. These consonants remain
clearly recognizable no matter what vowels appear or disappear
between them, or what prefixes and suffixes may be added. The
characteristic core of the word, stripped of its mutations, is called
the "triliteral root." A student learns, for example, that variations
of the idea "to kill" cluster around the unpronounceable abstraction [qtl],[2] which has no independent existence but which can
be detected in these related forms meaning "they killed:"

	HEBREW	ARAMAIC	ARABIC	ETHIOPIAN
Imperfect	yiqtəlū	yiqtəlūn	yaqtulu	yəqattəlū
Perfect	qātəlū	qətal(ū)	qatalū	qatalu

Nouns related to verbs show the same three-pillared structure of
consonants. In Hebrew the present-tense root form meaning "reign-

---

[2] The phonetic symbol [q] stands for a consonant resembling [k], but
spoken much deeper in the throat.

ing as king" is [moːleːχ]; "to be or become king" is [mɔːlaχ]; "to make one king" is [mɔlaχ]; "a king" is [meleχ], plural [məlɔχiːm]; and "kingdom" is [maləχuːs]. The consonantal abstraction of the root is [mlχ].[3] These examples are sufficient to clarify a persistent and very easily recognized trait in Semitic.

▶ Hamitic Languages

Contiguous with parts of Semitic territory and rather similar to Semitic in structure are the languages of the Hamitic group. They were named from the second son of that early navigator, Noah. Ancient Egyptian (known historically since 4000 B.C.) belonged to it, and produced in turn the Coptic or neo-Egyptian language which continued to be spoken down to the seventeenth century of our era. This Hamitic tongue has one of the longest careers so far as records are concerned. Akin to it are surviving dialects of Berber, spoken in scattered communities across the north of Africa as far as the Canary Islands, and also the Cushite languages bordering the Red Sea: Bedja, Somali, Saho, and Afar.

There is good reason to suppose that Hamitic and Semitic are themselves differentiations of an original linguistic unity called Hamito-Semitic by specialists. For one thing, Old Egyptian shows a marked preference for triliteral consonant roots, as a glance at its grammar will show, even though biliteral consonant roots are also common. Moreover, there are a few phonological traits common to the combined group, and one or two grammatical usages which appear to come from a common source. The peoples concerned have been neighbors from time immemorial. It is not unlikely that the idioms now spoken by them had a single origin. There has been quite enough time during and before recorded history for the multiple ramifications to occur.

▶ Sudanese and Bantu Groups

The rest of Africa is occupied almost entirely by two large groups, somewhat loosely defined: the Sudanese (generally southwest of the Hamitic belt) and Bantu (south of Sudanese). Though the field of African Negro languages has been comparatively neg-

---

[3] It may be noticed in passing that in certain of the Semitic languages a consonant is modified in pronunciation if it comes after a vowel. In Hebrew and Aramaic, for instance, an older [k] became [χ] in such a position. An earlier form of the verbal root [m¹χ] appears in the word [malkaː], "queen."

lected, the study of these two major groups has already revealed
evidence of common origin from a single language before the
cleavage into these two major divisions. Research is hampered, of
course, by an almost complete absence of written texts before modern times. (The study of Indo-European reveals clearly how illuminating and decisive an ancient text can be in determining
family relationships among languages.) Even today, however,
Bantu and Sudanese agree in classifying nouns grammatically according to the class of objects they represent, each class being
marked off by an affixed syllable to designate it. Parent Bantu, for
instance, probably had a prefix *mu-*, usually reserved for human
beings. An example is *mu-na* ("child") in the Duzala dialect. Other
prefixes were *ba-*, *gu-*, *mi-*. Sudanese uses such class prefixes for
nouns too. Bantu and Sudanese also inflect their verbs to show
aspects of action rather than time relations which we consider so
very important. A Bantu verb shows completeness, negation, emphasis, continuity, and other relations, but not very many temporal
ones. *Na-pula* means "I desire" in Duala, and *na-puli*, "I desired";
other inflexions are: *na-si-pula*, "I desire not"; *na-pulise*, "I cause
to desire"; *na-pulana*, "I desire because of something." Phonology
and vocabulary mark off Bantu as distinct from its northern neighbor in Sudan, but it may well be that underlying similarities will be
increasingly revealed in this domain too.

▶ Altaic Languages

Returning to the Balkans and the Near East we find another huge
family of languages represented by one, Turkish, spoken within
the very portals of Europe. The broad term for Turkish and its
relatives is Altaic. It includes three main divisions: Turkic, Mongol,
and Tunguz. These extend from the southeast of Europe (Istanbul)
through the Volga district and Turkey, through Azerbaijan, Ana-
tolia, and the Caucasian districts, to Mongolia and the Tunguz-
Manchu region around the Yenisei River. Among the Turkic subdivisions are the groups in the east or Altai region (including
Yakut); the Central Asian groups; the western one (including Tatar
in the Volga district and Kirghiz); and the southern (Turcoman,
Anatolian, Caucasian Turkic dialects, etc.).

The Mongolian subdivision centers in Mongolia, showing little
diffusion outside the political boundaries of the country. Tunguz

is spoken east of the Yenisei River, while Manchu, a close relative, is limited to the valleys of the Khurkha and Sungari rivers. It is being replaced by Chinese.

A common trait which links these widely sundered languages is the principle of vowel harmony, which also marks Finno-Ugric, as we have seen. There are other characters of a general phonological nature which can be found in all of them. An example of the vowel harmony is a pair of compounds from the Osmanli dialect (spoken in the Balkans):

öl-dür-mä-yälim,	"let us not kill."
otur-ma-yalïm,	"let us not stay seated."

Notice that in the first word, the first syllable began with a front vowel, so that all the following vowels—including those of the first person plural suffix—had to be fronted. In some, this front quality is indicated by two dots over the vowel. The second group began with [o], a back vowel, and as a consequence the following syllables also show lowered vowels. Even the [i] is lowered to [ï], and the [l] preceding it is lowered from its front position. (The sign [ł] represents an *l*-sound made with the back of the tongue instead of the tip.) These subtle gradations of sound within the phrasal unit are practiced automatically by the vast numbers of people who speak Turkic-Mongolian-Tunguz as well as those who employ Finno-Ugric, making a very imposing total in all.

▶ *Sino-Tibetan Languages*

In the Far East there is another inclusive group employed by an imposing section of humanity, namely the Sino-Tibetan languages. The subdivisions are Chinese, Tai, and Tibeto-Burman, covering a belt from China on the east to the Tibetan highlands of India, and dipping down into Siam. The characteristic word-form in all these languages is an uninflected monosyllable which shows its role in the sentence by position only. Yet there are traces of dissyllabic roots and inflectional forms which must have been common in the parent language. To a very limited degree English may be compared to Sino-Tibetan languages, since we too depend on word order to show relationships in the sentence; but of course we use many other devices as well.

Musical pitch is an important feature of all these languages. It may change the meaning of a word, since many syllables otherwise complete homonyms (that is, identical) are distinguished by high or low pitch alone. It is as if we distinguished between "sea" and "see" by giving one a high and the other a low tone. There is evidence that originally high pitch accompanied syllables beginning with a voiceless consonant, so that *tai* would necessarily be spoken—or, rather, intoned—higher than *dai;* but many intricate sound changes throughout the centuries have obscured this neat correlation.

▶ Malay-Polynesian Groups

The Malay-Polynesian belt, including peoples in the Dutch East Indies, Philippines, Malay Peninsula, Madagascar, Hawaii, and small Pacific archipelagos, reveals the close connection of its members with one another to the most casual observation. They make use of roots of two syllables and employ a variety of prefixes, suffixes, and infixes; yet their nouns are innocent of inflection to show gender and number. In Hawaiian, original consonants have been slurred away in so many positions that the language has become a tissue of vowels held together by a minimum of consonants in initial and intervocalic positions.

▶ American Indian Families

Across the Pacific we come once more to the two American continents where a pair of Indo-European languages, English and Spanish (together with Portuguese) dominate official life. They have displaced but not yet eliminated completely an enormously diversified series of Indian languages, extending from the Arctic to the Antarctic. Some families of these have been carefully studied, but the variety is so great that we are in no position to make hypotheses concerning underlying unities. Specialists differ widely in their estimates of the numbers of groups showing so little similarity at present as to appear to be independent. Emigration, conquest, cultural interpenetration, and merging have done much to confuse the picture. The reader will recognize the names of some of the larger groups in North America, such as the Algonquian, Iroquoian, Muskogean, Siouan, and Uto-Aztecan. Eskimo, which is spoken in the north of Canada, is now considered to be a relative of Nenets (Samoyedic) in the Uralic group which includes Finno-Ugric.

▶ *Australian, Caucasian, and Dravidian Families. Korean and Japanese*

In this rapid encirclement of the globe several important linguistic territories have been omitted, either because they have been too little charted for even the most summary description, or because they were too unified or too limited to illustrate ramified family relationships. The native languages of Australia are, for instance, a treasure-house of unexplored mystery. The region of the Caucasus Mountains presents a bewildering complexity of diversified tongues spoken by fairly small groups, neighbors to one another, many of which are mutually unintelligible. Of these, one, Georgian, achieved literary expression at a comparatively early date (fourth century A.D.), but others have remained practically unknown outside their own territory. (Now that they are being recorded in print there will be a basis for comparative study.) In India, the Dravidian dialects represent a large but shrinking language group which antedated the conquering Indo-European Sanskrit in the Indus Valley, and has retreated before it. India, the Malay Peninsula, and the Siamese territory include linguistic patches or "islands" designated as Austro-Asiatic, grouped together on the basis of parallelisms in vocabulary and word-formation.[4] Korean and Japanese, both languages associated with high cultures, resemble each other in vocabulary and general grammatical forms, but the relations of the two are not entirely clarified despite arguments to prove their kinship. Both have impersonal verbs and uninflected nouns; both depend largely on word order to indicate relationships within the sentence.

There is much work still to be done in charting the unknown or little known territories of human speech. If we can judge from experience in the past, we may expect that further relationships may be discovered by the comparative method, and that groups

[4] Father Wilhelm Schmidt has tried to prove their generic relation to Malay-Polynesian. This hypothesis is described by Przyluski as "grandiose— but fragile."

hitherto thought to be isolated will have relatives discovered for them, sometimes in lands quite far away. Indo-European linguistics was launched on its triumphant way by the discovery of a most distant émigré member of the family in India. The agreeable experience of perceiving unity beneath diversity has rewarded linguists so often that they have some justification for expecting it to be repeated in the future.

▶ *Single or Multiple Origin of Speech?*

Already the question has often been asked: "Do we know enough to decide whether all languages, the world over, had a single origin? Is *every* language related to every other?"

It is a fascinating question. The mere possibility of unified origin for all human speech appeals strongly to the imagination. Here indeed would be a most gratifying satisfaction for our natural desire to simplify our understanding of the universe about us by reducing the number of categories under which we conceive of it. There is also something aesthetically grandiose about the thought that the vast symphony of all languages and dialects was elaborated, so to speak, from a single theme.

In the early days of linguistic science, the presuppositions were naturally in favor of monogenesis of speech, because the story of the Garden of Eden, whether understood literally or not, exerted a strong influence on investigators. Then under the spell of Darwinism there was a reaction to a belief in polygenesis, likewise often expressed in dogmatic terms. Analogies were drawn and misapplied in linguistic science, for which Darwin himself should not be blamed. The chief exponent of linguistic polygenesis was Friedrich Müller, who assumed that the "speech" of animals must have developed gradually into human speech, so gradually indeed that man must have been a diversified type long before the evolution was completed, "and herewith," he argued, "we may be said to have an *a priori* postulate, from the point of view of the history of evolution, of the derivation of human speech (as an ideational and conceptional language based on sounds) from several mutually independent sources."

Today most authors are extremely cautious when they touch upon the unrecoverable epoch when speech originated. They usually avoid committing themselves on the question as to whether this happened once or several times in various parts of the world. In any case, they say, the answer is unimportant, even irrelevant, for the solution of problems significant for us today.

Nevertheless a few individual writers are willing to commit themselves. Alfredo Trombetti, for instance, has presented a lengthy, ambitious argument for monogenesis, fortified with many concrete illustrations. On the basis of extremely wide and detailed study, Trombetti builds up a scheme including wider and wider groups and families of languages, making use of surviving similarities in numerals, pronominal forms, and the like. Such structural words are apt to be conservative of their form, and they are not readily borrowed from one language by another in most cases. He records similarities between numerals in Sudanese-Bantu and Munda-Khmer of the Austro-Asiatic group; between pronouns in Hamitic-Semitic, Dravidian, Munda, and Polynesian; between numerals in Indo-Chinese and Uralic (he says "Ural-Altaic"); between verbs in Dakota (American Indian) and Georgian (in the Caucasian Territory). He observes that the greatest similarities are to be found between groups most widely separated on the periphery of a huge circle having its center in India. Therefore he deduces that India was the home and starting point for all races as well as all languages. It is true that Trombetti produces some astonishing parallelisms. But one becomes suspicious of them when one reflects upon the great mobility of language: its proneness to change and transformation. After observing the behavior of vowels and consonants over the very short span of recorded history, one begins to suspect that two words that look alike now are probably unrelated for that very reason—unless they belong to two subgroups in demonstrably close generic relation, and also mean approximately the same thing. English "book" and German *Buch* are indeed cognates, but it is quite accidental that Quiché *buj* or *vuj* (also pronounced [buχ], but with a loose *b*) means the same thing. We know too little about the early history of the languages outside of Indo-European and Hamito-Semitic to commit ourselves too far on the matter of ultimate relationships. For one thing, change operates very slowly in some groups and with almost dizzying rapidity in others. We must allow for this in estimating the value of Trombetti's parallels. The question about a single origin for the diverse tongues of mankind must be tabled until we know more of their earlier forms; and that may be—forever.

PRELIMINARY SKETCH*

Otto Jespersen

It will be my endeavour in this volume to characterize the chief peculiarities of the English language, and to explain the growth and significance of those features in its structure which have been of permanent importance. The older stages of the language, interesting as their study is, will be considered only in so far as they throw light either directly or by way of contrast on the main characteristics of present-day English, and an attempt will be made to connect the teachings of linguistic history with the chief events in the general history of the English people so as to show their mutual bearings on each other and the relation of language to national character. The knowledge that the latter conception is a very difficult one to deal with scientifically, as it may easily tempt one into hasty generalizations, should make us wary, but not deter us from grappling with problems which are really both interesting and important. My plan will be, first to give a rapid sketch of the language of our own days, so as to show how it strikes a foreigner— a foreigner who has devoted much time to the study of English, but who feels that in spite of all his efforts he is only able to look at it as a foreigner does, and not exactly as a native would[. . . .]

It is, of course, impossible to characterize a language in one formula; languages, like men, are too composite to have their whole essence summed up in one short expression. Nevertheless, there is one expression that continually comes to my mind whenever I think of the English language and compare it with others: it seems to me positively and expressly *masculine*, it is the language of a grown-up man and has very little childish or feminine about it. A great many things go together to produce and to confirm that impression, things phonetical, grammatical, and lexical, words and turns that are found, and words and turns that are not found, in the language. In dealing with the English language one is often reminded of the characteristic English hand-writing; just as an

English lady will nearly always write in a manner that in any other country would only be found in a man's hand, in the same manner the language is more manly than any other language I know.

First I shall mention the sound system. The English consonants are well defined; voiced and voiceless consonants stand over against each other in neat symmetry, and they are, as a rule, clearly and precisely pronounced. You have none of those indistinct or half-slurred consonants that abound in Danish, for instance (such as those in hade, hage, livlig), where you hardly know whether it is a consonant or a vowel-glide that meets the ear. The only thing that might be compared to this in English, is the r when not followed by a vowel, but then this has really given up definitely all pretensions to the rank of a consonant, and is (in the pronunciation of the South of England) either frankly a vowel (as in here) or else nothing at all (in hart, etc.). Each English consonant belongs distinctly to its own type, a t is a t, and a k is a k, and there an end. There is much less modification of a consonant by the surrounding vowels than in some other languages, thus none of that palatalization of consonants which gives an insinuating grace to such languages as Russian. The vowel sounds, too, are comparatively independent of their surroundings, and in this respect the language now has deviated widely from the character of Old English and has become more clear-cut and distinct in its phonetic structure, although, to be sure, the diphthongization of most long vowels (in ale, whole, eel, who, phonetically eil, houl, ijl, huw) counteracts in some degree this impression of neatness and evenness.

Besides these characteristics, the full nature of which cannot, perhaps, be made intelligible to any but those familiar with phonetic research, but which are still felt more or less instinctively by everybody hearing the language spoken, there are other traits whose importance can with greater ease be made evident to anybody possessed of a normal ear.

To bring out clearly one of these points I select at random, by way of contrast, a passage from the language of Hawaii: 'I kona hiki ana aku ilaila ua hookipa ia mai la oia me ke aloha pumehana loa.' Thus it goes on, no single word ends in a consonant, and a group of two or more consonants is never found. Can anyone be in doubt that even if such a language sound pleasantly and be full of music and harmony, the total impression is childlike and effeminate? You do not expect much vigour or energy in a people speaking such a language; it seems adapted only to inhabitants of sunny regions where the soil requires scarcely any labour on the part of man to yield him everything he wants, and where life therefore does not bear the stamp of a hard struggle against nature and against fellow-creatures. In a lesser degree we find the same phonetic structure in such languages as Italian and Spanish; but how different are our Northern tongues. English has no lack of words ending in two or more consonants—I am speaking, of course, of the pronunciation, not of the spelling—*age, hence, wealth, tent, tempt, tempts, months, helped, feasts,* etc., etc., and thus requires, as well as presupposes, no little energy on the part of the speakers. That many suchlike consonant groups do not tend to render the language beautiful, one is bound readily to concede; however, it cannot be pretended that their number in English is great enough to make the language harsh or rough. While the fifteenth century greatly increased the number of consonant groups by making the *e* mute in *monthes, helped,* etc., the following centuries, on the contrary, lightened such groups as *-ght* in *night, thought* (where the 'back-open' consonant as German *ch* is still spoken in Scotch) and the initial *kn-, gn-* in *know, gnaw,* etc. Note also the disappearance of *l* in *alms, folk,* etc., and of *r* in *hard, court,* etc.; the final consonant groups have also been simplified in *comb* and the other words in *-mb* (whereas *b* has been retained in *timber*) and in the exactly parallel group *-ng,* for instance in *strong,* where now only one consonant is heard after the vowel, a consonant partaking of the nature of *n* and of *g,* but identical with neither of them; formerly it was followed by a real *g,* which has been retained in *stronger.*

In the first ten stanzas of Tennyson's *Locksley Hall,* three hundred syllables, we have only thirty-three words ending in two consonants, and two ending in three, certainly no excessive number, especially if we take into account the nature of the groups, which are nearly all of the easiest kind (-dz: *comrades, Pleiads;* -mz: *gleams, comes;* -nz: *robin's, man's, turns;* -ns: *distance, science;* -ks: *overlooks;* -ts: *gets, thoughts;* -kts: *tracts, cataracts;* -zd: *reposed, closed;* -st: *rest, West, breast, crest;* -st: *burnish'd;* -nd: *sound, around, moorland, behind, land;* -nt: *want, casement, went, present;* -ld: *old, world;* -lt: *result;* -lf: *himself;* -pt: *dipt*). Thus, we may perhaps characterize English, phonetically speaking, as possessing male energy, but not brutal force. The accentual system points in the same direction, as will be seen below.

The Italians have a pointed proverb: *Le parole son femmine e i fatti son maschi.* If briefness, conciseness and terseness are characteristic of the style of men, while women as a rule are not such economizers of speech, English is more masculine than most languages. We see this in a great many ways. In grammar it has got rid of a great many superfluities found in earlier English as well as in most cognate languages, reducing endings, etc. to the shortest forms possible and often doing away with endings altogether. Where German has, for instance, *alle diejenigen wilden tiere, die dort leben,* so that the plural idea is expressed in each word separately (apart, of course, from the adverb), English has 'all the wild animals that live there,' where *all,* the article, the adjective, and the relative pronoun are alike incapable of receiving any mark of the plural number; the sense is expressed with the greatest clearness imaginable, and all the unstressed endings -*e* and -*en,* which make most German sentences so drawling, are avoided.

Rimes based on correspondence in the last syllable only of each line (as *bet, set; laid, shade*) are termed male rimes, as opposed to feminine rimes, where each line has two corresponding syllables, one strong and one weak (as *better, setter; lady, shady*). It is true that these names, which originated in France, were not at first meant to express any parallelism with the characteristics of the two sexes, but arose merely from the grammatical fact that the weak -*e* was the ending of the feminine gender (grande, etc.). But the designations are not entirely devoid of symbolic significance; there is really more of abrupt force in a word that ends with a strongly stressed syllable, than in a word where the maximum of force is followed by a weak ending. 'Thanks' is harsher and less polite than the two-syllabled 'thank you.' English has undoubtedly gained in force, what it has possibly lost in elegance, by reducing so many words of two syllables to monosyllables. If it had not been for the great number of long foreign, especially Latin, words, English would have approached the state of such monosyllabic languages as Chinese. Now one of the best Chinese scholars, G. v. d. Gabelentz, somewhere remarks that an idea of the condensed power of the monosyllabism found in old Chinese may be gathered from Luther's advice to a preacher '*Geh rasch 'nauf, tu's Maul auf, hör bald auf.*' He might with equal justice have reminded us of many English sentences. 'First come, first served' is much more vigorous than the French '*premier venu, premier moulu*' or '*le premier venu engrène,*' the German 'Wer *zuerst kommt, mahlt zuerst*' and especially than the Danish '*den der kommer først til mølle, får først malet.*' Compare also 'no cure, no pay,' 'haste makes waste, and waste makes want,' 'live and learn,' 'Love no man: trust no man: speak ill of no man to his face; nor well of any man behind his back' (Ben Jonson), 'to meet, to know, to love, and then to part' (Coleridge), 'Then none were for the party; Then all were for the state; Then the great man help'd the poor, And the poor man, loved the great' (Macaulay).

It will be noticed, however,—and the quotations just given serve to exemplify this, too—that it is not every collocation of words of one syllable that produces an effect of strength, for a great many of the short words most frequently employed are not stressed at all and therefore impress the ear in nearly the same way as prefixes and suffixes do. There is nothing particularly vigorous in the following passage from a modern novel: 'It was as if one had met part of one's self one had lost for a long time,' and in fact most people hearing it read aloud would fail to notice that it consisted of nothing but one-syllable words. Such sentences are not at all rare in colloquial prose, and even in poetry they are found oftener than in most languages, for instance:—

> And there a while it bode; and if a man
> Could touch or see it, he was heal'd at once,
> By faith, of all his ills.
>
> (Tennyson, *The Holy Grail.*)

But then, the weakness resulting from many small connecting words is to some extent compensated in English by the absence of the definite article in a good many cases where other languages think it indispensable, e.g., 'Merry Old England'; 'Heaven and Earth'; 'life is short'; 'dinner is ready'; 'school is over'; 'I saw him at church'; and this peculiarity delivers the language from a number of those short 'empty words,' which when accumulated cannot fail to make the style somewhat weak and prolix.

Business-like shortness is also seen in such convenient abbreviations of sentences as abound in English, for instance, 'While fighting in Germany he was taken prisoner' (= while he was fighting). 'He would not answer when spoken to.' 'To be left till called for.'

'Once at home, he forgot his fears.' 'We had no idea what to do.' 'Did they run? Yes, I made them' (= made them run). 'Shall you play tennis to-day? Yes, we are going to. I should like to, but I can't.' 'Dinner over, he left the house.' Such expressions remind one of the abbreviations used in telegrams; they are syntactical correspondencies to the morphological shortenings that are also of such frequent occurrence in English: cab for cabriolet, bus for omnibus, photo for photograph, phone for telephone, and innumerable others.

This cannot be separated from a certain sobriety in expression. As an Englishman does not like to use more words or more syllables than are strictly necessary, so he does not like to say more than he can stand to. He dislikes strong or hyperbolical expressions of approval or admiration; 'that isn't half bad' or 'she is rather good-looking' are often the highest praises you can draw out of him, and they not seldom express the same warmth of feeling that makes a Frenchman ejaculate his *charmant* or *ravissante* or *adorable*. German *kolossal* or *pyramidal* can often be correctly rendered by English *great* or *biggish*, and where a Frenchman uses his adverbs *extrêmement* or *infiniment*, an Englishman says only *very* or *rather* or *pretty*. '*Quelle horreur!*' is 'That's rather a nuisance.' '*Je suis ravi de vous voir*' is 'Glad to see you,' etc. An Englishman does not like to commit himself by being too enthusiastic or too distressed, and his language accordingly grows sober, too sober perhaps, and even barren when the object is to express emotions. There is in this trait a curious mixture of something praiseworthy, the desire to be strictly true without exaggerating anything or promising more than you can perform, and on the other hand of something blameworthy, the idea that it is affected, or childish and effeminate, to give vent to one's feelings, and the fear of appearing ridiculous by showing strong emotions. But this trait is certainly found more frequently in men than in women, so I may be allowed to add this feature of the English language to the signs of masculinity I have collected.

Those who use many strong words to express their likes or dislikes will generally also make an extensive use of another linguistic appliance, namely violent changes in intonation. Their voices will now suddenly rise to a very high pitch and then as suddenly fall to low tones. An excessive use of this emotional tonic accent is characteristic of many savage nations; in Europe it is found much more in Italy than in the North. In each nation it seems as if it were more employed by women than by men. Now, it has often been observed that the English speak in a more monotonous way than most other nations, so that an extremely slight rising or lowering of the tone indicates what in other languages would require a much greater interval. *'Les Anglais parlent extrêmement bas,'* says H. Taine (*Notes sur l'Angleterre*, p. 66). *'Une société italienne, dans laquelle je me suis fourvoyé par hasard, m'a positivement étourdi; je m'étais habitué à ce ton modéré des voix anglaises.'* Even English ladies are in this respect more restrained than many men belonging to other nations:

> She had the low voice of your English dames,
> Unused, it seems, to need rise half a note
> To catch attention.
>
> (Mrs. Browning, *Aurora Leigh*.)

If we turn to other provinces of the language we shall find our impression strengthened and deepened.

It is worth observing, for instance, how few diminutives the language has and how sparingly it uses them. English in this respect forms a strong contrast to Italian with its *-ino* (*ragazzino, fratellino,* originally a double diminutive), *-ina* (*donnina*), *-etto* (*giovinetto*), *-etta* (*oretta*), *-ello, -ella* (*asinello, storiella*) and other endings, German with its *-chen* and *-lein,* especially South German with its eternal *-le,* Dutch with its *-je,* Russian, Magyar, and Basque with their various endings. The continual recurrence of these endings without any apparent necessity tends to produce the impression that the speakers are innocent, childish, genial beings with no great business capacities or seriousness in life. But in English there are very few of these fondling-endings; *-let* is in the first place a comparatively modern ending, very few of the words in which it is used go back more than a hundred years; and then its extensive use in modern times is chiefly due to the naturalists who want it to express in a short and precise manner certain small organs (*budlet* Darwin; *bladelet* Todd; *conelet* Dana; *bulblet* Gray; *leaflet, fruitlet, featherlet,* etc.)—an employment of the diminutive which is as far removed as possible from the terms of endearment found in other languages. The endings *-kin* and *-ling* (*princekin, princeling*) are not very frequently used and generally express contempt or derision. Then, of course, there is *-y, -ie* (*Billy, Dicky,* *auntie, birdie,* etc.) which corresponds exactly to the fondling-suffixes of other languages; but its application in English is restricted to the nursery and it is hardly ever used by grown-up people except in speaking to children. Besides, this ending is more Scotch than English, and the Scotch with all their deadly earnestness, especially in religious matters, are, perhaps, in some respects more childlike than the English.

The business-like, virile qualities of the English language also manifest themselves in such things as word-order. Words in English do not play at hide-and-seek, as they often do in Latin, for instance, or in German, where ideas that by right belong together are widely sundered in obedience to caprice or, more often, to a rigorous grammatical rule. In English an auxiliary verb does not stand far from its main verb, and a negative will be found in the immediate neighbourhood of the word it negatives, generally the verb (auxiliary). An adjective nearly always stands before its noun; the only really important exception is when there are qualifications added to it which draw it after the noun so that the whole complex serves the purpose of a relative clause: 'a man every way prosperous and talented' (Tennyson), 'an interruption too brief and isolated to attract more notice' (Stevenson). And the same regularity is found in modern English word-order in other respects as well. A few years ago I made my pupils calculate statistically various points in regard to word-order in different languages. I give here only the percentage in some modern authors of sentences in which the subject preceded the verb and the latter in its turn preceded its object (as in 'I saw him' as against 'Him I saw, but not her' or 'Whom did you see?'):—

Shelley, prose 89, poetry 85.
Byron, prose 93, poetry 81.
Macaulay, prose 82.
Carlyle, prose 87.
Tennyson, poetry 88.
Dickens, prose 91.
Swinburne, poetry 83.
Pinero, prose 97.

For the sake of comparison I mention that one Danish prose-writer (J. P. Jacobsen) had 82, a Danish poet (Drachmann) 61,

Goethe (poetry) 30, a modern German prose writer (Tovote) 31, Anatole France 66, Gabriele d'Annunzio 49 per cent of the same word-order. That English has not always had the same regularity, is shown by the figure for *Beowulf* being 16, and for King Alfred's prose 40. Even if I concede that our statistics did not embrace a sufficient number of extracts to give fully reliable results, still it is indisputable that English shows more regularity and less caprice in this respect than most or probably all cognate languages, without however, attaining the rigidity found in Chinese, where the percentage in question would be 100 (or very near it). English has not deprived itself of the expedient of inverting the ordinary order of the members of a sentence when emphasis requires it, but it makes a more sparing use of it than German and the Scandinavian languages, and in most cases it will be found that these languages emphasize without any real necessity, especially in a great many every-day phrases: '*dēr har jeg ikke vēret,*' '*dort bin ich nicht gewesen,*' 'I haven't been there'; '*det kan jeg ikke,*' '*das kann ich nicht,*' 'I can't do that.' How superfluous the emphasis is, is best shown by the usual phrase, '*det veed jeg ikke,*' '*das weiss ich nicht,*' where the Englishman does not even find it necessary to state the object at all: 'I don't know.' Note also that in English the subject precedes the verb after most introductory adverbs: 'now he comes'; 'there he goes,' while German and Danish have, and English had till a few centuries ago, the inverted order: '*jetzt kommt er,*' '*da geht sie*'; '*nu kommer han*'; '*dēr gar hun*'; 'now comes he,' 'there goes she.' Thus order and consistency signalize the modern stage of the English language.

No language is logical in every respect, and we must not expect usage to be guided always by strictly logical principles. It was a frequent error with the older grammarians that whenever the actual grammar of a language did not seem conformable to the rules of abstract logic they blamed the language and wanted to correct it. Without falling into that error we may, nevertheless, compare different languages and judge them by the standard of logic, and here again I think that, apart from Chinese, which has been described as pure applied logic, there is perhaps no language in the civilized world that stands so high as English. Look at the use of the tenses; the difference between the past *he saw* and the composite perfect *he has seen* is maintained with great consistency as compared with the similarly formed tenses in Danish, not to speak of German, so that one of the most constant faults committed by English-speaking Germans is the wrong use of these forms ('Were you in Berlin?' for 'Have you been in (or to) Berlin?,' 'In 1815 Napoleon has been defeated at Waterloo' for 'was defeated'). And then the comparatively recent development of the expanded (or 'progressive') tenses has furnished the language with the wonderfully precise and logically valuable distinction between 'I write' and 'I am writing,' 'I wrote' and 'I was writing.' French has something similar in the distinction between le passé défini (*j'écrivis*) and *l'imparfait* (*j'écrivais*), but on the one hand the former tends to disappear, or rather has already disappeared in the spoken language, at any rate in Paris and in the northern part of the country, so that *j'ai écrit* takes its place and the distinction between 'I wrote' and 'I have written' is abandoned; on the other hand the distinction applies only to the past while in English it is carried through all tenses. Furthermore, the distinction as made in English is superior to the similar one found in the Slavonic languages, in that it is made uniformly in all verbs and in all tenses by means of the same device (*am -ing*), while the Slavonic languages employ a much more complicated system of prepositions and derivative endings, which has almost to be learned separately for each new verb or group of verbs.

In praising the logic of the English language we must not lose sight of the fact that in most cases where, so to speak, the logic of facts or of the exterior world is at war with the logic of grammar, English is free from the narrow-minded pedantry which in most languages sacrifices the former to the latter or makes people shy of saying or writing things which are not 'strictly grammatical.' This is particularly clear with regard to number. *Family* and *clergy* are, grammatically speaking, of the singular number; but in reality they indicate a plurality. Most languages can treat such words only as singulars, but in English one is free to add a verb in the singular if the idea of unity is essential, and then to refer to this unit as *it*, or else to put the verb in the plural and use the pronoun *they*, if the idea of plurality is predominant. It is clear that this liberty of choice is often greatly advantageous. Thus we find sentences like these, 'As the clergy are or are not what they ought to be, so are the rest of the nation' (Miss Austen), or 'the whole race of man (sing.) proclaim it lawful to drink wine' (De Quincey), or 'the club all know that he is a disappointed man' (the same). In 'there are no end of people here that I don't know' (George Eliot) *no end* takes the verb in the plural because it is equivalent to 'many,' and when Shelley writes in one of his letters 'the Quarterly are going to review me' he is thinking of the Quarterly (Review) as a whole staff of writers. Inversely, there is in English a freedom paralleled nowhere else of expressing grammatically a unity consisting of several parts, of saying, for instance, 'I do not think I ever spent a more delightful three weeks' (Ch. Darwin), 'for a quiet twenty minutes,' 'another United States,' *cf.* also 'a fortnight' (originally a fourteen-night); 'three years is but short' (Shakespeare), 'sixpence was offered him' (Ch. Darwin), 'ten minutes is heaps of time' (E. F. Benson), etc., etc.

A great many other phenomena in English show the same freedom from pedantry, as when passive constructions such as 'he was taken no notice of' are allowed, or when adverbs or prepositional complexes may be used attributively as in 'his then residence,' 'an almost reconciliation' (Thackeray), 'men invite their out-College friends' (Steadman), 'smoking his before-breakfast pipe' (Conan Doyle), 'in his threadbare, out-at-elbow shooting-jacket' (G. du Maurier), or when even whole phrases or sentences may be turned into a kind of adjective, as in 'with a quite at home kind of air' (Smedley), 'in the pretty diamond-cut-diamond scene between Pallas and Ulysses' (Ruskin), 'a little man with a puffy Say-nothing-to-me-, -or-I'll-contradict-you sort of countenance' (Dickens), 'With an I-turn-the-crank-of-the-Universe air' (Lowell), 'Rose is simply self-willed; a "she will" or "she won't" sort of little person' (Meredith). Although such combinations as the last-mentioned are only found in more or less jocular style, they show the possibilities of the language, and some expressions of a similar order belong permanently to the language, for instance, 'a would-be artist,' 'a stay-at-home man,' 'a turn-up collar.' Such things—and they might be easily multiplied—are inconceivable in such a language as French, where everything is condemned that does not conform to a definite set of rules laid down by grammarians. The French language is like the stiff French garden of Louis XIV, while the English is like an English park, which is laid out seemingly without any definite plan, and in which you are allowed to walk everywhere according to your own fancy without having to fear a stern keeper enforcing rigorous regulations. The English language would not have been what it is if the English had not been for centuries great respecters of the liberties of each individual and if everybody had not been free to strike out new paths for himself.

This is seen, too, in the vocabulary. In spite of the efforts of several authors of high standing, the English have never suffered an Academy to be instituted among them like the French or Italian Academies, which had as one of their chief tasks the regulation of the vocabulary so that every word not found in their Dictionaries was blamed as unworthy of literary use or distinction. In England every writer is, and has always been, free to take his words where he chooses, whether from the ordinary stock of everyday words, from native dialects, from old authors, or from other languages, dead or living. The consequence has been that English dictionaries comprise a larger number of words than those of any other nation, and that they present a variegated picture of terms from the four quarters of the globe. Now, it seems to be characteristic of the two sexes in their relation to language that women move in narrower circles of the vocabulary, in which they attain to perfect mastery so that the flow of words is always natural and, above all, never needs to stop, while men know more words and always want to be more precise in choosing the exact word with which to render their idea, the consequence being often less fluency and more hesitation. It has been statistically shown that a comparatively greater number of stammerers and stutterers are found among men (boys) than among women (girls). Teachers of foreign languages have many occasions to admire the ease with which female students express themselves in another language after so short a time of study that most men would be able to say only few words hesitatingly and falteringly, but if they are put to the test of translating a difficult piece either from or into the foreign language, the men will generally prove superior to the women. With regard to their native language the same difference is found, though it is perhaps not so easy to observe. At any rate our assertion is corroborated by the fact observed by every student of languages that novels written by ladies are much easier to read and contain much fewer difficult words than those written by men. All this seems to justify us in setting down the enormous richness of the English vocabulary to the same masculinity of the English nation which we have now encountered in so many various fields.

To sum up: The English language is a methodical, energetic, business-like and sober language, that does not care much for finery and elegance, but does care for logical consistency and is opposed to any attempt to narrow-in life by police regulations and strict rules either of grammar or of lexicon. As the language is, so also is the nation,

> For words, like Nature, half reveal
> And half conceal the Soul within.
>
> (Tennyson.)

CHANGES IN THE ENGLISH LANGUAGE*

J. N. Hook and E. G. Mathews

▶ *Examples of Old English*

At first glance a selection from Old English appears to be in a foreign tongue. More careful scrutiny reveals that some of the words are almost the same as ours, that others have undergone considerable change, and that still others have vanished. Modern English has lost some of the grammatical constructions that formerly existed.

Here is the Lord's Prayer in the Old English (West Saxon) version of approximately a thousand years ago:

Fæder ūre þū þe eart on heofonum sī þīn nama gehālgod. Tō becume þīn rīce. Gewurþe ðīn willa on eorðan swā swā on heofonum. Ūrne gedæghwāmlīcan hlāf syle ūs tō dæg. And forgyf ūs ūre gyltas swā swā wē forgyfað ūrum gyltendum. And ne gelæd þū ūs on costnunge ac ālys ūs of yfele. Sōþlīce.

Detailed comment on these few lines would fill many pages; here we shall look at only a few words and constructions. Word order was much less fixed in Old English than it is today: notice the Old English forms of *Father our* and *be thy name hallowed* as examples. Case endings are used with nouns, as in *heofonum* (heaven), *eorðan* (earth), *gyltas* (debts), and *gyltendum* (debtors). Adjectives had to agree in case, number, and gender with their nouns: *ūre, ūrne,* and *ūrum* are today simply our. The word *rīce* is now translated as *kingdom,* but it is actually a cognate of *Reich* which survives in German. The symbols þ (thorn) and ð (eth) were both used for *th.* Since Old English times some words have

---

been reduced in the number of syllables: *gehālgod* (hallowed), *gedæghwāmlīcan* (daily), *forgyfað* (forgive). Spelling was much more phonetic than that of today; in general, there were no silent letters. In pronunciation, vowel sounds were more similar to those found in modern continental languages than to those in Modern English; and consonant sounds were not much different from those of Modern English. Punctuation marks other than periods were not used very systematically by the scribes.

As a second example consider the following lines from the epic poem *Beowulf*. The manuscript is generally believed to be in the hand of a scribe of the late tenth century. This passage tells of King Hrothgar's sorrow over the killing of his friend and follower by a hideous demon:

Hrothgar spoke
Hrōðgar maþelode

defender of the Scyldings
helm Scyldinga:

Not ask thou about happiness.
Ne frīn þū æfter sælum

Sorrow is renewed
Sorh is genīwod

Of the Danes for the people
Denigea lēodum.

Dead is Aeschere
Dēad is Æschere

Irmenlaf's
Yrmenlāfes

elder brother
yldra brōþor

my confidant
mīn rūnwita

and my counselor
ond mīn rǣdbora

shoulder-companion
eaxlgestealla

when we in battle
ðonne wē on orlege

head protected
hafelan weredon

when clashed together troops
þonne hniton fēþan

boar-helmets struck
eoferas cnysedan

Such should hero be
Swylc scolde eorl wesan

nobleman good from old times
æþeling ǣrgōd

as Aeschere was.
swylc Æschere wæs.

Even the literal translation of this passage does not seem very clear today. A more free translation might go like this: "Hrothgar, the defender of the Scyldings, spoke: 'Do not ask about happiness, because sorrow has come again to the Danish people. Aeschere is dead. He was Irmenlaf's older brother and my confidant and counselor. He stood at my shoulder when in battle we protected our heads and hewed the boar-helmets as troops clashed. Every hero should be as Aeschere was, a nobleman good to recall from old times.' "

Notice, in comparing these translations, how word order has changed. Observe also how large a proportion of the Old English words have dropped out of the language. Some of them remain, however, in recognizable form: *helm* is a cousin of our *helmets*, *æfter* is *after*, *dēad* has changed only its pronunciation, *yldra brōþor* is still recognizable, *þonne* has become *then*, *wē* and *is* are unchanged in spelling, *scolde* is similar to *should*, *eorl* has altered its meaning and become *earl*, *ærgōd* contains the ancestors of *ere* and *good*, and *wæs* is obviously *was*.

Inflectional endings are much more important in Old English than in Modern; for example, *Scyldinga* (genitive plural) requires here a three-word translation, *of the Scyldings;* and *lēodum* also requires either a three-word translation, *for* (or *to*) *the people*, or a revised word order. The endings of such words as *rūnwita*, *fēþan*, and *eoferas* help, along with the context, to show whether the word is to be regarded as a subject or an object. In Modern English we depend more upon word order and upon "function words" such as prepositions than we do upon inflections.

Old English grammar may be made a subject for special study. Here you have seen illustrated only a few of its most obvious characteristics.

▶ *Example of Middle English*

When we move forward about four hundred years, from the late tenth to the late fourteenth century, we see that the language has changed rather drastically. Here are lines from the Prologue of Chaucer's *Canterbury Tales*, describing the squire, son of the knight:

With him ther was his sone a yong Squyer
    (lover)   (aspirant to knighthood)
A lovyere and a lusty bacheler
                 (curly) (as if)
With lokkes crulle as they were leyd in presse.

Of twenty yeer of age he was I gesse.

. . . .

(Embroidered)   (meadow)
Embrouded was he, as it were a mede
                    (flowers)
Al ful of fresshe floures whyte and rede.
                              (playing the flute)
Singinge he was or floyting al the day.
He was as fresh as is the month of May.
Short was his goune with sleves long and wyde.
                              (excellently)
Wel coude he sitte on hors and faire ryde.
                                        (compose the words)
He coude songes make and wel endyte
(Joust)   (draw)
Juste and eek daunce and wel purtreye and wryte.
    (hotly)   (in the night-time)
So hote he lovede that by nightertale
He sleep namore than dooth a nightingale.

This passage is closer to Modern English in word order than most Old English was. Only in two or three places, such as "He coude songes make," does the order seem very strange to us. Inflectional endings of Middle English were considerably reduced from Old English. In a noun an -s or -es usually signified either a genitive singular or any case of the plural. (The battle between an -s and an -en plural was almost decided by Chaucer's time, although in a few words such as *oxen* the -en plural never surrendered.) Adjectival forms had in general been reduced to two, one for the "strong" singular, and a second for the strong plural and the "weak" singular and plural. Verbs were somewhat simplified also; in the past tense no distinction was retained between singular and plural or between first, second, and third person, and the past tense and past participle were often identical, as they are in most verbs today.

Of all the things that have happened to English, the reduction of inflectional endings and the increased inflexibility of word order have been most important in giving the language its modern characteristics. Although these changes were not completed in Middle

English and will never be completed while the language lives, they were far advanced by the year 1500, a date chosen rather arbitrarily as the beginning of Modern English.

▶ *Some of the Developments in Modern English*

Since 1500 English word order has become still more fixed, and living inflections have been reduced to seven: an -*s* or -*es* plural for nearly all nouns, an -*s* ending for most third person singular verbs in the present tense, an -*ed* ending for most verbs in the past tense, an -*ing* form for verbs, a special past participle for some verbs, an -*er* ending for the comparative degree of many adjectives and some adverbs, and an -*est* ending for the superlative degree of the same words.

In other ways grammar has changed only slightly. Representative of the many comparatively small changes are the use of *do* in questions (*Does he consent?* rather than Elizabethan *Consents he?*) and the growth in frequency of the progressive tenses. (*He was speaking*, for instance, often replacing *He spoke*). Steadily increasing reliance upon prepositional phrases, greater employment of subordinate clauses, the increase in verb-adverb (or verb-preposition) combinations ("I ran into an old friend"), and a tendency to use almost any word as more than one part of speech—these are but a few of the Modern English developments that later will be treated in more detail.

In the eighteenth century some grammarians, failing to recognize the inevitability of linguistic change, strove to stop or at least retard it. They believed that change in a language is undesirable; since Latin was the most highly regarded language, and since Latin had not changed much in fifteen hundred years or so, change must be bad. (Those who held this theory failed to realize that Latin would probably have changed a great deal if it had not become a dead language, and that in monks' Latin it actually did change considerably.) They believed also that the loss of inflections should be stopped to prevent further "deterioration."

The results of the efforts of these few grammarians may be illustrated by referring to a couple of pronouns and a few verbs. The distinction between *who* and *whom*, which is not essential for clarity, was erratically observed during the eighteenth century. But under pressure from prescriptive grammarians, teachers and editors began to insist upon strict maintenance of *whom* as an object. Several verbs, including *blow, know,* and *throw,* were moving toward a "weak" or "regular" past tense and past participle: *blow, blowed, blowed,* and so on. They were thus following other verbs that had made the shift without hurting the language: as examples, *help* once had *healp* as one past form and *holpen* as the past participle; *climb* had *clamb* and *clumben; chew* had *ceaw* and *cowen.* Certainly *blowed* would be no worse than *climbed* or *chewed,* but the prescribers wanted no more "deterioration." As a result of their efforts and those of their intellectual descendants the use of *blowed, knowed,* and *throwed* may even today keep an able person from being employed for a white collar position.

Similarly, in the eighteenth century, a tendency toward identical forms for past tense and past participle was noticeable. The verb *sing* was tending toward *sing, sung, sung; write* toward *write, wrote, wrote.* The original title of Thomas Gray's most famous poem was "Elegy Wrote in a Country Church-yard." But once more the reactionaries went to work, and the schools ever since have insisted upon different forms for the past tense and past participle of *drink, give, ride, shrink, sing, sink, write,* and other verbs. How many million child-hours have been spent on mastering these forms is beyond calculation. Totally false conceptions of "correctness" have resulted from this wasted effort.

Perhaps the most noticeable change that has occurred since 1500 is not in grammar but in vocabulary. Through borrowings from dead Latin, dead Greek, and most of the important living languages of the world, English has multiplied its store of words manyfold. Since no one can precisely define what a word is, no one can say how many words are now in the language. One clue to the number is that unabridged dictionaries have about 600,000 entries. But since no lexicographer would claim that his dictionary lists every existing word in the language, the total may be much larger.

▶ Why the Language Has Changed

A language changes because things happen to people. If we could imagine the impossible—a society in which nothing happened— there would be no changes in language. But except possibly in a cemetery, things are constantly happening to people: they eat, drink, sleep, talk, make love, meet strangers, struggle against natural perils, and fight against one another. They slowly adapt their language to meet the changing conditions of their lives. Although the changes made in one generation may be small, those made in a dozen generations may enormously affect the language. The big and little phases of history—fashions, fads, inventions, the influence of a leader, a war or two, an invasion or two, travel to a foreign land, the demands of business intercourse—may alter a language so much that a Rip Van Winkle who slept two or three hundred years might have trouble in making himself understood when he awoke. Even in a relatively quiet society, linguistic change proceeds inexorably.

Think, if you will, of the English language as a river. Its headwaters are the closely interrelated Teutonic languages of the Angles, Saxons, and Jutes, who lived mainly in the northern part of what is now Germany. They provided the basic grammatical structure of the language that we call English; they provided most of its linguistic heritage; they provided its basic words, the common everyday words that still are the most important in our simple communications. But to the basic elements brought in by these Teutonic peoples many additions have been made.

When the Teutons began invading and settling in the British Isles in 449 A.D., they found in possession the Celts, who previously had been pushed about by Roman soldiers for several centuries. The Teutons pushed the Celts about some more, finally tending to localize them in what we now call Ireland, Wales, and parts of Scotland. But the Teutonic language was influenced somewhat by the Celtic and indirectly by the Latin which the Celts had fragmentarily learned. So in English we have words of Celtic ancestry such as *brat, cairn,* and *crag,* and the place names *Aberdeen* (*aber* = river mouth), *Avon* (river), *Caerleon, Cardiff, Carlyle* (*caer* or *car* = fortress), *Dundee, Dunbarton, Dunbar* (*dun* = hill), *Inchcape* (*inch* = island), *Kildare, Kilpatrick* (*kill* = church). And as a result of the early and indirect Latin tributary (which existed on the Continent even before the invasions of Britain) we have *wall* and *street* and *port,* words that give promise of enduring even longer than the Roman constructions that they name; and we have place names: Roman *Londinium* (originally Celtic) is now *London, Eboracum* (also once Celtic) has undergone considerable transformation to appear as *York,* and Latin *castra,* a military camp, appears both in England and the United States in *Lancaster, Worcester, Leicester, Gloucester, Chester, Dorchester, Rochester.* Thus Latin and Celtic are early tributaries of English.

By the end of the sixth century Latin was to renew its influence upon English. In 597 Roman missionaries began coming to the

British Isles in an attempt to Christianize the inhabitants. They introduced such church words as *altar, creed, mass,* and *nun* and some homely words such as *beet, pine, cheese,* and *cup.* Some of the words that the priests brought over had been borrowed by Latin from Greek: *bishop, deacon, martyr, church, devil, priest, monk, pope, psalm, dish,* and *plum.* So once more a double tributary entered the river of the English language.

In the seventh and most of the eighth centuries the Anglo-Saxon inhabitants of the British Isles lived a relatively peaceful existence—simple by modern standards, but maybe happier than a more complex society can be. But starting in about 790, "Northmen" or Danes began to invade the islands. They were rough and vigorous; in 793, "the heathen men miserably destroyed God's church at Lindisfarne with rapine and slaughter," a contemporary account says. The forays grew into expeditions; the Danes began to colonize; Alfred the Great for a while paid them tribute but then organized military forces and compelled the invaders to sign a peace treaty. One of the terms of the treaty was that the Danes accept Christianity. Since the chief difference between the Danes and Anglo-Saxons had been in religion, this concession meant that the two groups, already speaking kindred and often mutually intelligible languages, would merge. However, attacks by new groups of Danes, not covered by the treaty, continued, and early in the eleventh century a Danish king, Cnut, ruled in England.

It is often difficult to separate the linguistic contributions of the Danes from the closely related Anglo-Saxon, but apparently we owe to Danish such words as *fellow, husband, law, wrong,* and a number of words with an *sk* sound, as *skill, scale, scare, skirt* (*shirt,* a cognate form, is from Anglo-Saxon), *skin, sky, score,* and *bask.* Numerous English place names are Danish in origin. Danish *thwaite* (piece of ground) appears in many names such as *Stonethwaite, Hallthwaite; thorp* (village) is in names like *Lowthorpe* and *Northorpe; by* (town) is in *Derby, Kirby, Selby, Whitby,* etc.; *toft* (a clearing) is in *Lowestoft.*

The next big tributary came from north via east. Northmen, later called Normans, had begun moving into France at about the time that the Danes invaded England. They were flexible people who adopted French as their language, changing it somewhat in the process. They made of Normandy one of the most vigorous and ambitious states of Europe. In 1066, after the death of England's Edward the Confessor, the Duke of Normandy decided that

he would attempt to gain the crown of his late cousin, and at
Hastings he earned the more glorious title of William the Conqueror. His people moved into the British Isles, relegated natives
to the rank of second-class citizens, and eventually concentrated
their grip upon England as they lost their continental footholds.

Now began the period of greatest linguistic turmoil that English
has known. England was a country of two languages: the Norman
French of the ruling classes and the English of the conquered. The
Bishop of Worcester was deposed in 1095 because he was "an
idiot who did not know French." French was used in the churches,
in the courts, in important business transactions, and in the schools.
But inevitably the two groups had to meet. A French landowner
had to give instructions to his tenants; an English farmer or smith
had to try to sell his goods or his skills; intermarriage became frequent. Each group picked up words from the other. However, just
as American occupation troops learned only the rudiments of German, Italian, and Japanese after World War II, the Normans did
not learn the intricacies of English nor did the English learn the
intricacies of Norman French. Each group learned only the fundamentals.

Before the Norman conquest there had been signs that grammatical inflections were being reduced—the dative and accusative
cases, for instance, were blending their forms. But the coming of
the Normans seems to have expedited such change. At any rate,
after the Normans had been in England for about three centuries,
English inflections were not nearly so numerous.

The two groups gradually blended. So did their vocabularies,
and to a much smaller extent their grammar, although the impact
of Norman French upon English was less than one might think.
But partly as a result of that impact, and more largely as a result
of other, less tangible causes, grammatical gender was replaced
by natural gender, word order became less free as inflections were
reduced, pronunciations changed, and many words from Norman
French, French, and Latin entered the language.

Chaucer's contemporary, John Gower, in the fourteenth century wrote three major works—one in English, one in French, and
one in Latin. He chose three languages because he was not sure
which language would become standard in England, and he
wanted one of his works to be in the language that endured. Had
he lived fifty years later, he would have had no difficulty in seeing
that English was going to be the winner.

During the Renaissance two more large tributaries entered English. These, of course, were in the form of additional Latin and Greek contributions. Thousands of words came into the English vocabulary during this period, including huge numbers of relatively useless terms that lived briefly and were then buried in soon-to-be-forgotten graves. English spellings were also influenced by the new interest in the Classical languages. Learned men perhaps foolishly proclaimed that the orthography of English words should reveal their Latin backgrounds. They therefore recommended the spellings *debt* and *doubt,* even though the *b*'s in these words were not pronounced, and even though the French, from whom the English had borrowed both words, had already dropped the *b*'s that existed in Latin. A number of words with *tion,* like *nation,* had also been taken from the French, which often used a phonetically accurate *c* instead of *t;* in English the sound in question was pronounced as *s* or *sh,* but Renaissance scholars insisted that the Latin *t* be retained. Many other of our present illogical spellings may be attributed to the scholars of the Renaissance.

During the Renaissance period and later, the feeling grew that English grammar should be described in the terminology of Latin grammar. Sometimes that procedure was not objectionable, for many elements of the two languages were similar. But when the grammarians insisted upon finding in English everything that existed in Latin, when they made of Latin a procrustean bed into which English must be in some way fitted, and when they ignored the fact that English was basically a Teutonic and not an Italic language, they did irreparable harm to many generations of persons who wanted to acquire a clear understanding of the structure and peculiarities of the language.

Since the Renaissance, many small tributaries have enlarged the stream of English. These cannot be listed in chronological order. Latin has kept appearing, as have French and Greek. Italian has contributed many of the technical terms of music. Dutch has given sailing terms like *ahoy, boom, deck, hoist, skipper, sloop,* and *yacht.* Spanish has given, directly or indirectly, miscellaneous words like *matador, vanilla, armada, alligator,* and *mosquito.* North American Indian has contributed such words as *hominy, Mississippi* (an Algonquin word meaning "big river," not "Father of Waters"), *moccasin, moose, opossum, papoose, pemmican, raccoon, skunk, squaw, toboggan, tomahawk, wampum,* and *wigwam.*

Among other contributing languages, with one or two representative words from each, have been Bengali (*bungalow*); Persian (*azure*); Slavic (*polka, vampire, mammoth*); Hebrew (*amen, hallelujah, behemoth*); Hungarian (*goulash*); Tartar (*khan*); Malay (*amuck, gong, cockatoo*); Indian (*rajah, nabob, khaki, yogi*); Australian (*boomerang, kangaroo*); South American Indian (*alpaca, condor, jaguar, quinine*); Polynesian (*taboo, tattoo*); African (*gumbo, mumbo jumbo, okra*). Even Chinese has given us some words (*tea, typhoon, chop suey*, and *chow mein*); Chinese pidgin English has contributed the familiar *chop-stick;* Japanese has given us *tycoon, kimono, judo*, and *ju-jitsu*.

The borrowing has of course gone the other way, also, although the details need not concern us here. English and American gastronomic and athletic terms, for instance, have been incorporated in many European languages. An American can use the terms *cocktail* and *beefsteak* with satisfactory results in almost any European restaurant.

Why did English change? Simply because many things happened to many people in many countries. Had the Angles, Saxons, and Jutes moved southeast instead of southwest, the language of the British Isles might never have been Teutonic. Had Harold defeated William the Conqueror at Hastings in 1066, the language of today might have been considerably different, perhaps more complicated in morphology, more simple in syntax. Had the English been stay-at-homes, their language might have lacked some of the versatility, the expressiveness, and the color that we believe it now has.

CHANGING MEANINGS AND VALUES OF WORDS*

Stuart Robertson and Frederic G. Cassidy

The study of meaning in language is called Semasiology or Semantics. The latter term, however, has recently been used widely to refer to what is properly called General Semantics, a study allied

* From Stuart Robertson and Frederic G. Cassidy, *The Development of Modern English*, Second Edition, ©, 1954, by Prentice-Hall, Inc., Englewood Cliffs, N.J. Reprinted by permission.

more closely to the field of philosophy than to that of linguistics, and which therefore will not be dealt with [here]. The term *Semantics* nevertheless has application within the field of linguistics; there it is limited at present to the description of the meanings which words or other units of language convey, and, when these are seen historically, also to the various types of meaning-change that occur.

But the word "meaning" itself poses difficult problems. What is the meaning of "meaning"? We all recognize that language is a give-and-take of speech-signals, a series of stimuli by speakers and responses by hearers; also that some non-linguistic stimuli produce linguistic responses, and *vice versa*. (Thus a kiss may produce the response "Darling!"—and *vice versa*.) When the hearer of a linguistic stimulus responds to it in some predictable way, we say, in common parlance, that he has "understood" the speaker. But we are by no means certain—here we must throw ourselves upon the psychologists—what goes on inside the hearer's nervous system between his hearing of the words and his response to them. The student of language therefore limits himself to an investigation of the parts of the process which are clearly accessible, and with which he can deal with some degree of objectivity. Less and less do linguists raise the question of "ideas" or "concepts" in the mind; today they generally define meaning as simply the situation out of which language comes and the response that it elicits.

If this is meaning, how does it change? It is clear that, for speakers of the same language, there must be a large measure of consistency in the response to linguistic signals—otherwise, communication would be impossible. Nevertheless, since no two situations can ever be exactly alike, there is always some area of variation, and over a period of time the increment of slight variations will alter the reference of the linguistic signal. Let us take an example. Since meaning involves both the situation out of which a word comes (which makes the speaker say it) and the hearer's response, every speech situation is complex, with many components. But the relative prominence of these components will not always be the same. When the word *green* is first said it ordinarily brings a response in terms of color; but if the context concerns a fruit, this primary element of color may become associated with a secondary element—unripeness. Repetition may then establish this association until the element of unripeness becomes more prominent than that of color—so much so that it becomes possible to say, without fear of misunderstanding, "Blackberries are red when they are green."

Every new focus of prominence, once established, may beget others: when fruit and young people are associated, the element of unripeness may be paralleled with inexperience, and the latter may then assume primary prominence in such a statement as, "Those freshmen are pretty green." Thus a series of shifts in focus, from one element in a situation to others, will produce shifts in meaning—or "new meanings"—for words. In this example, *green* has acquired two new meanings and lost none; but many a word, after shifting, has lost its first meaning entirely. Indeed, over the centuries meanings grow and decay in a surprising variety of ways, the chief of which we are to examine in this chapter.

Yet before proceeding we must give attention to one more point. Even though it is generally recognized that meanings change, many people still cling, curiously enough, to the quite contradictory notion that words all have "true" meanings, that changes somehow take us away from the "true" meaning, and that the way to find out what a word "really means" is to find out what it once meant. This is particularly true in respect to borrowed words in English, the belief evidently being that the meaning of the word in contemporary English and the meaning of the Latin or Greek word from which the English word is derived must be one and the same. A little reflection should show that an appeal to etymology in order to establish the present meaning of the word is as untrustworthy as an appeal to spelling in order to establish its present pronunciation. And for a reason that is almost exactly parallel: change of *meaning* is likely to have altered the etymological sense, which is thereby rendered archaic or obsolete, just as change of *sound* is likely to be unrecorded in the "antiquarian" spelling that so frequently characterizes Modern English. The study of etymology has great value and interest—a point to which we shall later return—but its usefulness in settling the question of what a word means is subject to considerable qualification.

Let us see what results when one ignores the idea that a word may change its meaning, and appeals to its etymology in order to determine its present meaning. A handbook of only twenty-odd years ago on "correct English" sets forth the following dictum: "*Dilapidated* . . . Said of a building or other structure. But the word is from the Latin *lapis*, a stone, and cannot properly be used of any but a stone structure." One might just as reasonably argue that because *candidate* is related to the Latin *candidus* (white), it cannot properly be used of an aspirant for political office unless he is clothed in a suit of white material. More clearly even, one might protest that *holiday* properly describes Christmas or Easter, but should never be used of Independence Day or Labor Day; or that *bonfire* should not be applied except where the combustible material is bone. These arguments are not much more grotesque than some that have been seriously maintained in defense of an etymological crotchet, while ignoring the fact of change of meaning. Indeed, one who argues on this basis is a victim of the "etymological fallacy."

The fact is that what a word once meant is not necessarily what it now means; the etymological meaning has often died out, and a quite new development is the living descendant. This is particularly true of words in common or popular use. Words, after all, are for the most part purely conventional symbols. They mean only what those who are using them agree to make them mean. Exactly the same principles apply to "learned" words, but because their traditional users have generally known the language from which they were borrowed, or of whose elements they were composed, they have tended to preserve the etymological meaning— indeed, it is conventional to use such words with an eye to their source; thus they are less prone to alterations of meaning than are popular words. It is in this way, incidentally, that a cultural tradition holds in check, to some extent, the constant tendency of language to change.[1]

Change of meaning, however, though usually unpredictable, is not utterly arbitrary; as we shall see in a moment, it often proceeds along familiar paths. Furthermore, though it takes place in all languages, it does not proceed at the same rate even in related ones. If we look at cognate words in English and German, for example, which might have been expected to have the same meaning, we often find them widely different, and the difference is most commonly the result of some radical change of sense in the English word. Opposite instances can be found, admittedly, in which the English word has stood still and the German one changed;

---

[1] Some of this holding in check is unconscious, some conscious.

yet it is usually the latter which is conservative. Examples of this characteristic English shift in meaning are the following: *Schlagen* and *slay* are originally the same word, but the German word retains the general meaning of "smite" or "strike" while the English word has become narrowed to mean "strike with fatal consequences" or "kill."[2] *Knabe* is the cognate in German of Old English *cnapa* or *cnafa*, and has the same meaning, "boy"; but Modern English *knave* has a radically different one; the German *Tier* means any kind of animal, as did the cognate Old English *deor*, but in Modern English *deer* means one particular kind of animal.

▶ *Generalization and Specialization*

One very common type of change is that in which the "area" of the meaning is changed. When a word that has referred broadly or inclusively begins instead to refer narrowly or exclusively, this is an example of "specialization" of meaning; the contrary is called "generalization." Interestingly enough, the same word may undergo both processes at different stages of the development of its meaning. *Go*, for example, is a verb of motion that seems as general as possible in meaning, and presumably this is also the basic meaning; early in its history in English, however, it must have specialized, for Old English *gān* sometimes means "walk," and in Middle English *ryde* or *gon* (ride or walk) is a familiar formula. Although the present meaning is the generalized one, the specialization "walk" was still possible in the late seventeenth century, as we see in these phrases from Bunyan: "I am resolved to run when I can, to go when I cannot run, and to creep when I cannot go."

Borrowed words are quite as likely as native ones to undergo such transformations in meaning. *Virtue* is connected with Latin *vir* (man). Thus, *virtue* first meant "manliness" in general; but its meaning later specialized to stand for the manly quality most in demand in the military state, namely "fortitude" or "warlike prowess"—the meaning familiar in Caesar's *Commentaries*. But a still later Latin meaning is more comprehensive, and it was this very general meaning that was attached to *virtue* when it was borrowed in English through French. One possible specialization was "power," as in "Virtue had gone out of him," or even "magical

2 The Latin word *caedere*, though unrelated to English *slay*, has undergone exactly the same specialization of meaning.

power," as in "the virtue of the spell" or Milton's "virtuous ring and glass." More commonly, however, the word in English retained a general sense of "noble quality"—though more and more with reference to moral rather than to mental or physical characteristics. But another specialization limits its application to women; for example, "All the sons were brave, and all the daughters virtuous," where *virtuous* is equivalent to "chaste." "A woman's virtue" will today be interpreted in only the last sense. A curious evolution, indeed, when one recalls that the etymological meaning is "manliness."

The foregoing are particularly striking examples, but hundreds of others could be cited. We find generalization in such everyday words as *picture*, once restricted, as the etymology would suggest (compare: the *Picts*, "painted ones"), to a *painted* representation of something seen, but now applicable to photograph, crayon drawing, and so forth; *butcher*, who once slew one animal only, the goat (French *bouc*); the verb *sail*, which has been transferred to *steam* navigation, just as *drive* has been transferred to self-propelled vehicles; *injury*, which once was limited to "injustice"; *zest*, which meant "bit of lemon-peel"; *chest*, which usually meant "coffin"—"He is now deed and nayled in his cheste";[3] *pen*, which meant "feather," but which is now much more likely to mean a writing implement tipped with metal than a quill; *quarantine*, from which the original meaning of a "forty" days' isolation has quite disappeared; and *companion*, which has likewise lost the etymological sense of "one who (shares) bread with" another.

But generalization of meaning does not always stay within bounds; under some conditions the meaning becomes so broad that, in extreme cases, there is hardly any meaning left. We have a whole set of words, used conversationally when we either do not know, or cannot remember, or perhaps will not take the trouble to search for a more precise term: the *what-you-may-call-it* kind of word—*thingumabob, doohickey, jigger,* and so on. Not so long ago *gadget* was imported into the U.S. from England, and has found a very hearty welcome into this company.

Another type, in which generalization goes even farther, has aroused strong opposition from guardians of literary style, who realize that emptiness and "jargon" result from the indiscriminate

---

[3] Chaucer's clerk, speaking of Petrarch (*Clerk's Prologue*, line 30).

use of "words that mean little or nothing, but may stand for almost anything": such words are *thing, business, concern, condition, matter, article, circumstance*. As we all recognize at once, these are words that have a fairly exact sense, but which also have acquired the ability to fit into a wide variety of everyday contexts, in which their meaning becomes extremely vague—in fact, almost wholly dependent on the context. The word *deal* is the current American favorite in this group, its gamut of meaning running all the way from perfectly favorable ("Your job sounds like a pretty fine deal") to thoroughly unfavorable ("I won't take part in any of his deals"). This word serves the purpose, and is going through the same general sort of development, that *proposition* did a generation ago.

Even more frequent than generalization, and even more readily illustrated in numberless familiar instances, is the opposite process of specialization. *Steorfan* is an Old English word, cognate with the German *sterben,* which meant "die"; but the standard Modern English meaning ("starve") is a specialized one, namely "die from hunger." Another specialization, "die from cold," is found in certain Modern English dialects: "[he] . . . bid her come . . . sit close by the fire: he was sure she was starved" is from the Yorkshire dialect of *Wuthering Heights* (Chapter XXX). The older meaning of *meat* was "food" in general, as one might suspect from the archaic phrase *meat and drink* and from the compound *sweetmeat.* It is interesting to observe, incidentally, that the German cognate for *flesh, Fleisch,* suggests first of all the specialized sense of "meat"; this is the present meaning, too, of French *viande,* while the English *viands* retains the general sense of "food." *Coast* is a borrowing, through French, from a Latin word for "side" or "rib" (compare Modern English *intercostal*), and once meant "border" or "frontier"—the "coast of Bohemia" was not always an absurdity. But *coast* in present use not only has the usual specialization "seashore"; as employed in the eastern United States, it means specifically "Pacific coast." *Shore,* on the other hand, means, in parts of the east at any rate, "Atlantic shore."[4] In some of the same localities, however, "eastern shore" means what elsewhere

---

4 In Philadelphia it is often used in a still more specific sense, "southern New Jersey shore"; it sometimes bears a yet more localized signification: "Atlantic City," which occurs repeatedly in the headlines of Philadelphia newspapers.

would have to be expanded into "eastern shore of the Chesapeake in Maryland," just as in part of New England "the cape" means definitely "Cape Cod." *Token* formerly had the broad meaning "sign," but was long ago specialized to mean a physical thing that is a sign (of something)—as in *love token*, or the metal tokens used on streetcars or buses.

An *undertaker* once could undertake to do anything; nowadays he only undertakes to manage funerals. So, to people in general, *doctor* stands only for *doctor of medicine*. *Liquor*, which once was synonymous with *liquid*, is now definitely specialized. *Reek*, like the German *rauchen*, once had the broad meaning "smoke," as it still has in the Scotch dialect; but the standard Modern English use limits it quite definitely to unpleasant exhalations. *Disease* meant "discomfort"—"lack of ease" in general. *Girl* meant "young person" (of either sex). The limitation of *corpse* to "dead body" made it necessary to re-borrow the word in its Modern French form *corps* for another possible meaning of "body," and to make occasional use of the original Latin, *corpus*, for still another sense, "complete collection of writings." *Corn*, in general American use, will be immediately understood as "Indian corn" or "maize." But the word itself once meant simply "grain," and so, in other parts of the English-speaking world, it is differently specialized—in Scotland, to mean "oats," and in England "wheat." Keats's allusion to "Ruth amid the alien corn" probably calls up, to many American readers, a very different picture from what the poet had in mind.

What are the factors that account for specialization of meaning? One is, of course, that localities and groups of people have their own specialized associations for words that otherwise may convey a broader meaning. It has been well remarked that "every man is his own specializer." *Pipe*, for example, calls up different ideas in the mind of the smoker, the plumber, and the organist. *Ring* may be thought of in connection with jewelry, opera, politics, or pugilism—even though, in the last connection, the "squared circle" has long since superseded the original truly circular shape. Quite apart from particular or local specializations, however, there are a great many words whose meaning has become specialized for nearly everybody. A second factor that helps to account for both generalization and specialization is the fading of the etymological significance of the word. Thus, to illustrate the one point, *arrive* [<Lat. *ad* (to) + *ripa* (shore)] originally applied to the end of a

voyage only, and was used without the preposition, since this was included in the word. Milton's "ere he arrive the happy isle" illustrates a use that is in strict accord with the etymology of the word. When, however, consciousness of the Latin parts that made up the word was weakened, it was no longer used transitively, but in the phrase "arrive at," and with the more generalized application to the end of any journey.

Yet another factor is the competition among synonymous words. The borrowing of the Latin *animal* and the French *beast* meant that, with the native *deer,* English would have possessed three exactly synonymous terms for one idea; it is obviously in the interest of economy that *deer* should have specialized to mean one particular species of animal rather than "animal" in general, and that *beast* should have acquired connotations that limit its sphere. *Bird* and *fowl, dog* and *hound, boy* and *knave, chair* and *stool* are further instances of words that were once synonyms but that have been differentiated in meaning here by the specialization of the second term of each pair.

A further remark about generalization and specialization is suggested by some of the words just alluded to. The degree of specialization which a language exhibits seems to depend on cultural need. In a culture in which the coconut is essential—as in Polynesia—an extremely complex vocabulary is said to have grown up, with different terms for many stages of ripeness of the fruit. So also, the Eskimos have different terms for falling snow, snow on the ground, snow packed hard like ice, slushy snow, wind-driven flying snow, and other kinds. Many similar examples could be cited, for the language of peoples of undeveloped culture appear to be particularly rich in specialized terms. At one time in the course of the English language it must have seemed desirable to speakers to make verbal distinctions in connection with groups of animals—mostly those of interest to farmers and hunters. An elaborate set of what are called "company terms" was accordingly developed, some (but by no means all) of which survive today. The better known ones include a *herd* or a *drove* of cattle, but of a *flock* of sheep (or birds), a *school* of fish, a *pack* of wolves (or hounds), a *covey* of partridges, and a *swarm* of bees. But there are others far more esoteric, such as *nye* of pheasants, *cete* of badgers, *sord* of mallards, *wisp* of snipe, *doylt* of tame swine, *gaggle* of geese, *harras* of horses, and *kennel* of raches. There is a similar profusion of names for the same animal (*cow, heifer, bull, calf, steer,* and *ox*), the young of various animals (*puppy, kitten, kid, calf, colt, lamb,* and so forth), and the male and female of the same species (*gander* and *goose, drake* and *duck, horse* and *mare, cock* and *hen, dog* and *bitch*). The need for a generic term is of course particularly felt here, and it is supplied, not quite satisfactorily, by the convention of making either the name of the male (*horse* and *dog*) or of the female (*cow, duck,* and *goose*), or even that of the young of the species (*chicken* and *pig*), perform a larger duty.

▶ *Elevation and Degradation*

If generalization and specialization may be said to involve a change in the "area" of meaning, elevation and degradation[5] involve the rising or falling of meaning in a scale of values. Thus a word which once denominated something bad (or at least neutral) but comes to refer to something good, has undergone *elevation* of meaning; the reverse of this process, obviously, represents a *degradation* of meaning.

And here a word of warning: we must not confuse the linguistic signal with the thing it stands for, though that error is too often made. It is not the word as such which is bad or good, or which becomes elevated or degraded, but only the meaning which society chooses to put upon it. As we shall see, society often reverses itself in the course of time, and words which were once disapproved may become "respectable," while others that had social favor may lose it. This would not be possible if the value were inherent in the word. With this in mind, then, let us illustrate degradation of meaning.

Many terms that are now descriptive of moral depravity were once quite without this suggestion. *Lust,* for example, meant simply "pleasure," as in German; *wanton* was "untaught"; *lewd* was merely "ignorant," "lerned and lewed" being a phrase commonly standing for "clergy and laity"; *immoral* was "not customary"; *vice,* "flaw"; *hussy,* "housewife"; *wench,* "young girl"; and *harlot,* "fellow" (of either sex). In a similar way, words that impute rascality have often been thoroughly innocent labels:

[5] Elevation is also called *aggradation* or *amelioration,* and degradation is also called *degeneration* or *pejoration.*

villain, for example, was "farm laborer"; *counterfeiter,* "imitator" or "copyist"; *pirate* (at least in its earlier Greek sense), "one who adventures or tries"; *buccaneer,* "one who smokes meat"; *ringleader,* simply "leader" (in a good or a neutral sense); *varlet, knave,* and *imp* meant merely "boy"; and *sly, crafty,* and *cunning* all implied the compliment "skilful." A perennial form of humor—the city man's ridicule of the countryman—is witnessed in the degradation of such nouns as *peasant, boor* (compare German *Bauer* and Dutch *Boer),* and *churl,* and in the frequent implication of such adjectives as *bucolic, rural, rustic,* and *provincial.*

When a word may be applied in two possible ways, one favorable or complimentary and the other the reverse, it is extremely likely that it will specialize in the less desirable sense. Thus, *suggestive* is likely to mean only "evilly suggestive," though it may still mean "informative" or "illuminating," and though the noun *suggestion* has escaped any such specialization—just as the verb *to harbor* is limited to unworthy or illegal concealment (as in "harboring a criminal" or "harboring thoughts of revenge"), while the noun *harbor* retains the old broad and literal meaning of "haven." *Asylum,* through association with the idea of "refuge for the insane," has followed a course like that of the verb *harbor.* A *libel,* in Middle English and early Modern English, was simply a "brief bit of writing" (from Lat. *libellum,* little book); now it is definitely limited to something malicious or defamatory. *Doom* once meant "judgment"; now it means only "condemnation." *Reek,* as we have seen, can now stand only for unpleasant distillations; *stink* and *stench* have specialized in the same way from a formerly neutral meaning, and *smell* and even *odor* seem likely to follow their lead. A *smirk* was once merely a smile, without the suggestion of affectation. One could formerly *resent* benefits as well as injuries, and *retaliate* for favors as well as slights; compare with the present meanings of these words the ordinary implications of the phrase "get even with" or "get square with."

On the other hand, instances of words that have traveled an opposite path, from the humble to the exalted, or from the base to the refined, are not far to seek. The institution of chivalry brought about the elevation of *knight* (youth) and *squire* (shield-bearer); and *chivalry* itself was invested by the Romantic Revival with a glamor that the word (as we see from its source, Fr. *cheval,* horse) did not originally possess. "Romantic" ideas in the late eighteenth and early nineteenth centuries were similarly responsible for the gain in dignity of such words as *bard,* once a term of contempt like *vagabond; minstrel,* once applicable to juggler and buffoon as well as musician; and *enthusiasm,* in the earlier eighteenth century akin to *fanaticism.* Like *knight,* other terms for rank or position have had the good fortune to take on added prestige when the offices for which they stood changed their character, and when their own etymological meanings were forgotten. Such is the history of *marshal* (originally, "horse-servant"), *chamberlain* (room-attendant), *minister* (servant), *constable* (stable-attendant), *governor* (pilot), and *steward* (sty-guardian). It is true that in a number of these words the extent of the elevation fluctuates: *marshal* is a less dignified title when it is applied to the lone policeman of an American village than when it is applied to the highest ranking officers of the English or the French army; there is a similar variation between the American and the British connotations for *constable,* just as *steward* may suggest a club attendant as well as the Lord High Steward of England, or even the royal dynasty of the *Stewarts* (or *Stuarts*); likewise, *governor* may mean the *warden* of an English prison or the chief administrative officer of one of our American states. On the whole, however, the fact that any present implication of these words represents a gain in dignity over the etymological one is patent enough. So too it is with a number of political and religious labels: *Tory, Whig, Puritan, Quaker,* and *Methodist* are well-known examples of names that were originally applied in contempt but that have taken on dignified associations (though, to some, *Puritan* and perhaps *Tory* still convey a derisive significance). Archbishop Trench long ago pointed out that the influence of Christianity elevated *angel* from merely "messenger," *martyr* from "witness," and *paradise* from "park," through the Biblical application to the abode of our first parents (as in *Paradise Lost* and "*earthly* paradise") to the "blisful wait-place of faithful departed spirits." Miscellaneous further illustrations of elevation are *pretty* from an early meaning "sly," through "clever," to something approaching "beautiful"; *nice* from an etymological meaning "ignorant," through its earliest English sense "foolish," and later ones like "particular," to its present broad and vague colloquial meaning of "pleasant" or "acceptable"; and *fond* from "foolish" to "affectionate."

The usual view of degradation and elevation has been that the downward path is far the more common. Despite McKnight's protest to the effect that elevation has been less noticed simply because it is less dramatic, there seems to be every reason to agree with the general verdict. Examples of elevation, after all, are far less easy to find than examples of degradation, which indeed meet us at every turn. Besides, most of the words that have been cited as undergoing elevation fall into a few obvious categories, while the types of degradation are extremely various. The truth of the matter would appear to be that degradation has been more noticed not because it is more spectacular but simply because it is omnipresent, as elevation is not. Why should this be so, and why should the use of words be made difficult by a lurking leer, a hint of unpleasant connotation that makes a word that appears to be absolutely right in denotation impossible for a given occasion? It is hard to escape the conclusion that there is a disagreeable commentary on human nature here. How difficult it is for superlatives to retain their superlative force—because the general tendency is to apply them on light occasion and hence to weaken their meaning! So *fair* comes to mean "passable," and indeed it is often equivalent to "not good"; and *quite* has passed, in its usual American application at least, from "entirely" or "completely" to "moderately." The tendency to procrastinate finds illustration in a whole series of words or phrases—*by and by, presently, anon, immediately, directly,* and *soon* itself—that have "slowed up," changing their meaning from "now" or "at once" to "soon" or "after a time." It is scarcely a far-fetched interpretation to see in the narrowing of *demure* to apply to *mock* modesty, of *genteel* to *spurious* gentility, of *sophistication* to *worldly* wisdom, of *egregious* to *notoriety* rather than fame, of *sanctimonious* to *pretended* holiness, and of *grandiose* to *tinsel* (itself an example of degradation) grandeur—to see in all these, and dozens of others that might be mentioned, the workings of human motives like suspicion, contempt, and general pessimism.

▶ *Euphemism*

With degradation is often associated the widespread tendency in language to avoid the direct word by employing a pleasant, neutral, or even meaningless substitute, which is described as its "euphemism" (from Greek words meaning "well" and "speak"). Peoples of all times and places have apparently felt that to pronounce certain holy or ominous words is to tempt Providence. On the other hand, the god, demon, or monster that is feared may be propitiated, if not by silence, at any rate by circumlocution or by deliberately misapplied compliment. Thus the Greeks called the Furies the *Eumenides* (literally, the "well-minded" ones); the Irish peasantry prefer to avoid the term *fairies* and to employ instead *gentry, little people,* or *good people;* and many primitive races have had elaborate verbal taboos that prevent the direct naming of animals that are feared and persons that are either venerated or despised.

Most striking, perhaps, of such reticences and equivocations (in language after language) are the euphemisms for ideas associated with death. Instead of the verb *die,* we substitute *pass away* or *on,*[6] *breathe one's last, succumb, expire, depart this life, be taken* or *called, to go to a better world,* or *go west* (the favorite euphemism in the first World War, curiously parallel to the Greek conception of the *Hesperides,* or Western Isles, the abode of the dead). In the second World War, *replacements* was officially changed to *reinforcements,* since the former term carried the unpleasant suggestion that somebody had been hurt or killed. The *dead* person is alluded to as the *lost,* the *deceased, departed, defunct,* or the like. Sometimes the idea of the verb is veiled in such jocose phrases as *kick the bucket, push up the daisies,* and *pass in one's checks.* Likewise, *death* itself is more obscurely alluded to by generalized terms like *end, passing, departure,* and *dissolution;* and *kill* is avoided in favor of *settle, do for, remove, destroy,* or (in lower strata of speech) *knock off, bump off, take for a ride, put on the spot,* or the like. Dictators both before and since the second World War have cynically *liquidated* their enemies. (In George Orwell's horribly prophetic novel *1984,* enemies of the regime are *vaporized.*) The superstitious origin of these euphemisms seems evident in the fact that many speakers simply cannot allude to an imminent death by saying, "If he should die. . . ." It is as though merely to pronounce the word would bring about the dreaded possibility. Instead of "If he should die," they say "If he shouldn't recover," "If he shouldn't come back," or—vaguest of all in the words themselves, but nevertheless perfectly clear in the meaning intended—"If anything should happen to him."

One means of veiling the distressing truth is to employ a term

---

[6] In Old English, *gefaran* and *forþfaran* were used in this way, as in German *fahren* and *vergehen* are used, and in French *passer, trépasser,* and even *partir* or *s'en aller.*

that is not immediately intelligible, one that requires, in fact, something like translation. In place of plain words, therefore, we frequently have elaborate—usually borrowed rather than native— synonyms for ideas linked to death and disaster. *Casualty, suicide, mortality, obituary, accident,* and *fatality* have clearly originated in this way. *Cemetery* was once itself a euphemism (literally, "sleeping place"), but it has come to be felt as too direct in its implication of "burial ground"; hence we have *memorial park,* or occasionally *necropolis*—"city of the dead," to be sure, but decently veiled in the Greek equivalents. *Undertaker* was apparently a euphemistic shortening of *funeral undertaker,* but it came to mean what it undertook to conceal; hence *funeral director* was evolved, and more recently *mortician.* The last of course is distinctly American, for this kind of squeamishness (combined, perhaps, with a greater love of the pompous) has gone farther here than in England. So too are *casket* for *coffin,* and *funeral car* for *hearse* distinctively American euphemisms, as are also such elegancies as *mortuary chapel* and *funeral parlors.* The ultimate attempt to avoid the discomfort of this subject, however, is surely *funeral home!*

Not that euphemism is always to be ridiculed: on some occasions to soften the brutal reality is surely the part of taste and tact. But the effect of the process is to weaken the force of the euphemistic substitute, and often to lead in turn, as has already been indicated, to the degradation of that word. Thus *insane* (not healthy) begins as a polite evasion of the ugly truth; but it comes to have a direct and unequivocal meaning, so that other euphemisms must be resorted to—*simple, mental case,* and (formerly) *innocent* and *natural*[7] —to make good the loss caused by degradation. Words associated with insanity, it may be observed in passing, afford a peculiarly fertile field for the study of change of meaning in general; not only euphemism, degradation, and specialization, but also irony, metaphor, humor, superstition, and pedantry are to be observed here as active forces. *Sǣlig* in Old English meant "happy" or "blessed" (a sense largely retained by Modern German *selig*); but Middle English and Modern English *silly* came, through an ironical application, to mean first "innocent" or "harmless"—the disguised

---

[7] A frequent Shakespearean meaning; it survives in dialect much later. In French, incidentally, *simple* and *innocent* (and in German *einfältig*) have gone exactly the same way.

Archimago refers to himself as "silly old man"[8]—and finally "feeble-minded" or "half-witted" (themselves, frequently enough, euphemistic softenings of more accurately descriptive terms). *Crazy* is a jocose metaphor, literally equivalent to "cracked," a word that is itself a slang term for "insane." *Insane,* incidentally, is chronologically before *crazy,* since it is a Renaissance euphemism for earlier terms like *wood* and *mad* (the latter now colloquially transferred to anger rather than insanity, and somewhat stilted in its earlier application). In Old English, the equivalents of modern *dizzy* and *giddy* were the usual adjectives implying a lack of sense; according to Bradley, "the prehistoric meaning of both seems to have been 'possessed by a god.'" *Foolish,* along with *crazy* and *mad,* largely superseded *dizzy* and *giddy* in their Old English meanings; the source of *fool*—a Middle English borrowing of French *fol,* in turn a slangy application of Latin *follis* (windbag)—is also interesting. Other words of this group that may be mentioned are *idiot* (in Greek and in early Modern English "private person"), in which the application to one mentally deficient seems an unusually farfetched bit of euphemism; *imbecile,* of unknown origin, but meaning "weak" in general before it meant "weak-minded"; *moron,* a Greek borrowing which literally means "fool"; and *cretin,* from a French word which was originally a dialectal variant of *chrétien* (Christian). The foregoing list, it may be added, by no means exhausts the catalog of terms that betray an effort to gloss over a dreadful fact. Unfortunately there are still many people who seem to believe that to get rid of something undesirable one has only to give it a new name.

Equally interesting, are the distortions in language, sometimes called "minced forms," that result when the human impulse to swear is held in check by religious or social prohibitions. The usual compromise is a word or phrase that suggests rather than states, that at once approaches the forbidden and shies away from it. Thus, *God* becomes *gad, damn* becomes *darn,* and *God-damned*[9] becomes *dod-burned, goldurned,* and so forth. Further distortions of the sacred name are *goodness, gosh, gorry, Godfrey,* and *golly;*

---

[8] *Faery Queen,* Book I, Canto I, stanza 30.

[9] *God-darned,* put by Galsworthy into the mouth of Hallorsen, the American professor in *Maid in Waiting,* London (Heinemann), 1932, is as unrealistic as the conversation of Americans in British novels so often is. No American ever euphemizes only one syllable of this word.

and older oaths like *'Oddsbodkins* (for "God's little body"), *'Sblood* (God's blood), and *Zounds* (God's wounds). *Jesus* is suggested by the Elizabethan *Gis* (now *Jeez*), and by the modern *Geewhiz, Jerusalem*, and "for *Pete's* sake"; *Christ* is alluded to in *Cripes*, "for the love of *Mike*," and the otherwise meaningless "O for *crying* out loud"; *Jimminy Crickets* and the more recent *Jeepers Creepers* attempt to combine the two. A curious exhibition indeed, of the human desire to sin combined with want of courage!

A form of euphemism to which passing reference has already been made is that in which the motive is prudery—often accompanied by ostentation. The result is what Mr. Fowler has happily termed the *genteelism*, and defined as "the substituting, for the ordinary natural word that first suggests itself to the mind, of a synonym that is thought to be less soiled by the lips of the common herd, less familiar, less plebeian, less vulgar, less improper, less apt to come unhandsomely between the wind and our nobility." Some of Mr. Fowler's examples are rather British than American— *serviette* for *napkin, paying guest* (still further euphemized to *p.g.*) for *boarder*, and *coal-vase* for *coal-scuttle;* but others are more American than British—*expectorate* for *spit*, particularly. On the whole, indeed, an American must regretfully concede that the tendency both to be mealy-mouthed and to be pompous has gone farther in the United States than in England—though it is probably true that Englishmen are prone to exaggerate the difference.[10] Still, if Mr. Fowler can cite one pompous genteelism like *chiropodist* for *corn-cutter*, an American has no difficulty in citing dozens that are all too familiar to him: for a very few samples, *junior executive* for *clerk, exodontist* for *tooth-puller, custodian* for *janitor, realtor* for *real estate agent*, and *heating engineer* for *plumber*. The American passion for sonorous titles, even when the position in question is not particularly impressive, is further attested by such neologisms as *receptionist, beautician*, and *cosmetician*. H. L. Mencken has recently recorded *stripteuse* and *ecdysiast* as professional euphemisms for *strip-teaser*.

---

[10] In *Jesting Pilate*, Garden City (Doubleday, Doran), 1926, Aldous Huxley remarks on the "revaluation of values . . . (for the worse)" that has taken place in the United States. This revaluation he finds to be symbolized in the commercialization and degradation of such words as *service*, and the pretentious use of *mortician, casket*, and so forth—all as a result of the "humbug" necessary to maintain the democratic hypothesis that all men are equal.

Of a rather different type of genteelism, that in which squeamishness rather than ostentation is the more prominent motive force, a few words may be added. There have always been certain taboos associated with parts of the body and their clothing. Though the Victorian preference for *limb* over *leg* (even when referring to a chicken or a piano) seems to the present generation the height of ridiculous prudery, the tendency to avoid the plain name in speaking of certain other parts of the body is of course still active, and—what may perhaps be illustrated with less offense to the conventions in question—the names for the more personal and intimate garments are likely also to be genteel euphemisms. Thus *shirt* and *drawers* (for women's use) give way to words like *vest* and *panties; petticoat,* a sufficiently innocuous term meaning "little coat," yields to *slip* or to *skirt* (curiously enough, itself a doublet of and evidently a euphemistic substitute for *shirt,* since it is the Scandinavian variant of the Anglo-Saxon word); while *underwear* or *underclothing* as the general term is superseded by the more elegant French borrowing *lingerie* or some such equivalent as *intimate wear.* Moreover, if the garments in question have been worn, it is no longer proper to refer to them as *dirty,* and still less, as our distant ancestors would have done without a qualm, as *filthy* or *foul;* no, *dirty clothes* have given way to *soiled linen.* We are not quite so far removed as we may at first suppose from the atmosphere of that period in French society when *shirt* was alluded to by an elaborate circumlocution meaning "the constant companion of the dead and living."

It is true that for a generation or so there has been a cult of calling a spade a spade, and further, as someone has remarked, of inserting as many spades as possible into the conversation—what James Truslow Adams referred to pungently as "the mucker pose." Yet there are conventional limits even to this. Less restraint in speaking plainly of sex and morals is curiously accompanied by a frequent timidity in referring to the ills and unpleasantnesses that flesh is heir to. Thus *halitosis,* the happy discovery of purveyors of mouth-washes, has found a wider usefulness, and *bad breath* is taboo; just as *acute indigestion* some time ago replaced the old-fashioned *belly-ache.* The advertisers would likewise have us suffer from *comedones* instead of *blackheads,* from *conjunctivitis* instead of a *sty* (in the eye), and from *alopecia* instead of *baldness.* Their efforts have been crowned with financial success, for they have not only given dignity to many a homely malady, but the imposing Latin and Greek names play on people's fears associated with the unknown. In modern conversation on the subjects of sex and morals the obscure jargon of Freudian psychoanalysis serves a similar purpose of euphemism, lending at the same time a sense of importance and mystery to the abnormal. Likewise birth, as well as death, is often a subject for euphemistic substitution, *to be born* giving way to *see the light of day, come into the world,* and so forth. The prenatal state is even less likely to be referred to plainly; as in the age of Victoria, a pregnant woman is still too often referred to as being *in the family way* or, with coyest reticence, as *expecting.* Euphemism, in this field as in others, is neither dead nor dying.

▶ *Hyperbole*

Allied to euphemistic substitution, and likewise springing from dissatisfaction with the plain word, is the use of hyperbole or exaggeration. The most familiar illustrations are the adjectives and adverbs that indicate approval or disapproval. In the one group are terms like *grand, superb, gorgeous, magnificent, perfect,* and *unique* (the last two logically absolute, but nevertheless often qualified by *more* and *most*); in the other group are such words as *horrible, dreadful, outrageous, horrid, frightful, awful,* and— *lousy,* the adjective of the moment, the curious result of such incongruous motives as the will to call a spade a spade, the wish to shock by the use of the forbidden, and the desire to be emphatic. The point is, of course, that all the adjectives cited have their own distinctive meanings and serve admirably for exceptional occasions of various sorts; but they are by no means reserved for these exceptional occasions, with the result that their distinctive qualities are inevitably weakened. When the strong word is used on light occasion its strength begins to be dissipated, and when the fitting moment for it actually arrives it will no longer serve; familiarity has bred contempt in the hearer, and one must begin again to find a new "strong word."

One consequence is that the adjective of weakened force is frequently bolstered by an adverb that strives to restore its pristine vigor—but cannot do so long, for hyperbole has entered into *its* employment too. *Very* (truly) has, through overuse, become so weakened that *very good* may easily convey less of praise than an obviously sincere *good.* Expressions like *absolutely unique* and *awfully disgusting* betray a double hyperbole in their very aspect. There is nothing new, incidentally, about the hyperbolic qualifier: phrases like *monstrous agreeable, marvellous fine,* and *vastly pretty* merely anticipate by two or three centuries other phrases like *frightfully agreeable, wonderfully fine,* and *amazingly pretty.* Investigation of other aspects of hyperbole—for example, in terms of courteous address and in titles—would serve to strengthen one's feeling that, like euphemism, its effect upon the vocabulary is a powerful one, in the present as it has been in the past.

THE AMERICAN LANGUAGE*

H. L. Mencken

The first Englishman to notice an Americanism sneered at it aloofly, thus setting a fashion that many of his countrymen have been following ever since. He was one Francis Moore, a ruffian who came out to Georgia with Oglethorpe in 1735, and the word that upset him was *bluff,* in the sense of "a cliff or headland with a broad precipitous face." He did not deign to argue against it; he simply dismissed it as "barbarous," apparently assuming that all Englishmen of decent instincts would agree with him. For nearly a century they seem to have done so, and *bluff* lingered sadly below the salt. When it was printed at all in Great Britain it was set off by sanitary quotation marks, or accompanied by other hints of deprecation, as *rubberneck, hot spot* and *nerts* are accompanied today. But then, in 1830, the eminent Sir Charles Lyell used it shamelessly in the first volume of his monumental "Principles of Geology," and from that day to this it has been a perfectly respectable if somewhat unfamiliar word in England, with a place in every dictionary.

Its history is the history of almost countless other Americanisms. They have been edging their way into English since early colonial times, and, for more than a century past, in constantly increasing volume, but I can't recall one that didn't have to run a

* From *The Yale Review,* March, 1936, pp. 538–552. Copyright, 1936, by Alfred A. Knopf, Inc., and reprinted by permission.

gantlet of opposition in the motherland, at times verging upon the frantic. After the Revolution, that opposition took on the proportions of a holy war. Never an American book came out that the English reviewers did not belabor its vocabulary violently. The brunt of the attack, of course, had to be borne by the poetasters of the era—for example, Joel Barlow, whose "Columbiad" (1807) loosed a really terrifying geyser of abuse. But even the most serious writers got their share—among them, Jefferson, John Marshall, Noah Webster, and John Quincy Adams. Jefferson's crime was that he had invented the verb *to belittle*. It was, one may argue plausibly, a very logical, useful, and perhaps even nifty word, and seventy-five years later the prissy Anthony Trollope was employing it without apology. But when Jefferson ventured to use it in his "Notes on Virginia" (1787) "The London Review" tossed and raged in a manner befitting the discovery of a brace of duelling pistols beneath the cope of the Archbishop of Canterbury, and for several years following its dudgeon was supported virtuously by most of the other reviews. "What an expression!" roared the "London." "It may be an elegant one in Virginia, but for our part, all we can do is to *guess* at its meaning. For shame, Mr. Jefferson! Freely, good sir, will we forgive all your attacks, impotent as they are illiberal, upon our national character; but for the future spare—O spare, we beseech you, our mother-tongue!"

The underscoring of *guess* was a fling in passing at another foul Americanism. It was the belief of most Englishmen then, as it is today, that the use of the verb in the sense of *to suppose* or *assume* originated in this country. It is actually to be found, in that meaning precisely, in "Measure For Measure" and "Henry VI"; nay, in Chaucer, Wycliffe, and Gower. But such historical considerations have never daunted the more ardent preservers of the King's English. When a word acquires an American flavor it becomes anathema to them, even though it may go back to Boadicea. *To advocate* offers an instructive example. It appeared in English in the dark backward and abysm of time, but during the eighteenth century it seems to have dropped out of general use, though Burke used it. Towards the end of the century it came into vogue in this country, and soon it made its way back to the land of its birth. It was received with all the honors proper to an invasion of Asiatic cholera. The reviews denounced it as loutish, "Gothic," and against God, and lumped it with *to compromit* and *to happify* as proof

that civilization was impossible in America, and would be so for-
evermore. Even Benjamin Franklin, returning from England in
1789, was alarmed into begging Noah Webster to "reprobate" it,
along with *to notice, to progress,* and *to oppose.* There is no record
of Noah's reply, but it is most unlikely that he did any reprobating,
for when he began to make dictionaries he included all four verbs,
and they have been listed in every considerable dictionary published since, whether in this country or in England.

The leader of the heroic struggle to keep Americanisms out of
Britain, in its early stages, was the celebrated William Gifford,
editor of "The Quarterly Review." Gifford was a killer in general
practice, and his savage assaults on Wordsworth, Shelley, and Keats
are still unpleasantly remembered. He was the first magazine
editor in history to make the trade pay, and when he died in 1828
he left £25,000 and was buried in Westminster Abbey. One of his
major specialties was the villainousness of everything American,
from politics to table manners and from theology to speechways.
Among the allegations that he either made himself or permitted
his contributors to make were these: (*a*) that the Americans employed naked colored women to wait upon them at table, (*b*) that
they kidnapped Scotsmen, Irishmen, Hollanders, and Welshmen
and sold them into slavery, and (*c*) that they were planning to
repudiate the English language altogether, and adopt Hebrew in
its place. This last charge, as it flew from tongue to tongue, acquired variorum readings. One of them made the new American
language an Indian dialect, another made it Greek, and a third
was to the effect that the people of Britain would be forced to
acquire Greek, thus leaving English to the wicked will of the
barbaric Yankees. It all sounds idiotic to-day, but in 1814 it was
taken quite seriously by many Englishmen. Gifford was a tyranni-
cal editor and so vastly enjoyed slashing his contributors' copy that
Southey once denounced him as "a butcherly review-gelder." But
anything that was against the damyankee passed his eye unscathed,
and he piled up accusations in a manner so shameless that "The
North American Review" was moved to protest that if the tirade
went on it would "turn into bitterness the last drops of good-will
towards England that exist in the United States."

In the early Twenties of that century there was some amelioration, and when Gifford retired from the "Quarterly" in 1824, voices
that were almost conciliatory began to be heard. They heaped

praises on Niagara Falls, found something to commend in Cooper's "Spy," and even had kind words for the speed and luxuriousness of American canalboats. But my most diligent researches have failed to unearth anything complimentary to the American language. It continued to be treated as a grotesque and immoral gibberish, full of uncouth terms and at war with all the canons of English. Every British traveller who came to these shores between the War of 1812 and the Civil War had something to say about the neologisms his ears and eyes encountered on his tour, and nearly all were constrained to deplore them. Captain Basil Hall, who was here in 1827 and 1828, went about in a palpitating daze, confounded and outraged by the signs on American places of business. *Clothing Store* he interpreted after long thought, and *Flour and Feed Store* after prayer and soul-searching, but what on earth was a *Leather and Finding Store?* Captain Thomas Hamilton, who followed five years later, found it impossible to penetrate to "the precise import" of *Dry-Goods Store*, and when he encountered an establishment offering *Hollow Ware, Spiders, and Fire-Dogs* he gave up in despair.

Hall was not one to take it lying down. He decided to call upon Noah Webster, whose American Dictionary of the English Language had just come out, to find out what the Yankees meant by using the mother tongue so cruelly. Webster shocked him by arguing stoutly that "his country-men had not only a right to adopt new words, but were obliged to modify the language to suit the novelty of the circumstances, geographical and political, in which they were placed." The great lexicographer "who taught millions to spell but not one to sin" went on to observe judicially that it was "quite impossible to stop the progress of language—it is like the course of the Mississippi, the motion of which, at times, is scarcely perceptible; yet even then it possesses a momentum quite irresistible. Words and expressions will be forced into use in spite of all the exertions of all the writers in the world."

"But surely," persisted Hall, "such innovations are to be deprecated?"

"I don't think that," replied old Noah. "If a word becomes universally current in America, where English is spoken, why should it not take its station in the language?"

"Because," declared Hall with magnificent pertinacity, "there are words enough already."

This heroic dogma is still heard in England, where even native novelties are commonly opposed violently, and not infrequently strangled at birth. There seems to be, in the modern Englishman, very little of that ecstasy in word-making which so prodigiously engrossed his Elizabethan forebears. Shakespeare alone probably put more new words into circulation than all the English writers since Carlyle, and they were much better ones. The ideal over there to-day is not picturesque and exhilarating utterance, but correct and reassuring utterance, and one of its inevitable fruits is that bow-wow jargon which Sir Arthur Quiller-Couch describes in "On the Art of Writing" as "the medium through which boards of government, county councils, syndicates, committees, commercial firms, express the processes as well as the conclusions of their thought, and so voice the reason of their being." It is, at its worst, at least in accord with what are taken to be the principles of English grammar, and at its best it shows excellent manners and even a kind of mellifluous elegance; indeed, the English, taking one with another, may be said to write much better than we do—at all events by the standards of the schoolmaster. But what they write is seldom animated by anything properly describable as bounce. It lacks novelty, variety, audacity. There is little juice in it. The reader confronted by it is treated politely and lulled pleasantly, but he seldom enjoys the enchantment of surprise. That diligent search for new and racy locutions which occupied so much of the work day of Walt Whitman and William Dean Howells alike, and is practised so assiduously by scores of saucy Andersons and Hemingways, Sandburgs and Saroyans to-day, is carried on across the ocean by only a few extravagant eccentrics, virtually all of whom— for example, James Joyce and Ezra Pound—are non- and even anti-Englishmen. The hundred-per-cent English writers, save when they stoop to conscious wickedness, seldom depart very far from the jargon of Quiller-Couch. It is by no means a monopoly of the classes he named, nor is it reserved for solemn occasions. I find it also in my favorite English weekly, the "News of the World," which is devoted principally to sports, the theatres, and the more scabrous varieties of crime, and is probably a far better mirror of England than the "Times." When the "News of the World" reports the downfall of a rural dean or a raid on a Mayfair night club, the thing is done in a style so tight and brittle that nothing to match it is discoverable in this country, at least outside the pages

of "The Homiletic Review." "When we want to freshen our
speech," Mrs. Virginia Woolf was lately saying, "we borrow from
American—*poppycock, rambunctious, flip-flop, booster, good mixer.*
All the expressive, ugly, vigorous slang which creeps into use
among us, first in talk, later in writing, comes from across the
Atlantic."

But whether slang or something better, it always encounters opposition—sometimes merely sullen, but at other times extremely
violent. At more or less regular intervals, war upon the invasion is
declared formally, and there ensues a long uproar, with the papers
full of choleric letters to the editor. One such sharpening of activity
was loosed early in 1933, when the chief constable of Wallasey, a
suburb of Liverpool, reported in alarm that his policemen were
being called *cops* by the tougher youngsters of the place, and
otherwise insulted with blasphemies picked up from American
movies. "*Oh-yeahs,*" he said, "are frequent in answer to charges,
and we are promised *shoots-up in the burg* [*sic*] and threatened to
be *bumped off.*" Half the amateur publicists who took a hand in
the discussion which followed, advocated using the cat on the
offenders, and the other half demanded that American movies be
barred from England as intolerable public menaces, like cattle infected with foot-and-mouth disease. As usual, the debate ended in
philological futilities. Was *oh yeah* actually English, even bad English, insane English? Or was it only an American borrowing from
one of the dialects of the savage Red Indians, or maybe from
Polish, Pennsylvania Dutch, Gullah, Yiddish, or some other such
godless and anti-British lingo? No matter! *Oh yeah* continues to
flourish from the Lizard to Unst, and with it *cop* flourishes too.
The latter, in fact, has swept upward from the level of bad boys
baiting constables to that of bishops following their transcendental
occasions. Even before the chief constable of Wallasey sounded
his cry of "Wolf!" a right reverend father in God had been charged
before the Farnham (Surrey) magistrates with applying *speed-cop*
on a public road to a member of the *mobile police.* Overhauled in
his car, so the testimony went, he had demanded, "Are you a
speed-cop?" His Lordship denied with some heat that he had used
the term, or anything else so unseemly, but the magistrates apparently concluded that he must have let it slip, for they took a
serious view of his very modest adventure in speeding, fined him
£10, and suspended his driving license for three months. I give

his name and dignities as a warning to lesser evildoers. He was the Right Reverend Cyril Henry Gelding-Bird, D.D. (Oxon.), Assistant Bishop of Guildford and Archdeacon of Dorking, and a man previously unknown to the police.

Whenever an Americanism comes publicly into question in England, there are efforts to track down its etymology, and sometimes the theories offered are extremely bizarre. In January, 1935, for example, the London "Morning Post" opened its columns to a furious and fantastic discussion of the verb-phrase, to get his goat. I content myself with one of the explanations: "Among the Negroes in Harlem it is the custom for each household to keep a goat to act as general scavenger. Occasionally one man will steal another's goat, and the household débris then accumulates to the general annoyance." The truth is that to get his goat seems to be of French origin, and in the form of prendre sa chèvre, philological genealogists have traced it back to the year 1585. But whatever is strange and upsetting is put down, in England, to the hellish ingenuity of Americans—save, of course, when genuine Americanisms are claimed as really English. This last happens often enough to give what may be called a cockeyed aspect to the perennial pother. In 1934 even the learned Dr. C. T. Onions, one of the editors of the great Oxford Dictionary, succumbed to the madness by offering to find in the dictionary any alleged Americanism that a reporter for the London "Evening News" could name. The reporter began discreetly with fresh (in the sense of saucy), to figure (in the sense of to believe or conclude), and to grill (in the sense of to question), and Dr. Onions duly found them all. But when the reporter proceeded to bunkum, the learned editor had to forget conveniently that its progenitor was the thoroughly American buncombe, when rake-off followed he had to admit that the earliest example in the dictionary was from an American work, and when boloney and nerts were hurled at him he blew up with a bang.

Here, of course, Dr. Onions and his interlocutor ended on the level of slang, but there is no telling where they would be if they could be translated to the year 2036. Boloney, like to belittle, has the imprimatur of an eminent tribune of the people, and is quite as respectable, philologically speaking, as buncombe, gerrymander, pork barrel, filibuster, carpetbagger, gag rule, or on the fence. All these came into American from the argot of politics, and got only frowns from the schoolmarm, but they are all quite sound Ameri-

can to-day, and most of them have gone into English. As for *nerts,*
it seems to be but one more member of an endless dynasty of
euphemisms, beginning with *zounds* and coming down to *son-of-
a-gun, gee,* and *darn. Darn,* like *nerts,* is an Americanism, and Dr.
Louise Pound has demonstrated that it descends from *eternal,*
which first turned into *tarnal* and then lost its tail and borrowed the
head of *damn.* I have heard a bishop use it freely in private discourse, with a waggish sprinkling of actual *damns. Son-of-a-gun* is
now so feeble and harmless that the Italians in America use it as a
satirical designation for native Americans, who seem to them to
fall far behind the Italian talent for profanity and objurgation. It is,
I believe, a just criticism. Some time ago I was engaged by a
magazine to do an article on American and English swearwords.
After two or three attempts I had to give it up, for I found that
neither branch of our ancient Frisian tongue could show anything
worthy of serious consideration. The antinomians of England stick
to two or three banal obscenities, one of which, *bloody,* is obscene
only formally, and we Americans seldom get beyond variations of
hell and *damn.* A single Neapolitan boatman could swear down the
whole population of Anglo-Saxondom.

Bloody is perfectly innocuous in the United States, and it may be
innocuous in England also on some near to-morrow—or even more
disreputable than it is to-day. There is no predicting the social
career of words. Dr. Leonard Bloomfield says that even "our word
whore, cognate with the Latin *carus* (dear), must have been at one
time a polite substitute for some term now lost." Prophecy fails just
as dismally when propriety does not come into question. Shakespeare's numerous attempts to introduce new words, some of them
his own inventions and others borrowed from the slang of the Bank-
side, failed almost as often as they succeeded. He found ready
takers for *courtship, lonely, sportive, multitudinous, hubbub* and
bump, but his audiences would have none of *definement,* in the
sense of description, or of *citizen* as an adjective, and both seem
strange and uncouth to us to-day, though all the others are as
familiar and as decorous as *cat* or *rat.* When John Marston used
strenuous in 1599 it was attacked by Ben Jonson as barbarous, but
a dozen years later it had got into Chapman's Homer, and by 1670
it was being used by Milton. It remained perfectly respectable until
1900, when Theodore Roosevelt announced the Strenuous Life.
Both the idea and the term struck the American fancy, and in a

little while the latter passed into slang, and was worn so threadbare that all persons of careful speech sickened of it. To this day it carries a faintly ridiculous connotation, and is seldom used seriously. But by 1975 it may be restored to the dignity of *psychopath* or *homoousian*. No one can say yes with any confidence, and no one can say no. "Even the greatest purist," observes Robert Lynd, "does not object to the inclusion of *bogus* in a literary English vocabulary, though a hundred years ago it was an American slang word meaning an apparatus for coining false money. *Carpetbagger* and *bunkum* are other American slang words that have naturalized themselves in English speech, and *mob* is an example of English slang that was once as vulgar as *photo*."

Three Americanisms borrowed by English to one Briticism come into American! The true score, I suspect, is even more favorable to the Yankee as word-maker. Down to 1820, according to Sir William Craigie, the trans-Atlantic trade in neologisms ran mainly westward, but then it began to shift, and to-day it is very heavily eastward. It would be difficult to recall a dozen British inventions that have entered the common American vocabulary since the World War, but the number of Americanisms taken into English must run to hundreds, and perhaps even to thousands. The American movie and talkie, of course, have been responsible for the introduction of many of them, but there is something beyond that, and something more fundamental. They are adopted in England simply because England has nothing to offer in competition with them—that is, nothing so apt or pungent, nothing so good. His Lordship of Guildford did not apply *speed-cop* to that *mobile policeman* as a voluntary act of subversion, born of a desire to shock and insult the realm; he let it slip for the single reason that it was an irresistibly apposite and satisfying term. And so with all the other Americanisms that challenge and consume their British congeners. They win fairly on palpable points and by every rule of the game. Confronted by the same novelty, whether in object or in situation, the Americans always manage to fetch up a name for it that not only describes it but also illuminates it, whereas the English, since the Elizabethan stimulant oozed out of them, have been content merely to catalogue it. There was a brilliant exemplification of the two approaches in the early days of railways. The English, having to name the wedge-shaped fender that was put in front of the first locomotives, called it a *plough*, which was almost exactly what it

was, but the Americans gave it the bold and racy appellation of
cow-catcher. For the casting which guides the wheels from one
rail to another the English coined the depressingly obvious name of
crossing-plate; the Americans, setting their imaginations free,
called it a *frog.* The same sharp contrast appears every time there is
a call for a new word to-day. The American *movie* is obviously
much better than the English *cinema;* it is even better English. So
is *radio* better than *wireless,* though it may be Latin, and *job-holder*
better than *public servant,* though it is surely literal enough, and
shock absorber vastly better than *anti-bounce clip,* and *highball*
than *whisky and soda,* and *bouncer* than *chucker-out,* and *chain
store* than *multiple shop,* and *string bean* than *French bean,* and
union suit than *combination.* Confronting the immensely American
rubberneck, Dr. J. Y. T. Greig of Newcastle could only exclaim
"one of the best words ever coined!" And in the face of *lounge
lizard,* Horace Annesley Vachell fell silent like Sir Isaac Newton on
the seashore, overwhelmed by the solemn grandeur of the linguistic
universe.

One finds in current American all the characters and tendencies
that marked the rich English of Shakespeare's time—an eager borrowing of neologisms from other languages, a bold and often
very ingenious use of metaphor, and a fine disdain of the barri-
cades separating the parts of speech. The making of new words
is not carried on only, or even principally, to fill gaps in the vocabulary; indeed, one may well agree with Captain Hall that "there
are words enough already." It is carried on because there survives
in the American something that seems to have faded out of the
Englishman: an innocent joy in word-making for its own sake, a
voluptuous delight in the vigor and elasticity of the language. The
search for the *mot juste* is an enterprise that is altogether too
pedantic for him; he much prefers to solve his problem by non-
Euclidian devices. *Hoose-gow* was certainly not necessary when it
appeared, for we already had a large repertory of synonyms for
jail. But when the word precipitated itself from the Spanish *juz-
gado* somewhere along the Rio Grande it won quick currency, and
in a little while it was on the march through the country, and soon
or late, I suppose, it will produce its inevitable clipped forms,
hoose and *gow,* and its attendant adjective and verb. *Corral,* which
entered by the same route in the Forties of the last century, had
hatched a verb before the Civil War, and that verb, according to

Webster's New International (1934) now has four separate and distinct meanings. *Bummer,* coming in from the German, is now clipped to *bum,* and is not only noun, verb, and adjective but also adverb. *Buncombe,* borrowed by the English as *bunkum,* has bred *bunco* and *bunk* at home, both of which rove the parts of speech in a loose and easy way, and the last of which has issue in the harsh verb to *debunk,* still under heavy fire in England.

The impact of such lawless novelties upon the more staid English of the motherland is terrific. The more they are denounced as heathen and outlandish, the quicker they get into circulation. Nor do they prosper only on the level of the vulgate, and among careless speakers. There are constant complaints in the English newspapers about their appearance in the parliamentary debates, and even in discourses from the sacred desk, and they begin to show themselves also in *belles-lettres,* despite the English dislike of new ways of writing. Their progress, in fact, is so widespread and so insidious that they often pop up in the diatribes that revile them; the Englishman, conquered at last, can no longer protest against Americanisms without using them. Moreover, they are now supported actively by a definitely pro-American party of writers and scholars, and though it is still small in numbers, at least compared to the patriot band, it shows some distinguished names. The late Robert Bridges, Poet Laureate, was an active member of it, and among its other adherents are Wyndham Lewis, Edward Shanks, Richard Aldington, and Sir John Foster Fraser. Sir William Craigie, perhaps the first of living lexicographers, is so greatly interested in the American form of English that he has spent the years since 1925 in a scientific examination of it, and will presently begin the publication of an elaborate dictionary. If only because of the greater weight of the population behind it, it seems destined to usurp the natural leadership of British English, and to determine the general course of the language hereafter. But its chief advantage in this struggle is really not the numerical one, but the fact that its daring experiments and iconoclasms lie in the grand tradition of English, and are signs of its incurable normalcy and abounding vigor.

How far it will move away from the theorizing of grammarians and the policing of schoolmarms remains to be seen. They still make valiant efforts to curb its wayward spirit, but with gradually diminishing success. When, a few years ago, the late Sterling A.

Leonard of the University of Wisconsin submitted a long series of their admonitions to a committee of educated Americans, including many philologians, he found that opinion was against them on that high level almost as decidedly as it was on lower ones. His judges favored scores of forms that the school grammars and popular handbooks of usage still condemn. Since then a more direct attack upon the conservative position has been made by Dr. Robert C. Pooley of the same university. He shows that some of the rules laid down with most assurance by pedants have no support in either history or logic, and are constantly violated by writers of unquestionable authority. There have even been rumblings of revolt in the conservative camp. The late George Philip Krapp of Columbia, who was surely anything but a radical, was of the opinion that English would undergo profound changes in the United States, and that many of them would be of such a character that its very grammatical structure would be shaken. Dr. George O. Curme of Northwestern University is another eminent grammarian who warns his colleagues that the rules they cherish have no genuine authority, and must be overhauled from time to time. Once they steel themselves to that sacrifice of their professional dignity, he says, "it will give a thrill to English-speaking students to discover that the English language does not belong to the schoolteacher but belongs to them, and that its future destiny will soon rest entirely in their hands."

Dr. Curme is always careful to think and speak of American as no more than a variation of English. But it must be obvious that, in late years, the tail has begun a vigorous wagging of the dog. "The facts that we ought to realize," says Edward Shanks to his fellow Britons, "and that we ignore when we talk loftily about Americanisms, are that America is making a formidable contribution to the development of our language, and that all our attempts to reject that contribution will in the long run be vain."

On Dictionaries and the Current Condition of the Language

Preface to A DICTIONARY OF THE ENGLISH LANGUAGE [1755]

Samuel Johnson

It is the fate of those who toil at the lower employments of life, to be rather driven by the fear of evil, than attracted by the prospect of good; to be exposed to censure, without hope of praise; to be disgraced by miscarriage, or punished for neglect, where success would have been without applause, and diligence without reward.

Among these unhappy mortals is the writer of dictionaries; whom mankind have considered, not as the pupil, but the slave of science, the pionier of literature, doomed only to remove rubbish and clear obstructions from the paths through which Learning and Genius press forward to conquest and glory, without bestowing a smile on the humble drudge that facilitates their progress. Every other authour may aspire to praise; the lexicographer can only hope to escape reproach, and even this negative recompense has been yet granted to very few.

I have, notwithstanding this discouragement, attempted a dictionary of the *English* language, which, while it was employed in the cultivation of every species of literature, has itself been hitherto neglected; suffered to spread, under the direction of chance, into wild exuberance; resigned to the tyranny of time and fashion; and exposed to the corruptions of ignorance, and caprices of innovation.

When I took the first survey of my undertaking, I found our speech copious without order, and energetick without rules: whereever I turned my view, there was perplexity to be disentangled, and confusion to be regulated; choice was to be made out of boundless variety, without any established principle of selection; adulterations were to be detected, without a settled test of purity; and modes of expression to be rejected or received, without the suffrages of any writers of classical reputation or acknowledged authority.

Having therefore no assistance but from general grammar, I applied myself to the perusal of our writers; and noting whatever might be of use to ascertain or illustrate any word or phrase, accumulated in time the materials of a dictionary, which, by degrees, I reduced to method, establishing to myself, in the progress of the work, such rules as experience and analogy suggested to me; experience, which practice and observation were continually increasing; and analogy, which, though in some words obscure, was evident in others.

In adjusting the ORTHOGRAPHY, which has been to this time unsettled and fortuitous, I found it necessary to distinguish those irregularities that are inherent in our tongue, and perhaps coeval with it, from others which the ignorance or negligence of later writers has produced. Every language has its anomalies, which, though inconvenient, and in themselves once unnecessary, must be tolerated among the imperfections of human things, and which require only to be registered, that they may not be increased, and ascertained, that they may not be confounded: but every language has likewise its improprieties and absurdities, which it is the duty of the lexicographer to correct or proscribe.

As language was at its beginning merely oral, all words of necessary or common use were spoken before they were written; and while they were unfixed by any visible signs, must have been spoken with great diversity, as we now observe those who cannot read catch sounds imperfectly, and utter them negligently. When this wild and barbarous jargon was first reduced to an alphabet, every penman endeavoured to express, as he could, the sounds which he was accustomed to pronounce or to receive, and vitiated in writing such words as were already vitiated in speech. The powers of the letters, when they were applied to a new language, must have been vague and unsettled, and therefore different hands would exhibit the same sound by different combinations.

From this uncertain pronunciation arise in a great part the various dialects of the same country, which will always be observed to grow fewer, and less different, as books are multiplied; and from this arbitrary representation of sounds by letters, proceeds that diversity of spelling observable in the *Saxon* remains, and I suppose in the first books of every nation, which perplexes or destroys analogy, and produces anomalous formations, that, being once incorporated, can never be afterward dismissed or reformed.

Of this kind are the derivatives *length* from *long*, *strength* from *strong*, *darling* from *dear*, *breadth* from *broad*, from *dry*, *drought*, and from *high*, *height*, which *Milton*, in zeal for analogy, writes *highth; Quid te exempta juvat spinis de pluribus una* (Horace, *Epistles*, II. ii. 212); to change all would be too much, and to change one is nothing.

This uncertainty is most frequent in the vowels, which are so capriciously pronounced, and so differently modified, by accident or affectation, not only in every province, but in every mouth, that to them, as is well known to etymologists, little regard is to be shewn in the deduction of one language from another.

Such defects are not errours in orthography, but spots of barbarity impressed so deep in the *English* language, that criticism can never wash them away: these, therefore, must be permitted to remain untouched; but many words have likewise been altered by accident, or depraved by ignorance, as the pronunciation of the vulgar has been weakly followed; and some still continue to be variously written, as authours differ in their care or skill: of these it was proper to enquire the true orthography, which I have always considered as depending on their derivation, and have therefore referred them to their original languages: thus I write *enchant*, *enchantment*, *enchanter*, after the *French*, and *incantation* after the *Latin*; thus *entire* is chosen rather than *intire*, because it passed to us not from the *Latin integer*, but from the *French entier*.

Of many words it is difficult to say whether they were immediately received from the *Latin* or the *French*, since at the time when we had dominions in *France,* we had *Latin* service in our churches. It is, however, my opinion, that the *French* generally supplied us; for we have few *Latin* words, among the terms of domestick use, which are not *French;* but many *French,* which are very remote from *Latin.*

Even in words of which the derivation is apparent, I have been often obliged to sacrifice uniformity to custom; thus I write, in compliance with a numberless majority, *convey* and *inveigh, deceit* and *receipt, fancy* and *phantom;* sometimes the derivative varies from the primitive, as *explain* and *explanation, repeat* and *repetition.*

Some combinations of letters having the same power are used indifferently without any discoverable reason of choice, as in *choak, choke; soap, sope; fewel, fuel,* and many others; which I have sometimes inserted twice, that those who search for them under either form, may not search in vain.

In examining the orthography of any doubtful word, the mode of spelling by which it is inserted in the series of the dictionary, is to be considered as that to which I give, perhaps not often rashly, the preference. I have left, in the examples, to every authour his own practice unmolested, that the reader may balance suffrages, and judge between us: but this question is not always to be determined by reputed or by real learning; some men, intent upon greater things, have thought little on sounds and derivations; some, knowing in the ancient tongues, have neglected those in which our words are commonly to be sought. Thus *Hammond* writes *feciblebness* for *feasibleness,* because I suppose he imagined it derived immediately from the *Latin;* and some words, such as *dependant, dependent; dependance, dependence,* vary their final syllable, as one or another language is present to the writer.

In this part of the work, where caprice has long wantoned without controul, and vanity sought praise by petty reformation, I have endeavoured to proceed with a scholar's reverence for antiquity, and a grammarian's regard to the genius of our tongue. I have attempted few alterations, and among those few, perhaps the greater part is from the modern to the ancient practice; and I hope I may be allowed to recommend to those, whose thoughts have been perhaps employed too anxiously on verbal singularities, not to disturb, upon narrow views, or for minute propriety, the orthography of their fathers. It has been asserted, that for the law to be *known,* is of more importance than to be *right.* Change, says *Hooker,* is not made without inconvenience, even from worse to better. There is in constancy and stability a general and lasting advantage, which will always overbalance the slow improvements of gradual correction. Much less ought our written language to comply with the corruptions of oral utterance, or copy that which every variation of time or place makes different from itself, and imitate those changes, which will again be changed, while imitation is employed in observing them.

This recommendation of steadiness and uniformity does not proceed from an opinion, that particular combinations of letters have much influence on human happiness; or that truth may not be successfully taught by modes of spelling fanciful and erroneous: I am not yet so lost in lexicography, as to forget that *words are the daughters of earth, and that things are the sons of heaven.* Language is only the instrument of science, and words are but the signs of ideas: I wish, however, that the instrument might be less apt to decay, and that signs might be permanent, like the things which they denote.

In settling the orthography, I have not wholly neglected the pronunciation, which I have directed, by printing an accent upon the acute or elevated syllable. It will sometimes be found, that the accent is placed by the author quoted, on a different syllable from that marked in the alphabetical series; it is then to be understood, that custom has varied, or that the authour has, in my opinion, pronounced wrong. Short directions are sometimes given where the sound of letters is irregular; and if they are sometimes omitted, defect in such minute observations will be more easily excused, than superfluity.

In the investigation both of the orthography and signification of words, their ETYMOLOGY was necessarily to be considered, and they were therefore to be divided into primitives and derivatives. A primitive word, is that which can be traced no further to any *English* root; thus *circumspect, circumvent, circumstance, delude, concave,* and *complicate,* though compounds in the *Latin,* are to us primitives. Derivatives are all those that can be referred to any word in *English* of greater simplicity.

The derivatives I have referred to their primitives, with an accuracy sometimes needless; for who does not see that *remoteness* comes from *remote, lovely* from *love, concavity* from *concave,* and *demonstrative* from *demonstrate?* but this grammatical exuberance the scheme of my work did not allow me to repress. It is of great importance in examining the general fabrick of a language, to trace one word from another, by noting the usual modes of derivation and inflection; and uniformity must be preserved in systematical works, though sometimes at the expence of particular propriety.

Among other derivatives I have been careful to insert and elucidate the anomalous plurals of nouns and preterites of verbs, which in the *Teutonick* dialects are very frequent, and though familiar to those who have always used them, interrupt and embarrass the learners of our language.

The two languages from which our primitives have been derived are the *Roman* and *Teutonick:* under the *Roman* I comprehend the *French* and provincial tongues; and under the *Teutonick* range the *Saxon, German,* and all their kindred dialects. Most of our polysyllables are *Roman,* and our words of one syllable are very often *Teutonick.*

In assigning the *Roman* original, it has perhaps sometimes happened that I have mentioned only the *Latin,* when the word was borrowed from the *French:* and considering myself as employed only in the illustration of my own language, I have not been very careful to observe whether the *Latin* word be pure or barbarous, or the *French* elegant or obsolete.

For the *Teutonick* etymologies, I am commonly indebted to *Junius* and *Skinner,* the only names which I have forborn to quote when I copied their books; not that I might appropriate their labours or usurp their honours, but that I might spare a perpetual repetition by one general acknowledgment. Of these, whom I ought not to mention but with the reverence due to instructors and benefactors, *Junius* appears to have excelled in extent of learning, and *Skinner* in rectitude of understanding. *Junius* was accurately skilled in all the northern languages, *Skinner* probably examined the ancient and remoter dialects only by occasional inspection into dictionaries; but the learning of *Junius* is often of no other use than to show him a track by which he may deviate from his purpose, to which *Skinner* always presses forward by the shortest way. *Skinner* is often ignorant, but never ridiculous: *Junius* is always full of knowledge; but his variety distracts his judgment, and his learning is very frequently disgraced by his absurdities.

The votaries of the northern muses will not perhaps easily restrain their indignation, when they find the name of *Junius* thus degraded by a disadvantageous comparison; but whatever reverence is due to his diligence, or his attainments, it can be no criminal degree of censoriousness to charge that etymologist with want of judgment, who can seriously derive *dream* from *drama,* because *life is a drama, and a drama is a dream,* and who declares with a tone of defiance, that no man can fail to derive *moan* from μόνος, *monos, single* or *solitary,* who considers that grief naturally loves to be *alone.*

Our knowledge of the northern literature is so scanty, that of words undoubtedly *Teutonick* the original is not always to be found in any ancient language; and I have therefore inserted *Dutch* or *German* substitutes, which I consider not as radical but parallel, not as the parents, but sisters of the *English.*

The words which are represented as thus related by descent or cognation, do not always agree in sense; for it is incident to words, as to their authours, to degenerate from their ancestors, and to change their manners when they change their country. It is sufficient, in etymological enquiries, if the senses of kindred words be found such as may easily pass into each other, or such as may both be referred to one general idea.

The etymology, so far as it is yet known, was easily found in the volumes where it is particularly and professedly delivered; and, by proper attention to the rules of derivation, the orthography was soon adjusted. But to COLLECT the WORDS of our language was a task of greater difficulty: the deficiency of dictionaries was immediately apparent; and when they were exhausted, what was yet wanting must be sought by fortuitous and unguided excursions into books, and gleaned as industry should find, or chance should offer it, in the boundless chaos of a living speech. My search, however, has been either skillful or lucky; for I have much augmented the vocabulary.

As my design was a dictionary, common or appellative, I have omitted all words which have relation to proper names; such as *Arian, Socinian, Calvinist, Benedictine, Mahometan;* but have retained those of a more general nature, as *Heathen, Pagan.*

Of the terms of art I have received such as could be found either in books of science or technical dictionaries: and have often inserted, from philosophical writers, words which are supported perhaps only by a single authority, and which being not admitted into general use, stand yet as candidates or probationers, and must depend for their adoption on the suffrage of futurity.

The words which our authours have introduced by their knowledge of foreign languages, or ignorance of their own, by vanity or wantonness, by compliance with fashion or lust of innovation, I have registred as they occurred, though commonly only to censure them, and warn others against the folly of naturalizing useless foreigners to the injury of the natives.

I have not rejected any by design, merely because they were unnecessary or exuberant; but have received those which by different writers have been differently formed, as *viscid*, and *viscidity*, *viscous*, and *viscosity*.

Compounded or double words I have seldom noted, except when they obtain a signification different from that which the components have in their simple state. Thus *highwayman*, *woodman*, and *horsecourser*, require an explanation; but of *thieflike* or *coachdriver* no notice was needed, because the primitives contain the meaning of the compounds.

Words arbitrarily formed by a constant and settled analogy, like diminutive adjectives in *ish*, as *greenish*, *bluish*, adverbs in *ly*, as *dully*, *openly*, substantives in *ness*, as *vileness*, *faultiness*, were less diligently sought, and sometimes have been omitted, when I had no authority that invited me to insert them; not that they are not genuine and regular offsprings of *English* roots, but because their relation to the primitive being always the same, their signification cannot be mistaken.

The verbal nouns in *ing*, such as the *keeping* of the *castle*, the *leading* of the *army*, are always neglected, or placed only to illustrate the sense of the verb, except when they signify things as well as actions, and have therefore a plural number, as *dwelling*, *living*; or have an absolute and abstract signification, as *colouring*, *painting*, *learning*.

The participles are likewise omitted, unless, by signifying rather habit or quality than action, they take the nature of adjectives; as a *thinking* man, a man of prudence; a *pacing* horse, a horse that can pace: these I have ventured to call *participial adjectives*. But neither are these always inserted, because they are commonly to be understood, without any danger of mistake, by consulting the verb.

Obsolete words are admitted, when they are found in authours not obsolete, or when they have any force or beauty that may deserve revival.

As composition is one of the chief characteristicks of a language, I have endeavoured to make some reparation for the universal negligence of my predecessors, by inserting great numbers of compounded words, as may be found under *after, fore, new, night, fair,* and many more. These, numerous as they are, might be multiplied, but that use and curiosity are here satisfied, and the frame of our language and modes of our combination amply discovered.

Of some forms of composition, such as that by which *re* is prefixed to note *repetition,* and *un* to signify *contrariety* or *privation,* all the examples cannot be accumulated, because the use of these particles, if not wholly arbitrary, is so little limited, that they are hourly affixed to new words as occasion requires, or is imagined to require them.

There is another kind of composition more frequent in our language than perhaps in any other, from which arises to foreigners the greatest difficulty. We modify the signification of many verbs by a particle subjoined; as to *come off,* to escape by a fetch; to *fall on,* to attack; to *fall off,* to apostatize; to *break off,* to stop abruptly; to *bear out,* to justify; to *fall in,* to comply; to *give over,* to cease; to *set off,* to begin a course or journey; to *take off,* to copy; with innumerable expressions of the same kind, of which some appear wildly irregular, being so far distant from the sense of the simple words, that no sagacity will be able to trace the steps by which they arrived at the present use. These I have noted with great care; and though I cannot flatter myself that the collection is complete, I believe I have so far assisted the students of our language, that this kind of phraseology will be no longer insuperable; and the combinations of verbs and particles, by chance omitted, will be easily explained by comparison with those that may be found.

Many words yet stand supported only by the name of *Bailey, Ainsworth, Philips,* or the contracted *Dict.* for *Dictionaries* subjoined; of these I am not always certain that they are read in any book but the works of lexicographers. Of such I have omitted many, because I had never read them; and many I have inserted, because they may perhaps exist, though they have escaped my notice: they are, however, to be yet considered as resting only upon the credit of former dictionaries. Others, which I considered as useful, or know to be proper, though I could not at present support them by authorities, I have suffered to stand upon my own attestation, claiming the same privilege with my predecessors of being sometimes credited without proof.

The words, thus selected and disposed, are grammatically considered; they are referred to the different parts of speech; traced, when they are irregularly inflected, though their various terminations; and illustrated by observations, not indeed of great or striking importance, separately considered, but necessary to the elucidation of our language, and hitherto neglected or forgotten by *English* grammarians.

That part of my work on which I expect malignity most frequently to fasten, is the *Explanation;* in which I cannot hope to satisfy those, who are perhaps not inclined to be pleased, since I have not always been able to satisfy myself. To interpret a language by itself is very difficult; many words cannot be explained by synonimes, because the idea signified by them has not more than one appellation; nor by paraphrase, because simple ideas cannot be described. When the nature of things is unknown, or the notion unsettled and indefinite, and various in various minds, the words by which such notions are conveyed, or such things denoted, will be ambiguous and perplexed. And such is the fate of hapless lexicography, that not only darkness, but light, impedes and distresses it; things may be not only too little, but too much known, to be happily illustrated. To explain, requires the use of terms less abstruse than that which is to be explained, and such terms cannot always be found; for as nothing can be proved but by supposing something intuitively known, and evident without proof, so nothing can be defined but by the use of words too plain to admit a definition.

Other words there are, of which the sense is too subtle and evanescent to be fixed in a paraphrase; such are all those which are by the grammarians termed *expletives,* and, in dead languages, are suffered to pass for empty sounds, of no other use than to fill a verse, or to modulate a period, but which are easily perceived in living tongues to have power and emphasis, though it be sometimes such as no other form of expression can convey.

My labour has likewise been much increased by a class of verbs too frequent in the *English* language, of which the signification is so loose and general, the use so vague and indeterminate, and the senses detorted so widely from the first idea, that it is hard to trace them through the maze of variation, to catch them on the brink of utter inanity, to circumscribe them by any limitations, or interpret them by any words of distinct and settled meaning; such are *bear, break, come, cast, full, get, give, do, put, set, go, run, make, take, turn, throw.* If of these the whole power is not accurately delivered, it must be remembered, that while our language is yet living, and variable by the caprice of every one that speaks it, these words are hourly shifting their relations, and can no more be ascertained in a dictionary, than a grove, in the agitation of a storm, can be accurately delineated from its picture in the water.

The particles are among all nations applied with so great latitude, that they are not easily reducible under any regular scheme of explication: this difficulty is not less, nor perhaps greater, in *English*, than in other languages. I have laboured them with diligence, I hope with success; such at least as can be expected in a task, which no man, however learned or sagacious, has yet been able to perform.

Some words there are which I cannot explain, because I do not understand them; these might have been omitted very often with little inconvenience, but I would not so far indulge my vanity as to decline this confession: for when *Tully* owns himself ignorant whether *lessus*, in the twelve tables, means a *funeral song*, or *mourning garment;* and *Aristotle* doubts whether οὐρεὺς in the Iliad signifies a *mule*, or *muleteer*, I may surely, without shame, leave some obscurities to happier industry, or future information.

The rigour of interpretative lexicography requires that *the explanation, and the word explained, should be always reciprocal;* this I have always endeavoured, but could not always attain. Words are seldom exactly synonimous; a new term was not introduced, but because the former was thought inadequate: names, therefore, have often many ideas, but few ideas have many names. It was then necessary to use the proximate word, for the deficiency of single terms can very seldom be supplied by circumlocution; nor is the inconvenience great of such mutilated interpretations, because the sense may easily be collected entire from the examples.

In every word of extensive use, it was requisite to mark the progress of its meaning, and show by what gradations of intermediate sense it has passed from its primitive to its remote and accidental signification; so that every foregoing explanation should tend to that which follows, and the series be regularly concatenated from the first notion to the last.

This is specious, but not always practicable; kindred senses may be so interwoven, that the perplexity cannot be disentangled, nor any reason be assigned why one should be ranged before the other. When the radical idea branches out into parallel ramifications, how can a consecutive series be formed of senses in their nature collateral? The shades of meaning sometimes pass imperceptibly into each other; so that though on one side they apparently differ, yet it is impossible to mark the point of contact. Ideas of the same race, though not exactly alike, are sometimes so little different, that no words can express the dissimilitude, though the mind easily perceives it, when they are exhibited together; and sometimes there is such a confusion of acceptations, that discernment is wearied, and distinction puzzled, and perseverance herself hurries to an end, by crouding together what she cannot separate.

These complaints of difficulty will, by those that have never considered words beyond their popular use, be thought only the jargon of a man willing to magnify his labours, and procure veneration to his studies by involution and obscurity. But every art is obscure to those that have not learned it: this uncertainty of terms, and commixture of ideas, is well known to those who have joined philosophy with grammar; and if I have not expressed them very clearly, it must be remembered that I am speaking of that which words are insufficient to explain.

The original sense of words is often driven out of use by their metaphorical acceptations, yet must be inserted for the sake of a regular origination. Thus I know not whether *ardour* is used for *material heat*, or whether *flagrant*, in *English*, ever signifies the same with *burning;* yet such are the primitive ideas of these words, which are therefore set first, though without examples, that the figurative senses may be commodiously deduced.

Such is the exuberance of signification which many words have obtained, that it was scarcely possible to collect all their senses; sometimes the meaning of derivatives must be sought in the mother term, and sometimes deficient explanations of the primitive may be supplied in the train of derivation. In any case of doubt or difficulty, it will be always proper to examine all the words of the same race; for some words are slightly passed over to avoid repetition, some admitted easier and clearer explanation than others, and all will be better understood, as they are considered in greater variety of structures and relations.

All the interpretations of words are not written with the same skill, or the same happiness: things equally easy in themselves, are not all equally easy to any single mind. Every writer of a long work commits errours, where there appears neither ambiguity to mislead, nor obscurity to confound him; and in a search like this, many felicities of expression will be casually overlooked, many convenient parallels will be forgotten, and many particulars will admit improvement from a mind utterly unequal to the whole performance.

But many seeming faults are to be imputed rather to the nature of the undertaking, than the negligence of the performer. Thus some explanations are unavoidably reciprocal or circular, as *hind, the female of the stag; stag, the male of the hind:* sometimes easier words are changed into harder, as *burial* into *sepulture* or *interment, drier* into *desiccative, dryness* into *siccity* or *aridity, fit* into *paroxysm;* for the easiest word, whatever it be, can never be translated into one more easy. But easiness and difficulty are merely relative, and if the present prevalence of our language should invite foreigners to this dictionary, many will be assisted by those words which now seem only to increase or produce obscurity. For this reason I have endeavoured frequently to join a *Teutonick* and *Roman* interpretation, as to CHEER, to *gladden,* or *exhilarate,* that every learner of *English* may be assisted by his own tongue.

The solution of all difficulties, and the supply of all defects, must be sought in the examples, subjoined to the various senses of each word, and ranged according to the time of their authours.

When first I collected these authorities, I was desirous that every quotation should be useful to some other end than the illustration of a word; I therefore extracted from philosophers principles of science; from historians remarkable facts; from chymists complete processes; from divines striking exhortations; and from poets beautiful descriptions. Such is design, while it is yet at a distance from execution. When the time called upon me to range this accumulation of elegance and wisdom into an alphabetical series, I soon discovered that the bulk of my volumes would fright away the student, and was forced to depart from my scheme of including all that was pleasing or useful in *English* literature, and reduce my transcripts very often to clusters of words, in which scarcely any meaning is retained; thus to the weariness of copying, I was condemned to add the vexation of expunging. Some passages I have yet spared, which may relieve the labour of verbal searches, and intersperse with verdure and flowers the dusty desarts of barren philology.

The examples, thus mutilated, are no longer to be considered as conveying the sentiments or doctrine of their authours; the word for the sake of which they are inserted, with all its appendant clauses, has been carefully preserved; but it may sometimes happen, by hasty detruncation, that the general tendency of the sentence may be changed: the divine may desert his tenets, or the philosopher his system.

Some of the examples have been taken from writers who were never mentioned as masters of elegance or models of stile; but words must be sought where they are used; and in what pages, eminent for purity, can terms of manufacture or agriculture be found? Many quotations serve no other purpose, than that of proving the bare existence of words, and are therefore selected with less scrupulousness than those which are to teach their structures and relations.

My purpose was to admit no testimony of living authours, that I might not be misled by partiality, and that none of my contemporaries might have reason to complain; nor have I departed from this resolution, but when some performance of uncommon excellence excited my veneration, when my memory supplied me, from late books, with an example that was wanting, or when my heart, in the tenderness of friendship, solicited admission for a favourite name.

So far have I been from any care to grace my pages with modern decorations, that I have studiously endeavoured to collect examples and authorities from the writers before the restoration, whose works I regard as *the wells of English undefiled,* as the pure sources of genuine diction. Our language, for almost a century, has, by the concurrence of many causes, been gradually departing from its original *Teutonick* character, and deviating towards a *Gallick* structure and phraseology, from which it ought to be our endeavour to recal it, by making our ancient volumes the groundwork of stile, admitting among the additions of later times, only such as may supply real deficiencies, such as are readily adopted by the genius of our tongue, and incorporate easily with our native idioms.

But as every language has a time of rudeness antecedent to perfection, as well as of false refinement and declension, I have been cautious lest my zeal for antiquity might drive me into times too remote, and croud my book with words now no longer understood. I have fixed *Sidney's* work for the boundary, beyond which I make few excursions. From the authours which rose in the time of *Elizabeth,* a speech might be formed adequate to all the purposes of use and elegance. If the language of theology were extracted from *Hooker* and the translation of the Bible; the terms of natural knowledge from *Bacon;* the phrases of policy, war, and navigation from *Raleigh;* the dialect of poetry and fiction from *Spenser* and *Sidney;* and the diction of common life from *Shakespeare,* few ideas would be lost to mankind, for want of *English* words, in which they might be expressed.

It is not sufficient that a word is found, unless it be so combined as that its meaning is apparently determined by the tract and tenour of the sentence; such passages I have therefore chosen, and when it happened that any authour gave a definition of a term, or such an explanation as is equivalent to a definition, I have placed his authority as a supplement to my own, without regard to the chronological order, that is otherwise observed.

Some words, indeed, stand unsupported by any authority, but they are commonly derivative nouns or adverbs, formed from their primitives by regular and constant analogy, or names of things seldom occurring in books, or words of which I have reason to doubt the existence.

There is more danger of censure from the multiplicity than paucity of examples; authorities will sometimes seem to have been accumulated without necessity or use, and perhaps some will be found, which might, without loss, have been omitted. But a work of this kind is not hastily to be charged with superfluities: those quotations, which to careless or unskillful perusers appear only to repeat the same sense, will often exhibit, to a more accurate examiner, diversities of signification, or, at least, afford different shades of the same meaning: one will shew the word applied to persons, another to things; one will express an ill, another a good, and a third a neutral sense; one will prove the expression genuine from an ancient authour; another will shew it elegant from a modern: a doubtful authority is corroborated by another of more credit; an ambiguous sentence is ascertained by a passage clear and determinate; the word, how often soever repeated, appears with new associates and in different combinations, and every quotation contributes something to the stability or enlargement of the language.

When words are used equivocally, I receive them in either sense; when they are metaphorical, I adopt them in their primitive acceptation.

I have sometimes, though rarely, yielded to the temptation of exhibiting a genealogy of sentiments, by shewing how one authour copied the thoughts and diction of another: such quotations are indeed little more than repetitions, which might justly be censured, did they not gratify the mind, by affording a kind of intellectual history.

The various syntactical structures occurring in the examples have been carefully noted; the licence or negligence with which many words have been hitherto used, has made our stile capricious and indeterminate; when the different combinations of the same word are exhibited together, the preference is readily given to propriety, and I have often endeavoured to direct the choice.

Thus have I laboured by settling the orthography, displaying the analogy, regulating the structures, and ascertaining the signification of *English* words, to perform all the parts of a faithful lexicographer: but I have not always executed my own scheme, or satisfied my own expectations. The work, whatever proofs of diligence and attention it may exhibit, is yet capable of many improvements: the orthography which I recommend is still controvertible, the etymology which I adopt is uncertain, and perhaps frequently erroneous; the explanations are sometimes too much contracted, and sometimes too much diffused, the significations are distinguished rather with subtilty than skill, and the attention is harrassed with unnecessary minuteness.

The examples are too often injudiciously truncated, and perhaps sometimes, I hope very rarely, alleged in a mistaken sense; for in making this collection I trusted more to memory, than, in a state of disquiet and embarrassment, memory can contain, and purposed to supply at the review what was left incomplete in the first transcription.

Many terms appropriated to particular occupations, though

necessary and significant, are undoubtedly omitted; and of the words most studiously considered and exemplified, many senses have escaped observation.

Yet these failures, however frequent, may admit extenuation and apology. To have attempted much is always laudable, even when the enterprize is above the strength that undertakes it: To rest below his own aim is incident to every one whose fancy is active, and whose views are comprehensive; nor is any man satisfied with himself because he has done much, but because he can conceive little. When first I engaged in this work, I resolved to leave neither words nor things unexamined, and pleased myself with a prospect of the hours which I should revel away in feasts of literature, with the obscure recesses of northern learning, which I should enter and ransack; the treasures with which I expected every search into those neglected mines to reward my labour, and the triumph with which I should display my acquisitions to mankind. When I had thus enquired into the original words, I resolved to show likewise my attention to things; to pierce deep into every science, to enquire the nature of every substance of which I inserted the name, to limit every idea by a definition strictly logical, and exhibit every production of art or nature in an accurate description, that my book might be in place of all other dictionaries whether appellative or technical. But these were the dreams of a poet doomed at last to wake a lexicographer. I soon found that it is too late to look for instruments, when the work calls for execution, and that whatever abilities I had brought to my task, with those I must finally perform it. To deliberate whenever I doubted, to enquire whenever I was ignorant, would have protracted the undertaking without end, and, perhaps, without much improvement; for I did not find by my first experiments, that what I had not of my own was easily to be obtained: I saw that one enquiry only gave occasion to another, that book referred to book, that to search was not always to find, and to find was not always to be informed; and that thus to persue perfection, was, like the first inhabitants of Arcadia, to chace the sun, which, when they had reached the hill where he seemed to rest, was still beheld at the same distance from them.

I then contracted my design, determining to confide in myself, and no longer to solicit auxiliaries, which produced more incumbrance than assistance: by this I obtained at least one advantage, that I set limits to my work, which would in time be ended, though not completed.

Despondency has never so far prevailed as to depress me to negligence; some faults will at last appear to be the effects of anxious diligence and persevering activity. The nice and subtle ramifications of meaning were not easily avoided by a mind intent upon accuracy, and convinced of the necessity of disentangling combinations, and separating similitudes. Many of the distinctions which to common readers appear useless and idle, will be found real and important by men versed in the school philosophy, without which no dictionary shall ever be accurately compiled, or skilfully examined.

Some senses however there are, which, though not the same, are yet so nearly allied, that they are often confounded. Most men think indistinctly, and therefore cannot speak with exactness; and consequently some examples might be indifferently put to either signification: this uncertainty is not to be imputed to me, who do not form, but register the language; who do not teach men how they should think, but relate how they have hitherto expressed their thoughts.

The imperfect sense of some examples I lamented, but could not remedy, and hope they will be compensated by innumerable passages selected with propriety, and preserved with exactness; some shining with sparks of imagination, and some replete with treasures of wisdom.

The orthography and etymology, though imperfect, are not imperfect for want of care, but because care will not always be successful, and recollection or information come too late for use.

That many terms of art and manufacture are omitted, must be frankly acknowledged; but for this defect I may boldly allege that it was unavoidable: I could not visit caverns to learn the miner's language, nor take a voyage to perfect my skill in the dialect of navigation, nor visit the warehouses of merchants, and shops of artificers, to gain the names of wares, tools and operations, of which no mention is found in books; what favourable accident, or easy enquiry brought within my reach, has not been neglected; but it had been a hopeless labour to glean up words, by courting living information, and contesting with the sullenness of one, and the roughness of another.

To furnish the academicians *della Crusca* with words of this kind, a series of comedies called *la Fiera,* or *the Fair,* was professedly written by *Buonaroti;* but I had no such assistant, and therefore was content to want what they must have wanted likewise, had they not luckily been so supplied.

Nor are all words which are not found in the vocabulary, to be lamented as omissions. Of the laborious and mercantile part of the people, the diction is in a great measure casual and mutable; many of their terms are formed for some temporary or local convenience, and though current at certain times and places, are in others utterly unknown. This fugitive cant, which is always in a state of increase or decay, cannot be regarded as any part of the durable materials of a language, and therefore must be suffered to perish with other things unworthy of preservation.

Care will sometimes betray to the appearance of negligence. He that is catching opportunities which seldom occur, will suffer those to pass by unregarded, which he expects hourly to return; he that is searching for rare and remote things, will neglect those that are obvious and familiar: thus many of the most common and cursory words have been inserted with little illustration, because in gathering the authorities, I forbore to copy those which I thought likely to occur whenever they were wanted. It is remarkable that, in reviewing my collection, I found the word SEA unexemplified.

Thus it happens, that in things difficult there is danger from ignorance, and in things easy from confidence; the mind, afraid of greatness, and disdainful of littleness, hastily withdraws herself from painful searches, and passes with scornful rapidity over tasks not adequate to her powers, sometimes too secure for caution, and again too anxious for vigorous effort; sometimes idle in a plain path, and sometimes distracted in labyrinths, and dissipated by different intentions.

A large work is difficult because it is large, even though all its parts might singly be performed with facility; where there are many things to be done, each must be allowed its share of time and labour, in the proportion only which it bears to the whole; nor can it be expected, that the stones which form the dome of a temple, should be squared and polished like the diamond of a ring.

Of the event of this work, for which, having laboured it with so much application, I cannot but have some degree of parental fondness, it is natural to form conjectures. Those who have been per-

suaded to think well of my design, will require that it should fix
our language, and put a stop to those alterations which time and
chance have hitherto been suffered to make in it without opposition. With this consequence I will confess that I flattered myself
for a while; but now begin to fear that I have indulged expectation
which neither reason nor experience can justify. When we see men
grow old and die at a certain time one after another, from century
to century, we laugh at the elixir that promises to prolong life to a
thousand years; and with equal justice may the lexicographer be
derided, who being able to produce no example of a nation that
has preserved their words and phrases from mutability, shall
imagine that his dictionary can embalm his language, and secure
it from corruption and decay, that it is in his power to change
sublunary nature, and clear the world at once from folly, vanity,
and affectation.

With this hope, however, academies have been instituted, to
guard the avenues of their languages, to retain fugitives, and re-
pulse intruders; but their vigilance and activity have hitherto been
vain; sounds are too volatile and subtile for legal restraints; to
enchain syllables, and to lash the wind, are equally the undertakings of pride, unwilling to measure its desires by its strength.
The *French* language has visibly changed under the inspection of
the academy; the stile of *Amelot's* translation of Father *Paul* is
observed by *Le Courayer* to be *un peu passé;* and no *Italian* will
maintain that the diction of any modern writer is not perceptibly
different from that of *Boccace, Machiavel,* or *Caro.*

Total and sudden transformations of a language seldom happen;
conquests and migrations are now very rare: but there are other
causes of change, which, though slow in their operation, and invisible in their progress, are perhaps as much superiour to human
resistance, as the revolutions of the sky, or intumescence of the
tide. Commerce, however necessary, however lucrative, as it de-
praves the manners, corrupts the language; they that have frequent intercourse with strangers, to whom they endeavour to
accommodate themselves, must in time learn a mingled dialect,
like the jargon which serves the traffickers on the *Mediterranean*
and *Indian* coasts. This will not always be confined to the exchange, the warehouse, or the port, but will be communicated by
degrees to other ranks of the people, and be at last incorporated
with the current speech.

There are likewise internal causes equally forcible. The language most likely to continue long without alteration, would be that of a nation raised a little, and but a little above barbarity, secluded from strangers, and totally employed in procuring the conveniences of life; either without books, or, like some of the *Mahometan* countries, with very few: men thus busied and unlearned, having only such words as common use requires, would perhaps long continue to express the same notions by the same signs. But no such constancy can be expected in a people polished by arts, and classed by subordination, where one part of the community is sustained and accommodated by the labour of the other. Those who have much leisure to think, will always be enlarging the stock of ideas, and every increase of knowledge, whether real or fancied, will produce new words, or combinations of words. When the mind is unchained from necessity, it will range after convenience; when it is left at large in the fields of speculation, it will shift opinions; as any custom is disused, the words that expressed it must perish with it; as any opinion grows popular, it will innovate speech in the same proportion as it alters practice.

As by the cultivation of various sciences, a language is amplified, it will be more furnished with words deflected from original sense; the geometrician will talk of a courtier's zenith, or the excentrick virtue of a wild hero, and the physician of sanguine expectations and phlegmatick delays. Copiousness of speech will give opportunities to capricious choice, by which some words will be preferred, and others degraded; vicissitudes of fashion will enforce the use of new, or extend the signification of known terms. The tropes of poetry will make hourly encroachments, and the metaphorical will become the current sense: pronunciation will be varied by levity or ignorance, and the pen must at length comply with the tongue; illiterate writers will at one time or other, by publick infatuation, rise into renown, who, not knowing the original import of words, will use them with colloquial licentiousness, confound distinction, and forget propriety. As politeness increases, some expressions will be considered as too gross and vulgar for the delicate, others as too formal and ceremonious for the gay and airy; new phrases are therefore adopted, which must, for the same reasons, be in time dismissed. *Swift*, in his petty treatise on the *English* language, allows that new words must sometimes be introduced, but proposes that none should be suffered to become obsolete. But what makes a word obsolete, more than general agreement to forbear it? and how shall it be continued, when it conveys an offensive idea, or recalled again into the mouths of mankind, when it has once become unfamiliar by disuse, and unpleasing by unfamiliarity?

There is another cause of alteration more prevalent than any other, which yet in the present state of the world cannot be obviated. A mixture of two languages will produce a third distinct from both, and they will always be mixed, where the chief part of education, and the most conspicuous accomplishment, is skill in ancient or in foreign tongues. He that has long cultivated another language, will find its words and combinations croud upon his memory; and haste and negligence, refinement and affectation, will obtrude borrowed terms and exotick expressions.

The great pest of speech is frequency of translation. No book was ever turned from one language into another, without imparting something of its native idiom; this is the most mischievous and comprehensive innovation; single words may enter by thousands, and the fabrick of the tongue continue the same, but new phraseology changes much at once; it alters not the single stones of the building, but the order of the columns. If an academy should be established for the cultivation of our stile, which I, who can never wish to see dependance multiplied, hope the spirit of *English* liberty will hinder or destroy, let them, instead of compiling grammars and dictionaries, endeavour, with all their influence, to stop the licence of translatours, whose idleness and ignorance, if it be suffered to proceed, will reduce us to babble a dialect of *France*.

If the changes that we fear be thus irresistible, what remains but to acquiesce with silence, as in the other insurmountable distresses of humanity? It remains that we retard what we cannot repel, that we palliate what we cannot cure. Life may be lengthened by care, though death cannot be ultimately defeated: tongues, like governments, have a natural tendency to degeneration; we have long preserved our constitution, let us make some struggles for our language.

In hope of giving longevity to that which its own nature forbids to be immortal, I have devoted this book, the labour of years, to the honour of my country, that we may no longer yield the palm of philology, without a contest, to the nations of the continent. The chief glory of every people arises from its authours: whether

I shall add any thing by my own writings to the reputation of *English* literature, must be left to time: much of my life has been lost under the pressures of disease; much has been trifled away; and much has always been spent in provision for the day that was passing over me; but I shall not think my employment useless or ignoble, if by my assistance foreign nations, and distant ages, gain access to the propagators of knowledge, and understand the teachers of truth; if my labours afford light to the repositories of science, and add celebrity to *Bacon*, to *Hooker*, to *Milton*, and to *Boyle*.

When I am animated by this wish, I look with pleasure on my book, however defective, and deliver it to the world with the spirit of a man that has endeavoured well. That it will immediately become popular I have not promised to myself: a few wild blunders, and risible absurdities, from which no work of such multiplicity was ever free, may for a time furnish folly with laughter, and harden ignorance in contempt; but useful diligence will at last prevail, and there never can be wanting some who distinguish desert; who will consider that no dictionary of a living tongue ever can be perfect, since while it is hastening to publication, some words are budding, and some falling away; that a whole life cannot be spent upon syntax and etymology, and that even a whole life would not be sufficient; that he, whose design includes whatever language can express, must often speak of what he does not understand; that a writer will sometimes be hurried by eagerness to the end, and sometimes faint with weariness under a task, which *Scaliger* compares to the labours of the anvil and the mine; that what is obvious is not always known, and what is known is not always present; that sudden fits of inadvertency will surprize vigilance, slight advocations will seduce attention, and casual eclipses of the mind will darken learning; and that the writer shall often in vain trace his memory at the moment of need, for that which yesterday he knew with intuitive readiness, and which will come uncalled into his thoughts tomorrow.

In this work, when it shall be found that much is omitted, let it not be forgotten that much likewise is performed; and though no book was ever spared out of tenderness to the authour, and the world is little solicitous to know whence proceeded the faults of that which it condemns; yet it may gratify curiosity to inform it, that the *English Dictionary* was written with little assistance of the learned, and without any patronage of the great; not in the soft obscurities of retirement, or under the shelter of academick bowers, but amidst inconvenience and distraction, in sickness and in sorrow. It may repress the triumph of malignant criticism to observe, that if our language is not here fully displayed, I have only failed in an attempt which no human powers have hitherto completed. If the lexicons of ancient tongues, now immutably fixed, and comprised in a few volumes, be yet, after the toil of successive ages, inadequate and delusive; if the aggregated knowledge, and co-operating diligence of the *Italian* academicians, did not secure them from the censure of *Beni;* if the embodied criticks of *France,* when fifty years had been spent upon their work, were obliged to change its oeconomy, and give their second edition another form, I may surely be contented without the praise of perfection, which, if I could obtain, in this gloom of solitude, what would it avail me? I have protracted my work till most of those whom I wished to please have sunk into the grave, and success and miscarriage are empty sounds: I therefore dismiss it with frigid tranquillity, having little to fear or hope from censure or from praise.

Preface to WEBSTER'S THIRD NEW

INTERNATIONAL DICTIONARY*

Philip B. Gove

WEBSTER'S THIRD NEW INTERNATIONAL DICTIONARY is a completely new work, redesigned, restyled, and reset. Every line of it is new. This latest unabridged Merriam-Webster is the eighth in a series which has its beginning in Noah Webster's *American Dictionary of the English Language,* 1828. On Webster's death in 1843 the unsold copies and publishing rights of his dictionary were acquired by George and Charles Merriam, who in 1847 brought out a revision edited by Noah Webster's son-in-law, Professor Chauncey A. Goodrich of Yale College. The 1847 edition became the first Merriam-

Webster unabridged dictionary.[1] G. & C. Merriam Company now offers WEBSTER'S THIRD NEW INTERNATIONAL DICTIONARY to the English-speaking world as a prime linguistic aid to interpreting the culture and civilization of today, as the first edition served the America of 1828.

As the number of students in school and college jumps to ever-increasing heights, the quantity of printed matter necessary to their education increases too. Not only are more words used more often with these increases; words must be used more economically and more efficiently both in school and out. More and more do people undertaking a new job, practicing a new hobby, or developing a new interest turn to how-to pamphlets, manuals, and books for both elementary instruction and advanced guidance. Where formerly they had time to learn by doing, they now need to begin by reading and understanding what has been recorded. A quick grasp of the meanings of words becomes necessary if one is to be successful. A dictionary opens the way to both formal learning and to the daily self-instruction that modern living requires. It is the key also to the daily newspaper and to a vast number of other periodicals that demand our attention. This edition has been prepared with a constant regard for the needs of the high school and college student, the technician, and the periodical reader, as well as of the scholar and professional. It undertakes to provide for the changes in public interest in all classes of words as manifested by what people want to read, discuss, and study. The dictionary more than ever is the indispensable instrument of understanding and progress.

G. & C. Merriam Company have produced this THIRD NEW INTERNATIONAL at a cost of over $3,500,000. The budgetary and technical planning underlying its production has been directed and coordinated since 1953 by the Company's president, Mr. Gordon J. Gallan. His activity, understanding, and cooperation have contributed indispensably to its editorial completion and have made possible the maintenance of a Merriam-Webster permanent office

---

[1] The successors in the Merriam-Webster series are *American Dictionary of the English Language,* popularly known as the *Unabridged,* 1864, edited by Dr. Noah Porter, president of Yale College; *Webster's International Dictionary,* 1890, Noah Porter, editor in chief; *Webster's New International Dictionary,* 1909, Dr. William Torrey Harris, U. S. Commissioner of Education, editor in chief, and F. Sturges Allen, general editor; *Webster's New International Dictionary, Second Edition,* 1934, Dr. William Allan Neilson, president of Smith College, editor in chief, and Dr. Thomas A. Knott, general editor.

staff constituted according to need. This staff is in effect a faculty which specializes in different branches of knowledge much as a small college faculty does. Listed among the resident editors are a mathematician, a physicist, a chemist, a botanist, a biologist, a philosopher, a political scientist, a comparative religionist, a classicist, a historian, and a librarian as well as philologists, linguists, etymologists, and phoneticians whose specialty is the English language itself. Their academic affiliations and their degrees can be seen one by one in the "Merriam-Webster Editorial Staff" [. . .]. Besides the office staff over two hundred other scholars and specialists have served as outside consultants in supplementary reviewing, revising, and submitting new definitions in subjects in which they are authorities. [. . .]

In conformity with the principle that a definition, to be adequate, must be written only after an analysis of usage, the definitions in this edition are based chiefly on examples of usage collected since publication of the preceding edition. Members of the editorial staff began in 1936 a systematic reading of books, magazines, newspapers, pamphlets, catalogs, and learned journals. By the time of going to press the collection contained just under 4,500,000 such new examples of recorded usage, to be added to more than 1,665,000 citations already in the files for previous editions. Further, the citations in the indispensable many-volume *Oxford English Dictionary*, the new citations in Sir William Craigie's four-volume *Dictionary of American English* and Mitford M. Mathews' two-volume *Dictionary of Americanisms*, neither of which was available to the editors of the preceding edition, and the uncounted citations in dozens of concordances to the Bible and to works of English and American writers and in numerous books of quotations push the citation background for the definitions in this dictionary to over ten million. This figure does not include freely consulted text matter in the office library of reference books. Nor does it include thousands of textbooks in the private and academic libraries of the editors and consultants, nor books consulted in the Springfield City Library whose librarians have generously given the editorial staff ready and frequent access to its large and valuable word-hoard.

While dictionaries of special subjects, glossaries, indexes, and checklists are collected and examined to verify the existence of special words, no word has been entered in this dictionary merely on the authority of another dictionary, special or general, and no definition in this dictionary has been derived from any other dictionary (except, of course, Merriam-Webster predecessors). Learned and industrial organizations have created numerous committees of nomenclature to collect, define, and standardize the terminology in their fields. Some of the staff editors serve as advisory members of such committees. Nevertheless prescriptive and canonical definitions have not been taken over nor have recommendations been followed unless confirmed by independent investigation of usage borne out by genuine citations.

The primary objective of precise, sharp defining has been met through development of a new dictionary style based upon completely analytical one-phrase definitions throughout the book. Since the headword in a definition is intended to be modified only by structural elements restrictive in some degree and essential to each other, the use of commas either to separate or to group has been severely limited, chiefly to units in apposition or in series. The new defining pattern does not provide for a predication which conveys further expository comment. Instead of encyclopedic treatment at one place of a group of related terms, each term is defined at its own place in the alphabet. Every phrase in lowercase roman type following a heavy black colon and running to the next heavy colon or to a divisional number or letter is a complete definition of one sense of the word to which it is attached. Defining by synonym is carefully avoided by putting all unqualified or undifferentiated terms in small capital letters. Such a term in small capitals should not be considered a definition but a cross-reference to a definition of equivalent meaning that can be substituted for the small capitals.

A large number of verbal illustrations mostly from the mid-twentieth century has been woven into the defining pattern with a view to contributing considerably to the user's interest and understanding by showing a word used in context. The illustration is often a brief combination of words that has actually been used in writing and when this is so the illustration is attributed to its author or source. More than 14,000 different authors are quoted for their use of words or for the structural pattern of their words but not for their opinions or sentiments.

A number of other features are (1) the recognition and separate entry (with part-of-speech label) of verb-plus-adverb compounds (as *run down*) that function like one-word verbs in every way except for having a separable suffix, (2) the recognition (by using the label *n* for noun) that substantive open compounds (as *clothes moth*) belong in the same class as nouns written solid or hyphened, (3) the recognition (by using the label *often attrib*) of nouns that often function as adjectives but otherwise do not behave like the class of adjectives, (4) the indication (by inserting suffix-symbols, as -S or -ES, -ED/-ING/-S or -ES, -ER/-EST) of the inflectional forms of nouns, verbs, adjectives, and adverbs at which the forms are not written out in full, (5) the recognition (by beginning entries with a lowercase letter and by inserting either the label *cap, usu cap, often cap,* or *sometimes cap*) that words vary considerably in capitalization according to circumstances and environment, (6) the recognition (by not using at all the status label *colloquial*) that it is impossible to know whether a word out of context is colloquial or not, and (7) the incorporation of abbreviations alphabetically in the main vocabulary.

In continuation of Merriam-Webster policy the editors of this new edition have held steadfastly to the three cardinal virtues of dictionary making: accuracy, clearness, and comprehensiveness. Whenever these qualities are at odds with each other, accuracy is put first and foremost, for without accuracy there could be no appeal to WEBSTER'S THIRD NEW INTERNATIONAL as an authority. Accuracy in addition to requiring freedom from error and conformity to truth requires a dictionary to state meanings in which words are in fact used, not to give editorial opinion on what their meanings should be.

In the editorial striving for clearness the editors have tried to make the definitions as readable as possible. Even so, the terminology of many subjects contains words that can be adequately and clearly explained only to those who have passed through preliminary stages of initiation, just as a knowledge of algebra is prerequisite for trigonometry. A dictionary demands of its user much understanding and no one person can understand all of it. Therefore there is no limit to the possibilities for clarification. Somewhat paradoxically a user of the dictionary benefits in proportion to his effort and knowledge, and his contribution is an essential part of the process of understanding even though it may involve only a willingness to look up a few additional words.

Comprehensiveness requires maximum coverage with a minimum of compromise. The basic aim is nothing less than coverage of the current vocabulary of standard written and spoken English. At the same time the scientific and technical vocabulary has been considerably expanded to keep pace with progress especially in physical science (as in electronics, nuclear physics, statistics, and soil science), in technology (as in rocketry, communications, automation, and synthetics), in medicine, and in the experimental phases of natural science. Therefore space has been found not only for new terms but also for new uses of old terms, for English like other living languages is in a metabolic process of constant change. The changes affect not only word stock but meaning, syntax, morphology, and pronunciation.

The demands for space have made necessary a fresh judgment on the claims of many parts of the old vocabulary. This dictionary is the result of a highly selective process in which discarding material of insubstantial or evanescent quality has gone hand in hand with adding terms that have obtained a place in the language. It confines itself strictly to generic words and their functions, forms, sounds, and meanings as distinguished from proper names that are not generic. Selection is guided by usefulness, and usefulness is determined by the degree to which terms most likely to be looked for are included. Many obsolete and comparatively useless or obscure words have been omitted. These include in general words that had become obsolete before 1755 unless found in well-known major works of a few major writers.

In definitions of words of many meanings the earliest ascertainable meaning is given first. Meanings of later derivation are arranged in the order shown to be most probable by dated evidence and semantic development. This arrangement applies alike to all meanings whether standard, technical, scientific, historical, or obsolete. No definitions are grouped alphabetically by subject labels. In fact this edition uses very few subject labels. It depends upon the definition for incorporating necessary subject orientation.

The pronunciation editor is Mr. Edward Artin. This edition shows as far as possible the pronunciations prevailing in general cultivated conversational usage, both informal and formal, throughout the English-speaking world. It does not attempt to dictate what that usage should be. It shows a wide variety of acceptable pronunciations based on a large file of transcriptions made by attentive listening to actual educated speech in all fields and in all parts of the country—the speech of those expecting to be completely understood by their hearers. The facility with which such speech can be checked today by television, radio, and recordings has made it possible to show more representative and more realistic pronunciations than in the past.

To this end the Merriam-Webster pronunciation key has been revised. Many of the symbols of preceding editions have been retained, some with slight alteration, a few substitutions have been made, and some symbols that have outlived their usefulness have been dropped altogether. It is still fundamentally a diacritical key that makes use of many of the conventions of English spelling and is based on the principles that every distinct significant sound should have a distinct symbol to represent it and that no sound should be represented in more than one way. The elimination of symbols for all nonsignificant differences in sound makes it possible for transcriptions to convey to speakers in different parts of the English-speaking world sounds proper to their own speech. The new pronunciation alphabet is designed to represent clearly the standard speech of educated Americans.

It should be clearly understood that in striving to show realistic pronunciations definite limitations are fixed by the very nature of a dictionary. Each word must be isolated and considered apart from its place in connected spoken discourse. It is impracticable to show in a dictionary many kinds of variations—rising or falling pitch, syllabic emphasis or lack of emphasis, contraction or prolongation of sounds—to which the pronunciation of a word is susceptible under the influence of other words temporarily associated with it. [. . .]

The etymologist for this edition is Dr. Charles R. Sleeth. In the etymologies the aim has been to retrace step by step the line of transmission by which the words have come down to modern English from the language in which they are first recorded. The present work adheres in this respect to the sound general principles governing the presentation of word histories in previous editions and indeed applies them with a consistency that has not previously been attained. With particular care it traces back to Middle English every word which is recorded in Middle English; also it carefully distinguishes the age of borrowings from French by giving the source language as Old French if the word came into English before 1300, as Middle French if it came into English between 1300 and 1600, and as French only if it came into English in the seventeenth century or later.

The etymologies fall into four general groups based on the origins of English words. Native words (as *hound*) that have been in the language as long as it has existed are traced back first through Middle English to Old English and then to Germanic languages other than English and to Indo-European languages other than Germanic. Old and well-established borrowings (as *chief, add,* and *dialect*) that have been in English since medieval or Renaissance times and come from languages, usually French, Latin, or often indirectly Greek, which belong, like English, to the Indo-European language family are traced back through their immediate source to their ultimate source in as much detail as native words. Many more recent borrowings (as *éclair, anile, hubris, sforzando, lariat, dachshund, smorgasbord, galore, muzhik,* and *karma*) are incorporated into the network of Indo-European etymology more thoroughly than in earlier dictionaries by going beyond the immediate source to either a list of cognates or a cross-reference to another entry. Borrowings (as *bushido, tepee, sheikh, sampan,* and *taboo*) from non-Indo-European languages are traced to the immediate source and analyzed into their parts if in the source language they are compounds or derivatives.

In the modern technical vocabulary of the sciences it is difficult if not impossible to adhere strictly to the principle of tracing step by step the line of transmission of a word, because such vocabulary has expanded rapidly in numerous fields and has been transmitted freely across language boundaries. Very few works of reference give full or systematic information about the language of origin of technical terms in any one field, and consequently it is impossible for the etymological staff of a general dictionary to garner and present such information about the technical terms of all fields. The present work attempts a new solution of this problem by introducing the label ISV (for International Scientific Vocabulary), for use in the etymology of such words when their language of origin is not positively ascertainable but they are known to be current in at least one language other than English. [. . .] Some ISV words (like *haploid*) have been created by taking a word with a rather general and simple meaning from one of the languages of antiquity, usually Latin or Greek, and conferring upon it a very specific and complicated meaning for the purposes of modern scientific discourse. More typically, however, ISV words are compounds or derivatives, made up of constituents that can be found entered in their own alphabetical position with their own ulterior etymology, again generally involving Latin or Greek. In either case an ISV etymology as given in the present work incorporates the word into the system of Indo-European etymology as well as if the immediate source language were known and stated. At the same time, use of ISV avoids the often untenable implication that the word in question was coined in English, and recognizes that the word as such is a product of the modern world and gets only its raw materials, so to speak, from antiquity.

The scheme of biological classification used has been concerted in consultation between Dr. Mairé Weir Kay, staff biologist, and specialists in the several divisions of taxonomy. It is planned to coordinate in the broadest way with current professional usage and specifically avoids undue reliance on any single school or system. The total taxonomic coverage is far more extensive than this characterization might imply and is designed to include and link with the preferred scheme both historically important though now disused terminology and the more important terms pertinent to divergent schools of professional thought (as in the question of whether the leguminous plants constitute one or several families).

Words that are believed to be trademarks have been investigated in the files of the United States Patent Office. Those that were originally trademarks before being taken over generically by usage and becoming lexical are recognized as such. The inclusion of any word in this dictionary is not, however, an expression of the publishers' opinion on whether or not it is subject to proprietary rights. Indeed, no definition in this dictionary is to be regarded as affecting the validity of any trademark.

This dictionary has a vocabulary of over 450,000 words. It would have been easy to make the vocabulary larger although the book, in the format of the preceding edition, could hardly hold any more pages or be any thicker. By itself, the number of entries is, however, not of first importance. The number of words available is always far in excess of and for a one-volume dictionary many times the number that can possibly be included. To make all the changes mentioned only to come out with the same number of pages and the same number of vocabulary entries as in the preceding edition would allow little or no opportunity for new words and new senses. The compactness and legibility of Times Roman, a typeface new to Merriam-Webster dictionaries, have made possible more words to a line and more lines to a column than in the preceding edition, and a larger size page makes a better proportioned book.

The preparation of this edition has absorbed 757 editor-years. This figure does not include the time of typists, photocopiers, and clerical assistants or the time of over 200 consultants. The book appears, like its predecessor, after more than ten years of active full-time preparation. It is hardly necessary to observe that no one editor could harmonize all the diverse and disparate matter by reading and criticizing every line or even determine and keep firm control over editorial policy, nor could an editorial board of fixed membership. Instead the editor in chief has used his editors one by one and has delegated multiple responsibilities to them individually as occasion required. In this way members of the Merriam-Webster staff have been grouped and regrouped to form hundreds of task forces performing simultaneously thousands of missions. The editor can say with gratitude and relief that the accomplishment is not a one-man dictionary. "What individual," asks Noah Webster in his preface, "is competent to trace to their source, and define in all their various applications, popular, scientific, and technical, sixty or seventy thousand words!"

WEBSTER'S THIRD NEW INTERNATIONAL DICTIONARY is a collaborative effort. Without the cooperation of the scholarly, scientific, and technical world, the specialized guidance of our outside consultants, and the ingenuity of the compositors and printers, G. & C. Merriam Company and its permanent editorial staff could not have brought the work to its successful culmination. Those most deeply involved with overall responsibility deserve special mention here. Three associate editors, Mr. Artin, Dr. Kay, and Dr. Sleeth, have already been named in this preface. Among others who have shared large responsibilities are these associate editors: Miss Anne M. Driscoll, Dr. Philip H. Goepp, Mr. Hubert P. Kelsey, Dr. Howard G. Rhoads, and Dr. H. Bosley Woolf; two assistant editors, Miss Ervina E. Foss and Mrs. Laverne W. King; and the departmental secretary, Mrs. Christine M. Mullen.

It is now fairly clear that before the twentieth century is over every community of the world will have learned how to communicate with all the rest of humanity. In this process of intercommunication the English language has already become the most important language on earth. This new Merriam-Webster unabridged is the record of this language as it is written and spoken. It is offered with confidence that it will supply in full measure that information on the general language which is required for accurate, clear, and comprehensive understanding of the vocabulary of today's society.

THE STRING UNTUNED *

Dwight MacDonald

The third edition of Webster's New International Dictionary (Unabridged), which was published last fall by the G. & C. Merriam Co., of Springfield, Massachusetts, tells us a good deal about the changes in our cultural climate since the second edition appeared, in 1934. The most important difference between Webster's Second (hereafter called 2) and Webster's Third (or 3) is that 3 has accepted as standard English a great many words and expressions to which 2 attached warning labels: *slang, colloquial, erroneous, incorrect, illiterate.* My impression is that most of the words so labelled in the 1934 edition are accepted in the 1961 edition as perfectly normal, honest, respectable citizens. Between these dates in this country a revolution has taken place in the study of English grammar and usage, a revolution that probably represents an advance in scientific method but that certainly has had an unfortunate effect on such nonscientific activities as the teaching of English and the making of dictionaries—at least on the making of this particular dictionary. This scientific revolution has meshed gears with a trend toward permissiveness, in the name of democracy, that is debasing our language by rendering it less precise and thus less effective as literature and less efficient as communication.

It is felt that it is snobbish to insist on making discriminations—the very word has acquired a Jim Crow flavor—about usage. And it is assumed that true democracy means that the majority is right. This feeling seems to me sentimental and this assumption unfounded.

There have been other recent dictionaries calling themselves "unabridged," but they are to Webster's 3 as a welterweight is to a heavyweight. 3 is a massive folio volume (thirteen inches by nine and a half by four) that weighs thirteen and a half pounds, contains four hundred and fifty thousand entries—an "entry" is a word plus its definition—in 2,662 pages, cost three and a half million dollars to produce, and sells for $47.50 up, according to binding. The least comparable dictionary now in print is the New Webster's Vest Pocket Dictionary, which bears on its title page the charmingly frank notation, "This dictionary is not published by the original publishers of Webster's Dictionary or by their successors." It measures five and a half inches by two and a half by a half, weighs two and a quarter ounces, has two hundred and thirty-nine pages, and costs thirty-nine cents. The only English dictionary now in print that *is* comparable to 3 is the great Oxford English Dictionary, a unique masterpiece of historical research that is as important in the study of the language as the King James Bible has been in the use of the language. The O.E.D. is much bigger than 3, containing sixteen thousand four hundred pages in thirteen folio volumes. It is bigger because its purpose is historical as well as definitive; it traces the evolution of each word through the centuries, illustrating the changes in meaning with dated quotations. The latest revision of the O.E.D. appeared in 1933, a year before Webster's 2 appeared. For the language as it has developed in the last quarter of a century, there is no dictionary comparable in scope to 3.

The editor of 2, Dr. William A. Neilson, president of Smith College, followed lexical practice that had obtained since Dr. Johnson's day and assumed there was such a thing as correct English and that it was his job to decide what it was. When he felt he had to include a substandard word because of its common use, he put it in, but with a warning label: *Slang, Dial.,* or even bluntly *Illit.* His approach was normative and his dictionary was an authority that pronounced on which words were standard English and which were not. Bets were decided by "looking it up in the dictionary."

It would be hard to decide bets by appealing to 3, whose editor of fifteen years' standing, Dr. Philip Gove, while as dedicated a scholar as Dr. Neilson, has a quite different approach. A dictionary, he writes, "should have no traffic with . . . artificial notions of correctness or superiority. It must be descriptive and not prescriptive." Dr. Gove and the other makers of 3 are sympathetic to the school of language study that has become dominant since 1934. It is sometimes called Structural Linguistics and sometimes, rather magnificently, just Modern Linguistic Science. Dr. Gove gives its basic concepts as:

1. Language changes constantly.
2. Change is normal.
3. Spoken language is the language.
4. Correctness rests upon usage.
5. All usage is relative.

While one must sympathize with the counterattack the Structural Linguists have led against the tyranny of the schoolmarms and the purists, who have caused unnecessary suffering to generations of schoolchildren over such matters as *shall* v. *will* and the *who-whom* syndrome—someone has observed that the chief result of the long crusade against "It's me" is that most Americans now say "Between you and I"—it is remarkable what strange effects have been produced in 3 by following Dr. Gove's five little precepts, reasonable as each seems taken separately. Dr. Gove conceives of his dictionary as a recording instrument rather than as an authority; in fact, the whole idea of authority or correctness is repulsive to him as a lexical scientist. The question is, however, whether a purely scientific approach to dictionary-making may not result in greater evils than those it seeks to cure.

When one compares 2 and 3, the first difference that strikes one is that 2 is a work of traditional scholarship and hence oriented toward the past, while 3—though in many ways more scholarly, or at least more academic, than 2—exhales the breezy air of the present. This is hardly surprising, since the new school of linguistics is non-historical, if not anti-historical. Henry Luce's *Time* rather than Joseph Addison's *Spectator* was the hunting ground for 3's illus-

trative quotations. There is a four-and-a-half-page list of consultants. Its sheer bulk is impressive—until one begins to investi-
gate. One can see why James W. Perry had to be consulted on
Non-numerical Computer Applications and Margaret Fulford on
Mosses and Liverworts, but it seems overdoing it to have two consultants on both Hardware and Salvation Army, and some people
might even question one apiece on Soft Drinks, Boy Scouts, Camp
Fire Girls, and Girl Guiding, as well as the enrolling of Mr. Arthur
B. LaFar, formerly president of the Angostura-Wuppermann bit-
ters company, as consultant on Cocktails. Such padding is all the
more odd, considering that the editors of 3 have forgotten to appoint anybody in Philosophy, Political Theory, or Theatre. The old-
fashioned 2 had six consultants on Catholic Church and Protestant
Churches. 3 has only one, on Catholic Church. But it also has one
on Christian Science, a more up-to-date religion.

The G. & C. Merriam Co. has been publishing Webster's dictionaries since 1847, four years after Noah Webster died. Work on
3 began the day 2 went to press, but it gathered real momentum
only fifteen years ago, when Dr. Gove began building up his staff
of lexicographers. The first step was to sort out the words of 2 into
a hundred and nine categories, so that specialized-definition writers
could deal with them. It took five women two and a half years to do
this. (" 'If seven maids with seven mops swept it for a half a year,
Do you suppose,' the Walrus said, 'That they could get it clear?' "—
Lewis Carroll.) After that, all that had to be done was to write new
definitions for most of the three hundred and fifty thousand entries
that were taken over from 2, to select and write a hundred thousand
new entries, to collect four and a half million quotations illustrating
word usage, and to distribute them among the definition writers.
The scope of the operation may be suggested by the fact that in
chemistry alone the lexicographers gathered two hundred and fifty
thousand quotations and took six and a half years to write the
definitions. After that, it was up to the Lakeside Press, of Chicago,
to set type from a manuscript that was as bristling with revisions and
interlineations, mostly in longhand, as a Proust manuscript. At first
they gave the printers clean, retyped copy, but they soon found
that the extra step produced an extra crop of errors. The printing
was done by the Riverside Press, of Cambridge, Massachusetts, a
long-established firm, like Merriam, whose dictionaries it has been
printing for almost a century. But antiquity is relative. There is no

one at Riverside like the compositor at Oxford's Clarendon Press who began setting type for the O.E.D. in 1884 and was still at it when the last volume came off the presses in 1928.

In seeking out and including all the commonly used words, especially slang ones, the compilers of 3 have been admirably diligent. Their definitions, in the case of meanings that have arisen since 1900 or so, are usually superior (though, because of the tiny amount of a dictionary it is possible to read before vertigo sets in, all generalizations must be understood to be strictly impressionistic). They have also provided many more quotations (this is connected with the linguistic revolution), perhaps, indeed, too many more. It is quite true, as the promotional material for 3 claims, that this edition goes far beyond what is generally understood by the term "revision" and may honestly be termed a new dictionary. But I should advise the possessors of the 1934 edition to think carefully before they turn it in for the new model. Although the publishers have not yet destroyed the plates of 2, they do not plan to keep it in print, which is a pity. There are reasons, which will presently appear, that buyers should be given a choice between 2 and 3, and that, in the case of libraries and schools, 3 should be regarded as an up-to-date supplement to 2 rather than a replacement of it.

Quantitative comparison between 2 and 3 must be approached cautiously. On the surface, it is considerably in 2's favor: 3,194 pages v. 2,662. But although 2 has six hundred thousand entries to 3's four hundred and fifty thousand, its entries are shorter; and because 3's typography is more compact and its type page larger, it gets in almost as much text as 2. The actual number of entries dropped since 2 is not a hundred and fifty thousand but two hundred and fifty thousand, since a hundred thousand new ones have been added. This incredible massacre—almost half the words in the English language seem to have disappeared between 1934 and 1961—is in fact incredible. For the most part, the dropped entries fall into very special categories that have less to do with the language than with methods of lexicography. They are: variants; "nonce words," like *Shakespearolatry* ("excessive reverence or devotion to Shakespeare"), which seemed a good idea at the time, or for the nonce, but haven't caught on; a vast number of proper names, including nearly every one in both the King James and the Douay Bibles; foreign terms; and obsolete or archaic words. This last category is a large one, since 2 includes "all the literary and most of the technical and scientific words and meanings in the period of Modern English beginning with the year 1500," plus all the words in Chaucer, while 3, in line with its modernization program, has advanced the cut-off date to 1755. A great many, perhaps most, of the entries dropped from 2 were in a section of small type at the foot of each page, a sort of linguistic ghetto, in which the editors simply listed "fringe words"—the definitions being limited to a synonym or often merely a symbol—which they thought not important enough to put into the main text. 3 has either promoted them to the text or, more frequently, junked them.

Some examples of the kinds of word that are in 2 but not in 3 are: *arrousement, aswowe* (in a swoon), *dethronize, devoration* (act of devouring), *disagreeance, mummianize* (mummify), *noyous* (annoying), *punquetto* (strumpet), *ridiculize,* and *subsign* (subscribe). Two foreign words that one might expect to find in 3 were left out because of insufficient "backing;" i.e., the compilers didn't find enough usages to justify inclusion. They were *Achtung* and *niet;* the researchers must have skipped spy movies and Mclotovian diplomacy. *Pot holder* was left out, after considerable tergiversating, because (a) for some reason the compilers found little backing for it, and (b) it was held to be self-explanatory (though considering some of the words they put in . . .). If it had been considered to be a single word, it would have been admitted, since one rule they followed was: No word written solid is self-explanatory.

The hundred thousand new entries in 3 are partly scientific or technical terms, partly words that have come into general use since 1934. The sheer quantity of the latter is impressive. English is clearly a living, growing language, and in this portion of their task the compilers of 3 have done an excellent job. Merriam-Webster has compiled some interesting lists of words in 3 that are not in 2. Some of the political ones are:

character assassination	loyalty oath
desegregation	McCarthyism
freedom of speech	segregated
globalize	red-baiting
hatemonger	shoo-in
integrationist	sit-in
welfare capitalism	subsistence economy

Among the new entries in the cocktail-party area are:

club soda	name-dropping
elbow bending	pub crawler
gate-crasher	quick one
glad-hander	rumpot
good-time Charlie	silent treatment
Irish coffee	table-hop
jungle juice	yakety-yak

The most important new aspect of 3, the rock on which it has been erected, is the hundred thousand illustrative quotations—known professionally as "citations" or "cites"—drawn from fourteen thousand writers and publications. (Another hundred thousand "usage examples" were made up by the compilers.) Most of the cites are from living writers or speakers, ranging from Winston Churchill, Edith Sitwell, Jacques Maritain, J. Robert Oppenheimer, and Albert Schweitzer to Billy Rose, Ethel Merman, James Cagney, Burl Ives, and Ted Williams. Many are from publications, extending from the Dictionary of American Biography down to college catalogues, fashion magazines, and the annual report of the J. C. Penney Company. The hundred thousand cites were chosen from a collection of over six million, of which a million and a half were already in the Merriam-Webster files; four and a half million were garnered by Dr. Gove and his staff. (The O.E.D. had about the same number of cites in its files—drawn mostly from English literary classics—but used a much larger proportion of them, almost two million, which why it is five or six times as long as 3.) For years everybody in the office did up to three hours of reading a day—the most, it was found, that was possible without attention lag. Dr. Gove presently discovered a curious defect in this method: the readers tended to overlook the main meanings of a word and concentrate on the peripheral ones; thus a hundred and fifty cite slips were turned in for *bump* as in burlesque stripping but not one for *bump* as in a road. To compensate for this, he created a humbler task force, whose job it was to go through the gutted carcasses of books and magazines after the first group had finished with them and arbitrarily enter on a slip one word—plus its context—in the first sentence in the fourth line from the top of each surviving page. The percentage of useful slips culled by this method approximated the percentage of useful slips made out by the readers who had used their brains. Unsettling.

The cites in 2 are almost all from standard authors. Its cite on *jocund* is from Shakespeare; 3's is from Elinor Wylie. Under *ghastly* 2 has cites from Gray (two), Milton (three), Poe, Wordsworth, Shakespeare, Shelley, Hawthorne, and—as a slight concession to modernity—Maurice Hewlett. 3 illustrates *ghastly* with cites from Louis Bromfield, Macaulay, Thackeray, Thomas Herbert, Aldous Huxley, H. J. Laski, D. B. Chidsey, and J. C. Powys. For *debonair*, 2 has Milton's "buxom, blithe and debonair," while 3 has H. M. Reynolds' "gay, brisk and debonair." One may think, as I do, that 3 has dropped far too many of the old writers, that it has overemphasized its duty of recording the current state of the language and skimped its duty of recording the past that is still alive (Mr. Reynolds would hardly have arrived at his threesome had not Mr. Milton been there before). A decent compromise would have been to include both, but the editors of 3 don't go in for compromises. They seem imperfectly aware of the fact that the past of a language is part of its present, that tradition is as much a fact as the violation of tradition.

The editors of 3 have labored heroically on pronunciation, since one of the basic principles of the new linguistic doctrine is that Language is Speech. Too heroically, indeed. For here, as in other aspects of their labors, the editors have displayed more valor than discretion. Sometimes they appear to be lacking in common sense. The editors of 2 found it necessary to give only two pronunciations for *berserk* and two for *lingerie*, but 3 seems to give twenty-five for the first and twenty-six for the second. (This is a rough estimate; the system of notation is very complex. Dr. Gove's pronunciation editor thinks there are approximately that number but says that he is unable to take the time to be entirely certain.) Granted that 2 may have shirked its duty, one may still find something compulsive in the amplitude with which 3 has fulfilled its obligations. Does anybody except a Structural Linguist need to know that much? And what use is such plethora to a reader who wants to know how to pronounce a word? The new list of pronunciation symbols in 3 is slightly shorter than the one in 2 but also—perhaps for that reason—harder to understand. 2 uses only those nice old familiar letters of the alphabet, with signs over them to indicate long and short and so on. (It also repeats its pronunciation guide at the foot of each page, which is handy; 3 does not, to save space and dollars, so one has to flop over as much as thirteen and a half pounds of printed matter to refer back to the one place the guide appears.) 3 also uses the alphabet, but there is one catastrophic exception. This is an upside-down "e," known in the trade as a "schwa," which stands for a faint, indistinct sound, like the "e" in *quiet,* that is unnervingly common and that can be either "a," "e," "i," "o," or "u," according to circumstance. Things get quite lively when you trip over a schwa. *Bird* is given straight as *bûrd* in 2, but in 3 it is *bərd, bə̄d,* and *bəid.* This last may be boid, but I'm not sure. Schwa trouble. ("Double, double schwa and trouble." —*Shakespeare.*)

Almost all 3's pictures are new or have been redrawn in a style that is superior to 2's—clearer and more diagrammatic. The new cut of "goose," with no less than twenty-four parts clearly marked, is a special triumph. The other animal illustrations, from *aardvark* to *zebu,* are less picturesque but more informative than those in 2. The illustrations are—rightly—chosen for utility rather than orna- ment. On facing pages we have pictures of *coracles, corbel,* and *corbiesteps,* all definitely needed, though, on another, *pail* might have been left to the imagination. One of the few illustrations repeated from 2 is *digestive organs,* and a fine bit of uncompromis- ing realism it is, too.

I notice no important omissions in 3. *Namby-pamby* is in. How- ever, it was coined—to describe the eighteenth-century Ambrose Philips' insipid verses—not "by some satirists of his time" but by just one of them, Henry Carey, whose celebrated parody of Philips is entitled "Namby-Pamby." *Bromide* is in ("a conventional and commonplace or tiresome person"), but not the fact that Gelett Burgess invented it. Still, he gets credit for *blurb* and *goop.* *Ab- stract expressionism* is in, but *Tachism* and *action painting* are not. The entries on Marxist and Freudian terms are skimpy. *Id* is in, but without citations and with too brief a definition. *Ego* is defined as Fichte, Kant, and Hume used it but not as Freud did. The dis- tinction between *unconscious* and *subconscious* is muffed; the first is adequately defined and the reader is referred to the latter; look- ing that up, he finds "The mental activities just below the threshold of consciousness; *also:* the aspect of the mind concerned with such activities that is an entity or a part of the mental apparatus overlapping, equivalent to, or distinct from the unconscious." I can't grasp the nature of something that is overlapping, equivalent to, *or* distinct from something else. While *dialectical materialism* and *charisma* (which 2 treats only as a theological term, although Max Weber had made the word common sociological currency long before 1934) are in, there is no *mass culture,* and the full entry for the noun *masses* is "pl. of mass." There is no reference to Marx or even to Hegel under *reify,* and under *alienation* the closest 3 comes to this important concept of Marxist theory is "the state of being alienated or diverted from normal function," which is illustrated by "alienation of muscle." Marx is not mentioned in the very brief definition of *class struggle.*

The definitions seem admirably objective. I detected only one major lapse:

> McCarthyism—a political attitude of the mid-twentieth century closely allied to know-nothingism and characterized chiefly by opposition to elements held to be subversive and by the use of tactics involving personal attacks on individuals by means of widely publicized indiscriminate allegation *esp.* on the basis of unsubstantiated charges.

I fancy the formulator of this permitted himself a small, dry smile as he leaned back from his typewriter before trudging on to *McClellan saddle* and *McCoy* (the real). I'm not complaining, but I can't help remembering that the eponymous hero of *McCarthyism* wrote a little book with that title in which he gave a rather different definition. The tendentious treatment of *McCarthyism* contrasts with the objectivity of the definition of *Stalinism,* which some of us consider an even more reprehensible *ism:* "The political, economic and social principles and policies associated with Stalin; *esp:* the theory and practice of communism developed by Stalin from Marxism-Leninism." The first part seems to me inadequate and the second absurd, since Stalin never had a theory in his life. The definitions of *democratic* and *republican* seem fair: "policies of broad social reform and internationalism in foreign affairs" v. "usu. associated with business, financial, and some agricultural interests and with favoring a restricted governmental role in social and economic life." Though I wonder what the Republican National Committee thinks.

One of the most painful decisions unabridgers face is what to do about those obscene words that used to be wholly confined to informal discourse but that of late, after a series of favorable court decisions, have been cropping up in respectable print. The editors of 2, being gentlemen and scholars, simply omitted them. The editors of 3, being scientists, were more conscientious. All the chief four- and five-letter words are here, with the exception of perhaps the most important one. They defend this omission not on lexical grounds but on the practical and, I think, reasonable ground that its inclusion would have stimulated denunciations and boycotts. There are, after all, almost half a million other words in their dictionary—not to mention an investment of three and a half million dollars—and they reluctantly decided not to imperil the whole enterprise by insisting on that word.

Two useful features of 2 were omitted from 3: the gazetteer of place names and the biographical dictionary. They were left out partly to save money—they took up a hundred and seventy-six pages, and the biographical dictionary had to be brought up to date with each new printing—and partly because Dr. Gove and his colleagues, more severe than the easygoing editors of 2, considered such items "encyclopedic material" and so not pertinent to a dictionary. The force of this second excuse is weakened because although they did omit such encyclopedic features of 2 as the two pages on *grasses,* they put in a page-an-a-half table of currencies under *money* and three and a half pages of *dyes.* It is also worth noting that Merriam-Webster added a new item to its line in 1943 —the Webster's Biographical Dictionary. While I quite understand the publishers' reluctance to give away what their customers would otherwise have to buy separately, I do think the biographical dictionary should have been included—from the consumer's point of view, at any rate.

However, the editors have sneaked in many proper names by the back door; that is, by entering their adjectival forms. *Walpolian* means "1: of, relating to, or having the characteristics of Horace Walpole or his writings," and "2: of, relating to, or having the characteristics of Robert Walpole or his political policies," and we get the death dates of both men (but not the birth dates), plus the information that Horace was "Eng. man of letters" and Robert "Eng. statesman" (though it is not noted that Horace was Robert's son). This method of introducing proper names produces odd results. Raphael is in (*Raphaelesque, Raphaelism, Raphaelite*), as are Veronese (*Veronese green*) and Giotto and Giorgione and

Michelangelo, but not Tintoretto and Piero della Francesca, because they had the wrong kind of names. Caravaggio had the right kind, but the editors missed him, though *Caravaggesque* is as frequently used in art criticism as *Giottesque*. All the great modern painters, from Cézanne on, are omitted, since none have appropriate adjectives. Yeats is in (*Yeatsian*) but not Eliot, Pound, or Frost (why not Frosty?). Sometimes one senses a certain desperation, as when *Smithian* is used to wedge in Adam Smith. *Menckenian* and *Menckenese* get an inch each, but no *Hawthornean*, no *Melvillesque*, no *Twainite*. All the twentieth-century presidents are in—Eisenhower by the skin of *Eisenhower jacket* —except Taft and Truman and Kennedy. Hoover has the most entries, all dispiriting: *Hoover apron* and *Hooverize,* because he was food administrator in the First World War; *Hooversville,* for the depression shanty towns; *Hoovercrat,* for a Southern Democrat who voted for him in 1928; and *Hooverism.*

This brings up the matter of capitalization. 2 capitalized proper names; 3 does not, with one exception. There may have been some esoteric reason of typographical consistency. Whatever their reasons, the result is that they must cumbersomely and forever add *usu. cap.* (Why *usu.* when it is *alw?*) The exception is *God,* which even these cautious linguisticians couldn't quite bring themselves to label *usu. cap. Jesus* is out because of adjectival deficiency, except for *Jesus bug,* a splendid slang term, new to me, for the waterbug ("fr. the allusion to his walking on the water," the "his" being firmly lower case). He does get in via His second name, which, luckily, has given us a rather important adjective, *usu. cap.*

At first glance, 3's typography is cleaner and more harmonious. Dr. Gove estimates that the editors eliminated two million commas and periods (as after adj., n., and v.), or eighty pages' worth. A second glance shows a major and, from a utilitarian point of view, very nearly a fatal defect. Words that have more than one meaning—and many have dozens—are much easier to follow in 2, which gives a new paragraph to each meaning, than in 3, which runs the whole entry as one superparagraph. ("What! Will the line stretch out to the crack of doom?"—*Shakespeare.*) Thus 2 not only starts each new meaning of *cut* with a paragraph but also puts in an italicized heading: *Games & Sports, Bookbinding, Card Playing, Motion Pictures.* In 3 one has to look through a solid paragraph of nine inches, and there are no headings. The most extreme example

I found was 3's entry on the transitive verb *take,* which runs on for a single paragraph two feet eight inches long, in which the twenty-one main meanings are divided only by boldfaced numerals; there follow, still in the same paragraph, four inches of the intransitive *take,* the only sign of this gearshifting being a tiny printer's squiggle. *Take* is, admittedly, quite a verb. The Oxford English Dictionary gives sixty-three meanings in nine feet, but they are spaced out in separate paragraphs, as in the mere foot and a half that 2 devotes to *take.*

A second glance also suggests second thoughts about the richness of citations in 3. Often it seems *plethoric,* even *otiose* ("lacking use or effect"). The chief reason 3's entries on multiple-meaning words are so much longer than 2's is that it has so many more citations. Many are justified and do indeed enrich our sense of words, but a good thing can be overdone. The promotional material for 3 mentions the treatment of *freeze* as an improvement, but does anybody really need such illustrative richness as:

> 6a: to make (as the face) expressionless [with instructions to recognize no one; and in fact he did *freeze* his face up when an old acquaintance hailed him—Fletcher Pratt] [a look of incredulity *froze* his face . . . and his eyes went blank with surprise—Hamilton Basso] b. to preserve rigidly a particular expression on [he still sat, his face *frozen* in shame and misery—Agnes S. Turnbull]

The question is rhetorical.

One of the problems of an unabridger is where completeness ends and madness begins. The compilers of 2 had a weakness for such fabrications as *philomuse, philomythia* ("devotion to legends . . . sometimes, loquaciousness"), *philonoist* ("a seeker of knowledge"), *philophilosophos* ("partial to philosophers"), *philopolemic, philopornist* ("a lover of harlots"), and *philosopheress* (which means not only a woman philosopher, like Hannah Arendt, but a philosopher's wife, like Xantippe). These are omitted by the compilers of 3, though they could not resist *philosophastering* ("philosophizing in a shallow or pretentious manner"). But why do we need *nooky* ("full of nooks") or *name-caller* ("one that habitually engages in name-calling") or all those "night" words, from *night clothes*—"garments worn in bed," with a citation from Jane Welsh Carlyle, of all people—through *nightdress, nightgear, nightgown, nightrobe, nightshirt,* and *nightwear?* What need of *sea boat* ("a boat adapted to the open sea") or *sea captain* or *swimming pool* ("a pool suitable for swimming," lest we imagine it is a pool that swims) or *sunbath* ("exposure to sunlight"—"or to a sun lamp," they add cautiously) or *sunbather* ("one that takes sunbaths")? Why *kittenless* ("having no kitten")? Why need we be told that *white-faced* is "having the face white in whole or in part"? Or that *white-handed* is "having white hands"? (They missed *whitelipped*.)

Then there are those terrible negative prefixes, which the unwary unabridger gets started on and slides down with sickening momentum. 3 has left out many of 2's absurdities: *nonborrower, nonnervous, non-Mohammedan, non-Welsh, non-walking.* But it adds some of its own: *nonscientist, nonphilatelic, non-inbred, non-drying* (why no *nonwetting?*), *nonbank* ("not being or done by a bank"), and many other nonuseful and nonsensical entries. It has thirty-four pages of words beginning with *un-,* and while it may seem carping to object to this abundance, since the O.E.D. has three hundred and eight such pages, I think, given the difference in purpose, that many may be challenged. A reasonably bright child of ten will not have to run to Daddy's Unabridged to find the meaning of *unreelable* ("incapable of being wound on a reel"), *unlustrous* ("lacking luster"), and *unpowdered* ("not powdered"). And if it's for unreasonably dumb children, why omit *unspinnable, unshining,* and *unsanded?*

For a minor example of gnostimania, or scholar's knee, see the treatment of numbers. Every number from *one* to *ninety-nine* is entered and defined, also every numerical adjective. Thus when the reader hits *sixty* he goes into a skid fifteen inches long. *Sixty* ("being one more than 59 in number") is followed by the pronoun ("60 countable persons or things not specified but under consideration and being enumerated") and the noun ("six tens: twice 30: 12 fives," etc.). Then comes *sixty-eight* ("being one more than 67 in number") and *sixty-eighth* ("being number 68 in a countable series"), followed by *sixty-fifth, sixty-first,* and so on. The compilers of 2 dealt with the *sixty* problem in a mere two entries totalling an inch and a half. But the art of lexicography has mutated into a "science" since then. ("*Quotation mark* . . . sometimes used to enclose . . . words . . . in an . . . ironical . . . sense . . . or words for which a writer offers a slight apology.") In reading 3 one sometimes feels like a subscriber who gets two hundred and thirty-eight copies of the May issue because the addressing machine got stuck, and it doesn't make it any better to know that the operators jammed it on purpose.

My complaint is not that 3 is all-inclusive—that is, unabridged—but that *pedantry* is not a synonym of *scholarship*. I have no objection to the inclusion of such pomposities, mostly direct translations from the Latin, as *viridity* (greenness), *presbyopic* (far-sighted because of old age), *vellication* (twitching), *pudency* (modesty), and *vulnerary* (wound-healing). These are necessary if only so that one can read James Gould Cozzens' "By Love Possessed," in which they all occur, along with many siblings. And in my rambles through these 2,662 pages I have come across many a splendid word that has not enjoyed the popularity it deserves. I think my favorites are *pilpul*, from the Hebrew *to search*, which means "critical analysis and hairsplitting; casuistic argumentation;" *dysphemism*, which is the antonym of *euphemism* (as, *axle grease* for *butter* or *old man* for father), *subfusc*, from the Latin *subfuscus*, meaning brownish, which is illustrated with a beautiful citation from Osbert Sitwell ("the moment when the word Austerity was to take to itself a new subfusc and squalid twist of meaning")—cf. the more familiar *subacid*, also well illustrated with "a little subacid kind of . . . impatience," from Laurence Sterne; *nanism*, which is the antonym of *gigantism; mesocracy*, which is the form of government we increasingly have in this country; and *lib-lab*, which means a Liberal who sympathizes with Labor—I wish the lexicographers had not restored the hyphen I deleted when I imported it from England twenty years ago. One might say, and in fact I will say, that H. L. Mencken, whose prose was dysphemistic but never subfusc, eschewed pilpul in expressing his nanitic esteem for lib-lab mesocracy. Unfortunately, 3 omits 2's *thob* ("to think according to one's wishes"), which someone made up from *think-opinion-believe*, or else I could also have noted Mencken's distaste for thobbery.

Dr. Gove met the problem of *ain't* head on in the best traditions of Structural Linguistics, labelling it—reluctantly, one imagines—*substandard* for *have not* and *has not*, but giving it, unlabelled, as a contraction of *am not, are not*, and *is not*, adding "though disapproved by many and more common in less educated speech, used orally in most parts of the U.S. by many cultivated speakers esp. in the phrase ain't I." This was courageous indeed; when Dr. C. C. Fries, the dean of Structural Linguists today, said, at a meeting of the Modern Language Association several years ago, that *ain't* was not wholly disreputable, a teapot tempest boiled up in the press. When Dr. Gove included a reference to the entry on *ain't* in the press announcement of 3, the newspapers seethed again, from the Houston *Press* ("IT AIN'T UNCOUTH TO SAY AIN'T NOW") to the San Francisco *Examiner* ("AIN'T BAD AT ALL—IN NEWEST REVISED DICTIONARY") and the *World-Telegram* ("IT JUST AIN'T TRUE THAT AIN'T AIN'T IN THE DICTIONARY"). But moral courage is not the only quality a good lexicographer needs. Once the matter of education and culture is raised, we are right back at the nonscientific business of deciding what is correct—*standard* is the modern euphemism—and this is more a matter of a feeling for language (what the trade calls *Sprachgefühl*) than of the statistics on which Dr. Gove and his colleagues seem to have chiefly relied. For what Geiger counter will decide who is in fact educated or cultivated? And what adding machine will discriminate between *ain't* used because the speaker thinks it is standard English and *ain't* used because he wants to get a special effect? "Survival must have quality, or it ain't worth a bean," Thornton Wilder recently observed. It doesn't take much *Sprachgefühl* to recognize that Mr. Wilder is here being a mite folksy and that his effect would be lost if *ain't* were indeed "used orally in most parts of the U.S. by many cultivated speakers." Though I regret that the nineteenth-century schoolteachers without justification deprived us of *ain't* for *am not*, the deed was done, and I think the *Dial.* or *Illit.* with which 2 labels all uses of the word comes closer to linguistic fact today.

The pejorative labels in 2 are forthright: *colloquial, erroneous, incorrect, illiterate.* 3 replaces these self-explanatory terms with two that are both fuzzier and more scientific-sounding: *substandard* and *nonstandard.* The first "indicates status conforming to a pattern of linguistic usage that exists throughout the American language community but differs in choice of word or form from that of the prestige group in that community," which is academese for "Not used by educated people." *Hisself* and *drowned* are labelled *substand.*, which sounds better than *erron.*—more democratic. *Nonstandard* "is used for a very small number of words that can hardly stand without some status label but are too widely current in reputable context to be labelled *substand.*" *Irregardless* is given as an example, which for me again raises doubts about the compilers' notion of a reputable context. I think 2's label for the word, *erron. or humorous,* more accurate.

The argument has now shifted from whether a dictionary should be an authority as against a reporter (in Dr. Gove's terms, prescriptive v. descriptive) to the validity of the prescriptive guidance that 3 does in fact give. For Dr. Gove and his colleagues have not ventured to omit all qualitative discriminations; they have cut them down drastically from 2, but they have felt obliged to include many. Perhaps by 1988, if the Structural Linguists remain dominant, there will be a fourth edition, which will simply record, without labels or warnings, all words and non-words that are used widely in "the American language community," including such favorites of a former President as *nucular* (warfare), *inviduous,* and *mischievious.* But it is still 1962, and 3 often does discriminate. The trouble is that its willingness to do so has been weakened by its scientific conscience, so that it palters and equivocates; this is often more misleading than would be the omission of all discriminations.

One drawback to the permissive approach of the Structural Linguists is that it impoverishes the language by not objecting to errors if they are common enough. ("And how should I presume?" —*T. S. Eliot.*) There is a natural tendency among human beings, who are *by def.* fallible, to confuse similar-sounding words. "One look at him would turn you nauseous," Phil Silvers said on television one night, as better stylists have written before. Up to now, dictionaries have distinguished *nauseous* (causing nausea) from *nauseated* (experiencing nausea); 2 labels *nauseous* in the sense of experiencing nausea *obs.,* but it is no longer *obs.* It is simply *erron.,* a fact you will not learn from 3, which gives as its first definition, without label, "affected with or inclining to nausea." So the language is *balled up* and *nauseous* is telescoped into *nauseated* and nobody knows who means which exactly. The magisterial Fowler—magisterial, that is, until the Structural Linguists got to work—has an entry on Pairs & Snares that makes sad reading now. He calls *deprecate* and *depreciate* "one of the altogether false pairs," but 3 gives the latter as a synonym of the first. It similarly blurs the distinction between Fowler's *forcible* ("effected by force") and *forceful* ("full of force"), *unexceptional* ("constituting no exception to the general rule") and *unexceptionable* ("not open or liable to objection," which is quite a different thing). A Pair &

Snare Fowler doesn't give is *disinterested* (impartial) and *un-interested* (not interested); 2 lists the *uninterested* sense of *disinterested* but adds, *"now rare;"* even such permissive lexicographers as Bergen and Cornelia Evans, in their "Dictionary of Contemporary American Usage," state firmly, "Though *disinterested* was formerly a synonym for *uninterested*, it is not now so used." But 3 gives *disinterested* as a synonym of *uninterested*.

Each such confusion makes the language less efficient, and it is a dictionary's job to *define* words, which means, literally, to set limits to them. 3 still distinguishes *capital* from *capitol* and *principle* from *principal*, but how many more language-community members must join the present sizable band that habitually confuses these words before they go down the drain with the others? Perhaps nothing much is lost if almost everybody calls Frankenstein the monster rather than the man who made the monster, even though Mrs. Shelley wrote it the other way, but how is one to deal with the *bimonthly* problem? 2 defines it as "once in two months," which is correct. 3 gives this as the first meaning and then adds, gritting its teeth, "sometimes: twice a month." (It defines *biweekly* as "every two weeks" and adds "2: twice a week.") It does seem a little awkward to have a word that can mean every two weeks *or* every eight weeks, and it would have been convenient if 3 had compromised with scientific integrity enough to replace its perfectly accurate *sometimes* with a firm *erroneous*. But this would have implied authority, and authority is the last thing 3's modest recorders want. ("Let this cup pass from me."—*New Testament*.)

The objection is not to recording the facts of actual usage. It is to failing to give the information that would enable the reader to decide which usage he wants to adopt. If he prefers to use *deprecate* and *depreciate* interchangeably, no dictionary can prevent him, but at least he should be warned. Thus 3 has under *transpire*—"4: to come to pass; happen, occur." 2 has the same entry, but it is followed by a monitory pointing hand: "*transpire* in this sense has been disapproved by most authorities on usage, although the meaning occurs in the writings of many authors of good standing." Fair enough. I also prefer 2's handling of the common misuse of *infer* to mean *imply*—"5: loosely and erroneously, to imply." 3 sounds no warning, and twice under *infer* it advises "compare imply." Similarly, 2 labels the conjunctive *like* "illiterate" and "incorrect," which it is, adding that "in the works of

careful writers [it] is replaced by *as.*" 3 accepts it as standard,
giving such unprepossessing citations as "impromptu programs
where they ask questions much like I do on the air—Art Linkletter"
and "wore his clothes like he . . . afraid of getting dirt on them—
St. Petersburg (Fla.) Independent." *Enthuse* is labelled *colloq.* in
2 but not in 3. It still sounds *colloq.* if not *godawf.* to me, nor am
I impressed by 3's citations, from writers named L. G. Pine and
Lawrence Constable and from a trade paper called *Fashion Acces-
sories.* Or consider the common misuse of *too* when *very* is meant,
as "I was not too interested in the lecture." 2 gives this use but
labels it *colloq.* 3 gives it straight and cites Irving Kolodin: "an
episodic work without too consistent a texture;" Mr. Kolodin
probably means "without a very consistent texture," but how does
one know he doesn't mean "without an excessively consistent [or
monotonous] texture"? In music criticism such ambiguities are not
too helpful.

In dealing with words that might be considered slang, 2 uses
the label wherever there is doubt, while 3 leans the other way.
The first procedure seems to me more sensible, since no great harm
is done if a word is left waiting in the antechamber until its pretensions to being standard have been thoroughly tested (as long as
it is admitted into the dictionary), while damage may be done if it
is prematurely admitted. Thus both 2 and 3 list such women's-
magazine locutions as *galore, scads, scrumptious,* and *too-too,* but
only 2 labels them slang. (Fowler's note on *galore* applies to them
all: "Chiefly resorted to by those who are reduced to relieving the
dullness of matter by oddity of expression.") Thus *rummy, spang* (in
the middle of), and *nobby* are in both, but only 2 calls them slang.

Admittedly, the question is most difficult. Many words begin
as slang and then rise in the world. Dean Swift, a great purist,
objected to *mob* (from the Latin *mobile vulgus*), *banter, bully,* and
sham; he also objected to *hyp,* which has disappeared as slang for
hypochondriac, and *rep,* which persists for reputation but is still
labelled slang even in 3. Some slang words have survived for
centuries without bettering themselves, like the Jukes and the
Kallikaks. *Dukes* (fists) and *duds* (clothes) are still slang, although
they go back to the eighteenth and the sixteenth century, re-
spectively.

The definition of *slang* in 3 is "characterized primarily by connotations of extreme informality . . . coinages or arbitrarily changed

words, clipped or shortened forms, extravagant, forced, or facetious figures of speech or verbal novelties usu. experiencing quick popularity and relatively rapid decline into disuse." A good definition (Dr. Gove has added that slang is "linguistically self-conscious"), but it seems to have been forgotten in making up 3, most of whose discriminations about slang strike me as arbitrary. According to 3, *scram* is not slang, but *vamoose* is. "*Goof* 1" ("to make a mistake or blunder") is not slang, but "*goof* 2" ("to spend time idly or foolishly") is, and the confusion is compounded when one finds that Ethel Merman is cited for the non-slang *goof* and James T. Farrell for the slang *goof*. "*Floozy* 1" ("an attractive young woman of loose morals") is standard, but "*floozy* 2" ("a dissolute and sometimes slovenly woman") is slang. Can even a Structural Linguist make such fine distinctions about such a word? The many synonyms for *drunk* raise the same question. Why are *oiled, pickled,* and *boiled* labelled slang if *soused* and *spiflicated* are not? Perhaps cooking terms for *drunk* are automatically slang, but why?

I don't mean to *imply* (see *infer*) that the compilers of 3 didn't give much thought to the problem. When they came to a doubtful word, they took a staff poll, asking everybody to check it, after reviewing the accumulated cites, as either slang or standard. This resulted in *cornball's* being entered as slang and *corny's* being entered as standard. Such scientific, or quantitative, efforts to separate the goats from the sheep produced the absurdities noted above. Professor Austin C. Dobbins raised this point in *College English* for October, 1956:

> But what of such words as *boondoggle, corny, frisk, liquidate, pinched, bonehead, carpetbagger, pleb, slush fund,* and *snide?* Which of these words ordinarily would be considered appropriate in themes written by cultivated people? According to the editors of the ACD [the American College Dictionary, the 1953 edition, published by Random House] the first five of these are slang; the second five are established usage. To the editors of WNCD [Webster's New Collegiate Dictionary, published by Merriam-Webster in the same year] the first five of these words represent established usage; the second five are slang. Which authority is the student to follow?

Mr. Dobbins is by no means hostile to Structural Linguistics, and his essay appears in a recent anthology edited by Dr. Harold B. Allen, of the University of Minnesota, an energetic proponent of the new school. "Perhaps the answer," Mr. Dobbins concludes, "is to advise students to study only one handbook, consult one dictionary, listen to one instructor. An alternate suggestion, of course, is for our textbooks more accurately to base their labels upon studies of usage." Assuming the first alternative is ironical, I would say the second is impractical unless the resources of a dozen Ford Foundations are devoted to trying to decide the matter scientifically—that is, statistically.

Short of this Land of Cockaigne, where partridges appear in the fields ready-roasted, I see only two logical alternatives: to label all doubtful words slang, as 2 does, or to drop the label entirely, as I suspect Dr. Gove would have liked to do. Using the label sparingly, if it is not to produce bizarre effects, takes a lot more *Sprachgefühl* than the editors of 3 seem to have possessed. Thus *horse* as a verb ("to engage in horseplay") they accept as standard. The citations are from Norman Mailer ("I never horse around much with the women") and J. D. Salinger ("I horse around quite a lot, just to keep from getting bored"). I doubt whether either Mr. Mailer or Mr. Salinger would use *horse* straight; in these cites, I venture, it is either put in the mouth of a first-person narrator or used deliberately to get a colloquial effect. Slang is concise and vivid—*jalopy* has advantages over *dilapidated automobile*—and a few slang terms salted in a formal paragraph bring out the flavor. But the user must know he *is* using slang, he must be aware of having introduced a slight discord into his harmonics, or else he coarsens and blurs his expression. This information he will not, for the most part, get from 3. I hate to think what monstrosities of prose foreigners and high-school students will produce if they take 3 seriously as a guide to what is and what is not standard English.

Whenever the compilers of 3 come up against a locution that some (me, or I) might consider simply wrong, they do their best, as Modern Linguists and democrats, to be good fellows. The softening-up process begins with substituting the euphemistic *substandard* for 2's blunt *erroneous* and *illiterate*. From there it expands into several forms. *Complected* (for *complexioned*) is *dialect* in 2, *not often in formal use* in 3. *Learn* (for teach) is *now a vulgarism* in 2, *now chiefly substand.* in 3. (*Chiefly* is the thin end of the wedge, implying that users of standard English on occasion exclaim, "I'll learn you to use bad English!") *Knowed* is listed as the past of *known,* though *broke* is labelled substandard for *broken*—another of those odd discriminations. Doubtless they counted noses, or citation slips, and concluded that "Had I but knowed!" is standard while "My heart is broke" is substandard.

(To be entirely fair, perhaps compulsively so: If one reads carefully the five closely printed pages of Explanatory Notes in 3, and especially paragraphs 16.0 through 16.6 (twelve inches of impenetrable lexical jargon), one finds that light-face small capitals means a cross-reference, and if one looks up KNOW—which is given after *knowed* in light-face small capitals—one does find that *knowed* is dialect. This is not a very practical or sensible dictionary, one concludes after such scholarly labors, and one wonders why Dr. Gove and his editors did not think of labelling *knowed* as substandard right where it occurs, and one suspects that they wanted to slightly conceal the fact or at any rate to put off its exposure as long as decently possible.)

The systematic softening or omitting of pejorative labels in 3 could mean: (1) we have come to use English more loosely, to say the least, than we did in 1934; or (2) usage hasn't changed, but 3 has simply recorded The Facts more accurately; or (3) the notion of what is a relevant Fact has changed between 2 and 3. I suspect it is mostly (3), but in any case I cannot see *complected* as anything but *dialected.*

In 1947 the G. & C. Merriam Co. published a little book entitled "Noah's Ark"—in reference to Noah Webster, who began it all—celebrating its first hundred years as the publisher of Webster dictionaries. Toward the end, the author, Robert Keith Leavitt, rises to heights of eloquence which have a tinny sound now that "Webster" means not 2 but 3:

> This responsibility to the user is no light matter. It has, indeed, grown heavier with every year of increasing acceptance of Webster. Courts, from the United States Supreme Court down, rely on the *New International's* definitions as a sort of common law: many a costly suit has hinged on a Webster definition, and many a citizen has gone behind prison bars or walked out onto the streets a free man, according to the light Webster put upon his doings. The statute law itself is not infrequently phrased by legislators in terms straight out of Webster. Most daily newspapers and magazines, and nearly all the books that come off the press, are edited and printed in accordance with Websterian usage. Col-

leges and schools make the *New International* their standard, and, for nearly half a century, students have dug their way through pedantic obscurity with the aid of the *Collegiate*. In business offices the secretary corrects her boss out of Webster and the boss holds customers and contractors alike in line by citing how Webster says it shall be done. In thousands upon thousands of homes, youngsters lying sprawled under the table happily absorb from Webster information which teachers have striven in vain to teach them from textbooks. Clear through, indeed, to the everyday American's most trivial and jocose of doings, Webster is the unquestioned authority.

While this picture is a bit idyllic—Clarence Barnhart's American College Dictionary, put out by Random House, is considered by many to be at least as good as the Webster Collegiate—it had some reality up to 1961. But as of today, courts that Look It Up In Webster will often find themselves little the wiser, since 3 claims no authority and merely records, mostly deadpan, what in fact every Tom, Dick, and Harry is now doing—in all innocence—to the language. That freedom or imprisonment should depend on 3 is an alarming idea. The secretary correcting her boss, if he is a magazine publisher, will collide with the unresolved *bimonthly* and *biweekly* problem, and the youngsters sprawled under the table will happily absorb from 3 the information that *jerk* is standard for "a stupid, foolish, naïve, or unconventional person." One imagines the themes: "Dr. Johnson admired Goldsmith's literary talent although he considered him a jerk." The editors of the New Webster's Vest Pocket Dictionary, thirty-nine cents at any cigar store, label *jerk* as *coll.* But then they aren't Structural Linguists.

The reviews of 3 in the lay press have not been enthusiastic. *Life* and the *Times* have both attacked it editorially as a "say-as-you-go" dictionary that reflects "the permissive school" in language study. The usually solemn editorialists of the *Times* were goaded to unprecedented wit:

> A passel of double-domes at the G. & C. Merriam Company joint in Springfield, Mass. [the editorial began], have been confabbing and yakking for twenty-seven years—which is not intended to infer that they have not been doing plenty work—and now they have finalized Webster's Third New International Dictionary, Unabridged, a new edition of that swell and esteemed word book.

Those who regard the foregoing paragraph as acceptable English prose will find that the new Webster's is just the dictionary for them.

But the lay press doesn't always prevail. The irreverent may call 3 "Gove's Goof," but Dr. Gove and his editors are part of the dominant movement in the professional study of language—one that has in the last few years established strong beachheads in the National Council of Teachers of English and the College English Association. One may grant that for the scientific study of language the Structural Linguistic approach is superior to that of the old grammarians, who overestimated the importance of logic and Latin, but one may still object to its transfer directly to the teaching of English and the making of dictionaries. As a scientific discipline, Structural Linguistics can have no truck with value or standards. Its job is to deal only with The Facts. But in matters of usage, the evaluation of The Facts is important, too, and this requires a certain amount of general culture, not to mention common sense—commodities that many scientists have done brilliantly without but that teachers and lexicographers need in their work.

The kind of thinking responsible for 3 is illustrated by Dr. Gove's riposte, last week, to the many unfavorable reviews of his dictionary: "The criticisms involve less than one per cent of the words in the dictionary." This quantitative approach might be useful to novelists who get bad reviews. It is foolproof here; a reviewer who tried to meet Dr. Gove's criterion and deal with a sizable proportion of 3's words—say ten per cent—would need forty-five thousand words just to list them, and if his own comments averaged ten words apiece he would have to publish his five-hundred-thousand-word review in two large volumes. Some odd thinking gets done up at the old Merriam-Webster place in Springfield.

Dr. Gove's letter to the *Times* objecting to its editorial was also interesting. "The editors of *Webster's Third New International Dictionary* are not amused by the ingenuity of the first paragraph of your editorial," it began loftily, and continued, "Your paragraph obscures, or attempts to obscure, the fact that there are so many different degrees of standard usage that dictionary definitions cannot hope to distinguish one from another by status labelling." (But the *Times'* point was precisely that the editors did make such distinctions by status labelling, only they were the wrong distinctions; i.e., by omitting pejorative labels they accepted as standard words that, in the opinion of the *Times*, are not standard.) There followed several pages of citations in which Dr. Gove showed that the *Times* itself had often used the very words it objected to 3's including as standard language. "If we are ever inclined to the linguistic pedantry that easily fails to distinguish moribund traditions from genuine living usage [the adjectives here are perhaps more revealing than Dr. Gove intended] we have only to turn to the columns of the *Times*," Dr. Gove concluded. The *Times* is the best newspaper in the world in the gathering and printing of news, but it has never been noted for stylistic distinction. And even if it were, the exigencies of printing a small book every day might be expected to drive the writers and editors of a newspaper into usages as convenient as they are sloppy —usages that people with more time on their hands, such as the editors of an unabridged dictionary, might distinguish from standard English.

There are several reasons that it is important to maintain standards in the use of a language. English, like other languages, is beautiful when properly used, and beauty can be achieved only by attention to form, which means setting limits, or de-fining, or dis-criminating. Language expresses the special, dis-tinctive quality of a people, and a people, like an individual, is to a large extent defined by its past—its traditions—whether it is conscious of this or not. If the language is allowed to shift too rapidly, without challenge from teachers and lexicographers, then the special character of the American people is blurred, since it tends to lose its past. In the same way a city loses its character if too much of it is torn down and rebuilt too quickly. "Languages are the pedigrees of nations," said Dr. Johnson.

The effect on the individual is also unfortunate. The kind of permissiveness that permeates 3 (the kind that a decade or two ago was more common in progressive schools than it is now) results, oddly, in less rather than more individuality, since the only way an individual can "express himself" is in relation to a social norm—in the case of language, to standard usage. James Joyce's creative distortions of words were possible only because he had a perfect ear for orthodox English. But if the very idea of form, or standards, is lacking, then how can one violate it? It's no fun to use *knowed* for *known* if everybody thinks you're just trying to be standard.

Counting cite slips is simply not the way to go about the delicate business of deciding these matters. If nine-tenths of the citizens of the United States, including a recent President, were to use *inviduous,* the one-tenth who clung to *invidious* would still be right, and they would be doing a favor to the majority if they continued to maintain the point. It is perhaps not democratic, according to some recent users, or abusers, of the word, to insist on this, and the question comes up of who is to decide at what point change— for language does indeed change, as the Structural Linguists insist —has evolved from *slang, dial., erron.,* or *substand.* to *standard.* The decision, I think, must be left to the teachers, the professional writers, and the lexicographers, and they might look up Ulysses' famous defense of conservatism in Shakespeare's "Troilus and Cressida":

> The heavens themselves, the planets and this centre
> Observe degree, priority and place,
> Insisture, course, proportion, season, form,
> Office and custom in all line of order. . . .
> Take but degree away, untune that string,
> And, hark, what discord follows! Each thing meets
> In mere oppugnancy. The bounded waters
> Should lift their bosoms higher than the shores
> And make a sop of all this solid globe.
> Strength should be lord of imbecility
> And the rude son should strike his father dead.
> Force should be right, or rather right and wrong
> (Between whose endless jar justice resides)
> Should lose their names, and so should justice too.
> Then every thing includes itself in power,
> Power into will, will into appetite
> And appetite, a universal wolf,
> So doubly seconded with will and power,
> Must make perforce a universal prey
> And, last, eat up himself. . . .

Dr. Johnson, a dictionary-maker of the old school, defined *lexicographer* as "a harmless drudge." Things have changed. Lexicographers may still be drudges, but they are certainly not harmless. They have untuned the string, made a sop of the solid structure of English, and encouraged the language to eat up himself.

THE DICTIONARY AS A BATTLEFRONT:
ENGLISH TEACHERS' DILEMMA*

Mario Pei

For some years, there have been more and more insistent rumblings from all sorts of quarters concerning the quality of the
English imparted in our schools and colleges. Graduates of our
educational institutions, the critics have charged, do not know how
to spell, punctuate, or capitalize; to divide a thought concept into
phrases, sentences, and paragraphs; or to express themselves,
either in speech or writing, in the sort of English that is meaningful and acceptable. As a single sample of the many complaints
that have been voiced, I may cite a friend who is a high official in
WNBC-TV: "Recently we interviewed over a hundred college
graduates to fill a post calling for a knowledge of good English.
Not one of them made the grade. None of them knew the rules of
good writing, and none of them could express himself or herself
in clear, simple, forthright English sentences."

The blame for this state of affairs has consistently been put upon
two branches of the educational world: the teachers of English
and the progressive educationists. Books such as "Why Johnny
Can't Read" are indictments of modern educational practice. A
cultured lay writer, J. Donald Adams of the New York *Times Book
Review,* said in his column of December 20, 1959:

> If more parents who were themselves the recipients of a decent
> education could be made aware of the asinine statements about
> the teaching of the English language which are being spewed forth
> by today's educational theorists, there would be an armed uprising
> among the Parent-Teacher Associations all over the United States.
> It would be an uprising armed by common sense and hot in-
> dignation, and it would demand and get the scalps of those
> so-called educators whose indefensible doctrines are rapidly pro-
> ducing a generation of American illiterates. . . . The root respon-
> sibility for the decline in standards of English rests, I think, with

* From *Saturday Review,* July 21, 1962. By permission of the author
and the publisher.

the teachers of English in our primary and secondary schools, and even more so, with the teachers of education who produced them. . . . There is an organization called the National Council of Teachers of English, whose attitudes and activities constitute one of the chief threats to the cultivation of good English in our schools.

What critics of present-day methods of teaching English have in the past failed to realize is that the responsibility for the situation lies deeper than the departments of English and the teachers' colleges. The practices of both are merely a reflection of the philosophy and theories of a school of linguistics that is in turn linked with a school of cultural anthropology of the equalitarian persuasion whose views color far more than the teaching of languages in general or English in particular.

As far back as 1948, in a New York *Herald Tribune* book review, Bernard De Voto came out with a blast at the cultural anthropologists for assuming that methods that seem to work with the Ubangi and the Trobriand Islanders will produce dependable results when applied to the English or Americans. But his was a voice crying in the wilderness. Few people were sufficiently specialized, or interested, to perceive the link between theories presented in scholarly books on anthropology or linguistics and practices that affect the daily lives of all of us.

It was only with the appearance of the new third edition of "Webster's Unabridged International Dictionary" late in 1961 that the issues at stake, at least for what concerns language, became clear to the cultured, educated layman of America. For this there was a deep, underlying reason that reaches down to the grass roots of our mores.

The English language, as is well known, has no set standard and no accepted authority, in the sense that countries such as France, Italy, and Spain have language academies that undertake to tell the speakers what is and what is not good standard practice. Since the days of Dr. Johnson, who refused to embalm the language and thereby destroy liberty, English speakers have submitted to the Doctrine of Usage rather than to the Voice of Authority. But usage has its own canons. In Britain, something called the King's (or Queen's) English has been enshrined over and above local dialects that range from London's Cockney to super-cultivated Oxford, and from the harsh speech of the North Country to the mellifluous accents of Kent. In America there is no President's American, but there is the Dictionary. From the time of Noah Webster, Americans have been wont to dip into a dictionary, the more unabridged the better, to settle questions of usage and proper practice.

It may be stressed at this point that at no time did the compilers of the various editions of the Merriam-Webster, the most comprehensive dictionary of America, set themselves up as authorities or arrogate the right to tell the people what was right and what was wrong in the matter of language. All they did was to record prevailing usage among the more educated classes. They listed and described plenty of variant regional pronunciations and words. They recorded, too, speech-forms of the lower classes, carefully labeling them "colloquial," "substandard," "vulgar," or "slang." This was not meant to prescribe or proscribe the use of certain forms, but merely to inform the reader as to the distribution of their occurrence. The attitude of the earlier lexicographers seemed to be: "Go ahead and use this form if you want to; but if you do, don't complain if someone says you are using a slang term."

The new 1961 edition of the Merriam-Webster has many features to commend it. Not only does it list the multitude of new terms, technological and otherwise, that have entered the language in recent years; it also has the merit of listing, with full definitions and examples, word combinations that have acquired special connotations not inherent in their component parts. The older Webster's defines both "guilt" and "association"; but the new Webster's also gives you "guilt by association." This means that the new edition is a handier tool than the older.

But the new edition makes one startling innovation which has recommended itself to the attention of all reviewers and of the general public as well. It blurs to the point of obliteration the older distinction between standard, substandard, colloquial, vulgar, and slang. "Ain't," it says, is now used by many cultivated speakers; "who" in the accusative function and "me" after a copulative verb are of far more frequent occurrence than "whom" and "I," and, by implication, should be preferred. This viewpoint goes right down the line. It led the editor of the New York *Times* to compose a passage that starts:

A passel of double-domes at the G. & C. Merriam Company joint in Springfield, Mass., have been confabbing and yakking for twenty-seven years—which is not intended to infer that they have not been doing plenty work—and now they have finalized Webster's Third New International Dictionary, Unabridged, a new edition of that swell and esteemed word book.

Those who regard the foregoing paragraph as acceptable English prose will find that the new Webster's is just the dictionary for them.

There is more: the older Webster's, insofar as it gave citations, used only established authors, recognized masters of the language. The new Webster's cites profusely from people who are in the public eye, but who can hardly be said to qualify as shining examples of fine speaking or writing. This leads another critic to complain that Churchill, Maritain, Oppenheimer, and Schweitzer are ranged as language sources side by side with Billy Rose, Ethel Merman, James Cagney, and Ted Williams; Shakespeare and Milton with Polly Adler and Mickey Mantle.

Dr. Gove's defense, fully presented in the pages of the same New York *Times* that had thundered editorially against his product, is both able and forthright: a dictionary's function, he said in substance, is to record the language, not to judge or prescribe it. Language, like practically everything else, is in a state of constant flux. It is not responsible to expect it to remain static, to retain unchanged forms that were current at one period but are no longer current today. We have changed our point of view in many fields; why not in language? His defense is, in a sense, a counterattack against the forces of purism, conservatism, and reaction. Why disguise the true function of a dictionary by turning it into a tool of prescriptivism, a fortress of a language traditionalism that no one today really wants? Language, after all, is what people speak, not what someone, be it even Webster, thinks they ought to speak.

This both clarifies and restricts the issue. But an issue still remains. Should a dictionary be merely a record of what goes on in language (all language, both high and low), or should it also be not so much a prescriptive tool as a guide for the layman, to not merely what *is* usage, but what is the *best* usage?

A speaking community that has been accustomed for the better part of two centuries to rely upon the dictionary to settle questions of usage balks at finding all usage now set on an identical plane. The contention of the objectors is that there are different, clearly identifiable levels of usage, which it is the duty of the dictionary to define. Without necessarily using the terms "correct" and "incorrect," they still would like to see a distinction made between what is better and what is worse.

In opposition to their stand, the new philosophy, linguistic and otherwise, seems to be summed up in this formula: "What is is good, simply because it is." Good and bad, right and wrong, correct and incorrect no longer exist. Any reference to any of these descriptive adjectives is a value judgment, and unworthy of the scientific attitude, which prescribes that we merely observe and catalogue the facts, carefully refraining from expressing either judgment or preference.

This relativistic philosophy, fully divorced from both ethics and esthetics, is said to be modern, sophisticated, and scientific. Perhaps it is. Some claim that its fruits are to be seen in present-day moral standards, national, international, and personal, as well as in modern so-called art, music, literature, and permissive education.

But we are concerned here only with its reflections on the language. The appearance of the new Webster's International has had several major effects. It has brought the question of permissiveness in language squarely to the attention of millions of educated laymen, who use the dictionary and refer to it for guidance. Without forcing a renunciation of Anglo-American reliance on usage rather than on the Voice of Authority, it has brought into focus the paramount question: "Whose usage? That of the cultivated speakers, or that of the semiliterates?" Finally, it has for the first time brought forth, into the view of the general public, those who are primarily responsible for the shift in attitude and point of view in matters of language—not the ordinary classroom teachers of English, not the educationists of the teachers colleges, but the followers of the American, anthropological, descriptive, structuralistic school of linguistics, a school which for decades has been preaching that one form of language is as good as another; that there is no such thing as correct or incorrect so far as native speakers of the language are concerned; that at the age of five anyone who is not deaf or idiotic has gained a full mastery of his language; that we must not try to correct or improve language, but must leave it alone; that the only language activity worthy of the name is speech on the colloquial, slangy, even illiterate plane; that writing is a secondary, unimportant activity which cannot be dignified with the name of language; that systems of writing serve only to disguise the true nature of language; and that it would be well if we completely refrained from teaching spelling for a number of years.

If these pronouncements come as a novelty to some of my readers, it is the readers themselves who are at fault. The proponents of these language theories certainly have made no mystery about them; they have been openly, even vociferously advancing them for years, and this can easily be documented from their voluminous writings.

The real novelty of the situation lies in the fact that, through the publication of the new Webster's—compiled in accordance with these principles—the principles themselves and their original formulators, rather than their effects upon the younger generations, now come to the attention of the general public. Lay reviewers generally display their complete awareness.

Dwight MacDonald, reviewing the new Webster extensively in the March 10, 1962 *New Yorker*, after claiming that the "scientific" revolution in linguistics has meshed gears with a trend toward permissiveness, in the name of democracy, that is debasing our language by rendering it less precise and thus less effective as communication, goes on to say:

> Dr. Gove and the other makers of 3 are sympathetic to the school of language—one that has in the last few years established strong times called Structural Linguistics and sometimes, rather magnificently, just Modern Linguistic Science. . . . Dr. Gove and his editors are part of the dominant movement in the professional study of language—one that has in the last few years established strong beachheads in the National Council of Teachers of English and the College English Association. . . . As a scientific discipline, Structural Linguistics can have no truck with values or standards. Its job is to deal only with The Facts.

Max S. Marshall, Professor of Microbiology at the University of California, writing in *Science*, March 2, 1962, says in part:

> Opposed to [believers in a standard of quality in English] with several ringleaders at the head, is a group which goes back some thirty years, but has been actively proselytizing only in relatively recent years. These are the advocates of 'observing precisely what happens when native speakers speak.' These are the self-styled structural linguists, presenting language in a way so foreign that it might be imposed before users of the language discover its existence. . . . Gove declares himself flatly on the side of the structural linguists, calmly assuming, as do their ringleaders, that they are about to take over.

The principles of the American school of linguistics described above may come as a shock to some, but there is no need to be shocked. They are based upon definitely observable historical facts. Language invariably changes. Within our own personal experience we have noticed certain forms and expressions once considered slangy turning into regularly accepted parts of the standard language.

All that the American school of linguistics advocates is that we accept the process of change in language and submit gracefully to its inevitability. If we persist in hanging on to language forms and concepts that are antiquated and superceded, then we are merely subscribing to what they call "the superstitions of the past." We should be forward-looking, and progressive-minded. We renounce imperialism and colonialism in international relations, and admit nations like Ghana and the Congo to full equality with the established countries of Europe; by the same token, we should view the languages of the Arapahoes and the Zulus as being of equal importance with Latin and French. We believe in democracy and majority rule in political elections. Then, if a majority of the speakers of American English use "ain't," "knowed," "I'll learn you," "I laid on the bed," "who did you see," "between you and I," "like a cigarette should," these forms are by definition standard usage, and the corresponding minority forms, though sanctioned by traditional grammars, are, if not incorrect, at least obsolescent.

It may be argued, as does our Professor of Microbiology in *Science,* that "weighing the speech of casual speakers with no pretense of expertness on the same IBM card as usages of topnotch writers of past and present is an example of what the modern linguist calls 'science.' Tabulation is not science. Public opinion polls do not settle questions of science, or even of right and wrong. . . . If the guttersnipes of language do more talking than professors of English they get proportionally more votes."

But the structuralistic linguists can easily reply that language is a matter of habit and convention, not of dogma or esthetics, and that if the basic purpose of semantic communication is achieved, it matters little what linguistic form is used. In engineering, calculations as to stresses and structures must be precise and correct, under penalty of seeing the bridge collapse. In medicine, correct dosage is essential, under penalty of seeing your patient die. But in language, the use of a substandard for a standard form seldom leads to irreparable consequences; at the most, as picturesquely stated by a leader of the school, you may not be invited to tea again.

On the other hand, members of the American school of linguistics are not always consistent in the application of their democratic and equalitarian principles. In reply to his critics, Dr. Gove remarked that while comments in lay newspapers and magazines had generally been unfavorable, the learned journals had not yet reviewed the new edition. The implication seemed to be that favorable reviews from a few members of his own clique, read and approved by a small circle of professional structuralistic linguists, would more than offset the generally unfavorable reaction of newspapers like the New York *Times* and magazines like the *New Yorker,* which appeal to large audiences of cultivated laymen. This not only puts the process of democracy into reverse; it comes close to setting up a hierarchy of professional linguists acting as the Voice of Authority for a recalcitrant majority of educated people.

There is no doubt in my mind that widespread localisms, slang, vulgarisms, colloquialisms, even obscenities and improprieties, should be duly noted in a comprehensive dictionary, whose first duty is to record what goes on in the field of language. Should such forms be labeled and described for what they are, not in a spirit of condemnation, but merely for the guidance of the reader? That, too, seems reasonable. If this procedure helps to slow up the inevitable process of language change by encouraging the speakers to use what the older dictionaries call standard forms, and discouraging them from using substandard forms, this impresses me as a distinct advantage. Too rapid and too widespread language change is a hindrance to communications. It lends itself to confusion and misunderstanding. The use of a more or less uniform standard by all members of the speaking community is desirable in the interests of efficiency rather than of esthetics. There is no question that within the next 500 years the English language, along with all other languages spoken today, will be so changed as to be practically unrecognizable. This will happen whether we like it or not. But need we deliberately hasten and amplify the process? Between sudden revolution and stolid reaction there is a middle ground of sound conservatism and orderly change.

Also, without being puristic to the point of ejecting "ain't" and kindred forms from a dictionary of recorded usage, it might be worth while to recognize the existence of a standard language, neither literary nor slangy, which has acceptance and is understood practically everywhere in the country, even if everybody does not use it. Such phrases as "Them dogs is us'uns" and "I'll call you up without I can't," which an American structural linguist claims are good, meaningful language to him, merely because they are uttered by some native American speakers, definitely do not form part of that standard language. By all means let us record them for our own information and amusement, but let us not try to palm them off on the public on the general ground that the native speaker can do no wrong, and that "correct" and "incorrect" are terms that can be legitimately applied only to the speech of foreigners attempting to use English.

Language is something more than a heritage of sentimental value. It is an indispensable tool of communication and exchange of ideas. The more standardized and universal it is, the more effective it is. The more it is allowed to degenerate into local and class forms, the less effective it becomes. It may be perfectly true that in the past language has been allowed to run its own sweet, unbridled course, with the chips falling where they might. We are now in an age where we no longer believe in letting diseases and epidemics run their natural course, but take active, artificial means to control them. In fact, we endeavor to control natural, physical, and sociological phenomena of all descriptions, from floods to business cycles, from weather to diet, from the monetary system to racial relations. Is it unreasonable for us, far from leaving our language alone, as advocated by the American school of linguistics, to wish to channel it in the directions where it will prove of maximum efficiency for its avowed function, which is that of semantic transfer?

For the concern of that other burning question, standards of writing, as apart from standards of speech, ought we not to recognize that until such a time as tapes, recordings, dictaphones and spoken films altogether replace our system of written communications, the latter should be viewed and treated with respect? Again, we need not let ourselves be led too far afield by purely literary or esthetic considerations. The written language, in a modern civilization, is practically on a par with speech as a communications tool. It is incongruous to see our American structuralistic linguists devote so much painstaking attention to phonetic phenomena like pitch, stress, intonation, and juncture, to the fine distinctions between "a light housekeeper" and "a lighthouse keeper," "an iceman" and "a nice man," and yet shrug their shoulders at correct spelling, punctuation, and capitalization. More misunderstandings have occurred over misplaced commas than over misplaced junctures, and a wrong spelling can be just as fatal as a wrong intonation.

Perhaps the time has come, in language as in other fields, for the return of reason, and its ascendancy over dogma, whether the latter be of the puristic or of the structuralistic variety.

Above all, there is need for sound, scientific consideration of *all* the facts of language, not merely that portion which happens to suit the tastes and inclinations of a small group. Language is more than a set of phonemes, morphemes, junctures, and stresses. It also happens to be our most important instrument of semantic transfer, and the common possession of all of us. If democracy means anything, we, the speakers, have the right to have our say as to how it shall be viewed and used, and not be forced to subscribe to the prescriptive excesses of what the European professor of linguistics describes as "the God's Truth School."

AN ENGLISH TEACHER ANSWERS MARIO PEI[*]

Margaret K. Bonney

Mario Pei's article "The Dictionary as a Battlefront" reflects the concern of a great many responsible citizens who are genuinely worried that this thing labeled "linguistics" is not only presiding over but contributing directly to the demise of the English language by abandoning standards of right and wrong. Educated people who love the language most are afraid that linguistics is encouraging lawlessness; thoughtful parents who want their children educated well are afraid of the consequences of abandoning traditional grammar. Pei rightly says that the publication of the "Third New International Dictionary," based as it is on linguistic

[*] From *Saturday Review*, September 15, 1962. By permission of the author and the publisher.

principles, has brought the subject of linguistics into even greater prominence. I believe his article also reflects certain mental confusion and some errors of fact which I should like to clarify. As an English teacher in a public school, I am committed to training young people in the knowledge and use of the language which I, too, love. Contrary to Pei's assumption, I believe this training can be best accomplished by basing my teaching on the findings of the linguistic and behavioral scientists.

Let us look first at just what Pei does say, and then try to isolate the areas of confusion and error.

First, he attributes the current lack of language ability in college graduates not to English teachers, or educationists who teach English teachers, but to the "philosophy and theories of a school of linguistics." Now precisely whom is he accusing? There have been isolated publications over a period of 200 years by linguists who took an objective view of the nature of English, but in America activity of the sort which we catalogue generally as the new science of linguistics is only about thirty years old. Leonard Bloomfield published his "Language" in 1933; Fries published a significant work in 1940, "The Structure of English." These constitute a scientific look at the structure of English and might qualify as theories, but hardly as philosophies. There have been many other books like these which present objective data from research, such as those by Chomsky and Raven McDavid, Nelson Francis, Trager and Smith, etc. These men are linguistic scientists and may be the "school of linguistics" Pei refers to, since he specifically eliminates professors and school teachers. Their work has all been published since 1930. Pei infers that their theorizing has influenced the schools of education, hence the teaching in colleges, high schools, and elementary schools; thus it is responsible for the present sorry state.

It is indeed true that linguistic facts and theories are being taught in graduate schools and in many summer institutes for teachers throughout the country; this new thinking is beginning to be reflected in the teaching of English in colleges and in lower schools, but that this thinking is *already* reflected in sufficient numbers of schools to have affected the skills of many graduates simply is not so. I know of one school system in the East with a linguistically oriented curriculum—Westport, Connecticut—in grades K–12, but this new curriculum was put into effect not more than three or four years ago. In the Boston area, the Newton and Concord school systems have made a start; Lexington expects to revise its English department along linguistic lines over the period of the next year and a half. Professor William G. Moulton of Princeton cites an article written in 1954 which states that at the time there were only 260 persons in this country who practiced structural linguistics. It would seem, therefore, that most of today's college graduates are the products of traditional and conservative methods and can't possibly be the products of language-centered curricula, simply because linguistics hasn't been practiced in the schools long enough. If our young people are poorly trained in English, it cannot yet be said that the fault lies with the linguistic scientists. Only time will tell if this will ever be so.

Pei also asserts that this school of linguistics has no standards of right and wrong in the use of English, that the new dictionary is the symbol of this lack of standards, and that the "followers of the school of linguistics" subscribe to a permissive doctrine based on the work of the linguists. We have assumed this school to mean linguistic scientists like Fries and Chomsky. Now what is the proper activity for a scientist in any field? His research involves observation of data, not judgment as to whether it is good or bad. When Raven McDavid reports that in Ohio people say "farhead" and in Massachusetts they say "forehead," he is reporting what he has found to be so. Standards of right and wrong do not apply. To say that speakers in Ohio are wrong, or that they speak bad English is as ridiculous as to say, "My eyes are blue; yours are brown. All eyes should be blue; therefore, you are wrong to have brown eyes." Pei says "Them dogs is us'uns," is not good English because it is not standard English; the linguistic scientist will be quick to agree it is not standard, but whether it is good or bad is irrelevant. Standard here assumes a different meaning from "standards of right and wrong"; standard English is that used by most of middle-class America. We will have more to say later about what is good English when we discuss the nature of the language.

If the linguistic scientist's proper job is to theorize and make observations about the language, it might be profitable to look for a moment at some of the observations he has made. What are some of the facts of language he would like us to notice? The matter of different dialects in different geographical areas we have already mentioned. If we observe that people in Massachusetts pronounce "forehead" differently than do Ohioans, what inferences can we draw? If "farhead" is characteristic of one person and reflects his geographical environment, "us'uns" is characteristic of another. Each person of each environment has a characteristic dialect which belongs to his region. It does not follow that one is bad, much less wrong.

Another quickly made observation is that of social levels of usage. There is a level of usage suitable to each social situation, and it is fairly closely adhered to by speakers. The high school student who brings his teen-age dialect into the schoolroom will cause mirth. Not only does each individual command more than one level—Have you ever heard a ten-year-old answer the phone in his most adult manner?—but he may consciously change from one identified with a lower social status to one typical of a higher because he wishes to be associated with people who talk that way. It is not difficult to think of cases, for example, of people born in uneducated, lower-income environments who become educated leaders—and change their dialects radically to suit their new social status. One's dialect is learned from emulating the sounds in the environment, and not from precepts and rules. The child talks as his family talks; the adolescent talks like other adolescents; the coal miner talks like other coal miners. A person changes his dialect usually by willing himself to do so, generally because of a wish to change his environment or status. This has important implications for the English teacher.

These two observations of the linguistic scientists, that language has dialects and levels, lead us to their very basic theory that language is primarily speech and that the written word is a form of speech and therefore secondary. Now to say something is primary means that it has a quality of firstness in some sort of relative, numerical order, as primary, secondary, and tertiary—which we seldom use of course. Children go to primary school first, then to secondary school next. This does not mean that primary school is more important in any sense than secondary school, or that secondary school is unimportant. Analogously, when the linguistic scientists say "Language is primarily speech," it cannot follow that writing therefore is unimportant. To say that all linguistic scientists consider writing unimportant is wrong. Fries, the structural linguist, has written a major work based on writing, "American English Grammar."

Perhaps the most controversial theories of the linguistic scientists pertain to grammar. The linguistic scientist uses the term "grammar" to label a theory or a systematic description of how a language operates. There are several kinds of theories of grammar at the moment, ranging from the traditional through the structural, the transformational, to the tagmemic. The linguists point out that no one grammar is a universal grammar, that each language has its own, and that in no case is a grammar prescriptive, or logical, or absolute. It is a description of the structure and operational procedures of a particular language. Here again the linguist remains in the scientist's domain of reporting what he finds to be so with no pretensions to value judgments. One's use of language is right or wrong only as it follows or violates the inherent rules of the language.

Perhaps "rule" is a misleading word to use here. A rule is a statement laid down in a prescriptive fashion by some authority, such as game rules in tennis: if the server's ball lands outside the stated area in the opposite court, the server does not gain a point. Another case would be in a school situation: when the bell rings, the teacher must stop talking and dismiss her class. However, if I wish to use my dishwasher, I must be sure the water is connected, but I would not say I was breaking the rules of dishwashers. Using language is like using dishwashers in this respect: the user is governed by the nature of the thing he is using. The use of the word "rules" in relation to grammar is a hangover from traditional grammar, in which an outside authority in the form of a school teacher or a textbook writer issued a collection of injunctions about how the language should be used, with the added inference that a person was wrong if he violated any one of the injunctions. If the teacher said, "All pronouns coming after the verb 'to be' must be in the nominative case," then a speaker was wrong if he said, "It is me." The linguistic scientist will observe reliably that a greater majority of Americans say "It is me" than say "It is I." He does not remark at all on which is "right."

However, in commenting on the innate structure of the language, the linguistic scientist will note, for example, that a certain subclass of verbs, say a transitive verb like "catch," is always and invariably followed by a noun phrase. One cannot say, "He caught several large foolish." This, the linguist would say, is wrong, a violation of the inherent nature of the language. Similarly, you have to have the water turned on to work the dishwasher. But this isn't really a "rule." In fact, let's not talk about "rules of grammar" any more because there aren't any, in the usual sense. Let's call them "operating principles."

Now someone will justifiably remark, "Why bother to say that 'He caught several large foolish' is wrong—nobody would make that kind of mistake anyway." And this is true; no native speaker would because, as the linguists say, a native speaker handles his language with marvelous ease by the time he is five years old. But is this saying that children never do anything with language that is incorrect? No it's not; they make such errors as: "The number of persons involved in those dreadful accidents over the holidays were greater than last year's."

It is seldom safe to play the prophet, but whereas "I" and "me" are becoming acceptable as interchangeable pronouns after the verb "to be," I doubt that verbs will ever cease to correspond in number with their subjects, because, if they did, ambiguity would set in at once. The dishwasher would not work very well.

Teaching English is only seldom the teaching of right and wrong; it is changing levels of usage where appropriate, leading from, but not condemning, the student's own level to a higher level; in writing, from an oral level to a more literary level. It is the teaching of discipline and control of the language structure, first to recognize it, then to be able to use and manipulate it; it is the teaching of taste in selection. It is not dogmatic and full of rules to be obeyed; it is a search, by trial and error, that leads to self-confidence and creativity and sweep. As there are operating principles to become familiar with, so there are levels of better or worse sentence structure, word choice, phraseology, and organization; but the possibilities of the choices available in the use of English are so vast that it is rarely a question of right and wrong. Standards of what is better or worse are the responsibility of the teacher and are a matter of taste. To label this "permissiveness" with the word's connotation of a regrettable loosening of authority is not to grasp the nature of the English teacher's job.

Perhaps here we should ask what is good taste, or conversely, what could be considered as debasing the language? Pei gives a careful answer in saying that language is debased when it is less precise and effective as communication. Where can we look for an example of precise and effective communication? Would he consider some current journalism by Robert Coughlin in *Life*?

Who Khrushchev is, he himself has made all too evident: a rough-and-tumble fellow ever ready to gouge an eye or put a knee in the groin, a rambunctious apostle of materialism, a master dissembler and propagandist with a flair for the unexpected—an exciting, rude, somehow grotesquely charming, thoroughly alarming old ruffian.

—October 31, 1960, page 82

For effective communication that is also precise, can he better this advertisement: "BOAC *jets* you there."?

My taste approves of these samples—I find the language dynamic, persuasive, and charming. Another might, of course, feel that this is letting language run its course "like a disease." Or perhaps it is evidence of debasement. The point is, if these examples can be accepted as good, how did these writers do it? Do the samples conform to the prescriptive rules of Latinate grammar, or have they emerged from a free, confident use of language? To teach young people to use their language with confidence, it is well not to keep telling them how wrong their particular use is; to teach them to use it creatively they must be allowed to try everything out; to use it freely they must be freed from prescriptive injunctions. Pei admits the fact of language change, but inexplicably he wants to control change by keeping it static, making it conform to rules he and "the community" think are right.

The teacher, then, can base her objectives and methods on the findings of the linguistic scientist. He records the facts of the language; she teaches the facts as grammar, and she also teaches taste.

The matter of what makes language good or poor extends naturally into a further discussion of what language is to people. Pei believes language to be the tool of communication, that it therefore should be standardized for efficiency, and that "a standardized language is a good language." I wish to add that language is much, much more than this, and that, in Pei's own words, "there is need for sound consideration of *all* [emphasis his] the facts."

In addition to being a more or less efficient instrument of semantic transfer, language is the individual's personal equipment by means of which he organizes the world around him into principles and concepts; it is his means of coping with external reality. He must be able to use this equipment with confidence, to use it freely so he can live and act freely. If you hedge in his language, you hedge in his development, because, as the psychologists point out, language behavior is not one among many, but an all-pervasive activity. The world—everything—outside us comes to us in a confusion of limitless numbers of impressions provoking endless associations. One of the ways man tries to achieve order out of this chaos is through his language. It is with words that the infant labels objects in his environment. They serve him as handles with which he begins quickly to manipulate his environment. This gives him a hold. The young child who talks to his toys and then talks back for them is ordering his world, not trying to communicate anything. This verbalizing becomes internal and silent—except for teen-age telephone conversations—but continues to be the process whereby the individual reduces reality to chunks he can manage.

And once he has it in words, the reality is more his to control as he wishes. An indication of whether or not a student fully understands, or knows, a particular concept is evidenced in his ability to verbalize it. As Gilbert Ryle suggests, if he knows it well, he has "practiced" the verbalization many times and can use it freely and quickly in any context. Language then is order and control, as well as communication.

If one accepts these facts established by psychologists about the nature of language, does it follow that standardizing it as Pei wishes is desirable? By "standardize," we will mean attempting to force language to conform to established forms—to be recorded in a large and widely read dictionary—and to restrain and discourage its free use.

As an English teacher, this assignment to hold the line and maintain the status quo would fall in my lap, and I would resign. To freeze my student's use of language by restriction and inhibition would be to try to freeze his development, and this I would not do. He needs to grow, to move about with increasing confidence, to develop more courage to try more new ideas, in short to go forward. If he is stuck, if he thinks in clichés, this ingrained habit of using the same words in the same connotation acts as a window shade that shuts off the denotation of the words, and he is thereby limited. A student who is allowed to remain in a word-using rut is dealing with empty symbols. Therefore, if we want active, searching, inquiring minds capable of coping with new problems as they arise, we should train them to constantly use new words in new ways. I want to teach students to think straight: to read accurately and make statements clearly; to be able to verbalize their environment: to say or write an opinion, an idea, a concept so they gain control of it; to have confidence in their own words because this is themselves. I want to lead them to ever higher levels of abstractions through increasing skill in manipulating their language, as in using grammar stylistically, in using metaphor, and in the development of individual style. I believe this type of linguistic training will lead to forceful, effective people who are able to cope with problems of life as they find them. I believe that one's ability to cope with problems requiring decisions that lead to action is in proportion to his ability to formulate apprehensions into words. In its written form this is English composition and the domain of the English teacher.

Each person has something that is uniquely his own, of which his dialect is the expression. He will learn to respect and value himself when his teachers respect and value him in the form of the words he uses, oral or written. A young person must have this self-respect to grow confident and stable. A composition is a tentative publication of the student's effort to organize the chaotic collection of impressions in his mind. It has to be valued as being a more or less successful effort than a previous one; it is simply inappropriate to apply standards of right and wrong.

In pursuing her age-old trade of bending the twig, the English teacher becomes a guardian of American English by keeping the way open for change, adaptation, and any additions. Because of this flexibility, English is the useful tool that it is, spoken by rapidly increasing numbers of the earth's population. With the advent of Telstar, a recent issue of *Newsweek* reported one writer who thinks English may well become the one international language. Far from presiding over a terminal "whimper" then, the linguistic and behavioral scientists with their colleagues in colleges and schools are showing the way to a more precise understanding of a great national asset and to a reinvigorating use of it. This is probably the greatest thing that has happened to English since Shakespeare put the free talk of common people into an art form.

On Style and the Uses of the Language

CORRUPTION OF OUR ENGLISH TONGUE

From THE TATLER [1710]

Richard Steele

The following letter has laid before me many great and manifest evils in the world of letters which I had overlooked; but they open to me a very busy scene, and it will require no small care and application to amend errors which are become so universal. The affectation of politeness is exposed in this epistle with a great deal of wit and discernment; so that whatever discourses I may fall into hereafter upon the subjects the writer treats of, I shall at present lay the matter before the world, without the least alteration from the words of my correspondent.

To Isaac Bickerstaff, Esquire.

Sir,

There are some abuses among us of great consequence, the reformation of which is properly your province; though, as far as I have been conversant in your papers, you have not yet considered them. These are, the deplorable ignorance that for some years hath reigned among our English writers, the great depravity of our taste, and the continual corruption of our style. I say nothing here of those who handle particular sciences, divinity, law, physic, and the like; I mean the traders in history and politics, and the *belles lettres;* together with those by whom books are not translated, but, as the common expressions are, 'done out of' French, Latin, or other language, and 'made English.' I cannot but observe to you, that until of late years a Grub Street book was always bound in sheepskin, with suitable print and paper, the price never above a shilling, and taken off wholly by common tradesmen or country pedlars; but now they appear in all sizes and shapes, and in all places. They are handed about from lapfuls in every coffee-house to persons of quality; are shown in Westminster Hall and the Court of Requests. You may see them gilt, and in royal paper of five or six hundred pages, and rated accordingly. I would engage to furnish you with a catalogue of English books published within the compass of seven years past, which at the first hand would cost you a hundred pounds, wherein you shall not be able to find ten lines together of common grammar or common sense.

These two evils, ignorance and want of taste, have produced a third; I mean the continual corruption of our English tongue, which, without some timely remedy, will suffer more by the false refinements of twenty years past, than it hath been improved in the foregoing hundred. And this is what I design chiefly to enlarge upon, leaving the former evils to your animadversion.

But instead of giving you a list of the last refinements crept into our language, I here send you the copy of a letter I received, some time ago, from a most accomplished person in this way of writing; upon which I shall make some remarks. It is in these terms:

'Sir,

'I *cou'd n't* get the things you sent for all *about Town—I thôt* to *ha* come down myself, and then *I'd h' brot'um;* but I *ha'nt don't,* and I believe I *can't do't,* that's *Pozz*—Tom begins to *gi' mself* airs, because *he's* going with the *Plenipo's*— 'Tis said the French King will *bamboozl us agen,* which causes many speculations. The *Jacks* and others of that *Kidney* are very *uppish,* and *alert upon't,* as you may see by their *Phizz's*— Will Hazard has got the *hipps,* having lost *to the Tune* of five *hundr'd* pound, *tho'* he understands play very well, *no Body better.* He has *promis't* me upon *rep,* to leave off play; but you know 'tis a weakness *he's* too apt to *give into, tho'* he has as much wit as any man, *no Body more.* He has

lain *incog* ever since— The *mob's* very quiet with us now—I believe
you *thôt* I *banter'd* you in my last, like a *country put*— I *shan't*
leave town this month, *etc.'*

This letter is in every point an admirable pattern of the present
polite way of writing; nor is it of less authority for being an epistle.
You may gather every flower in it, with a thousand more of equal
sweetness, from the books, pamphlets, and single papers offered
us every day in the coffee-houses. And these are the beauties introduced to supply the want of wit, sense, humour, and learning,
which formerly were looked upon as qualifications for a writer.
If a man of wit, who died forty years ago, were to rise from the
grave on purpose, how would he be able to read this letter? And
after he had got through that difficulty, how would he be able to
understand it? The first thing that strikes your eye is the breaks at
the end of almost every sentence; of which I know not the use,
only that it is a refinement, and very frequently practised. Then
you will observe the abbreviations and elisions, by which consonants of most obdurate sound are joined together, without one
softening vowel to intervene; and all this only to make one syllable
of two, directly contrary to the example of the Greeks and Romans,
altogether of the Gothic strain, and a natural tendency towards
relapsing into barbarity, which delights in monosyllables, and
uniting mute consonants, as it is observable in all the northern languages. And this is still more visible in the next refinement, which
consists in pronouncing the first syllable in a word that has many,
and dismissing the rest, such as 'phizz, hipps, mob, pozz, rep,'
and many more, when we are already overloaded with monosyllables, which are the disgrace of our language. Thus we cram one
syllable, and cut off the rest, as the owl fattened her mice after she
had bit off their legs to prevent them from running away; and if
ours be the same reason for maiming our words, it will certainly
answer the end; for I am sure no other nation will desire to borrow
them. Some words are hitherto but fairly split, and therefore only
in their way to perfection, as Incog, and Plenipo. But in a short
time, it is to be hoped, they will be further docked to Inc, and Plen.
This reflection has made me of late years very impatient for a
peace, which I believe would save the lives of many brave words,
as well as men. The war has introduced abundance of polysyllables, which will never be able to live many more campaigns,

'speculations, operations, preliminaries, ambassadors, palisadoes, communication, circumvallation, battalions,' as numerous as they are, if they attack us too frequently in our coffee-houses, we shall certainly put them to flight, and cut off the rear.

The third refinement, observable in the letter I send you, consists in the choice of certain words invented by some pretty fellows, such as 'banter, bamboozle, country put, and kidney,' as it is there applied; some of which are now struggling for the vogue, and others are in possession of it. I have done my utmost for some years past, to stop the progress of 'mob' and 'banter,' but have been plainly borne down by numbers, and betrayed by those who promised to assist me.

In the last place, you are to take notice of certain choice phrases scattered through the letter, some of them tolerable enough, until they were worn to rags by servile imitators. You might easily find them though they were not in a different print, and therefore I need not disturb them.

These are the false refinements in our style which you ought to correct; first, by argument and fair means, but if those fail, I think you are to make use of your authority as Censor, and by an annual *Index Expurgatorius* expunge all words and phrases that are offensive to good sense and condemn those barbarous mutilations of vowels and syllables. In this last point the usual pretence is that they spell as they speak: a noble standard for language! to depend upon the caprice of every coxcomb, who, because words are the clothing of our thoughts, cuts them out and shapes them as he pleases, and changes them oftener than his dress. I believe all reasonable people would be content that such refiners were more sparing in their words and liberal in their syllables; and upon this head I should be glad you would bestow some advice upon several young readers in our churches, who, coming up from the university full fraught with admiration of our town politeness, will needs correct the style of their prayer-books. In reading the absolution, they are very careful to say 'Pardons and Absolves'; but in the prayer for the Royal Family, it must be *endue'um, enrich'um, prosper'um,* and *bring'um.* Then in their sermons they use all the modern terms of art, 'sham, banter, mob, bubble, bully, cutting, shuffling, and palming'; all which, and many more of the like stamp, as I have heard them often in the pulpit from such young sophisters, so I have read them in some of 'those sermons that have made most noise of late.' The design, it seems, is to avoid the dreadful imputation of pedantry; to show us that they know the town, understand men and manners, and have not been poring upon old unfashionable books in the university.

I should be glad to see you the instrument of introducing into our style that simplicity which is the best and truest ornament of most things in life, which the politer ages always aimed at in their building and dress, *simplex munditiis,* as well as their productions of wit. It is manifest that all new affected modes of speech, whether borrowed from the court, the town, or the theatre, are the first perishing parts in any language; and, as I could prove by many hundred instances, have been so in ours. The writings of Hooker, who was a country clergyman, and of Parsons the Jesuit, both in the reign of Queen Elizabeth, are in a style that, with very few allowances, would not offend any present reader, and are much more clear and intelligible than those of Sir Harry Wotton, Sir Robert Naunton, Osborn, Daniel the historian, and several others who writ later; but being men of the court, and affecting the phrases then in fashion, they are often either not to be understood, or appear perfectly ridiculous.

What remedies are to be applied to these evils I have not room to consider, having, I fear, already taken up most of your paper. Besides, I think it is our office only to represent abuses, and yours to redress them. I am with great respect,

Sir,
Your, etc.

LEARNING TO WRITE [1789]

Benjamin Franklin

A question was once, somehow or other, started between Collins and me, of the propriety of educating the female sex in learning, and their abilities for study. He was of the opinion that it was improper, and that they were naturally unequal to it. I took the contrary side, perhaps a little for dispute's sake. He was naturally more eloquent, had a ready plenty of words; and sometimes, as I thought, bore me down more by his fluency than by the strength of his reasons. As we parted without settling the point, and were not to see one another again for some time, I sat down to put my arguments in writing, which I copied fair and sent to him. He answered, and I replied. Three or four letters of a side had passed, when my father happened to find my papers and read them. Without entering into the discussion, he took occasion to talk to me about the manner of my writing; observed that, though I had the advantage of my antagonist in correct spelling and pointing (which I owed to the printing-house), I fell far short in elegance of expression, in method and in perspicuity, of which he convinced me by several instances. I saw the justice of his remarks, and thence grew more attentive to the manner in writing, and determined to endeavor at improvement.

About this time I met with an odd volume of the *Spectator*. It was the third. I had never before seen any of them. I thought the writing excellent, and wished, if possible, to imitate it. With this view I took some of the papers, and, making short hints of the sentiment in each sentence, laid them by a few days, and then, without looking at the book, tried to complete the papers again, by expressing each hinted sentiment at length, and as fully as it had been expressed before, in any suitable words that should come to hand. Then I compared my *Spectator* with the original, discovered some of my faults, and corrected them. But I found I wanted a stock of words, or a readiness in recollecting and using them, which I thought I should have acquired before that time if I had gone on making verses; since the continual occasion for words of the same import, but of different length, to suit the measure, or of different sound for the rhyme, would have laid me under a constant necessity of searching for variety, and also have tended to fix that variety in my mind, and make me master of it. Therefore I took some of the tales and turned them into verse; and, after a time, when I had pretty well forgotten the prose, turned them back again. I also sometimes jumbled my collections of hints into confusion, and after some weeks endeavored to reduce them into the best order, before I began to form the full sentences and complete the paper. This was to teach me method in the arrangement of thoughts. By comparing my work afterwards with the original, I

discovered many faults and amended them; but I sometimes had
the pleasure of fancying that, in certain particulars of small import,
I had been lucky enough to improve the method or the language,
and this encouraged me to think I might possibly in time come to
be a tolerable English writer, of which I was extremely ambitious.

ON FAMILIAR STYLE [1821]

William Hazlitt

It is not easy to write a familiar style. Many people mistake a
familiar for a vulgar style, and suppose that to write without
affectation is to write at random. On the contrary, there is nothing
that requires more precision, and, if I may so say, purity of expression, than the style I am speaking of. It utterly rejects not only all
unmeaning pomp, but all low, cant phrases, and loose, unconnected, *slipshod* allusions. It is not to take the first word that offers,
but the best word in common use; it is not to throw words together
in any combinations we please, but to follow and avail ourselves
of the true idiom of the language. To write a genuine familiar or
truly English style, is to write as any one would speak in common
conversation, who had a thorough command and choice of words,
or who could discourse with ease, force, and perspicuity, setting
aside all pedantic and oratorical flourishes. Or to give another
illustration, to write naturally is the same thing in regard to common conversation, as to read naturally is in regard to common
speech. It does not follow that it is an easy thing to give the true
accent and inflection to the words you utter, because you do not
attempt to rise above the level of ordinary life and colloquial
speaking. You do not assume indeed the solemnity of the pulpit,
or the tone of stage-declamation: neither are you at liberty to
gabble on at a venture, without emphasis or discretion, or to resort
to vulgar dialect or clownish pronunciation. You must steer a
middle course. You are tied down to a given and appropriate
articulation, which is determined by the habitual associations between sense and sound, and which you can only hit by entering
into the author's meaning, as you must find the proper words and

style to express yourself by fixing your thoughts on the subject you have to write about. Any one may mouth out a passage with a theatrical cadence, or get upon stilts to tell his thoughts: but to write or speak with propriety and simplicity is a more difficult task. Thus it is easy to affect a pompous style, to use a word twice as big as the thing you want to express: it is not so easy to pitch upon the very word that exactly fits it. Out of eight or ten words equally common, equally intelligible, with nearly equal pretensions, it is a matter of some nicety and discrimination to pick out the very one, the preferableness of which is scarcely perceptible, but decisive. The reason why I object to Dr. Johnson's style is, that there is no discrimination, no variety in it. He uses none but "tall, opaque words," taken from the "first row of the rubric":—words with the greatest number of syllables, or Latin phrases with merely English terminations. If a fine style depended on this sort of arbitrary pretension, it would be fair to judge of an author's elegance by the measurement of his words, and the substitution of foreign circumlocutions (with no precise associations) for the mother-tongue. How simple it is to be dignified without ease, to be pompous without meaning! Surely, it is but a mechanical rule for avoiding what is low to be always pedantic and affected. It is clear you cannot use a vulgar English word, if you never use a common English word at all. A fine tact is shewn in adhering to those which are perfectly common, and yet never falling into any expressions which are debased by disgusting circumstances, or which owe their signification and point to technical or professional allusions. A truly natural or familiar style can never be quaint or vulgar, for this reason, that it is of universal force and applicability, and that quaintness and vulgarity arise out of the immediate connection of certain words with coarse and disagreeable, or with confined ideas. The last form what we understand by cant or slang phrases. —To give an example of what is not very clear in the general statement. I should say that the phrase To cut with a knife, or To cut a piece of wood, is perfectly free from vulgarity, because it is perfectly common: but to cut an acquaintance is not quite unexceptionable, because it is not perfectly common or intelligible, and has hardly yet escaped out of the limits of slang phraseology. I should hardly therefore use the word in this sense without putting it in italics as a license of expression, to be received cum grano salis. All provincial or bye-phrases come under the same mark of reprobation

—all such as the writer transfers to the page from his fireside or a particular *coterie,* or that he invents for his own sole use and convenience. I conceive that words are like money, not the worse for being common, but that it is the stamp of custom alone that gives them circulation or value. I am fastidious in this respect, and would almost as soon coin the currency of the realm as counterfeit the King's English. I never invented or gave a new and unauthorized meaning to any word but one single one (the term *impersonal* applied to feelings) and that was in an abstruse metaphysical discussion to express a very difficult distinction. I have been (I know) loudly accused of revelling in vulgarisms and broken English. I cannot speak to that point: but so far I plead guilty to the determined use of acknowledged idioms and common elliptical expressions. I am not sure that the critics in question know the one from the other, that is, can distinguish any medium between formal pedantry and the most barbarous solecism. As an author, I endeavour to employ plain words and popular modes of construction, as were I a chapman and dealer, I should common weights and measures.

The proper force of words lies not in the words themselves, but in their application. A word may be a fine-sounding word of an unusual length, and very imposing from its learning and novelty, and yet in the connection in which it is introduced, may be quite pointless and irrelevant. It is not pomp or pretension, but the adaptation of the expression to the idea that clenches a writer's meaning:—as it is not the size or glossiness of the materials, but their being fitted each to its place, that gives strength to the arch; or as the pegs and nails are as necessary to the support of the building as the large timbers, and more so than the mere shewy, unsubstantial ornaments. I hate any thing that occupies more space than it is worth. I hate to see a load of band-boxes go along the street, and I hate to see a parcel of big words without any thing in them. A person who does not deliberately dispose of all his thoughts alike in cumbrous draperies and flimsy disguises, may strike out twenty varieties of familiar everyday language, each coming somewhat nearer to the feeling he wants to convey, and at last not hit upon that particular and only one, which may be said to be identical with the exact impression in his mind. This would seem to shew that Mr. Cobbett is hardly right in saying that the first word that occurs is always the best. It may be a very good one; and yet a better may present itself on reflection or from time to time. It should be suggested naturally, however, and spontaneously, from a fresh and lively conception of the subject. We seldom succeed by trying at improvement, or by merely substituting one word for another that we are not satisfied with, as we cannot recollect the name of a place or person by merely plaguing ourselves about it. We wander farther from the point by persisting in a wrong scent, but it starts up accidentally in the memory when we least expected it, by touching some link in the chain of previous association.

There are those who hoard up and make a cautious display of nothing but rich and rare phraseology;—ancient medals, obscure coins, and Spanish pieces of eight. They are very curious to inspect; but I myself would neither offer nor take them in the course of exchange. A sprinkling of archaisms is not amiss; but a tissue of obsolete expressions is more fit *for keep than wear*. I do not say I would not use any phrase that had been brought into fashion before the middle or the end of the last century; but I should be shy of using any that had not been employed by any approved author during the whole of that time. Words, like clothes, get old-fashioned, or mean and ridiculous, when they have been for some time laid aside. Mr. Lamb is the only imitator of old English style I can read with pleasure; and he is so thoroughly imbued with the spirit of his authors, that the idea of imitation is almost done away. There is an inward unction, a marrowy vein both in the thought and feeling, an intuition, deep and lively, of his subject that carries off any quaintness or awkwardness arising from an antiquated style and dress. The matter is completely his own, though the manner is assumed. Perhaps his ideas are altogether so marked and individual, as to require their point and pungency to be neutralised by the affectation of a singular but traditional form of conveyance. Tricked out in the prevailing costume, they would probably seem more startling and out of the way. The old English authors, Burton, Fuller, Coryate, Sir Thomas Browne, are a kind of mediator between us and the more eccentric and whimsical modern, reconciling us to his peculiarities. I do not, however, know how far this is the case or not, till he condescends to write like one of us. I must confess that what I like best of his papers under the signature of Elia (still I do not presume, amidst such excellence, to decide what is most excellent) is the account of *Mrs. Battle's Opinions on Whist*, which is also the most free from obsolete allusions and turns of expressions—

A well of native English undefiled.

To those acquainted with his admired prototypes, these *Essays* of the ingenious and highly gifted author have the same sort of charm and relish, that Erasmus's *Colloquies* or a fine piece of modern Latin have to the classical scholar. Certainly, I do not know any borrowed pencil that has more power or felicity of execution than the one of which I have here been speaking.

It is as easy to write a gaudy style without ideas, as it is to spread a pallet of shewy colours, or to smear in a flaunting transparency. "What do you read?"—"Words, words, words."—"What is the matter?"—"*Nothing*," it might be answered. The florid style is the reverse of the familiar. The last is employed as an unvarnished medium to convey ideas; the first is resorted to as a spangled veil to conceal the want of them. When there is nothing to be set down but words, it costs little to have them fine. Look through the dictionary, and cull out a *florilegium*, rival the *tulipomania*. *Rouge* high enough, and never mind the natural complexion. The vulgar, who are not in the secret, will admire the look of preternatural health and vigour; and the fashionable, who regard only appearances, will be delighted with the imposition. Keep to your sounding generalities, your tinkling phrases, and all will be well. Swell out an unmeaning truism to a perfect tympany of style. A thought, a distinction is the rock on which all this brittle cargo of verbiage splits at once. Such writers have merely *verbal* imaginations, that retain nothing but words. Or their puny thoughts have dragon-wings, all green and gold. They soar far above the vulgar failing of the *Sermo humi obrepens*—their most ordinary speech is never short of an hyperbole, splendid, imposing, vague, incomprehensible, magniloquent, a cento of sounding common-places. If some of us, whose "ambition is more lowly," pry a little too narrowly into nooks and corners to pick up a number of "unconsidered trifles," they never once direct their eyes or lift their hands to seize on any but the left-off finery of poetic extravagance, transmitted down through successive generations of barren pretenders. If they criticise actors and actresses, a huddled phantasmagoria of feather, spangles, floods of light, and oceans of sound float before their morbid sense, which they paint in the style of Ancient Pistol. Not a glimpse can you get of the merits or defects of the performers: they are hidden in a profusion of barbarous epithets and wilful rhodomontade. Our hypercritics are not thinking of these little fantoccini beings—

That strut and fret their hour upon the stage—

but of tall phantoms of words, abstractions, *genera* and *species*, sweeping clauses, periods that unite the Poles, forced alliterations, astounding antitheses—

And on their pens *Fustian* sits plumed.

If they describe kings and queens, it is an Eastern pageant. The Coronation at either House is nothing to it. We get at four repeated images—a curtain, a throne, a sceptre, and a foot-stool. These are with them the wardrobe of a lofty imagination; and they turn their servile strains to servile uses. Do we read a description of pictures? It is not a reflection of tones and hues which "nature's own sweet and cunning hand laid on," but piles of precious stones, rubies, pearls, emeralds, Golconda's mines, and all the blazonry of art. Such persons are in fact besotted with words, and their brains are turned with the glittering, but empty and sterile phantoms of things. Personifications, capital letters, seas of sunbeams, visions of glory, shining inscriptions, the figures of a transparency, Britannia with her shield, or Hope leaning on an anchor, make up their stock in trade. They may be considered as *hieroglyphical* writers. Images stand out in their minds isolated and important merely in themselves, without any ground-work of feeling—there is no context in their imaginations. Words affect them in the same way, by the mere sound, that is, by their possible, not by their actual application to the subject in hand. They are fascinated by first appearances, and have no sense of consequences. Nothing more is meant by them than meets the ear: they understand or feel nothing more than meets the eye. The web and texture of the universe, and of the heart of man, is a mystery to them: they have no faculty that strikes a chord in unison with it. They

cannot get beyond the daubings of fancy, the varnish of sentiment.
Objects are not linked to feelings, words to things, but images
revolve in splendid mockery, words represent themselves in their
strange rhapsodies. The categories of such a mind are pride and
ignorance—pride in outside show, to which they sacrifice every
thing, and ignorance of the true worth and hidden structure both
of words and things. With a sovereign contempt for what is
familiar and natural, they are the slaves of vulgar affection—of a
routine of high-flown phrases. Scorning to imitate realities, they
are unable to invent any thing, to strike out one original idea.
They are not copyists of nature, it is true; but they are the poorest
of all plagiarists, the plagiarists of words. All is far-fetched, dear-
bought, artificial, oriental in subject and allusion: all is mechanical,
conventional, vapid, formal, pedantic in style and execution. They
startle and confound the understanding of the reader, by the remoteness and obscurity of their illustrations: they soothe the ear
by the monotony of the same everlasting round of circuitous metaphors. They are the *mock-school* in poetry and prose. They
flounder about between fustian in expression, and bathos in sentiment. They tantalise the fancy but never reach the head nor touch
the heart. Their Temple of Fame is like a shadowy structure raised
by Dulness to Vanity, or like Cowper's description of the Empress
of Russia's palace of ice, as "worthless as in shew 'twas glittering"—

It smiled, and it was cold!

From A WEEK ON THE CONCORD AND

MERRIMAC RIVERS [1849]

Henry David Thoreau

A perfectly healthy sentence, it is true, is extremely rare. For the
most part we miss the hue and fragrance of the thought, as if we
could be satisfied with the dews of the morning or evening without
their colors, or the heavens without their azure. The most attractive sentences are, perhaps, not the wisest, but the surest and
roundest. They are spoken firmly and conclusively, as if the
speaker had a right to know what he says, and if not wise, they

have at least been well learned. Sir Walter Raleigh might well be studied if only for the excellence of his style, for he is remarkable in the midst of so many masters. There is a natural emphasis in his style, like a man's tread, and a breathing space between the sentences, which the best of modern writing does not furnish. His chapters are like English parks, or say rather like a western forest, where the larger growth keeps down the underwood, and one may ride on horse-back through the openings. All the distinguished writers of that period, possess a greater vigor and naturalness than the more modern.—for it is allowed to slander our own time,— and when we read a quotation from one of them in the midst of modern authors, we seem to have come suddenly upon a greener ground, a greater depth and strength of soil. It is as if a green bough were laid across the page, and we are refreshed as by the sight of fresh grass in mid-winter or early spring. You have constantly the warrant of life and experience in what you read. The little that is said is eked out by implication of the much that was done. The sentences are verduous and blooming as evergreen and flowers, because they are rooted in fact and experience, but our false and florid sentences have only the tints of flowers without their sap or roots. All men are really most attracted by the beauty of plain speech, and they even write in a florid style in imitation of this. They prefer to be misunderstood rather than to come short of its exuberance. Hussein Effendi praised the epistolary style of Ibrahim Pasha to the French traveller Botta, because of "the difficulty of understanding it; there was," he said, "but one person at Jidda who was capable of understanding and explaining the Pasha's correspondence." A man's whole life is taxed for the least thing well done. It is its net result. Every sentence is the result of a long probation. Where shall we look for standard English, but to the words of a standard man? The word which is best said came nearest to not being spoken at all, for it is cousin to a deed which the speaker could have better done. Nay, almost it must have taken the place of a deed by some urgent necessity, even by some misfortune, so that the truest writer will be some captive knight, after all. And perhaps the fates had such a design, when, having stored Raleigh so richly with the substance of life and experience, they made him a fast prisoner, and compelled him to make his words his deeds, and transfer to his expression the emphasis and sincerity of his action.

Men have a respect for scholarship and learning greatly out of proportion to the use they commonly serve. We are amused to read how Ben Jonson engaged, that the dull masks with which the royal family and nobility were to be entertained, should be "grounded upon antiquity and solid learning." Can there be any greater reproach than an idle learning? Learn to split wood, at least. The necessity of labor and conversation with many men and things, to the scholar is rarely well remembered; steady labor with the hands, which engrosses the attention also, is unquestionably the best method of removing palaver and sentimentality out of one's style, both of speaking and writing. If he has worked hard from morning till night, though he may have grieved that he could not be watching the train of his thoughts during that time, yet the few hasty lines which at evening record his day's experience will be more musical and true than his freest but idle fancy could have furnished. Surely the writer is to address a world of laborers, and such therefore must be his own discipline. He will not idly dance at his work who has wood to cut and cord before nightfall in the short days of winter; but every stroke will be husbanded, and ring soberly through the wood; and so will the strokes of that scholar's pen, which at evening record the story of the day, ring soberly, yet cheerily, on the ear of the reader, long after the echoes of his axe have died away. The scholar may be sure that he writes the tougher truth for the calluses on his palms. They give firmness to the sentence. Indeed, the mind never makes a great and successful effort without a corresponding energy of the body. We are often struck by the force and precision of style to which hardworking men, unpractised in writing, easily attain, when required to make the effort. As if plainness, and vigor, and sincerity, the ornaments of style, were better learned on the farm and in the workshop than in the schools. The sentences written by such rude hands are nervous and tough, like hardened thongs, the sinews of the deer, or the roots of the pine. As for the graces of expression, a great thought is never found in a mean dress; but though it proceed from the lips of the Woloffs, the nine Muses and the three Graces will have conspired to clothe it in fit phrase. Its education has always been liberal, and its implied wit can endow a college. The scholar might frequently emulate the propriety and emphasis of the farmer's call to his team, and confess that if that were written it would surpass his labored sentences. Whose are the truly *labored* sentences? From the weak and flimsy periods of the politician and literary man, we are glad to turn even to the description of work, the simple record of the month's labor in the farmer's almanac, to restore our tone and spirits. A sentence should read as if its author, had he held a plow instead of a pen, could have drawn a furrow deep and straight to the end. The scholar requires hard and serious labor to give an impetus to his thought. He will learn to grasp the pen firmly so, and wield it gracefully and effectively, as an axe or a sword.

FENIMORE COOPER'S LITERARY OFFENSES [1895]

Mark Twain

The Pathfinder and *The Deerslayer* stand at the head of Cooper's novels as artistic creations. There are others of his works which contain parts as perfect as are to be found in these, and scenes even more thrilling. Not one can be compared with either of them as a finished whole.

The defects in both of these tales are comparatively slight. They were pure works of art.—*Prof. Lounsbury.*

The five tales reveal an extraordinary fullness of invention. . . . One of the very greatest characters in fiction, Natty Bumppo . . .

The craft of the woodsman, the tricks of the trapper, all the delicate art of the forest, were familiar to Cooper from his youth up.—*Prof. Brander Matthews.*

Cooper is the greatest artist in the domain of romantic fiction yet produced by America.—*Wilkie Collins.*

It seems to me that it was far from right for the Professor of English Literature in Yale, the Professor of English Literature in Columbia, and Wilkie Collins to deliver opinions on Cooper's literature without having read some of it. It would have been much more decorous to keep silent and let persons talk who have read Cooper.

Cooper's art has some defects. In one place in *Deerslayer,* and in the restricted space of two-thirds of a page, Cooper has scored

114 offenses against literary art out of a possible 115. It breaks the record.

There are nineteen rules governing literary art in the domain of romantic fiction—some say twenty-two. In *Deerslayer* Cooper violated eighteen of them. These eighteen require:

1. That a tale shall accomplish something and arrive somewhere. But the *Deerslayer* tale accomplishes nothing and arrives in the air.

2. They require that the episodes of a tale shall be necessary parts of the tale and shall help to develop it. But as the *Deerslayer* tale is not a tale and accomplishes nothing and arrives nowhere, the episodes have no rightful place in the work, since there was nothing for them to develop.

3. They require that the personages in a tale shall be alive, except in the case of corpses, and that always the reader shall be able to tell the corpses from the others. But this detail has often been overlooked in the *Deerslayer* tale.

4. They require that the personages in a tale, both dead and alive, shall exhibit a sufficient excuse for being there. But this detail also has been overlooked in the *Deerslayer* tale.

5. They require that when the personages of a tale deal in conversation, the talk shall sound like human talk, and be talk such as human beings would be likely to talk in the given circumstances, and have a discoverable meaning, also a discoverable purpose and a show of relevancy, and remain in the neighborhood of the subject in hand, and be interesting to the reader, and help out the tale, and stop when the people cannot think of anything more to say. But this requirement has been ignored from the beginning of the *Deerslayer* tale to the end of it.

6. They require that when the author describes the character of a personage in his tale, the conduct and conversation of that personage shall justify said description. But this law gets little or no attention in the *Deerslayer* tale, as Natty Bumppo's case will amply prove.

7. They require that when a personage talks like an illustrated, gilt-edged, tree-calf, hand-tooled, seven-dollar Friendship's Offering in the beginning of a paragraph, he shall not talk like a Negro minstrel in the end of it. But this rule is flung down and danced upon in the *Deerslayer* tale.

8. They require that crass stupidities shall not be played upon the reader as "the craft of the woodsman, the delicate art of the

forest," by either the author or the people in the tale. But this rule is persistently violated in the *Deerslayer* tale.

9. They require that the personages of a tale shall confine themselves to possibilities and let miracles alone; or, if they venture a miracle, the author must so plausibly set it forth as to make it look possible and reasonable. But these rules are not respected in the *Deerslayer* tale.

10. They require that the author shall make the reader feel a deep interest in the personages of his tale and in their fate, and that he shall make the reader love the good people in the tale and hate the bad ones. But the reader of the *Deerslayer* tale dislikes the good people in it, is indifferent to the others, and wishes they would all get drowned together.

11. They require that the characters in a tale shall be so clearly defined that the reader can tell beforehand what each will do in a given emergency. But in the *Deerslayer* tale this rule is vacated.

In addition to these large rules there are some little ones. These require that the author shall:

12. *Say* what he is proposing to say, not merely come near it.

13. Use the right word, not its second cousin.

14. Eschew surplusage.

15. Not omit necessary details.

16. Avoid slovenliness of form.

17. Use good grammar.

18. Employ a simple and straightforward style.

Even these seven are coldly and persistently violated in the *Deerslayer* tale.

Cooper's gift in the way of invention was not a rich endowment but such as it was he liked to work it, he was pleased with the effects, and indeed he did some quite sweet things with it. In his little box of stage-properties he kept six or eight cunning devices, tricks, artifices for his savages and woodsmen to deceive and circumvent each other with, and he was never so happy as when he was working these innocent things and seeing them go. A favorite one was to make a moccasined person tread in the tracks of the moccasined enemy, and thus hide his own trail. Cooper wore out barrels and barrels of moccasins in working that trick. Another stage-property that he pulled out of his box pretty frequently was his broken twig. He prized his broken twig above all the rest of his effects, and worked it the hardest. It is a restful chapter in any book of his when somebody doesn't step on a dry twig and alarm all the reds and whites for two hundred yards around. Every time a Cooper person is in peril and absolute silence is worth four dollars a minute, he is sure to step on a dry twig. There may be a hundred handier things to step on but that wouldn't satisfy Cooper. Cooper requires him to turn out and find a dry twig, and if he can't do it, go and borrow one. In fact, the Leatherstocking Series ought to have been called the Broken Twig Series.

I am sorry there is not room to put in a few dozen instances of the delicate art of the forest, as practised by Natty Bumppo and some of the other Cooperian experts. Perhaps we may venture two or three samples. Cooper was a sailor, a naval officer; yet he gravely tells us how a vessel, driving toward a lee shore in a gale, is steered for a particular spot by her skipper because he knows of an *undertow* there which will hold her back against the gale and save her. For just pure woodcraft, or sailorcraft, or whatever it is, isn't that neat? For several years Cooper was daily in the society of artillery and he ought to have noticed that when a cannon-ball strikes the ground it either buries itself or skips a hundred feet or so, skips again a hundred feet or so, and so on till finally it gets tired and rolls. Now in one place he loses some "females"—as he always calls women—in the edge of a wood near a plain at night in a fog, on purpose to give Bumppo a chance to show off the delicate art of the forest before the reader. These mislaid people are hunting for a fort. They hear a cannon-blast, and a cannon-ball presently comes rolling into the wood and stops at their feet. To the females this suggests nothing. The case is very different with the admirable Bumppo. I wish I may never know peace again if he doesn't strike out promptly and *follow the track* of that cannon-ball across the plain through the dense fog and find the fort. Isn't it a daisy? If Cooper had any real knowledge of Nature's ways of doing things, he had a most delicate art in concealing the fact. For instance: one of his acute Indian experts, Chingachgook (pronounced Chicago, I think), has lost the trail of a person he is tracking through the forest. Apparently that trail is hopelessly lost. Neither you nor I could ever have guessed out the way to find it. It was very different with Chicago. Chicago was not stumped for long. He turned a running stream out of its course and there, in the slush in its old bed, were that person's moccasin tracks. The current did not wash them away, as it would have done in all other like cases—no, even the eternal laws of Nature have to vacate when Cooper wants to put up a delicate job of woodcraft on the reader.

We must be a little wary when Brander Matthews tells us that Cooper's books "reveal an extraordinary fullness of invention." As a rule, I am quite willing to accept Brander Matthews's literary judgments and applaud his lucid and graceful phrasing of them, but that particular statement needs to be taken with a few tons of salt. Bless your heart, Cooper hadn't any more invention than a horse, and I don't mean a high-class horse, either, I mean a clothes-horse. It would be very difficult to find a really clever "situation" in Cooper's books, and still more difficult to find one of any kind which he has failed to render absurd by his handling of it. Look at the episodes of "the caves"; and at the celebrated scuffle between Maqua and those others on the tableland a few days later; and at Hurry Harry's queer water-transit from the castle to the ark; and at Deerslayer's half-hour with his first corpse; and at the quarrel between Hurry Harry and Deerslayer later; and at—But choose for yourself, you can't go amiss.

If Cooper had been an observer his inventive faculty would have worked better; not more interestingly but more rationally, more plausibly. Cooper's proudest creations in the way of "situations" suffer noticeably from the absence of the observer's protecting gift. Cooper's eye was splendidly inaccurate. Cooper seldom saw anything correctly. He saw nearly all things as through a glass eye, darkly. Of course a man who cannot see the commonest little every-day matters accurately is working at a disadvantage when he is constructing a "situation." In the *Deerslayer* tale Cooper has a stream which is fifty feet wide where it flows out of a lake; it presently narrows to twenty as it meanders along for no given reason, and yet when a stream acts like that it ought to be required to explain itself. Fourteen pages later the width of the brook's outlet from the lake has suddenly shrunk thirty feet and become "the narrowest part of the stream." This shrinkage is not accounted for. The stream has bends in it, a sure indication that it has alluvial banks and cuts them, yet these bends are only thirty and fifty feet long. If Cooper had been a nice and punctilious observer he would have noticed that the bends were oftener nine hundred feet long than short of it.

Cooper made the exit of that stream fifty feet wide in the first place for no particular reason; in the second place, he narrowed it to less than twenty to accommodate some Indians. He bends a "sapling" to the form of an arch over this narrow passage and conceals six Indians in its foliage. They are "laying" for a settler's scow or ark which is coming up the stream on its way to the lake; it is being hauled against the stiff current by a rope whose stationary end is anchored in the lake; its rate of progress cannot be more than a mile an hour. Cooper describes the ark, but pretty obscurely. In the matter of dimensions "it was little more than a modern canalboat." Let us guess, then, that it was about one hundred and forty feet long. It was of "greater breadth than common." Let us guess, then, that it was about sixteen feet wide. This leviathan had been prowling down bends which were but a third as long as itself and scraping between banks where it had only two feet of space to spare on each side. We cannot too much admire this miracle. A low-roofed log dwelling occupies "two-thirds of the ark's length"—a dwelling ninety feet long and sixteen feet wide, let us say, a kind of vestibule train. The dwelling has two rooms, each forty-five feet long and sixteen feet wide, let us guess. One of them is the bedroom of the Hutter girls, Judith and Hetty; the other is the parlor in the daytime, at night it is papa's bed-chamber. The ark is arriving at the stream's exit now, whose width has been reduced to less than twenty feet to accommodate the Indians—say to eighteen. There is a foot to spare on each side of the boat. Did the Indians notice that there was going to be a tight squeeze there? Did they notice that they could make money by climbing down out of that arched sapling and just stepping aboard when the ark scraped by? No, other Indians would have noticed these things but Cooper's Indians never notice anything. Cooper thinks they are marvelous creatures for noticing but he was almost always in error about his Indians. There was seldom a sane one among them.

The ark is one hundred and forty feet long; the dwelling is ninety feet long. The idea of the Indians is to drop softly and secretly from the arched sapling to the dwelling as the ark creeps along under it at the rate of a mile an hour, and butcher the family. It will take the ark a minute and a half to pass under. It will take the ninety-foot dwelling a minute to pass under. Now, then, what did the six Indians do? It would take you thirty years

to guess and even then you would have to give up, I believe.
Therefore, I will tell you what the Indians did. Their chief, a person of quite extraordinary intellect for a Cooper Indian, warily
watched the canal-boat as it squeezed along under him and when
he had got his calculations fined down to exactly the right shade,
as he judged, he let go and dropped. And *missed the house!* That
is actually what he did. He missed the house and landed in the
stern of the scow. It was not much of a fall, yet it knocked him
silly. He lay there unconscious. If the house had been ninety-seven
feet long he would have made the trip. The fault was Cooper's,
not his. The error lay in the construction of the house. Cooper
was no architect.

There still remained in the roost five Indians. The boat has
passed under and is now out of their reach. Let me explain what
the five did—you would not be able to reason it out for yourself.
No. 1 jumped for the boat but fell in the water astern of it. Then
No. 2 jumped for the boat but fell in the water still farther astern
of it. Then No. 3 jumped for the boat and fell a good way astern
of it. Then No. 4 jumped for the boat and fell in the water *away*
astern. Then even No. 5 made a jump for the boat—for he was a
Cooper Indian. In the matter of intellect, the difference between
a Cooper Indian and the Indian that stands in front of the cigar-
shop is not spacious. The scow episode is really a sublime burst of
invention but it does not thrill, because the inaccuracy of the
details throws a sort of air of fictitiousness and general improb-
ability over it. This comes of Cooper's inadequacy as an observer.

The reader will find some examples of Cooper's high talent for
inaccurate observation in the account of the shooting-match in
The Pathfinder.

A common wrought nail was driven lightly into the target, its
head having been first touched with paint.

The color of the paint is not stated—an important omission, but
Cooper deals freely in important omissions. No, after all, it was
not an important omission, for this nail-head is *a hundred yards
from* the marksmen and could not be seen by them at that distance,
no matter what its color might be. How far can the best eyes see
a common house-fly? A hundred yards? It is quite impossible.
Very well, eyes that cannot see a house-fly that is a hundred yards
away cannot see an ordinary nail-head at that distance, for the

size of the two objects is the same. It takes a keen eye to see a fly or a nail-head at fifty yards—one hundred and fifty feet. Can the reader do it?

The nail was lightly driven, its head painted, and game called. Then the Cooper miracles began. The bullet of the first marksman chipped an edge of the nail-head; the next man's bullet drove the nail a little way into the target—and removed all the paint. Haven't the miracles gone far enough now? Not to suit Cooper, for the purpose of this whole scheme is to show off his prodigy, Deerslayer-Hawkeye-Long-Rifle-Leatherstocking-Pathfinder-Bumppo before the ladies.

> "Be all ready to clench it, boys!" cried out Pathfinder, stepping into his friend's tracks the instant they were vacant. "Never mind a new nail; I can see that, though the paint is gone, and what I can see I can hit at a hundred yards, though it were only a mosquito's eye. Be ready to clench!"
>
> The rifle cracked, the bullet sped its way, and the head of the nail was buried in the wood, covered by the piece of flattened lead.

There, you see, is a man who could hunt flies with a rifle, and command a ducal salary in a Wild West show today if we had him back with us.

The recorded feat is certainly surprising just as it stands, but it is not surprising enough for Cooper. Cooper adds a touch. He has made Pathfinder do this miracle with another man's rifle; and not only that, but Pathfinder did not have even the advantage of loading it himself. He had everything against him, and yet he made that impossible shot, and not only made it but did it with absolute confidence, saying, "Be ready to clench." Now a person like that would have undertaken the same feat with a brickbat, and with Cooper to help he would have achieved it, too.

Pathfinder showed off handsomely that day before the ladies. His very first feat was a thing which no Wild West show can touch. He was standing with the group of marksmen, observing—a hundred yards from the target, mind; one Jasper raised his rifle and drove the center of the bull's-eye. Then the Quartermaster fired. The target exhibited no result this time. There was a laugh. "It's a dead miss," said Major Lundie. Pathfinder waited an impressive moment or two, then said in that calm, indifferent, know-it-all way of his, "No, Major, he has covered Jasper's bullet, as will be seen if anyone will take the trouble to examine the target."

Wasn't it remarkable! How *could* he see that little pellet fly through the air and enter that distant bullet-hole? Yet that is what he did, for nothing is impossible to a Cooper person. Did any of those people have any deep-seated doubts about this thing? No; for that would imply sanity and these were all Cooper people.

> The respect for Pathfinder's skill and for his *quickness* and *accuracy of sight* [the italics are mine] was so profound and general, that the instant he made this declaration the spectators began to distrust their own opinions, and a dozen rushed to the target in order to ascertain the fact. There, sure enough, it was found that the Quartermaster's bullet had gone through the hole made by Jasper's, and that, too, so accurately as to require a minute examination to be certain of the circumstance, which, however, was soon clearly established by discovering one bullet over the other in the stump against which the target was placed.

They made a "minute" examination; but never mind, how could they know that there were two bullets in that hole without digging the latest one out? for neither probe nor eyesight could prove the presence of any more than one bullet. Did they dig? No; as we shall see. It is the Pathfinder's turn now; he steps out before the ladies, takes aim, and fires.

But, alas! here is a disappointment, an incredible, an unimaginable disappointment—for the target's aspect is unchanged; there is nothing there but that same old bullet-hole!

> "If one dared to hint at such a thing," cried Major Duncan, "I should say that the Pathfinder has also missed the target!"

As nobody had missed it yet, the "also" was not necessary, but never mind about that for the Pathfinder is going to speak.

> "No, no, Major," said he, confidently, "that *would* be a risky declaration. I didn't load the piece, and can't say what was in it; but if it was lead, you will find the bullet driving down those of the Quartermaster and Jasper, else is not my name Pathfinder."

A shout from the target announced the truth of this assertion.

Is the miracle sufficient as it stands? Not for Cooper. The Path-finder speaks again, as he "now slowly advances toward the stage occupied by the females":

> "That's not all, boys, that's not all; if you find the target touched at all, I'll own to a miss. The Quartermaster cut the wood, but you'll find no wood cut by that last messenger."

The miracle is at last complete. He knew—doubtless *saw*—at the distance of a hundred yards—that his bullet had passed into the hole *without fraying the edges*. There were now three bullets in that one hole, three bullets embedded processionally in the body of the stump back of the target. Everybody knew this, somehow or other, and yet nobody had dug any of them out to make sure. Cooper is not a close observer but he is interesting. He is certainly always that, no matter what happens. And he is more interesting when he is not noticing what he is about than when he is. This is a considerable merit.

The conversations in the Cooper books have a curious sound in our modern ears. To believe that such talk really ever came out of people's mouths would be to believe that there was a time when time was of no value to a person who thought he had some-thing to say, when it was the custom to spread a two-minute remark out to ten, when a man's mouth was a rolling-mill and busied itself all day long in turning four-foot pigs of thought into thirty-foot bars of conversational railroad iron by attenuation, when subjects were seldom faithfully stuck to but the talk wan-dered all around and arrived nowhere, when conversations con-sisted mainly of irrelevancies with here and there a relevancy, a relevancy with an embarrassed look, as not being able to explain how it got there.

Cooper was certainly not a master in the construction of dia-logue. Inaccurate observation defeated him here as it defeated him in so many other enterprises of his. He even failed to notice that the man who talks corrupt English six days in the week must and will talk it on the seventh, and can't help himself. In the *Deer-slayer* story he lets Deerslayer talk the showiest kind of book-talk sometimes, and at other times the basest of base dialects. For in-stance, when some one asks him if he has a sweetheart, and if so where she abides, this is his majestic answer:

"She's in the forest—hanging from the boughs of the trees, in a
soft rain—in the dew on the open grass—the clouds that float about
in the blue heavens—the birds that sing in the woods—the sweet
springs where I slake my thirst—and in all the other glorious gifts
that come from God's Providence!"

And he preceded that, a little before, with this:

"It consarns me as all things that touches a fri'nd consarns a
fri'nd."

And this is another of his remarks:

"If I was Injin born, now, I might tell of this, or carry in the
scalp and boast of the expl'ite afore the whole tribe; or if my
inimy had only been a bear"—[and so on].

We cannot imagine such a thing as a veteran Scotch Com-
mander-in-Chief comporting himself in the field like a windy
melodramatic actor, but Cooper could. On one occasion Alice
and Cora were being chased by the French through a fog in the
neighborhood of their father's fort:

"*Point de quartier aux coquins!*" cried an eager pursuer, who
seemed to direct the operations of the enemy.
"Stand firm and be ready, my gallant 60ths!" suddenly exclaimed
a voice above them: "wait to see the enemy; fire low, and sweep the
glacis."
"Father! father," exclaimed a piercing cry from out the mist;
"it is I! Alice! thy own Elsie! spare, O! save your daughters!"
"Hold!" shouted the former speaker, in the awful tones of
parental agony, the sound reaching even to the woods, and rolling
back in solemn echo. " 'Tis she! God has restored me my children!
Throw open the sally-port; to the field, 60ths, to the field! pull
not a trigger, lest ye kill my lambs! Drive off these dogs of France
with your steel!"

Cooper's word-sense was singularly dull. When a person has a
poor ear for music he will flat and sharp right along without knowing it. He keeps near the tune, but it is *not* the tune. When a person
has a poor ear for words, the result is a literary flatting and sharp-
ing; you perceive what he is intending to say but you also perceive
that he doesn't *say* it. This is Cooper. He was not a word-musician.

His ear was satisfied with the *approximate* word. I will furnish some circumstantial evidence in support of this charge. My instances are gathered from half a dozen pages of the tale called *Deerslayer.* He uses "verbal" for "oral"; "precision" for "facility"; "phenomena" for "marvels"; "necessary" for "predetermined"; "unsophisticated" for "primitive"; "preparation" for "expectancy"; "rebuked" for "subdued"; "dependent on" for "resulting from"; "fact" for "condition"; "fact" for "conjecture"; "precaution" for "caution"; "explain" for "determine"; "mortified" for "disappointed"; "meretricious" for "factitious"; "materially" for "considerably"; "decreasing" for "deepening"; "increasing" for "disappearing"; "embedded" for "inclosed"; "treacherous" for "hostile"; "stood" for "stooped"; "softened" for "replaced"; "rejoined" for "remarked"; "situation" for "condition"; "different" for "differing"; "insensible" for "unsentient"; "brevity" for "celerity"; "distrusted" for "suspicious"; "mental imbecility" for "imbecility"; "eyes" for "sight"; "counteracting" for "opposing"; "funeral obsequies" for "obsequies."

There have been daring people in the world who claimed that Cooper could write English but they are all dead now—all dead but Lounsbury. I don't remember that Lounsbury makes the claim in so many words, still he makes it for he says that *Deerslayer* is a "pure work of art." Pure, in that connection, means faultless—faultless in all details—and language is a detail. If Mr. Lounsbury had only compared Cooper's English with the English which he writes himself—but it is plain that he didn't, and so it is likely that he imagines until this day that Cooper's is as clean and compact as his own. Now I feel sure, deep down in my heart, that Cooper wrote about the poorest English that exists in our language and that the English of *Deerslayer* is the very worst that even Cooper ever wrote.

I may be mistaken, but it does seem to me that *Deerslayer* is not a work of art in any sense; it does seem to me that it is destitute of every detail that goes to the making of a work of art; in truth, it seems to me that *Deerslayer* is just simply a literary *delirium tremens.*

A work of art? It has no invention; it has no order, system, sequence, or result; it has no lifelikeness, no thrill, no stir, no seeming of reality; its characters are confusedly drawn and by their acts and words they prove that they are not the sort of people the author claims that they are; its humor is pathetic; its pathos is funny; its conversations are—oh! indescribable; its love-scenes odious; its English a crime against the language.

Counting these out, what is left is Art. I think we must all admit that.

POLITICS AND THE ENGLISH LANGUAGE*

George Orwell

Most people who bother with the matter at all would admit that the English language is in a bad way, but it is generally assumed that we cannot by conscious action do anything about it. Our civilization is decadent, and our language—so the argument runs—must inevitably share in the general collapse. It follows that any struggle against the abuse of language is a sentimental archaism, like preferring candles to electric light or hansom cabs to aeroplanes. Underneath this lies the half-conscious belief that language is a natural growth and not an instrument which we shape for our own purposes.

Now, it is clear that the decline of a language must ultimately have political and economic causes: it is not due simply to the bad influence of this or that individual writer. But an effect can become a cause, reinforcing the original cause and producing the same effect in an intensified form, and so on indefinitely. A man may take to drink because he feels himself to be a failure, and then fail all the more completely because he drinks. It is rather the same thing that is happening to the English language. It becomes ugly and inaccurate because our thoughts are foolish, but the slovenliness of our language makes it easier for us to have foolish thoughts. The point is that the process is reversible. Modern English, especially written English, is full of bad habits which spread by imitation and which can be avoided if one is willing to take the necessary trouble. If one gets rid of these habits one can think more clearly, and to think clearly is a necessary first step towards political regeneration: so that the fight against bad English is not

* From *Shooting an Elephant and Other Essays* by George Orwell, copyright, 1945, 1946, 1949, 1950, by Sonia Brownell Orwell. Reprinted by permission of Harcourt, Brace & World, Inc.

frivolous and is not the exclusive concern of professional writers. I will come back to this presently, and I hope that by that time the meaning of what I have said here will have become clearer. Meanwhile, here are five specimens of the English language as it is now habitually written.

These five passages have not been picked out because they are especially bad—I could have quoted far worse if I had chosen— but because they illustrate various of the mental vices from which we now suffer. They are a little below the average, but are fairly representative samples. I number them so that I can refer back to them when necessary:

> (1) I am not, indeed, sure whether it is not true to say that the Milton who once seemed not unlike a seventeenth-century Shelley had not become, out of an experience ever more bitter in each year, more alien (*sic*) to the founder of that Jesuit sect which nothing could induce him to tolerate.
>
> Professor Harold Laski (Essay in *Freedom of Expression*)

> (2) Above all, we cannot play ducks and drakes with a native battery of idioms which prescribes such egregious collocations of vocables as the Basic *put up with* for *tolerate* or *put at a loss* for *bewilder*.
>
> Professor Lancelot Hogben (*Interglossa*)

> (3) On the one side we have the free personality; by definition it is not neurotic, for it has neither conflict nor dream. Its desires, such as they are, are transparent, for they are just what institutional approval keeps in the forefront of consciousness; another institutional pattern would alter their number and intensity; there is little in them that is natural, irreducible, or culturally dangerous. But *on the other side*, the social bond itself is nothing but the mutual reflection of these self-secure integrities. Recall the definition of love. Is not this the very picture of a small academic? Where is there a place in this hall of mirrors for either personality or fraternity?
>
> Essay on psychology in *Politics (New York)*

> (4) All the "best people" from the gentlemen's clubs, and all the frantic fascist captains, united in common hatred of Socialism and bestial horror of the rising tide of the mass revolutionary movement, have turned to acts of provocation, to foul incendiarism, to medieval legends of poisoned wells, to legalize their own de-

struction of proletarian organizations, and rouse the agitated petty-bourgeoisie to chauvinistic fervor on behalf of the fight against the revolutionary way out of the crisis.

Communist pamphlet

(5) If a new spirit *is* to be infused into this old country, there is one thorny and contentious reform which must be tackled, and that is the humanization and galvanization of the B.B.C. Timidity here will bespeak canker and atrophy of the soul. The heart of Britain may be sound and of strong beat, for instance, but the British lion's roar at present is like that of Bottom in Shakespeare's *Midsummer Night's Dream*—as gentle as any sucking dove. A virile new Britain cannot continue indefinitely to be traduced in the eyes, or rather ears, of the world by the effete languors of Langham Place, brazenly masquerading as "standard English." When the Voice of Britain is heard at nine o'clock, better far and infinitely less ludicrous to hear aitches honestly dropped than the present priggish, inflated, inhibited, school-ma'amish arch braying of blameless bashful mewing maidens.

Letter in *Tribune*

Each of these passages has faults of its own, but quite apart from avoidable ugliness, two qualities are common to all of them. The first is staleness of imagery; the other is lack of precision. The writer either has a meaning and cannot express it, or he inadvertently says something else, or he is almost indifferent as to whether his words mean anything or not. This mixture of vagueness and sheer incompetence is the most marked characteristic of modern English prose, and especially of any kind of political writing. As soon as certain topics are raised, the concrete melts into the abstract and no one seems able to think of turns of speech that are not hackneyed: prose consists less and less of *words* chosen for the sake of their meaning, and more and more of *phrases* tacked together like the sections of a prefabricated hen-house. I list below, with notes and examples, various of the tricks by means of which the work of prose-construction is habitually dodged:

> *Dying metaphors.* A newly-invented metaphor assists thought by evoking a visual image, while on the other hand a metaphor which is technically "dead" (e.g. *iron resolution*) has in effect reverted to being an ordinary word and can generally be used without loss of vividness. But in between these

two classes there is a huge dump of worn-out metaphors which have lost all evocative power and are merely used because they save people the trouble of inventing phrases for themselves. Examples are: *Ring the changes on, take up the cudgels for, toe the line, ride roughshod over, stand shoulder to shoulder with, play into the hands of, an axe to grind, grist to the mill, fishing in troubled waters, on the order of the day, Achilles' heel, swan song, hotbed.* Many of these are used without knowledge of their meaning (what is a "rift," for instance?), and incompatible metaphors are frequently mixed, a sure sign that the writer is not interested in what he is saying. Some metaphors now current have been twisted out of their original meaning without those who use them even being aware of the fact. For example, *toe the line* is sometimes written *tow the line.* Another example is *the hammer and the anvil,* now always used with the implication that the anvil gets the worst of it. In real life it is always the anvil that breaks the hammer, never the other way about: a writer who stopped to think what he was saying would be aware of this, and would avoid perverting the original phrase.

Operators, or *verbal false limbs.* These save the trouble of picking out appropriate verbs and nouns, and at the same time pad each sentence with extra syllables which give it an appearance of symmetry. Characteristic phrases are: *render inoperative, militate against, prove unacceptable, make contact with, be subjected to, give rise to, give grounds for, have the effect of, play a leading part* (role) *in, make itself felt, take effect, exhibit a tendency to, serve the purpose of, etc., etc.* The keynote is the elimination of simple verbs. Instead of being a single word, such as *break, stop, spoil, mend, kill,* a verb becomes a phrase, made up of a noun or adjective tacked on to some general-purposes verb such as *prove, serve, form, play, render.* In addition, the passive voice is wherever possible used in preference to the active, and noun constructions are used instead of gerunds (*by examination of* instead of *by examining*). The range of verbs is further cut down by means of the *-ize* and *de-* formations, and banal statements are given an appearance of profundity by means of the *not un-* formation. Simple conjunctions and prepositions are replaced by such phrases as *with respect to, having regard to, the fact that,* *by dint of, in view of, in the interests of, on the hypothesis that;* and the ends of sentences are saved from anti-climax by such resounding commonplaces as *greatly to be desired, cannot be left out of account, a development to be expected in the near future, deserving of serious consideration, brought to a satisfactory conclusion,* and so on and so forth.

Pretentious diction. Words like *phenomenon, element, individual* (as noun), *objective, categorical, effective, virtual, basis, primary, promote, constitute, exhibit, exploit, utilize, eliminate, liquidate,* are used to dress up simple statements and give an air of scientific impartiality to biased judgments. Adjectives like *epoch-making, epic, historic, unforgettable, triumphant, age-old, inevitable, inexorable, veritable,* are used to dignify the sordid processes of international politics, while writing that aims at glorifying war usually takes on an archaic color, its characteristic words being: *realm, throne, chariot, mailed fist, trident, sword, shield, buckler, banner, jackboot, clarion.* Foreign words and expressions such as *cul de sac, ancien régime, deus ex machina, mutatis mutandis, status quo, gleichschaltung, weltanschauung,* are used to give an air of culture and elegance. Except for the useful abbreviations *i.e., e.g.,* and *etc.,* there is no real need for any of the hundreds of foreign phrases now current in English. Bad writers, and especially scientific, political and sociological writers, are nearly always haunted by the notion that Latin or Greek words are grander than Saxon ones, and unnecessary words like *expedite, ameliorate, predict, extraneous, deracinated, clandestine, subaqueous* and hundreds of others constantly gain ground from their Anglo-Saxon opposite numbers.[1] The jargon peculiar to Marxist writing (*hyena, hangman, cannibal, petty bourgeois, these gentry, lackey, flunkey, mad dog, White Guard,* etc.) consists largely of words and phrases translated from Russian, German or French; but the normal way of coining a new word is to use a Latin or Greek root with the appropriate

---

[1] An interesting illustration of this is the way in which the English flower names which were in use till very recently are being ousted by Greek ones, *snap-dragon* becoming *antirrhinum, forget-me-not* becoming *myosotis,* etc. It is hard to see any practical reason for this change of fashion: it is probably due to an instinctive turning-away from the more homely word and a vague feeling that the Greek word is scientific.

affix and, where necessary, the *-ize* formation. It is often easier to make up words of this kind (*de-regionalize, impermissible, extramarital, non-fragmentary* and so forth) than to think of the English words that will cover one's meaning. The result, in general, is an increase in slovenliness and vagueness.

Meaningless words. In certain kinds of writing, particularly in art criticism and literary criticism, it is normal to come across long passages which are almost completely lacking in meaning.[2] Words like *romantic, plastic, values, human, dead, sentimental, natural, vitality,* as used in art criticism, are strictly meaningless, in the sense that they not only do not point to any discoverable object, but are hardly even expected to do so by the reader. When one critic writes, "The immediately striking thing about Mr. X's work is its peculiar deadness," the reader accepts this as a simple difference of opinion. If words like *black* and *white* were involved, instead of the jargon words *dead* and *living,* he would see at once that language was being used in an improper way. Many political words are similarly abused. The word *Fascism* has now no meaning except in so far as it signifies "something not desirable." The words *democracy, socialism, freedom, patriotic, realistic, justice,* have each of them several different meanings which cannot be reconciled with one another. In the case of a word like *democracy,* not only is there no agreed definition, but the attempt to make one is resisted from all sides. It is almost universally felt that when we call a country democratic we are praising it: consequently the defenders of every kind of regime claim that it is a democracy, and fear that they might have to stop using the word if it were tied down to any one meaning. Words of this kind are often used in a consciously dishonest way. That is, the person who uses them has his own private definition, but allows his hearer to think he means something quite different. Statements like *Marshal Petain was*

---

2 Example: "Comfort's catholicity of perception and image, strangely Whitmanesque in range, almost the exact opposite in aesthetic compulsion, continues to evoke that trembling atmospheric accumulative hinting at a cruel, an inexorably serene timelessness . . . Wrey Gardiner scores by aiming at simple bullseyes with precision. Only they are not so simple, and through this contented sadness runs more than the surface bittersweet of resignation."

(Poetry Quarterly.)

a true patriot, The Soviet Press is the freest in the world, The Catholic Church is opposed to persecution, are almost always made with intent to deceive. Other words used in variable meanings, in most cases more or less dishonestly, are: *class, totalitarian, science, progressive, reactionary, bourgeois, equality.*

Now that I have made this catalogue of swindles and perversions, let me give another example of the kind of writing that they lead to. This time it must of its nature be an imaginary one. I am going to translate a passage of good English into modern English of the worst sort. Here is a well-known verse from *Ecclesiastes:*

> I returned, and saw under the sun, that the race is not to the swift, nor the battle to the strong, neither yet bread to the wise, nor yet riches to men of understanding, nor yet favor to men of skill; but time and chance happeneth to them all.

Here it is in modern English:

> Objective consideration of contemporary phenomena compels the conclusion that success or failure in competitive activities exhibits no tendency to be commensurate with innate capacity, but that a considerable element of the unpredictable must invariably be taken into account.

This is a parody, but not a very gross one. Exhibit (3), above, for instance, contains several patches of the same kind of English. It will be seen that I have not made a full translation. The beginning and ending of the sentence follow the original meaning fairly closely, but in the middle the concrete illustrations—race, battle, bread—dissolve into the vague phrase "success or failure in competitive activities." This had to be so, because no modern writer of the kind I am discussing—no one capable of using phrases like "objective consideration of contemporary phenomena"—would ever tabulate his thoughts in that precise and detailed way. The whole tendency of modern prose is away from concreteness. Now analyze these two sentences a little more closely. The first contains 49 words but only 60 syllables, and all its words are those of everyday life. The second contains 38 words of 90 syllables: 18 of its words are from Latin roots, and one from Greek. The first sentence contains six vivid images, and only one phrase ("time and chance") that could be called vague. The second contains not a single fresh, arresting phrase, and in spite of its 90 syllables it gives only a shortened version of the meaning contained in the first. Yet without a doubt it is the second kind of sentence that is gaining ground in modern English. I do not want to exaggerate. This kind of writing is not yet universal, and out-crops of simplicity will occur here and there in the worst-written page. Still, if you or I were told to write a few lines on the uncertainty of human fortunes, we should probably come much nearer to my imaginary sentence than to the one from *Ecclesiastes*.

As I have tried to show, modern writing at its worst does not consist in picking out words for the sake of their meaning and inventing images in order to make the meaning clearer. It consists in gumming together long strips of words which have already been set in order by someone else, and making the results presentable by sheer humbug. The attraction of this way of writing is that it is easy. It is easier—even quicker, once you have the habit—to say *In my opinion it is a not unjustifiable assumption that* than to say *I think*. If you use ready-made phrases, you not only don't have to hunt about for words; you also don't have to bother with the rhythms of your sentences, since these phrases are generally so arranged as to be more or less euphonious. When you are composing in a hurry—when you are dictating to a stenographer, for instance, or making a public speech—it is natural to fall into a pretentious, Latinized style. Tags like *a consideration which we should do well to bear in mind* or *a conclusion to which all of us would readily assent* will save many a sentence from coming down with a bump. By using stale metaphors, similes and idioms, you save much mental effort at the cost of leaving your meaning vague, not only for your reader but for yourself. This is the significance of mixed metaphors. The sole aim of a metaphor is to call up a visual image. When these images clash—as in *The Fascist octopus has sung its swan song, the jackboot is thrown into the melting pot* —it can be taken as certain that the writer is not seeing a mental image of the objects he is naming; in other words he is not really thinking. Look again at the examples I gave at the beginning of this essay. Professor Laski (1) uses five negatives in 53 words. One of these is superfluous, making nonsense of the whole passage, and in addition there is the slip *alien* for *akin,* making further nonsense, and several avoidable pieces of clumsiness which increase the general vagueness. Professor Hogben (2) plays ducks and drakes with a battery which is able to write prescriptions, and, while disapproving of the everyday phrase *put up with*, is unwilling to look *egregious* up in the dictionary and see what it means. (3), if one takes an uncharitable attitude towards it, is simply meaningless: probably one could work out its intended meaning by reading the whole of the article in which it occurs. In (4), the writer knows more or less what he wants to say, but an accumulation of stale phrases chokes him like tea leaves blocking a sink. In (5), words and meaning have almost parted company. People who write in this manner usually have a general emotional meaning—they dislike one thing and want to express solidarity with another—but they are not interested in the detail of what they are saying. A scrupulous writer, in every sentence that he writes, will ask himself at least four questions, thus: What am I trying to say? What words will express it? What image or idiom will make it clearer? Is this image fresh enough to have an effect? And he will probably ask himself two more: Could I put it more shortly? Have I said anything that is avoidably ugly? But you are not obliged to go to all this trouble. You can shirk it by simply throwing your mind open and letting the ready-made phrases come crowding in. They will construct your sentences for you—even think your thoughts for you, to a certain extent—and at need they will perform the important service of partially concealing your meaning even from yourself. It is at this point that the special connection between politics and the debasement of language becomes clear.

In our time it is broadly true that political writing is bad writing. Where it is not true, it will generally be found that the writer is some kind of rebel, expressing his private opinions and not a "party line." Orthodoxy, of whatever color, seems to demand a lifeless, imitative style. The political dialects to be found in pamphlets, leading articles, manifestoes, White Papers and the speeches of under-secretaries do, of course, vary from party to party, but they are all alike in that one almost never finds in them a fresh, vivid, home-made turn of speech. When one watches some tired hack on the platform mechanically repeating the familiar phrases—*bestial, atrocities, iron heel, bloodstained tyranny, free peoples of the world, stand shoulder to shoulder*—one often has a curious feeling that one is not watching a live human being but some kind of dummy: a feeling which suddenly becomes stronger at moments when the light catches the speaker's spectacles and

turns them into blank discs which seem to have no eyes behind
them. And this is not altogether fanciful. A speaker who uses that
kind of phraseology has gone some distance towards turning himself into a machine. The appropriate noises are coming out of his
larynx, but his brain is not involved as it would be if he were
choosing his words for himself. If the speech he is making is one
that he is accustomed to make over and over again, he may be
almost unconscious of what he is saying, as one is when one utters
the responses in church. And this reduced state of consciousness,
if not indispensable, is at any rate favorable to political conformity.

In our time, political speech and writing are largely the defense
of the indefensible. Things like the continuance of British rule in
India, the Russian purges and deportations, the dropping of the
atom bombs on Japan, can indeed be defended, but only by arguments which are too brutal for most people to face, and which do
not square with the professed aims of political parties. Thus
political language has to consist largely of euphemism, question-
begging and sheer cloudy vagueness. Defenseless villages are
bombarded from the air, the inhabitants driven out into the countryside, the cattle machine-gunned, the huts set on fire with in-
cendiary bullets: this is called *pacification*. Millions of peasants
are robbed of their farms and sent trudging along the roads with
no more than they can carry: this is called *transfer of population*
or *rectification of frontiers*. People are imprisoned for years without trial, or shot in the back of the neck or sent to die of scurvy in
Arctic lumber camps: this is called *elimination of unreliable elements*. Such phraseology is needed if one wants to name things
without calling up mental pictures of them. Consider for instance
some comfortable English professor defending Russian totali-
tarianism. He cannot say outright, "I believe in killing off your
opponents when you can get good results by doing so." Probably,
therefore, he will say something like this:

> While freely conceding that the Soviet régime exhibits certain
> features which the humanitarian may be inclined to deplore, we
> must, I think, agree that a certain curtailment of the right to
> political opposition is an unavoidable concomitant of transitional
> periods, and that the rigors which the Russian people have been
> called upon to undergo have been amply justified in the sphere of
> concrete achievement.

The inflated style is itself a kind of euphemism. A mass of Latin words falls upon the facts like soft snow, blurring the outlines and covering up all the details. The great enemy of clear language is insincerity. When there is a gap between one's real and one's declared aims, one turns, as it were instinctively, to long words and exhausted idioms, like a cuttlefish squirting out ink. In our age there is no such thing as "keeping out of politics." All issues are political issues, and politics itself is a mass of lies, evasions, folly, hatred and schizophrenia. When the general atmosphere is bad, language must suffer. I should expect to find—this is a guess which I have not sufficient knowledge to verify—that the German, Russian and Italian languages have all deteriorated in the last ten or fifteen years as a result of dictatorship.

But if thought corrupts language, language can also corrupt thought. A bad usage can spread by tradition and imitation, even among people who should and do know better. The debased language that I have been discussing is in some ways very convenient. Phrases like *a not unjustifiable assumption, leaves much to be desired, would serve no good purpose, a consideration which we should do well to bear in mind,* are a continuous temptation, a packet of aspirins always at one's elbow. Look back through this essay, and for certain you will find that I have again and again committed the very faults I am protesting against. By this morning's post I have received a pamphlet dealing with conditions in Germany. The author tells me that he "felt impelled" to write it. I open it at random, and here is almost the first sentence that I see: "[The Allies] have an opportunity not only of achieving a radical transformation of Germany's social and political structure in such a way as to avoid a nationalistic reaction in Germany itself, but at the same time of laying the foundations of a cooperative and unified Europe." You see, he "feels impelled" to write—feels, presumably, that he has something new to say—and yet his words, like cavalry horses answering the bugle, group themselves automatically into the familiar dreary pattern. This invasion of one's mind by ready-made phrases (*lay the foundations, achieve a radical transformation*) can only be prevented if one is constantly on guard against them, and every such phrase anesthetizes a portion of one's brain.

I said earlier that the decadence of our language is probably curable. Those who deny this would argue, if they produced an argument at all, that language merely reflects existing social conditions, and that we cannot influence its development by any direct tinkering with words and constructions. So far as the general tone or spirit of a language goes, this may be true, but it is not true in detail. Silly words and expressions have often disappeared, not through any evolutionary process but owing to the conscious action of a minority. Two recent examples were *explore every avenue* and *leave no stone unturned*, which were killed by the jeers of a few journalists. There is a long list of fly-blown metaphors which could similarly be got rid of if enough people would interest themselves in the job; and it should also be possible to laugh the *not un-* formation out of existence,[3] to reduce the amount of Latin and Greek in the average sentence, to drive out foreign phrases and strayed scientific words, and, in general, to make pretentiousness unfashionable. But all these are minor points. The defense of the English language implies more than this, and perhaps it is best to start by saying what it does *not* imply.

To begin with, it has nothing to do with archaism, with the salvaging of obsolete words and turns of speech, or with the setting-up of a "standard English" which must never be departed from. On the contrary, it is especially concerned with the scrapping of every word or idiom which has outworn its usefulness. It has nothing to do with correct grammar and syntax, which are of no importance so long as one makes one's meaning clear, or with the avoidance of Americanisms, or with having what is called a "good prose style." On the other hand it is not concerned with fake simplicity and the attempt to make written English colloquial. Nor does it even imply in every case preferring the Saxon word to the Latin one, though it does imply using the fewest and shortest words that will cover one's meaning. What is above all needed is to let the meaning choose the word, and not the other way about. In prose, the worst thing one can do with words is to surrender them. When you think of a concrete object, you think wordlessly, and then, if you want to describe the thing you have been visualizing, you probably hunt about till you find the exact words that seem to fit it. When you think of something abstract you are more inclined to use words from the start, and unless you

---

[3] One can cure oneself of the *not un-* formation by memorizing this sentence: *A not unblack dog was chasing a not unsmall rabbit across a not ungreen field.*

make a conscious effort to prevent it, the existing dialect will come rushing in and do the job for you, at the expense of blurring or even changing your meaning. Probably it is better to put off using words as long as possible and get one's meaning as clear as one can through pictures or sensations. Afterwards one can choose —not simply *accept*—the phrases that will best cover the meaning, and then switch round and decide what impressions one's words are likely to make on another person. This last effort of the mind cuts out all stale or mixed images, all prefabricated phrases, needless repetitions, and humbug and vagueness generally. But one can often be in doubt about the effect of a word or a phrase, and one needs rules that one can rely on when instinct fails. I think the following rules will cover most cases:

(i) Never use a metaphor, simile or other figure of speech which you are used to seeing in print.

(ii) Never use a long word where a short one will do.

(iii) If it is possible to cut a word out, always cut it out.

(iv) Never use the passive where you can use the active.

(v) Never use a foreign phrase, a scientific word or a jargon word if you can think of an everyday English equivalent.

(vi) Break any of these rules sooner than say anything barbarous.

These rules sound elementary, and so they are, but they demand a deep change of attitude in anyone who has grown used to writing in the style now fashionable. One could keep all of them and still write bad English, but one could not write the kind of stuff that I quoted in these five specimens at the beginning of this article.

I have not here been considering the literary use of language, but merely language as an instrument for expressing and not for concealing or perverting thought. Stuart Chase and others have come near to claiming that all abstract words are meaningless, and have used this as a pretext for advocating a kind of political quietism. Since you don't know what Fascism is, how can you struggle against Fascism? One need not swallow such absurdities as this, but one ought to recognize that the present political chaos is connected with the decay of language, and that one can probably bring about some improvement by starting at the verbal end. If you simplify your English, you are freed from the worst follies of orthodoxy. You cannot speak any of the necessary dialects, and when you make a stupid remark its stupidity will be obvious, even to yourself. Political language—and with variations this is true of all political parties, from Conservatives to Anarchists—is designed to make lies sound truthful and murder respectable, and to give an appearance of solidity to pure wind. One cannot change this all in a moment, but one can at least change one's own habits, and from time to time one can even, if one jeers loudly enough, send some worn-out and useless phrase—some *jackboot, Achilles' heel, hotbed, melting pot, acid test, veritable inferno* or other lump of verbal refuse—into the dustbin where it belongs.

HOW TO WRITE AND BE READ*

Jacques Barzun

> Here and there a touch of good
> grammar for picturesqueness.
> —MARK TWAIN

Writing comes before reading, in logic and also in the public mind. No one cares whether you read fast or slow, well or ill, but as soon as you put pen to paper, somebody may be puzzled, angry, bored, or ecstatic; and if the occasion permits, your reader is almost sure to exclaim about the schools not doing their duty. This is the oldest literary tradition, of which here is a modern instance:—

WHAT KIND OF TEACHING IN THE PRIMARY SCHOOLS? BY "DISGUSTED"

Recently a letter came into my office from a boy who described himself as a first-year high school student. He wanted *infirmation* about *Africia,* because for his project in the social studies class he had *chozen Africia.* If we could not help him, *were* could he write? In closing, he was ours *sinceerly.* His handwriting was comparable to that of my 6-year-old nephew.

Too bad, but I am not alarmed. This student of "Africia" may or may not learn to spell: it is not nearly so important as his diction

* From *Teacher in America* by Jacques Barzun, by permission of Little, Brown and Co.–Atlantic Monthly Press. Copyright 1944, 1945, by Jacques Barzun.

and his sentence structure, which the plaintiff withheld, though they would have better enabled us to judge what the schools were really doing. What I fear about this boy is that when grown-up and provided with a secretary who can spell, he will write something like this:—

Dear Sir:—

   As you know, security prices have been advancing rapidly in the recent past *in belated recognition of the favorable fundamentals that exist.* [Italics mine]

What is decadent about this I shall shortly explain. Meantime, the fact should be faced squarely that good writing is and has always been extremely rare. I do not mean fine writing, but the simple, clear kind that everyone always demands—from others. The truth is that Simple English is no one's mother tongue. It has to be worked for. As an historian, I have plowed through state papers, memoirs, diaries, and letters, and I know that the ability to write has only a remote connection with either intelligence, or greatness, or schooling. Lincoln had no schooling yet became one of the great prose writers of the world. Cromwell went to Cambridge and was hardly ever able to frame an intelligible sentence. Another man of thought and action, Admiral Lord Howe, generally refrained from writing out his plan of battle, so as to save his captains from inevitable misunderstanding. Yet Howe managed to win the famous First of June by tactics that revolutionized the art, and led directly to Nelson's Trafalgar plan—itself a rather muddled piece of prose. Let us then start with no illusion of an imaginary golden age of writing.

Which leaves the problem of doing the best with what nature gives us. And here I have some convictions born of long struggle, with myself and with others. First, I pass by all considerations of penmanship and elementary spelling to remark only that I think it a mistake to start children writing on typewriters, and worse yet to let them grow up unable to do anything but print capitals.

Above the beginner's level, the important fact is that writing cannot be taught exclusively in a course called English Composition. Writing can only be taught by the united efforts of the entire teaching staff. This holds good of any school, college, or university. Joint effort is needed, not merely to "enforce the rules"; it is needed to insure accuracy in every subject. How can an answer

in physics or a translation from the French or an historical statement be called correct if the phrasing is loose or the key word
wrong? Students argue that the reader of the paper knows perfectly well what is meant. Probably so, but a written exercise is
designed to be read; it is not supposed to be a challenge to clair-
voyance. My Italian-born tailor periodically sends me a postcard
which runs: "Your clothes is ready and should come down for a fitting." I understand him, but the art I honor him for is cutting
cloth, not precision of utterance. Now a student in a college must
be inspired to achieve in all subjects the utmost accuracy of perception combined with the utmost artistry of expression. The two
merge and develop the sense of good workmanship, of preference
for quality and truth, which is the chief mark of the genuinely
educated man.

This is obviously a collective task, in which every department
and every faculty has a common stake. But it is not enough to give
notice that these are the faculty's sentiments. Even supposing that
all teachers were willing and able to exert vigilance over written
work, there would still be many practical problems of detail. And
first, what motive for writing well can the student be made to feel?
There is only one valid motive: the desire to be read. You will say
that most students have no urge either to write or to be read. True,
but (a) they know that they have to write and (b) most of them
want to be well thought of. They should accordingly be made to
see that reading the ordinary student paper can be a nuisance and
a bore to the teacher, and that the proper aim of writing should be
to make it a pleasure. This is another way of saying that most school
writing is bad because student and teacher play at writing and
reading instead of taking it seriously. The teacher expects second-
rate hokum and the student supplies it. Let the teacher assert his
rights just as the students do: in many college classes the men
protest—quite rightly—when they are asked to read a dull or ill-
organized book. Similarly, the instructor may warn the students
that when they turn in filler and padding, jargon and lingo, stuff
and nonsense, he will mark them down, not only in his grade book,
but in his violated soul.

Naturally, this conscious brutality must go with a helping hand;
in fact a revision of all usual practices is in order. The embargo on
hokum will already work a healthy elimination of bad prose. Then
the long Term Paper must be discarded and replaced with the short

essay, not more than five typewritten pages in length. Students always ask how long a final paper should be and they are absolutely right in believing that most instructors are impressed by mere bulk. But when one knows how difficult it is to articulate even three measly thoughts around a single point, it is folly to ask eighteen-year-olds to produce thirty- or forty-page monographs that shall be readable. What they produce is an uncarded mattress of quotations, paraphrase, "however's," and "Thus we see's." Size being aimed at, there is no time for rewriting or reordering the material culled from half a dozen books, and the main effort goes into the irrelevant virtues of neat typing, plentiful footnotes, and the mannerisms of scholarship.

The short paper—and I speak from a large pile accumulated over twelve years—aims and arrives at different ends. It answers the reader's eternal question: Just what are you trying to tell me? It is in that spirit that student writing must be read, corrected and if need be rewritten. When first presented, it must already be a second or third draft. The only reason I can think of for the somewhat higher average of good writing in France is that the *brouillon* is a national institution. The *brouillon* (literally: scrambled mess) is the first draft, and even the concierge writing to the police about anarchists on the third floor begins with a *brouillon,* later found by his heirs.

Of course it is no use telling an American boy or girl that the essay must be written, laid aside, and rewritten at least once before handing in: the innocents do not know what to do after their first painful delivery. So the simplest thing is to ask early in the term for a good five-page essay, which turns out to be pretty bad. This is fully annotated by the reader and turned back before the next one is called for. But the corrections on it are not merely the conventional *sp., ref., punc.,* and *awk.* which the writers have seen in their margins from the seventh grade on. The comments are intensely and painfully personal, being the responses that an alert reader would feel if he were encountering the essay in print. The result is that even the best students feel abashed, if not actually resentful. To which one can only say that they should resent the neglect in which their previous teachers have left them.

This neglect has not damaged their grammar so much as their vocabulary. Since the last thing any writer learns is the uses of words, it is no wonder if untutored youths of ability write like the stockbroker whom I quoted about "favorable fundamentals that exist"—spineless, vague, and incoherent prose. Indeed, the exact parallel comes this moment under my hand, taken from a very able student's report on Newman's *University Sketches:* "A University that rests on a firm financial foundation has the greater ability to unleash the minds of its students." Despite the difference in names, the stockbroker is that boy's putative father. Their failure comes from a like inattention to meaning—their own and that of the words they use.

This means that words and tone are the main things to be taught. Spelling, grammar, and punctuation do not precede but follow in the order of importance. They follow also quite naturally in the order of facility. Accordingly, the teacher-critic must slowly and carefully explain to the student what each word conveys in its particular context. I find that in the essay just cited I have written such comments as: "I can't follow—This repeats in disguise—'avocational fruit' suggests alligator pears: why?—We now have about eight 'problems' on hand: Begin!—What! more issues and problems? —Commercial lingo—Who is 'we'?—Why 'cradle':—Don't scold and trail off in this way—This is your point at last." In addition, images are changed, synonyms proposed, and bad sentences recast, sometimes in alternative ways, in order to show precisely how the original misleads and how clarity is to be reached.

Tone grows naturally out of diction, but the choice of words betrays feelings of which the young writer is usually unaware. "Are you pleading, denouncing, coaxing, or laughing? Do you back up this exaggeration? Why suddenly talk down, or turn pedant? If you want to change the mood inside the piece, you must modulate, otherwise your reader will stumble and you will lose him." The student who learns to quiz himself in this fashion over his first draft is learning not only something about English, about writing, and about thinking, but about the human heart as well.

At the risk of tediousness I repeat that what has to be done is to dramatize the relation between writer and reader. The blunt comments are just a device to break the spell of routine, and though they administer an unpleasant shock at first, they are also flattering. "Somebody cares about what I want to say." The teacher is no longer a paid detective hunting stray commas.

To point these lessons up in minute detail to a student of average powers is of course time-consuming—but what else is the teacher there for? Time spent on reading and writing, in any subject, is never a waste, and the reward almost always comes, often astonishingly great. The excitement aroused by the discovery that words live is like finding that you can balance on skates. A new world of motion and of feeling is opened out to the student, a source of some anguish balanced by lifelong delight. George Gissing writes somewhere that he saw an excursion steamer advertised as being "Replete with Ladies' Lavatories" and he comments on how many people could pass by the sign without a smile. My own favorite recollection is of a guarantee pasted on a modest shop window: "Hats fitted to the head exclusively"—fun in every ad and at the company's expense.

The pleasure to be taken in words is as innocent and satisfying as the moral effect is clear: unless words are used deftly to set the imagination on its travels, language, literature, conversation, and friendship are full of snares. Much of our modern anxiety about the tyranny of words and of our desire for foolproof Basic comes from the uneasy suspicion that we have lost the art of diction and with it the control over our own minds. This is more serious than it seems, for there is no doubt that the world outside the school largely checks what present instruction attempts, as we shall see. But having spoken of the imagination, let me first meet a likely objection to the advice here proposed. I can fancy some reader for whom school compositions were torture shaking a skeptical head and saying: "Most young children have very little to say and school assignments blot out even that little." I agree and the second great practical problem is, What to ask boys and girls to write about?

The don'ts are easy. Don't ask them for "A vacation experience," or "My most embarrassing moment," or "I am the Mississippi River." Such topics will only elicit the driest kind of hokum, though to be fair I must say that they are an improvement on the older practice of expecting infant moralizing and "What the flag means to me." Although as a child I enjoyed writing—history chiefly—I can remember the blankness of mind that overtook me when we had to do a *dissertation morale*. I still have a school text with some of those themes checked as having been done—for example: "The Faithful Dog.—A poor man has resolved to drown his dog. Thrown into the river, the dog tries to scramble up the bank, but his master lunges out to kill him with a stick. In so doing, he slips and falls. The dog saves him. Remorse of the owner."

I regret to say that French school life is stuffed with such thorns

as these, but I am not sure that the opposite "progressive" extreme
of turning children into researchers on their own is desirable either.
The eleven-year-old son of a friend of mine once told me that he
was writing a "project" on Papyrus. Why papyrus? Well, the class
had been "doing" Egypt and each child was assigned one aspect
of Egyptian civilization. Where was the information to come from?
From encyclopedias, museums, friends, and paper manufacturers—
hence such letters to strangers as the one about "Africia" quoted
earlier. As I see it, two things are wrong with this scheme. One is
that it gives a false freedom, the other is that it hardly trains in
the art of composing. Did this boy care at all about Egypt, let
alone about the technicalities of papyrology? A child should select
a topic that truly engages his interest. To eliminate pretense he
must be helped to do this by means of questions and suggestions.
At any age, it is very reassuring to be told that you don't really
want to write about the Tariff. After two or three casts a real subject emerges, satisfactory to both parties.

Next should come into play the single good feature of the
French dissertation, namely its furnishing a plan or program. Depending on the child's age a briefer or longer table of contents
should be set out for each theme, either in logically organized
form, or pell-mell for the student himself to disentangle. After all,
what is wanted is prose, not a riot of fancy. In my experience, even
examination questions are answered better when they consist of
five or six sentences outlining a topic for discussion. This means
further brevity should never be accounted a fault in itself. After
thirty, we can all spin tall tales, mostly secondhand, but students,
even of college age, have had very little conscious experience of
life or books and it is no wonder their minds are bone dry. One
should moreover keep in view the possibility that in some of them
brevity may come from genius. American schoolmarms who relate
the anecdote of Lincoln's "failure" with the Gettysburg Address
are just as likely to say at one glance, "Jane, this is too short." How
do they know? Perhaps they unwittingly agree with the Gettysburg
crowd that Everett's speech, being longer, was better.

Some secondary schools, particularly the private ones, require
the writing of verse as well as of prose. If the students are really
shown how to go about versifying and are not expected to be
"poetic," there is no harm in it. Verse writing is excellent practice
for the prose writer and the striving for correct rhythm and rhyme

gives the student of literature a feeling for words that may not otherwise be obtained. What can be done in this way before college by a gifted teacher has been shown by the experience of my friend, the poet Dudley Fitts, formerly at Choate and now at Andover. In collegiate circles, it is now well known that a freshman prepared under him is a literate, sometimes a polished writer, who can be safely allowed to skip into advanced work. No doubt Fitts has had his failures like all of us, but it is the successes we are looking for and that count in leavening the mass.

▶ *II*

I am not so foolish as to think that carrying out my few suggestions would get rid of illiterate A.B.'s. I am too conscious of my initial point about "Education," which is that the school does not work in a vacuum but rather in a vortex of destructive forces. As regards writing, we in the twentieth century must offset not only the constant influence of careless speech and the indifference of parents, but the tremendous output of jargon issuing from the new mechanical means at man's disposal. Worst of all, circumstances have conspired to put the most corrupting force at the very heart of the school system. It is not newspapers, radio scripts, and movies that spoil our tongue so much as textbooks, official documents, commencement speeches, and learned works.

The rise, at the turn of the century, of what James called "the softer pedagogy" is responsible for a debasement of language beyond all bounds of forgiveness. The desire to be kind, to sound new, to foster useful attitudes, to appear "scientific," and chiefly also the need to produce rapidly, account for this hitherto unheard-of deliquescence. In the victims, the softness goes to the very roots of the mind and turns it into mush. And among the "new" educators thus afflicted, the Progressive vanguard has naturally outstripped the rest. I shall not multiply examples from catalogues, reports, and speeches, though over the years, I have gathered a blush-making collection. I want only to identify the evil because it spreads like the plague.

It consists mainly of what our forefathers called "cant phrases," strung together without continuity, like wash on a line. At a faculty meeting, a teacher asks the Director of Admissions why there seem to be more music students applying than before. The Director replies, "Well, I should say that the forces undergirding the process are societal." Or a committee chairman wants to know what we do next. "I think," says the secretary, "that we should go on to institute actual implementation."

Teachers steeped in this medium are bound to ooze it out themselves, particularly if weekly and daily they receive official instructions like these: "Specify the kinds of change or permanence the student seems to crave, reject, or fear; the reasons given for liking-disliking, giving up-persistence; complaining-boasting. . . . It cannot be too strongly emphasized that the observations of characteristics associated with age and background are not being made in the general area of adolescent behavior but under specific and limited conditions—those set by the aims, emphases, and assumptions of one particular faculty. Moreover, the observations of what appear to be the interests of freshmen conceal a possible ambiguity. The term 'interests' may refer to fairly superficial interests in the sense of surprise, pleasure, enjoyment, which are comparatively temporary; or 'interests' may involve an awakening curiosity which leads to consistent inquiry along the lines of some project." The reader must imagine not merely a paragraph taken at random, but pages and pages of similar woolly abstractions, mimeographed at the rate of nine and one-half pounds per person per semester. If the words "specific" and "objective" were blotted out of the English language, Progressive Education would have to shut up . . . shop.

As for students in teachers' colleges, the long climb up the ladder of learning comes to mean the mastering of this ghoulish *Desperanto,* so that with the attainment of the M.A. degree, we get the following utterance:—

> In the proposed study I wish to describe and evaluate representative programs in these fields as a means of documenting what seems to me a trend of increasing concern with the role of higher education in the improvement of interpersonal and intergroup relations and of calling attention in this way to outstanding contributions in practice.

Some readers might think this quotation very learned and highbrow indeed. But in fact it says nothing definite. It only embodies the disinclination to think. This is a general truth, and nothing is more symptomatic of the whole jargon than the fantastic use and abuse it makes of the phrase "in terms of." The fact is worth a moment's attention. "In terms of" used to refer to things that had terms, like algebra. "Put the problem in terms of *a* and *b*." This makes sense. But in educational circles today "in terms of" means any connection between any two things. "We should grade students in terms of their effort"—that is, *for* or *according to* their effort. The *New York Public Library Bulletin* prints: "The first few months of employment would be easier . . . and more efficient in terms of service . . ."—that is, would yield more efficient service. But no one seems to care how or when or why his own two ideas are related. The gap in thought is plugged with "in terms of." I have been asked, "Will you have dinner with me, not tonight or tomorrow, but *in terms of* next week?" A modern Caesar would write: "All Gaul is to be considered in terms of three parts."

From this Educator's patois, easily the worst English now spoken, we ought to pass to the idiom of textbooks, since they are written either by educators or by teachers. Happily, there is a standard set by other books—trade books—and it is not true that all textbooks are as badly written as those on education. On the contrary, it is very encouraging that the leading ones in every field are usually well planned *and* well written. The success of Morison and Commager's *Growth of the American Republic* is only the most recent case in point. Students, nevertheless, are asked to read many ill-written books. There is no excuse for this, though it is by no means the only source of error. We must remember that students do not read only books; they read what every man reads, and this would do no harm—it does no harm—when the mind is trained to resilience by the kind of writing practice I have advocated.

Unfortunately, with the vast increase in public schooling since 1870, an entirely new notion of what is good English has come to prevail. Awakened by free schooling, the people have shown worthy intentions. They want to be right and even elegant, and so become at once suspicious of plainness and pedantic. They purchase all sorts of handbooks that make a fetish of spelling, of avoiding split infinitives, of saying "it is I" (with the common result of "between you and I")—in short, dwell on trivialities or vulgarisms which do not affect style or thought in the slightest. But with this intolerance towards crude and plain error goes a remarkable insensitivity to inflated nonsense. Most bad journalism is only highbrow verbosity, yet the popular mind continues to believe that the

pedantry which it likes is simple and the simplicity which it finds
hard is complex. Here is the opening of a serial thriller in a Boston
paper:—

> Strange things happen in Chinatown. But even that exotic and
> perverse district seldom presented drama as fantastic as the secret
> that hid among the silk and jade and porcelain splendors of the
> famous House of the Mandarin on Mulberry Lane.

There is a certain art in this, and I take note of "porcelain
splendors" as the *mot juste* for bathtubs on exhibit. But the passage
as a whole contains nothing but arty and highfalutin words, joined
by the good will of the reader rather than the mind of the writer.
Still, every newspaper reader feels he understands it. Take now a
well-known sentence composed of common words, all but two of
them single syllables: "If there are more trees in the world than
there are leaves on any one tree, then there must be at least two
trees with the same number of leaves." Read this aloud and almost
any listener will respond with "Huh? Say that again." For this sentence records a thought, and the Chinatown "drama" did not.

The close logic in the truly "simple" sentence makes the contrast
sharper, but it would be just as sharp between a feeling clearly put
and a feeble attempt to thrill. Thus there is a superstition that
the novels of Henry James are written in a "difficult style." Yet if
you examine them, you will find that the words and sentences—in
The Ambassadors for example—are in themselves quite usual. But
the feelings they convey are unusual and subtle, and require attention. At the same time they also compel it, which is all that an
artist takes pains for in writing.

Conversely, the only thing that can be asked of a writer is that
he should know his own meaning and present it as forcibly as he
can. The rule has not changed since Byron affirmed that "easy writing makes damned hard reading." Hence there is great value, as I
think, in having college graduates recognize good prose when they
see it, know that a tolerable paragraph must have gone through six
or seven versions, and be ready to follow athletically on the trail of
articulate thoughts, rather than look for the soapy incline to
muddled meaning.

One does not have to go very far for the enjoyment of precise
sinewy writing. The same newspaper that furnishes tripe for the
morning meal also brings such rarer tidbits as these: "They [the

robot bombs] are of much the same shape and size as a small fighter plane, with stubby wings. They come over with tails aglow from the propelling rocket force, like little meteors moving at a nightmare pace by dark, and by day like little black planes with tails afire." This is perfection; and here is poetry: "Mr. McCaffrey, himself the father of two children, *and therefore schooled in apprehension,* ran across the street . . . shouting a warning."

When the daily reporter, harried by falling bombs or hustled by a city editor, can write like this, it is depressing to return to agencies closer to the school and find verbal laziness encouraged and imbecility taken for granted. One publisher of reference works sends out a circular stressing the fact that his books give the pronunciation of "all difficult—'hard-to-say'—words." Is this where we are after fifty years of quasi-universal literacy? Is the word "difficult" so difficult that it has to be translated in its own sentence? The question is one for readers [. . .].

Recommended Readings

Several items not listed below are worthy of frequent reading and study. These include *The New English Dictionary on Historical Principles* and three journals, *College English, The Quarterly Journal of Speech,* and *College Composition and Communication.*

Aristotle. *The Art of Rhetoric,* trans. by John H. Freese. Cambridge, 1947.

Baldwin, Charles S. *Ancient Rhetoric and Poetic.* New York, 1924.

———. *Medieval Rhetoric and Poetic.* New York, 1928.

Baugh, Albert C. *History of the English Language.* New York, 1935.

Blair, Hugh. *Lectures on Rhetoric and Belles Lettres.* Edinburgh, 1783.

Bloomfield, Leonard. *Language.* New York, 1933.

Boulton, Marjorie. *The Anatomy of Prose.* London, 1954.

Britton, Karl. *Communication: A Philosophical Study of Language.* London, 1939.

Bryant, Donald, ed. *The Rhetorical Idiom.* Ithaca, 1958.

Campbell, George. *The Philosophy of Rhetoric,* ed. by Lloyd F. Bitzer. Carbondale, 1963.

Carroll, John B. *The Study of Language.* Cambridge, 1953.

Cassirer, Ernst. *Language and Myth,* trans. by Susanne K. Langer. New York, 1953.

Chase, Stuart. *The Power of Words.* New York, 1954.

Cicero. *On Oratory and Orators,* trans. by J. S. Watson. London, 1855.

Clark, Donald L. *Rhetoric and Poetic in the Renaissance.* New York, 1922.

——. *Rhetoric in Greco-Roman Education.* New York, 1957.

Cooper, Lane. *Theories of Style.* New York, 1923.

Crane, William G. *Wit and Rhetoric in the Renaissance.* New York, 1946.

Dobrée, Bonamy. *Modern Prose Style.* Oxford, 1956.

Evans, Bergen. *Comfortable Words.* New York, 1962.

Fogarty, Daniel. *Roots for a New Rhetoric.* New York, 1959.

Fowler, H. W. *A Dictionary of Modern English Usage.* Oxford, 1926.

—— and F. G. Fowler. *The King's English.* Oxford, 1951.

Fries, Charles C. *American English Grammar.* New York, 1940.

Graff, William. *Language and Languages.* New York, 1932.

Hayakawa, S. I. *Language in Thought and Action.* New York, 1940.

Hill, Archibald. *Introduction to Linguistics.* New York, 1958.

Hook, J. N. and E. G. Mathews. *Modern American Grammar and Usage.* New York, 1956.

Howell, W. S. *Logic and Rhetoric in England, 1500–1700.* Princeton, 1956.

Howes, Raymond F., ed. *Historical Studies of Rhetoric and Rhetoricians.* Ithaca, 1961.

Jespersen, Otto. *Growth and Structure of the English Language.* New York, 1923.

Kennedy, George. *The Art of Persuasion in Greece.* Princeton, 1963.

Krapp, George Philip. *The English Language in America.* New York, 1925.

Laird, Charlton. *The Miracle of Language.* New York, 1953.

McKnight, G. H. *Modern English in the Making.* New York, 1928.

——. *English Words and Their Background.* New York, 1923.

Marckwardt, Albert H. *American English.* Oxford, 1958.

Mencken, H. L. *The American Language.* New York, 1937.

Pei, Mario. *The Story of English.* New York, 1952.

Quiller-Couch, Arthur. *On the Art of Writing.* Cambridge, 1946.

Quintilian. *Institutes of Oratory.* London, 1875.

Roberts, Paul. *Understanding English.* New York, 1958.

Robertson, Stuart and Frederic G. Cassidy. *The Development of Modern English.* Englewood Cliffs, 1954.

Sapir, Edward. *Language: An Introduction to the Study of Speech.* New York, 1921.

Schlauch, Margaret. *The Gift of Tongues.* New York, 1942.

Stevenson, Robert Louis. *Essays in the Art of Writing.* London, 1905.

Weaver, Richard M. *The Ethics of Rhetoric.* Chicago, 1953.

Part Two

✵

ON THE
USES OF
LANGUAGE

Introduction

Although attendant studies, justifiable and valuable in their own right, frequently usurp his time, his talent, and his attention, the principal obligation of the student in a college composition course is to address himself to the problem of mastering the accumulation of methods and manners effective in prose composition, so that he may use those methods and others his wit will later disclose to him in fulfilling the public and private offices of an educated man. Failing this, the student sometimes allows himself to be preoccupied, for example, with niceties of grammar, punctuation, and spelling. No one can deny the necessity of studying such things, and no one can deny the responsibility of the college to put the mark on errors in grammar, punctuation, and spelling, especially since such errors in form usually in some way prohibit the full realization of rhetorical method. But continuous study of these matters, we can assume, is not within the province of the college course, which must proceed to its own work in method and style on the presupposition that the student is reasonably comfortable in his handling of these basic matters of form. Vital as they are, grammar, punctuation, and spelling do not provide the means for writing a literate essay.

Neither does study of the content of essays and other literary selections, the other common preoccupation of the freshman English student. The excitement of both contemporary and eternal issues and themes discoverable in this kind of study is of inestimable worth, naturally, and the evocation of intellectual excitement is a goal of education. Yet this study of issues and themes, while it should in all other courses of study be predominant, cannot substitute for study and practice of rhetorical, procedural, stylistic means for grasping and honestly manipulating those issues and themes.

The means of attack, then, the craft of prose writing, provides the subject matter and the form for Part II of this book. An accumulation of methods and manners, a body of reliable techniques, their worth long since proved, is available to the modern student. It is to these methods that the remainder of this book is devoted. Ignoring them, a good student may find for himself vital and efficacious ways of writing; but if he does so, he can only congratulate himself for arriving at regions others have long since explored and left behind. Assuming that native genius or untrained wit is sufficient to all occasions, almost always produces, Sir Joshua Reynolds once said, "either a vain confidence, or a sluggish despair, both equally fatal to all proficiency." The student is therefore exhorted to study the works of the great prose masters, their manner and their principles. He must study the world, to be sure, but let it be done with those masters in his company. "Consider them," Reynolds said, "as models which you are to imitate, and at the same time as rivals with whom you are to contend."

Diligent study of the works of distinguished prose masters will frequently provide the modern student with specific methods he will find effective in almost any situation where discourse is required of him. Where it does not give him specific methods, it will acquaint him, through illustrations, with vivid uses of the language and thus may suggest to him ways in which he may manage the language. Knowledge of these actual methods and acquaintance with a wide variety of excellent prose *may* be sufficient to an author's needs, but unquestionably *are* sufficient as a beginning. With reliable methods, an author has some dependable control of his work. With procedures at his command already proven by good writers, the young writer may shape his own perceptions; even if his wit and inspiration fail him, he may still produce effective discourse. It is only when a student has command of a wide variety of discursive methods that he may begin successfully to perform the offices of an educated man.

The methods and illustrations he learns from study of fine stylists are not, however, the end, but the beginning for a good writer, as arpeggios, augmented sevenths, and triads are the beginning for the composer and pianist, whether he be a combo or chamber music player. Once he is master of these methods, he is free. He is free to combine them, to extend them, to develop from them in whatever circumstances life and the obligations of an educated man may present. As in the Introduction to Part I, the first sentence of this discussion illustrates by its form the proper place of these rhetorical methods and the perspective from which they should be viewed. The sentence is complex, having first a dependent clause, then a main clause that includes a second dependent clause as predicate nominative, and concluding with two closely related dependent clauses. If we state it another way, we can see a minor antecedent statement, a major statement, and a minor consequent statement. Viewed in this way, the sentence in miniature states what seems an ideal sequence in the study of rhetoric and composition. Minor and antecedent, but necessary as is the first minor statement in the sentence, is the study of grammar, punctuation, and spelling. That antecedent assumed, the student progresses, as the sentence does, to the major concern, the study of rhetorical method. But just as the sentence continues with a forecast (minor only so far as this textbook is concerned) of what follows this study, so the student, when he masters his rhetoric, moves on to the confrontation of life.

The selections that follow illustrating methods and styles are whenever possible chosen from the works of long-acknowledged masters of English prose style in its varying forms. Some contemporary essays have been included that treat important or interesting current issues in good style. But most of what is identifiable as good in prose style has been identifiable for generations, made so by writers whose works have already passed the most crucial challenge of a writer's effectiveness, the test of time.

The arrangement of the selections deserves some explanation. The first four sections invite attention not to whole essays or to extended discursive methods, but to parts of essays and segments of method. These sections on Words, Sentences, Paragraphs, and Planning were designed to illustrate various approaches to these units of discourse and to demonstrate that in the part as in the whole, conscious deliberation is required to make a good writer, who must know that no word or sentence can be accidental, that all must be the writer's deliberate choice, and who must know that paragraphs and outlines must prepare the order and effect to be realized in the whole essay.

Following these are sections labeled Exposition, Argumentation,

Description, and Narration. There is nothing new or exciting about this nomenclature; the terms have been used for generations to name characteristic approaches to experience. Nor are the four terms inevitable. Writing does not necessarily divide into four basic kinds; nor should an arbitrary classification be forced upon written discourse. The four terms have been used and the four sections have been arranged to establish a focus for the study of method. Many essays, for example, could be classed as narrative, descriptive, or expository because their authors, to get desired effects and establish desired meaning, used several methods developed from various viewpoints. Or the essays might be classed differently according to another system of classification. An essay like Stevenson's "Pulvis et Umbra" might be studied as exposition or as description or as exhortation. But if we recognize that classification is meant only to assure convenience in study, we can derive definite advantages. If we call "Pulvis et Umbra" description, we will know that it achieves other effects as well, but we will be free to devote complete attention to those methods used for describing. The system of classification, thus, is used so that the student may watch the accumulation of different methods employed to gain different ends.

Each of the subsections begins with a brief note identifying and explaining the particular focus or method to be illustrated. After the first illustrative selection, the student will find, except in the sections on Words and Paragraphs, an analysis of the selection, a Commentary. The analysis is not meant to be definitive; it calls attention only to the method or problem under discussion and shows how it is worked out. Then follow other illustrations with Suggestions to be used as Study Guides. Finally the student will find suggested Writing Programs. These assignments, which suggest procedures, not subjects, will, if a student follows them from first to last, constitute a coherent writing program, calculated to provide practice for the student in what seem to be fundamental prose techniques accumulated logically through the sequence of sections. Throughout Part II where complete essays or long sections of essays appear, paragraphs are numbered for ease in reference in class or private study. (The number is in heavy type and stands away from the text.)

The bibliography that concludes Part II has two purposes. First, it offers a guide to the student who wants more illustrations or even just good reading. Second, by demonstrating an alternative method of classification using terms and types of writing the student will encounter daily, it is meant to show that the traditional classification used in this textbook is still useful and that modern, practical writing chores still demand the techniques of traditional usage.

The Right Word

☼

You must say precisely what you mean; coming near it, as you will discover, is not enough, unless, of course, you are content with coming close. But to say precisely what you mean is an arduous task. It is entirely unlikely that the right word will appear magically upon your page unless you have created the magic with deliberation. For there can be no other mode: deliberation must be your manner.

The words you use in writing must, to be sure, be correct and natural. Any decent writer will observe grammatical proprieties, unless he has a specific purpose for doing otherwise, as he might, for example, in dialogue. And any decent writer will use his own vocabulary, the words that are naturally and comfortably his. But correctness and naturalness, while they may be conditions of good writing, are not sufficient alone to make good writing. Preciseness is far more crucial in your choice of vocabulary.

The brief illustrations in the following section are meant to exemplify some of the writer's means to precision. They illustrate some of the characteristic ways in which words are used, some of the kinds of words writers use and the qualities those words have, and some of the extensions words are capable of.

Concrete and Abstract Words

A major problem the writer faces is finding the word so fitting that the meaning the writer puts into it and the meaning the reader takes from it coincide. The writer who is most successful in doing this is likely to be the writer who most consciously and consistently uses concrete words. The word with the clear, undisputed referent is likely to establish unambiguous meaning while the abstract word with no clear referent may not. With care, even ideas almost imponderable may be shown to a reader in the same everyday dress they usually wear. Even such imponderables are tangled in the way human beings behave, and probably the surest way to identify them is not by giving their abstract names but by singling out the concrete behavior, the specific actions, the particular objects among which they are tangled and out of which they rise. You may find it useful to refer to "Politics and the English Language" and "Fenimore Cooper's Literary Offenses" in Part I.

Yet our language includes many abstract words, and no one can sanely contend that they are useless. They *are* useless when employed where concrete words would work better. Used in explanation or description of human activity or in the discussion of ideas embedded in human activity, they cannot serve as satisfactorily as concrete words. But they do have their uses. In some theoretical discussions, in some evaluations or exhortations logically developing traditional knowledge, in some exercises in moral judgment, abstract words can be strikingly exact. Thought must proceed, Samuel Johnson once said, "from something *known,* done, or suffered; and must *produce* some action or event." And we must endeavor, he said in another place, "to see things as they are." Yet, as Johnson's own prose style beautifully attests, in an effort to discover the stability of truth, a good writer may seek to convey ideas in such a manner that their worth or lack of truth will be immediately and appealingly clear to the widest possible audience. To this end, some good writers, Johnson included, have sought to render universal truths in exact though abstract words.

From LETTER TO DOCTOR LEWIS *in*

HUMPHREY CLINKER [1771]

Tobias Smollett

The country is amazingly wild, especially toward the mountains, which are heaped upon the backs of one another, making a most stupendous appearance of savage nature, with hardly any signs of

cultivation, or even of population. All is sublimity, silence, and solitude. The people live together in glens or bottoms, where they are
sheltered from the cold and storms of winter; but there is a margin
of plain ground spread along the seaside, which is well inhabited,
and improved by the arts of husbandry; and this I take to be one
of the most agreeable tracts of the whole island; the sea not only
keeps it warm, and supplies it with fish, but affords one of the
most ravishing prospects in the whole world; I mean the appearance of the Hebrides, or Western Islands, to the number of three
hundred, scattered as far as the eye can reach, in the most agreeable confusion. As the soil and climate of the Highlands are but ill
adapted to the cultivation of corn, the people apply themselves
chiefly to the breeding and feeding of black cattle, which turn to
good account. Those animals run wild all the winter, without any
shelter or subsistence but what they can find among the heath.
When the snow lies so deep and hard that they cannot penetrate
to the roots of the grass, they make a diurnal progress, guided by a
sure instinct, to the seaside, at low water, where they feed on the
alga marina, and other plants that grow upon the beach. . . .

From THE HISTORY OF THE WORLD [1614]

Sir Walter Raleigh

For the rest, if we seek a reason of the succession and continuance
of this boundless ambition in mortal men, we may add to that
which hath been already said, that the kings and princes of the
world have always laid before them the actions, but not the ends,
of those great ones which preceded them. They are always transported with the glory of the one, but they never mind the misery of
the other, till they find the experience in themselves. They neglect
the advice of God, while they enjoy life, or hope it; but they follow
the counsel of Death upon his first approach. It is he that puts
into man all the wisdom of the world, without speaking a word,
which God, with all the words of his law, promises, or threats, doth
not infuse. Death, which hateth and destroyeth man, is believed;
God, which hath made him and loves him, is always deferred. *I
have considered,* saith Solomon, *all the works that are under the
sun, and, behold, all is vanity and vexation of spirit.* But who believes

it, till Death tells us? It was Death which, opening the conscience of Charles the Fifth, made him enjoin his son Philip to restore Navarre; and king Francis the First of France, to command that justice should be done upon the murderers of the Protestants in Merindol and Cabrieres, which till then he neglected. It is therefore Death alone that can suddenly make man to know himself. He tells the proud and insolent that they are but abjects and humbles them at the instant, makes them cry, complain, and repent, yea, even to hate their forepast happiness. He takes the account of the rich and proves him a begger, a naked begger, which hath interest in nothing but in the gravel that fills his mouth. He holds a glass before the eyes of the most beautiful, and makes them see therein their deformity and rottenness, and they acknowledge it.

O eloquent, just, and mighty Death! whom none could advise, thou hast persuaded; what none hath dared, thou hast done; and whom all the world hath flattered, thou only hast cast out of the world and despised; thou hast drawn together all the far-stretched greatness, all the pride, cruelty, and ambition of man, and covered it all over with these two narrow words, *Hic jacet!* . . . .

A YOUNG GENTLEMAN OF
THE UNIVERSITY [1628]

John Earle

[A young gentleman of the university] is one that comes there to wear a gown, and to say hereafter, he has been at the university. His father sent him thither because he heard there were the best fencing and dancing schools; from these he has his education, from his tutor the oversight. The first element of his knowledge is to be shown the colleges, and initiated in a tavern by the way, which hereafter he will learn of himself. The two marks of his seniority is the bare velvet of his gown, and his proficiency at tennis, where when he can once play a set, he is a freshman no more. His study has commonly handsome shelves, his books neat silk strings, which he shows to his father's man, and is loth to untie or take down for fear of misplacing. Upon foul days for recreation he retires thither, and looks over the pretty book his tutor reads to him,

which is commonly some short history, or a piece of *Euphormio;*
for which his tutor gives him money to spend next day. His main
loitering is at the library, where he studies arms and books of
honor, and turns a gentleman critic in pedigrees. Of all things he
endures not to be mistaken for a scholar, and hates a black suit
though it be made of satin. His companion is ordinarily some stale
fellow, that has been notorious for an ingle to gold hatbands,
whom he admires at first, afterwards scorns. If he have spirit or
wit he may light of better company, and may learn some flashes of
wit, which may do him knight's service in the country hereafter.
But he is now gone to the inns-of-court, where he studies to forget
what he learned before, his acquaintance and the fashion.

MATTHEW 7:1–14

1. Judge not, that ye be not judged.
2. For with what judgment ye judge, ye shall be judged: and
with what measure ye mete, it shall be measured to you again.
3. And why beholdest thou the mote that is in thy brother's eye,
but considerest not the beam that is in thine own eye?
4. Or how wilt thou say to thy brother, Let me pull out the mote
out of thine eye; and, behold, a beam *is* in thine own eye?
5. Thou hypocrite, first cast out the beam out of thine own eye;
and then shalt thou see clearly to cast out the mote out of thy
brother's eye.
6. Give not that which is holy unto the dogs, neither cast ye your
pearls before swine, lest they trample them under their feet, and
turn again and rend you.
7. Ask, and it shall be given you; seek, and ye shall find; knock,
and it shall be opened unto you:
8. For every one that asketh receiveth; and he that seeketh findeth;
and to him that knocketh it shall be opened.
9. Or what man is there of you, whom if his son ask bread, will he
give him a stone?
10. Or if he ask a fish, will he give him a serpent?
11. If ye then, being evil, know how to give good gifts unto your
children, how much more shall your Father which is in heaven give
good things to them that ask him?
12. Therefore all things whatsoever ye would that men should do
to you, do ye even so to them: for this is the law and the prophets.

13. Enter ye in at the strait gate: for wide *is* the gate, and broad *is* the way, that leadeth to destruction, and many there be which go in thereat:

14. Because strait *is* the gate, and narrow *is* the way, which leadeth unto life, and few there be that find it.

From OF EDUCATION [1644]

John Milton

I shall detain you now no longer in the demonstration of what we should not do, but straight conduct ye to a hillside, where I will point ye out the right path of a virtuous and noble education; laborious indeed at the first ascent, but else so smooth, so green, so full of goodly prospect and melodious sounds on every side, that the harp of Orpheus was not more charming. I doubt not but ye shall have more ado to drive our dullest and laziest youth, our stocks and stubs, from the infinite desire of such a happy nurture, than we have now to hale and drag our choicest and hopefullest wits to that asinine feast of sow-thistles and brambles which is commonly set before them as all the food and entertainment of their tenderest and most docile age. I call therefore a complete and generous education, that which fits a man to perform justly, skillfully, and magnanimously all the offices, both private and public, of peace and war. And how all this may be done between twelve and one and twenty, less time than is now bestowed in pure trifling at grammar and sophistry, is to be thus ordered. . . .

From AREOPAGITICA [1644]

John Milton

Good and evil we know in the field of this world grow up together almost inseparably; and the knowledge of good is so involved and interwoven with the knowledge of evil, and in so many cunning resemblances hardly to be discerned, that those confused seeds which were imposed upon Psyche as an incessant labor to cull out, and sort asunder, were not more intermixed. It was from out the rind of one apple tasted, that the knowledge of good and evil, as two twins cleaving together, leaped forth into the world.

And perhaps this is that doom which Adam fell into of knowing good and evil, that is to say, of knowing good by evil.

As therefore the state of man now is, what wisdom can there be to choose, what continence to forbear without the knowledge of evil? He that can apprehend and consider vice with all her baits and seeming pleasures, and yet abstain, and yet distinguish, and yet prefer that which is truly better, he is the true warfaring Christian. I cannot praise a fugitive and cloistered virtue, unexercised and unbreathed, that never sallies out and sees her adversary, but slinks out of the race where that immortal garland is to be run for, not without dust and heat. Assuredly we bring not innocence into the world, we bring impurity much rather: that which purifies us is trial, and trial is by what is contrary. That virtue therefore which is but a youngling in the contemplation of evil, and knows not the utmost that vice promises to her followers, and rejects it, is but a blank virtue, not a pure; her whiteness is but an excremental whiteness; which was the reason why our sage and serious poet Spenser, whom I dare be known to think a better teacher than Scotus or Aquinas, describing true temperance under the person of Guion, brings him in with his palmer through the cave of Mammon and the bower of earthly bliss, that he might see and know, and yet abstain.

Since therefore, the knowledge and survey of vice is in this world so necessary to the constituting of human virtue, and the scanning of error to the confirmation of truth, how can we more safely, and with less danger, scout into the regions of sin and falsity, than by reading all manner of tractates and hearing all manner of reason? And this is the benefit which may be had of books promiscuously read.

From DISCOURSE TWO [1769]

Sir Joshua Reynolds

I congratulate you on the honour which you have just received. I have the highest opinion of your merits, and could wish to show my sense of them in something which possibly may be more useful to you than barren praise. I could wish to lead you into such a course of study as may render your future progress answerable to your past improvement; and, whilst I applaud you for what has been done, remind you how much yet remains to attain perfection.

I flatter myself, that from the long experience I have had, and the unceasing assiduity with which I have pursued those studies, in which, like you, I have been engaged, I shall be acquitted of vanity in offering some hints to your consideration. They are indeed in a great degree founded upon my own mistakes in the same pursuit. But the history of errors, properly managed, often shortens the road to truth. And although no method of study that I can offer, will of itself conduct to excellence, yet it may preserve industry from being misapplied.

In speaking to you of the Theory of the Art, I shall only consider it as it has a relation to the *method* of your studies.

Dividing the study of painting into three distinct periods, I shall address you as having passed through the first of them, which is confined to the rudiments; including a facility of drawing any object that presents itself, a tolerable readiness in the management of colours, and an acquaintance with the most simple and obvious rules of composition.

This first degree of proficiency is, in painting, what grammar is in literature, a general preparation for whatever species of the art the student may afterwards choose for his more particular application. The power of drawing, modelling, and using colours, is very properly called the Language of the art; and in this language, the honours you have just received, prove you to have made no inconsiderable progress.

When the Artist is once enabled to express himself with some degree of correctness, he must then endeavour to collect subjects for expression; to amass a stock of ideas, to be combined and varied as occasion may require. He is now in the second period of study, in which his business is to learn all that has been known and done before his own time. Having hitherto received instructions from a particular master, he is now to consider the Art itself as his master. He must extend his capacity to more sublime and general instructions. Those perfections which lie scattered among various masters, are now united in one general idea, which is henceforth to regulate his taste, and enlarge his imagination. With a variety of models thus before him, he will avoid that narrowness and poverty of conception which attends a bigotted admiration of a single master,

and will cease to follow any favourite where he ceases to excel.
This period is, however, still a time of subjection and discipline.
Though the Student will not resign himself blindly to any single
authority, when he may have the advantage of consulting many,
he must still be afraid of trusting his own judgment, and of deviating into any track where he cannot find the footsteps of some
former master.

The third and last period emancipates the Student from subjection to any authority, but what he shall himself judge to be supported by reason. Confiding now in his own judgment, he will
consider and separate those different principles to which different
modes of beauty owe their original. In the former period he sought
only to know and combine excellence, wherever it was to be found,
into one idea of perfection: in this, he learns, what requires the
most attentive survey and the most subtle disquisition, to discriminate perfections that are incompatible with each other.

He is from this time to regard himself as holding the same rank
with those masters whom he before obeyed as teachers, and as
exercising a sort of sovereignty over those rules which have hitherto
restrained him. Comparing now no longer the performance of the
Art with each other, but examining the Art itself by the standard
of Nature, he corrects what is erroneous, supplies what is scanty,
and adds by his own observation what the industry of his predecessors may have yet left wanting to perfection. Having well established his judgment, and stored his memory, he may now without
fear try the power of his imagination. The mind that has been thus
disciplined, may be indulged in the warmest enthusiasm, and
venture to play on the borders of the wildest extravagance. The
habitual dignity which long converse with the greatest minds has
imparted to him, will display itself in all his attempts; and he will
stand among his instructors, not as an imitator, but a rival.

These are the different stages of the Art. But as I now address
myself particularly to those Students who have been this day rewarded for their happy passage through the first period, I can
with no propriety suppose they want any help in the initiatory
studies. My present design is to direct your view to distant excellence, and to show you the readiest path that leads to it. Of this
I shall speak with such latitude, as may leave the province of the
professor uninvaded; and shall not anticipate those precepts,
which it is his business to give, and your duty to understand.

It is indisputably evident that a great part of every man's life must be employed in collecting materials for the exercise of genius. Invention, strictly speaking, is little more than a new combination of those images which have been previously gathered and deposited in the memory: nothing can come of nothing: he who has laid up no materials, can produce no combinations.

A Student unacquainted with the attempts of former adventurers, is always apt to over-rate his own abilities; to mistake the most trifling excursions for discoveries of moment, and every coast new to him, for a new-found country. If by chance he passes beyond his usual limits, he congratulates his own arrival at those regions which they who have steered a better course have long left behind them.

From RAMBLER, NO. 154 [1751]

Samuel Johnson

The same method must be pursued by him who hopes to become eminent in any other part of knowledge. The first task is to search books, the next to contemplate nature. He must first possess himself of the intellectual treasures which the diligence of former ages has accumulated, and then endeavour to encrease them by his own collections.

The mental disease of the present generation, is impatience of study, contempt of the great masters of ancient wisdom, and a disposition to rely wholly upon unassisted genius and natural sagacity. The wits of these happy days have discovered a way to fame, which the dull caution of our laborious ancestors durst never attempt; they cut the knots of sophistry which it was formerly the business of years to untie, solve difficulties by sudden irradiations of intelligence, and comprehend long processes of argument by immediate intuition.

• SUGGESTIONS •

Compare the preceding passages with respect to their use of concrete and abstract words. In those passages where concrete words seem to predominate, note the frequency with which specific objects, persons, and actions are named, and note how often ideas and attitudes appearing in the work are given in terms of everyday experience, even in terms of concrete things that elicit sensory response. In those passages where abstract words seems to predominate, consider whether or not those abstractions are exact in their meaning. Finally, compare two of these passages (say those by Earle and Reynolds, or those by Smollett and Johnson), actually counting abstract and concrete words in each. This statistical evidence added to similar evidence to be obtained in the following sections should give you eventually the material necessary to characterize some different kinds of prose style.

Denotative and Connotative Values

Another way of discovering the difficulty in choosing the right word—hence, another way of preparing yourself for your own writing—is in recognizing the distinction between denotation and connotation. The writer who uses a word for its commonly agreed-upon meaning, for its primary definition, in other words, one who uses a word for a single, concrete meaning, is calling upon the word for its denotative value. His problem is to find the word that has the exact denotative value he wishes to offer, to determine, for example, whether he wants to use *fall* or *stumble, stagger* or *reel, build* or *erect.*

But our experiences are seldom isolated events. Words accumulate meanings and evoke associations in the reader. A writer cannot ignore the suggestive power words have, a power they acquire through the way in which they are commonly used or by association with a particular context. The word *doom,* for example, can hardly be used for a single, specific meaning because it has with time gathered to itself far too many implications: it is packed with suggestions of the long movement of time, of the slow manipulations of fate, of the very wrath of God. There may be compressed into even a concrete word whole ranges of meaning. The "ding-dong" of sound Faulkner mentions in one of the following passages is no mere bell. The writer who deliberately calls upon such packed meanings may find a kind of precision unlike concrete meaning. When he does so, he relies on the connotative value of words.

From THE JOURNAL [1769]

Thomas Gray

Oct: 3. W^d at S: E:; a heavenly day. rose at seven, and walk'd out under the conduct of my Landlord to *Borrodale*. the grass was cover'd with a hoar-frost, wch soon melted, & exhaled in a thin blewish smoke cross'd the meadows obliquely, catching a diversity of views among the hills over the lake & islands, & changing prospect at every ten paces, left *Cockshut* & *Castle-hill* (wch we formerly mounted) behind me, & drew near the foot of *Walla-crag*, whose bare & rocky brow, cut perpendicularly down above 400 feet, as I guess, awefully overlooks the way: our path here tends to the left, & the ground gently rising, & cover'd with a glade of scattering trees & bushes on the very margin of the water, opens both ways the most delicious view, that my eyes ever beheld. behind you are the magnificent heights of *Walla-crag;* opposite lie the thick hanging woods of Ld Egremont, & *Newland*-valley, with green & smiling fields embosom'd in the dark cliffs; to the left of the jaws of *Borodale*, with that turbulent Chaos of mountain behind mountain roll'd in confusion; beneath you, & stretching far away to the right, the shining purity of the *Lake*, just ruffled by the breeze enough to shew it is alive, reflecting rocks, woods, fields, & inverted tops of mountains, with the white buildings of *Keswick, Crosthwait*-church, & *Skiddaw* for a back ground at distance. oh Doctor! I never wish'd more for you; & pray think, how the glass played its part in such a spot, wch is called *Carf-close-reeds:* I chuse to set down these barbarous names, that any body may enquire on the place, & easily find the particular station, that I mean. this scene continues to *Barrow-gate*, & a little farther, passing a brook called *Barrow-beck*, we enter'd *Borrodale*. the crags, named *Lodoor-banks* now begin to impend terribly over your way; & more terribly, when you hear, that three years since an immense mass of rock tumbled at once from the brow, & bar'd all access to the dale (for this is the only road) till they could work their way thro' it. luckily no one was passing at the time of this fall; but down the side of the mountain, & far into the lake lie dispersed the huge fragments of this ruin in all shapes & in all directions. something farther we turn'd aside into a coppice, ascending a little in front of *Lodoor* water-fall. the height appears to be about 200 feet, the quantity of water not great, tho' (these three days excepted) it had rain'd daily in the hills for near two months before: but then the stream was nobly broken, leaping from rock to rock, & foaming with fury. on one side a towering crag, that spired up to equal, if not overtop, the neighbouring cliffs (this lay all in shade & darkness) on the other hand a rounder broader projecting hill shag'd with wood & illumined by the sun, wch glanced sideways on the upper part of the cataract. the force of the water wearing a deep channel in the ground hurries away to join the lake. we descended again, & passed the stream over a rude bridge. soon after we came under *Gowder-crag*, a hill more formidable to the eye & to the apprehension than that of *Lodoor;* the rocks atop, deep-cloven perpendicularly by the rains, hanging loose & nodding forwards, seem just starting from their base in shivers: the whole way down & the road on both sides is strew'd with piles of the fragments strangely thrown across each other & of a dreadful bulk. the place reminds one of those passes in the Alps, where the Guides tell you to move with speed, & say nothing, lest the agitation of the air should loosen the snows above, and bring down a mass, that would over-whelm a caravan. I took their counsel here and hasten'd on in silence.

From CIRCUS AT DAWN*

Thomas Wolfe

Talking in low excited voices we would walk rapidly back towards town under the rustle of September leaves, in cool streets just greyed now with that still, that unearthly and magical first light of day which seems suddenly to rediscover the great earth out of darkness, so that the earth emerges with an awful, a glorious sculptural stillness, and one looks out with a feeling of joy and disbelief,

---

as the first men on this earth must have done, for to see this happen is one of the things that men will remember out of life forever and think of as they die.

At the sculptural still square where at one corner, just emerging into light, my father's shabby little marble shop stood with a ghostly strangeness and familiarity, my brother and I would "catch" the first streetcar of the day bound for the "depot" where the circus was—or sometimes we would meet someone we knew, who would give us a lift in his automobile.

Then, having reached the dingy, grimy, rickety depot section, we would get out and walk rapidly across the tracks of the station yard, where we could see great flares and steamings from the engines, and hear the crash and bump of shifting freight cars, the swift sporadic thunders of a shifting engine, the tolling of bells, the sounds of great trains on the rails.

From SPECTATOR, no. 112 [1711]

Joseph Addison

As Sir Roger is landlord to the whole congregation, he keeps them in very good order, and will suffer nobody to sleep in it besides himself; for, if by chance he has been surprised into a short nap at sermon, upon recovering out of it he stands up and looks about him, and if he sees anybody else nodding, either wakes them himself, or sends his servant to them. Several other of the old knight's particularities break out upon these occasions; sometimes he will be lengthening out a verse in the Singing-Psalms half a minute after the rest of the congregation have done with it; sometimes, when he is pleased with the matter of his devotion, he pronounces "Amen" three or four times to the same prayer; and sometimes stands up when everybody else is upon their knees, to count the congregation, or see if any of his tenants are missing.

I was yesterday very much surprised to hear my old friend, in the midst of the service, calling out to one John Matthews to mind what he was about, and not disturb the congregation. This John Matthews, it seems, is remarkable for being an idle fellow, and at that time was kicking his heels for his diversion. This authority of

the knight, though exerted in that odd manner which accompanies
him in all circumstances of life, has a very good effect upon the
parish, who are not polite enough to see anything ridiculous in
his behavior; besides that the general good sense and worthiness
of his character makes his friends observe these little singularities
as foils that rather set off than blemish his good qualities.

As soon as the sermon is finished, nobody presumes to stir till
Sir Roger is gone out of the church. The knight walks down from
his seat in the chancel between a double row of his tenants, that
stand bowing to him on each side, and every now and then in-
quires how such an one's wife, or mother, or son, or father do,
whom he does not see at church—which is understood as a secret
reprimand to the person that is absent.

From PULVIS ET UMBRA [1892]

Robert Louis Stevenson

But take the Kosmos with a grosser faith, as our senses give it us.
We behold space sown with rotatory islands, suns and worlds and
the shards and wrecks of systems: some, like the sun, still blazing;
some rotting, like the earth; others, like the moon, stable in desolation. All of these we take to be made of something we call matter:
a thing no analysis can help us to conceive; to whose incredible
properties no familiarities can reconcile our minds. This stuff, when
not purified by the lustration of fire, rots uncleanly into something
we call life; seized through all its atoms with a pediculous malady;
swelling in tumors that become independent, sometimes even (by
an abhorrent prodigy) locomotory; one splitting into millions, millions cohering into one, as the malady proceeds through varying
stages. This vital putrescence of the dust, used as we are to it, yet
strikes us with occasional disgust, and the profusion of worms in a
piece of ancient turf, or the air of a marsh darkened with insects,
will sometimes check our breathing so that we aspire for cleaner
places. But none is clean: the moving sand is infected with lice; the
pure spring, where it bursts out of the mountain, is a mere issue of
worms; even in the hard rock the crystal is forming.

From AN ESSAY OF DRAMATIC POESY [1668]

John Dryden

To begin, then, with Shakespeare. He was the man who of all modern, and perhaps ancient poets, had the largest and most comprehensive soul. All the images of Nature were still present to him, and he drew them, not laboriously, but luckily; when he describes anything, you more than see it, you feel it too. Those who accuse him to have wanted learning, give him the greater commendation: he was naturally learned; he needed not the spectacles of books to read Nature; he looked inwards, and found her there. I cannot say he is everywhere alike; were he so, I should do him injury to compare him with the greatest of mankind. He is many times flat, insipid; his comic wit degenerating into clenches, his serious swelling into bombast. But he is always great, when some great occasion is presented to him; no man can say he ever had a fit subject for his wit, and did not then raise himself as high above the rest of poets, ...

From NOBEL PRIZE SPEECH [1950]

William Faulkner

Until he relearns these things, he will write as though he stood among and watched the end of man. I decline to accept the end of man. It is easy enough to say that man is immortal simply because he will endure: that when the last ding-dong of doom has clanged and faded from the last worthless rock hanging tideless in the last red and dying evening, that even then there will still be one more sound: that of his puny inexhaustible voice, still talking. I refuse to accept this. I believe that man will not merely endure: he will prevail. He is immortal, not because he alone among creatures has an inexhaustible voice, but because he has a soul, a spirit capable of compassion and sacrifice and endurance. The poet's, the writer's, duty is to write about these things. It is his privilege to help man endure by lifting his heart, by reminding him of the courage and honor and hope and pride and compassion and pity and sacrifice which have been the glory of his past. The poet's voice need not merely be the record of man, it can be one of the props, the pillars to help him endure and prevail.

• SUGGESTIONS •

Determine which of the preceding selections seem to depend more upon denotation, which upon connotation. Examine the latter to discover what kind of mood, what kind of implication the author is seeking to bring to the language beyond literal meaning. Return then to the selections you examined in the preceding section and examine them in the light of denotative-connotative usage, adding this to your evidence for characterizing style.

Figurative Usage

Words accumulate more than their dictionary meanings, or other than their dictionary meanings, in a rather special way when a writer deliberately sets aside the literal meaning for figurative meaning or when the writer adds to a literal meaning some figurative implication. Figurative language is not merely ornamental, embroidered to writing. It is, rather, a kind of shorthand writers have by which they can say more in few words than would otherwise be possible. It is functional; it is a way of compressing meaning into brief space and involving the reader's emotional reactions in the written work. When Walpole describes a mountain descent as "steep and rough as O————'s father's face, over which, you know, the devil walked with hobnails in his shoes," we can know, without his saying it, that the descent is almost perpendicular, that it is pitted and probably boulder-strewn and hatched with ravines, and that it is of such roughness and awfulness that it suggests the very grandeur of evil. But be warned: figurative language is vivid, colorful, and concise; but nothing mars work more than using figurative expressions that have already been used.

From LETTER TO RICHARD WEST [1739]

Horace Walpole

So, as the song says, we are in fair Italy! I wonder we are; for on the very highest precipice of Mount Cenis, the devil of discord, in the similitude of sour wine, had got amongst our Alpine savages, and set them a-fighting with Gray and me in the chairs; they rushed him by me on a crag, where there was scarce room for a cloven foot. The least slip had tumbled us into such a fog, and such an eternity, as we should never have found our way out of again. We were eight days in coming hither from Lyons; the four last in crossing the Alps. Such uncouth rocks, and such uncomely inhabitants! My dear West, I hope I shall never see them again! At the foot of Mount Cenis we were obliged to quit our chaise, which was taken all to pieces and loaded on mules; and we were carried in low armchairs on poles, swathed in beaver bonnets, beaver gloves, beaver stockings, muffs, and bear-skins. When we came to the top, behold the snows fallen! and such quantities, and con- ducted by such heavy clouds that hung glouting, that I thought we could never have waded through them. The descent is two leagues, but steep and rough as O———'s father's face, over which, you know, the devil walked with hobnails in his shoes. But the dexterity and nimbleness of the mountaineers are inconceivable: they run with you down steeps and frozen precipices, where no man as men are now, could possibly walk. . . .

PSALMS 23

1. The LORD *is* my shepherd; I shall not want.
2. He maketh me to lie down in green pastures: he leadeth me beside the still waters.
3. He restoreth my soul: he leadeth me in the paths of righteous- ness for his name's sake.
4. Yea, though I walk through the valley of the shadow of death, I will fear no evil: for thou art with me; thy rod and thy staff they comfort me.

5. Thou preparest a table before me in the presence of mine enemies: thou anointest my head with oil; my cup runneth over.
6. Surely goodness and mercy shall follow me all the days of my
life: and I will dwell in the house of the LORD for ever.

From MEDITATION XVII [1624]

John Donne

Perchance he for whom this bell tolls may be so ill, as that he
knows not it tolls for him; and perchance I may think myself so
much better than I am, as that they who are about me, and see
my state, may have caused it to toll for me, and I know not that.
The church is catholic, universal, so are all her actions; all that she
does belongs to all. When she baptizes a child, that action concerns me; for that child is thereby connected to that head which is
my head too, and ingrafted into that body whereof I am a member.
And when she buries a man, that action concerns me: all mankind
is of one author, and is one volume; when one man dies, one chapter is not torn out of the book, but translated into a better language;
and every chapter must be so translated; God employs several
translators; some pieces are translated by age, some by sickness,
some by war, some by justice; but God's hand is in every translation, and his hand shall bind up all our scattered leaves again for
that library where every book shall lie open to one another. As
therefore the bell that rings to a sermon calls not upon the preacher
only, but upon the congregation to come, so this bell calls us all;
but how much more me, who am brought so near the door by this
sickness. There was a contention as far as a suit (in which both
piety and dignity, religion and estimation, were mingled), which
of the religious orders should ring to prayers first in the morning;
and it was determined, that they should ring first that rose earliest.
If we understand aright the dignity of this bell that tolls for our
evening prayer, we would be glad to make it ours by rising early, in
that application, that it might be ours as well as his, whose indeed
it is. The bell doth toll for him that thinks it doth; and though it
intermit again, yet from that minute that that occasion wrought
upon him, he is united to God. Who casts not up his eye to the

sun when it rises? but who takes off his eye from a comet when that breaks out? Who bends not his ear to any bell which upon any occasion rings? but who can remove it from that bell which is passing a piece of himself out of this world? No man is an island, entire of itself; every man is a piece of the continent, a part of the main. If a clod be washed away by the sea, Europe is the less, as well as if a promontory were, as well as if a manor of thy friend's or of thine own were: any man's death diminishes me, because I am involved in mankind, and therefore never send to know for whom the bell tolls; it tolls for thee.

I CORINTHIANS 13

1. Though I speak with the tongues of men and of angels, and have not charity, I am become *as* sounding brass, or a tinkling cymbal.

2. And though I have *the gift of* prophecy, and understand all mysteries, and all knowledge; and though I have all faith, so that I could remove mountains, and have not charity, I am nothing.

3. And though I bestow all my goods to feed *the poor*, and though I give my body to be burned, and have not charity, it profiteth me nothing.

4. Charity suffereth long, *and* is kind; charity envieth not; charity vaunteth not itself, is not puffed up,

5. Doth not behave itself unseemly, seeketh not her own, is not easily provoked, thinketh no evil;

6. Rejoiceth not in the iniquity, but rejoiceth in the truth;

7. Beareth all things, believeth all things, hopeth all things, endureth all things.

8. Charity never faileth: but whether *there be* prophecies, they shall fail; whether *there be* tongues, they shall cease; whether *there be* knowledge, it shall vanish away.

9. For we know in part, and we prophesy in part.

10. But when that which is perfect is come, then that which is in part shall be done away.

11. When I was a child, I spake as a child, I understood as a child, I thought as a child: but when I became a man, I put away childish things.

12. For now we see through a glass, darkly; but then face to face: now I know in part; but then shall I know even as also I am known. 13. And now abideth faith, hope, charity, these three; but the greatest of these *is* charity.

• **SUGGESTIONS** •

Identify the figures of speech used in these selections, and write an analysis of the figurative language of Psalms 23 indicating the effectiveness and propriety of the figurative usage. Examine the passages you studied earlier for figurative language, adding this to the evidence you have accumulated.

Economical Usage

A word is right if it expresses precisely the meaning you wish expressed in a given situation. It says in one word what would require several less exacting ones. Thus the right word is the economical word, and the writer who is exacting in his selection is not usually in danger of writing sentences and paragraphs that contain unnecessary words, words that do not advance the meaning in any way. Since the writers represented in this book are not usually guilty of this error, the following selections are from amateur writers whose control of their craft is not yet sufficient to enable them to avoid using words they do not need to use.

STUDENT ESSAY I

As I sat in the shadows of a stadium that once played a memorable role in my high school career, I watched the bonfire now surrounded by the present gleeful youth of my old school. As if in a time machine my memories carried me back to the days when I was young and jubilant in my devotion to this school.

The chants of the throng as led by the gay and jovial cheerleaders echoed in the stillness of the night, closing the span of time between my world of yesterday and today. Many were the lithesome figures swaying to and fro to the rhythm of the drum beat in the background. The enthusiastic cheers coming from the large group of loyal supporters of the most prominent football team in the history of the school made such a deafening roar that it seemed to shake the nearby buildings.

A hush fell over the excited crowd as the first strains of the highly-respected alma mater were rendered by the ever-faithful band. Reverence prevailed over the entire group until the last note faded away. A short-lived silence reigned just before the thunderous fight song filled the air. At this signal the crowd dispersed, each to his own way.

STUDENT ESSAY II

It was a cool, cloudy Friday morning in April. The calm of the early morning was gratifying to my friend, Frank, and me, as we started on our long awaited fishing trip.

We woke up early that morning and could hardly wait to start plugging away at the large mouth blacks we knew were hiding in the cave at Nigger's Bluff.

We loaded up Frank's poor excuse for an automobile and were just about to drive off when I heard the ever-familiar echo of my dog's barking. Telling Frank that I could not leave my dog, Tippy, behind, I opened the door and with one happy bound he jumped in and we were on our way at last.

Our happy trio arrived at Nigger's Bluff at six o'clock, and we were soon nestled in the broad shoals of the cove. The water was still, shimmering bright, like a fresh glass of champagne, and not a sound could be heard for miles around. Frank was the first to throw his line into the water. He arched it high and gracefully. It slid into the clear water with a dull "thunk." He started reeling in his line ever so carefully and cautiously, as if he were about to put the finishing touches on a great hand-painted masterpiece. Every part of our bodies was tensed, ready for the action of the first strike. But to our surprise, nothing happened. That run of bad luck continued throughout the morning and into the early afternoon.

I suggested we return to the car, pack some food, and take a hike through the peaceful countryside. Frank was against the idea, as he knew that this was bear country. I assured him that no harm would come to either of us. Frank consented, after much deliberation, and we started on our way through the calm countryside.

After hiking several miles Frank and I came upon some tracks we thought to be those of a large wildcat. We set Tippy on the trail of this animal and he raced ahead with great delight. When he got about two hundred yards from us, he stopped and let out a number of high-pitched yelps. Frank and I ran to see what he had caught and were surprised to see what it was. We saw that the tracks were really those of a bear cub. We caught the cub after a few minutes of quick maneuvering.

Just then we heard a sound of rustling leaves and snapping twigs. I saw the hair on Tippy's back rise as if someone had just placed him on a hot electrical wire. Frank and I wheeled around and our glance was quickly met by that of an enraged female grizzly. I was sure I saw a small flame of hate flickering in her bloodshot eyes as she rushed for us. Cold pangs of fear, like thousands of sharp pins, ran through my body, as I watched the bear bowl Frank over with one hasty slap of her big paw. A dull, sickening sensation crept over me as I had no idea what to do.

Tippy was suddenly a ball of fury as he jumped between the frenzied bear and Frank. Shaking off the nauseating fear that had gripped me, I utilized all of my power and put Frank on my shoulder. I carried him to the safety of a close rock formation, and watched the battle still raging between the dog and the bear. Tippy was darting back and forth, nipping at the bear's nose, but still managing to keep out of her reach. The bear gave one desperate lunge, but Tippy dodged and raced quickly away. The bear, sensing no more trouble, gathered the cub to her side and disappeared into the woods.

Frank was coming to and was obviously in pain as thick, red blood was spurting from a gaping wound in his arm. I helped him back to the car, where my heroic dog was waiting for us. Putting them both in the car, I headed directly for the nearest hospital. The doctor told me that Frank was a very lucky boy not to have lost his arm.

Frank was discharged from the hospital in two weeks and I

went to visit him at his home. He told me that he would go fishing with me again, but if I ever got the idea to go hiking again, it would be by myself.

• SUGGESTION •

Examine these selections for inexact words and for unnecessary words.

A Writing Program

1. Early in your first semester in composition class write an essay or two using topics agreed upon by you and your instructor. Preserve these essays for use in applying some of the methods suggested by illustrations in this and following sections of the book.

2. From those included in this section select three or four passages that differ markedly and write passages of your own in imitation. Maintain the same sorts of sentence structure, and try to maintain the same concrete-abstract, denotative-connotative, literal-figurative balance that is maintained in the originals.

3. If you have written a preliminary essay, examine and revise it now, using the illustrations in this section as a guide. Delete all unnecessary words, change those that are inexact, eliminate figurative expressions unless they are fresh, substitute concrete for abstract terms unless the abstraction is clearly unavoidable, and check to be sure you have not allowed implied meanings to intrude inappropriately.

4. Using the evidence you have collected through this section, write a short analysis of one writer's style.

The Right Sentence

☼

The basic structural unit in writing, the sentence, is itself a composition, though in miniature. Although the needs of literary art sometimes require spasmodic or otherwise ill-formed expression, a good sentence is formed, finished thought, delivered with calculated skill. This means, among other things, that the writer must guarantee grammatical accuracy, pleasant sound, and logical arrangement of the parts of the sentence.

You are now presumably capable of writing a sentence that is grammatically accurate. The examples in this section illustrate methods of clarifying meaning in the sentence and methods of diversifying sentence structure to maintain reader interest. The specific stylistic methods illustrated are subordination, coordination, balance, parallelism, loose and periodic construction, and some procedures for effecting transition.

Subordination

Tight control of the technique of subordination is the clearest sign that a writer is master of his prose and the surest evidence that a writer is a literate, educated man. Subordination requires deliberation, and a good complex or compound-complex sentence reflects the judicious exercise of critical intelligence. Hence effective subordination indicates educated control of subject matter by its educated control of the sentences delivering that subject matter. A writer cannot properly lump together ideas that do not belong together; neither can he properly separate what does belong together. What he can do is find the stylistic means of revealing what the relationship between ideas is—and subordination is the best means for the realization of this purpose, for quite simply it is a method of showing in a sentence that one idea is more important than other related ideas and that there is some relationship between the major and the minor ideas.

Subordination also is a major stylistic device in another way. Since the sentence in which subordination occurs distinguishes major from minor ideas, a writer can use this distinction to diversify the structure and movement of his sentences. He can, for example, compose sentences that build toward a climax by arranging all dependent elements first in the sentence, withholding the independent element until the last. Deliberate placing of the independent clause provides a writer many alternatives for the arrangement of his sentence.

From THE CROSS OF GOLD SPEECH [1896]

William Jennings Bryan

Our ancestors, when but three millions in number, had the courage to declare their political independence of every other nation; shall we, their descendants, when we have grown to seventy millions, declare that we are less independent than our forefathers? No, my friends, that will never be the verdict of our people. Therefore, we care not upon what lines the battle is fought. If they say bimetallism is good, but that we cannot have it until other nations help us, we reply that, instead of having a gold standard because England has, we will restore bimetallism, and then let England have bimetallism because the United States has it. If they dare to come out in the open field and defend the gold standard as a good thing, we will fight them to the uttermost. Having behind us the producing masses of this nation and the world, supported by the commercial interests, the laboring interests, and the toilers everywhere, we will answer their demand for a gold standard by saying to them: You shall not press down upon the brow of labor this crown of thorns, you shall not crucify mankind upon a cross of gold.

• COMMENTARY •

Notice how the movement of the sentences in this selection reinforces the meaning of the passage. The first sentence states two major ideas, which act as a call, a summons to the audience. The second sentence states the position to be taken, and Bryan attracts our attention to it by making it the shortest sentence in this passage that concludes his famous speech. Then observe particularly the movement of the fourth, fifth, and sixth sentences. Each begins with a long dependent construction and culminates in a statement of the major idea, which in each case supports or restates the position already announced. Our attention is thus led through the supporting material to a climax in the major idea in each of the last three sentences. The movement can be traced as follows:

1. SUMMONS TO A POSITION
2. THE POSITION TO BE TAKEN
3. CONSEQUENCE OF THAT POSITION
4. adverse circumstances to be overcome—DETERMINATION
5. adverse circumstances to be overcome—DETERMINATION
6. adverse circumstances to be overcome—DETERMINATION TO HOLD POSITION

From DISCOURSE FOUR [1771]

Sir Joshua Reynolds

On the whole, it seems to me that there is but one presiding principle which regulates, and gives stability to every art. The works, whether of poets, painters, moralists, or historians, which are built upon general nature, live for ever; while those which depend for their existence on particular customs and habits, a partial view of nature, or the fluctuation of fashion, can only be coeval with that which first raised them from obscurity. Present time and future may be considered as rivals, and he who solicits the one must expect to be discountenanced by the other.

From DISCOURSE SIX [1774]

Sir Joshua Reynolds

The purport of this discourse, and, indeed, of most of my other discourses, is to caution you against that false opinion, but too prevalent among artists, of the imaginary power of native genius, and its sufficiency in great works. This opinion, according to the temper of mind it meets with, almost always produces, either a vain confidence, or a sluggish despair, both equally fatal to all proficiency.

Study therefore the great works of the great masters, for ever. Study as nearly as you can, in the order, in the manner, and on the principles, on which they studied. Study nature attentively, but always with those masters in your company; consider them as models which you are to imitate, and at the same time as rivals with whom you are to contend.

From DISCOURSE TWO [1769]

Sir Joshua Reynolds

There is one precept, however, in which I shall only be opposed by the vain, the ignorant, and the idle. I am not afraid that I shall repeat it too often. You must have no dependence on your own genius. If you have great talents, industry will improve them; if you have but moderate abilities, industry will supply their deficiency. Nothing is denied to well directed labour: nothing is to be obtained without it. Not to enter into metaphysical discussion on the nature or essence of genius, I will venture to assert, that assiduity unabated by difficulty, and a disposition eagerly directed to the object of its pursuit, will produce effects similar to those which some call the result of *natural powers*.

From SPECTATOR, no. 62 [1711]

Joseph Addison

As *true wit* generally consists in this resemblance and congruity of ideas, *false wit* chiefly consists in the resemblance and congruity sometimes of single letters, as in anagrams, chronograms, lipograms, and acrostics; sometimes of syllables, as in echoes and doggerel rhymes; sometimes of words, as in puns and quibbles;

and sometimes of whole sentences or poems, cast into the figures of eggs, axes, or altars. Nay, some carry the notion of wit so far as to ascribe it even to external mimicry, and to look upon a man as an ingenious person, that can resemble the tone, posture, or face of another.

As true wit consists in the resemblance of ideas, and false wit in the resemblance of words, according to the foregoing instances, there is another kind of wit which consists partly in the resemblance of ideas and partly in the resemblance of words; which for distinction sake I shall call mixed wit. This kind of wit is that which abounds in Cowley more than in any other author that ever wrote. Mr. Waller has likewise a great deal of it. Mr. Dryden is very sparing in it. Milton had a genius much above it. Spenser is in the same class with Milton. The Italians, even in their epic poetry, are full of it. Monsieur Boileau, who formed himself upon the ancient poets, has everywhere rejected it with scorn. If we look after mixed wit among the Greek writers, we shall find it nowhere but in the epigrammatists. There are indeed some strokes of it in the little poem ascribed to Musaeus, which by that, as well as many other marks, betrays itself to be a modern composition. If we look into the Latin writers, we find none of this mixed wit in Vergil, Lucretius, or Catullus; very little in Horace, but a great deal of it in Ovid, and scarce anything else in Martial.

From FIRST INAUGURAL ADDRESS [1801]

Thomas Jefferson

Called upon to undertake the duties of the first executive office of our country, I avail myself of the presence of that portion of my fellow-citizens which is here assembled to express my grateful thanks for the favor with which they have been pleased to look toward me, to declare a sincere consciousness that the task is above my talents, and that I approach it with those anxious and awful presentiments which the greatness of the charge and the weakness of my powers so justly inspire. A rising nation, spread over a wide and fruitful land, traversing all the seas with the rich productions of their industry, engaged in commerce with nations who feel power and forget right, advancing rapidly to destinies beyond the reach of mortal eye—when I contemplate these transcendent objects, and see the honor, the happiness, and the hopes of this beloved country committed to the issue and the auspices of this day, I shrink from the contemplation, and humble myself before the magnitude of the undertaking. Utterly, indeed, should I despair did not the presence of many whom I here see remind me that in the other high authorities provided by our Constitution I shall find resources of wisdom, of virtue, and of zeal on which to rely under all difficulties. To you, then, gentlemen, who are charged with the sovereign functions of legislation, and to those associated with you, I look with encouragement for that guidance and support which may enable us to steer with safety the vessel in which we are all embarked amidst the conflicting elements of a troubled world.

From AN APOLOGY FOR POETRY [1580]

Sir Philip Sidney

Our tragedies and comedies not without cause cried out against, observing rules neither of honest civility nor skilful poetry. Excepting *Gorboduc* (again I say of those that I have seen), which notwithstanding as it is full of stately speeches and well-sounding phrases, climbing to the height of Seneca his style, and as full of notable morality, which it doeth most delightfully teach, and so obtain the very end of poesy; yet, in truth, it is very defectious in the circumstances, which grieves me, because it might not remain as an exact model of all tragedies. For it is faulty both in place and time, the two necessary companions of all corporal actions. For where the stage should always represent but one place, and the uttermost time presupposed in it should, both by Aristotle's precept and common reason, but one day; there is both many days and many places inartificially imagined.

From PRAYERS AND MEDITATIONS [1784]

Samuel Johnson

O Lord, my Maker and Protector, who hast graciously sent me into this world to work out my salvation, enable me to drive from me all such unquiet and perplexing thoughts as may mislead or hinder me in the practice of those duties which Thou hast required. When I behold the works of thy hands, and consider the course of thy providence, give me grace always to remember that thy thoughts are not my thoughts, nor thy ways my ways. And while it shall please Thee to continue me in this world, where much is to be done, and little to be known, teach me, by thy Holy Spirit, to withdraw my mind from unprofitable and dangerous enquiries, from difficulties vainly curious, and doubts impossible to be solved. Let me rejoice in the light which Thou hast imparted, let me serve Thee with active zeal and humble confidence, and wait with patient expectation for the time in which the soul which Thou receivest shall be satisfied with knowledge. Grant this, O Lord, for Jesus Christ's sake. Amen.

• SUGGESTIONS •

Examine the sentence structure in each of the preceding selections to discover, first, the extent of variation in sentence types for diversity and interest, second, the extent of variation in the placement of the independent construction and, if possible, the reason for the placement of these constructions, and, third, the relationships (for example, cause-effect, condition) between the major and minor constructions.

Coordination, Balance, and Parallelism

As the preceding section may illustrate, a sentence will fail if the author lumps ideas together without discrimination; it will fail if the author does not keep together ideas that belong together though one is more important than the others. But style and effect may also suffer if the author fails to bring together ideas related *and* equal in importance. The means for doing this is coordination.

Coordination, like subordination usually viewed as primarily a grammatical feature of sentences, is a major stylistic technique. It is the basic method for designating equality of ideas. The selections that follow illustrate various effects gained through careful coordination. They also illustrate some special features of coordination, the balanced construction, and the parallel construction. The balanced construction offers equal ideas in exactly identical constructions, as in this sentence from Macaulay's description of the Puritan: "He prostrated himself in the dust before his Maker; but he set his foot on the neck of his king." The parallel construction is a specialized form of coordination and balance; it is the setting together of a series of related phrases in similar grammatical patterns.

LETTER TO LORD CHESTERFIELD [1755]

Samuel Johnson

I have been lately informed, by the proprietor of *The World*, that two papers, in which my Dictionary is recommended to the Publick, were written by your Lordship. To be so distinguished, is an honour, which, being very little accustomed to favours from the great, I know not well how to receive, or in what terms to acknowledge.

When, upon some slight encouragement, I first visited your Lordship, I was overpowered, like the rest of mankind, by the enchantment of your address; and could not forbear to wish that I might boast myself *le vainqueur du vainqueur de la terre;*—that I might obtain that regard for which I saw the world contending; but I found my attendance so little encouraged, that neither pride nor modesty would suffer me to continue it. When I had once addressed your Lordship in publick, I had exhausted all the art of pleasing which a retired and uncourtly scholar can possess. I had done all that I could; and no man is well pleased to have his all neglected, be it ever so little.

Seven years, my Lord, have now past, since I waited in your outward rooms, or was repulsed from your door; during which time I have been pushing on my work through difficulties, of which it is useless to complain, and have brought it, at last, to the verge of publication, without one act of assistance, one word of encouragement, or one smile of favour. Such treatment I did not expect, for I never had a Patron before.

The shepherd in Virgil grew at last acquainted with Love, and found him a native of the rocks.

Is not a Patron, my Lord, one who looks with unconcern on a man struggling for life in the water, and, when he has reached ground, encumbers him with help? The notice which you have been pleased to take of my labours, had it been early, had been kind; but it has been delayed till I am indifferent, and cannot enjoy it; till I am solitary, and cannot impart it; till I am known, and do not want it. I hope it is no very cynical asperity not to confess obligations where no benefit has been received, or to be unwilling that the Publick should consider me as owing that to a Patron, which Providence has enabled me to do for myself.

Having carried on my work thus far with so little obligation to any favourer of learning, I shall not be disappointed though I should conclude it, if less be possible, with less; for I have been long wakened from that dream of hope, in which I once boasted myself with so much exultation, my Lord,

your Lordship's most humble,
most obedient servant.

• **COMMENTARY** •

Examination of one sentence from this letter may be sufficient to show the benefits of coordination. The next-to-last paragraph is particularly devastating in its effect because of the long parallel sentence. The reasons for Johnson's animosity toward Chesterfield are piled up in one sentence, and by presenting them in parallel constructions, Johnson is at once able to create a sense of relentlessness and, by the sonorous sound of the rhythmic parallels, to exalt his personal animosity into universal scorn. The sentence may be understood in its parallel construction in this way:

The notice which you have been
pleased to take of my labours,   had it been early,
                                   had been kind;

                                   but

                                   till I am indifferent, and cannot enjoy it;
it has been delayed   till I am solitary, and cannot impart it;
                                   till I am known, and do not want it.

ECCLESIASTES 3:1–11

1. To every *thing there is* a season, and a time to every purpose under the heaven:
2. A time to be born, and a time to die; a time to plant, and a time to pluck up *that which is* planted;
3. A time to kill, and a time to heal; a time to break down, and a time to build up;
4. A time to weep, and a time to laugh; a time to mourn, and a time to dance;
5. A time to cast away stones, and a time to gather stones together; a time to embrace, and a time to refrain from embracing;
6. A time to get, and a time to lose; a time to keep, and a time to cast away;
7. A time to rend, and a time to sew; a time to keep silence, and a time to speak;
8. A time to love, and a time to hate; a time of war, and a time of peace.
9. What profit hath he that worketh in that wherein he laboureth?
10. I have seen the travail, which God hath given to the sons of men to be exercised in it.
11. He hath made every *thing* beautiful in his time: also he hath set the world in their heart, so that no man can find out the work that God maketh from the beginning to the end.

MATTHEW 5:1–10

1. And seeing the multitudes, he went up into a mountain: and when he was set, his disciples came unto him:

2. And he opened his mouth, and taught them, saying,

3. Blessed *are* the poor in spirit: for theirs is the kingdom of heaven.

4. Blessed *are* they that mourn: for they shall be comforted.

5. Blessed *are* the meek: for they shall inherit the earth.

6. Blessed *are* they which do hunger and thirst after righteousness: for they shall be filled.

7. Blessed *are* the merciful: for they shall obtain mercy.

8. Blessed *are* the pure in heart: for they shall see God.

9. Blessed *are* the peacemakers: for they shall be called the children of God.

10. Blessed *are* they which are persecuted for righteousness' sake: for theirs is the kingdom of heaven.

From PREFACE, 1717

Alexander Pope

I confess it was want of consideration that made me an author; I writ because it amused me; I corrected because it was as pleasant to me to correct as to write; and I published because I was told I might please such as it was a credit to please. To what degree I have done this, I am really ignorant; I had too much fondness for my productions to judge of them at first, and too much judgment to be pleased with them at last. But I have reason to think they can have no reputation which will continue long, or which deserves to do so: for they have always fallen short not only of what I read of others, but even of my own Ideas of Poetry.

From PULVIS ET UMBRA [1892]

Robert Louis Stevenson

What a monstrous specter is this man, the disease of agglutinated dust, lifting alternate feet or lying drugged with slumber; killing, feeding, growing, bringing forth small copies of himself; grown upon with hair like grass, fitted with eyes that move and glitter in his face; a thing to set children screaming; and yet looked at nearlier, known as his fellows know him, how surprising are his attributes! Poor soul, here for so little, cast among so many hardships, filled with desires so incommensurate and so inconsistent, savagely surrounded, savagely descended, irremediably condemned to prey upon his fellow lives: who would have blamed him had he been of a piece with his destiny and a being merely barbarous? And we look and behold him instead filled with imperfect virtues: infinitely childish, often admirably valiant, often touchingly kind; sitting down, amidst his momentary life, to debate of right and wrong and the attributes of the deity; rising up to do battle for an egg or die for an idea; singling out his friends and his mate with cordial affection; bringing forth in pain, rearing with long-suffering solicitude, his young. To touch the heart of his mystery, we find in him one thought, strange to the point of lunacy: the thought of duty; the thought of something owing to himself, to his neighbor, to his God: an ideal of decency, to which he would rise if it were possible; a limit of shame, below which, if it be possible, he will not stoop.

From PREFACE TO SHAKESPEARE [1765]

Samuel Johnson

Nothing can please many, and please long, but just representations of general nature. Particular manners can be known to few, and therefore few only can judge how nearly they are copied. The irregular combinations of fanciful invention may delight a-while, by that novelty of which the common satiety of life sends us all in quest; but the pleasures of sudden wonder are soon exhausted, and the mind can only repose on the stability of truth.

. . . .

The force of his comick scenes has suffered little diminution from the changes made by a century and a half, in manners or in words. As his personages act upon principles arising from genuine passion, very little modified by particular forms, their pleasures and vexations are communicable to all times and to all places: they are natural, and therefore durable; the adventitious peculiarities of personal habits, are only superficial dies, bright and pleasing for a little while, yet soon fading to a dim tinct, without any remains of former lustre; but the discriminations of true passion are the colours of nature; they pervade the whole mass, and can only perish with the body that exhibits them. The accidental compositions of heterogeneous modes are dissolved by the chance which combined them; but the uniform simplicity of primitive qualities neither admits increase, nor suffers decay. The sand heaped by one flood is scattered by another, but the rock always continues in its place. The stream of time, which is continually washing the dissoluble fabricks of other poets, passes without injury by the adamant of *Shakespeare.*

• SUGGESTIONS •

Study the preceding passages to discover examples of balanced and parallel coordinate constructions. Note how dependent constructions are made coordinate.

Loose and Periodic Constructions

To diversify his sentence structure and at the same time to emphasize his meaning clearly, a writer can vary from loose to periodic constructions. One fault amateur writing often reveals is simple monotony, which may result when the writer without conscious care uses too many sentences of the same grammatical type following the standard subject-verb-complement pattern. This can be overcome by shifting from time to time from this typically loose construction to periodic construction. In a loose sentence, the principal sentence elements come at or near the beginning, with modifying dependent elements coming last. The periodic sentence withholds one or more of the principal elements until the end of the sentence, achieving a kind of climactic effect. This, in addition to adding some variety to please the reader, also serves to emphasize meaning, for it forces the reader forward through the sentence to the main item at the end.

From PREFACE TO SHAKESPEARE [1765]

Samuel Johnson

That praises are without reason lavished on the dead, and that the honours due only to excellence are paid to antiquity, is a complaint likely to be always continued by those, who, being able to add nothing to truth, hope for eminence from the heresies of paradox; or those, who, being forced by disappointment upon consolatory expedients, are willing to hope from posterity what the present age refuses, and flatter themselves that the regard which is yet denied by envy, will be at last bestowed by time.

Antiquity, like every other quality that attracts the notice of mankind, has undoubtedly votaries that reverence it, not from reason, but from prejudice. Some seem to admire indiscriminately whatever has been long preserved, without considering that time has sometimes co-operated with chance; all perhaps are more willing to honour past than present excellence; and the mind contemplates genius through the shades of age, as the eye surveys the sun through artificial opacity. The great contention of criticism is to find the faults of the moderns, and the beauties of the ancients. While an author is yet living we estimate his powers by his worst performance, and when he is dead we rate them by his best.

To works, however, of which the excellence is not absolute and definite, but gradual and comparative; to works not raised upon principles demonstrative and scientifick, but appealing wholly to observation and experience, no other test can be applied than length of duration and continuance of esteem. What mankind have long possessed they have often examined and compared, and if they persist to value the possession, it is because frequent comparisons have confirmed opinion in its favour. As among the works of nature no man can properly call a river deep or a mountain high, without the knowledge of many mountains and many rivers; so in the productions of genius, nothing can be stiled excellent till it has been compared with other works of the same kind.

• COMMENTARY •

Twice in this passage Johnson leads the reader through a long sentence to a key point at the end, the first time to stress the point of a contrast, the second time to stress the point of a comparison.

The first two paragraphs are given to Johnson's account of irrational and prejudiced praise of the works of the ancients. To show the contrast between this irrational praise and the just praise that some ancient works deserve, and to point up that contrast emphatically, he leads us through the first sentence of the third paragraph to the culminating point that explains the *real* means by which ancient works come to deserve praise. He reiterates that point in the second sentence of the third paragraph, and then once again in the third sentence shifts to a periodic construction. Using an analogy to show how men come to discover merit in works of art, he takes us first through the known element in the analogy, to come at the last again to the less known and thus to stress again the point he has already made.

From OF STUDIES [1625]

Sir Francis Bacon

Studies serve for delight, for ornament, and for ability. Their chief use for delight, is in privateness and retiring; for ornament, is in discourse; and for ability, is in the judgment and disposition of business. For expert men can execute, and perhaps judge of particulars, one by one; but the general counsels, and the plots and marshalling of affairs, come best from those that are learned. To spend too much time in studies is sloth; to use them too much for ornament, is affectation; to make judgment wholly by their rules, is the humour of a scholar. They perfect nature, and are perfected by experience: for natural abilities are like natural plants, that need proyning by study; and studies themselves do give forth directions too much at large, except they be bounded in by experience. Crafty men contemn studies, simple men admire them, and wise men use them; for they teach not their own use; but that is a wisdom without them, and above them, won by observation.

Read not to contradict and confute; nor to believe and take for granted; nor to find talk and discourse; but to weigh and consider. Some books are to be tasted, others to be swallowed, and some few to be chewed and digested; that is, some books are to be read only in parts; others to be read, but not curiously; and some few to be read wholly, and with diligence and attention.

From THE EMANCIPATION PROCLAMATION [1863]

Abraham Lincoln

That on the first day of January, in the year of our Lord one thousand eight hundred and sixty-three, all persons held as slaves within any state or designated part of a state, the people whereof shall then be in rebellion against the United States, shall be then, thenceforward, and forever, free; and the Executive Government of the United States, including the military and naval authority thereof, will recognize and maintain the freedom of such persons, and will do no act or acts to repress such persons, or any of them, in any efforts they may make for their actual freedom. . . .

And by virtue of the power and for the purpose aforesaid, I do order and declare that all persons held as slaves within said designated states and parts of states are, and henceforward shall be, free; and that the Executive Government of the United States, including the military and naval authorities thereof, will recognize and maintain the freedom of said persons.

And I hereby enjoin upon the people so declared to be free to abstain from all violence, unless in necessary self-defense; and I recommend to them that, all cases when allowed, they labor faithfully for reasonable wages.

And I further declare and make known that such persons, of suitable condition, will be received into the armed service of the United States to garrison forts, positions, stations, and other places, and to man vessels of all sorts in said service.

From SELF-RELIANCE [1841]

Ralph Waldo Emerson

Whoso would be a man, must be a nonconformist. He who would gather immortal palms must not be hindered by the name of goodness, but must explore if it be goodness. Nothing is at last sacred but the integrity of your own mind. Absolve you to yourself, and you shall have the suffrage of the world. I remember an answer which when quite young I was prompted to make to a valued adviser who was wont to importune me with the dear old doctrines of the church. On my saying, "What have I to do with the sacredness of traditions, if I live wholly from within?" my friend suggested—"But these impulses may be from below, not from above." I replied, "They do not seem to me to be such; but if I am the Devil's child, I will live then from the Devil." No law can be sacred to me but that of my nature. Good and bad are but names very readily transferable to that or this; the only right is what is after my constitution; the only wrong what is against it. A man is to carry himself in the presence of all opposition as if every thing were titular and ephemeral but he. I am ashamed to think how easily we capitulate to badges and names, to large societies and dead institutions. Every decent and well-spoken individual affects and sways me more than is right. I ought to go upright and vital, and speak of rude truth in all ways. If malice and vanity wear the coat of philanthropy, shall that pass? If an angry bigot assumes this bountiful cause of Abolition, and comes to me with his last news from Barbadoes, why should I not say to him, "Go love thy infant; love thy wood-chopper; be good-natured and modest; have that grace; and never varnish your hard, uncharitable ambition with this incredible tenderness for black folk a thousand miles off. Thy love afar is spite at home." Rough and graceless would be such greeting, but truth is handsomer than the affectation of love. Your goodness must have some edge to it—else it is none. The doctrine of hatred must be preached, as the counteraction of the doctrine of love, when that pules and whines. I shun father and mother and wife and brother when my genius calls me. I would write on the lintels of the door-post, *Whim.* I hope it is somewhat better than whim at last, but we cannot spend the day in explanation. Expect me not to show cause why I seek or why I exclude company. Then again, do not tell me, as a good man did to-day, of my obligation to put all poor men in good situations. Are they *my* poor? I tell thee, thou foolish philanthropist, that I grudge the dollar, the dime, the cent I give to such men as do not belong to me and to whom I do not belong. There is a class of persons to whom by all spiritual affinity I am bought and sold; for them I will go to prison if need be; but your miscellaneous popular charities; the education at college of fools; the building of meeting-houses to the vain end to which many now stand; alms to sots, and the thousand-fold Relief Societies; though I confess with shame I sometimes succumb and give the dollar, it is a wicked dollar, which by and by I shall have the manhood to withhold.

From SECOND INAUGURAL ADDRESS [1865]

Abraham Lincoln

One eighth of the whole population was colored slaves, not distributed generally over the Union, but localized in the southern part of it. These slaves constituted a peculiar and powerful interest. All knew that this interest was somehow the cause of the war. To strengthen, perpetuate, and extend this interest was the object for which the insurgents would rend the Union even by war, while the Government claimed no right to do more than to restrict the territorial enlargement of it. Neither party expected for the war the magnitude or the duration which it has already attained. Neither anticipated that the *cause* of the conflict might cease with or even before the conflict itself should cease. Each looked for an easier triumph, and a result less fundamental and astounding. Both read the same Bible and pray to the same God, and each invokes His aid against the other. It may seem strange that any men should dare to ask a just God's assistance in wringing their bread from the sweat of other men's faces, but let us judge not, that we be not judged. The prayers of both could not be answered. That of neither has been answered fully. The Almighty has His own purposes. "Woe unto the world because of offenses; for it must needs be that offenses come, but woe to that man by whom the offense cometh." If we shall suppose that American slavery is one of those offenses which, in the providence of God, must needs come, but which, having continued through His appointed time, He now wills to remove, and that He gives to both North and South this terrible war as the woe due to those by whom the offense came, shall we discern therein any departure from those divine attributes which the believers in a living God always ascribe to Him? Fondly do we hope, fervently do we pray, that this mighty scourge of war may speedily pass away. Yet, if God wills that it continue until all the wealth piled by the bondman's two hundred and fifty years of unrequited toil shall be sunk, and until every drop of blood drawn with the lash shall be paid by another drawn with the sword, as was said three thousand years ago, so still it must be said, "The judgments of the Lord are true and righteous altogether."

With malice toward none, with charity for all, with firmness in the right as God gives us to see the right, let us strive on to finish the work we are in, to bind up the nation's wounds, to care for him who shall have borne the battle and for his widow and his orphan, to do all which may achieve and cherish a just and a lasting peace among ourselves and with all nations.

From SPEECH ON BECOMING PRIME MINISTER [1940]

Winston S. Churchill

In this crisis I hope I may be pardoned if I do not address the House at any length today. I hope that any of my friends and colleagues, or former colleagues, who are affected by the political reconstruction, will make all allowance for any lack of ceremony with which it has been necessary to act. I would say to the House, as I said to those who have joined this Government: "I have nothing to offer but blood, toil, tears, and sweat."

We have before us an ordeal of the most grievous kind. We have before us many, many long months of struggle and of suffering. You ask, What is our policy? I will say: "It is to wage war, by sea, land and air, with all our might and with all the strength that God can give us: to wage war against a monstrous tyranny, never surpassed in the dark, lamentable catalogue of human crime. That is our policy." You ask, What is our aim? I can answer in one word: Victory—victory at all cost, victory in spite of all terror, victory however long and hard the road may be; for without victory there is no survival. Let that be realized; no survival for the British Empire; no survival for all that the British Empire has stood for; no survival for the urge and impulse of the ages, that mankind will move forward towards its goal. But I take up my task with buoyancy and hope. I feel sure that our cause will not be suffered to fail among men. At this time I feel entitled to claim the aid of all, and I say, "Come, then, let us go forward together with our united strength."

* SUGGESTIONS *

Study these passages to observe the distinction between loose and periodic construction. Note particularly how different writers vary their constructions, and note the frequency of periodic sentences.

Transitional Sentences

Smooth continuity, one quality of good writing, is a subject for discussion and illustration later in this book, where larger patterns of continuity are under consideration. But the sentence alone can act as an effective transitional device, linking paragraph to paragraph or section to section by bringing into the sentence what has been and what will be in the discussion at hand. The following selections illustrate several methods of effecting easy transition from one unit of writing to the next.

From WHAT HAPPENED TO COMMON SENSE?*

Calvin D. Linton

Common sense! That ultimate sovereign so praised by the Age of Reason, so ardently looked to in an earlier age as the unassailable arbiter, believed to be so inevitably right once artificial pressures of prejudice and emotion are removed, so hopeful because it is "common" (universally distributed), so comforting in the very sound of the word "sense"—this sovereign has fled murmuring, and with it many rays of light. Psychologists have kicked it out, declaring—in Huck Finn's phrase—that "it's not a circumstance" compared to the subconscious, where the real work goes on. Logicians have pointed out that common sense must be self-authenticating—it must, so to speak, take itself on faith. And that spoils all the fun at the outset. But most of all, worst of all, most ultimately annihilating of all, is the forced abandonment of common sense by that pinnacle of our contemporary pride, science.

This is a controversial statement, so I run for cover to one quali-fied to speak. Huston Smith of the Massachusetts Institute of Technology said [ADVENTURES OF THE MIND: THE REVOLUTION IN WESTERN THOUGHT, *The Saturday Evening Post*, August 29, 1961]: "The problems the new physics poses for man's sense of order cannot be resolved by refinements in scale. Instead they appear to point to a radical disjunction between the way things behave and every possible way in which we might try to visualize them. How, for example, are we to picture an electron traveling two or more different routes through space concurrently or passing from orbit to orbit without traversing the space between them at all? . . . It is such enigmas which are causing physicists like P. W. Bridg-man of Harvard to suggest that 'the structure of nature may even-tually be such that our processes of thought do not correspond to it sufficiently to permit us to think about it at all. . . . We have reached the limit of the vision, namely, that we live in a sympa-thetic world in that it is comprehensible by our minds.'"

These are appalling words. Their implications are so vast that

* From *The Saturday Evening Post*, April 28, 1962. By permission of Calvin D. Linton.

we cannot, at the moment of reading them, begin to grasp their significance.

But to some extent we all acknowledge their truth. Who among us would think for a moment of refuting some new discovery of science by arguing that it simply "does not make sense"? The day when we could, with Dr. Samuel Johnson, refute Berkeley's subjective idealism by kicking a stone is long past. Kick if we wish, but our sole reward is a sore toe.

For example, we have read recently of the discovery of yet another subatomic particle, the omega. And we read that some physicists believe that *protons* may contain as many subatomic particles as the ninety-odd chemical elements which, it was thought, compose all matter. The omega itself may turn out to have complicated structures of its own, and two of the discoverers of the omega, Dr. Luis W. Alvarez and Dr. M. L. Stevenson, declare that there may *never* be an end of this incredible process of peeling one layer from another.

Who among us would deny this on the grounds that it violates plain common sense? Or who would dare contradict the scientist who tells us that if all the space in each atom of the human body were squeezed out, the remaining matter would be invisibly small but would still register 170 pounds—or whatever—on the scales? Presumably the omega is true, the neutrino is true, the relative amount of space in the atom is true—but the layman can know neither the truth nor the possible falsity for himself. He must take such things—as people of the Middle Ages are alleged to have done—on the word of the acknowledged authority. Thus is the soil of gullibility plowed and ready for rich seeding, either by truth or by falsehood.

Blind faith in authority in the realm of the arts is even easier to illustrate. Here is a single sentence from a piece of authoritative art criticism which appeared in *Art News* and was quoted in *The New Yorker*: "He (the artist) pictures the stultified intricacy of tension at the plasmic level; his prototypical zygotes and somnolent somatomes inhabit a primordial lagoon where impulse is an omnidirectional drift and isolation is the consequence of an inexplicable exogamy." For all its own desperate problems, ignorance permits a healthy disbelief in such semantic idiocy; excessive sophistication, on the other hand, compels acceptance—on faith. The author, after all, must be an authority or he could not write that way.

Note carefully the effect that the first sentence in Linton's paragraphs frequently has: it commonly is typically a bipartite construction, one part of which brings into play the ideas of the previous paragraph, the second part of which forecasts the ideas of the new paragraph. The first paragraph climaxes with the assertion that we have abandoned common sense. The first sentence of the second paragraph, then, links the two: "This is a controversial statement, so I run for cover to one qualified to speak." *This* and *statement* in the first clause clearly refer to the climactic sentence of the preceding paragraph, while Linton's turning to an authority in the second clause anticipates the quotation that takes up the rest of the second paragraph.

The first sentences of the third and fourth paragraphs perform similar functions. *These* and *words* at the beginning of the third paragraph link the new paragraph to the long quotation that takes up most of the second paragraph. The sentence opening the fourth paragraph, "But to some extent we all acknowledge their truth," also has the Janus effect. *Their* refers back to the antecedent *words* in the preceding paragraph, and the suggestion that we all acknowledge this truth forecasts the discussion that follows.

Similar effects can be found with each pair of paragraphs. Consider, for example, how the idea of authority is used to link the last two paragraphs.

From RESEARCH REVISITED: SCHOLARSHIP AND THE FINE ART OF TEACHING*

Donald H. Reiman

Legitimate contributions to scholarship and criticism are irreplaceable tools of the conscientious classroom teacher. Asked to present, at least in his younger days, everything from *King Lear* to *Lucky Jim* and "The Wanderer" to "The Windhover," he must

* From *College English*, October, 1961. Reprinted with permission of the National Council of Teachers of English and Professor Donald H. Reiman.

rely on the specialized study of other teacher-scholars for an adequate understanding of these varied works. Only within a relatively narrow sphere can the average teacher hope for such mastery of an author's works that he can repay through original contributions to knowledge the bank of scholarship from which he borrows so freely.

Of even greater value than scholarship-in-general to the individual teacher, however, is his own research. Growth is the only sign of life in the world of the intellect, and intellectual curiosity is the lifeblood of the educated man. The teacher who remains *satisfied* with guesses, with half-answers, or even with the honest and necessary "I don't know" forfeits the respect of his students and colleagues alike. And the ultimate test of his quality of mind is whether or not he can contribute to teachers' or students' understanding of literature, in writing that will bear the scrutiny of his peers. Our love for knowledge, our enthusiasm for the mind's adventure, and our eagerness to grapple with life's great issues are the most valuable gifts we can bequeath to our society. A teacher who merely repeats what he has been told or what he has read can seldom generate the electric spark that will jump the gap between him and his students. The rigor of disciplined study does, however, generate that energy, and the excitement of personal discovery can transmit that enthusiasm.

Dedication to the ideals of the intellect and a willingness to sacrifice something of self for the promotion of knowledge have been hallmarks of the best teachers I have known, and although personal limitations interpose themselves, I am convinced that most productive scholars are better, not worse, teachers for their scholarly passion. Consider the alternative: a man of great intellect but somewhat introverted personality who concentrates on methods of teaching or superficial preparations for classes, rather than on deep knowledge of a field, is a teacher twice as self-conscious and half as effective because he is acutely aware that his mastery of the subject is inadequate. Buttressed, however, by the confidence that personal discovery brings, such men can become stimulating teachers as well as valuable contributors to the scholarly world.

What I have been saying is, of course, that although we should recognize effective teaching as the desired end, productive research is one of the best means to it. Now arises the question of those abuses which have recently come under fire. How does one prevent a teacher from short-changing his students by over-emphasizing his personal investigations to the detriment of preparation in other areas and interest in the students themselves? And how does one lessen the tendency of researchers to publish anything they can, whether or not it is stimulating, sound, or useful? Let me say first that these abuses do not seem to me any more widespread than abuses of another kind in schools where there is no emphasis upon publication. I have known graduate students who declared that they wanted to teach in college so that they would have more time free to play golf and travel. I have known teachers whose contempt for the intellectual adventures of scholarship was matched only by their disinterest in their students. Without responsible administration neither the pressurized publish-or-perish system nor the *laissez faire* approach will foster dedicated teaching.

From RAMBLER, no. 25 [1750]

Samuel Johnson

There are some vices and errors, which, though often fatal to those in whom they are found, have yet, by the universal consent of mankind, been considered as entitled to some degree of respect, or have, at least, been exempted from contemptuous infamy, and condemned by the severest moralists with pity rather than detestation.

A constant and invariable example of this general partiality will be found in the different regard which has always been shown to rashness and cowardice, two vices, of which, though they may be conceived equally distant from the middle point, where true fortitude is placed, and may equally injure any publick or private interest, yet the one is never mentioned without some kind of veneration, and the other always considered as a topick of unlimited and licentious censure, on which all the virulence of reproach may be lawfully exerted.

The same distinction is made, by the common suffrage, between profusion and avarice, and, perhaps, between many other opposite vices: and, as I have found reason to pay great regard to the voice of the people, in cases where knowledge has been forced upon them by experience, without long deductions or deep researches, I am inclined to believe that this distribution of respect, is not without some agreement with the nature of things; and that in the faults, which are thus invested with extraordinary privileges, there are generally some latent principles of merit, some possibilities of future virtue, which may, by degrees, break from obstruction, and by time and opportunity be brought into act.

It may be laid down as an axiom, that it is more easy to take away superfluities than to supply defects; and, therefore, he that is culpable, because he has passed the middle point of virtue, is always accounted a fairer object of hope, than he who fails by falling short. The one has all that perfection requires, and more, but the excess may be easily retrenched; the other wants the qualities requisite to excellence, and who can tell how he shall obtain them? We are certain that the horse may be taught to keep pace with his fellows, whose fault is that he leaves them behind. We know that a few strokes of the axe will lop a cedar; but what arts of cultivation can elevate a shrub?

To walk with circumspection and steadiness in the right path, at an equal distance between the extremes of error, ought to be the constant endeavour of every reasonable being; nor can I think those teachers of moral wisdom much to be honoured as benefactors to mankind, who are always enlarging upon the difficulty of our duties, and providing rather excuses for vice, than incentives to virtue.

But, since to most it will happen often, and to all sometimes, that there will be a deviation towards one side or the other, we ought always to employ our vigilance, with most attention, on that enemy from which there is greatest danger, and to stray, if we must stray, towards those parts from whence we may quickly and easily return.

Among other opposite qualities of the mind, which may become dangerous, though in different degrees, I have often had occasion to consider the contrary effects of presumption and despondency; of heady confidence, which promises victory without contest, and heartless pusillanimity, which shrinks back from the thought of great undertakings, confounds difficulty with impossibility, and considers all advancement towards any new attainment as irreversibly prohibited.

Presumption will be easily corrected. Every experiment will teach caution, and miscarriages will hourly shew, that attempts are not always rewarded with success. The most precipitate ardour will, in time, be taught the necessity of methodical gradation, and preparatory measures; and the most daring confidence be convinced that neither merit, nor abilities, can command events.

It is the advantage of vehemence and activity, that they are always hastening to their own reformation; because they incite us to try whether our expectations are well grounded, and therefore detect the deceits which they are apt to occasion. But timidity is a disease of the mind more obstinate and fatal; for a man once persuaded, that any impediment is insuperable, has given it, with respect to himself, that strength and weight which it had not before. He can scarcely strive wih vigour and perseverance, when he has no hope of gaining the victory; and since he never will try his strength, can never discover the unreasonableness of his fears.

There is often to be found in men devoted to literature, a kind of intellectual cowardice, which whoever converses much among them, may observe frequently to depress the alacrity of enterprise, and, by consequence, to retard the improvement of science. They have annexed to every species of knowledge some chimerical character of terror and inhibition, which they transmit, without much reflexion, from one to another; they first fright themselves, and then propagate the panic to their scholars and acquaintance. One study is inconsistent with a lively imagination, another with a solid judgment; one is improper in the early parts of life, another requires so much time, that it is not to be attempted at an advanced age; one is dry and contracts the sentiments, another is diffuse and overburdens the memory; one is insufferable to taste and delicacy, and another wears out life in the study of words, and is useless to a wise man, who desires only the knowledge of things.

• **SUGGESTION** •

Demonstrate how transition is accomplished in these passages.

A Writing Program

---

1. Write sentences imitating the patterns in these selections. The passages from Bryan, Reynolds, Johnson, and Ecclesiastes would furnish especially good models.

2. Return now to the preliminary essays you wrote; re-examine them with the help of the suggestions made in this section. If you discover, as you very well may, that subordination rarely occurs, that you have used coordinate constructions excessively without using balanced or parallel constructions, that you have used loose sentences almost exclusively, then you probably have good reason to revise again. Rewrite your essay giving deliberate attention to the kinds and shapes of sentences.

The Right Paragraph

From the sentence onward, every step in writing requires composition. The sentence demands a kind of composition, and the paragraph is not just a happy covey of sentences. It is the writer's discovery of order and meaning, on however small a scale; it is a variously useful or pleasant strength shored by pertinent material in pertinent sequence. It is testimony of the peculiar bond between writer and reader: in the paragraph the writer can take the reader nearer where he must be; the reader can see where the writer has been. If a sentence is an act of judgment, perhaps a paragraph is an act of faith, an operation signifying that the decisions and judgments delivered in sentences when brought together in good order can tell meaning that is and prophesy meaning yet to be.

The passages that follow, each illustrating some *special* problem or problems in paragraphing, demonstrate some of the *general* necessities of paragraphing. If they are good paragraphs, as most of them are, you will discover that they are *unified* and *coherent*. They will be unified if the author has successfully excluded all irrelevant material and if he has successfully arranged his paragraphs so that minor but necessary points are made subordinate to more important points in the development. They will be coherent if minor and major steps in the development coalesce so that the reader can follow the development without break in continuity.

Some features of the other sections of this book do not appear here. Other sections contain a Commentary following the first selection and Suggestions regarding the rest. In this section, where each kind of paragraph development is labeled and illustrated, this did not seem necessary.

The first and last paragraphs in an essay deserve special attention, for you must first seize and then relinquish the reader's attention forcefully, yet naturally. The first paragraph bears the burden of attracting an audience to the essay in the first place. It cannot do this unless it accomplishes one or more of several effects. The first paragraph can demonstrate the author's authority for saying what he has to say, or it can serve to establish the author's benevolent attitude toward his audience, informing that audience that the essay is offered sincerely and generously for its entertainment or enlightenment, or it can attract the audience's attention by any vivid anecdote, any tale that will arouse curiosity, any striking statement that is not excessively obvious, or by any other method that will catch attention.

The last paragraph must so conclude the essay that the reader knows the essay has been concluded, brought well to a full, sensible stop, with no wires left unconnected, with no issues left unfaced. Writers have found an almost infinite number of ways to do this. Sometimes the last paragraph is used for a summary of the more telling points of the essay. Sometimes the last paragraph is used to reiterate the main point, and sometimes the main point is withheld until the end for climactic effect. Where appropriate, the last paragraph is sometimes used for a call to action of some kind.

Opening Paragraphs

From WHAT HAPPENED TO COMMON SENSE?

Calvin D. Linton

We live in the best-educated age in human history. It also may well be the most gullible. Gullibility is not a matter of *what* one believes, but of *why*. The modern educated man undoubtedly believes more true things than his predecessors. He has more to choose from. After all, our fund of knowledge doubled between 1900 and 1950, we are told; it doubled again between 1950 and 1960; and it is expected to redouble by 1963.

From A PRIMER OF EXISTENTIALISM*

Gordon E. Bigelow

For some years I fought the word by irritably looking the other way whenever I stumbled across it, hoping that like dadaism and some of the other "isms" of the French *avant garde* it would go away if I ignored it. But existentialism was apparently more than the picture it evoked of uncombed beards, smoky basement cafés, and French beatniks regaling one another between sips of absinthe with brilliant variations on the theme of despair. It turned out to be of major importance to literature and the arts, to philosophy and theology, and of increasing importance to the social sciences. To learn more about it, I read several of the self-styled introductions to the subject, with the baffled sensation of a man who reads a critical introduction to a novel only to find that he must read the novel before he can understand the introduction. Therefore, I should like to provide here something most discussions of existentialism take for granted, a simple statement of its basic characteristics. This is a reckless thing to do because there are several kinds of existentialism and what one says of one kind may not be true of another, but there is an area of agreement, and it is this common ground that I should like to set forth here. We should not run into trouble so long as we understand from the outset that the six major themes outlined below will apply in varying degrees to particular existentialists. A reader should be able to go from here to the existentialists themselves, to the more specialized critiques of them, or be able to recognize an existentialist theme or coloration in literature when he sees it.

* From *College English*, December, 1961. Reprinted with permission of the National Council of Teachers of English and Professor Gordon Bigelow.

From PUBLISH AND PERISH*

Lester Hurt

The other day I happened to hear a senior professor of our faculty not too politely admonishing a younger member of the English department for his failure to publish. As a scholar himself, as a professor who exercises considerable power in the college hierarchy, and as a man who is concerned about the standards and reputation of the institution, the senior professor was perhaps within his rights to call his younger colleague to task. Indeed, as I listened, my own withers were not entirely unwrung; I ruefully had to confess to myself that I, too, had spent too much time with beer and Beethoven, too many hours with tennis and Toynbee, too many evenings with students and Schopenhauer, while neglecting to write up and send on the rounds my observations about water symbolism in the novels of William Faulkner—a subject well known to the students in my course in the modern novel but not yet decently embalmed in the pages of the scholarly journals, to the public credit of my chairman, the university which granted my doctorate, and the college which pays my salary.

From TO THE DAMNATION OF DEANS†

John Ciardi

I leaned on my first lectern in January of 1940 as a new-minted instructor at the University of Kansas City. After a shade under four years with the Army Air Corps, beginning in 1942, I taught for seven years at Harvard as an instructor and then for eight years more at Rutgers, ending up as a full-chicken professor of English, a post and tenure I resigned last June.

* From *College English*, October, 1961. Reprinted by permission of the National Council of Teachers of English and Professor Lester Hurt.

† From *Saturday Review*, March 24, 1962. By permission of the author and publisher.

From SELF-RELIANCE [1841]

Ralph Waldo Emerson

I read the other day some verses written by an eminent painter which were original and not conventional. The soul always hears an admonition in such lines, let the subject be what it may. The sentiment they instil is of more value than any thought they may contain. To believe your own thought, to believe that what is true for you in your private heart is true for all men—that is genius. Speak your latent conviction, and it shall be the universal sense; for the inmost in due time becomes the outmost, and our first thought is rendered back to us by the trumpets of the Last Judgment. Familiar as the voice of the mind is to each, the highest merit we ascribe to Moses, Plato and Milton is that they set at naught books and traditions, and spoke not what men, but what *they* thought. A man should learn to detect and watch that gleam of light which flashes across his mind from within, more than the lustre of the firmament of bards and sages. Yet he dismisses without notice his thought, because it is his. In every work of genius we recognize our own rejected thoughts; they come back to us with a certain alienated majesty. Great works of art have no more affecting lesson for us than this. They teach us to abide by our spontaneous impression with good-humored inflexibility then most when the whole cry of voices is on the other side. Else to-morrow a stranger will say with masterly good sense precisely what we have thought and felt all the time, and we shall be forced to take with shame our own opinion from another.

Concluding Paragraphs

From LIFE OF RICHARD SAVAGE [1744]

Samuel Johnson

This relation will not be wholly without its use, if those who languish under any part of his sufferings shall be enabled to fortify their patience by reflecting that they feel only those afflictions from which the abilities of Savage did not exempt him; or those who, in confidence of superior capacities or attainments, disregard the common maxims of life, shall be reminded that nothing will supply the want of prudence; and that negligence and irregularity, long continued, will make the knowledge useless, wit ridiculous, and genius contemptible.

From SINNERS IN THE HANDS OF AN

ANGRY GOD [1741]

Jonathan Edwards

Therefore let every one that is out of Christ now awake and fly from the wrath to come. The wrath of Almighty God is now undoubtedly hanging over great part of this congregation. Let every one fly out of Sodom. *"Haste and escape for your lives, look not behind you, escape to the mountain, lest ye be consumed."*

From FIRST INAUGURAL ADDRESS [1801]

Thomas Jefferson

Relying then on the patronage of your good-will, I advance with obedience to the work, ready to retire from it whenever you become sensible how much better choice it is in your power to make. And may that Infinite Power which rules the destinies of the universe lead our councils to what is best, and give them a favorable issue for your peace and prosperity.

From PULVIS ET UMBRA [1892]

Robert Louis Stevenson

And as we dwell, we living things, in our isle of terror and under the imminent hand of death, God forbid it should be man the erected, the reasoner, the wise in his own eyes—God forbid it should be man that wearies in well-doing, that despairs of un-

rewarded effort, or utters the language of complaint. Let it be
enough for faith, that the whole creation groans in mortal frailty,
strives with unconquerable constancy: surely not all in vain.

Transitional Paragraphs

Sentences alone, as you have seen, can establish continuity between units in an essay. Paragraphs are also sometimes used for
this purpose. When this happens, the single paragraph is not
designed to develop a topic of its own, but to fasten together what
precedes and what follows, by, for example, summarizing preceding remarks and outlining those to come. For obvious reasons,
this use of paragraphs may be more likely to occur in speeches,
where the audience must be kept aware of what transpires, and
in essays developing complex subjects, where the audience has to
be kept informed about the process of development.

From WHAT HAPPENED TO COMMON SENSE?

Calvin D. Linton

These are appalling words. Their implications are so vast that we
cannot, at the moment of reading them, begin to grasp their significance.

From AREOPAGITICA [1644]

John Milton

If ye be thus resolved, as it were injury to think ye were not, I
know not what should withhold me from presenting ye with a
fit instance wherein to show both that love of truth which ye
eminently profess, and that uprightness of your judgment which
is not wont to be partial to yourselves; by judging over again that
Order which ye have ordained *to regulate Printing: that no book,
pamphlet, or paper shall be henceforth printed, unless the same
be first approved and licensed by such,* or at least one of such as

shall be thereto appointed. For that part which preserves justly every man's copy to himself, or provides for the poor, I touch not, only wish they be not made pretences to abuse and persecute honest and painful men, who offend not in either of these particulars. But that other clause licensing books, which we thought had died with his brother *quadragesimal* and *matrimonial* when the prelates expired, I shall now attend with such a homily as shall lay before ye, first, the inventors of it to be those whom ye will be loth to own; next, what is to be thought in general of reading, whatever sort the books be; and that this Order avails nothing to the suppressing of scandalous, seditious, and libellous books, which were mainly intended to be suppressed. Last, that it will be primely to the discouragement of all learning, and the stop of truth, not only by dis-exercising and blunting our abilities in what we know already, but by hindering and cropping the discovery that might be yet made both in religious and civil wisdom.

From FIRST INAUGURAL ADDRESS [1861]

Abraham Lincoln

That there are persons in one section or another who seek to destroy the Union at all events and are glad of any pretext to do it I will neither affirm nor deny; but if there be such, I need address no word to them. To those, however, who really love the Union may I not speak?

Patterns of Paragraph Development

There is probably no man alive who can look at every paragraph and announce unequivocally, "It is developed thus and so; it follows this, that or the other pattern." If you should happen to meet such a man, you would probably do well to speak brusquely and pass on, for he is likely a monster.

But while it may be monstrous to suppose that every paragraph follows some pre-established pattern, a great many good paragraphs do just that, and it would be just as monstrous to ignore the practice of good writers who have found that some basic paragraph patterns work strikingly well.

Some of these methods are quite simple. If the subject is such as to make the method usable, a paragraph can be based on plain *chronological* development. Or if again the subject makes it appropriate, a paragraph can be arranged by some *spatial* organization, so that the movement in the paragraph is from one place to other places in some sensible order. Or paragraphs can reflect general characteristics of speaking, either blurting out the main point first and then offering evidence, as in the *support* paragraph, or withholding the main point until last and providing the evidence first, as in the *climax* paragraph.

Other methods are somewhat more involved, but they are just as natural and just as useful since they are only reproductions of common ways of thinking. A basic technique for paragraph development is simply *illustration*, where the author uses the paragraph entirely to give examples of a point made in a preceding or following paragraph. Or if the subject at hand calls for explanation of how something came about, a paragraph can be arranged so as to show chronological *process*. Another basic pattern for the paragraph is *definition*, where the author in whatever order best suits his case, defines a term by putting it into a general class and then showing how it differs from other members of that class. Or an author can base his paragraph upon *comparison*, explaining his topic by showing its similarities to something better known or upon *contrast*, explaining his topic by showing how it differs from something better known. *Classification* is still another basic pattern, allowing an author to explain his topic by resolving it into its parts. For many topics a *cause-effect* movement can also be useful. These patterns lend themselves to many variations, and doubtless others remain yet unnamed.

* **CHRONOLOGICAL DEVELOPMENT**

From A STUDENT ESSAY

Johann Sebastian Bach was born in the lovely old town of Eisenach, Germany, on March 21, 1685. When Bach was ten years old, his father died and he went to live with his brother, also a musician. It was difficult to get music in those days; Bach used to copy his brother's music by the moonlight. Bach was forced to leave Eisenach, and he journeyed to Luneberg where he became a chorister at St. Michael's. There he learned the clavichord, the organ, the violin, and also the rudiments of composition. His desire for musical training was so great that he often walked long distances to hear famous musicians; he once walked two hundred and twenty-five miles to hear the blind organist, Buxtehude, play.

From SPECTATOR, no. 329 [1712]

Joseph Addison

We were immediately conducted into the little chapel on the right hand. Sir Roger, planting himself at our historian's elbow, was very attentive to every thing he said, particularly to the account he gave us of the lord who had cut off the King of Morocco's head. Among several other figures, he was very well pleased to see the statesman Cecil upon his knees; and, concluding them all to be great men, was conducted to the figure which represents that martyr to good housewifery, who died by the prick of a needle. Upon our interpreter telling us that she was a maid of honor to Queen Elizabeth, the Knight was very inquisitive into her name and family; and, after having regarded her finger for some time, "I wonder," says he, "that Sir Richard Baker has said nothing of her in his Chronicle."

• SPATIAL DEVELOPMENT

From A STUDENT ESSAY

The morning air was fresh and invigorating as we arrived at the beautiful spot in southern Canada, which we called our fishing lake. The cool lake breeze was whistling through the pine trees as we began to try our luck at fishing. As we sat there, we could see the rolling hills, covered with beautiful green pine, rise and fall as they left the lake's shore. By noon no one had caught a thing, and so we stopped for lunch, which we ate on a high rock overlooking the lake. After lunch we went back down to the lake, where we impatiently resumed our fishing task. By two o'clock we still had not caught anything, and we were about ready to leave. Just then a fish struck on my hook and pulled me into three feet of water. It took me over thirty minutes to reel it in. I was shocked when I saw what I had caught. The fish was a record-breaking Northern Pike, weighing twenty-two pounds and being over four feet in length. My father took a picture of me holding the fish with the clear blue water of the lake in the background.

From SPECTATOR, no. 116 [1711]

Joseph Addison

This, with my aversion to leaping hedges, made me withdraw to a rising ground, from whence I could have the picture of the whole chase, without the fatigue of keeping in with the hounds. The hare immediately threw them above a mile behind her: but I was pleased to find that instead of running straight forward, or in hunter's language, "flying the country," as I was afraid she might have done, she wheeled about, and described a sort of circle round the hill where I had taken my station, in such a manner as gave me a very distinct view of the sport. I could see her first pass by, and the dogs some time afterwards unravelling the whole track she had made, and following her through all her doubles. I was at the same time delighted in observing that deference which the rest of the pack paid to each particular hound, according to the character he had acquired amongst them: if they were at fault, and an old hound of reputation opened but once, he was immediately followed by the whole cry; while a raw dog, or one who was a noted liar, might have yelped his heart out, without being taken notice of.

• SUPPORT DEVELOPMENT

From CIVIL DISOBEDIENCE [1849]

Henry David Thoreau

I heartily accept the motto,—"That government is best which governs least;" and I should like to see it acted up to more rapidly and systematically. Carried out, it finally amounts to this, which also I believe,—"That government is best which governs not at all;" and when men are prepared for it, that will be the kind of government which they will have. Government is at best but an expedient; but most governments are usually, and all governments are sometimes, inexpedient. The objections which have been brought against a standing army, and they are many and weighty, and deserve to prevail, may also at last be brought against a standing government. The standing army is only an arm of the standing government. The government itself, which is only the mode which the people have chosen to execute their will, is equally liable to be abused and perverted before the people can act through it. Witness the present Mexican war, the work of comparatively a few individuals using the standing government as their tool; for, in the outset, the people would not have consented to this measure.

From AREOPAGITICA [1644]

John Milton

As therefore the state of man now is, what wisdom can there be to choose, what continence to forbear without the knowledge of evil? He that can apprehend and consider vice with all her baits and seeming pleasures, and yet abstain, and yet distinguish, and yet prefer that which is truly better, he is the true warfaring Christian. I cannot praise a fugitive and cloistered virtue, unexercised and unbreathed, that never sallies out and sees her adversary, but slinks out of the race where that immortal garland is to be run for, not without dust and heat. Assuredly we bring not innocence into the world, we bring impurity much rather: that which purifies us is trial, and trial is by what is contrary. That virtue therefore which is but a youngling in the contemplation of evil, and knows not the utmost that vice promises to her followers, and rejects it, is but a blank virtue, not a pure; her whiteness is but an excremental whiteness; which was the reason why our sage and serious poet Spenser, whom I dare be known to think a better teacher than Scotus or Aquinas, describing true temperance under the person of Guion, brings him in with his palmer through the cave of Mammon and the bower of earthly bliss, that he might see and know, and yet abstain.

• CLIMAX DEVELOPMENT

From WHAT HAPPENED TO COMMON SENSE?

Calvin D. Linton

Common sense! That ultimate sovereign so praised by the Age of Reason, so ardently looked to in an earlier age as the unassailable arbiter, believed to be so inevitably right once artificial pressures of prejudice and emotion are removed, so hopeful because it is "common" (universally distributed), so comforting in the very sound of the word "sense"—this sovereign has fled murmuring, and with it many rays of light. Psychologists have kicked it out, declaring—in Huck Finn's phrase—that "it's not a circumstance" compared to the subconscious, where the real work goes on. Logicians have pointed out that common sense must be self-authenticating— it must, so to speak, take itself on faith. And that spoils all the fun at the outset. But most of all, worst of all, most ultimately annihilating of all, is the forced abandonment of common sense by that pinnacle of our contemporary pride, science.

From OF EDUCATION [1644]

John Milton

I shall detain you now no longer in the demonstration of what we should not do, but straight conduct ye to a hillside, where I will point ye out the right path of a virtuous and noble education; laborious indeed at the first ascent, but else so smooth, so green, so full of goodly prospect and melodious sounds on every side, that the harp of Orpheus was not more charming. I doubt not but ye shall have more ado to drive our dullest and laziest youth, our stocks and stubs, from the infinite desire of such a happy nurture, than we have now to hale and drag our choicest and hopefullest wits to that asinine feast of sow-thistles and brambles which is commonly set before them as all the food and entertainment of their tenderest and most docible age. I call therefore a complete and generous education that which fits a man to perform justly, skillfully, and magnanimously all the offices, both private and public, of peace and war. And how all this may be done between twelve and one and twenty, less time than is now bestowed in pure trifling at grammar and sophistry, is to be thus ordered.

• DEVELOPMENT BY ILLUSTRATION

From WHAT HAPPENED TO COMMON SENSE?

Calvin D. Linton

Blind faith in authority in the realm of the arts is even easier to illustrate. Here is a single sentence from a piece of authoritative art criticism which appeared in *Art News* and was quoted in *The New Yorker:* "He (the artist) pictures the stultified intricacy of tension at the plasmic level; his prototypical zygotes and somnolent somatomes inhabit a primordial lagoon where impulse is an omnidirectional drift and isolation is the consequence of an inexplicable exogamy." For all its own desperate problems, ignorance permits a healthy disbelief in such semantic idiocy; excessive sophistication, on the other hand, compels acceptance—on faith. The author, after all must be an authority or he could not write that way.

From A STUDENT ESSAY

A sandpile, while it provides exciting entertainment for the children, may break a father's back and a mother's heart. On the afternoon when I finished our sandpile, I called the children out, and they came in eight- and five- and two-year-old fury to the urgent matter of excavation. Listening and watching from the kitchen window, we did not hear the usual rages and roars, only the business-like exchange of instructions for this hole, that road, and yonder cave. Watching their squatted concentration we knew again how large and free is the child's world, and I could see my

wife's eyes grow misty seeing their straight backs, arms hooked
over bent knees. She very nearly cried, but remembered that I was
supposed to empty the trash. I tried to get up, discovered that at
least three of my vertebrae had gotten fastened together a new
way from the digging and found that though I was not in a chair,
I was still in the posture. And so I very nearly cried. A balding
goblin, I started out the door, only to meet face to face—I was
broken, please remember—with the unholy three who sought a
spoon, a big spoon, and a drink and brought on seat and knee
and face and hand the entire top surface of the sandpile in a
massive transfer of topsoil from outside to in. And so my wife
very nearly cried again.

• DEVELOPMENT BY PROCESS ANALYSIS

From A STUDENT ESSAY

Getting a sandpile built can sometimes be exacting business. In
order to get ours ready this summer, my wife and children started
last September, all four of them knowing by now that I am
hesitant to undertake physical labor of even the tenderest sort.
So they mentioned it along ever so often, during Christmas holidays got me to inquire about the price of sand, mentioned it some
more, at Easter encouraged me to find some boards for siding,
and early in June hinted that the summer might be over with no
sandpile for all they could tell. Circumstances and conscience per-
mitting no further delay, I borrowed a shovel the first week in
June, a wheelbarrow the second week, bought a small pick the
third week, and in the fourth week got under way when my oldest
daughter asked if she could go visit a friend across town who *had*
a sandpile. Not liking this kind of thing very much, I firmly resolved to do the whole affair in one day to have it done. We had
agreed to dig about twelve inches down in the arranged plot,
board the sides, and then pile in the dirt. I started digging at
eight in the morning. At nine I thought perhaps a little water
might soften the soil for digging, and having wet it down, thought
I had better wait a little while until it dried to just the right consistency. After I had gotten the children out of the mud and
helped clean them up—after all, the mud *was* my doing—I started
to dig again.

• DEVELOPMENT BY DEFINITION

From TO THE DAMNATION OF DEANS*

John Ciardi

My nostalgic notion of the true college was of an absolute and self-determining body of scholar-teachers. They are the faculty. They are appointed for their distinction and responsibility. And they, by discussion and vote, set the college policy, which is then passed on as formulated to a variety of clerk known as a dean. The duty of such clerks is to count the paper clips and add up the totals as instructed, leaving the faculty free for the important business of gathering information, of thinking about it, and of transmitting the information, the thought, and the method of thinking to students.

From A STUDENT ESSAY

A sandpile is a bunch of dirt. But all in one place and circumscribed by board, cement, or other restraining materials, it is the setting for children's cavorting, the occasion for dad's dexterity in arranging it, and otherwise the source of parental pouting. Composed of sifted sand, forty-seven toy soldiers, eight trucks, one tractor, one road-grader, three spoons, one shovel, and innumerable incidental children, both indigent and immigrant, a sandpile, unlike other bunches of dirt, is informed by the vision of children.

* From *Saturday Review*, March 24, 1962. By permission of the author and publisher.

● **DEVELOPMENT BY COMPARISON OR CONTRAST**

From THE LIFE OF POPE [1781]

Samuel Johnson

Poetry was not the sole praise of either, for both excelled likewise in prose; but Pope did not borrow his prose from his predecessor. The style of Dryden is capricious and varied, that of Pope is cautious and uniform; Dryden obeys the motions of his own mind, Pope constrains his mind to his own rules of composition. Dryden is sometimes vehement and rapid; Pope is always smooth, uniform, and gentle. Dryden's page is a natural field, rising into inequalities, and diversified by the varied exuberance of abundant vegetation; Pope's is a velvet lawn, shaven by the scythe, and levelled by the roller.

Of genius, that power which constitutes a poet; that quality without which judgement is cold and knowledge is inert; that energy which collects, combines, amplifies, and animates—the superiority must, with some hesitation, be allowed to Dryden. It is not to be inferred that of this poetical vigour Pope had only a little, because Dryden had more, for every other writer since Milton must give place to Pope; and even of Dryden it must be said that if he has brighter paragraphs, he has not better poems. Dryden's performances were always hasty, either excited by some external occasion, or extorted by domestick necessity; he composed without consideration, and published without correction. What his mind could supply at call, or gather in one excursion, was all that he sought, and all that he gave. The dilatory caution of Pope enabled him to condense his sentiments, to multiply his images, and to accumulate all that study might produce, or chance might supply. If the flights of Dryden therefore are higher, Pope continues longer on the wing. If of Dryden's fire the blaze is brighter, of Pope's the heat is more regular and constant. Dryden often surpasses expectation, and Pope never falls below it. Dryden is read with frequent astonishment, and Pope with perpetual delight.

From A STUDENT ESSAY

The careless observer may conclude that a sandpile is like any other pile of sand, such as, for example, the truck-dumped pile awaiting the concrete mixer alongside the membraned structure that will be a new dormitory. He will see that the sandpile, like the sand for cement mixing, is usually sifted and free of any more than dime-size pebbles. He will see that the sandpile, like the other sand, is limited and solitary, set off from other areas of the same material. He will see that they share the same colors and the same texture. And he will see that like most things here on earth, they both are perpetually shifting. But if he sees only this, he does not understand sandpiles, for a sandpile is a cultural fact of sedimentary significance quite unlike the builder's pile of sand. The builder's pile is after all only a means to an end, partial constituent of other means to other ends. A sandpile is a thing in itself, an end, sand made entire in castle, road, cave, and fort. Watchers of sandpiles know that while other sand may find use in the exercise of one man's vision articulated in another man's blueprint, and finding form in the construction of a third, a sandpile is vision whole and unimpeded, world on top of world, world beneath world, the formed fancy of that great philosopher, the child.

● DEVELOPMENT BY CLASSIFICATION

From PUBLISHING AND PROFESSIONALISM IN ENGLISH DEPARTMENTS*

William Van O'Connor

In using the term productive scholar I have in mind three kinds of writers, (1) the poet, dramatist or fiction writer, (2) the critic, and (3) the research scholar. The critic and the scholar are not always

* From *College English,* October, 1961. Reprinted with permission of the National Council of Teachers of English and Professor William Van O'Connor.

separable, and sometimes the creative writer takes a turn at writing criticism—but for our present purposes we can consider each to be separate. They are the three productive types currently found in English departments. Each of them looks at literature through truly professional eyes. They are initiates, or, in Stephen Crane's term, they are *interpreters*.

From CIVIL DISOBEDIENCE [1849]

Henry David Thoreau

The mass of men serve the state thus, not as men mainly, but as machines, with their bodies. They are the standing army, and the militia, jailors, constables, posse comitatus, etc. In most cases there is no free exercise whatever of the judgment or of the moral sense; but they put themselves on a level with wood and earth and stones; and wooden men can perhaps be manufactured that will serve the purpose as well. Such command no more respect than men of straw or a lump of dirt. They have the same sort of worth only as horses and dogs. Yet such as these even are commonly esteemed good citizens. Others—as most legislators, politicians, lawyers, ministers, and office-holders—serve the state chiefly with their heads; and, as they rarely make any moral distinctions, they are as likely to serve the Devil, without *intending* it, as God. A very few, as heroes, patriots, martyrs, reformers in the great sense, and *men,* serve the state with their consciences also, and so necessarily resist it for the most part; and they are commonly treated as enemies by it. A wise man will only be useful as a man, and will not submit to be "clay," and "stop a hole to keep the wind away," but leave that office to his dust at least.

From A STUDENT ESSAY

Watchers of sandpiles, you see, know that not all sandpiles are alike. They know that there are sandpiles in public playgrounds, they know that the beach is a haven of other public sandpiles, and they know that at last there are SANDPILES, though proficiency in sandpile-watching may demonstrate the existence of other classes. The expert knows that the sandpile in the public playground has the same composition as any in private yards, save for the greater incidence of rocks, toy soldiers, spoons, and shovels, but he also knows that it doesn't permit that sovereign sense the child has in his own domain. The expert also understands that the beach sandpile, composed much like that in the public playground but for a new ingredient, shells, and a new sense, the sound of ocean which makes forts all the more desirable in sand, likewise forbids the exercise of monarchy except temporarily. But he who knows sandpiles, knows that the private sandpile in the backyard is an empire untroubled except by brothers and sisters and occasional friends, and they can be managed when the vision is strong.

• DEVELOPMENT BY CAUSAL ANALYSIS

From DISCOURSE ONE [1769]

Sir Joshua Reynolds

The principal advantage of an Academy is, that, beside furnishing able men to direct the Student, it will be a repository for the great examples of the Art. These are the materials on which Genius is to work, and without which the strongest intellect may be fruitlessly or deviously employed. By studying these authentick models, that idea of excellence which is the result of the accumulated experience of past ages, may be at once acquired, and the tardy and obstructed progress of our predecessors may teach us a shorter and easier way. The Student receives, at one glance, the principles which many Artists have spent their whole lives in ascertaining; and, satisfied with their effect, is spared the painful investigation by which they came to be known and fixed. How many men of great natural abilities have been lost to this nation, for want of these advantages! They never had an opportunity of seeing those masterly efforts of genius, which at once kindle the whole soul, and force it into sudden and irresistible approbation.

From A STUDENT ESSAY

Because my wife had a sandpile and enjoyed it and because I didn't have a sandpile and missed it, we agreed that the children should have a sandpile. Perhaps, in a maze of fancy I could even say that long ago in the West Texas of the thirties, I found a need for sandpiles, in the midst of the long copper-black dust storms envisioning restrained and controlled sand. And perhaps long ago in her West Texas of the thirties she knew a freedom in her sandpile, a freedom transferable even to city and cement in its sandy form. Perhaps. But wife shakes her head. She knows that sandpiles have their own myriad pasts fitting each child's conceit, and she knows that I could not be stirred to shovel and haul by even such whimsy as this, and she knows that I built a sandpile because the oldest asked for one and the middle asked for one and the youngest had a falling-down fit when she could not break through the rocky soil of our yard.

A Writing Program

---

1. Write several paragraphs of each type illustrated here.

2. Return to the preliminary essays you wrote and examine your paragraphing. Determine whether or not each of your paragraphs develops its own topic (or serves some special purpose such as transition), whether or not the method of development in each paragraph is appropriate to the topic, and whether or not the method of development clearly relates each paragraph to the general subject. You may well have sufficient evidence to prompt still another revision.

Planning the Complete Essay

☼

Any student knows how to make his essay follow his outline closely—he writes the essay first. Still, if words and sentences and paragraphs are to coalesce, as they must if meaning is to be found, something has to happen between the conception of an idea followed by the collection of materials to give it body and the rendition of that idea. What has to happen—and this may be the most demanding of all the disciplines that go into good writing—may very well take as much time as the actual writing, and may take more time. What has to happen is a plan.

You may wish to trust to your wit and its present insights, or to some sweet singing inspiration, and let words splatter out their meaning on the page. And they just might; they might splatter out a developing pattern of thought. If they should, you can count yourself lucky—but you cannot call yourself consistent, for you will not be able to depend on successfully splattering every time. What you can depend on is a competent plan that has been developed rationally.

The Muse, after all, may not come trippingly every time the demands of education, profession, citizenship, or conviction require that you write. Until she comes, or in the event that she comes not at all, there are reliable procedures for planning a rational discourse. They require considerable calculation and deliberation, which may seem inimical to fine writing; but even divine furor and brilliant inspiration are only beginnings that must be developed through disciplined craftsmanship.

Make no mistake: planning does require that calculation and deliberation, for it is not accomplished when you have decided upon a subject and arranged the parts of your discussion in your mind. It is more demanding—and in the long run more rewarding.

Planning an essay properly means forecasting *completely* every step you will take, every paragraph you will write, every connection you will try to establish between thoughts. To tire further a worn cliché, your plan or outline serves as the skeleton of your work, and more; it is the complete skeleton, not just the neck bone and cranium, and to fulfill its function properly it must also be provided with the ligaments that connect the bones. In effect, a plan or outline should be so thorough that one has only to add illustrative material (shall we call it the fatty tissue that makes curves?) to create an essay.

There are, no doubt, many ways to organize an essay competently. This section suggests and illustrates three specific ways to do it. Each is designed to provide the writer with control over his work before he starts to write, to forecast all the steps of his discourse and their connections. Each will work in almost any situation; mastering each should therefore give you three ways out when you are asked or led to write. The last given here is an ancient method, and essays long a part of our heritage are used to illustrate it. The first two do not have the sanction of tradition; though they lack that, they are yet reliable methods, as the anonymous student essays will perhaps illustrate. One last section is given to special problems of organization, coherence, and transition.

A Plan for Short Essays

You are presumably familiar with a number of methods of developing paragraphs, many of which were discussed and illustrated in the preceding section. Knowledge of these procedures in paragraphing can be used to good advantage in planning short essays. Indeed, to plan a short essay (perhaps less than ten paragraphs), one has only to combine paragraphs judiciously. If, for example, a writer uses one of the standard procedures for paragraphing as his ruling method, he can develop each of the paragraphs in his essay according to the immediate needs and yet so manage each that it serves as a step in the ruling procedure.

Suppose you are asked to write a short essay explaining some term, say, for example, the term "honor system" as it is understood at your college. Such a task might very well call for a definition.

Using the pattern of a definition as your ruling method and remembering that this calls usually for, first, a statement of the term to be defined; second, classification of that term; and, third, differentiation of that term from all other members of the same class, you can very easily and logically develop a three-paragraph essay, each paragraph of which will satisfy one of these demands. The first paragraph, developed by illustration, states the term to be defined. If you develop the second paragraph by comparison, you have in effect performed the second step, for you will show similarities between your subject and other things of the same class. Developing the third paragraph by contrast, you can then fulfill the final requirement of a logical definition by showing how your subject differs from other things of the same class. Each paragraph is thus developed in its own way, and at the same time each serves as one part of a unified whole.

The possibilities for such combinations of paragraphs according to the requirements of one central method are almost endless. For a further example: if your subject should involve cause-effects sequences, consider how easily three paragraphs developed by illustration, a fourth developed by process analysis, and a fifth developed by definition coalesce to form just such a cause-effect sequence.

Several specific advantages arise from use of this method. First of all, by knowing before you begin to write how many paragraphs you will have and what their relationship to each other will be, you are given a degree of deliberate control over your work. Second, since you will already have worked out how each paragraph is to be developed before beginning to write, you should be assured that each will be decently and logically handled. Third, since you will already know how the paragraphs fit together, you should be assured of at least a reasonably well-unified essay; knowing that a ruling method brings your paragraphs together logically should further guarantee that transitions between paragraphs will be relatively easy.

LOST, ALIENATED, AND ESTRANGED

A Student Essay

1   I get upset easily. Third grade teachers intimidate me, and
so do ministers and bus drivers and my mother. I was afraid when
I went to school, and even now I am very nervous when I go to my
children's school for the fall carnival. I have always been fright-
ened and upset by science, particularly vectors and things like
that, and space being bent—maybe clear back next door, for all
I know. When I was drafted, a lot of things bothered me for
about two years. It has been like that all along, being upset and
all by clerks and first one thing and then another, most recently by
my own children, who lurk, watching every day to see whether
I make out as a parent.

2   That is how I happened to be lost. It all gets worse when
I'm face to face with authority. Well, anyway, it all started when
I had to fill out some kind of form in high school. One section
asked for place of birth. Now I was born in a farmhouse several
miles outside Jayton, Texas, but I didn't think I had room to put
all that down and it didn't seem like they would want all that
anyway, so I put down Jayton as the place of my birth. I waited
for some weeks expecting to be called to the principal's office
and made to put it right, but nothing happened. Then I was
drafted, and there was another form to fill out. But this time it was
the United States Army, and I felt that Jayton just wouldn't do. I
thought at least one official somewhere would know, what with
statistics and all, that Jayton is in one county and the little farmhouse where I was born is in the neighboring county. I couldn't
put down Jayton, but I couldn't put down any town in the other
county either because you don't mess around with the United
States Army. I finally just put down Stonewall County, where the
little house was. That bothered me too. For one thing, it was
presumptuous. But it goes on. While I was in the Army I got
married. A thing that has the sanction of church, state, and my
wife is a thing to be careful with, and there was another form to
fill out before we could get the marriage license. This time I put
all my faith in authority and announced that the place of my
birth was Aspermont, Texas. I have never been in Aspermont

except to pass through, but since that is the county seat of the county in which the little farmhouse is located, I somehow felt that I must be recorded there. And I think there is a real nice statue of a Confederate soldier in front of the courthouse there. Then later we had a son, and they wanted to know where I was born when they gave him a birth certificate. This time, in sheer bravado at my escape for all these years, and in my pride at being a father, I threw caution to the winds and wrote down that the place of my birth was Spur, Texas. I never lived in Spur either, but it seemed like more people would have heard of it. Spur had a rodeo once and a swimming pool made of concrete, and was once headquarters for a big ranch. It was a kind of status symbol, you see, and I had sold out.

3   And that is how it all came about. That is how I got lost. Now I know, after all these years, that herself has been going around filling out forms too, and she isn't too familiar with that part of West Texas, and all these years she's been putting down places for me like Spur and Stamford and Lubbock and all, and what I've done she has helped with, as she vowed to, and as far as I know, no one on earth knows for sure where I was born. My parents could say, I think, but we don't talk about it much any more.

• COMMENTARY •

This short essay illustrates another advantage in outlining by combining paragraphs. Judicious selection of the ruling method appropriate to your subject and of the methods to be used in each paragraph that will show the steps in that ruling method should give you a plan so sufficiently thorough and continuous that it requires only illustrations to become an essay, as was the case here.

The title of this short piece, the first sentence of the second paragraph, and the first two sentences of the third paragraph give us a clue to its structure. Something has happened to the author, and he wishes to explain here how it came about. Analysis of the essay shows that the three paragraphs combine appropriately enough to form a cause-effect sequence.

The first paragraph, developed by illustration, establishes the original causes for the present predicament, fear and intimidation. The second paragraph, developed by chronological process, shows how in the course of this process a number of immediate causes for the predicament arise. The final paragraph, which is developed by a cause-effect sequence itself, states finally the effects of what has gone before. The first two paragraphs are given to cause, the last to effect.

EARLY PREJUDICE AGAINST THE NEGRO

A Student Essay

1   When I was eight my family moved to Little Rock, Arkansas. Since I was rather young, I had not come in contact with the Negro, and therefore did not have any definite opinions about him. Arkansas seemed an anti-Negro state, and when we moved there they were having some trouble with Negro riots and the school situation. The state I was in started me thinking more about the Negro.

2   I soon found many friends my age in Little Rock. I also soon learned that most of my friends were against the Negro, and that in most cases, this opposition had become hatred of the Negro. This also stimulated my thinking about the Negro.

3   The day finally came when I made direct contact with a Negro boy. He approached me, and without saying a word, knocked me down. Then he began beating on me, as if I were his worst enemy. My first direct contact with the Negro was over, and my feelings toward them were now quite definite.

4   Because of this process that occurred in my early life, I became so prejudiced against the Negro that I took many years to forget this prejudice once and for all. It was not just one of these steps that brought about my prejudice, but rather a combination of all of them.

WASTEFULNESS IN THE UNITED STATES

A Student Essay

1   The rise of industrialization, capitalism, and mass production in the United States has brought tremendous amounts of wastefulness among the people of this resource-abundant country.

"Planned obsolescence" has become a key factor in the making of modern-day products of all kinds. Wastefulness is found everywhere from the factory to the home.

2   The factory is an important part of our society today. It mass produces items of all shapes and sizes to be sent out to the people of our country. But today there is a key factor in the minds of designers and manufacturers of these products. This key factor is referred to by Vance Packard as "planned obsolescence." "Planned obsolescence" is the manufacturing of a product so that it will break down at a given time, usually closely determined by the designer of the product. Manufacturers today want their products to break down after a certain period of use. They feel that this wastefulness has to be because if they manufacture a product that will last for years and years, they are going to run themselves out of business from lack of consumers. Therefore they produce a car which will only have three good years in it or make a washing machine which will break down after two years' use. Through "planned obsolescence" they keep their sales booming by making the consumer come back year after year for a new model. "Planned obsolescence" is wastefulness because it creates a continuous throwing away process.

3   There is a huge amount of wastefulness found in the modern-day, mass-producing factory. Millions upon millions of identical products are produced weekly by a single factory. Are all of these products consumed? If not, where do the products go that are not consumed? Very definitely all that is manufactured is not consumed. And most of the time what is not consumed, which makes up a large part of what is produced, is thrown away. Not used again the next year, but merely thrown away as though our resources were endless.

4   The home is also a place where wastefulness can be found in abundance. A tin can is opened, the contents poured out, and the rest thrown away to be buried or burned. In many Oriental countries that tin can, which we throw away, is valuable beyond many Americans' imagination. But to us, with our endless wealth, it is merely a useless object to be gotten rid of. Another example of wastefulness found in the home can be seen when a person buys a bottle of glue or a can of whipped cream. Sure everyone thinks he is getting his money's worth, but manufacturers make the brush just long enough to use three-fourths of a bottle of glue, and they

make sure the can of whipped cream seems empty when it still is half full. One would be surprised to see how many people throw away a bottle of glue still a fourth full, because they are too lazy to put out a little extra effort to get the rest. These examples may seem trite, but they all add up to a huge amount of wastefulness going on in the United States today.

5   There is quite a difference between the modern-day American and an American who lived before mass production in the age of the craftsman. Back in the days when the craftsman could make a decent living, wastefulness was unheard of. People saved practically everything and cherished items which are readily thrown away today. There was just no wastefulness to speak of. It was a society which took great pride in their work and in what they owned. How can a person today take pride in what he owns? He usually does not keep it long enough even to get acquainted with it.

6   What will be the overall effect of this age of wastefulness now upon us? One effect might be that we will become so wasteful that we will start buying one-day products. Wear a suit one day and throw it away the next. Buy a car one day and trade it away the next. When and where will this wastefulness stop? I think the answer to this question lies in our natural resources which are being used up very readily. No one seems to realize that there is just so much as far as natural resources are concerned, and that when they are gone we must go also. Oh, but surely synthetic products will be made which are twice as good as the products of today. I would just as soon not take that chance.

• SUGGESTIONS •

Examine these two brief student essays to see which of the standard paragraph forms dictates each one's general pattern. Consider whether the ruling method seems appropriate to the subject and whether each paragraph properly accomplishes its purpose as a part of the general plan.

A Plan for Short and Intermediate Essays

Ever since you were in high school you have probably been periodically pestered by English teachers or others of that ilk telling you that a sound way to write an essay is to begin by knowing what you are going to do. They may have told you that one way to determine exactly what you are going to do in the essay is to work out a careful thesis statement. Such a thesis statement, formulated with care, is the basis for a second calculated outline procedure.

It should be understood at the outset that composing the kind of thesis statement necessary to plan an essay is no easy task. A one-sentence statement may indeed take more time than you may have been accustomed to devoting to entire outlines, for the thesis sentence should be an exact miniature of the essay to come, forecasting very part of the essay. To begin with, this thesis sentence should have only one independent clause. This is necessary to guarantee that your essay to follow develops only one central idea. Making your thesis sentence complex (rather than compound) is a means of unifying your essay. Having determined the one major point to be stated in your independent clause, you can then arrange your supporting points in a series of dependent constructions. These dependent constructions can be arranged around the independent statement in the order in which you wish to present your supporting points. Thus, for example, if you wish to build toward a climax, you can arrange the dependent constructions first in the sentence, withholding the main clause until the end. An essay carefully following such a thesis should build toward its main point at the end.

When the thesis sentence is completely composed, then you can convert each portion of this sentence into a sentence in its own right. Each of these sentences then becomes the topic sentence for a paragraph in the essay. These sentences can be arranged much as the thesis sentence was. Each should be either complex or simple, to assure that you have only one key point, with supporting points grouped appropriately around the topic idea.

The advantages of this plan are fairly easy to see. The deliberation necessary to compose your thesis sentence and topic sentences properly may help you to get slowed down and spend the necessary time in preparation *before* you start to write. The plan enables you to know before you write how many paragraphs you will have, what each of them is to do, and how they fit together. If you know how your paragraphs fit together from scrutiny of your thesis sentence, then the problem of managing continuity and transition will be more easily solved. Finally, if you have worked out the plan thoroughly, you can probably create a decent essay by supplying concrete illustrations to what you already have.

This plan, as the title of this subsection indicates, is primarily designed for short or medium-length essays, anything longer requiring an unwieldy thesis sentence. It can, however, be successfully used in long essays. If you employ, because of your own inclination or your instructor's, the traditional Roman-numeral, capital-letter, Arabic-numeral outline, this plan can be used to develop each Roman-numeral main heading.

HOW TO COACH A BASEBALL TEAM

A Student Essay

THESIS SENTENCE: If one satisfies certain prerequisites, including some knowledge of the rules, he may very well find himself coaching a baseball team of ten year olds, which will involve observing certain procedures in practice and in games and fulfilling such responsibilities as inducing sportsmanship.

TOPIC SENTENCE #1: There are certain prerequisites one has to satisfy before he undertakes such a coaching job.

TOPIC SENTENCE #2: One of these prerequisites is some knowledge of the rules.

TOPIC SENTENCE #3: Once I had apparently satisfied the prerequisites, I was then faced first with arranging proper procedures for practice.

TOPIC SENTENCE #4: When all of this is done, then I am faced with the actual games.

TOPIC SENTENCE #5: Through it all, there are certain responsibilities that a coach just has to accept.

TOPIC SENTENCE #6: Probably the major responsibility is inducing good sportsmanship.

(In the essay that follows, the thesis sentence and the topic sentences are italicized.)

1   Sometimes I wonder how it all came about, how I came to be owned, body, soul, and torn muscle, by the Alice Carlson Cubs. Sometimes late at night when I can't sleep because my legs ache, or early in the morning when I can't get up because my back is stiff, or in the middle of the day when I grow nauseated from the heat, sometimes I think it isn't real, that I've lost my mind and am suffering psychotic illusions. Other times I think it is all too real and I am already on earth being punished for sins I haven't even committed yet. Still other times, when the schedule gives us a day off and I can rest for a moment and be rational, I feel a little better about it all. *After all, I tell myself, if one satisfies certain prerequisites, including some knowledge of the rules, he may very well find himself coaching a baseball team of ten year olds, which will involve observing certain procedures in practice and in games, and fulfilling such responsibilities as inducing sportsmanship.*
2   *There are, of course, certain prerequisites one has to satisfy before he undertakes such a coaching job.* These requirements are not, however, what the uninitiated may expect. In a sane and proper world one would expect a coach to be a man with a keen interest in boys, a man of some athletic inclination and accomplishment, and a man dedicatedly believing in the importance of a sound body to house a sound mind. But a Ten-and-Under League is a world neither sane nor proper. Were these the requirements, I would have failed, for I satisfy none of them. Little boys, nearly hopeless in the singular, are intolerable in the plural. I can cite no spectacular accomplishments in athletics for myself, though I am given to watching baseball on the television. And I am by nature unequivocally opposed to exercise. Obviously, then, these are not the real requirements. The real requirements are only three: that one know a little something about baseball, that he have a son who wants to be on a team, and that he be available.

The first two I readily confess to; the third everyone assumes, for I am a schoolteacher, and everyone knows that they don't do anything in the summer or very much anytime.

3   *One of these prerequisites, I have said, is some knowledge of the rules.* Actually, there wasn't a very strenuous examination to see if I did know them. When the first game began and I sent nine boys out to play, the supervisors seemed satisfied and went away. And there I was, alone with them. Since, I have been troubled frequently about these rules. I think probably I did know most of them and they lingered quietly in the back of my mind. But some things I forgot. One team got two of our boys out because they didn't touch all of the bases. They both had gotten hits long enough to be home runs (that is, any hit that goes to the outfield) and were so overcome and kind of jumping up and down as they ran that they missed one of the bases and the other team got them out. I think I knew that they were supposed to touch all the bases, but I don't believe I had mentioned it to them. I believe I must have thought that they would be lucky to get around without falling down, much less worrying about bases and things like that.

4   So I try not to worry too much. The boys think I satisfy the requirements, and since there is so much else that I get upset about, I just try not to think about it. *Once I had apparently satisfied the prerequisites, I was then faced with arranging proper procedures for practice.* The Cubs practice on Mondays and Thursdays at 4:00, and that's bad enough with the heat and all, but that seems to bother me more than it does them. If I can get them there, there are always some things we have to work on. I yell a lot to get their attention. I insist that they can't all pitch. I try to get one of the bigger boys to catch. I remind them that they don't need to wear their uniforms to practice. I yell once in a while all along through the practice. I spend most of the time trying to get them to watch where the ball is. This is very important. We practice base running. This is very important too. Pitchers in this league are not known for their tight control. They walk many of the batters, and if the boys can run the bases well and know what to do, they make lots of runs. We won one game without ever getting a hit. Finally, at practice, I let them have batting practice, and I have to pitch because our pitchers can't throw near the plate consistently enough for the batters to practice hitting, and this

hurts because I am the slack-muscled type. I expect I have left something out, but that just means that this is a pretty accurate record of practice, since I nearly always forget something there too.

5   *Anyway, when all of this is done, then I am faced with the actual games.* Of course there's less to do at the games because the boys do the playing and they're alone out on the field. But there are some things that I have to do. I have to see to it that the boys get to the ball field, and I have to get there myself with the equipment, and it's quite heavy. Then I have to restrain them until the game starts and find out where the nearest restroom is because some of them get too excited. Then I have to go out in the stands and beg some man to umpire for us. It has to be a new man every time because once a man has done it, he's not likely to try it again. Sometimes catchers in our league don't catch but about a third of the pitches, and umpires get a little jumpy, and anyway they have to squat way over to get down even with the strike zone and that makes their legs knot up. When the game gets started and the Cubs are at bat, I try to get them to bat in order, and when they are out in the field I stand in the dugout and yell.

6   *Through it all, there are certain responsibilities that a coach just has to accept.* I have to go by and pick up boys that don't have rides. I have to sort of watch out for when their families go on vacation and hope that we always have nine boys left. Every time I get a chance I try to scrounge up some more umpires, and I'm always scouting for the location of restrooms near baseball fields.

7   *Probably the major responsibility, however, is inducing good sportsmanship.* I do my best, but it is very hard because when we lose I get mad myself. I teach them that they are not supposed to yell at the umpire. This is pretty easy; I encourage them in this a great deal. They think it's because of good sportsmanship, but actually it's because I'm hoping that if everybody is nice, the man who is umpiring will do it again. In the interests of sportsmanship every once in a while I shout "Good play there" to one of the players on the other team, and I console our players when they strike out. When the game is over, I get the boys to go over and either congratulate or console the other team. As for myself, when we win I get pretty expansive and very sportsman-like. When we lose, I yell some and then go home and pout.

The outline given with the essay eliminates the need for much commentary. Obviously, the thesis sentence requires considerable time and care in its composition, but just as obviously, once it is done, the essay is *completely* planned. The author here has used an introductory paragraph that provides some background and includes the thesis sentence, as shown by the *italics*. After that he has followed the plan shown, and one could probably assume that, since his plan was done and his continuity more or less assured, he was free to devote his whole energies to providing *specific* illustrations and to working on the manner of his presentation.

MY GOALS IN LIFE

A Student Essay

(A) *thesis sentence*

Although when I was younger I thought the only real goal in life was to achieve fame and fortune, my main goals now are getting a good education, getting a good job, marrying and raising a family, practicing fair play and honest business, the most important goal being to strive to do my best at achieving my goals.

(B) *topic sentence outline*

1. I first thought that the only goal in life was achieving fame and fortune.
2. My first goal is getting a good college education.
3. My second goal is getting a good job.
4. My third goal is marrying and raising a family.
5. My fourth goal is practicing fair play and honest business.
6. My most important goal is to do my best and strive my hardest to achieve my goals.

1   When I was young I had goals completely different from those I have today. I thought that the only real goal in life was achieving fame and fortune. I used to think of myself as someday being a famous business tycoon, who would rule the industrial world.

2   My thoughts toward my main goals in life have changed drastically since then. I have but a few goals in life, but I think they are important. My first goal is getting a good college education. This is of vital importance if I am to amount to anything. With a good college foundation I can achieve my goals.

3   My second goal is getting a good job once I finish my college education. I do not mean the highest paying job necessarily, but rather one that I will be satisfied with and can do my best at.

4   Another of my goals in life is marrying and raising a family. But it is important that this should be done after I get my job and am settled in it. Then I will be sure that my wife and children will have the proper atmosphere in which to live.

5   Another goal I will strive for is practicing fair play and honesty in my business. If one businessman wants to get ahead by cheating, it is up to him. As for me, I would just as soon earn my living through cooperation with other people.

6   Finally, I see one main goal in life which is of extreme importance. This is the goal I call striving to do my best at achieving my goals. What good are goals to a man if he is not going to work at achieving them? Maybe some men will never achieve their goals, but if they sought to achieve them, and actually did their best, then their satisfaction deserves to be as great as any man's.

THE FARM PROBLEM IN THE U.S.

A Student Essay

1   Ever since the administration of Franklin D. Roosevelt, the United States government has been gaining more and more controls in farming until the farmer no longer has the freedom to raise crops as he chooses. The farmer is bound by quotas on most of his produce, and even so much of his land must be turned over to soil bank or left for legumes.

2   Although business began in our country with the independent retailer, it was large industries that made our economy what it is today. The only thing the government did to retard this growth was to restrict business from getting so large that it could destroy all other businesses, charge unfair prices to the consumer,

and demand work from employees at substandard wages. But in the farm program the government has not allowed big farming to become part of our agricultural system. The government has made it possible, by enormous subsidization, to pay the small farmer enough for *not farming* that he has been able to stay on his farm. If free enterprise were in effect in our farm program, the small farmer would have to sell out to the big farmer and prepare himself for another occupation or hire himself as a tenant farmer. In this way, the large farmers would control the market by supply and demand; the government would not need to set quotas. In this way, the government would not put out almost $8 billion a year for grain storage, subsidization of the small farmer, and bureaucracy. Farming would demand educated men with an understanding of business and agricultural methods. They would recognize where they would lose money by over-production and what new crops would bring in greater profits; if prices were not high, this large business would cover the low profits. This type of free business would lower the artificially high prices which now exist because of government minimum price guarantees and would open U.S. agriculture to world competition.

3   Farmers are beginning to recognize their deplorable situation, and they are starting to do something about it. The most significant action taken so far by the farmer has been the rejection of the Kennedy wheat referendum last May 21. This referendum would enable the government to appropriate $700 million through taxes to pay the farmer anywhere from $50 to $15,000 for *farming less.* If the farmers voted yes, it would mean more idle fields, tighter government controls, and possibly more money for the individual farmer; if the farmers voted no, it would mean lower price supports, but more freedom to farm. The government put up a tremendous propaganda barrage to get the farmer to vote for the referendum; this included mailing absentee ballots to the farmers in some areas along with favorable literature to make him vote yes. However, the referendum was soundly defeated—not one major wheat state voted in favor of it. This was the first of thirteen referenda to be turned down. The president of the Farmer's Union, the only one of the six major farming unions to oppose the referendum, remarked, "This is the turning point in the battle against Big Government."

4   *Business Week* magazine calls our farm program ". . . in-

defensible from an economic point of view." The magazine further notes, "American consumers pay artificially high prices to support the program but the government is giving away surplus—free. . . . We have priced ourselves out of the world market." This surplus, if placed in freight cars, would make two continuous lines from New York City to San Francisco. To help pay for this and the other costs of the farm program the government appropriated $7.5 billion in 1963—if the referendum had passed, the 1964 cost would be almost $8.5 billion. What is most ironical about all this spending is that the farmer doesn't get much of this money. Our bureaucracy in Washington and in the several states amounts to one government farm administrator for every eleven farmers. An example of how expensive this is is in our corn quota program; it costs the government $27 to avoid production of a one dollar bushel of corn. It has also been shown that those areas where the farmers cooperate the most get the most allotments from Washington. A further example of the "indefensible" program is the "Crime of Stanley Yankus." Stanley Yankus was fined right off his farm for growing a small amount of wheat grain to feed his chickens. We may certainly wonder what kind of men are in control of our policies with examples like these: a top aide of Agricultural Secretary Orville Freeman put this sign up at a South Dakota fair referring to the farm situation, "FREE ENTERPRISE WRECKED THIS TRAIN."

5   Henry Hezlitt, deploring the farm situation, offers this solution: Before anything can be done the surpluses must be sold. Sell to each farmer an allotment of the surplus and he may accept it and sell it on the free world market, or reject it and the government will sell it for him and pay the difference in the price to him and the market selling price (the farmer's allotted price would be very small). When this has been done, the government must gradually get out of the farming business. With the money the government saves, the small farmers may be trained to take their place among our labor forces. These men won't be hard pressed because most of them own farms valued at at least $150 per acre. With this change the government will be saving $8 billion a year in about five years and will be making huge sums from taxes on large farmers and on the world trade. If this could be accomplished, the government would once again return to its constitutional position in our free society.

TOO MUCH LEISURE

A Student Essay

1   Everyone in the United States today loves and cherishes his leisure hours. Everyone looks forward to getting off from that rough six-, seven-, or maybe even eight-hour day and going home to relax with a good newspaper. And on the week-ends everyone flocks to the beaches, the movie theaters, and the baseball parks. There is nothing wrong with leisure time in a working man's life, but how much leisure time does he need?

2   I think there is too much leisure in today's society. I have worked at many good, full-time summer jobs, where I have put in nine and ten hours a day for six days a week. I looked forward to my leisure time, and I couldn't have got along without it. But I also believed in working a long hard day, so that I would at least deserve the leisure hours that I got. Many men today, and the number is growing, do not even work a long enough day to deserve any leisure time. None of them seem to realize the harm it is doing to them and future generations.

3   A very good example of excess leisure can be found by looking at the labor unions, who want shorter working days. Some are only working six-hour days at ridiculously high pay scales. And they are even trying to get these hours cut, and at the same time to get higher salaries. What more do they want? When will they be satisfied; at a five-, four-, or three-hour working day?

4   Society in the future will be greatly affected by this rise in the number of leisure hours. People will become lazy, incompetent, and will not be able to act for themselves unless they are told what to do by their labor unions. If only people of today could realize this, future generations could know the satisfaction of work. The more leisure time people acquire for themselves, the lazier they are going to get. How can anything else result? A person who works so little of the time and plays so much of the time is bound to become lazy. And when a worker becomes lazy, his mind wanders, and he loses interest in his work. This leads to incompetent workmanship, which our society has too much of already. A sort of "chain reaction" occurs, starting with too much

leisure time and going through the worker to the product, which ends up with the consumer. There are also going to rise in the future strong labor unions, which will have so much control over the workers, that they will be lost unless they are told what to do at all times. We have strong labor unions today, but they will be nothing compared with these labor unions of the future. There goes man's freedom. We will return to a Middle Age feudalism system, where man will be ruled over by a lord, who will be the head of the labor union. Man will be told when to work, what to work at, and how much to produce. He can hardly say he has freedom when this occurs.

5   What can be done about this growing problem of too much leisure time? Is there a solution, or has it already gone too far out of hand? I see no solution until people begin to realize the harm that can be done by too much leisure. Nor do I think a solution will be found, because I honestly do not think that people want to find the harm that can be done by too much leisure. All they think about is fun and relaxation. Work is a bore and a burden. Can no one be satisfied? I will be proud to say, I did a full and worthwhile day's work.

• SUGGESTIONS •

These student essays are offered as illustrations of a way of planning essays, not as illustrations of the finest prose style and artistic competence. Each has the virtue of being decently and logically planned, which can be a major accomplishment. The first is given with the plan upon which it is based. It is a simple, very brief essay, which serves only to indicate that planning beforehand guarantees some logical development and continuity. For the second and third essays the outlines have not been given. After examining these two essays see if you can determine their thesis sentences and the topic sentences that were developed from the theses.

A Plan for Longer Essays

For organizing longer essays, you may find the method of the classical oration useful. There is no reason why this system should not be employed; it has been successfully developed and used for two thousand years. Cicero followed a plan like this, as did Milton, Dryden, and countless other major prose stylists of our culture. It is in many respects easier to use than the standard Roman-numeral outline because it shows the relationship among parts more clearly.

The first step in this plan is the *exordium* or *proem.* This is the introduction, and it is the occasion for you to attract the attention of your audience, to establish your authority for saying what you have to say, and to arouse the sympathy of your audience. The second step, or *narratio,* is the presentation of any pertinent background material for the subject at hand. The third step, or *propositio,* is approximately the same as the thesis statement. It is a statement of the specific point you hope to explain or to prove. When that is clear, the next step is the *partitio,* which typically announces the divisions of the subject to be discussed and in effect explains the procedure you are going to follow. Then you can proceed to the *confirmatio,* which is the body of your discussion, the support for your proposition, and which is likely to be the largest part of your essay. If your approach is argumentative, you may then offer the section called the *reprehensio,* or refutation of opposing positions. The final step is the *peroratio,* or general conclusion. It should be understood that while this sequence of steps is probably the most common, the parts of the plan may be re-arranged to serve your interests if you wish to get some special effect. And this plan has a further—and lovely—advantage; traditionally this system allows for digressions. The *digressio* should make this method of organizing especially attractive.

Examples of the use of this plan other than those which follow include Milton's *Areopagitica,* his essay "Of Education," Dryden's "Essay of Dramatic Poesy," Wordsworth's Preface to *Lyrical Ballads,* and many others. It has the sanction of long and brilliant use.

ON THE ADVISABLENESS OF IMPROVING
NATURAL KNOWLEDGE [1866]

Thomas Henry Huxley

1   This time two hundred years ago—in the beginning of January, 1866—those of our forefathers who inhabited this great

and ancient city, took breath between the shocks of two fearful calamities, one not quite past, although its fury had abated; the other to come.

2 Within a few yards of the very spot on which we are assembled, so the tradition runs, that painful and deadly malady, the plague, appeared in the latter months of 1664; and, though no new visitor, smote the people of England, and especially of her capital, with a violence unknown before, in the course of the following year. The hand of a master has pictured what happened in those dismal months; and in that truest of fictions, *The History of the Plague Year,* Defoe shows death, with every accompaniment of pain and terror, stalking through the narrow streets of old London, and changing their busy hum into a silence broken only by the wailing of the mourners of fifty thousand dead; by the woeful denunciations and mad prayers of fanatics; and by the madder yells of despairing profligates.

3 But, about this time in 1666, the death rate had sunk to nearly its ordinary amount; a case of plague occurred only here and there, and the richer citizens who had flown from the pest had returned to their dwellings. The remnant of the people began to toil at the accustomed round of duty, or of pleasure; and the stream of city life bid fair to flow back along its old bed, with renewed and uninterrupted vigor.

4 The newly kindled hope was deceitful. The great plague, indeed, returned no more; but what it had done for the Londoners, the great fire, which broke out in the autumn of 1666, did for London; and, in September of that year, a heap of ashes and the indestructible energy of the people were all that remained of the glory of five-sixths of the city within the walls.

5 Our forefathers had their own ways of accounting for each of these calamities. They submitted to the plague in humility and in penitence, for they believed it to be the judgment of God. But towards the fire they were furiously indignant, interpreting it as the effect of the malice of man—as the work of the Republicans, or of the Papists, according as their prepossessions ran in favor of loyalty or of Puritanism.

6 It would, I fancy, have fared but ill with one who, standing where I now stand, in what was then a thickly-peopled and fashionable part of London, should have broached to our ancestors the doctrine which I now propound to you—that all their hypotheses were alike wrong; that the plague was no more, in their sense,

a Divine judgment, than the fire was the work of any political, or of any religious sect; but that they were themselves the authors of both plague and fire, and that they must look to themselves to prevent the recurrence of calamities, to all appearance so peculiarly beyond the reach of human control—so evidently the result of the wrath of God, or of the craft and subtlety of an enemy.

7   And one may picture to oneself how harmoniously the holy cursing of the Puritan of that day would have chimed in with the unholy cursing and the crackling wit of the Rochesters and Sedleys, and with the revilings of the political fanatics, if my imaginary plain dealer had gone on to say that, if the return of such misfortunes were ever rendered impossible, it would not be in virtue of the victory of the faith of Laud, or of that of Milton; and, as little, by the triumph of republicanism, as by that of monarchy. But that the one thing needful for compassing this end was that the people of England should second the efforts of an insignificant corporation, the establishment of which, a few years before the epoch of the great plague and the great fire, had been as little noticed, as they were conspicuous.

8   Some twenty years before the outbreak of the plague a few calm and thoughtful students banded themselves together for the purpose, as they phrased it, of "improving natural knowledge." The ends they proposed to attain cannot be stated more clearly than in the words of one of the founders of the organization:

9   "Our business was (precluding matters of theology and state affairs) to discourse and consider of philosophical inquiries, and such as related thereunto: as Physick, Anatomy, Geometry, Astronomy, Navigation, Staticks, Magneticks, Chymicks, Mechanicks, and Natural Experiments; with the state of these studies and their cultivation at home and abroad. We then discoursed of the circulation of the blood, the valves in the veins, the venae lacteae, the lymphatic vessels, the Copernican hypothesis, the nature of comets and new stars, the satellites of Jupiter, the oval shape (as it then appeared) of Saturn, the spots on the sun and its turning on its own axis, the inequalities and selenography of the moon, the several phases of Venus and Mercury, the improvement of telescopes and grinding of glasses for that purpose, the weight of air, the possibility or impossibility of vacuities and nature's abhorrence thereof, the Torricellian experiment in quicksilver, the

descent of heavy bodies and the degree of acceleration therein, with diverse other things of like nature, some of which were then but new discoveries, and others not so generally known and embraced as now they are; with other things appertaining to what hath been called the New Philosophy, which from the times of Galileo at Florence, and Sir Francis Bacon (Lord Verulam) in England, hath been much cultivated in Italy, France, Germany, and other parts abroad, as well as with us in England."

10   The learned Dr. Wallis, writing in 1696, narrates in these words, what happened half a century before, or about 1645. The associates met at Oxford, in the rooms of Dr. Wilkins, who was destined to become a bishop; and subsequently coming together in London, they attracted the notice of the king. And it is a strange evidence of the taste for knowledge which the most obviously worthless of the Stuarts shared with his father and grandfather, that Charles the Second was not content with saying witty things about his philosophers, but did wise things with regard to them. For he not only bestowed upon them such attention as he could spare from his poodles and his mistresses, but, being in his usual state of impecuniosity, begged for them of the Duke of Ormond; and, that step being without effect, gave them Chelsea College, a charter, and a mace: crowning his favors in the best way they could be crowned, by burdening them no further with royal patronage or state interference.

11   Thus it was that the half-dozen young men, studious of the "New Philosophy," who met in one another's lodgings in Oxford or in London, in the middle of the seventeenth century, grew in numerical and in real strength, until, in its latter part, the "Royal Society for the Improvement of Natural Knowledge" had already become famous, and had acquired a claim upon the veneration of Englishmen, which it has ever since retained, as the principal focus of scientific activity in our islands, and the chief champion of the cause it was formed to support.

12   It was by the aid of the Royal Society that Newton published his *Principia*. If all the books in the world, except the *Philosophical Transactions,* were destroyed, it is safe to say that the foundations of physical science would remain unshaken, and that the vast intellectual progress of the last two centuries would be largely, though incompletely, recorded. Nor have any signs of halting or of decrepitude manifested themselves in our own times.

As in Dr. Wallis's days, so in these, "our business is, precluding theology and state affairs, to discourse and consider of philosophical inquiries." But our "Mathematick" is one which Newton would have to go to school to learn; our "Staticks, Mechanicks, Magneticks, Chymicks, and Natural Experiments" constitute a mass of physical and chemical knowledge, a glimpse at which would compensate Galileo for the doings of a score of inquisitorial cardinals; our "Physick" and "Anatomy" have embraced such infinite varieties of being, have laid open such new worlds in time and space, have grappled, not unsuccessfully, with such complex problems, that the eyes of Vesalius and of Harvey might be dazzled by the sight of the tree that has grown out of their grain of mustard seed.

13   The fact is perhaps rather too much, than too little, forced upon one's notice, nowadays, that all this marvelous intellectual growth has a no less wonderful expression in practical life; and that, in this respect, if in no other, the movement symbolized by the progress of the Royal Society stands without a parallel in the history of mankind.

14   A series of volumes as bulky as the *Transactions* of the Royal Society might possibly be filled with the subtle speculations of the schoolmen; not improbably, the obtaining a mastery over the products of medieval thought might necessitate an even greater expenditure of time and of energy than the acquirement of the "New Philosophy"; but though such work engrossed the best intellects of Europe for a longer time than has elapsed since the great fire, its effects were "writ in water," so far as our social state is concerned.

15   On the other hand, if the noble first President of the Royal Society could revisit the upper air and once more gladden his eyes with a sight of the familiar mace, he would find himself in the midst of a material civilization more different from that of his day than that of the seventeenth was from that of the first century. And if Lord Brouncker's native sagacity had not deserted his ghost, he would need no long reflection to discover that all these ships, these railways, these telegraphs, these factories, these printing presses, without which the whole fabric of modern English society would collapse into a mass of stagnant and starving pauperism—that all these pillars of our State are but the ripple and the bubbles upon the surface of that great spiritual stream, the

springs of which, only, he and his fellows were privileged to see; and seeing, to recognize as that which it behoved them above all things to keep pure and undefiled.

16 It may not be too great a flight of imagination to conceive our noble *revenant* not forgetful of the great troubles of his own day, and anxious to know how often London had been burned down since his time, and how often the plague had carried off its thousands. He would have to learn that, although London contains tenfold the inflammable matter that it did in 1666; though, not content with filling our rooms with woodwork and light draperies, we must needs lead inflammable and explosive gases into every corner of our streets and houses, we never allow even a street to burn down. And if he asked how this had come about, we should have to explain that the improvement of natural knowledge had furnished us with dozens of machines for throwing water upon fires, any one of which would have furnished the ingenious Mr. Hooke, the first "curator and experimenter" of the Royal Society, with ample materials for discourse before half a dozen meetings of that body; and that, to say truth, except for the progress of natural knowledge, we should not have been able to make even the tools by which these machines are constructed. And, further, it would be necessary to add that, although severe fires sometimes occur and inflict great damage, the loss is very generally compensated by societies, the operations of which have been rendered possible only by the progress of natural knowledge in the direction of mathematics, and the accumulation of wealth in virtue of other natural knowledge.

17 But the plague? My Lord Brouncker's observation would not, I fear, lead him to think that Englishmen of the nineteenth century are purer in life, or more fervent in religious faith, than the generation which could produce a Boyle, an Evelyn, and a Milton. He might find the mud of society at the bottom instead of at the top, but I fear that the sum total would be as deserving of swift judgment as at the time of the Restoration. And it would be our duty to explain once more, and this time not without shame, that we have no reason to believe that it is the improvement of our faith, nor that of our morals, which keeps the plague from our city; but, again, that it is the improvement of our natural knowledge.

18 We have learned that pestilences will only take up their

abode among those who have prepared unswept and ungarnished residences for them. Their cities must have narrow, unwatered streets, foul with accumulated garbage. Their houses must be ill-drained, ill-lighted, ill-ventilated. Their subjects must be ill-washed, ill-fed, ill-clothed. The London of 1665 was such a city. The cities of the East, where plague has an enduring dwelling, are such cities. We, in later times, have learned somewhat of nature, and partly obey her. Because of this partial improvement of our natural knowledge and of that fractional obedience, we have no plague; because that knowledge is still very imperfect and that obedience yet incomplete, typhus is our companion and cholera our visitor; but it is not presumptuous to express the belief that, when our knowledge is more complete and our obedience the expression of our knowledge, London will count her centuries of freedom from typhus and cholera, as she now gratefully reckons her two hundred years of ignorance of that plague, which swooped upon her thrice in the first half of the seventeenth century.

19   Surely, there is nothing in these explanations which is not fully borne out by the facts? Surely, the principles involved in them are now admitted among the fixed beliefs of all thinking men? Surely, it is true that our countrymen are less subject to fire, famine, pestilence, and all the evils which result from a want of command over and due anticipation of the course of nature, than were the countrymen of Milton; and health, wealth, and well-being are more abundant with us than with them? But no less certainly is the difference due to the improvement of our knowledge of nature, and the extent to which that improved knowledge has been incorporated with the household words of men, and has supplied the springs of their daily actions.

20   Granting for a moment, then, the truth of that which the depreciators of natural knowledge are so fond of urging, that its improvement can only add to the resources of our material civilization; admitting it to be possible that the founders of the Royal Society themselves looked for no other reward than this, I cannot confess that I was guilty of exaggeration when I hinted, that to him who had the gift of distinguishing between prominent events and important events, the origin of a combined effort on the part of mankind to improve natural knowledge might have loomed larger than the Plague and have outshone the glare of the Fire; as a something fraught with a wealth of beneficence to mankind,

in comparison with which the damage done by those ghastly evils would shrink into insignificance.

21   It is very certain that for every victim slain by the plague, hundreds of mankind exist and find a fair share of happiness in the world by the aid of the spinning jenny. And the great fire, at its worst, could not have burned the supply of coal, the daily working of which, in the bowels of the earth, made possible by the steam pump, gives rise to an amount of wealth to which the millions lost in old London are but as an old song.

22   But spinning jenny and steam pump are, after all, but toys, possessing an accidental value; and natural knowledge creates multitudes of more subtle contrivances, the praises of which do not happen to be sung because they are not directly convertible into instruments for creating wealth. When I contemplate natural knowledge squandering such gifts among men, the only appropriate comparison I can find for her is, to liken her to such a peasant woman as one sees in the Alps, striding ever upward, heavily burdened, and with mind bent only on her home; but yet, without effort and without thought, knitting for her children. Now stockings are good and comfortable things, and the children will undoubtedly be much better for them; but surely it would be short-sighted, to say the least of it, to depreciate this toiling mother as a mere stocking-machine—a mere provider of physical comforts?

23   However, there are blind leaders of the blind, and not a few of them, who take this view of natural knowledge, and can see nothing in the bountiful mother of humanity but a sort of comfort-grinding machine. According to them, the improvement of natural knowledge always has been, and always must be synonymous with no more than the improvement of the material resources and the increase of the gratifications of men.

24   Natural knowledge is, in their eyes, no real mother of mankind, bringing them up with kindness, and, if need be, with sternness in the way they should go, and instructing them in all things needful for their welfare; but a sort of fairy godmother, ready to furnish her pets with shoes of swiftness, swords of sharpness, and omnipotent Aladdin's lamps, so that they may have telegraphs to Saturn, and see the other side of the moon, and thank God they are better than their benighted ancestors.

25   If this talk were true, I, for one, should not greatly care

to toil in the service of natural knowledge. I think I would just as soon be quietly chipping my own flint ax, after the manner of my forefathers a few thousand years back, as be troubled with the endless malady of thought which now infests us all, for such reward. But I venture to say that such views are contrary alike to reason and to fact. Those who discourse in such fashion seem to me to be so intent upon trying to see what is above nature, or what is behind her, that they are blind to what stares them in the face, in her.

26   I should not venture to speak thus strongly if my justification were not to be found in the simplest and most obvious facts—if it needed more than an appeal to the most notorious truths to justify my assertion, that the improvement of natural knowledge, whatever direction it has taken, and however low the aims of those who may have commenced it—has not only conferred practical benefits on men, but, in so doing, has effected a revolution in their conceptions of the universe and of themselves, and has profoundly altered their modes of thinking and their views of right and wrong. I say that natural knowledge, seeking to satisfy natural wants, has found the ideas which can alone still spiritual cravings. I say that natural knowledge, in desiring to ascertain the laws of comfort, has been driven to discover those of conduct, and to lay the foundations of a new morality.

27   Let us take these points separately; and, first, what great ideas has natural knowledge introduced into men's minds?

28   I cannot but think that the foundations of all natural knowledge were laid when the reason of man first came face to face with the facts of nature; when the savage first learned that the fingers of one hand are fewer than those of both; that it is shorter to cross a stream than to head it; that a stone stops where it is unless it be moved, and that it drops from the hand which lets it go; that light and heat come and go with the sun; that sticks burn away in a fire; that plants and animals grow and die; that if he struck his fellow savage a blow he would make him angry, and perhaps get a blow in return; while if he offered him a fruit he would please him, and perhaps receive a fish in exchange. When men had acquired this much knowledge, the outlines, rude though they were, of mathematics, of physics, of chemistry, of biology, of moral, economical, and political science, were sketched. Nor did the germ of religion fail when science began to bud.

Listen to words which, though new, are yet three thousand years old:

> . . . When in heaven the stars about the moon
> Look beautiful, when all the winds are laid,
> And every height comes out, and jutting peak
> And valley, and the immeasurable heavens
> Break open to their highest, and all the stars
> Shine, and the shepherd gladdens in his heart.

But, if the half-savage Greek could share our feelings thus far, it is irrational to doubt that he went further, to find, as we do, that upon that brief gladness there follows a certain sorrow—the little light of awakened human intelligence shines so mere a spark amidst the abyss of the unknown and unknowable; seems so insufficient to do more than illuminate the imperfections that cannot be remedied, the aspirations that cannot be realized, of man's own nature. But in this sadness, this consciousness of the limitation of man, this sense of an open secret which he cannot penetrate, lies the essence of all religion; and the attempt to embody it in the forms furnished by the intellect is the origin of the higher theologies.

29   Thus it seems impossible to imagine but that the foundations of all knowledge—secular or sacred—were laid when intelligence dawned, though the superstructure remained for long ages so slight and feeble as to be compatible with the existence of almost any general view respecting the mode of governance of the universe. No doubt, from the first, there were certain phenomena which, to the rudest mind, presented a constancy of occurrence, and suggested that a fixed order ruled, among them at any rate. I doubt if the grossest of fetish worshippers ever imagined that a stone must have a god within it to make it fall, or that a fruit had a god within it to make it taste sweet. With regard to such matters as these, it is hardly questionable that mankind from the first took strictly positive and scientific views.

30   But, with respect to all the less familiar occurrences which present themselves, uncultured man, no doubt, has always taken himself as a standard of comparison, as the center and measure of the world; nor could he well avoid doing so. And finding that his apparently uncaused will has a powerful effect in giving rise to many occurrences, he naturally enough ascribed other and

greater events to other and greater volitions, and came to look
upon the world and all that therein is, as the product of the volitions of persons like himself, but stronger, and capable of being
appeased or angered, as he himself might be smoothed or irritated.
Through such conceptions of the plan and working of the universe
all mankind have passed, or are passing. And we may now consider what has been the effect of the improvement of natural
knowledge on the views of men who have reached this stage, and
who have begun to cultivate natural knowledge with no desire
but that of "increasing God's honor and bettering man's estate."

31   For example: what could seem wiser, from a mere material point of view, more innocent from a theological one, to an
ancient people, than that they should learn the exact succession
of the seasons, as warnings for their husbandmen; or the position
of the stars, as guides to their rude navigators? But what has grown
out of this search for natural knowledge of so merely useful a
character? You all know the reply. Astronomy—which of all sciences has filled men's minds with general ideas of a character most
foreign to their daily experience, and has, more than any other,
rendered it impossible for them to accept the beliefs of their
fathers. Astronomy—which tells them that this so vast and seemingly solid earth is but an atom among atoms, whirling, no man
knows whither, through illimitable space; which demonstrates that
what we call the peaceful heaven above us, is but that space,
filled by an infinitely subtle matter whose particles are seething
and surging, like the waves of an angry sea; which opens up to us
infinite regions where nothing is known, or ever seems to have
been known, but matter and force, operating according to rigid
rules; which leads us to contemplate phenomena the very nature
of which demonstrates that they must have had a beginning, and
that they must have an end, but the very nature of which also
proves that the beginning was, to our conceptions of time, infinitely remote, and that the end is as immeasurably distant.

32   But it is not alone those who pursue astronomy who ask
for bread and receive ideas. What more harmless than the attempt
to lift and distribute water by pumping it; what more absolutely
and grossly utilitarian? But out of pumps grew the discussions
about nature's abhorrence of a vacuum; and then it was discovered
that nature does not abhor a vacuum, but that air has weight; and
that notion paved the way for the doctrine that all matter has

weight, and that the force which produces weight is co-extensive with the universe—in short, to the theory of universal gravitation and endless force. And learning how to handle gases led to the discovery of oxygen and to modern chemistry, and to the notion of the indestructibility of matter.

33   Again, what simpler, or more absolutely practical, than the attempt to keep the axle of a wheel from heating when the wheel turns round very fast? How useful for carters and gig drivers to know something about this; and how good were it, if any ingenious person would find out the cause of such phenomena, and thence educe a general remedy for them. Such an ingenious person was Count Rumford; and he and his successors have landed us in the theory of the persistence or indestructibility of force. And in the infinitely minute, as in the infinitely great, the seekers after natural knowledge of the kinds called physical and chemical, have everywhere found a definite order and succession of events which seem never to be infringed.

34   And how has it fared with "Physick" and Anatomy? Have the anatomist, the physiologist, or the physician, whose business it has been to devote themselves assiduously to that eminently practical and direct end, the alleviation of the sufferings of mankind—have they been able to confine their vision more absolutely to the strictly useful? I fear they are the worst offenders of all. For if the astronomer has set before us the infinite magnitude of space, and the practical eternity of the duration of the universe; if the physical and chemical philosophers have demonstrated the infinite minuteness of its constituent parts, and the practical eternity of matter and of force; and if both have alike proclaimed the universality of a definite and predicable order and succession of events, the workers in biology have not only accepted all these, but have added more startling theses of their own. For, as the astronomers discover in the earth no center of the universe, but an eccentric speck, so the naturalists find man to be no center of the living world, but one amidst endless modifications of life; and as the astronomer observes the mark of practically endless time set upon the arrangements of the solar system, so the student of life finds the records of ancient forms of existence peopling the world for ages, which, in relation to human experience, are infinite.

35   Furthermore, the physiologist finds life to be as depend-

ent for its manifestation on particular molecular arrangements as any physical or chemical phenomenon; and, wherever he extends his researches, fixed order and unchanging causation reveal themselves, as plainly as in the rest of nature.

36   Nor can I find that any other fate has awaited the germ of Religion. Arising, like all other kinds of knowledge, out of the action and interaction of man's mind, with that which is not man's mind, it has taken the intellectual coverings of Fetishism or Polytheism; of Theism or Atheism; of Superstition or Rationalism. With these, and their relative merits and demerits, I have nothing to do; but this it is needful for my purpose to say, that if the religion of the present differs from that of the past, it is because the theology of the present has become more scientific than that of the past; because it has not only renounced idols of wood and idols of stone, but begins to see the necessity of breaking in pieces the idols built up of books and traditions and fine-spun ecclesiastical cobwebs; and of cherishing the noblest and most human of man's emotions, by worship "for the most part of the silent sort" at the altar of the Unknown and Unknowable.

37   Such are a few of the new conceptions implanted in our minds by the improvement of natural knowledge. Men have acquired the ideals of the practically infinite extent of the universe and of its practical eternity; they are familiar with the conception that our earth is but an infinitesimal fragment of that part of the universe which can be seen; and that, nevertheless, its duration is, as compared with our standards of time, infinite. They have further acquired the idea that man is but one of innumerable forms of life now existing on the globe, and that the present existences are but the last of an immeasurable series of predecessors. Furthermore, every step they have made in natural knowledge has tended to extend and rivet in their minds the conception of a definite order of the universe—which is embodied in what are called, by an unhappy metaphor, the laws of nature—and to narrow the range and loosen the force of men's belief in spontaneity, or in changes other than such as arise out of that definite order itself.

38   Whether these ideas are well or ill founded is not the question. No one can deny that they exist, and have been the inevitable outgrowth of the improvement of natural knowledge. And if so, it cannot be doubted that they are changing the form of men's most cherished and most important convictions.

39   And as regards the second point—the extent to which the improvement of natural knowledge has remodeled and altered what may be termed the intellectual ethics of men—what are among the moral convictions most fondly held by barbarous and semi-barbarous people?

40   They are the convictions that authority is the soundest basis of belief; that merit attaches to a readiness to believe; that the doubting disposition is a bad one, and skepticism a sin; that when good authority has pronounced what is to be believed, and faith has accepted it, reason has no further duty. There are many excellent persons who yet hold by these principles, and it is not my present business, or intention, to discuss their views. All I wish to bring clearly before your minds is the unquestionable fact that the improvement of natural knowledge is affected by methods which directly give the lie to all these convictions, and assume the exact reverse of each to be true.

41   The improver of natural knowledge absolutely refuses to acknowledge authority, as such. For him, skepticism is the highest of duties; blind faith the one unpardonable sin. And it cannot be otherwise, for every great advance in natural knowledge has involved the absolute rejection of authority, the cherishing of the keenest skepticism, the annihilation of the spirit of blind faith; and the most ardent votary of science holds his firmest convictions, not because the men he most venerates hold them; not because their verity is testified by portents and wonders; but because his experience teaches him that whenever he chooses to bring these convictions into contact with their primary source, nature—whenever he thinks fit to test them by appealing to experiment and to observation—nature will confirm them. The man of science has learned to believe in justification, not by faith, but by verification.

42   Thus, without for a moment pretending to despise the practical results of the improvement of natural knowledge, and its beneficial influence on material civilization, it must, I think, be admitted that the great ideas, some of which I have indicated, and the ethical spirit which I have endeavored to sketch, in the few moments which remained at my disposal, constitute the real and permanent significance of natural knowledge.

43   If these ideas be destined, as I believe they are, to be more and more firmly established as the world grows older; if that spirit be fated, as I believe it is, to extend itself into all departments of human thought, and to become co-extensive with the

range of knowledge; if, as our race approaches its maturity, it discovers, as I believe it will, that there is but one kind of knowledge and but one method of acquiring it; then we, who are still children, may justly feel it our highest duty to recognize the advisableness of improving natural knowledge, and so to aid ourselves and our successors in our course towards the noble goal which lies before mankind.

· COMMENTARY ·

The first two paragraphs here act as *proem* or *exordium*. Huxley introduces the two great calamities that came to London and uses the first, the plague, to set the stage for the extensive background material that is to follow. Paragraphs three through eighteen then provide the background or *narratio*. Here he uses the two calamities and the disputes about their causes to prepare for his proposition. Included in this section, along with discussion of the controversies over fancied and real causes for fire and plague, is a brief account of the early history of the Royal Society.

Bringing his background to a close with paragraph eighteen, in which he summarizes the advance of knowledge to the present, Huxley then moves into the development of his *propositio*. This works out from paragraph nineteen, culminating in paragraph twenty-six, where Huxley states his main point, that as science seeks to satisfy natural wants, it finds the great ideas.

The two paragraphs which follow (twenty-seven and twenty-eight) function as the *partitio*, as Huxley forecasts discussion of the two parts of his proposition. Paragraphs twenty-nine through thirty-six comprise his *confirmatio*, as he piles up illustrations to show that man in the search for bread found ideas as well. In his *reprehensio* (paragraphs thirty-seven through forty-one) he continues to assert the importance of improving natural knowledge, but here he does so partly by denying opposing viewpoints stemming from authority or tradition. This section closes with the famous statement (paragraph forty-one) of the value of skepticism. The last two paragraphs form his *peroratio*; there is no *digressio*.

AN ARGUMENT AGAINST ABOLISHING

CHRISTIANITY [1708]

Jonathan Swift

1   I am very sensible what a Weakness and Presumption it is, to reason against the general Humour and Disposition of the World. I remember it was with great Justice, and a due Regard to the Freedom both of the Publick and the Press, forbidden upon severe Penalties to write or discourse, or lay Wagers against the *Union,* even before it was confirmed by Parliament: Because that was looked upon as a Design to oppose the Current of the People; which besides the Folly of it, is a manifest Breach of the Fundamental Law, that makes this Majority of Opinion the Voice of God. In like Manner, and for the very same Reasons, it may perhaps be neither safe nor prudent to argue against the Abolishing of Christianity, at a Juncture when all Parties appear so unanimously determined upon the Point; as we cannot but allow from their Actions, their Discourses, and their Writings. However, I know not how, whether from the Affectation of Singularity, or the Perverseness of human Nature; but so it unhappily falls out, that I cannot be entirely of this Opinion. Nay, although I were sure an Order were issued out for my immediate Prosecution by the Attorney-General; I should still confess, that in the present Posture of our Affairs at home or abroad, I do not yet see the absolute Necessity of extirpating the Christian Religion from among us.

2   This perhaps may appear too great a Paradox, even for our wise and paradoxical Age to endure: Therefore I shall handle it with all Tenderness, and with the utmost Deference to that great and profound Majority, which is of another Sentiment.

3   And yet the Curious may please to observe, how much the Genius of a Nation is liable to alter in half an Age: I have heard it affirmed for certain by some very old People, that the contrary Opinion was even in their Memories as much in Vogue as the other is now; and, that a Project for the Abolishing of Christianity would then have appeared as singular, and been thought as absurd, as it would be at this Time to write or discourse in its Defence.

4   Therefore I freely own, that all Appearances are against

me. The System of the Gospel, after the Fate of other Systems, is generally antiquated and exploded; and the Mass or Body of the common People, among whom it seems to have had its latest Credit, are now grown as much ashamed of it as their Betters: Opinions, like Fashions always descending from those of Quality to the middle Sort, and thence to the Vulgar, where at length they are dropt and vanish.

5   But there I would not be mistaken; and must therefore be so bold as to borrow a Distinction from the Writers on the other Side, when they make a Difference between nominal and real *Trinitarians.* I hope, no Reader imagines me so weak to stand up in the Defence of *real* Christianity; such as used in primitive Times (if we may believe the Authors of those Ages) to have an Influence upon Mens Belief and Actions: To offer at the Restoring of that, would indeed be a wild Project; it would be to dig up Foundations; to destroy at one Blow *all* the Wit, and *half* the Learning of the Kingdom; to break the entire Frame and Constitution of Things; to ruin Trade, extinguish Arts and Sciences with the Professors of them; in short, to turn our Courts, Exchanges and Shops into Desarts: And would be full as absurd as the Proposal of *Horace,* where he advises the *Romans,* all in a Body, to leave their City, and seek a new Seat in some remote Part of the World, by Way of Cure for the Corruption of their Manners.

6   Therefore, I think this Caution was in it self altogether unnecessary, (which I have inserted only to prevent all Possibility of cavilling) since every candid Reader will easily understand my Discourse to be intended only in Defence of *nominal* Christianity; the other having been for some Time wholly laid aside by general Consent, as utterly inconsistent with our present Schemes of Wealth and Power.

7   But why we should therefore cast off the Names and Title of Christians, although the general Opinion and Resolution be so violent for it; I confess I cannot (with Submission) apprehend the Consequence necessary. However, since the Undertakers propose such wonderful Advantages to the Nation by this Project; and advance many plausible Objections against the System of Christianity; I shall briefly consider the Strength of both; fairly allow them their greatest Weight, and offer such Answers as I think most reasonable. After which I will beg leave to shew what Inconveniencies may possibly happen by such an Innovation, in the present Posture of our Affairs.

8   *First,* One great Advantage proposed by the Abolishing
of Christianity is, That it would very much enlarge and establish
Liberty of Conscience, that great Bulwark of our Nation, and of
the *Protestant* Religion, which is still too much limited by *Priest-
Craft,* notwithstanding all the good Intentions of the Legislature;
as we have lately found by a severe Instance. For it is confidently
reported, that two young Gentlemen of great Hopes, bright Wit,
and profound Judgment, who upon a thorough Examination of
Causes and Effects, and by the meer Force of natural Abilities,
without the least Tincture of Learning; having made a Discovery,
that there was no God, and generously communicating their
Thoughts for the Good of the Publick; were some Time ago, by an
unparalleled Severity, and upon I know not what *obsolete* Law,
broke *only* for *Blasphemy.* And as it hath been wisely observed;
if Persecution once begins, no Man alive knows how far it may
reach, or where it will end.

9   In Answer to all which, with Deference to wiser Judgments; I think this rather shews the Necessity of a *nominal* Religion among us. Great Wits love to be free with the highest
Objects; and if they cannot be allowed a *God* to revile or renounce; they will *speak Evil of Dignities,* abuse the Government,
and reflect upon the Ministry; which I am sure, few will deny
to be of much more pernicious Consequence; according to the
Saying of *Tiberius; Deorum offensa Diis curae.* As to the particular
Fact related, I think it is not fair to argue from one Instance;
perhaps another cannot be produced; yet (to the Comfort of all
those, who may be apprehensive of Persecution) Blasphemy we
know is freely spoke a Million of Times in every Coffee-House
and Tavern, or where-ever else *good Company* meet. It must be
allowed indeed, that to break an *English Free-born* Officer only
for Blasphemy, was, to speak the gentlest of such an Action, a
very high Strain of absolute Power. Little can be said in Excuse
for the General; perhaps he was afraid it might give Offence to
the Allies, among whom, for ought I know, it may be the Custom
of the country to believe a God. But if he argued, as some have
done, upon a mistaken Principle, that an Officer who is guilty of
speaking Blasphemy, may, some Time or other, proceed so far
as to raise a Mutiny; the Consequence is, by no Means, to be admitted: For, surely the Commander of an *English* Army is like to
be but ill obeyed, whose Soldiers fear and reverence him as little
as they do a Deity.

10   It is further objected against the Gospel System, that it
obliges Men to the Belief of Things too difficult for Free-Thinkers,
and such who have shaken off the Prejudices that usually cling
to a confined Education. To which I answer, that Men should be
cautious how they raise Objections, which reflect upon the Wisdom of the Nation. Is not every Body freely allowed to believe
whatever he pleaseth; and to publish his Belief to the World whenever he thinks fit; especially if it serve to strengthen the Party
which is in the Right? Would any indifferent Foreigner, who
should read the Trumpery lately written by *Asgill, Tindall, Toland,
Coward,* and Forty more, imagine the Gospel to be our Rule of
Faith, and confirmed by Parliaments? Does any Man either believe, or say he believes, or desire to have it thought that he says
he believes one Syllable of the Matter? And is any Man worse
received upon that Score; or does he find his Want of *Nominal*
Faith a Disadvantage to him, in the Pursuit of any Civil, or Military Employment? What if there be an old dormant Statute or
two against him? Are they not now obsolete, to a Degree, that
Empson and *Dudley* themselves, if they were now alive, would
find it impossible to put them in Execution?

11   It is likewise urged, that there are, by Computation, in
this Kingdom, above ten Thousand Parsons; whose Revenues
added to those of my Lords the Bishops, would suffice to maintain, at least, two Hundred young Gentlemen of Wit and Pleasure,
and Free-thinking; Enemies to Priest-craft, narrow Principles,
Pedantry, and Prejudices; who might be an Ornament to the
Court and Town: And then again, so great a Number of able
(bodied) Divines might be a Recruit to our Fleet and Armies.
This, indeed, appears to be a Consideration of some Weight:
But then, on the other Side, several Things deserve to be considered likewise: As, First, Whether it may not be thought necessary, that in certain Tracts of Country, like what we call Parishes,
there should be *one* Man at least, of Abilities to read and write.
Then, it seems a wrong Computation, that the Revenues of the
Church throughout this Island, would be large enough to maintain two Hundred young Gentlemen, or even Half that Number,
after the present refined Way of Living; that is, to allow each
of them such a Rent, as, in the modern Form of Speech, would
make them *easy.* But still, there is in this Project a greater Mischief behind; and we ought to beware of the Woman's Folly, who

killed the Hen, that every Morning laid her a Golden Egg. For, pray, what would become of the Race of Men in the next Age, if we had nothing to trust to, besides the scrophulous consumptive Productions furnished by our Men of Wit and Pleasure; when having squandered away their Vigour, Health, and Estates; they are forced, by some disagreeable Marriage, to piece up their broken Fortunes, and entail Rottenness and Politeness on their Posterity? Now, here are ten Thousand Persons reduced by the wise Regulations of *Henry* the Eighth, to the Necessity of a low Diet, and moderate Exercise, who are the only great Restorers of our Breed; without which, the Nation would, in an Age or two, become but one great Hospital.

12   Another Advantage proposed by the abolishing of Christianity, is, the clear Gain of one Day in Seven, which is now entirely lost, and consequently the Kingdom one Seventh less considerable in Trade, Business, and Pleasure; beside the Loss to the Publick of so many stately Structures now in the Hands of the Clergy; which might be converted into Theatres, Exchanges, Market-houses, common Dormitories, and other publick Edifices.

13   I hope I shall be forgiven a hard Word, if I call this a perfect Cavil. I readily own there hath been an old Custom, Time out of Mind, for People to assemble in the Churches every *Sunday*, and that Shops are still frequently shut; in order, as it is conceived, to preserve the Memory of that antient Practice; but how this can prove a Hindrance to Business, or pleasure, is hard to imagine. What if the Men of Pleasure are forced, one Day in the Week, to game at home, instead of the *Chocolate-House?* Are not the *Taverns* and *Coffee-Houses* open? Can there be a more convenient Season for taking a Dose of Physick? Are fewer Claps got upon *Sundays* than other Days? Is not that the chief Day for Traders to sum up the Accounts of the Week; and for Lawyers to prepare their Briefs? But I would fain know how it can be pretended, that the Churches are misapplied. Where are more Appointments and Rendezvouzes of Gallantry? Where more Care to appear in the foremost Box with greater Advantage of Dress? Where more Meetings for Business? Where more Bargains driven of all Sorts? And where so many Conveniences, or Incitements to sleep?

14   There is one Advantage, greater than any of the foregoing, proposed by the abolishing of Christianity; that it will utterly extinguish Parties among us, by removing those factious

Distinctions of High and Low Church, of *Whig* and *Tory, Presby-*
terian and *Church-of-England;* which are now so many grievous
Clogs upon publick Proceedings, and dispose Men to prefer the
gratifying themselves, or depressing their Adversaries, before the
most important Interest of the State.

15   I confess, if it were certain that so great an Advantage
would redound to the Nation by this Expedient, I would submit
and be silent: But, will any Man say, that if the Words *Whoring,*
Drinking, Cheating, Lying, Stealing, were, by Act of Parliament,
ejected out of the *English* Tongue and Dictionaries; we should
all awake next Morning chaste and temperate, honest and just,
and Lovers of Truth. Is this a fair Consequence? Or if the Physi-
cians would forbid us to pronounce the Words *Pox, Gout, Rheuma-*
tism, and *Stone;* would that Expedient serve like so many Talis-
mans to destroy the Diseases themselves? Are Party and Faction
rooted in Mens Hearts no deeper than Phrases borrowed from
Religion; or founded upon no firmer Principles? And is our Language so poor, that we cannot find other Terms to express them?
Are Envy, Pride, Avarice and Ambition, such ill Nomenclators,
that they cannot furnish Appellations for their Owners? Will not
Heydukes and *Mamalukes, Mandarins,* and *Potshaws,* or any
other Words formed at Pleasure, serve to distinguish those who
are in the *Ministry* from others, who *would be in* it *if they could?*
What, for Instance, is easier than to vary the Form of Speech;
and instead of the Word *Church,* make it a Question in Politicks,
Whether the Monument be in Danger? Because Religion was nearest at Hand to furnish a few convenient Phrases; is our Invention
so barren, we can find no Others? Suppose, for Argument Sake,
that the *Tories* favoured *Margarita,* the *Whigs* Mrs. *Tofts,* and the
Trimmers Valentini; would not *Margaritians, Toftians,* and *Valen-*
tinians, be very tolerable Marks of Distinction? The *Prasini* and
Veneti, two most virulent Factions in Italy, began (if I remember
right) by a Distinction of Colours in Ribbonds; which we might
do, with as good a Grace, about the Dignity of the *Blue* and the
Green; and would serve as properly to divide the Court, the
Parliament, and the Kingdom between them, as any Terms of Art
whatsoever, borrowed from Religion. Therefore, I think there is
little Force in this Objection against *Christianity;* or Prospect of
so great an Advantage as is proposed in the Abolishing of it.

16   It is again objected, as a very absurd, ridiculous Custom,

that a Set of Men should be suffered, much less employed, and hired to bawl one Day in Seven, against the Lawfulness of those Methods most in Use towards the Pursuit of Greatness, Riches, and Pleasure; which are the constant Practice of all Men alive on the other Six. But this Objection is, I think, a little unworthy so refined an Age as ours. Let us argue this Matter calmly. I appeal to the Breast of any polite Free-Thinker, whether in the Pursuit of gratifying a predominant Passion, he hath not always felt a wonderful Incitement, by reflecting it was a Thing forbidden: And therefore we see, in order to cultivate this Taste, the Wisdom of the Nation hath taken special Care, that the Ladies should be furnished with Prohibited Silks, and the Men with prohibited Wine: And, indeed, it were to be wished, that the Pleasures of the Town; which, for want of such Expedients, begin already, as I am told, to flag and grow languid; giving way daily to cruel Inroads from the Spleen.

17   It is likewise proposed, as a great Advantage to the Publick, that if we once discard the System of the Gospel, all Religion will, of Course, be banished for ever; and consequently along with it, those grievous Prejudices of Education; which, under the Names of Virtue, Conscience, Honour, Justice, and the like, are so apt to disturb the Peace of human Minds; and the Notions whereof are so hard to be eradicated by right Reason, or Free-thinking, sometimes during the whole Course of our Lives.

18   Here, first, I observe how difficult it is to get rid of a Phrase, which the World is once grown fond of, although the Occasion that first produced it, be entirely taken away. For several Years past, if a Man had but an ill-favoured Nose, the Deep-Thinkers of the Age would, some way or other, contrive to impute the Cause to the Prejudice of his Education. From this Fountain are said to be derived all our foolish Notions of Justice, Piety, Love of our Country; all our Opinions of God, or a future State, Heaven, Hell, and the like: And there might formerly, perhaps, have been some Pretence for this Charge. But so effectual Care hath been since taken, to remove those Prejudices by an entire Change in the Methods of Education; that (with Honour I mention it to our polite Innovators) the young Gentlemen, who are now on the Scene, seem to have not the least Tincture left of those Infusions, or String of those Weeds; and, by Consequence, the Reason for abolishing *Nominal* Christianity upon that Pretext, is wholly ceased.

19   For the rest, it may perhaps admit a Controversy, whether the Banishing of all Notions of Religion whatsoever, would be convenient for the Vulgar. Not that I am in the least of Opinion with those, who hold Religion to have been the Invention of Politicians, to keep the lower Part of the World in Awe, by the Fear of invisible Powers; unless Mankind were then very different from what is now: For I look upon the Mass, or Body of our People here in *England*, to be as Free-Thinkers, that is to say, as stanch Unbelievers, as any of the highest Rank. But I conceive some scattered Notions about a superior Power to be of singular Use for the common People, as furnishing excellent Materials to keep Children quiet, when they grow peevish; and providing Topicks of Amusement in a tedious Winter Night.

20   Lastly, It is proposed as a singular Advantage, that the Abolishing of Christianity, will very much contribute to the uniting of *Protestants*, by enlarging the Terms of Communion, so as to take in all Sorts of *Dissenters;* who are now shut out of the Pale upon Account of a few Ceremonies, which all Sides confess to be Things indifferent: That this alone will effectually answer the great Ends of a Scheme for Comprehension, by opening a large noble Gate, at which all Bodies may enter; whereas the chaffering with *Dissenters,* and dodging about this or the other Ceremony, is but like opening a few Wickets, and leaving them at jar, by which no more than one can get in at a Time, and that not without stooping and sideling, and squeezing his Body.

21   To all this I answer, That there is one darling Inclination of Mankind, which usually affects be a Retainer to Religion, although she be neither its Parent, its Godmother, or its Friend; I mean the Spirit of Opposition, that lived long before Christianity, and can easily subsist without it. Let us, for Instance, examine wherein the Opposition of Sectaries among us consists; we shall find Christianity to have no Share in it at all. Does the Gospel any where prescribe a starched squeezed Countenance, a stiff formal Gait, a Singularity of Manners and Habit, or any affected Modes of Speech, different from the reasonable Part of Mankind? Yet, if Christianity did not lend its Name, to stand in the Gap, and to employ or divert these Humours, they must of Necessity be spent in Contraventions to the Laws of the Land, and Disturbance of the publick Peace. There is a Portion of Enthusiasm assigned to every Nation, which if it hath not proper Objects to

work on, will burst out, and set all in a Flame. If the Quiet of a State can be bought by only flinging Men a few Ceremonies to devour, it is a Purchase no wise Man would refuse. Let the Mastiffs amuse themselves about a Sheep-skin stuffed with Hay, provided it will keep them from worrying the Flock. The Institution of Convents abroad, seems in one Point a Strain of great Wisdom; there being few Irregularities in human Passions, that may not have recourse to vent themselves in some of those Orders; which are so many Retreats for the Speculative, the Melancholy, the Proud, the Silent, the Politick and the Morose, to spend themselves, and evaporate the noxious Particles; for each of whom, we in this Island are forced to provide a several Sect of Religion, to keep them quiet. And whenever Christianity shall be abolished, the Legislature must find some Expedient to employ and entertain them. For what imports is, how large a Gate you open, if there will be always left a Number, who place a Pride and a Merit in refusing to enter?

22   Having thus considered the most important Objections against Christianity, and the chief Advantages proposed by the Abolishing thereof; I shall not with equal Deference and Submission to wiser Judgments as before, proceed to mention a few Inconveniences that may happen, if the Gospel should be repealed; which perhaps the projectors may not have sufficiently considered.

23   And first, I am very sensible how much the Gentlemen of Wit and Pleasure are apt to murmur, and be choqued at the sight of so many daggled-tail Parsons, who happen to fall in their Way, and offend their Eyes: But at the same Time these wise Reformers do not consider what an Advantage and Felicity it is, for great Wits to be always provided with Objects of Scorn and Contempt, in order to exercise and improve their Talents, and divert their Spleen from falling on each other, or on themselves; especially when all this may be done without the least imaginable *Danger to their Persons.*

24   And to urge another Argument of a parallel Nature: If Christianity were once abolished, how would the Free-Thinkers, the strong Reasoners, and the Men of profound Learning be able to find another Subject so calculated in all Points whereon to display their Abilities. What wonderful Productions of Wit should we be deprived of, from those whose Genius, by continual Prac-

tice hath been wholly turned upon Raillery and Invectives against Religion; and would therefore never be able to shine or distinguish themselves upon any other Subject. We are daily complaining of the great Decline of Wit among us; and would we take away the greatest, perhaps the only Topick we have left? Who would ever have suspected *Asgill* for a Wit, or *Toland* for a Philosopher, if the inexhaustible Stock of Christianity had not been at hand to provide them with Materials? What other Subject through all Art or Nature could have produced *Tindal* for a profound Author, or furnished him with Readers? It is the wise Choice of the Subject that alone adorns and distinguishes the Writer. For had an hundred such Pens as these been employed on the Side of Religion, they would have immediately sunk into Silence and Oblivion.

25   Nor do I think it wholly groundless, or my Fears altogether imaginary; that the Abolishing of Christianity may perhaps bring the Church in Danger; or at least put the Senate to the Trouble of another Securing Vote. I desire, I may not be mistaken; I am far from presuming to affirm or think, that the Church is in Danger at present, or as Things now stand; but we know not how soon it may be so, when the Christian Religion is repealed. As plausible as this Project seems, there may a dangerous Design lurk under it. Nothing can be more notorious, than that the *Atheists, Deists, Socinians, Anti-Trinitarians,* and other Subdivisions of Free-Thinkers, are Persons of little Zeal for the present Ecclesiastical Establishment: Their declared Opinion is for repealing the Sacramental Test; they are very indifferent with regard to Ceremonies; nor do they hold the *Jus Divinum* of Episcopacy. Therefore this may be intended as one politick Step towards altering the Constitution of the Church Established, and setting up *Presbytery* in the stead; which I leave to be further considered by those at the Helm.

26   In the last Place, I think nothing can be more plain, than that by this Expedient, we shall run into the Evil we chiefly pretend to avoid; and that the Abolishment of the Christian Religion, will be the readiest Course we can take to introduce Popery. And I am the more inclined to this Opinion, because we know it hath been the constant Practice of the *Jesuits* to send over Emissaries, with Instructions to personate themselves Members of the several prevailing Sects amongst us. So it is recorded, that they have at sundry Times appeared in the Guise of *Presbyterians, Anabaptists,*

PLANNING THE COMPLETE ESSAY

Independents, and *Quakers,* according as any of these were most
in Credit: So, since the Fashion hath been taken up of exploding
Religion, the *Popish* Missionaries have not been wanting to mix
with the Free-Thinkers; among whom, *Toland,* the great Oracle of
the *Anti-Christians,* is an *Irish* Priest, the Son of an *Irish* Priest;
and the most learned and ingenious Author of a Book, called the
Rights of the Christian Church, was in a proper Juncture, reconciled to the *Romish* Faith; whose true Son, as appears by an
Hundred Passages in his Treatise, he still continues. Perhaps I
could add some others to the Number; but the Fact is beyond
Dispute; and the Reasoning they proceed by, is right: For, supposing Christianity to be extinguished, the People will never be
at Ease, till they find out some other Method of Worship; which
will as infallibly produce Superstition, as this will end in *Popery.*

27   And therefore, if notwithstanding all I have said, it shall
still be thought necessary to have a Bill brought in for repealing
Christianity; I would humbly offer an Amendment, that instead
of the Word *Christianity,* may be put *Religion* in general; which
I conceive, will much better answer all the good Ends proposed by
the Projectors of it. For, as long as we leave in Being a God, and
his Providence, with all the necessary Consequences, which curious and inquisitive Men will be apt to draw from such Premises;
we do not strike at the Root of the Evil, although we should ever
so effectually annihilate the present Scheme of the Gospel. For,
of what Use is Freedom of Thought, if it will not produce Freedom of Action; which is the sole End, how remote soever, in
Appearance, of all Objections against Christianity? And therefore,
the Free-Thinkers consider it as a Sort of Edifice, wherein all
the Parts have such a mutual Dependance on each other, that if
you happen to pull out one single Nail, the whole Fabrick must
fall to the Ground. This was happily expressed by him, who had
heard of a Text brought for Proof of the Trinity, which in an
antient Manuscript was differently read; he thereupon immediately took the Hint, and by a sudden Deduction of a long *Sorites,*
most logically concluded; Why, if it be as you say, I may safely
whore and drink on, and defy the Parson. From which, and many
the like Instances easy to be produced, I think nothing can be more
manifest, than that the Quarrel is not against any particular Points
of hard Digestion in the Christian System; but against Religion in
general; Which, by laying Restraints on human Nature, is supposed the great Enemy to the Freedom of Thought and Action.

28   Upon the whole; if it shall still be thought for the Benefit of Church and State, that Christianity be Abolished; I conceive, however, it may be more convenient to defer the Execution to a Time of Peace; and not venture in this Conjuncture to disoblige our Allies; who, as it falls out, are all Christians; and many of them, by the Prejudices of their Education, so bigotted, as to place a Sort of Pride in the Appellation. If, upon being rejected by them, we are to trust to an Alliance with the *Turk*, we shall find our selves much deceived: For, as he is too remote, and generally engaged in War with the *Persian* Emperor; so his People would be more scandalized at our Infidelity, than our Christian Neighbours. Because, the *Turks* are not only strict Observers of religious Worship; but, what is worse, believe a God; which is more than is required of us, even while we preserve the Name of Christians.

29   To conclude: Whatever some may think of the great Advantages to Trade, by this favourite Scheme; I do very much apprehend, that in six Months Time, after the Act is past for the Extirpation of the Gospel, the Bank and *East-India* Stock may fall, at least, One *per* Cent. And, since that is Fifty Times more than ever the Wisdom of our Age thought fit to venture for the *Preservation* of Christianity, there is no Reason we should be at so great a Loss, merely for the Sake of *destroying* it.

• SUGGESTION •

Analyze this essay to show its organization in terms of the classical oration.

Coherence and Transition in Planning

If you develop a logical plan for any essay you are going to write, using either one of the methods recommended in the preceding sections or a method recommended by your instructor, and if that plan is complete, you will already have taken major precautions to insure coherence and smooth transitions. Careful planning should assure first that your essay will develop one major idea, thus maintaining coherence; it should assure in the second place that you know how the parts of your essay will fit together, thus providing a built-in method of accomplishing transitions. Still it is important that you remain aware of the various other means of effecting sure continuity. The selections that follow will illustrate some of these means: use of standard transitional expressions, repetition of key words, pronoun reference, and others.

GETTYSBURG ADDRESS [1863]

Abraham Lincoln

1   Fourscore and seven years ago our fathers brought forth on this continent a new nation, conceived in liberty, and dedicated to the proposition that all men are created equal.

2   Now we are engaged in a great civil war, testing whether that nation, or any nation so conceived and so dedicated, can long endure. We are met on a great battlefield of that war. We have come to dedicate a portion of that field as a final resting-place for those who here gave their lives that that nation might live. It is altogether fitting and proper that we should do this.

3   But, in a larger sense, we cannot dedicate—we cannot consecrate—we cannot hallow—this ground. The brave men, living and dead, who struggled here, have consecrated it far above our poor power to add or detract. The world will little note nor long remember what we say here, but it can never forget what they did here. It is for us, the living, rather, to be dedicated here to the unfinished work which they who fought here have thus far so nobly advanced. It is rather for us to be here dedicated to the great task remaining before us—that from these honored dead we take increased devotion to that cause for which they gave the last full measure of devotion; that we here highly resolve that these dead shall not have died in vain; that this nation, under God, shall have a new birth of freedom; and that government of the people, by the people, for the people, shall not perish from the earth.

• COMMENTARY •

The first paragraph establishes some of the key terms and ideas that help to provide continuity through the rest of the speech. The word "Now," which begins the second paragraph, connects the first two paragraphs by establishing the time-contrast, and "we," the subject of the first sentence in the second paragraph, also shows this in its contrast with "our fathers" in the first paragraph. The phrases "that nation," "so conceived," and "so dedicated" in this same sentence by repetition connect it with the first paragraph.

The second sentence of the second paragraph is related closely to the first by the words "that war," which refer to "a great civil war" in the first sentence. In the third sentence, the words "that field" refer to "battlefield" in the second sentence and thus keep the line of development perfectly clear. In the same way "here" in this third sentence again refers to the battlefield, as "that nation," again by repetition, connects this sentence with the first sentence in this second paragraph. In the fourth sentence of this paragraph, the last word, "this," refers us to "We have come to dedicate a portion of that field" in the third sentence.

The first word of the first sentence in the third paragraph, "But," a simple transitional device, once again establishes a contrast with the preceding paragraph and forecasts Mr. Lincoln's assertion that though they have met for that purpose, they "cannot dedicate" this battlefield. The words "this ground" at the end of the first sentence serves to keep us conscious still of the place, the battlefield. Throughout the rest of this final paragraph several key words and concepts maintain the continuity of the piece: repeated use of some form of the word *dedicate;* continual reference through pronouns to the "brave men" mentioned in the second sentence; repeated use of the transitional word *rather* to establish the contrast; use of the "unfinished work" to establish the "task remaining before us"; and in the last sentence use of "that cause," "this nation," and "new birth" to bring the audience back, re-dedicated, to the ideas the address begins with.

The beauty and compactness of Mr. Lincoln's prose style, only one quality of which is touched on here, should be apparent to you if for no other reason than that even a tentative commentary is longer than the address. If the commentary seems a monument of the "making molehills out of mountains" prose style, remember that this is one of the ways those of us who are not mountain climbers find out what mountains are made of.

RAMBLER, no. 154 [1751]

Samuel Johnson

1   The direction of *Aristotle* to those that study politicks, is, first to examine and understand what has been written by the ancients upon government; then to cast their eyes round upon the

world, and consider by what causes the prosperity of communities is visibly influenced, and why some are worse, and others better administered.

2   The same method must be pursued by him who hopes to become eminent in any other part of knowledge. The first task is to search books, the next to contemplate nature. He must first possess himself of the intellectual treasures which the diligence of former ages has accumulated, and then endeavour to encrease them by his own collections.

3   The mental disease of the present generation, is impatience of study, contempt of the great masters of ancient wisdom, and a disposition to rely wholly upon unassisted genius and natural sagacity. The wits of these happy days have discovered a way to fame, which the dull caution of our laborious ancestors durst never attempt; they cut the knots of sophistry which it was formerly the business of years to untie, solve difficulties by sudden irradiations of intelligence, and comprehend long processes of argument by immediate intuition.

4   Men who have flattered themselves into this opinion of their own abilities, look down on all who waste their lives over books, as a race of inferior beings condemned by nature to per-petual pupillage, and fruitlessly endeavouring to remedy their barrenness by incessant cultivation, or succour their feebleness by subsidiary strength. They presume that none would be more in-dustrious than they, if they were not more sensible of deficiencies, and readily conclude, that he who places no confidence in his own powers, owes his modesty only to his weakness.

5   It is however certain that no estimate is more in danger of erroneous calculations than those by which a man computes the force of his own genius. It generally happens at our entrance into the world, that by the natural attraction of similitude, we asso-ciate with men like ourselves young, sprightly, and ignorant, and rate our accomplishments by comparison with theirs; when we have once obtained an acknowledged superiority over our acquaint-ances, imagination and desire easily extend it over the rest of mankind, and if no accident forces us into new emulations, we grow old, and die in admiration of ourselves.

6   Vanity, thus confirmed in her dominion, readily listens to the voice of idleness, and sooths the slumber of life with continual dreams of excellence and greatness. A man elated by confidence in his natural vigour of fancy and sagacity of conjecture, soon con-

cludes that he already possesses whatever toil and enquiry can confer. He then listens with eagerness to the wild objections which folly has raised against the common means of improvement; talks of the dark chaos of indigested knowledge; describes the mischievous effects of heterogeneous sciences fermenting in the mind; relates the blunders of lettered ignorance; expatiates on the heroick merit of those who deviate from prescription, or shake off authority; and gives vent to the inflations of his heart by declaring that he owes nothing to pedants and universities.

7   All these pretensions, however confident, are very often vain. The laurels which superficial acuteness gains in triumphs over ignorance unsupported by vivacity, are observed by *Locke* to be lost whenever real learning and rational diligence appear against her; the sallies of gaiety are soon repressed by calm confidence, and the artifices of subtilty are readily detected by those who having carefully studied the question, are not easily confounded or surprised.

8   But though the contemner of books had neither been deceived by others nor himself, and was really born with a genius surpassing the ordinary abilities of mankind; yet surely such gifts of providence may be more properly urged as incitements to labour, than encouragements to negligence. He that neglects the culture of ground, naturally fertile, is more shamefully culpable than he whose field would scarcely recompence his husbandry.

9   Cicero remarks, that not to know what has been transacted in former times is to continue always a child. If no use is made of the labours of past ages, the world must remain always in the infancy of knowledge. The discoveries of every man must terminate in his own advantage, and the studies of every age be employed on questions which the past generation had discussed and determined. We may with as little reproach borrow science as manufactures from our ancestors; and it is as rational to live in caves till our own hands have erected a palace, as to reject all knowledge of architecture, which our understandings will not supply.

10   To the strongest and quickest mind it is far easier to learn than to invent. The principles of arithmetick and geometry may be comprehended by a close attention in a few days; yet who can flatter himself that the study of a long life would have enabled him to discover them, when he sees them yet unknown to so many

nations, whom he cannot suppose less liberally endowed with natural reason, than the *Grecians* or *Egyptians?*

11 Every science was thus far advanced towards perfection, by the emulous diligence of contemporary students, and the gradual discoveries of one age improving on another. Sometimes unexpected flashes of instruction were struck out by the fortuitous collision of happy incidents, or an involuntary concurrence of ideas, in which the philosopher to whom they happened had no other merit than that of knowing their value, and transmitting unclouded to posterity that light which had been kindled by causes out of his power. The happiness of these casual illuminations no man can promise to himself, because no endeavours can procure them; and therefore, whatever be our abilities or application, we must submit to learn from others what perhaps would have lain hid for ever from human penetration, had not some remote enquiry brought it to view; as treasures are thrown up by the ploughman and the digger in the rude exercise of their common occupations.

12 The man whose genius qualifies him for great undertakings, must at least be content to learn from books the present state of human knowledge; that he may not ascribe to himself the invention of arts generally known; weary his attention with experiments of which the event has been long registered; and waste, in attempts which have already succeeded or miscarried, that time which might have been spent with usefulness and honour upon new undertakings.

13 But though the study of books is necessary, it is not sufficient to constitute literary eminence. He that wishes to be counted among the benefactors of posterity, must add by his own toil to the acquisitions of his ancestors, and secure his memory from neglect by some valuable improvement. This can only be effected by looking out upon the wastes of the intellectual world, and extending the power of learning over regions yet undisciplined and barbarous; or by surveying more exactly her antient dominions, and driving ignorance from the fortresses and retreats where she skulks undetected and undisturbed. Every science has its difficulties which yet call for solution before we attempt new systems of knowledge; as every country has its forests and marshes, which it would be wise to cultivate and drain, before distant colonies are projected as a necessary discharge of the exuberance of inhabitants.

14   No man ever yet became great by imitation. Whatever hopes for the veneration of mankind must have invention in the design or the execution; either the effect must itself be new, or the means by which it is produced. Either truths hitherto unknown must be discovered, or those which are already known enforced by stronger evidence, facilitated by clearer method, or ellucidated by brighter illustrations.

15   Fame cannot spread wide or endure long that is not rooted in nature, and manured by art. That which hopes to resist the blast of malignity, and stand firm against the attacks of time, must contain in itself some original principle of growth. The reputation which arises from the detail or transposition of borrowed sentiments, may spread for a while, like ivy on the rind of antiquity, but will be torn away by accident or contempt, and suffered to rot unheeded on the ground.

• SUGGESTIONS •

Examine this essay to determine how continuity is maintained. If you find no other satisfactory way of proceeding, perhaps you could arrange your discussion in the manner of the Commentary following the Gettysburg Address.

A Writing Program

1. Formulate several plans for essays using the first method suggested here. Vary the ruling method, using a different form in each plan, and vary the types of paragraphs you use. On the agreement of your instructor, use these plans, or perhaps just the best one, for an essay you will write later.

2. Formulate several plans for essays using the second method suggested here. Develop a number of thesis-sentence and topic-sentence outlines, some of which you can use for later essays.

3. Formulate several plans for essays using the third method suggested here. You might do this by listing under each of the headings the ideas and information to be offered in that section.

Exposition

✳

For some kinds of writing, specific strategies may be suggested to accomplish specific effects. Some problems in description and argumentation, for example, and even in narration, may be neatly and sometimes elegantly worked out through use of established procedures. For expository writing, which may very well be required of you more often than any other kind, this may not be true. This does not necessarily mean that expository writing is more difficult than other kinds; it only means that because its range is so wide and its needs therefore so varied there may not be many clearly defined and commonly accepted methods for you to follow.

And the range is wide. Exposition—the vehicle for explaining what is unknown, inadequately known, or mistakenly known—includes many of our practical, most of our theoretical discourses; it is both the expression of judgment and the means to further judgment. As a wise man once said, "the province of exposition extends from autobiographical explanation of self to objective views of the universe, from exploration of personal and immediate experience to rationalizations of world history. So distant are its boundaries, embracing man's daydreams, ideas, and activities, that it is rather an empire than a province." In this whole wide range, each subject necessarily determines an appropriate method (just as an appropriate method determines what a subject really is).

If, then, there is a strategy for exposition, it can only be said to reside in the possibilities available to you in unifying the methods already suggested (see the sections on sentence and paragraph style and on planning) and the methods yet to be suggested (see the sections following this). Patterns of definition and subordination, of comparison and parallelism, of contrast and coordination—in short, all of the methods so far illustrated—may be fused in exposition; in the same manner you will find that the subjects for exposition may also demand descriptive, narrative, or argumentative effects.

The selections that follow are intended to illustrate various procedures in exposition and various problems to be encountered. Their arrangement is not inevitable; it may be justified only perhaps because it seems to reflect natural interest, beginning as it does with the self and ending with ideas.

Autobiographical Essays

One of the earliest full-length essays you may be asked to write in college is an autobiographical essay, a variety of self-analysis. It is in one respect at least the simplest writing task you will be given, for here, if nowhere else, information is available, even copious.

This is not to say that information about yourself is stacked around in bundles, waiting only to be sorted and shown. Information is there, but you may not be always fully awake to it, fully conscious of it, as Thoreau suggests in the selection from his work that follows. Good autobiographical writing will probably demand of you complete honesty, as most good things do; it will require of you a deliberate effort to reveal yourself—and we are all disposed usually rather to conceal than to reveal. But this kind of writing is revelation; you must remember this, for while the needs of autobiography may require narration, you will not be able always to substitute narration of what you have done for exposition of what you are. An essay is after all an effort to do something; there is no point in bothering with it unless you make it worth the doing.

Your time and your place and what you have been and are will have to determine how you proceed. Perhaps the one piece of advice that might be useful is that you decide what you are going to essay, that is, settle upon a thesis (something you seek to explain about yourself) and follow its commitment, developing your plan and your essay in such a way as best to fulfill what your thesis-commitment requires.

The selections that follow, each a species of self-revelation, form a kind of progression. Those by Samuel Johnson are entirely private revelations, meditations not necessarily meant for publication. The selection from *Walden* begins with private revelation and makes of that privacy a public comment. The selection from Lincoln is an entirely public revelation, so designed, and reveals his privacy only indirectly.

From MEDITATIONS

Samuel Johnson

April 21, 1764, 3 in the morning.

1   My indolence, since my last reception of the Sacrament, has sunk into grosser sluggishness, and my dissipation spread into wilder negligence. My thoughts have been clouded with sensuality; and, except that from the beginning of this year I have in some measure forborn excess of strong drink, my appetites have predominated over my reason. A kind of strange oblivion has overspread me, so that I know not what has become of the last year; and perceive that incidents and intelligence pass over me without leaving any impression.

2   This is not the life to which heaven is promised. I purpose to approach the altar again to-morrow. Grant, O Lord, that I may receive the Sacrament with such resolutions of a better life as may by thy grace be effectual, for the sake of Jesus Christ. Amen.

Sept. 18, 1771, 9 at night.

1   I am now come to my sixty-third year. For the last year I have been slowly recovering both from the violence of my last illness and, I think, from the general disease of my life. My breath is less obstructed, and I am more capable of motion and exercise. My mind is less encumbered, and I am less interrupted in mental employment. Some advances I hope have been made towards regularity. I have missed church since Easter only two Sundays, both which I hope I have endeavoured to supply by attendance on divine worship in the following week. Since Easter, my evening devotions have been lengthened. But indolence and indifference has been neither conquered nor opposed. No plan of study has been pursued or formed, except that I have commonly read every week, if not on Sunday, a stated portion of the New Testament in

Greek. But what is most to be considered, I have neither attempted
nor formed any scheme of life by which I may do good, and please
God.

2   One great hindrance is want of rest; my nocturnal complaints grow less troublesome towards morning; and I am tempted
to repair the deficiencies of the night. I think, however, to try to
rise every day by eight, and to combat indolence as I shall obtain
strength. Perhaps Providence has yet some use for the remnant of
my life.

[Undated]

1   Almighty and everlasting God, whose mercy is over all thy
works, and who hast no pleasure in the death of a sinner, look with
pity upon me, succour and preserve me; enable me to conquer evil
habits, and surmount temptations. Give me grace so to use the degree of health which Thou has restored to my mind and body, that
I may perform the task Thou shalt yet appoint me. Look down, O
gracious Lord, upon my remaining part of life; grant, if it please
Thee, that the days few or many which Thou shalt yet allow me,
may pass in reasonable confidence, and holy tranquillity. Withhold
not thy Holy Spirit from me, but strengthen all good purposes, till
they shall produce a life pleasing to Thee. And when Thou shalt
call me to another state, forgive me my sins, and receive me to
happiness, for the sake of Jesus Christ our Lord. Amen.

2   Safely brought us, &c.

[March] *30, Easter Day (1777), Imâ mane.*

1   The day is now come again, in which, by a custom which
since the death of my wife I have by the divine assistance always
observed, I am to renew the great covenant with my Maker and
my Judge. I humbly hope to perform it better. I hope for more
efficacy of resolution, and more diligence of endeavour. When I
survey my past life, I discover nothing but a barren waste of time,
with some disorders of body, and disturbances of the mind very
near to madness, which I hope He that made me, will suffer to
extenuate many faults, and excuse many deficiencies. Yet much
remains to be repented and reformed. I hope that I refer more to
God than in former times, and consider more what submission is
due to his dispensations. But I have very little reformed my practical life; and the time in which I can struggle with habits cannot

be now expected to be long. Grant, O God, that I may no longer resolve in vain, or dream away the life which thy indulgence gives me, in vacancy and uselessness.

GOOD FRIDAY [1779] 11 P.M.

1   I am now to review the last year, and find little but dismal vacuity, neither business nor pleasure; much intended, and little done. My health is much broken; my nights afford me little rest. I have tried opium, but its help is counter-balanced with great disturbance; it prevents the spasms, but it hinders sleep. O God, have mercy on me.

2   Last week I published the Lives of the Poets, written, I hope, in such a manner as may tend to the promotion of piety.

3   In this last year I have made little acquisition; I have scarcely read any thing. I maintain Mrs. [Desmoulins] and her daughter. Other good of myself I know not where to find, except a little charity.

4   But I am now in my seventieth year; what can be done, ought not to be delayed.

• COMMENTARY •

These selections are among some meditations written in Johnson's private notebooks; they were not designed as publishable essays, yet they are remarkable exercises in self-analysis. Only very briefly does Johnson narrate events and activities; almost his whole attention is given to his explanation of his present conditions, and very little seems to have been concealed in these selections. The first selection is given entirely to a brief account of his capacities and his disposition. The second does undertake some brief review of events of the past year, but the purpose of this review is expository, as the last sentence of the first paragraph reveals: "But what is most to be considered, I have neither attempted nor formed any scheme of life by which I may do good, and please God." The third selection is a summation, but again its intent is clearly expository; the review of the past year in the last selection serves only to reinforce his revelations.

A characteristic feature of Johnson's style is especially suited to the kind of self-analysis and revelation given here. Coordinate constructions —which may occur as paired or parallel independent or dependent con-

structions, or frequently as triplet constructions—are frequent in Johnson's prose; he uses them to bring as wide as possible a range of experience and insight into the disciplining bounds of one sentence. Here he
uses such constructions frequently to bring into his meditations the full
scope of his analytical insights. In the second selection, for example, he
explains that "no plan of study has been pursued or formed," and con-
fesses that he has "neither attempted nor formed any scheme of life"
by which he may do good. In the fourth selection he hopes for

more efficacy of resolution,
and
more diligence of endeavour.

A sentence in the second selection illustrates this method best: "But
indolence and indifference has been neither conquered nor opposed."

From WALDEN [1854]

Henry David Thoreau

1   The millions are awake enough for physical labor; but
only one in a million is awake enough for effective intellectual
exertion, only one in a hundred millions to a poetic or divine life.
To be awake is to be alive. I have never yet met a man who was
quite awake. How could I have looked him in the face?

2   We must learn to reawaken and keep ourselves awake, not
by mechanical aids, but by an infinite expectation of the dawn,
which does not forsake us in our soundest sleep. I know of no
more encouraging fact than the unquestionable ability of man to
elevate his life by a conscious endeavor. It is something to be able
to paint a particular picture, or to carve a statue, and so to make
a few objects beautiful; but it is far more glorious to carve and
paint the very atmosphere and medium through which we look,
which morally we can do. To affect the quality of the day, that is
the highest of arts. Every man is tasked to make his life, even in
its details, worthy of the contemplation of his most elevated and
critical hour. If we refused, or rather used up, such paltry information as we get, the oracles would distinctly inform us how this
might be done.

3   I went to the woods because I wished to live deliberately,
to front only the essential facts of life, and see if I could not learn

what it had to teach, and not, when I came to die, discover that I
had not lived. I did not wish to live what was not life, living is so
dear; nor did I wish to practice resignation, unless it was quite
necessary. I wanted to live deep and suck out all the marrow of
life, to live so sturdily and Spartan-like as to put to rout all that was
not life, to cut a broad swath and shave close, to drive life into a
corner, and reduce it to its lowest terms, and, if it proved to be
mean, why then to get the whole and genuine meanness of it, and
publish its meanness to the world; or if it were sublime, to know it
by experience, and be able to give a true account of it in my next
excursion. For most men, it appears to me, are in a strange uncertainty about it, whether it is of the devil or of God, and have
somewhat hastily concluded that it is the chief end of man here to
"glorify God and enjoy him forever."

4   Still we live meanly, like ants; though the fable tells us
that we were long ago changed into men; like pygmies we fight
with cranes; it is error upon error, and clout upon clout, and our
best virtue has for its occasion a superfluous and evitable wretched-
ness. Our life is frittered away by detail. An honest man has hardly
need to count more than his ten fingers, or in extreme cases he may
add his ten toes, and lump the rest. Simplicity, simplicity, simplicity! I say, let your affairs be as two or three, and not a hundred
or a thousand; instead of a million count half a dozen, and keep
your accounts on your thumb-nail. In the midst of this chopping
sea of civilized life, such are the clouds and storms and quicksands
and thousand-and-one items to be allowed for, that man has to
live, if he would not founder and go to the bottom and not make
his port at all, by dead reckoning, and he must be a great calcu-
lator indeed who succeeds. Simplify, simplify. Instead of three
meals a day, if it be necessary eat but one; instead of a hundred
dishes, five; and reduce other things in proportion. Our life is like
a German Confederacy, made up of petty states, with its boundary
forever fluctuating, so that even a German cannot tell you how it
is bounded at any moment. The nation itself, with all its so-called
internal improvements, which, by the way are all external and
superficial, is just such an unwieldy and overgrown establishment,
cluttered with furniture and tripped up by its own traps, ruined
by luxury and heedless expense, by want of calculation and a
worthy aim, as the million households in the land; and the only
cure for it, as for them, is in rigid economy, a stern and more than

Spartan simplicity of life and elevation of purpose. It lives too fast.
Men think that it is essential that the *Nation* have commerce, and
export ice, and talk through a telegraph, and ride thirty miles an
hour, without a doubt, whether *they* do or not; but whether we
should live like baboons or like men, is a little uncertain. If we
do not get out sleepers, and forge rails, and devote days and nights
to the work, but go to tinkering upon our *lives* to improve *them*,
who will build railroads? And if railroads are not built, how shall
we get to heaven in season? But if we stay at home and mind our
business, who will want railroads? Each one is a man, an Irish-
man, or a Yankee man. The rails are laid on them, and they are
covered with sand, and the cars run smoothly over them. They are
sound sleepers, I assure you. And every few years a new lot is
laid down and run over; so that, if some have the pleasure of riding
on a rail, others have the misfortune to be ridden upon. And when
they run over a man that is walking in his sleep, a supernumerary
sleeper in the wrong position, and wake him up, they suddenly
stop the cars, and make a hue and cry about it, as if this were an
exception. I am glad to know that it takes a gang of men for every
five miles to keep the sleepers down and level in their beds as it
is, for this is a sign that they may sometime get up again.

5   Why should we live with such hurry and waste of life?
We are determined to be starved before we are hungry. Men say
that a stitch in time saves nine, and so they take a thousand stitches
to-day to save nine tomorrow. As for *work*, we haven't any of any
consequence. We have the Saint Vitus's dance, and cannot possibly keep our heads still. If I should only give a few pulls at the
parish bell-rope, as for a fire, that is, without setting the bell,
there is hardly a man on his farm in the outskirts of Concord, notwithstanding that press of engagements which was his excuse so
many times this morning, nor a boy, nor a woman, I might almost
say, but would forsake all and follow that sound, not mainly to
save property from the flames, but, if we will confess the truth,
much more to see it burn, since burn it must, and we, be it known,
did not set it on fire,—or to see it put out, and have a hand in it, if
that is done as handsomely; yes, even if it were the parish church
itself. Hardly a man takes a half-hour's nap after dinner, but when
he wakes he holds up his head and asks, "What's the news?" as if
the rest of mankind had stood his sentinels. Some give directions to
be waked every half-hour, doubtless for no other purpose; and

then, to pay for it, they tell what they have dreamed. After a night's sleep the news is as indispensable as the breakfast. "Pray tell me anything new that has happened to a man anywhere on this globe,"—and he reads it over his coffee and rolls, that a man has had his eyes gouged out this morning on the Wachito River; never dreaming the while that he lives in the dark unfathomed mammoth cave of this world, and has but the rudiment of an eye himself.

• SUGGESTIONS •

Thoreau voices the aspirations of what he would be rather than the revelation of what he has been; this means among other things that while Johnson looked primarily inward, Thoreau looks at himself against a large background. From your examination of this selection, explain its general movement or plan and determine the propriety of the rather frequent short sentences and the rhetorical questions. By comparison to the private revelations of the Johnson selections, what is there about the style of this piece that makes it a public statement?

AUTOBIOGRAPHY [1859]

Abraham Lincoln

1   I was born February 12, 1809, in Hardin County, Kentucky. My parents were both born in Virginia, of undistinguished families—second families, perhaps I should say. My mother, who died in my tenth year, was of a family of the name of Hanks, some of whom now reside in Adams, and others in Macon County, Illinois. My paternal grandfather, Abraham Lincoln, emigrated from Rockingham County, Virginia, to Kentucky about 1781 or 1782, where a year or two later he was killed by the Indians, not in battle, but by stealth, when he was laboring to open a farm in the forest. His ancestors, who were Quakers, went to Virginia from Berks County, Pennsylvania. An effort to identify them with the New England family of the same name ended in nothing more definite than a similarity of Christian names in both families, such as Enoch, Levi, Mordecai, Solomon, Abraham, and the like.

2   My father, at the death of his father, was but six years
of age, and he grew up literally without education. He removed
from Kentucky to what is now Spencer County, Indiana, in my
eighth year. We reached our new home about the time the state
came into the Union. It was a wild region, with many bears and
other wild animals still in the woods. There I grew up. There were
some schools, so called, but no qualification was ever required of
a teacher beyond "readin', writin', and cipherin'," to the rule of
three. If a straggler supposed to understand Latin happened to
sojourn in the neighborhood, he was looked upon as a wizard.
There was absolutely nothing to excite ambition for education. Of
course, when I came of age I did not know much. Still, somehow,
I could read, write, and cipher to the rule of three, but that was
all. I have not been to school since. The little advance I now have
upon this store of education, I have picked up from time to time
under the pressure of necessity.

3   I was raised to farm work, which I continued till I was
twenty-two. At twenty-one I came to Illinois, Macon County.
Then I got to New Salem, at that time in Sangamon, now in Menard
County, where I remained a year as a sort of clerk in a store. Then
came the Black Hawk War; and I was elected a captain of volun-
teers, a success which gave me more pleasure than any I have had
since. I went the campaign, was elated, ran for the legislature the
same year (1832), and was beaten—the only time I ever have been
beaten by the people. The next and three succeeding biennial
elections I was elected to the legislature. I was not a candidate
afterward. During this legislative period I had studied law, and
removed to Springfield to practice it. In 1846 I was once elected to
the lower House of Congress. Was not a candidate for reëlection.
From 1849 to 1854, both inclusive, practiced law more assiduously than ever before. Always a Whig in politics; and generally
on the Whig electoral tickets, making active canvasses. I was losing
interest in politics when the repeal of the Missouri Compromise
aroused me again. What I have done since that is pretty well
known.

4   If any personal description of me is thought desirable, it
may be said I am, in height, six feet four inches, nearly; lean in
flesh, weighing on an average one hundred and eighty pounds;
dark complexion, with coarse black hair and gray eyes. No other
marks or brands recollected.

This brief account was written for campaign purposes in 1859. Helpful to your evaluation of the piece would be some account of the appropriateness of the relatively short sentences. It would also be helpful if you could account for the pacing of the selection, that is, the amount of space and time given to the various periods of his life. A good part of this is simple chronological narration. Is the narration used for expository purposes?

Biographical Essays

Biographical writing, like autobiography, as the written history of a person's life or of a portion of his life, is usually narrative in form. But as the selections in the preceding section illustrate, the needs of both autobiography and biography frequently require exposition, revelation of the subject's character.

To reveal oneself, as in autobiography, is difficult enough; to reveal another is yet more demanding. Perhaps the greatest biography in English, Boswell's *Life of Samuel Johnson,* succeeded in part because Boswell had access to the kind of material most of us, in more casual writing assignments, cannot hope to have. Boswell knew Johnson for more than twenty years and for most of that time was deliberately collecting the materials for his biography. He learned through their friendship of Johnson's early years, recorded Johnson's conversations, and "spared no pains in obtaining materials concerning him."

Though you will not be asked now to undertake anything of such scope, indeed, will probably be writing only about a moment or two in your subject's life, you can profit from Boswell's model. "Indeed I cannot conceive," he says, "a more perfect mode of writing any man's life, than not relating all the most important events of it in their order, but interweaving what he privately wrote, and said, and thought; by which mankind are enabled as it were to see him live, and to 'live o'er each scene' with him, as he actually advanced through the several stages of his life." And Samuel Johnson himself warned of the dangers in writing only from personal knowledge; if the writer does so, he said, "there is danger lest his interest, his fear, his gratitude, or his tenderness overpower his fidelity, and tempt him to conceal, if not to invent."

Personal knowledge of your subject may well be insufficient. It may be insufficient for the reasons Johnson mentioned; it may be plainly insufficient, not providing you material you will need. To overcome such threatening insufficiency, you do have at your disposal various indices to character, and, as you are no longer writing about yourself, you can be more dispassionate in using them. Careful study of what a man does is one such index to his character. The reactions of others to him and their remarks about him provide other indices. Finally, his own words reveal him, though not, perhaps, as clearly as his actions and the responses of others to him.

The following selections are of two kinds. The first, from Boswell, are biographical expositions of one particular person. But since the necessities of education may also demand that you scrutinize types of men, the second group of selections illustrates methods of dealing with man in general, or with types of men.

From THE LIFE OF SAMUEL JOHNSON [1791]

James Boswell

▶ *Boswell's First Call on Johnson*

1   He received me very courteously; but, it must be confessed that his apartment, and furniture, and morning dress, were sufficiently uncouth. His brown suit of clothes looked very rusty; he had on a little old shrivelled unpowdered wig, which was too small for his head; his shirt-neck and knees of his breeches were loose; his black worsted stockings, ill drawn up; and he had a pair of unbuckled shoes by way of slippers. But all these slovenly particularities were forgotten the moment that he began to talk. Some gentlemen, whom I do not recollect, were sitting with him; and when they went away, I also rose; but he said to me, "Nay, don't go."—"Sir," said I, "I am afraid that I intrude upon you. It is benevolent to allow me to sit and hear you." He seemed pleased with this compliment, which I sincerely paid him, and answered, "Sir, I am obliged to any man who visits me."—I have preserved the following short minute of what passed this day.

2   "Madness frequently discovers itself merely by unnecessary deviation from the usual modes of the world. My poor friend Smart showed the disturbance of his mind, by falling upon his knees, and saying his prayers in the street, or in any other unusual place. Now although, rationally speaking, it is greater madness not to pray at all, than to pray as Smart did, I am afraid there are so many who do not pray, that their understanding is not called in question."

3   Concerning this unfortunate poet, Christopher Smart, who was confined in a mad-house, he had, at another time, the following conversation with Dr. Burney.—BURNEY. "How does poor Smart do, Sir: is he likely to recover?" JOHNSON. "It seems as if his mind had ceased to struggle with the disease; for he grows fat upon it." BURNEY. "Perhaps, Sir, that may be from want of exercise." JOHNSON. "No, Sir; he has partly as much exercise as he used to have, for he digs in the garden. Indeed, before his confinement, he used for exercise to walk to the alehouse; but he was *carried* back again. I did not think he ought to be shut up. His infirmities were not noxious to society. He insisted on people praying with him; and I'd as lief pray with Kit Smart as anyone else. Another charge was, that he did not love clean linen; and I have no passion for it."

4   Johnson continued. "Mankind have a great aversion to intellectual labor; but even supposing knowledge to be easily attainable, more people would be content to be ignorant than would take even a little trouble to acquire it.

5   "The morality of an action depends on the motive from which we act. If I fling half a crown to a beggar with intention to break his head, and he picks it up and buys victuals with it, the physical effect is good; but, with respect to me, the action is very wrong. So, religious exercises, if not permitted with an intention to please God, avail us nothing. As our Savior says of those who perform them from other motives, 'Verily they have their reward.' "

6   Talking of Garrick, he said, "He is the first man in the world for sprightly conversation."

7   When I rose a second time, he again pressed me to stay, which I did.

8   He told me that he generally went abroad at four in the afternoon, and seldom came home till two in the morning. I took the liberty to ask if he did not think it wrong to live thus, and not

make more use of his great talents. He owned it was a bad habit.
On reviewing, at the distance of many years, my journal of this
period, I wonder how, at my first visit, I ventured to talk to him
so freely, and that he bore it with so much indulgence.

9   Before we parted, he was so good as to promise to favor
me with his company one evening at my lodgings; and, as I took
my leave, shook me cordially by the hand. It is almost needless to
add, that I felt no little elation at having now so happily established
an acquaintance of which I had been so long ambitious[. . . .]

▶ Relish for Good Eating

1   At supper this night he talked of good eating with uncommon satisfaction. "Some people," said he, "have a foolish way of
not minding, or pretending not to mind, what they eat. For my part,
I mind my belly very studiously, and very carefully; for I look
upon it, that he who does not mind his belly, will hardly mind
anything else." He now appeared to me *Jean Bull philosophe,* and
he was for the moment, not only serious, but vehement. Yet I
have heard him, upon other occasions, talk with great contempt of
people who were anxious to gratify their palates; and the 206th
number of his *Rambler* is a masterly essay against gulosity. His
practice, indeed, I must acknowledge, may be considered as casting
the balance of his different opinions upon this subject; for I never
knew any man who relished good eating more than he did. When
at table, he was totally absorbed in the business of the moment;
his looks seemed riveted to his plate; nor would he, unless when in
very high company, say one word, or even pay the least attention to
what was said by others, till he had satisfied his appetite; which
was so fierce, and indulged with such intenseness, that while in the
act of eating, the veins of his forehead swelled, and generally a
strong perspiration was visible. To those whose sensations were
delicate, this could not but be disgusting; and it was doubtless not
very suitable to the character of a philosopher, who should be distinguished by self-command. But it must be owned that Johnson,
though he could be rigidly *abstemious,* was not a *temperate* man
either in eating or drinking. He could refrain, but he could not
use moderately. He told me that he had fasted two days without
inconvenience, and that he had never been hungry but once. They
who beheld with wonder how much he eat upon all occasions,
when his dinner was to his taste, could not easily conceive what
he must have meant by hunger; and not only was he remarkable for

the extraordinary quantity which he eat, but he was, or affected to be, a man of very nice discernment in the science of cookery. He used to descant critically on the dishes which had been at table where he had dined or supped, and to recollect very minutely what he had liked. I remember when he was in Scotland, his praising "Gordon's palates" (a dish of palates at the Honorable Alexander Gordon's), with a warmth of expression which might have done honor to more important subjects. "As for Maclaurin's imitation of *made dish*, it was a wretched attempt." He about the same time was so much displeased with the performances of a nobleman's French cook, that he exclaimed with vehemence, "I'd throw such a rascal into the river"; and he then proceeded to alarm a lady at whose house he was to sup, by the following manifesto of his skill: "I, Madam, who live at a variety of good tables, am a much better judge of cookery than any person who has a very tolerable cook, but lives much at home; for his palate is gradually adapted to the taste of his cook; whereas, Madam, in trying by a wider range, I can more exquisitely judge." When invited to dine, even with an intimate friend, he was not pleased if something better than a plain dinner was not prepared for him. I have heard him say on such an occasion, "This was a good dinner enough, to be sure; but it was not a dinner to *ask* a man to." On the other hand, he was wont to express, with great glee, his satisfaction when he had been entertained quite to his mind. One day when he had dined with his neighbor and landlord, in Bolt Court, Mr. Allen, the printer, whose old housekeeper had studied his taste in everything, he pronounced this eulogy: "Sir, we could not have had a better dinner, had there been a *Synod of Cooks.*"

2   While we were left by ourselves, after the Dutchman had gone to bed, Dr. Johnson talked of that studied behavior which many have recommended and practiced. He disapproved of it; and said, "I never considered whether I should be a grave man, or a merry man, but just let inclination, for the time, have its course."

▶ *Johnson's Peculiarities*

1   About this time he was afflicted with a very severe return of the hypochondriac disorder which was ever lurking about him. He was so ill as, notwithstanding his remarkable love of company, to be entirely averse to society, the most fatal symptom of that malady. Dr. Adams told me that as an old friend he was admitted

to visit him, and that he found him in a deplorable state, sighing, groaning, talking to himself, and restlessly walking from room to room. He then used this emphatical expression of the misery which he felt: "I would consent to have a limb amputated to recover my spirits."

2   Talking to himself was, indeed, one of his singularities ever since I knew him. I was certain that he was frequently uttering pious ejaculations; for fragments of the Lord's Prayer had been distinctly overheard. His friend Mr. Thomas Davies, of whom Churchill says, "That Davies hath a very pretty wife," when Dr. Johnson muttered "lead us not into temptation," used with waggish and gallant humor to whisper Mrs. Davies, "You, my dear, are the cause of this."

3   He had another particularity, of which none of his friends ever ventured to ask an explanation. It appeared to me some super-stitious habit which he had contracted early, and from which he had never called upon his reason to disentangle him. This was his anxious care to go out or in at a door or passage by a certain num-ber of steps from a certain point, or at least so as that either his right or his left foot (I am not certain which) should constantly make the first actual movement when he came close to the door or passage. Thus I conjecture: for I have upon innumerable occa-sions observed him suddenly stop, and then seem to count his steps with a deep earnestness; and when he had neglected or gone wrong in this sort of magical movement, I have seen him go back again, put himself in a proper posture to begin the ceremony, and, having gone through it, break from his abstraction, walk briskly on, and join his companion. A strange instance of something of this nature, even when on horseback, happened when he was in the Isle of Skye. Sir Joshua Reynolds has observed him to go a good way about rather than cross a particular alley in Leicester Fields; but this Sir Joshua imputed to his having had some disagreeable recollection associated with it.

4   That the most minute singularities which belonged to him, and made very observable parts of his appearance and manner, may not be omitted, it is requisite to mention that while talking or even musing as he sat in his chair, he commonly held his head to one side towards his right shoulder, and shook it in a tremulous manner, moving his body backwards and forwards, and rubbing his left knee in the same direction with the palm of his hand. In the intervals of articulating he made various sounds with his mouth,

sometimes as if ruminating, or what is called chewing the cud, sometimes giving a half whistle, sometimes making his tongue play backwards from the roof of his mouth, as if clucking like a hen, and sometimes protruding it against his upper gums in front, as if pronouncing quickly under his breath *too, too, too*; all this accompanied sometimes with a thoughtful look, but more frequently with a smile. Generally when he had concluded a period in the course of a dispute, by which time he was a good deal exhausted by violence and vociferation, he used to blow out his breath like a whale. This I suppose was a relief to his lungs; and seemed in him to be a contemptuous mode of expression, as if he had made the arguments of his opponent fly like chaff before the wind.

5   I am fully aware how very obvious an occasion I here give for the sneering jocularity of such as have no relish of an exact likeness; which to render complete, he who draws it must not disdain the slightest strokes. But if witlings should be inclined to attack on this account, let them have the candor to quote what I have offered in my defense[. . . .]

▶ *Kindness*

1   Johnson's love of little children, which he discovered upon all occasions, calling them "pretty dears," and giving them sweetmeats, was an undoubted proof of the real humanity and gentleness of his disposition.

2   His uncommon kindness to his servants, and serious concern, not only for their comfort in this world, but their happiness in the next, was another unquestionable evidence of what all who were intimately acquainted with him knew to be true.

3   Nor would it be just, under this head, to omit the fondness which he showed for animals which he had taken under his protection. I never shall forget the indulgence with which he treated Hodge, his cat; for whom he himself used to go out and buy oysters, lest the servants having that trouble should take a dislike to the poor creature. I am, unluckily, one of those who have an antipathy to a cat, so that I am uneasy when in the room with one; and I own, I frequently suffered a good deal from the presence of this same Hodge. I recollect him one day scrambling up Dr. Johnson's breast, apparently with much satisfaction, while my friend smiling and half-whistling, rubbed down his back, and pulled him by the tail; and when I observed he was a fine cat,

saying, "Why yes, Sir, but I have had cats whom I liked better than this"; and then as if perceiving Hodge to be out of countenance, adding, "but he is a very fine cat, a very fine cat indeed."

4   This reminds me of the ludicrous account which he gave Mr. Langton, of the despicable state of a young gentleman of good family. "Sir, when I heard of him last, he was running about town shooting cats." And then in a sort of kindly reverie, he bethought himself of his own favorite cat, and said, "But Hodge shan't be shot; no, no, Hodge shall not be shot."

▶ *Johnson's Funeral*

1   A few days before his death, he had asked Sir John Hawkins, as one of his executors, where he should be buried; and on being answered, "Doubtless, in Westminster Abbey," seemed to feel a satisfaction, very natural to a poet; and indeed in my opinion very natural to every man of any imagination, who has no family sepulcher in which he can be laid with his fathers. Accordingly, upon Monday, December 20, his remains were deposited in that noble and renowned edifice; and over his grave was placed a large blue flag-stone, with this inscription:

SAMUEL JOHNSON, LL.D.
Obiit XIII *die Decembris,*
ANNO DOMINI
M.DCC.LXXXIV.
Aetatis suae LXXV.

2   His funeral was attended by a respectable number of his friends, particularly such of the members of the Literary Club as were then in town; and was also honored with the presence of several of the Reverend Chapter of Westminster. Mr. Burke, Sir Joseph Banks, Mr. Windham, Mr. Langton, Sir Charles Bunbury, and Mr. Coleman, bore his pall. His school-fellow, Dr. Taylor, performed the mournful office of reading the burial service.

3   I trust, I shall not be accused of affectation, when I declare, that I find myself unable to express all that I felt upon the loss of such a "guide, philosopher, and friend." I shall, therefore, not say one word of my own, but adopt those of an eminent friend, which he uttered with an abrupt felicity, superior to all studied compositions: "He has made a chasm, which not only nothing can

fill up, but which nothing has a tendency to fill up.—Johnson is dead.—Let us go to the next best:—there is nobody; no man can be said to put you in mind of Johnson."[. . .]

• COMMENTARY •

Observation of the kind of material Boswell offers may be useful for your writing. The first selection given depends for its effect primarily upon Johnson's actions and words. His reception of the relative stranger, Boswell, on his first visit reveals his gentleness, and his words, especially in the anecdote about Kit Smart, tell us volumes, revealing his straight-forwardness and his honest, unassuming acceptance of a friend.

Boswell's own honesty and his efforts to picture his subject completely are manifest in the second selection, where he depends primarily upon Johnson's manners and actions to reveal him. What they reveal, not especially attractive to some people, is part of an accumulating revelation, for if in some respects to some people his manners seem uncouth, they are a feature of his unswerving honesty and unwavering forthrightness. Again in the third selection Boswell shows us Johnsonian features that are not all complimentary, and here he relies on actions to reveal the man. But if you must write about some person, explaining him to an audience, the person is presumably worth explaining (else why bother), and if he is worth explaining, he is worth explaining truthfully. Boswell's revelation of Johnson's peculiarities in this selection is indeed one of the excellencies of his work, as similar revelation would adorn any writing you may do. For your audience cannot really know your subject unless you show him to them specifically, in the very flesh, his moles revealed as well as his major philanthropies, his profundities shown, to be sure, but not to the exclusion of his casual kindnesses and trivial pleasures. For this reason, the fourth selection on Johnson and his cat is as revealing as an account of his literary theory might be. Throughout the selections, it is just such candid glimpses that reveal the man.

JOB 14

1. MAN *that is* born of a woman *is* of few days, and full of trouble.
2. He cometh forth like a flower, and is cut down: he fleeth also as a shadow and continueth not.

3. And dost thou open thine eyes upon such an one, and bringest me into judgment with thee?

4. Who can bring a clean *thing* out of an unclean? not one.

5. Seeing his days *are* determined, the number of his months *are* with thee, thou hast appointed his bounds that he cannot pass;

6. Turn from him, that he may rest, till he shall accomplish, as an hireling, his day.

7. For there is hope of a tree, if it be cut down, that it will sprout again, and that the tender branch thereof will not cease.

8. Though the root thereof wax old in the earth, and the stock thereof die in the ground;

9. *Yet* through the scent of water it will bud, and bring forth boughs like a plant.

10. But man dieth, and wasteth away: yea, man giveth up the ghost, and where *is* he?

11. As the waters fail from the sea, and the flood decayeth and drieth up:

12. So man lieth down, and riseth not: till the heavens *be* no more, they shall not awake, nor be raised out of their sleep.

13. O that thou wouldest hide me in the grave, that thou wouldest keep me secret, until thy wrath be past, that thou wouldest appoint me a set time, and remember me!

14. If a man die, shall he live *again?* all the days of my appointed time will I wait, till my change come.

15. Thou shalt call, and I will answer thee: thou wilt have a desire to the work of thine hands.

16. For now thou numberest my steps: dost thou not watch over my sin?

17. My transgression *is* sealed up in a bag, and thou sewest up mine iniquity.

18. And surely the mountain falling cometh to nought, and the rock is removed out of his place.

19. The waters wear the stones: thou washest away the things which grow *out* of the dust of the earth and thou destroyest the hope of man.

20. Thou prevailest for ever against him, and he passeth: thou changest his countenance, and sendest him away.

21. His sons come to honour, and he knoweth *it* not; and they are brought low, but he perceiveth *it* not of them.

22. But his flesh upon him shall have pain, and his soul within him shall mourn.

This selection, obviously, is devoted not to a particular man, but to the very state of man. Since you will at some time in your career wish or need to offer some commentary upon the conditions of existence, it would be useful to examine here the *order* of these comments and to observe carefully how the general observations are made concrete.

THE GOOD SCHOOLMASTER [1642]

Thomas Fuller

There is scarce any profession in the commonwealth more necessary which is so slightly performed. The reasons whereof I conceive to be these: First, young scholars make this calling their refuge, yea, perchance, before they have taken any degree in the university, commence schoolmasters in the country, as if nothing else were required to set up his profession but only a rod and a ferula. Secondly, others who are able use it only as a passage to better preferment, to patch the rents in their present fortune till they can provide a new one, and betake themselves to some more gainful calling. Thirdly, they are disheartened from doing their best with the miserable reward which in some places they receive, being masters to the children and slaves to their parents. Fourthly, being grown rich, they grow negligent, and scorn to touch the school but by the proxy of an usher. But see how well our schoolmaster behaves himself.

1. His genius inclines him with delight to his profession. Some men had as lief be schoolboys as schoolmasters, to be tied to the school as Cooper's Dictionary and Scapula's Lexicon are chained to the desk therein; and though great scholars, and skilful in other arts, are bunglers in this: but God of his goodness hath fitted several men for several callings, that the necessity of church and state, in all conditions, may be provided for. So that he who beholds the fabric thereof may say, God hewed out this stone, and appointed it to lie in this very place, for it would fit none other so well, and here it doth most excellent. And thus God moldeth some for a schoolmaster's life, undertaking it with desire and delight, and discharging it with dexterity and happy success.

2. He studies his scholars' natures as carefully as they their books; and ranks their dispositions into several forms. And though it may seem difficult for him in a great school to descend to all particulars, yet experienced schoolmasters may quickly make a grammar of boys' natures, and reduce them all, saving some few exceptions, to these general rules:

(a) Those that are ingenious and industrious. The conjunction of two such planets in a youth presage much good unto him. To such a lad a frown may be a whipping, and a whipping a death; yea, where their master whips them once, shame whips them all the week after. Such natures he useth with all gentleness.

(b) Those that are ingenious and idle. These think, with the hare in the fable, that, running with snails (so they count the rest of their schoolfellows), they shall come soon enough to the post, though sleeping a good while before their starting. Oh, a good rod would finely take them napping!

(c) Those that are dull and diligent. Wines, the stronger they be, the more lees they have when they are new. Many boys are muddy-headed till they be clarified with age, and such afterwards prove the best. Bristol diamonds are both bright and squared and pointed by nature, and yet are soft and worthless; whereas orient ones in India are rough and rugged naturally. Hard, rugged, and dull natures of youth acquit themselves afterwards the jewels of the country, and therefore their dullness at first is to be borne with, if they be diligent. That schoolmaster deserves to be beaten himself who beats nature in a boy for a fault. And I question whether all the whippings in the world can make their parts, which are naturally sluggish, rise one minute before the hour nature hath appointed.

(d) Those that are invincibly dull and negligent also. Correction may reform the latter, not amend the former. All the whetting in the world can never set a razor's edge on that which hath no steel in it. Such boys he consigneth over to other professions. Shipwrights and boatmakers will choose those crooked pieces of timber which other carpenters refuse. Those may make excellent merchants who will not serve for scholars.

3. He is able, diligent, and methodical in his teaching; not leading them rather in a circle than forwards. He minces his precepts for children to swallow, hanging clogs on the nimbleness of his own soul, that his scholars may go along with him.

4. He is and will be known to be an absolute monarch in his

school. If cockering mothers proffer him money to purchase their sons an exemption from his rod (to live as it were in a peculiar, out of their master's jurisdiction), with disdain he refuseth it, and scorns the late custom, in some places, of commuting whipping into money, and ransoming boys from the rod at a set price. If he hath a stubborn youth, correction-proof, he debaseth not his authority by contesting with him, but fairly, if he can, puts him away before his obstinacy hath affected others.

5. He is moderate in inflicting deserved correction. Many a schoolmaster better answereth the name παιδοτρίβης than παιδαγωγός rather tearing his scholars' flesh with whipping than giving them good education. No wonder if his scholars hate the muses, being presented unto them in the shapes of fiends and furies. Junius complains *de insolenti carnificina* of his schoolmaster, by whom *conscindebatur flagris septies aut octies in dies singulos*. Yea, hear the lamentable verses of poor Tusser, in his own Life:

> From Paul's I went, to Eton sent,
> To learn straightways the Latin phrase,
> Where fifty-three stripes given to me
> At once I had.

> For fault but small, or none at all,
> It came to pass thus beat I was;
> See, Udal, see the mercy of thee
> To me, poor lad.

Such an Orbilius mars more scholars than he makes: their tyranny hath caused many tongues to stammer, which spake plain by nature, and whose stuttering at first was nothing else but fears quavering on their speech at their master's presence; and whose mauling them about their heads hath dulled those who in quickness exceeded their master.

6. He makes his school free to him who sues to him *in forma pauperis*. And surely learning is the greatest alms that can be given. But he is a beast who because the poor scholar cannot pay him wages, pays the scholar in his whipping. Rather are diligent lads to be encouraged with all excitements to learning. This minds me of what I have heard concerning Mr. Bust, that worthy late schoolmaster of Eton, who would never suffer any wandering begging scholar, such as justly the statute hath ranked in the forefront of rogues, to come into his school, but would thrust him out

with earnestness (however privately charitable unto him) lest his schoolboys should be disheartened from their books, by seeing some scholars, after their studying in the university, preferred to beggary.

7. He spoils not a good school to make thereof a bad college, therein to teach his scholars logic. For besides that logic may have an action of trespass against grammar for encroaching on her liberties, syllogisms are solecisms taught in the school, and oftentimes they are forced afterwards in the university to unlearn the fumbling skill they had before.

8. Out of his school he is no whit pedantical in carriage or discourse; contenting himself to be rich in Latin, though he doth not jingle with it in every company wherein he comes.

To conclude, let this amongst other motives make schoolmasters careful in their place, that the eminencies of their scholars have commended the memories of their schoolmasters to posterity, who otherwise in obscurity had altogether been forgotten. Who had ever heard of R. Bond in Lancashire, but for the breeding of learned Ascham his scholar; or of Hartgrave in Brundley school, in the same county, but because he was the first to teach worthy Dr. Whitaker? Nor do I honor the memory of Mulcaster for anything so much as for his scholar, that gulf of learning, Bishop Andrews. This made the Athenians, the day before the great feast of Theseus their founder, to sacrifice a ram to the memory of Conidas his schoolmaster that first instructed him.

· SUGGESTIONS ·

This is a character sketch of a type, clearly not of an individual. For benefit to your own writing, it would be well once again to see how this character sketch has been organized and to note what prevents its being entirely generalization.

Explanation of Things

Most *things* are irrelevant to the well-being of the human spirit, and yet we must know about them. We must know about them to know what we clutter and surround ourselves with, to know what usurps our strength, to know what preoccupies our mental energies, to know what we work with, and for. Understanding things, in other words, however trivial they may be, may help us to know ourselves as well as the world around us.

If the subject itself does not immediately suggest to you a way of developing what you have to say, the procedures suggested earlier for developing paragraphs can be particularly helpful. Definition, for example, would help in the explanation of many things, and process analysis could be useful in explaining any mechanism or institution. Both methods could help, and both methods could provide a controlling pattern for an entire essay. The same is true of the other methods suggested, illustration, comparison, contrast, causal analysis, classification, and description.

SPECTATOR, NO. 18 [1711]

Joseph Addison

Wednesday, March 21, 1710/11.

1   It is my design in this paper to deliver down to posterity a faithful account of the Italian opera, and of the gradual progress which it has made upon the English stage: for there is no question but our great-grandchildren will be very curious to know the reason why their forefathers used to sit together like an audience of foreigners in their own country, and to hear whole plays acted before them in a tongue which they did not understand.

2   *Arsinoe* was the first opera that gave us a taste of Italian music. The great success this opera met with produced some attempts for forming pieces upon Italian plans, which should give a more natural and reasonable entertainment than what can be met with in the elaborate trifles of that nation. This alarmed the poetasters and fiddlers of the town, who were used to deal in more ordinary kind of ware; and therefore laid down an established rule, which is received as such to this day, *that nothing is capable of being well set to music, that is not nonsense.*

3   This maxim was no sooner received but we immediately fell to translating the Italian operas; and as there was no great danger of hurting the sense of those extraordinary pieces, our authors would often make words of their own which were entirely

foreign to the meaning of the passages they pretended to translate;
their chief care being to make the numbers of the English verse
answer to those of the Italian, that both of them might go to the
same tune. Thus the famous song in *Camilla,*

Barbara si t' intendo, &c.
Barbarous woman, yes, I know your meaning,

which expresses the resentments of an angry lover, was translated
into that English lamentation,

Frail are a lover's hopes, &c.

And it was pleasant enough to see the most refined persons of the
British nation dying away and languishing to notes that were filled
with a spirit of rage and indignation. It happened also very frequently, where the sense was rightly translated, the necessary
transposition of words, which were drawn out of the phrase of one
tongue into that of another, made the music appear very absurd
in one tongue that was very natural in the other. I remember an
Italian verse that ran thus word for word,

And turn'd my rage into pity:

which the English for rhyme sake translated,

And into pity turn'd my rage.

By this means the soft notes that were adapted to *pity* in the
Italian fell upon the word *rage* in the English, and the angry
sounds that were turned to *rage* in the original were made to express *pity* in the translation. It oftentimes happened likewise that
the finest notes in the air fell upon the most insignificant words in
the sentence. I have known the word *and* pursued through the
whole gamut, have been entertained with many a melodious *the,*
and have heard the most beautiful graces, quavers, and divisions
bestowed upon *then, for,* and *from;* to the eternal honor of our
English particles.

4   The next step to our refinement was the introducing of
Italian actors into our opera; who sung their parts in their own
language, at the same time that our countrymen performed theirs
in our native tongue. The king or hero of the play generally spoke
in Italian, and his slaves answered him in English: the lover frequently made his court, and gained the heart of his princess, in a

language which she did not understand. One would have thought it very difficult to have carried on dialogues after this manner without an interpreter between the persons that conversed together; but this was the state of the English stage for about three years.

5   At length the audience grew tired of understanding half of the opera and therefore, to ease themselves entirely of the fatigue of thinking, have so ordered it at present that the whole opera is performed in an unknown tongue. We no longer understand the language of our own stage; insomuch that I have often been afraid, when I have seen our Italian performers chattering in the vehemence of action, that they have been calling us names, and abusing us among themselves; but I hope, since we do put such an entire confidence in them, they will not talk against us before our faces, though they may do it with the same safety as if it were behind our backs. In the meantime, I cannot forbear thinking how naturally an historian who writes two or three hundred years hence, and does not know the taste of his wise forefathers, will make the following reflection: *In the beginning of the eighteenth century the Italian tongue was so well understood in England that operas were acted on the public stage in that language.*

6   One scarce knows how to be serious in the confutation of an absurdity that shows itself at the first sight. It does not want any great measure of sense to see the ridicule of this monstrous practice; but what makes it the more astonishing, it is not the taste of the rabble, but of persons of the greatest politeness, which has established it.

7   If the Italians have a genius for music above the English, the English have a genius for other performances of a much higher nature, and capable of giving the mind a much nobler entertainment. Would one think it was possible (at a time when an author lived that was able to write the *Phaedra and Hippolytus*) for a people to be so stupidly fond of the Italian opera as scarce to give a third day's hearing to that admirable tragedy? Music is certainly a very agreeable entertainment, but if it would take the entire possession of our ears, if it would make us incapable of hearing sense, if it would exclude arts that have a much greater tendency to the refinement of human nature, I must confess I would allow it no better quarter than Plato has done, who banishes it out of his commonwealth.

8   At present, our notions of music are so very uncertain that we do not know what it is we like; only, in general, we are transported with anything that is not English. So if it be of a foreign growth, let it be Italian, French, or High Dutch, it is the same thing. In short, our English music is quite rooted out and nothing yet planted in its stead.

9   When a royal palace is burnt to the ground, every man is at liberty to present his plan for a new one; and though it be but indifferently put together, it may furnish several hints that may be of use to a good architect. I shall take the same liberty in a following paper, of giving my opinion upon the subject of music; which I shall lay down only in a problematical manner, to be considered by those who are masters in the art.

• COMMENTARY •

Addison's expository method in this paper on opera (which, incidentally, may come as a surprise to those who thought their distaste for opera was unique) is forecast in his first sentence: "It is my design in this paper to deliver down to posterity a faithful account of the Italian opera, and of the gradual progress which it has made upon the English stage. . . ." The sentence indicates that the paper will be developed largely in the manner of a process analysis (see section on paragraph development).

Paragraph two explains the first step in this process, the arrival and success of the first Italian opera, and the consequent maxim established, "that nothing is capable of being well set to music, that is not nonsense." Paragraph three explains the following step: "This maxim was no sooner received but we immediately fell to translating the Italian operas." The rest of the paragraph is given to discussion and illustration of what Addison regards as the absurdities resulting from translations. Paragraph four follows with the next logical step, the introduction of Italian actors and the production of bilingual operas. The fifth paragraph brings the process to a conclusion—in Addison's view a ridiculous one—that "At length the audience grew tired of understanding half the opera and therefore, to ease themselves entirely of the fatigue of thinking, have so ordered it at present that the whole opera is performed in an unknown tongue."

The remaining paragraphs of the paper constitute Addison's commentary on this process. Paragraphs seven and eight in this group are developed by cause-effect analysis.

OF STUDIES [1625]

Sir Francis Bacon

Studies serve for delight, for ornament, and for ability. Their chief use for delight, is in privateness and retiring; for ornament, is in discourse; and for ability, is in the judgment and disposition of business. For expert men can execute, and perhaps judge of particulars, one by one; but the general counsels, and the plots and marshalling of affairs, come best from those that are learned. To spend too much time in studies is sloth; to use them too much for ornament, is affectation; to make judgment wholly by their rules, is the humour of a scholar. They perfect nature, and are perfected by experience: for natural abilities are like natural plants, that need proyning by study; and studies themselves do give forth directions too much at large, except they be bound in by experience. Crafty men contemn studies, simple men admire them, and wise men use them; for they teach not their own use; but that is a wisdom without them, and above them, won by observation. Read not to contradict and confute; nor to believe and take for granted; nor to find talk and discourse; but to weigh and consider. Some books are to be tasted, others to be swallowed, and some few to be chewed and digested; that is, some books are to be read only in parts; others to be read, but not curiously; and some few to be read wholly, and with diligence and attention. Some books also may be read by deputy, and extracts made of them by others; but that would be only in the less important arguments, and the meaner sort of books; else distilled books are like common distilled waters, flashy things. Reading maketh a full man; conference a ready man; and writing an exact man. And therefore, if a man write little, he had need have a great memory; if he confer little, he had need have a present wit; and if he read little, he had need have much cunning, to seem to know that he doth not. Histories make men wise; poets witty; the mathematics subtile; natural philosophy deep; moral grave; logic and rhetoric able to contend. *Abeunt studia in mores.* Nay there is no stond or impediment in the wit, but may be wrought out by fit studies: like as diseases of the body may have appropriate exercises. Bowling is good for the stone and reins; shooting for the lungs and breast; gentle walking for the stomach; riding for the head; and the like. So if a man's wit be wandering let him study the mathematics; for in demonstrations, if his wit be called away never so little, he must begin again. If his wit be not apt to distinguish or find differences, let him study the Schoolmen; for they are *cymini sectores.* If he be not apt to beat over matters, and to call up one thing to prove and illustrate another, let him study the lawyer's cases. So every defect of the mind may have a special receipt.

• SUGGESTIONS •

This brief study makes extensive use of several of the methods of development suggested in the section on paragraph development. Analyze its coordinate and parallel constructions to show Bacon's employment of these methods. It might be useful to your understanding of his method actually to chart the essay, beginning with the three elements given in the first sentence.

SPECTATOR, NO. 81 [1711]

Joseph Addison

1   About the middle of last winter I went to see an opera at the theatre in the Hay Market, where I could not but take notice of two parties of very fine women, that had placed themselves in the opposite side boxes, and seemed drawn up in a kind of battle array one against another. After a short survey of them, I found they were patched differently; the faces on one hand being spotted on the right side of the forehead, and those upon the other on the left. I quickly perceived that they cast hostile glances upon one another; and that their patches were placed in those different situations, as party signals to distinguish friends from foes. In the middle boxes, between these two opposite bodies, were several ladies who patched indifferently on both sides of their faces, and seemed to sit there with no other intention but to see the opera. Upon inquiry I found, that the body of Amazons on my right hand

were Whigs, and those on my left Tories: and that those who had placed themselves in the middle boxes were a neutral party, whose faces had not yet declared themselves. These last however, as I afterwards found, diminished daily, and took their party with one side or the other; insomuch that I observed in several of them, the patches, which were before dispersed equally, are now all gone over to the Whig or Tory side of the face. The censorious say that the men, whose hearts are aimed at, are very often the occasions that one part of the face is thus dishonored, and lies under a kind of disgrace, while the other is so much set off and adorned by the owners; and that the patches turn to the right or to the left, according to the principles of the man who is most in favor. But whatever may be the motives of a few fantastical coquettes, who do not patch for the public good so much as for their own private advantage, it is certain, that there are several women of honor, who patch out of principle, and with an eye to the interest of their country. Nay, I am informed that some of them adhere so steadfastly to their party, and are so far from sacrificing their zeal for the public to their passion for any particular person, that in a late draught of marriage articles a lady has stipulated with her husband, that whatever his opinions are, she shall be at liberty to patch on which side she pleases.

2   I must here take notice, that Rosalinda, a famous Whig partisan, has most unfortunately a very beautiful mole on the Tory part of her forehead; which, being very conspicuous, has occasioned many mistakes, and given an handle to her enemies to misrepresent her face, as though it had revolted from the Whig interest. But whatever this natural patch may seem to intimate, it is well known that her notions of government are still the same. This unlucky mole, however, has misled several coxcombs: and like the hanging out of false colors, made some of them converse with Rosalinda in what they thought the spirit of her party, when on a sudden she has given them an unexpected fire, that has sunk them all at once. If Rosalinda is unfortunate in her mole, Nigranilla is as unhappy in a pimple, which forces her, against her inclinations, to patch on the Whig side.

3   I am told that many virtuous matrons, who formerly have been taught to believe that this artificial spotting of the face was unlawful, are now reconciled, by a zeal for their cause, to what they could not be prompted by a concern for their beauty. This

way of declaring war upon one another, puts me in mind of what
is reported of the tigress, that several spots rise in her skin when
she is angry, or, as Mr. Cowley says:—

> She swells with angry pride,
> And calls forth all her spots on ev'ry side.

When I was in the theatre the time above mentioned, I had the
curiosity to count the patches on both sides, and found the Tory
patches to be about twenty stronger than the Whig; but to make
amends for this small inequality, I the next morning found the
whole puppet-show filled with faces spotted after the Whiggish
manner. Whether or no the ladies had retreated hither in order to
rally their forces I cannot tell; but the next night they came in so
great a body to the opera, that they out-numbered the enemy.

4   This account of party patches will, I am afraid, appear im-
probable to those who live at a distance from the fashionable
world; but as it is a distinction of a very singular nature, and what
perhaps may never meet with a parallel, I think I should not have
discharged the office of a faithful Spectator, had not I recorded it.

5   I have, in former papers, endeavored to expose this party
rage in women, as it only serves to aggravate the hatred and
animosities that reign among men, and in a great measure deprives
the fair sex of those peculiar charms with which nature has en-
dued them.

6   When the Romans and Sabines were at war, and just upon
the point of giving battle, the women who were allied to both of
them interposed with so many tears and entreaties, that they prevented the mutual slaughter which threatened both parties, and
united them together in a firm and lasting peace.

7   I would recommend this noble example to our British
ladies at a time when their country is torn with so many unnatural
divisions, that, if they continue, it will be a misfortune to be born
in it. The Greeks thought it so improper for women to interest
themselves in competitions and contentions, that for this reason,
among others, they forbade them under pain of death to be present
at the Olympic games, notwithstanding these were the public
diversions of all Greece.

8   As our English women excel those of all nations in
beauty, they should endeavor to out-shine them in all other ac-

complishments proper to the sex, and to distinguish themselves as tender mothers and faithful wives, rather than as furious partisans. Female virtues are of a domestic turn. The family is the proper province for private women to shine in. If they must be showing their zeal for the public, let it not be against those who are perhaps of the same family, or at least of the same religion or nation, but against those who are the open, professed, undoubted enemies of their faith, liberty, and country. When the Romans were pressed with a foreign enemy, the ladies voluntarily contributed all their rings and jewels to assist the government under a public exigence; which appeared so laudable an action in the eyes of their countrymen, that from thenceforth it was permitted by a law to pronounce public orations at the funeral of a woman in the praise of the deceased person, which till that time was peculiar to men. Would our English ladies, instead of sticking on a patch against those of their own country, show themselves so truly public-spirited as to sacrifice every one her necklace against the common enemy, what decrees ought not to be made in favor of them!

• SUGGESTIONS •

Determine the principles of organization giving this essay its shape. You may find it useful to refer to the section on the classical oration (see section on planning the longer essay) in order to discover whether or not this is an abbreviated classical oration. Paragraph five may be seen to state a proposition; if so, is the rest of the piece arranged according to the classical method?

Explanation of Sequences

A glance back to one of the selections in the preceding section, *Spectator, No. 18*, will prepare you for the material in this. Fully half of that selection is given to explaining a subject by chronicling the process through which it became important. The management of such sequences is the subject of this section.

Because it is almost always arranged chronologically, exposition of sequences may seem inseparable from narrative writing, and there are some similarities between the two. Still, they are different forms, divergent manners of proceeding, lending themselves to different kinds of problems. One explains; the other dramatizes. Exposition takes us through a sequence to a meaning; its purpose is usually instruction in following steps or in understanding their result. The narrative writer is devoted not to abstracting instruction from a sequence of events, but to recording the passing moments of life.

Sequences in exposition are best handled—indeed are only handled—by extended process analysis. You are obligated, of course, to keep stages in the sequence straight, though not inevitably chronological. You may wish, for example, to speak first of the total meaning of the sequence and then back up to record the events comprising the sequence.

Chronology nevertheless remains the ruling pattern since you are explaining things that happen in a sequence of a certain significance. And since this is true, you will find it necessary to give some attention to the pacing of your chronology so that you spend your time on events of importance, minimizing those that are in the sequence but have no major importance for the whole.

HOW A GALLANT SHOULD BEHAVE HIMSELF

IN A PLAYHOUSE [1609]

Thomas Dekker

1   The theater is your poets' royal exchange, upon which their muses (that are not turned to merchants) meeting, barter away that light commodity of words for a lighter ware than words, plaudities, and the breath of the great beast; which, like the threatenings of two cowards, vanish all into air. Players and their factors, who put away the stuff, and make the best of it they possibly can (as indeed 'tis their parts so to do), your gallant, your courtier, and your captain had wont to be the soundest paymasters; and I think are still the surest chapmen; and these, by means that their heads are well stocked, deal upon this comical freight by the gross; when your groundling and gallery-commoner

buys his sport by the penny and, like a haggler, is glad to utter it again by retailing.

2   Sithence then the place is so free in entertainment, allowing a stool as well to the farmer's son as to your templar; that your stinkard has the selfsame liberty to be there in his tobacco fumes, which your sweet courtier hath; and that your carman and tinker claim as strong a voice in their suffrage, and sit to give judgment on the play's life and death, as well as the proudest momus among the tribes of critic; it is fit that he, whom the most tailors' bills do make room for, when he comes, should not be basely (like a viol) cased up in a corner.

3   Whether therefore the gatherers of the public or private playhouse stand to receive the afternoon's rent, let our gallant (having paid it) presently advance himself up to the throne of the stage. I mean not into the lord's room, which is now but the stage's suburbs; no, those boxes, by the iniquity of custom, conspiracy of waiting women and gentlemen ushers, that there sweat together, and the covetousness of sharers, are contemptibly thrust into the rear, and much new satin is there damned by being smothered to death in darkness. But on the very rushes where the comedy is to dance, yea, and under the state of Cambyses himself, must our feathered estridge, like a piece of ordnance, be planted, valiantly (because impudently) beating down the mews and hisses of the opposed rascality.

4   For do but cast up a reckoning, what large comings-in are pursed up by sitting on the stage. First a conspicuous eminence is gotten; by which means the best and most essential parts of a gallant (good clothes, a proportionable leg, white hand, the Persian lock, and a tolerable beard) are perfectly revealed.

5   By sitting on the stage you have a signed patent to engross the whole commodity of censure; may lawfully presume to be a girder; and stand at the helm to steer the passage of scenes; yet no man shall once offer to hinder you from obtaining the title of an insolent, overweening coxcomb.

6   By sitting on the stage, you may, without traveling for it, at the very next door ask whose play it is; and, by that quest of inquiry, the law warrants you to avoid much mistaking; if you know not the author, you may rail against him; and peradventure so behave yourself that you may enforce the author to know you.

7   By sitting on the stage, if you be a knight you may happily

get you a mistress; if a mere Fleet-street gentleman, a wife; but assure yourself, by continual residence, you are the first and principal man in election to begin the number of We Three.

8   By spreading your body on the stage, and by being a justice in examining of plays, you shall put yourself into such true scentical authority that some poet shall not dare to present his muse rudely upon your eyes, without having first unmasked her, rifled her, and discovered all her bare and most mystical parts before you at a tavern, when you most knightly shall, for his pains, pay for both their suppers.

9   By sitting on the stage, you may (with small cost) purchase the dear acquaintance of the boys; have a good stool for sixpence; at any time know what particular part any of the infants present; get your match lighted, examine the play-suits' lace, and perhaps win wagers upon laying 'tis copper, etc. And to conclude, whether you be a fool or a justice of peace, a cuckold or a captain, a lord-mayor's son or a dawcock, a knave or an under-sheriff; of what stamp soever you be, current or counterfeit, the stage, like time, will bring you to most perfect light and lay you open; neither are you to be hunted from thence, though the scarecrows in the yard hoot at you, hiss at you, spit at you, yea, throw dirt even in your teeth; 'tis most gentlemanlike patience to endure all this and to laugh at the silly animals; but if the rabble, with a full throat, cry, "Away with the fool," you were worse than a madman to tarry by it; for the gentleman and the fool should never sit on the stage together.

10   Marry, let this observation go hand in hand with the rest; or rather, like a country servingman, some five yards before them. Present not yourself on the stage (especially at a new play) until the quaking prologue hath (by rubbing) got color into his cheeks, and is ready to give the trumpets their cue that he's upon point to enter; for then it is time, as though you were one of the properties or that you dropped out of the hangings, to creep from behind the arras, with your tripos or three-footed stool in one hand and a teston mounted between a forefinger and a thumb in the other; for if you should bestow your person upon the vulgar when the belly of the house is but half full, your apparel is quite eaten up, the fashion lost, and the proportion of your body in more danger to be devoured than if it were served up in the counter amongst the poultry; avoid that as you would the bastome. It shall crown you

with rich commendation to laugh aloud in the midst of the most serious and saddest scene of the terriblest tragedy; and to let that clapper, your tongue, be tossed so high that all the house may ring of it. Your lords use it; your knights are apes to the lords, and do so too; your Inn-a-Court-man is zany to the knights, and (marry, very scurvily) comes likewise limping after it; be thou a beagle to them all, and never lin snuffing, till you have scented them; for by talking and laughing (like a plowman in a morris) you heap Pelion upon Ossa, glory upon glory; as first, all the eyes in the galleries will leave walking after the players and only follow you; the simplest dolt in the house snatches up your name, and when he meets you in the streets, or that you fall into his hands in the middle of a watch, his word shall be taken for you; he'll cry "He's such a gallant," and you pass. Secondly, you publish your temperance to the world, in that you seem not to resort thither to taste vain pleasures with a hungry appetite; but only as a gentleman to spend a foolish hour or two, because you can do nothing else; thirdly, you mightily disrelish the audience and disgrace the author; marry, you take up (though it be at the worst hand) a strong opinion of your own judgment, and enforce the poet to take pity of your weakness and, by some dedicated sonnet, to bring you into a better paradise only to stop your mouth.

11   If you can, either for love or money, provide yourself a lodging by the water side; for above the convenience it brings to shun shoulder-clapping and to ship away your cockatrice betimes in the morning, it adds a kind of state unto you to be carried from thence to the stairs of your playhouse; hate a sculler (remember that) worse than to be acquainted with one o' the scullery. No, your oars are your only sea-crabs, board them, and take heed you never go twice together with one pair; often shifting is a great credit to gentlemen; and that dividing of your fare will make the poor watersnakes be ready to pull you in pieces to enjoy your custom; no matter whether upon landing you have money or no; you may swim in twenty of their boats over the river upon ticket; marry, when silver comes in, remember to pay treble their fare, and it will make your flounder-catchers to send more thanks after you when you do not draw than when you do; for they know it will be their own another day.

12   Before the play begins, fall to cards; you may win or lose (as fencers do in a prize) and beat one another by confederacy,

yet share the money when you meet at supper; notwithstanding, to gull the ragamuffins that stand aloof gaping at you, throw the cards (having first torn four of five of them) round about the stage, just upon the third sound, as though you had lost; it skills not if the four knaves lie on their backs, and outface the audience; there's none such fools as dare take exception at them, because, ere the play go off, better knaves than they will fall into the company.

13   Now, sir, if the writer be a fellow that hath either epigrammed you, or hath had a flirt at your mistress, or hath brought either your feather, or your red beard, or your little leggs, etc., on the stage, you shall disgrace him worse than by tossing him in a blanket or giving him the bastinado in a tavern, if, in the middle of his play (be it pastoral or comedy, moral or tragedy), you rise with a screwed and discontented face from your stool to be gone; no matter whether the scenes be good or no; the better they are the worse do you distaste them; and, being on your feet, sneak not away like a coward, but salute all your gentle acquaintance that are spread either on the rushes or on stools about you, and draw what troop you can from the stage after you. The mimics are beholden to you for allowing them elbow-room; their poet cries, perhaps, "A pox go with you," but care not for that, there's no music without frets.

14   Marry, if either the company or indisposition of the weather bind you to sit it out, my counsel is then that you turn plain ape, take up a rush, and tickle the earnest ears of your fellow gallants, to make other fools fall a-laughing; mew at passionate speeches, blare at merry, find fault with the music, whew at the children's action, whistle at the songs; and above all, curse the sharers, that whereas the same day you bestowed forty shillings on an embroidered felt and feather (Scotch-fashion) for your mistress in the court or your punk in the city, within two hours after you encounter with the very same block on the stage, when the haberdasher swore to you the impression was extant but that morning.

15   To conclude, hoard up the finest play-scraps you can get, upon which your lean wit may most savorly feed, for want of other stuff, when the Arcadian and Euphuized gentlewomen have their tongues sharpened to set upon you; that quality (next to your shuttlecock) is the only furniture to a courtier that's but a

new beginner, and is but in his A B C of compliment. The next places that are filled, after the playhouses be emptied, are (or ought to be) taverns. Into a tavern then let us next march, where the brains of one hogshead must be beaten out to make up another.

• COMMENTARY •

With the exception of one step, this is an exposition of folly and silliness organized as a chronological record of a sequence. The major steps are as follows:

Step 1: the gallant is urged to advance to the "throne of the stage," the attendant advantages described in the following paragraphs (paragraphs 3–9)

Step 2: he is advised to wait until the prologue has begun for several good reasons (paragraph 10)

Step 3: he is urged to find lodging on the Thames near the theater with some fanfare—this step out of chronological order (paragraph 11)

Step 4: he is advised how to conduct himself before the play begins (paragraph 12)

Step 5: he is advised how to conduct himself during the play (paragraph 13)

Step 6: he is advised how to conduct himself if circumstances force him to stay for the entire play (paragraph 14)

Step 7: he is advised how to equip his mind for the theater and for the next stop, the tavern (paragraph 15)

The ordering of the process is simple and appropriate to the spectacle it reveals, following the gallant from his entrance to his prospective exit in straightforward chronological manner, except for step three. This step is out of place, but it is offered as a kind of afterthought and is not an essential part of the sequence.

The pacing is accurate, most space and time being given to the most crucial steps in the sequence. The first step in the sequence gets six paragraphs while the other steps get only one each; the first step in this sequence is obviously the critical event, and the various advantages attendant upon sitting on the stage are carefully, if whimsically, spelled out. Step two gets one paragraph just as the rest do, but it is a longer paragraph, important because it recommends specific activities for the gallant while he is upon the stage.

The first two paragraphs introduce the sequence.

SPECTATOR, no. 409 [1712]

Joseph Addison

1   Gracian very often recommends *the fine Taste* as the utmost perfection of an accomplished man. As this word arises very often in conversation, I shall endeavor to give some account of it, and to lay down rules how we may know whether we are possessed of it, and how we may acquire that fine taste of writing which is so much talked of among the polite world.

2   Most languages make use of this metaphor to express that faculty of the mind which distinguishes all the most concealed faults and nicest perfections in writing. We may be sure this metaphor would not have been so general in all tongues had there not been a very great conformity between that mental taste which is the subject of this paper and that sensitive taste which gives us a relish of every different flavor that affects the palate. Accordingly we find there are as many degrees of refinement in the intellectual faculty as in the sense which is marked out by this common denomination.

3   I knew a person who possessed the one in so great a perfection that after having tasted ten different kinds of tea, he would distinguish, without seeing the color of it, the particular sort which was offered him; and not only so, but any two sorts of them that were mixed together in an equal proportion; nay, he has carried the experiment so far as, upon tasting the composition of three different sorts, to name the parcels from whence the three several ingredients were taken. A man of a fine taste in writing will discern after the same manner, not only the general beauties and imperfections of an author, but discover the several ways of thinking and expressing himself which diversify him from all other authors, with the several foreign infusions of thought and language, and the particular authors from whom they were borrowed.

4   After having thus far explained what is generally meant by a fine taste in writing, and shown the propriety of the metaphor which is used on this occasion, I think I may define it to be *that faculty of the soul which discerns the beauties of an author with*

pleasure, and the imperfections with dislike. If a man would know whether he is possessed of this faculty; I would have him read over the celebrated works of antiquity, which have stood the test of so many different ages and countries; or those works among the moderns which have the sanction of the politer part of our contemporaries. If upon the perusal of such writings he does not find himself delighted in an extraordinary manner, or if, upon reading the admired passages in such authors, he finds a coldness and indifference in his thoughts, he ought to conclude, not (as is too usual among tasteless readers) that the author wants those perfections which have been admired in him, but that he himself wants the faculty of discovering them.

5   He should, in the second place, be very careful to observe whether he tastes the distinguishing perfections, or, if I may be allowed to call them so, the specific qualities of the author whom he peruses; whether he is particularly pleased with Livy for his manner of telling a story, with Sallust for his entering into those internal principles of action which arise from the characters and manners of the persons he describes, or with Tacitus for his displaying those outward motives of safety and interest which give birth to the whole series of transactions which he relates.

6   He may likewise consider how differently he is affected by the same thought which presents itself in a great writer from what he is when he finds it delivered by a person of an ordinary genius. For there is as much difference in apprehending a thought clothed in Cicero's language and that of a common author as in seeing an object by the light of a taper or by the light of the sun.

7   It is very difficult to lay down rules for the acquirement of such a taste as that I am here speaking of. The faculty must in some degree be born with us, and it very often happens that those who have other qualities in perfection are wholly void of this. One of the most eminent mathematicians of the age has assured me that the greatest pleasure he took in reading Vergil was in examining Aeneas his voyage by the map; as I question not but many a modern compiler of history would be delighted with little more in that divine author than the bare matters of fact.

8   But notwithstanding this faculty must in some measure be born with us, there are several methods for cultivating and improving it, and without which it will be very uncertain, and of little use to the person that possesses it. The most natural method

for this purpose is to be conversant among the writings of the most polite authors. A man who has any relish for fine writing either discovers new beauties or receives stronger impressions from the masterly strokes of a great author every time he peruses him: besides that, he naturally wears himself into the same manner of speaking and thinking.

9   Conversation with men of a polite genius is another method for improving our natural taste. It is impossible for a man of the greatest parts to consider anything in its whole extent, and in all its variety of lights. Every man, besides those general observations which are to be made upon an author, forms several reflections that are peculiar to his own manner of thinking; so that conversation will naturally furnish us with hints which we did not attend to, and make us enjoy other men's parts and reflections as well as our own. This is the best reason I can give for the observation which several have made, that men of great genius in the same way of writing seldom rise up singly, but at certain periods of time appear together and in a body; as they did at Rome in the reign of Augustus, and in Greece about the age of Socrates. I cannot think that Corneille, Racine, Molière, Boileau, La Fontaine, Bruyère, Bossu, or the Daciers would have written so well as they have done, had they not been friends and contemporaries.

10   It is likewise necessary for a man who would form to himself a finished taste of good writing to be well versed in the works of the best critics both ancient and modern. I must confess that I could wish there were authors of this kind, who, beside the mechanical rules which a man of very little taste may discourse upon, would enter into the very spirit and soul of fine writing, and show us the several sources of that pleasure which rises in the mind upon the perusal of a noble work. Thus although in poetry it be absolutely necessary that the unities of time, place, and action, with other points of the same nature, should be thoroughly explained and understood, there is still something more essential to the art, something that elevates and astonishes the fancy and gives a greatness of mind to the reader, which few of the critics besides Longinus have considered.

11   Our general taste in England is for epigram, turns of wit, and forced conceits, which have no manner of influence, either for the bettering or enlarging the mind of him who reads them, and have been carefully avoided by the greatest writers, both

among the ancients and moderns. I have endeavored in several of my speculations to banish this Gothic taste which has taken possession among us. I entertained the town for a week together with an essay upon wit, in which I endeavored to detect several of those false kinds which have been admired in the different ages of the world; and at the same time to show wherein the nature of true wit consists. I afterwards gave an instance of the great force which lies in a natural simplicity of thought to affect the mind of the reader, from such vulgar pieces as have little else besides this single qualification to recommend them. I have likewise examined the works of the greatest poet which our nation or perhaps any other has produced, and particularized most of those rational and manly beauties which give a value to that divine work. I shall next Saturday enter upon an essay on *the Pleasures of the Imagination,* which, though it shall consider that subject at large, will perhaps suggest to the reader what it is that gives a beauty to many passages of the finest writers both in prose and verse. As an undertaking of this nature is entirely new, I question not but it will be received with candor.

• **SUGGESTIONS** •

Determine the purpose of this essay, outline the work to show the stages in the process given, and analyze transitions which help to maintain continuity between steps in the process.

Explanation of Ideas

Be urged anew that native genius is inadequate to the requirements of education and citizenship and maturity. The great goal of education is the mastery of what the race knows; any man who has his wits knows that this is not literally possible, yet any man who has his wits can honor the quest by first of all submerging himself in study rather than trusting to what he already knows. Such trust, almost always misplaced, leads usually to foolish confidence in oneself, or to despair upon the inevitable discovery of that self's inadequacy. No task you will face, no obligation you will meet, demands more of you; some glimpse of its difficulty can be seen in the arduous task of first knowing, then explaining ideas.

To explain ideas well, a writer must recognize their appearance in the events, institutions, and experiences of life, but he must also avoid confusing them with the events, institutions, or experiences themselves. Even a casual reading of letters to editors in magazines and newspapers or of the magazines and newspapers themselves will discover frequent confusion of this kind. Writers not uncommonly treat things as if they were ideas, the Declaration of Independence as a document as if the document itself were the ideas contained, automobiles as if they were philosophies, fluoride compounds as if they were political ideologies.

To explain ideas well, a writer must also confine his work to manageable limits. Explaining ideas, which by their very intangibility are remote to us, requires knowing how to begin; it also requires recognizing the necessary limits of your treatment. Most such explanations can be rendered successfully only in terms of some immediately pertinent and specific situation, for only in this way can a beginning be found and limits be properly set. Any idea that is a subject for exposition must, in other words, be given a local habitation; nothing is worse—or more common—than an essay that only generalizes.

Many other reasons could be cited, not least of which is the primary ordeal of first knowing your subject before you ever begin to explain it. That task, presumably, you are presently and eternally engaged in.

THE NEW IMMORALITY*

Joseph Wood Krutch

1   The provost of one of our largest and most honored institutions told me not long ago that a questionnaire was distributed to his undergraduates and that 40 per cent refused to acknowledge that they believed cheating on examinations to be reprehensible.

* From *Saturday Review*, July 30, 1960. By permission of the author and publisher.

2 Recently a reporter for a New York newspaper stopped six people on the street and asked them if they would consent to take part in a rigged television quiz for money. He reported that five of the six said yes. Yet most of these five, like most of the college cheaters, would probably profess a strong social consciousness. They may cheat, but they vote for foreign aid and for enlightened social measures.

3 These two examples exhibit a paradox of our age. It is often said, and my observation leads me to believe it true, that our seemingly great growth in social morality has oddly enough taken place in a world where private morality—a sense of the supreme importance of purely personal honor, honesty, and integrity—seems to be declining. Beneficent and benevolent social institutions are administered by men who all too frequently turn out to be accepting "gifts." The world of popular entertainment is rocked by scandals. College students, put on their honor, cheat on examinations. Candidates for the Ph.D. hire ghost writers to prepare their theses.

4 But, one may object, haven't all these things always been true? Is there really any evidence that personal dishonesty is more prevalent than it always was?

5 I have no way of making a historical measurement. Perhaps these things are not actually more prevalent. What I do know is that there is an increasing tendency to accept and take for granted such personal dishonesty. The bureaucrat and disk jockey say, "Well, yes, I took presents, but I assure you that I made just decisions anyway." The college student caught cheating does not even blush. He shrugs his shoulders and comments: "Everybody does it, and besides, I can't see that it really hurts anybody."

6 Jonathan Swift once said: "I have never been surprised to find men wicked, but I have often been surprised to find them not ashamed." It is my conviction that though men may be no more wicked than they always have been, they seem less likely to be ashamed. If everybody does it, it must be right. Honest, moral, decent mean only what is usual. This is not really a wicked world, because morality means mores or manners and usual conduct is the only standard.

7 The second part of the defense, "it really doesn't hurt anybody" means it doesn't do that abstraction called society any harm. The harm it did the bribe-taker and the cheater isn't important;

it is purely personal. And personal as opposed to social decency doesn't count for much. Sometimes I am inclined to blame sociology for part of this paradox. Sociology has tended to lay exclusive stress upon social morality, and tended too often to define good and evil as merely the "socially useful" or its reverse.

8   What social morality and social conscience leave out is the narrower but very significant concept of honor—as opposed to what is sometimes called merely "social desirable conduct." The man of honor is not content to ask merely whether this or that will hurt society, or whether it is what most people would permit themselves to do. He asks, and he asks first of all, would it hurt him and his self-respect? Would it dishonor him personally?

9   It was a favorite and no doubt sound argument among early twentieth-century reformers that "playing the game" as the gentleman was supposed to play it was not enough to make a decent society. They were right; it is not enough. But the time has come to add that it is nevertheless indispensable. I hold that it is indeed inevitable that the so-called social conscience unsupported by the concept of personal honor will create a corrupt society. But suppose that it doesn't? Suppose that no one except the individual suffers from the fact that he sees nothing wrong in doing what everybody else does? Even so, I still insist that for the individual himself nothing is more important than this personal, interior sense of right and wrong and his determination to follow that rather than to be guided by what everybody does or merely the criterion of "social usefulness." It is impossible for me to imagine a good society composed of men without honor.

10   We hear it said frequently that what present-day men most desire is security. If that is so, then they have a wrong notion of what the real, the ultimate, security is. No one who is dependent on anything outside himself, upon money, power, fame, or whatnot, is or ever can be secure. Only he who possesses himself and is content with himself is actually secure. Too much is being said about the importance of adjustment and "participation in the group." Even cooperation, to give this thing its most favorable designation, is no more important than the ability to stand alone when the choice must be made between the sacrifice of one's own integrity and adjustment to or participation in group activity.

11   No matter how bad the world may become, no matter how much the mass man of the future may lose such of the virtues as he still has, one fact remains. If one person alone refuses to go

along with him, if one person alone asserts his individual and inner
right to believe in and be loyal to what his fellow men seem to
have given up, then at least he will still retain what is perhaps the
most important part of humanity.

• COMMENTARY •

The title of this selection identifies the idea discussed, but it is the first
paragraph that gives the idea its local habitation, thus setting the limits
to the discussion. The illustrations in paragraphs two and three help to
establish those limits, which are still more clearly defined in paragraph
five, where Krutch makes clear that he has no intention of setting this
problem in any long historical perspective. He is intent upon a current
phenomenon, which he explains by concrete illustrations, upon which
are founded his accumulating generalizations. On the basis of the
illustrations offered in the first four paragraphs, he contends in paragraph five that "there is an increasing tendency to accept and take for
granted . . . personal dishonesty." Using a further illustration and a
reference to Swift as a bridge, he then moves in paragraph six to a restatement of this conviction, "that though men may be no more wicked
than they always have been, they seem less likely to be ashamed."
Paragraphs six and seven are given to some account of the usual defenses for this "new immorality," the arguments that "everybody does
it" and that "it really doesn't hurt anybody." It seems clear enough that
these defenses are offered not so that he may refute them as in an argumentative discourse, but so that he may by analysis demonstrate that
the defense itself is a function of the "new immorality." The remaining
paragraphs, eight through eleven, follow patterns of development approximately identical. Each begins with a common assumption revealing
this immorality, only to conclude with corrective analysis of the assumption.

A PRIMER OF EXISTENTIALISM*

Gordon E. Bigelow

1   For some years I fought the word by irritably looking the
other way whenever I stumbled across it, hoping that like dadaism

* From *College English*, December, 1961. Reprinted with the permission
of the National Council of Teachers of English and Professor Gordon Bigelow.

and some of the other "isms" of the French *avant garde* it would
go away if I ignored it. But existentialism was apparently more
than the picture it evoked of uncombed beards, smoky basement
cafés, and French beatniks regaling one another between sips of
absinthe with brilliant variations on the theme of despair. It turned
out to be of major importance to literature and the arts, to philosophy and theology, and of increasing importance to the social
sciences. To learn more about it, I read several of the self-styled
introductions to the subject, with the baffled sensation of a man
who reads a critical introduction to a novel only to find that he
must read the novel before he can understand the introduction.
Therefore, I should like to provide here something most discussions of existentialism take for granted, a simple statement of its
basic characteristics. This is a reckless thing to do because there
are several kinds of existentialism and what one says of one kind
may not be true of another, but there is an area of agreement, and
it is this common ground that I should like to set forth here. We
should not run into trouble so long as we understand from the
outset that the six major themes outlined below will apply in varying degrees to particular existentialists. A reader should be able to
go from here to the existentialists themselves, to the more specialized critiques of them, or be able to recognize an existentialist
theme or coloration in literature when he sees it.

2   A word first about the kinds of existentialism. Like tran-
scendentalism of the last century, there are almost as many
varieties of this *ism* as there are individual writers to whom the
word is applied (not all of them claim it). But without being
facetious we might group them into two main kinds, the *ungodly*
and the *godly*. To take the ungodly or atheistic first, we would list
as the chief spokesmen among many others Jean-Paul Sartre,
Albert Camus, and Simone de Beauvoir. Several of this important
group of French writers had rigorous and significant experience
in the Resistance during the Nazi occupation of France in World
War II. Out of the despair which came with the collapse of their
nation during those terrible years they found unexpected strength
in the single indomitable human spirit, which even under severe
torture could maintain the spirit of resistance, the unextinguishable
ability to say "No." From this irreducible core in the human spirit,
they erected after the war a philosophy which was a twentieth-
century variation of the philosophy of Descartes. But instead of

saying "I think, therefore I am," they said "I can say No, therefore I exist." As we shall presently see, the use of the word "exist" is of prime significance. This group is chiefly responsible for giving existentialism its status in the popular mind as a literary-philosophical cult.

3   Of the godly or theistic existentialists we should mention first a mid-nineteenth-century Danish writer, Søren Kierkegaard; two contemporary French Roman Catholics, Gabriel Marcel and Jacques Maritain; two Protestant theologians, Paul Tillich and Nicholas Berdyaev; and Martin Buber, an important contemporary Jewish theologian. Taken together, their writings constitute one of the most significant developments in modern theology. Behind both groups of existentialists stand other important figures, chiefly philosophers, who exert powerful influence upon the movement—Blaise Pascal, Friedrich Nietzsche, Henri Bergson, Martin Heidegger, Karl Jaspers, among others. Several literary figures, notably Tolstoy and Dostoievsky, are frequently cited because existentialist attitudes and themes are prominent in their writings. The eclectic nature of this movement should already be sufficiently clear and the danger of applying too rigidly to any particular figure the general characteristics of the movement which I now make bold to describe:

▶ *1. Existence before Essence*

4   Existentialism gets its name from an insistence that human life is understandable only in terms of an individual man's existence, his particular experience of life. It says that a man *lives* (has existence) rather than *is* (has being or essence), and that every man's experience of life is unique, radically different from everyone else's and can be understood truly only in terms of his involvement in life or commitment to it. It strenuously shuns that view which assumes an ideal of Man or Mankind, a universal of human nature of which each man is only one example. It eschews the question of Greek philosophy, *"What is mankind?"* which suggests that man can be defined if he is ranged in his proper place in the order of nature; it asks instead the question of Job and St. Augustine, *"Who am I?"* with its suggestion of the uniqueness and mystery of each human life and its emphasis upon the subjective or personal rather than the objective or impersonal. From the outside a man appears to be just another natural creature; from the inside

he is an entire universe, the center of infinity. The existentialist insists upon this latter radically subjective view, and from this grows much of the rest of existentialism.

▶ 2. Reason is Impotent to Deal with the Depths of Human Life

5   There are two parts to this proposition—first, that human reason is relatively weak and imperfect, and second, that there are dark places in human life which are "non-reason" and to which reason scarcely penetrates. Since Plato, Western civilization has usually assumed a separation of reason from the rest of the human psyche, and has glorified reason as suited to command the non-rational part. The classic statement of this separation appears in the *Phaedrus*, where Plato describes the psyche in the myth of the chariot which is drawn by the white steeds of the emotions and the black unruly steeds of the appetites. The driver of the chariot is Reason who holds the reins which control the horses and the whip to subdue the surging black steeds of passion. Only the driver, the rational nature, is given human form; the rest of the psyche, the nonrational part, is given a lower, animal form. This separation and exaltation of reason is carried further in the allegory of the cave in the *Republic*. You recall the sombre picture of human life with which the story begins: men are chained in the dark in a cave, with their backs to a flickering firelight, able to see only uncertain shadows moving on the wall before them, able to hear only confused echoes of sounds. One of the men, breaking free from his chains, is able to turn and look upon the objects themselves and the light which casts the shadows; even, at last, he is able to work his way entirely out of the cave into the sunlight beyond. All this he is able to do through his reason; he escapes from the bondage of error, from time and change, from death itself, into the realm of changeless eternal ideas or Truth, and the lower nature which had chained him in darkness is left behind.

6   Existentialism in our time, and this is one of its most important characteristics, insists upon reuniting the "lower" or irrational parts of the psyche with the "higher." It insists that man must be taken in his wholeness and not in some divided state, that whole man contains not only intellect but also anxiety, guilt, and the will to power—which modify and sometimes overwhelm the reason. A man seen in this light is fundamentally ambiguous, if

not mysterious, full of contradictions and tensions which cannot be dissolved simply by taking thought. "Human life," said Berdyaev, "is permeated by underground streams." One is reminded of D. H. Lawrence's outburst against Franklin and his rational attempt to achieve moral perfection: "The Perfectability of Man! . . . The perfectability of which man? I am many men. Which of them are you going to perfect? I am not a mechanical contrivance. . . . It's a queer thing is a man's soul. It is the whole of him. Which means it is the unknown as well as the known. . . . The soul of man is a dark vast forest, with wild life in it." The emphasis in existentialism is not on idea but upon the thinker who has the idea. It accepts not only his power of thought, but his contingency and fallibility, his frailty, his body, blood, and bones, and above all his death. Kierkegaard emphasized the distinction between *subjective* truth (what a person *is*) and *objective* truth (what the person *knows*), and said that we encounter the true self not in the detachment of thought but in the involvement and agony of choice and in the pathos of commitment to our choice. This distrust of rational systems helps to explain why many existential writers in their own expression are paradoxical or prophetic or gnomic, why their works often belong more to literature than to philosophy.

▶ *3. Alienation or Estrangement*

7   One major result of the dissociation of reason from the rest of the psyche has been the growth of science, which has become one of the hallmarks of Western civilization, and an ever-increasing rational ordering of men in society. As the existentialists view them, the main forces of history since the Renaissance have progressively separated man from concrete earth existence, have forced him to live at ever higher levels of abstraction, have collectivized individual man out of existence, have driven God from the heavens, or what is the same thing, from the hearts of men. They are convinced that modern man lives in a fourfold condition of alienation: from God, from nature, from other men, from his own true self.

8   The estrangement from God is most shockingly expressed by Nietzsche's anguished cry, "God is dead," a cry which has continuously echoed through the writings of the existentialists, particularly the French. This theme of spiritual barrenness is a commonplace in literature of this century, from Eliot's "Hollow

Man" to the novels of Dos Passos, Hemingway, and Faulkner. It often appears in writers not commonly associated with the existentialists as in this remarkable passage from *A Story-Teller's Story*, where Sherwood Anderson describes his own awakening to his spiritual emptiness. He tells of walking alone late at night along a moonlit road when,

> I had suddenly an odd, and to my own seeming, a ridiculous desire to abase myself before something not human and so stepping into the moonlit road, I knelt in the dust. Having no God, the gods having been taken from me by the life about me, as a personal God has been taken from all modern men by a force within that man himself does not understand but that is called the intellect, I kept smiling at the figure I cut in my own eyes as I knelt in the road. . . .
>
> There was no God in the sky, no God in myself, no conviction in myself that I had the power to believe in a God, and so I merely knelt in the dust in silence and no words came to my lips.

In another passage Anderson wondered if the giving of itself by an entire generation to mechanical things was not really making all men impotent, if the desire for a greater navy, a greater army, taller public buildings, was not a sign of growing impotence. He felt that Puritanism and the industrialism which was its offspring had sterilized modern life, and proposed that men return to a healthful animal vigor by renewed contact with simple things of the earth, among them untrammeled sexual expression. One is reminded of the unkempt and delectable raffishness of Steinbeck's *Cannery Row* or of D. H. Lawrence's quasi-religious doctrine of sex, "blood-consciousness" and the "divine otherness" of animal existence.

9   Man's estrangement from nature has been a major theme in literature at least since Rousseau and the Romantic movement, and can hardly be said to be the property of existentialists. But this group nevertheless adds its own insistence that one of modern man's most urgent dangers is that he builds ever higher the brick and steel walls of technology which shut him away from a health-giving life according to "nature." Their treatment of this theme is most commonly expressed as part of a broader insistence that modern man needs to shun abstraction and return to "concreteness" or "wholeness."

10   A third estrangement has occurred at the social level and its sign is a growing dismay at man's helplessness before the great machine-like colossus of industrialized society. This is another major theme of Western literature, and here again, though they hardly discovered the danger or began the protest, the existentialists in our time renew the protest against any pattern or force which would stifle the unique and spontaneous in individual life. The crowding of men into cities, the subdivision of labor which submerges the man in his economic function, the burgeoning of centralized government, the growth of advertising, propaganda, and mass media of entertainment and communication—all the things which force men into Riesman's "Lonely Crowd"—these same things drive men asunder by destroying their individuality and making them live on the surface of life, content to deal with things rather than people. "Exteriorization," says Berdyaev, "is the source of slavery, whereas freedom is interiorization. Slavery always indicates alienation, the ejection of human nature into the external." This kind of alienation is exemplified by Zero, in Elmer Rice's play "The Adding Machine." Zero's twenty-five years as a bookkeeper in a department store have dried up his humanity, making him incapable of love, of friendship, of any deeply felt, freely expressed emotion. Such estrangement is often given as the reason for man's inhumanity to man, the explanation for injustice in modern society. In Camus' short novel, aptly called *The Stranger*, a young man is convicted by a court of murder. This is a homicide which he has actually committed under extenuating circumstances. But the court never listens to any of the relevant evidence, seems never to hear anything that pertains to the crime itself; it convicts the young man on wholly irrelevant grounds—because he had behaved in an unconventional way at his mother's funeral the day before the homicide. In this book one feels the same dream-like distortion of reality as in the trial scene in *Alice in Wonderland*, a suffocating sense of being enclosed by events which are irrational or absurd but also inexorable. Most disturbing of all is the young man's aloneness, the impermeable membrane of estrangement which surrounds him and prevents anyone else from penetrating to his experience of life or sympathizing with it.

11   The fourth kind of alienation, man's estrangement from his own true self, especially as his nature is distorted by an exaltation of reason, is another theme having an extensive history as a

major part of the Romantic revolt. Of the many writers who treat the theme, Hawthorne comes particularly close to the emphasis of contemporary existentialists. His Ethan Brand, Dr. Rappaccini, and Roger Chillingworth are a recurrent figure who represents the dislocation in human nature which results when an over-developed or misapplied intellect severs "the magnetic chain of human sympathy." Hawthorne is thoroughly existential in his concern for the sanctity of the individual human soul, as well as in his preoccupation with sin and the dark side of human nature, which must be seen in part as his attempt to build back some full-ness to the flattened image of man bequeathed to him by the Enlightenment. Whitman was trying to do this when he added flesh and bone and a sexual nature to the spiritualized image of man he inherited from Emerson, though his image remains diffused and attenuated by the same cosmic optimism. Many of the nine-teenth-century depictions of man represent him as a figure of power or of potential power, sometimes as daimonic, like Melville's Ahab, but after World War I the power is gone; man is not merely distorted or truncated, he is hollow, powerless, faceless. At the time when his command over natural forces seems to be un-limited, man is pictured as weak, ridden with nameless dread. And this brings us to another of the major themes of existentialism.

▶ *4. "FEAR AND TREMBLING," Anxiety*

12   At Stockholm when he accepted the Nobel Prize, William Faulkner said that "Our tragedy today is a general and universal physical fear so long sustained by now that we can even bear it. There are no longer problems of the spirit. There is only one question: When will I be blown up?" The optimistic vision of the Enlightenment which saw man, through reason and its extensions in science, conquering all nature and solving all social and political problems in a continuous upward spiral of Progress, cracked open like a melon on the rock of World War I. The theories which held such high hopes died in that sickening and unimaginable butchery. Here was a concrete fact of human nature and society which the theories could not contain. The Great Depression and World War II deepened the sense of dismay which the loss of these ideals brought, but only with the atomic bomb did this become an un-bearable terror, a threat of instant annihilation which confronted all men, even those most insulated by the thick crust of material goods and services. Now the most unthinking person could sense

that each advance in mechanical technique carried not only a chromium and plush promise of comfort but a threat as well.

13   Sartre, following Kierkegaard, speaks of another kind of anxiety which oppresses modern man—"The anguish of Abraham" —the necessity which is laid upon him to make moral choices on his own responsibility. A military officer in wartime knows the agony of choice which forces him to sacrifice part of his army to preserve the rest, as does a man in high political office, who must make decisions affecting the lives of millions. The existentialists claim that each of us must make moral decisions in our own lives which involve the same anguish. Kierkegaard finds that this necessity is one thing which makes each life unique, which makes it impossible to speculate or generalize about human life, because each man's case is irretrievably his own, something in which he is personally and passionately involved. His book *Fear and Trembling* is an elaborate and fascinating commentary on the Old Testament story of Abraham, who was commanded by God to sacrifice his beloved son Isaac. Abraham thus becomes the emblem of man who must make a harrowing choice, in this case between love for his son and love for God, between the universal moral law which says categorically, "thou shalt not kill," and the unique inner demand of his religious faith. Abraham's decision, which is to violate the abstract and collective moral law, has to be made not in arrogance but in fear and trembling, one of the inferences being that sometimes one must make an exception to the general law because he is (existentially) an exception, a concrete being whose existence can never be completely subsumed under any universal.

▶ 5. *The Encounter with Nothingness*

14   For the man alienated from God, from nature, from his fellow man and from himself, what is left at last but Nothingness? The testimony of the existentialists is that this is where modern man now finds himself, not on the highway of upward Progress toward a radiant Utopia but on the brink of a catastrophic preci- pice, below which yawns the absolute void, an uncompromised black Nothingness. In one sense this is Eliot's Wasteland inhabited by his Hollow Man, who is

> Shape without form, shade without color
> Paralyzed force, gesture without motion.

This is what moves E. A. Robinson's Richard Cory, the man who
is everything that might make us wish that we were in his place,
to go home one calm summer night and put a bullet through his
head.

15   One of the most convincing statements of the encounter
with Nothingness is made by Leo Tolstoy in "My Confession."
He tells how in good health, in the prime of life, when he had
everything that a man could desire—wealth, fame, aristocratic
social position, a beautiful wife and children, a brilliant mind and
great artistic talent in the height of their powers, he nevertheless
was seized with a growing uneasiness, a nameless discontent which
he could not shake or alleviate. His experience was like that of a
man who falls sick, with symptoms which he disregards as insignificant; but the symptoms return again and again until they
merge into a continuous suffering. And the patient suddenly is
confronted with the overwhelming fact that what he took for mere
indisposition is more important to him than anything else on
earth, that it is death! "I felt the ground on which I stood was
crumbling, that there was nothing for me to stand on, that what
I had been living for was nothing, that I had no reason for living.
. . . To stop was impossible, to go back was impossible; and it was
impossible to shut my eyes so as to see that there was nothing
before me but suffering and actual death, absolute annihilation."
This is the "Sickness Unto Death" of Kierkegaard, the despair in
which one wishes to die but cannot. Hemingway's short story, "A
Clean, Well-Lighted Place," gives an unforgettable expression of
this theme. At the end of the story, the old waiter climbs into bed
late at night saying to himself, "What did he fear? It was not fear
or dread. It was nothing which he knew too well. It was all a
nothing and a man was nothing too. . . . Nada y pues nada,
y nada y pues nada." And then because he has experienced the
death of God he goes on to recite the Lord's Prayer in blasphemous
despair: "Our Nothing who art in Nothing, nothing be thy
nothing . . ." And then the Ave Maria, "Hail nothing, full of
nothing . . ." This is stark, even for Hemingway, but the old
waiter does no more than name the void felt by most people in
the early Hemingway novels, a hunger they seek to assuage with
alcohol, sex, and violence in an aimless progress from bar to bed
to bull-ring. It goes without saying that much of the despair and
pessimism in other contemporary authors springs from a similar
sense of the void in modern life.

▶ *6. Freedom*

16   Sooner or later, as a theme that includes all the others, the existentialist writings bear upon freedom. The themes we have outlined above describe either some loss of man's freedom or some threat to it, and all existentialists of whatever sort are concerned to enlarge the range of human freedom.

17   For the avowed atheists like Sartre freedom means human autonomy. In a purposeless universe man is *condemned* to freedom because he is the only creature who is "self-surpassing," who can become something other than he is. Precisely because there is no God to give purpose to the universe, each man must accept individual responsibility for his own becoming, a burden made heavier by the fact that in choosing for himself he chooses for all men "the image of man as he ought to be." A man *is* the sum total of the acts that make up his life—no more, no less—and though the coward has made himself cowardly, it is always possible for him to change and make himself heroic. In Sartre's novel, *The Age of Reason,* one of the least likeable of the characters, almost overwhelmed by despair and self-disgust at his homosexual tendencies, is on the point of solving his problem by mutilating himself with a razor, when in an effort of will he throws the instrument down, and we are given to understand that from this moment he will have mastery over his aberrant drive. Thus in the daily course of ordinary life must men shape their becoming in Sartre's world.

18   The religious existentialists interpret man's freedom differently. They use much the same language as Sartre, develop the same theses concerning the predicament of man, but always include God as a radical factor. They stress the man of faith rather than the man of will. They interpret man's existential condition as a state of alienation from his essential nature which is God-like, the problem of his life being to heal the chasm between the two, that is, to find salvation. The mystery and ambiguity of man's existence they attribute to his being the intersection of two realms. "Man bears within himself," writes Berdyaev, "the image which is both the image of man and the image of God, and is the image of man as far as the image of God is actualized." Tillich describes salvation as "the act in which the cleavage between the essential being and the existential situation is overcome." Freedom here, as for Sartre, involves an acceptance of responsibility for choice and a *commitment* to one's choice. This is the meaning of faith, a faith like Abraham's, the commitment which is an agonizing sacrifice of one's own desire and will and dearest treasure to God's will.

19   A final word. Just as one should not expect to find in a particular writer all of the characteristics of existentialism as we have described them, he should also be aware that some of the most striking expressions of existentialism in literature and the arts come to us by indirection, often through symbols or through innovations in conventional form. Take the preoccupation of contemporary writers with time. In *The Sound and the Fury*, Faulkner both collapses and expands normal clock time, or by juxtapositions of past and present blurs time into a single amorphous pool. He does this by using various forms of "stream of consciousness" or other techniques which see life in terms of unique, subjective experience—that is, existentially. The conventional view of externalized life, a rational orderly progression cut into uniform segments by the hands of a clock, he rejects in favor of a view which sees life as opaque, ambiguous, and irrational—that is, as the existentialist sees it. Graham Greene does something like this in *The Power and the Glory*. He creates a scene isolated in time and cut off from the rest of the world, steamy and suffocating as if a bell jar had been placed over it. Through this atmosphere fetid with impending death and human suffering, stumbles the whiskey priest, lonely and confused, pursued by a police lieutenant who has experienced the void and the death of God.

20   Such expressions in literature do not mean necessarily that the authors are conscious existentialist theorizers, or even that they know the writings of such theorizers. Faulkner may never have read Heidegger—or St. Augustine—both of whom attempt to demonstrate that time is more within a man and subject to his unique experience of it than it is outside him. But it is legitimate to call Faulkner's views of time and life "existential" in this novel because in recent years existentialist theorizers have given such views a local habitation and a name. One of the attractions, and one of the dangers, of existential themes is that they become like Sir Thomas Browne's quincunx: once one begins to look for them, he sees them everywhere. But if one applies restraint and discrimination, he will find that they illuminate much of contemporary literature and sometimes the literature of the past as well.

• SUGGESTIONS •

Outline this essay and determine what use, if any, has been made of principles and procedures such as definition, classification, comparison, and others earlier discussed. Explain Bigelow's method for limiting his discourse.

PSALMS 103

1. Bless the LORD, O my soul: and all that is within me, *bless* his holy name.
2. Bless the LORD, O my soul, and forget not all his benefits:
3. Who forgiveth all thine iniquities; who healeth all thy diseases;
4. Who redeemeth thy life from destruction; who crowneth thee with lovingkindness and tender mercies;
5. Who satisfieth thy mouth with good *things; so that* thy youth is renewed like the eagle's.
6. The LORD executeth righteousness and judgment for all that are oppressed.
7. He made known his ways unto Moses, his acts unto the children of Israel.
8. The LORD *is* merciful and gracious, slow to anger, and plenteous in mercy.
9. He will not always chide: neither will he keep *his anger* for ever.
10. He hath not dealt with us after our sins; nor rewarded us according to our iniquities.
11. For as the heaven is high above the earth, *so* great is his mercy toward them that fear him.
12. As far as the east is from the west, *so* far hath he removed our transgressions from us.
13. Like as a father pitieth *his* children, *so* the LORD pitieth them that fear him.
14. For he knoweth our frame; he remembereth that we are dust.
15. *As for* man, his days *are* as grass: as a flower of the field, so he flourisheth.

16. For the wind passeth over it, and it is gone; and the place thereof shall know it no more.

17. But the mercy of the LORD *is* from everlasting to everlasting upon them that fear him, and his righteousness unto children's children;

18. To such as keep his covenant, and to those that remember his commandments to do them.

19. The LORD hath prepared his throne in the heavens; and his kingdom ruleth over all.

20. Bless the LORD, ye his angels, that excel in strength, that do his commandments, hearkening unto the voice of his word.

21. Bless ye the LORD, all *ye* his hosts; *ye* ministers of his, that do his pleasure.

22. Bless the LORD, all his works in all places of his dominion: bless the LORD, O my soul.

• SUGGESTIONS •

The conception that is the subject of this selection is perhaps the most difficult of all to explain, is, perhaps, inexplicable. Examine the selection to determine how the subject is brought into manageable confines. One bit of help: one feature that sets humanly understandable limits to the discussion is the indirect account of the attributes of God through the use, as in verses 5, 15, and 16, of specific, familiar human references.

A Writing Program

1. Write a short autobiographical revelation in the manner of Johnson's "Meditations."

2. Write an autobiographical account of your life to the present using Lincoln's sketch as a model.

3. Using as your subject someone whom you know intimately, for example your father, write a biographical essay, making sure that you exploit that intimate knowledge as, for example, Boswell does in the selection from *The Life of Johnson.*

4. Using a laboratory report or a progress report from one of your other courses as a foundation, write an essay explaining some mechanism, institution, or sequence.

5. Use one of the essays in the section on explaining sequences as a model for a "how-to-do-it" essay. *Spectator, No. 409,* for example, could provide a model for an essay on repairing a car.

6. Using the Bigelow essay as a model, write a "primer" on some other significant idea.

Argumentation

Through expository writing a man may offer the necessary explanations of his public and private life. But it also provides him the opportunity to say "This is the way things are," or "This is what I believe." It may be an objective interpretation, an attempt to furnish background for and explanation of a given subject, or it may be a subjective statement of opinion. Argumentative writing may also render objective interpretation and subjective opinion, but there is, in addition, a new element.

Argumentative writing, like argument itself, is the result of disagreement. It may offer objective interpretation and subjective opinion, but it does so in order to express a disagreement and, more important, to persuade an audience to adopt a new attitude, belief, position, or policy. This makes argumentative writing fundamentally different from exposition, and it exacts of the writer a more formal discipline, for one properly has to earn the right to convince others. Each man has the right to his own opinion, someone has said, but not every man has the right to have his opinion taken seriously. Here, perhaps more than anywhere else, "he who begins by presuming on his own sense, has ended his studies as soon as he has commenced them." Because of its nature, argumentative discourse demands of the writer frequent recourse to knowledge, experience, and tradition and conscious use of the meaning found there.

Because it deals with conflicting ideas, because it is designed to persuade, and because it necessarily relies on both the author's native wit and the knowledge he has acquired for this purpose, an argumentative essay is more likely than an expository essay to be developed in formal, recognizable stages. The order in which the stages are presented varies as the circumstances of the argument vary, and often an argumentative essay may be a full development of only one stage, but argumentative discourse may yet be said to consist of four primary parts.

The first of these is often introductory. It is necessary to determine exactly what the question being presented is and what issue is being argued. This first stage, often called the *location of the argument*, usually includes the author's statement of his position, the proposition he intends to prove. Frequently this preliminary section also offers definitions of any key terms that might be ambiguous. The second stage, often the most extensive, may be called the *establishment of a position*. It is here that the author is obliged to call upon all the resources, both public and private, that are available to him. We hear too much of men who would merely assert; the arguer who deserves to be heard is he who calls upon fact, authority, and the valid processes of his own reasoning for support of his position. Equally important in argument is the third stage, the *refutation*. Here the author may further demonstrate the wisdom of his position (he has already done so if he *proved* his original proposition) by revealing weaknesses in the argument of his opponent. This he may do in any number of ways. In the heat of argument, men not infrequently fail to observe the necessities of reason and judgment; we find them sometimes guilty of hasty generalizations, of false analogies, and of other classical fallacies—begging the question, ignoring the question, *non sequitur, post hoc ergo propter hoc*. Discovery of any of these fallacies, by weakening the opponent's arguments, strengthens one's own. A writer may sometimes find, too, that his opponent is loading or slanting his discourse, suggesting values in his argument without demonstrating them. Exposure of such slanted writing may aid the writer in strengthening his position. Finally, because he may very well want to leave his audience with his proposal clearly in mind, the writer of argument often presents a *formal conclusion*. This typically offers a brief summary of the argument or an emphatic restatement of the proposal and its most clear-cut merits.

Arguments may of course take many forms, depending on the nature of the controversy, the circumstances in which it takes place, and the goals sought. Probably the most common form is either an argument that includes all the steps mentioned above, or an argument that for special purposes develops only one of these steps. Thus, we may expect to find (1) ritual proposals or assertions, which may be only extended proposals; (2) full arguments giving proposal, proof, refutation, and conclusion; (3) confirmations, which may offer only a one-sided discussion; and (4) refutations, which are likely to be entirely devoted to attacks on other positions, negative statements where no positive proposal has been given. Each of these is illustrated and discussed in the following section.

Ritual Proposal

On special occasions, with special audiences met under special circumstances, the writer—or the speaker—has always been free to present his proposal by itself. If he can trust in the wisdom of his proposal, and if he can present the proposal appealingly, the writer or speaker may accomplish the end of argumentation, persuading his audience to accept his position, whether it calls for action or for changed thinking. When a proposal is presented alone, obviously no argument is developed, and indeed the controversy may only be implicit, as in the first selection below. Still, this procedure may be sufficient; it probably will be sufficient if the occasion is right, if the audience is sympathetic, and if the cause is just. It is all the more likely to be sufficient when it summons men out of indifference to a course of action they already believe in.

But this kind of presentation is demanding. Because he is not presenting evidence, the writer is obliged first of all, as he always is, to unswerving honesty and forthrightness. And the absence of evidence serves to place an unusual burden on the manner of presentation. Some of the best such arguments in our language are therefore hortatory, highly rhetorical, sometimes even rhythmic and repetitive—hence the title of this subsection.

A word of warning: Ritualistic assertions have fulfilled noble functions, but demagogues have used the same method. A persuasive speaker playing upon the sympathy of an audience—one thinks of Adolf Hitler, for example—may make base motives seem pure.

From THE BERLIN ADDRESS [1963]

John F. Kennedy

There are many people in the world who really don't understand —or say they don't—what is the great issue between the free world and the Communist world. Let them come to Berlin. There are some who say that Communism is the wave of the future. Let them come to Berlin. There are some who say in Europe and elsewhere, "We can work with the Communists." Let them come to Berlin. And there are even a few who say that it's true that Communism is an evil system but it permits us to make economic progress. *Lass sie nach Berlin kommen!*

• COMMENTARY •

Little comment is needed here. The occasion, as perhaps everyone knows by now, was right. Seldom has there been such immediate rapport between a speaker and his audience as there was when President Kennedy spoke in Berlin. He developed no argument, for there was no need. He named no issue, for there was no need. Given the place and the time and the audience, the speaker had only to propose that men of good will *see* the evidence around them. He did this largely by the force of the rhythmic passage given here, invoking all doubters with the refrain-like "Let them come to Berlin."

NOBEL PRIZE SPEECH [1950]

William Faulkner

1   I feel that this award was not made to me as a man but to my work—a life's work in the agony and sweat of the human spirit, not for glory and least of all for profit, but to create out of the materials of the human spirit something which did not exist

before. So this award is only mine in trust. It will not be difficult
to find a dedication for the money part of it commensurate with
the purpose and significance of its origin. But I would like to do
the same with the acclaim too, by using this moment as a pinnacle
from which I might be listened to by the young men and women
already dedicated to the same anguish and travail, among whom
is already that one who will some day stand here where I am
standing.

2   Our tragedy today is a general and universal physical fear
so long sustained by now that we can even bear it. There are no
longer problems of the spirit. There is only the question: when will
I be blown up? Because of this, the young man or woman writing
today has forgotten the problems of the human heart in conflict
with itself which alone can make good writing because only that
is worth writing about, worth the agony and the sweat.

3   He must learn them again. He must teach himself that the
basest of all things is to be afraid; and, teaching himself that,
forget it forever, leaving no room in his workshop for anything but
the old verities and truths of the heart, the old universal truths
lacking which any story is ephemeral and doomed—love and honor
and pity and pride and compassion and sacrifice. Until he does
so he labors under a curse. He writes not of love but of lust, of
defeats in which nobody loses anything of value, of victories without hope and worst of all without pity or compassion. His griefs
grieve on no universal bones, leaving no scars. He writes not of
the heart but of the glands.

4   Until he relearns these things he will write as though he
stood among and watched the end of man. I decline to accept the
end of man. It is easy enough to say that man is immortal simply
because he will endure; that when the last ding-dong of doom
has clanged and faded from the last worthless rock hanging tideless in the last red and dying evening, that even then there will
still be one more sound: that of his puny inexhaustible voice, still
talking. I refuse to accept this. I believe that man will not merely
endure: he will prevail. He is immortal, not because he alone
among creatures has an inexhaustible voice, but because he has a
soul, a spirit capable of compassion and sacrifice and endurance.
The poet's, the writer's, duty is to write about these things. It is
his privilege to help man endure by lifting his heart, by reminding
him of the courage and honor and hope and pride and compassion

and pity and sacrifice which have been the glory of his past. The poet's voice need not merely be the record of man, it can be one of the props, the pillars to help him endure and prevail.

• SUGGESTIONS •

The proposal here (and you should first determine what it is) is supported not by evidence but by the prose harmony of the assertion itself. Examination of two features of Faulkner's style here may be helpful to you. First consider the vocabulary itself, and note the frequency of words packed with the suggestions of time, tradition, and the long work man has done. Then consider the sentence structure, and note especially the effects he gets by coordination. One extension of this effect through coordination is the rhythmic quality achieved by similarities in sentence structure.

PSALMS 136

1. O give thanks unto the LORD; for he is good: for his mercy *endureth* for ever.

2. O give thanks unto the God of gods: for his mercy *endureth* for ever.

3. O give thanks unto the Lord of lords: for his mercy *endureth* for ever.

4. To him who alone doeth great wonders: for his mercy *endureth* for ever.

5. To him that by wisdom made the heavens: for his mercy *endureth* for ever.

6. To him that stretched out the earth above the waters: for his mercy *endureth* for ever.

7. To him that made great lights: for his mercy *endureth* for ever:

8. The sun to rule by day: for his mercy *endureth* for ever:

9. The moon and stars to rule by night: for his mercy *endureth* for ever.

10. To him that smote Egypt in their firstborn: for his mercy *endureth* for ever:

11. And brought out Israel from among them: for his mercy *endureth* for ever:

12. With a strong hand, and with a stretched out arm: for his mercy *endureth* for ever.

13. To him which divided the Red sea into parts: for his mercy *endureth* for ever:

14. And made Israel to pass through the midst of it: for his mercy *endureth* for ever:

15. But overthrew Pharaoh and his host in the Red sea: for his mercy *endureth* for ever.

16. To him which led his people through the wilderness: for his mercy *endureth* for ever.

17. To him which smote great kings: for his mercy *endureth* for ever:

18. And slew famous kings: for his mercy *endureth* for ever:

19. Sihon king of the Amorites: for his mercy *endureth* for ever:

20. And Og the king of Bashan: for his mercy *endureth* for ever:

21. And gave their land for an heritage: for his mercy *endureth* for ever:

22. *Even* an heritage unto Israel his servant: for his mercy *endureth* for ever.

23. Who remembered us in our low estate: for his mercy *endureth* for ever:

24. And hath redeemed us from our enemies: for his mercy *endureth* for ever.

25. Who giveth food to all flesh: for his mercy *endureth* for ever.

26. O give thanks unto the God of heaven: for his mercy *endureth* for ever.

MATTHEW 6:19–34

19. Lay not up for yourselves treasures upon earth, where moth and rust doth corrupt, and where thieves break through and steal:

20. But lay up for yourselves treasures in heaven, where neither moth nor rust doth corrupt, and where thieves do not break through nor steal:

21. For where your treasure is, there will your heart be also.

22. The light of the body is the eye: if therefore thine eye be single, thy whole body shall be full of light.

23. But if thine eye be evil, thy whole body shall be full of darkness. If therefore the light that is in thee be darkness, how great *is* that darkness!

24. No man can serve two masters: for either he will hate the one, and love the other; or else he will hold to the one, and despise the other. Ye cannot serve God and mammon.

25. Therefore I say unto you, Take no thought for your life, what ye shall eat, or what ye shall drink; nor yet for your body, what ye shall put on. Is not the life more than meat, and the body than raiment?

26. Behold the fowls of the air: for they sow not, neither do they reap, nor gather into barns; yet your heavenly Father feedeth them. Are ye not much better than they?

27. Which of you by taking thought can add one cubit unto his stature?

28. And why take ye thought for raiment? Consider the lilies of the field, how they grow; they toil not, neither do they spin:

29. And yet I say unto you, That even Solomon in all his glory was not arrayed like one of these.

30. Wherefore, if God so clothe the grass of the field, which to day is, and to morrow is cast into the oven, *shall he* not much more *clothe* you, O ye of little faith?

31. Therefore take no thought, saying, What shall we eat? or, What shall we drink? or, Wherewithal shall we be clothed?

32. (For after all these things do the Gentiles seek:) for your heavenly Father knoweth that ye have need of all these things.

33. But seek ye first the kingdom of God, and his righteousness; and all these things shall be added unto you.

34. Take therefore no thought for the morrow: for the morrow shall take thought for the things of itself. Sufficient unto the day *is* the evil thereof.

• SUGGESTIONS •

The first of these exhortations from the Bible, Psalms 136, summons the people to praise God for his mercy. Its effectiveness results partly from the repeated refrain, "for his mercy endureth forever," partly from the *concrete* evidence of his mercy. Perhaps the most notable stylistic feature of the second selection here, from Matthew, is the concreteness of the language. See if you can state the hortatory proposals embedded in each of these selections.

SPEECH ON BECOMING PRIME MINISTER [1940]

Winston S. Churchill

1   On Friday evening last I received His Majesty's Commission to form a new Administration. It was the evident wish and will of Parliament and the nation that this should be conceived on the broadest possible basis and that it should include all Parties, both those who supported the late Government and also the Parties of the Opposition. I have completed the most important part of this task. A War Cabinet has been formed of five Members, representing, with the Opposition Liberals, the unity of the nation. The three Party Leaders have agreed to serve, either in the War Cabinet or in high executive office. The three Fighting Services have been filled. It was necessary that this should be done in one single day, on account of the extreme urgency and rigor of events. A number of other key positions were filled yesterday, and I am submitting a further list to His Majesty tonight. I hope to complete the appointment of the principal Ministers during tomorrow. The appointment of the other Ministers usually takes a little longer, but I trust that, when Parliament meets again, this part of my task will be completed, and that the Administration will be complete in all respects.

2   I considered it in the public interest to suggest that the House should be summoned to meet today. Mr. Speaker agreed, and took the necessary steps, in accordance with the powers conferred upon him by the Resolution of the House. At the end of the proceedings today, the Adjournment of the House will be proposed until Tuesday, 21st May, with, of course, provision for earlier meeting if need be. The business to be considered during that week will be notified to Members at the earliest opportunity. I now invite the House, by the Resolution which stands in my name, to record its approval of the steps taken and to declare its confidence in the new Government.

3   To form an Administration of this scale and complexity is a serious undertaking in itself, but it must be remembered that we are in the preliminary stage of one of the greatest battles in history, that we are in action at many points in Norway and in Holland, that we have to be prepared in the Mediterranean, that the air battle is continuous, and that many preparations have to be made here at home. In this crisis I hope I may be pardoned if I do not address the House at any length today. I hope that any of my friends and colleagues, or former colleagues, who are affected by the political reconstruction, will make all allowance for any lack of ceremony with which it has been necessary to act. I would say to the House, as I said to those who have joined this Government: "I have nothing to offer but blood, toil, tears, and sweat."

4   We have before us an ordeal of the most grievous kind. We have before us many, many long months of struggle and of suffering. You ask, What is our policy? I will say: "It is to wage war, by sea, land, and air, with all our might and with all the strength that God can give us: to wage war against a monstrous tyranny, never surpassed in the dark, lamentable catalogue of human crime. That is our policy." You ask, What is our aim? I can answer in one word: Victory—victory at all costs, victory in spite of all terror, victory however long and hard the road may be; for without victory there is no survival. Let that be realized; no survival for the British Empire; no survival for all that the British Empire has stood for; no survival for the urge and impulse of the ages, that mankind will move forward towards its goal. But I take up my task with buoyancy and hope. I feel sure that our cause will not be suffered to fail among men. At this time I feel entitled to claim the aid of all, and I say, "Come, then, let us go forward together with our united strength."

• SUGGESTIONS •

Determine for yourself what it is that lends this piece its strength and dignity. A clue that you may find useful is the obvious difference between the first two and the last two paragraphs. The first two paragraphs are unassuming and matter-of-fact. The contrast between these and the final paragraphs may help you to measure the quality of the selection.

The Complete Presentation

The usual steps in a full argument have already been discussed in the first pages of this section. They are, in effect, only more or less formal articulations of procedures that occur in any argument, even the most impromptu, even the most violent. It is not uncommon in a bull-session argument to hear some one begin, "Well now, there's a lot to consider. . . ." What often follows is the *location of the argument*. Then, if the argument is heated, sometime during the session, he will have heard all he can stand and blurt out, "You don't know what you're talking about," which usually heralds the *refutation* (and may also remind us that one of the pleasures of written argument is the relative distance it puts between us and a punch in the nose). If he can still talk after that, he is likely to begin another pitch with "You've got to remember that . . . ," or "Don't you see . . . ," or "Everybody knows that . . . ," signals that he is about to try to *establish his position* as thoroughly as possible. The difference between this kind of argument and arguments you will feel compelled to write is that what one does in the bull session more or less accidentally, he now is asked to do with calm deliberation.

These steps, in whatever order, are also common in the formal research paper. There the writer usually seeks to offer formal, documented proof of his position. The student doing his first college research paper sometimes wonders, with all the evidence he has collected and with all the notes he has compiled, just what part of the work is really his. Perhaps it would help to remember, though of course it is an oversimplification, that in an argumentative research paper most of the footnotes are likely to occur in connection with the third step mentioned above.

SCIENCE AND CULTURE [1880]

Thomas Henry Huxley

1   Six years ago, as some of my present hearers may remember, I had the privilege of addressing a large assemblage of the inhabitants of this city, who had gathered together to do honor

to the memory of their famous townsman, Joseph Priestley; and, if any satisfaction attaches to posthumous glory, we may hope that the *manes* of the burnt-out philosopher were then finally appeased.

2   No man, however, who is endowed with a fair share of common sense, and not more than a fair share of vanity, will identify either contemporary or posthumous fame with the highest good; and Priestley's life leaves no doubt that he, at any rate, set a much higher value upon the advancement of knowledge, and the promotion of that freedom of thought which is at once the cause and the consequence of intellectual progress.

3   Hence I am disposed to think that, if Priestley could be amongst us today, the occasion of our meeting would afford him even greater pleasure than the proceedings which celebrated the centenary of his chief discovery. The kindly heart would be moved, the high sense of social duty would be satisfied, by the spectacle of well-earned wealth neither squandered in tawdry luxury and vainglorious show, nor scattered with the careless charity which blesses neither him that gives nor him that takes, but expended in the execution of a well-considered plan for the aid of present and future generations of those who are willing to help themselves.

4   We shall all be of one mind thus far. But it is needful to share Priestley's keen interest in physical science; and to have learned, as he had learned, the value of scientific training in fields of inquiry apparently far remote from physical science; in order to appreciate, as he would have appreciated, the value of the noble gift which Sir Josiah Mason has bestowed upon the inhabitants of the Midland district.

5   For us children of the nineteenth century, however, the establishment of a college under the conditions of Sir Josiah Mason's Trust, has a significance apart from any which it could have possessed a hundred years ago. It appears to be an indication that we are reaching the crisis of the battle, or rather of the long series of battles, which have been fought over education in a campaign which began long before Priestley's time, and will probably not be finished just yet.

6   In the last century, the combatants were the champions of ancient literature on the one side, and those of modern literature on the other; but, some thirty years ago, the contest became

complicated by the appearance of a third army, ranged round the banner of physical science.

7   I am not aware that anyone has authority to speak in the name of this new host. For it must be admitted to be somewhat of a guerilla force, composed largely of irregulars, each of whom fights pretty much for his own hand. But the impressions of a full private, who has seen a good deal of service in the ranks, respecting the present position of affairs and the conditions of a permanent peace, may not be devoid of interest; and I do not know that I could make a better use of the present opportunity than by laying them before you.

8   From the time that the first suggestion to introduce physical science into ordinary education was timidly whispered, until now, the advocates of scientific education have met with opposition of two kinds. On the one hand, they have been pooh-poohed by the men of business who pride themselves on being the representatives of practicality; while, on the other hand, they have been excommunicated by the classical scholars, in their capacity of Levites in charge of the ark of culture and monopolists of liberal education.

9   The practical men believed that the idol whom they worship—rule of thumb—has been the source of the past prosperity, and will suffice in the future welfare of the arts and manufactures. They were of opinion that science is speculative rubbish; that theory and practice have nothing to do with one another; and that the scientific habit of mind is an impediment, rather than an aid, in the conduct of ordinary affairs.

10   I have used the past tense in speaking of the practical men—for although they were very formidable thirty years ago, I am not sure that the pure species has not been extirpated. In fact, so far as mere argument goes, they have been subjected to such a *feu d'enfer* that it is a miracle if any have escaped. But I have remarked that your typical practical man has an unexpected resemblance to one of Milton's angels. His spiritual wounds, such as are inflicted by logical weapons, may be as deep as a well and as wide as a church door, but beyond shedding a few drops of ichor, celestial or otherwise, he is no whit the worse. So, if any of these opponents be left, I will not waste time in vain repetition of the demonstrative evidence of the practical value of science, but knowing that a parable will sometimes penetrate where syllogisms

fail to effect an entrance, I will offer a story for their consideration.

11   Once upon a time, a boy, with nothing to depend upon but his own vigorous nature, was thrown into the thick of the struggle for existence in the midst of a great manufacturing population. He seems to have had a hard fight, inasmuch as, by the time he was thirty years of age, his total disposable funds amounted to twenty pounds. Nevertheless, middle life found him giving proof of his comprehension of the practical problems he had been roughly called upon to solve, by a career of remarkable prosperity.

12   Finally, having reached old age with its well-earned surroundings of "honor, troops of friends," the hero of my story bethought himself of those who were making a like start in life, and how he could stretch out a helping hand to them.

13   After long and anxious reflection this successful practical man of business could devise nothing better than to provide them with the means of obtaining "sound, extensive, and practical scientific knowledge." And he devoted a large part of his wealth and five years of incessant work to this end.

14   I need not point the moral of a tale which, as the solid and spacious fabric of the Scientific College assures us, is no fable, nor can anything which I could say intensify the force of this practical answer to practical objections.

15   We may take it for granted then, that, in the opinion of those best qualified to judge, the diffusion of thorough scientific education is an absolutely essential condition of industrial progress; and that the college which has been opened today will confer an inestimable boon upon those whose livelihood is to be gained by the practice of the arts and manufactures of the district.

16   The only question worth discussion is, whether the conditions, under which the work of the college is to be carried out, are such as to give it the best possible chance of achieving permanent success.

17   Sir Josiah Mason, without doubt most wisely, has left very large freedom of action to the trustees, to whom he proposes ultimately to commit the administration of the college, so that they may be able to adjust its arrangements in accordance with the changing conditions of the future. But, with respect to three points, he has laid most explicit injunctions upon both administrators and teachers.

18   Party politics are forbidden to enter into the minds of

either, so far as the work of the college is concerned; theology is as sternly banished from its precincts; and finally, it is especially declared that the college shall make no provision for "mere literary instruction and education."

19   It does not concern me at present to dwell upon the first two injunctions any longer than may be needful to express my full conviction of their wisdom. But the third prohibition brings us face to face with those other opponents of scientific education, who are by no means in the moribund condition of the practical man, but alive, alert, and formidable.

20   It is not impossible that we shall hear this express exclusion of "literary instruction and education" from a college which, nevertheless professes to give a high and efficient education, sharply criticized. Certainly the time was that the Levites of culture would have sounded their trumpets against its walls as against an educational Jericho.

21   How often have we not been told that the study of physical science is incompetent to confer culture; that it touches none of the higher problems of life; and, what is worse, that the continual devotion to scientific studies tends to generate a narrow and bigoted belief in the applicability of scientific methods to the search after truth of all kinds? How frequently one has reason to observe that no reply to a troublesome argument tells so well as calling its author a "mere scientific specialist." And, as I am afraid it is not permissible to speak of this form of opposition to scientific education in the past tense, may we not expect to be told that this, not only omission, but prohibition, of "mere literary instruction and education" is a patent example of scientific narrow-mindedness?

22   I am not acquainted with Sir Josiah Mason's reasons for the action which he has taken; but if, as I apprehend is the case, he refers to the ordinary classical course of our schools and universities by the name of "mere literary instruction and education," I venture to offer sundry reasons of my own in support of that action.

23   For I hold very strongly by two convictions. The first is that neither the discipline nor the subject-matter of classical education is of such direct value to the student of physical science as to justify the expenditure of valuable time upon either; and the second is, that for the purpose of attaining real culture, an ex-

clusively scientific education is at least as effectual as an exclusively literary education.

24   I need hardly point out to you that these opinions, especially the latter, are diametrically opposed to those of the great majority of educated Englishmen, influenced as they are by school and university traditions. In their belief, culture is obtainable only by a liberal education; and a liberal education is synonymous, not merely with education and instruction in literature, but in one particular form of literature, namely, that of Greek and Roman antiquity. They hold that the man who has learned Latin and Greek, however little, is educated; while he who is versed in other branches of knowledge, however deeply, is a more or less respectable specialist, not admissible into the cultured caste. The stamp of the educated man, the university degree, is not for him.

25   I am too well acquainted with the generous catholicity of spirit, the true sympathy with scientific thought, which pervades the writing of our chief apostle of culture to identify him with these opinions; and yet one may cull from one and another of those epistles to the Philistines, which so much delight all who do not answer to that name, sentences which lend them some support.

26   Mr. Arnold tells us that the meaning of culture is "to know the best that has been thought and said in the world." It is the criticism of life contained in literature. That criticism regards "Europe as being, for intellectual and spiritual purposes, one great confederation, bound to a joint action and working to a common result; and whose members have, for their common outfit, a knowledge of Greek, Roman, and Eastern antiquity, and of one another. Special, local, and temporary advantages being put out of account, that modern nation will in the intellectual and spiritual sphere make most progress, which most thoroughly carries out this program. And what is that but saying that we too, all of us, as individuals, the more thoroughly we carry it out, shall make the more progress?"

27   We have here to deal with two distinct propositions. The first, that a criticism of life is the essence of culture; the second, that literature contains the materials which suffice for the construction of such criticism.

28   I think that we must all assent to the first proposition. For culture certainly means something quite different from learning or technical skill. It implies the possession of an ideal, and the

habit of critically estimating the value of things by comparison
with a theoretic standard. Perfect culture should supply a complete theory of life, based upon a clear knowledge alike of its
possibilities and of its limitations.

29   But we may agree to all this, and yet strongly dissent
from the assumption that literature alone is competent to supply
this knowledge. After having learned all that Greek, Roman, and
Eastern antiquity have thought and said, and all that modern
literatures have to tell us, it is not self-evident that we have laid
a sufficiently broad and deep foundation for that criticism of life
which constitutes culture.

30   Indeed, to anyone acquainted with the scope of physical
science, it is not at all evident. Considering progress only in the
"intellectual and spiritual sphere," I find myself wholly unable to
admit that either nations or individuals will really advance, if their
common outfit draws nothing from the stores of physical science.
I should say that an army, without weapons of precision and with
no particular base of operations, might more hopefully enter upon
a campaign on the Rhine, than a man, devoid of a knowledge of
what physical science has done in the last century, upon a criticism
of life.

31   When a biologist meets with an anomaly, he instinctively
turns to the study of development to clear it up. The rationale of
contradictory opinions may with equal confidence be sought in
history.

32   It is, happily, no new thing that Englishmen should
employ their wealth in building and endowing institutions for
educational purposes. But, five or six hundred years ago, deeds
of foundation expressed or implied conditions as nearly as possible
contrary to those which have been thought expedient by Sir Josiah
Mason. That is to say, physical science was practically ignored,
while a certain literary training was enjoined as a means to the
acquirement of knowledge which was essentially theological.

33   The reason of this singular contradiction between the
actions of men alike animated by a strong and disinterested desire
to promote the welfare of their fellows, is easily discovered.

34   At that time, in fact, if anyone desired knowledge beyond
such as could be obtained by his own observation, or by common
conversation, his first necessity was to learn the Latin language,
inasmuch as all the higher knowledge of the western world was

contained in works written in that language. Hence, Latin grammar, with logic and rhetoric, studied through Latin, were the fundamentals of education. With respect to the substance of the knowledge imparted through this channel, the Jewish and Christian Scriptures, as interpreted and supplemented by the Romish Church, were held to contain a complete and infallibly true body of information.

35   Theological dicta were, to the thinkers of those days, that which the axioms and definitions of Euclid are to the geometers of these. The business of the philosophers of the Middle Ages was to deduce from the data furnished by the theologians, conclusions in accordance with ecclesiastical decrees. They were allowed the high privilege of showing, by logical process, how and why that which the Church said was true, must be true. And if their demonstrations fell short of or exceeded this limit, the Church was maternally ready to check their aberrations; if need were by the help of the secular arm.

36   Between the two, our ancestors were furnished with a compact and complete criticism of life. They were told how the world began and how it would end; they learned that all material existence was but a base and insignificant blot upon the fair fact of the spiritual world, and that nature was, to all intents and purposes, the playground of the devil; they learned that the earth is the center of the visible universe, and that man is the cynosure of things terrestrial; and more especially was it inculcated that the course of nature had no fixed order, but that it could be, and constantly was, altered by the agency of innumerable spiritual beings, good and bad, according as they were moved by the deeds and prayers of men. The sum and substance of the whole doctrine was to produce the conviction that the only thing really worth knowing in this world was how to secure that place in a better which, under certain conditions, the Church promised.

37   Our ancestors had a living belief in this theory of life, and acted upon it in their dealings with education, as in all other matters. Culture meant saintliness—after the fashion of the saints of those days; the education that led to it was, of necessity, theological; and the way to theology lay through Latin.

38   That the study of nature—further than was requisite for the satisfaction of everyday wants—should have any bearing on human life was far from the thoughts of men thus trained. Indeed,

as nature had been cursed for man's sake, it was an obvious conclusion that those who meddled with nature were likely to come into pretty close contact with Satan. And, if any born scientific investigator followed his instincts, he might safely reckon upon earning the reputation, and probably upon suffering the fate, of a sorcerer.

39   Had the western world been left to itself in Chinese isolation, there is no saying how long this state of things might have endured. But, happily, it was not left to itself. Even earlier than the thirteenth century, the development of Moorish civilization in Spain and the great movement of the Crusades had introduced the leaven which, from that day to this, has never ceased to work. At first, through the intermediation of Arabic translations, afterwards by the study of the originals, the western nations of Europe became acquainted with the writings of the ancient philosophers and poets, and, in time, with the whole of the vast literature of antiquity.

40   Whatever there was of high intellectual aspiration or dominant capacity in Italy, France, Germany, and England, spent itself for centuries in taking possession of the rich inheritance left by the dead civilizations of Greece and Rome. Marvelously aided by the invention of printing, classical learning spread and flourished. Those who possessed it prided themselves on having attained the highest culture then within the reach of mankind.

41   And justly. For, saving Dante on his solitary pinnacle, there was no figure in modern literature at the time of the Renascence to compare with the men of antiquity; there was no art to compete with their sculpture; there was no physical science but that which Greece had created. Above all, there was no other example of perfect intellectual freedom—of the unhesitating acceptance of reason as the sole guide to truth and the supreme arbiter of conduct.

42   The new learning necessarily soon exerted a profound influence upon education. The language of the monks and schoolmen seemed little better than gibberish to scholars fresh from Virgil and Cicero, and the study of Latin was placed upon a new foundation. Moreover, Latin itself ceased to afford the sole key to knowledge. The student who sought the highest thought of antiquity, found only a second-hand reflection of it in Roman literature, and turned his face to the full light of the Greeks. And

after a battle, not altogether dissimilar to that which is at present being fought over the teaching of physical science, the study of Greek was recognized as an essential element of all higher education.

43   Thus the Humanists, as they were called, won the day; and the great reform which they effected was of incalculable service to mankind. But the Nemesis of all reformers is finality; and the reformers of education, like those of religion, fell into the profound, however common, error of mistaking the beginning for the end of the work of reformation.

44   The representatives of the Humanists, in the nineteenth century, take their stand upon classical education as the sole avenue to culture, as firmly as if we were still in the age of Renascence. Yet, surely, the present intellectual relations of the modern and the ancient worlds are profoundly different from those which obtained three centuries ago. Leaving aside the existence of a great and characteristically modern literature, of modern painting, and, especially, of modern music, there is one feature of the present state of the civilized world which separates it more widely from the Renascence than the Renascence was separated from the Middle Ages.

45   This distinctive character of our own times lies in the vast and constantly increasing part which is played by natural knowledge. Not only is our daily life shaped by it, not only does the prosperity of millions of men depend upon it, but our whole theory of life has long been influenced, consciously or unconsciously, by the general conceptions of the universe which have been forced upon us by physical science.

46   In fact, the most elementary acquaintance with the results of scientific investigation shows us that they offer a broad and striking contradiction to the opinion so implicitly credited and taught in the Middle Ages.

47   The notions of the beginning and the end of the world entertained by our forefathers are no longer credible. It is very certain that the earth is not the chief body in the material universe, and that the world is not subordinated to man's use. It is even more certain that nature is the expression of a definite order with which nothing interferes, and that the chief business of mankind is to learn that order and govern themselves accordingly. Moreover this scientific "criticism of life" presents itself to us with

different credentials from any other. It appeals not to authority, nor to what anybody may have thought or said, but to nature. It admits that all our interpretations of natural fact are more or less imperfect and symbolic, and bids the learner seek for truth not among words, but among things. It warns us that the assertion which outstrips evidence is not only a blunder but a crime.

48   The purely classical education advocated by the representatives of the Humanists in our day, gives no inkling of all this. A man may be a better scholar than Erasmus, and know no more of the chief causes of the present intellectual fermentation than Erasmus did. Scholarly and pious persons, worthy of all respect, favor us with allocutions upon the sadness of the antagonism of science to their medieval way of thinking, which betray an ignorance of the first principles of scientific investigation, an incapacity for understanding what a man of science means by veracity, and an unconsciousness of the weight of established scientific truths, which is almost comical.

49   There is no great force in the *tu quoque* argument, or else the advocates of scientific education might fairly enough retort upon the modern Humanists that they may be learned specialists, but that they possess no such sound foundation for a criticism of life as deserves the name of culture. And, indeed, if we were disposed to be cruel, we might urge that the Humanists have brought this reproach upon themselves, not because they are too full of the spirit of the ancient Greek, but because they lack it.

50   The period of the Renascence is commonly called that of the "Revival of Letters," as if the influences then brought to bear upon the mind of Western Europe had been wholly exhausted in the field of literature. I think it is very commonly forgotten that the revival of science, effected by the same agency, although less conspicuous, was not less momentous.

51   In fact, the few and scattered students of nature of that day picked up the clue to her secrets exactly as it fell from the hands of the Greeks a thousand years before. The foundations of mathematics were so well laid by them, that our children learn their geometry from a book written for the schools of Alexandria two thousand years ago. Modern astronomy is the natural continuation and development of the work of Hipparchus and of Ptolemy; modern physics of that of Democritus and of Archi-

medes; it was long before modern biological science outgrew the
knowledge bequeathed to us by Aristotle, by Theophrastus, and
by Galen.

52   We cannot know all the best thoughts and sayings of the
Greeks unless we know what they thought about natural phenomena. We cannot fully apprehend their criticism of life unless
we understand the extent to which that criticism was affected by
scientific conceptions. We falsely pretend to be the inheritors of
their culture, unless we are penetrated, as the best minds among
them were, with an unhesitating faith that the free employment
of reason, in accordance with scientific method, is the sole method
of reaching truth.

53   Thus I venture to think that the pretensions of our modern
Humanists to the possession of the monopoly of culture and to
the exclusive inheritance of the spirit of antiquity must be abated,
if not abandoned. But I should be very sorry that anything I have
said should be taken to imply a desire on my part to depreciate
the value of classical education, as it might be and as it sometimes
is. The native capacities of mankind vary no less than their opportunities; and while culture is one, the road by which one man
may best reach it is widely different from that which is most
advantageous to another. Again, while scientific education is yet
inchoate and tentative, classical education is thoroughly well
organized upon the practical experience of generations of teachers.
So that, given ample time for learning and estimation for ordinary
life, or for a literary career, I do not think that a young Englishman in search of culture can do better than follow the course
usually marked out for him, supplementing its deficiencies by his
own efforts.

54   But for those who mean to make science their serious
occupation; or who intend to follow the profession of medicine;
or who have to enter early upon the business of life; for all these,
in my opinion, classical education is a mistake; and it is for this
reason that I am glad to see "mere literary education and instruction" shut out from the curriculum of Sir Josiah Mason's
College, seeing that its inclusion would probably lead to the
introduction of the ordinary smattering of Latin and Greek.

55   Nevertheless, I am the last person to question the importance of genuine literary education, or to suppose that intellectual
culture can be complete without it. An exclusively scientific train-

ing will bring about a mental twist as surely as an exclusively literary training. The value of the cargo does not compensate for a ship's being out of trim; and I should be very sorry to think that the Scientific College would turn out none but lopsided men.

56   There is no need, however, that such a catastrophe should happen. Instruction in English, French, and German is provided, and thus the three greatest literatures of the modern world are made accessible to the student.

57   French and German, and especially the latter language, are absolutely indispensable to those who desire full knowledge in any department of science. But even supposing that the knowledge of these languages acquired is not more than sufficient for purely scientific purposes, every Englishman has, in his native tongue, an almost perfect instrument of literary expression; and, in his own literature, models of every kind of literary excellence. If an Englishman cannot get literary culture out of his Bible, his Shakespeare, his Milton, neither, in my belief, will the profoundest study of Homer and Sophocles, Virgil and Horace, give it to him.

58   Thus, since the constitution of the college makes sufficient provision for literary as well as for scientific education, and since artistic instruction is also contemplated, it seems to me that a fairly complete culture is offered to all who are willing to take advantage of it.

59   But I am not sure that at this point the "practical" man, scotched but not slain, may ask what all this talk about culture has to do with an institution, the object of which is defined to be "to promote the prosperity of the manufactures and the industry of the country." He may suggest that what is wanted for this end is not culture, nor even a purely scientific discipline, but simply a knowledge of applied science.

60   I often wish that this phrase, "applied science," had never been invented. For it suggests that there is a sort of scientific knowledge of direct practical use, which can be studied apart from another sort of scientific knowledge, which is of no practical utility, and which is termed "pure science." But there is no more complete fallacy than this. What people call applied science is nothing but the application of pure science to particular classes of problems. It consists of deductions from those general principles, established by reasoning and observation, which constitute pure science. No one can safely make these deductions until he has a firm grasp of the principles; and he can obtain that grasp only by

personal experience of the operations of observation and of reasoning on which they are founded.

61   Almost all the processes employed in the arts and manufactures fall within the range either of physics or of chemistry. In order to improve them, one must thoroughly understand them; and no one has a chance of really understanding them, unless he has obtained that mastery of principles and that habit of dealing with facts, which is given by long-continued and well-directed purely scientific training in the physical and the chemical laboratory. So that there really is no question as to the necessity of purely scientific discipline, even if the work of the college were limited by the narrowest interpretation of its stated aims.

62   And, as to the desirableness of a wider culture than that yielded by science alone, it is to be recollected that the improvement of manufacturing processes is only one of the conditions which contribute to the prosperity of industry. Industry is a means and not an end; and mankind work only to get something which they want. What that something is depends partly on their innate, and partly on their acquired, desires.

63   If the wealth resulting from prosperous industry is to be spent upon the gratification of unworthy desires, if the increasing perfection of manufacturing processes is to be accompanied by an increasing debasement of those who carry them on, I do not see the good of industry and prosperity.

64   Now it is perfectly true that men's views of what is desirable depend upon their characters; and that the innate proclivities to which we give that name are not touched by any amount of instruction. But it does not follow that even mere intellectual education may not, to an indefinite extent, modify the practical manifestation of the characters of men in their actions, by supplying them with motives unknown to the ignorant. A pleasure-loving character will have pleasure of some sort; but, if you give him the choice, he may prefer pleasures which do not degrade him to those which do. And this choice is offered to every man, who possesses in literary or artistic culture a never-failing source of pleasures, which are neither withered by age, nor staled by custom, nor embittered in the recollection by the pangs of self-reproach.

65   If the institution opened today fulfills the intention of its founder, the picked intelligences among all classes of the population of this district will pass through it. No child born in Birming-

ham, henceforward, if he have the capacity to profit by the
opportunities offered to him, first in the primary and other schools,
and afterwards in the Scientific College, need fail to obtain, not
merely the instruction, but the culture most appropriate to the
conditions of his life.

66   Within these walls, the future employer and the future
artisan may sojourn together for a while, and carry, through all
their lives, the stamp of the influences then brought to bear upon
them. Hence, it is not beside the mark to remind you, that the
prosperity of industry depends not merely upon the improvement
of manufacturing processes, not merely upon the ennobling of the
individual character, but upon a third condition, namely, a clear
understanding of the conditions of social life, on the part of both
the capitalist and the operative, and their agreement upon common
principles of social action. They must learn that social phenomena
are as much the expression of natural laws as any others; that no
social arrangements can be permanent unless they harmonize with
the requirements of social statics and dynamics; and that, in the
nature of things, there is an arbiter whose decisions execute themselves.

67   But this knowledge is only to be obtained by the application of the methods of investigation adopted in physical researches
to the investigation of the phenomena of society. Hence, I confess,
I should like to see one addition made to the excellent scheme of
education propounded for the college, in the shape of provision
for the teaching of sociology. For though we are all agreed that
party politics are to have no place in the instruction of the college;
yet in this country, practically governed as it is now by universal
suffrage, every man who does his duty must exercise political
functions. And, if the evils which are inseparable from the good
of political liberty are to be checked, if the perpetual oscillation
of nations between anarchy and despotism is to be replaced by
the steady march of self-restraining freedom; it will be because
men will gradually bring themselves to deal with political, as they
now deal with scientific questions; to be as ashamed of undue haste
and partisan prejudice in the one case as in the other; and to
believe that the machinery of society is at least as delicate as that
of a spinning-jenny, and as little likely to be improved by the
meddling of those who have not taken the trouble to master the
principles of its action.

68   In conclusion, I am sure that I make myself the mouth-
piece of all present in offering to the venerable founder of the
institution, which now commences its beneficent career, our con-
gratulations on the completion of his work, and in expressing the
conviction, that the remotest posterity will point to it as a crucial
instance of the wisdom which natural piety leads all men to ascribe
to their ancestors.

• COMMENTARY •

Huxley presents his argument for the importance of science in education and general culture using the traditional steps, but in an order different from that given in the introductory remarks. His argument, following
his introduction, proceeds first to his *refutation*, for reasons we will
see later, then to the formal *establishment of his position*, finally to a
conclusion.

The first seven paragraphs seem to constitute Huxley's *introduction*.
In paragraphs one through three he speaks of the occasion, the founding
of the new Science College by Sir Josiah Mason. Paragraphs four
through seven, with their brief account of the significance of the college
and of the value of scientific education, announce the impending argument and offer at least a preliminary *proposal* as Huxley contends that
in the "crisis of battle" over education, the time has come for science to
take its proper place.

He moves then into the *refutation*. We can see several reasons why
this would precede establishing his belief in the importance of science.
First of all, he has already prepared a natural transition into this part
of his discussion with his reference to the long series of battles over
education. In the context of those long battles, the very founding of
the Science College instigates argument. Further, presenting his refutation first enables him to show the background, sometimes inimical, out of
which science grew to its new proportions. This section of the piece,
which extends from paragraph eight through paragraph forty-four, is
divided in two parts, each considering one of the opponents of scientific
education. In paragraph eight Huxley names the two kinds of opposition, from men of business and from classical scholars. Paragraphs nine
through fifteen are then devoted to the first opponents, the men of business, whom Huxley can dismiss very briefly, for as he shows, their
opposition, once vigorous, has now waned, as the founding of the Science College by Sir Josiah Mason, a businessman, amply proves. The

policies announced by Mason on the founding of the college and given in paragraph eighteen affect the transition to Huxley's discussion of the second group of opponents. Mason's injunction against "mere literary instruction" serves to introduce the argument against classical scholars which follows in paragraphs nineteen through forty-four. The principal direction of Huxley's refutation is indicated in paragraph twenty-three.

The rest of the selection can be divided into *establishment of position* (paragraphs forty-five through fifty-eight) and *conclusion* (paragraphs fifty-nine through sixty-eight), though the material in the conclusion may also be seen as part of the proof of his argument. Two points bear the burden of his proof. The first (paragraphs forty-five through forty-nine) is that history shows the insufficiency of literary study. The second (paragraphs fifty through fifty-nine) is that the Renaissance, which the classicists hail as their great revival, also saw the revival and consequent burgeoning of scientific study.

The conclusion, which quite clearly enforces the proof, has as its primary strength the cardinal values of scientific study given in paragraphs sixty-two through sixty-seven. The concluding paragraph prophesies the laudatory response of posterity.

THE DECLARATION OF INDEPENDENCE [1776]

When in the Course of human events, it becomes necessary for one people to dissolve the political bands which have connected them with another, and to assume among the powers of the earth, the separate and equal station to which the Laws of Nature and of Nature's God entitle them, a decent respect to the opinions of mankind requires that they should declare the causes which impel them to the separation.—We hold these truths to be self-evident, that all men are created equal, that they are endowed by their Creator with certain unalienable Rights, that among these are Life, Liberty, and the pursuit of Happiness.—That to secure these rights, Governments are instituted among Men, deriving their just powers from the consent of the governed,—That whenever any Form of Government becomes destructive of these ends, it is the Right of the People to alter or to abolish it, and to institute new Government, laying its foundation on such principles and organizing its powers in such form, as to them shall seem most likely to effect their Safety and Happiness. Prudence, indeed, will dictate that Governments long established should not be changed for light and transient causes; and accordingly all experience hath shewn, that mankind are more disposed to suffer, while evils are sufferable, than to right themselves by abolishing the forms to which they are accustomed. But when a long train of abuses and usurpations, pursuing invariably the same Object evinces a design to reduce them under absolute Despotism, it is their right, it is their duty, to throw off such Government, and to provide Guards for their future security.—Such has been the patient sufferance of these Colonies; and such is now the necessity which constrains them to alter their former Systems of Government. The history of the present King of Great Britain is a history of repeated injuries and usurpations, all having in direct object the establishment of an absolute Tyranny over these States. To prove this, let Facts be submitted to a candid world.—He has refused his Assent to Laws, the most wholesome and necessary to the public good.—He has forbidden his Governors to pass Laws of immediate and pressing importance, unless suspended in their operation till his Assent should be obtained; and when so suspended, he has utterly neglected to attend to them.—He has refused to pass other Laws for the accommodation of large districts of people, unless those people would relinquish the right of Representation in the Legislature, a right inestimable to them and formidable to tyrants only.— He has called together legislative bodies at places unusual, uncomfortable, and distant from the depository of their public Records, for the sole purpose of fatiguing them into compliance with his measures.—He has dissolved Representative Houses repeatedly, for opposing with manly firmness his invasions on the right of the people.—He has refused for a long time, after such dissolutions, to cause others to be elected; whereby the Legislative powers, incapable of Annihilation, have returned to the People at large for their exercise; the State remaining in the mean time exposed to all the dangers of invasion from without, and convulsions within.—He has endeavoured to prevent the population of these States; for that purpose obstructing the Laws for Naturalization of Foreigners; refusing to pass others to encourage their migrations hither, and raising the conditions of new Appropriations of Lands.—He has obstructed the Administration of Justice, by refusing his Assent to Laws for establishing Judiciary powers.— He has made Judges dependent on his Will alone, for the tenure

of their offices, and the amount and payment of their salaries.—
He has erected a multitude of New Offices, and sent hither swarms
of Officers to harass our people, and eat out their substance.—He
has kept among us, in times of peace, Standing Armies without
the Consent of our legislatures.—He has affected to render the
Military independent of and superior to the Civil power.—He has
combined with others to subject us to a jurisdiction foreign to our
constitution, and unacknowledged by our laws; giving his Assent
to their Acts of pretended Legislation:—For quartering large
bodies of armed troops among us;—For protecting them, by a
mock Trial, from punishment for any Murders which they should
commit on the Inhabitants of these States:—For cutting off our
Trade with all parts of the world:—For imposing Taxes on us
without our Consent:—For depriving us in many cases, of the
benefits of Trial by Jury:—For transporting us beyond Seas to be
tried for pretended offences:—For abolishing the free System of
English Laws in a neighbouring Province, establishing therein
an Arbitrary government, and enlarging its Boundaries so as to
render it at once an example and fit instrument for introducing
the same absolute rule into these Colonies:—For taking away our
Charters, abolishing our most valuable Laws, and altering fundamentally the Forms of our Governments:—For suspending our
own Legislatures, and declaring themselves invested with power
to legislate for us in all cases whatsoever.—He has abdicated
Government here, by declaring us out of his Protection and
waging War against us.—He has plundered our seas, ravaged our
Coasts, burnt our towns, and destroyed the lives of our people.—
He is at this time transporting large Armies of foreign Mercenaries
to complete the works of death, desolation and tyranny, already
begun with circumstances of Cruelty & perfidy scarcely paralleled
in the most barbarous ages, and totally unworthy the Head of a
civilized nation.—He has constrained our fellow Citizens taken
Captive on the high Seas to bear Arms against their Country, to
become the executioners of their friends and Brethren, or to fall
themselves by their Hands.—He has excited domestic insurrections
amongst us, and has endeavoured to bring on the inhabitants of
our frontiers, the merciless Indian Savages, whose known rule of
warfare, is an undistinguished destruction of all ages, sexes and
conditions. In every stage of these Oppressions We have Peti-
tioned for Redress in the most humble terms. Our repeated Peti-
tions have been answered only by repeated injury. A Prince, whose

character is thus marked by every act which may define a Tyrant, is unfit to be the ruler of a free people. Nor have We been wanting in attentions to our British brethren. We have warned them from time to time of attempts by their legislature to extend an unwarrantable jurisdiction over us. We have reminded them of the circumstances of our emigration and settlement here. We have appealed to their native justice and magnanimity, and we have conjured them by the ties of our common kindred to disavow these usurpations, which would inevitably interrupt our connections and correspondence. They too have been deaf to the voice of justice and of consanguinity. We must, therefore, acquiesce in the necessity, which denounces our Separation, and hold them, as we hold the rest of mankind, Enemies in War, in Peace Friends.—

We, therefore, the Representatives of the United States of America, in General Congress, Assembled, appealing to the Supreme Judge of the world for the rectitude of our intentions, do, in the Name, and by the Authority of the good People of these Colonies, solemnly publish and declare, That these United Colonies are, and of Right ought to be Free and Independent States; that they are Absolved from all allegiance to the British Crown, and that all political connection between them and the State of Great Britain, is and ought to be totally dissolved; and that as Free and Independent States, they have full Power to levy War, conclude Peace, contract Alliances, establish Commerce, and to do all other Acts and Things which Independent States may of right do.—And for the support of this Declaration, with a firm reliance on the protection of divine Providence, we mutually pledge to each other our Lives, our Fortunes, and our sacred Honor.

• SUGGESTION •

Demonstrate the steps in the argument presented here.

Confirmation

The difference between the following selections, Confirmations, and those earlier, Ritual Proposals, may seem slight, may indeed be slight. However, there are some differences. The confirmation, which usually will contain only a proposal and support, or position and establishment of a position, is likely to be a more extended discussion than the ritual proposal. Where the proposal alone may depend on style for its effectiveness, we can usually expect the writer offering a confirmation to offer with his proposal some evidence, some show of the long processes of thought that created the proposal. Perhaps the greatest difference between the two may lie in the nature of the proposals they offer. The ritual proposal works best when it invokes response to what is already accepted. The confirmation probably will offer a little more room to work in; consequently the writer may undertake a new proposal or one not commonly accepted.

PUT POETS IN SPACE*

Norman Cousins

1   The idea of man in space is an explosion in the imagination. It shakes free the sense of wonder; it cracks open a vast area of the human potential; it confronts the intelligence with the prospect of an encounter with the infinite. But it also adds to the terror. Not terror from what is unknown about space but from what is known about man. These cosmic vehicles are the forerunners of space platforms carrying loaded nuclear pistols pointed at the head of man on earth. A great ascent has taken place without any corresponding elevation of ideas. Man has raised his station without raising his sights. He roams the heavens with the engines of hell.

2   No human being who ever lived was able to see more of the world than Yuri Gagarin. No human being was ever in a better position to reflect on human destiny. Yet at precisely the moment that he should have been asserting the cause of man he was asserting the cause of the nation. The one thing on earth that most needed to be left behind—the sense of the tribe—he had carried securely with him. A magnificent new vantage point was not enough to offset an old perspective. Into the center of the focused view came the national flag.

* From *Saturday Review,* April 29, 1961. By permission of the author and publisher.

3   This is not to say that there is anything wrong or unnatural about a surge of national pride over such an event. Nor is it strange that the reaction in the United States should have been registered so largely on the level of the national ego-hurt, with assurances from government that we were not too far behind. In the context of a struggle for world balance of power, for prestige, and for pre-eminence, every gain is bound to be posted on the competitive scoreboard. But at some point the human race must have its innings. An assessment must ultimately be made in terms of human development. In the end, it is not the nation but man who will have to account for the record of life on earth.

4   The heart of the problem is that the earth dwellers, whether they live in eastern or western hemispheres, have not prepared themselves adequately for the journey into space. We have directed our attention to machinery rather than motives. We have been concerned with blast-off when we should have been thinking about basic purpose. In a more general sense, our education bears all the marks of specific earth gravity. We have been part of the cosmos but we have tended to regard it as scenery rather than a total abode. Copernicus, Einstein, and Shapley notwithstanding, man still sees man as the center of the universe. We have cheapened our Gods by cutting them down to accessible size and separating them from a concept beyond infinity. It is as though we had been preparing for Beethoven by listening to hyenas.

5   The journey into space is, or should be, a sublime experience. The selection of astronauts ought not be confined to men in the military or in technology. Why not poets, philosophers, or theologians? If it is said that space has stern physical requirements, the problem can be met. There are strapping fellows among those who have demonstrated their capacity to think creatively and who have some convictions about the nature of man. One of the prime requisites for an astronaut is not just his ability to follow a specified procedure and to take measurements but to be able to be at one with a new environment. A space ship requires true perspective. This is nothing that can be imparted in a course on astronautics; it comes with the responsible development of intellect and insight. A respect for the human spirit may be even more important than a knowledge of centrifugal force. Moreover, a certain artistry is called for when man proposes to range the universe. It is an artistry both of personal response and

ability to communicate. For when the astronaut returns to earth his message should be more than an excited series of remarks on a fabulous journey. The returning messenger should have the ability to impart a sense of great new connections that may transform life as we have known it.

6   Men like Paul Tillich, Reinhold Niebuhr, Lewis Mumford, and Robert Frost may be too old to withstand the rigors of training for such an assignment, but at least they ought to be consulted on the younger men who may be equal to the job. In the meantime, the rest of us can try to prepare ourselves to accord a full measure of comprehension to the dimensions of a new age. There is something else we can do. We can try to chart a direction for human survival with at least as much concentration of effort as we are putting into a trip to the moon.

• COMMENTARY •

The proposal here is in the title of the selection, but this short essay is not merely an assertion. There is a logical progression through the first five paragraphs that culminates appropriately enough in a fuller statement of the proposal in the last paragraph. Paragraph one states a generalized contradiction: "A great ascent has taken place without any corresponding elevation of ideas." This, then, is given concrete form by the illustration in paragraph two, which renders the same idea but gives it a local habitation. The third paragraph brings the conception back to its general form; but something has been added. Where the generalization in the first paragraph presents only the contrast between capability and vision, the generalization in the third paragraph, while it restates that conception, does so on the strength of the illustration already given to lead into the second contrast, between the hopes of nations and the hopes of the race.

Cousins then can move more directly to his goal. The two contradictions, one general, the other still general but with a specific reference, enables him in paragraph four to get to "the heart of the problem" which is that "earth dwellers . . . have not prepared themselves adequately for the journey into space." He is able to support this primary contention with the contradictions he has already shown, and which he restates in the rest of the fourth paragraph: "We have directed our attention to machinery rather than motives." By contrast, he says in the fifth paragraph, "The journey into space is, or should be, a sublime experience." In such an experience, he says, "respect for the human spirit may be even more important than a knowledge of centrifugal force."

On the basis of this development Cousins proposes in the last paragraph that if we cannot send poets into space, we can seek to comprehend what we do.

CIVIL DISOBEDIENCE [1849]

Henry David Thoreau

1   I heartily accept the motto,—"That government is best which governs least;" and I should like to see it acted up to more rapidly and systematically. Carried out, it finally amounts to this, which also I believe,—"That government is best which governs not at all;" and when men are prepared for it, that will be the kind of government which they will have. Government is at best but an expedient; but most governments are usually, and all governments are sometimes, inexpedient. The objections which have been brought against a standing army, and they are many and weighty, and deserve to prevail, may also at last be brought against a standing government. The standing army is only an arm of the standing government. The government itself, which is only the mode which the people have chosen to execute their will, is equally liable to be abused and perverted before the people can act through it. Witness the present Mexican war, the work of comparatively a few individuals using the standing government as their tool; for, in the outset, the people would not have consented to this measure.

2   This American government,—what is it but a tradition, though a recent one, endeavoring to transmit itself unimpaired to posterity, but each instant losing some of its integrity? It has not the vitality and force of a single living man; for a single man can bend it to his will. It is a sort of wooden gun to the people themselves. But it is not the less necessary for this; for the people must have some complicated machinery or other, and hear its din, to satisfy that idea of government which they have. Governments show thus how successfully men can be imposed on, even impose

on themselves, for their own advantage. It is excellent, we must all allow. Yet this government never of itself furthered any enterprise, but by the alacrity with which it got out of its way. *It* does not keep the country free. *It* does not settle the West. *It* does not educate. The character inherent in the American people has done all that has been accomplished; and it would have done somewhat more, if the government had not sometimes got in its way. For government is an expedient by which men would fain succeed in letting one another alone; and, as has been said, when it is most expedient, the governed are most let alone by it. Trade and commerce, if they were not made of India-rubber, would never manage to bounce over the obstacles which legislators are continually putting in their way; and, if one were to judge these men wholly by the effects of their actions and not partly by their intentions, they would deserve to be classed and punished with those mischievous persons who put obstructions on the railroads.

3   But, to speak practically and as a citizen, unlike those who call themselves no-government men, I ask for, not at once no government, but *at once* a better government. Let every man make known what kind of government would command his respect, and that will be one step toward obtaining it.

4   After all, the practical reason why, when the power is once in the hands of the people, a majority are permitted, and for a long period continue, to rule is not because they are most likely to be in the right, nor because this seems fairest to the minority, but because they are physically the strongest. But a government in which the majority rule in all cases cannot be based on justice, even as far as men understand it. Can there not be a government in which majorities do not virtually decide right and wrong, but conscience?—in which majorities decide only those questions to which the rule of expediency is applicable? Must the citizen ever for a moment, or in the least degree, resign his conscience to the legislator? Why has every man a conscience, then? I think that we should be men first, and subjects afterward. It is not desirable to cultivate a respect for the law, so much as the right. The only obligation which I have a right to assume is to do at any time what I think right. It is truly enough said, that a corporation has no conscience; but a corporation of conscientious men is a corporation *with* a conscience. Law never made men a whit more just; and, by means of their respect for it, even the well-disposed are

daily made the agents of injustice. A common and natural result of an undue respect for law is, that you may see a file of soldiers, colonel, captain, corporal, privates, powder-monkeys, and all, marching in admirable order over hill and dale to the wars, against their wills, ay, against their common sense and consciences, which makes it very steep marching indeed, and produces a palpitation of the heart. They have no doubt that it is a damnable business in which they are concerned; they are all peaceably inclined. Now, what are they? Men at all? or small movable forts and magazines, at the service of some unscrupulous man in power? Visit the Navy-Yard, and behold a marine, such a man as an American government can make, or such as it can make a man with its black arts,—a mere shadow and reminiscence of humanity, a man laid out alive and standing, and already, as one may say, buried under arms with funeral accompaniments, though it may be,—

> "Not a drum was heard, not a funeral note,
>   As his corse to the rampart we hurried;
> Not a soldier discharged his farewell shot
>   O'er the grave where our hero we buried."

5   The mass of men serve the state thus, not as men mainly, but as machines, with their bodies. They are the standing army, and the militia, jailors, constables, posse comitatus, etc. In most cases there is no free exercise whatever of the judgment or of the moral sense; but they put themselves on a level with wood and earth and stones; and wooden men can perhaps be manufactured that will serve the purpose as well. Such command no more respect than men of straw or a lump of dirt. They have the same sort of worth only as horses and dogs. Yet such as these even are commonly esteemed good citizens. Others—as most legislators, politicians, lawyers, ministers, and office-holders—serve the state chiefly with their heads; and, as they rarely make any moral distinctions, they are as likely to serve the Devil, without *intending* it, as God. A very few, as heroes, patriots, martyrs, reformers in the great sense, and *men,* serve the state with their consciences also, and so necessarily resist it for the most part; and they are commonly treated as enemies by it. A wise man will only be useful as a man, and will not submit to be "clay," and "stop a hole to keep the wind away," but leave that office to his dust at least:—

> "I am too high-born to be propertied,
> To be a secondary at control,
> Or useful serving-man and instrument
> To any sovereign state throughout the world."

6   He who gives himself entirely to his fellow-men appears to them useless and selfish; but he who gives himself partially to them is pronounced a benefactor and philanthropist.

7   How does it become a man to behave toward this American government to-day? I answer, that he cannot without disgrace be associated with it. I cannot for an instant recognize that political organization as *my* government which is the *slave's* government also.

8   All men recognize the right of revolution; that is, the right to refuse allegiance to, and to resist, the government, when its tyranny or its inefficiency are great and unendurable. But almost all say that such is not the case now. But such was the case, they think, in the Revolution of '75. If one were to tell me that this was a bad government because it taxed certain foreign commodities brought to its ports, it is most probable that I should not make an ado about it, for I can do without them. All machines have their friction; and possibly this does enough good to counterbalance the evil. At any rate, it is a great evil to make a stir about it. But when the friction comes to have its machine, and oppression and robbery are organized, I say, let us not have such a machine any longer. In other words, when a sixth of the population of a nation which has undertaken to be the refuge of liberty are slaves, and a whole country is unjustly overrun and conquered by a foreign army, and subjected to military law, I think that it is not too soon for honest men to rebel and revolutionize. What makes this duty the more urgent is the fact that the country so overrun is not our own, but ours is the invading army.

9   Paley, a common authority with many on moral questions, in his chapter on the "Duty of Submission to Civil Government," resolves all civil obligation into expediency; and he proceeds to say, "that so long as the interest of the whole society requires it, that is, so long as the established government cannot be resisted or changed without public inconveniency, it is the will of God that the established government be obeyed, and no longer. . . . This principle being admitted, the justice of every particular case of

resistance is reduced to a computation of the quantity of the danger and grievance on the one side, and of the probability and expense of redressing it on the other." Of this, he says, every man shall judge for himself. But Paley appears never to have contemplated those cases to which the rule of expediency does not apply, in which a people, as well as an individual, must do justice, cost what it may. If I have unjustly wrested a plank from a drowning man, I must restore it to him though I drown myself. This, according to Paley, would be inconvenient. But he that would save his life, in such a case, shall lose it. This people must cease to hold slaves, and to make war on Mexico, though it cost them their existence as a people.

10   In their practice, nations agree with Paley; but does any one think that Massachusetts does exactly what is right at the present crisis?

> "A drab of state, a cloth-o'-silver slut,
> To have her train borne up, and her soul trail in the dirt."

Practically speaking, the opponents to a reform in Massachusetts are not a hundred thousand politicians at the South, but a hundred thousand merchants and farmers here, who are more interested in commerce and agriculture than they are in humanity, and are not prepared to do justice to the slave and to Mexico, *cost what it may.* I quarrel not with far-off foes, but with those who, near at home, coöperate with, and do the bidding of, those far away, and without whom the latter would be harmless. We are accustomed to say, that the mass of men are unprepared; but improvement is slow, because the few are not materially wiser or better than the many. It is not so important that many should be as good as you, as that there be some absolute goodness somewhere; for that will leaven the whole lump. There are thousands who are *in opinion* opposed to slavery and to the war, who yet in effect do nothing to put an end to them; who, esteeming themselves children of Washington and Franklin, sit down with their hands in their pockets, and say that they know not what to do, and do nothing; who even postpone the question of freedom to the question of free-trade, and quietly read the prices-current along with the latest advices from Mexico, after dinner, and, it may be, fall asleep over them both. What is the price-current of an honest man and patriot to-day? They hesitate, and they regret, and sometimes they petition; but they do nothing in earnest and with effect. They will wait, well disposed, for others to remedy the evil, that they may no longer have it to regret. At most, they give only a cheap vote, and a feeble countenance and God-speed, to the right, as it goes by them. There are nine hundred and ninety-nine patrons of virtue to one virtuous man. But it is easier to deal with the real possessor of a thing than with the temporary guardian of it.

11   All voting is a sort of gaming, like checkers or backgammon, with a slight moral tinge to it, a playing with right and wrong, with moral questions; and betting naturally accompanies it. The character of the voters is not staked. I cast my vote, perchance, as I think right; but I am not vitally concerned that that right should prevail. I am willing to leave it to the majority. Its obligation, therefore, never exceeds that of expediency. Even voting *for the right* is *doing* nothing for it. It is only expressing to men feebly your desire that it should prevail. A wise man will not leave the right to the mercy of chance, nor wish it to prevail through the power of the majority. There is but little virtue in the action of masses of men. When the majority shall at length vote for the abolition of slavery, it will be because they are indifferent to slavery, or because there is but little slavery left to be abolished by their vote. *They* will then be the only slaves. Only *his* vote can hasten the abolition of slavery who asserts his own freedom by his vote.

12   I hear of a convention to be held at Baltimore, or elsewhere, for the selection of a candidate for the Presidency, made up chiefly of editors, and men who are politicians by profession; but I think, what is it to any independent, intelligent, and respectable man what decision they may come to? Shall we not have the advantage of his wisdom and honesty, nevertheless? Can we not count upon some independent votes? Are there not many individuals in the country who do not attend conventions? But no: I find that the respectable man, so called, has immediately drifted from his position, and despairs of his country, when his country has more reason to despair of him. He forthwith adopts one of the candidates thus selected as the only *available* one, thus proving that he is himself *available* for any purposes of the demagogue. His vote is of no more worth than that of any unprincipled foreigner or hireling native, who may have been bought. O for a man

who is a *man,* and, as my neighbor says, has a bone in his back
which you cannot pass your hand through! Our statistics are at
fault: the population has been returned too large. How many *men*
are there to a square thousand miles in this country? Hardly one.
Does not America offer any inducement for men to settle here?
The American has dwindled into an Odd Fellow,—one who may
be known by the development of his organ of gregariousness, and
a manifest lack of intellect and cheerful self-reliance; whose first
and chief concern, on coming into the world, is to see that the
Almshouses are in good repair; and, before yet he has lawfully
donned the virile garb, to collect a fund for the support of the
widows and orphans that may be; who, in short, ventures to live
only by the aid of the Mutual Insurance company, which has
promised to bury him decently.

13   It is not a man's duty, as a matter of course, to devote
himself to the eradication of any, even the most enormous wrong;
he may still properly have other concerns to engage him; but it is
his duty, at least, to wash his hands of it, and, if he gives it no
thought longer, not to give it practically his support. If I devote
myself to other pursuits and contemplations, I must first see, at
least, that I do not pursue them sitting upon another man's
shoulders. I must get off him first, that he may pursue his contemplations too. See what gross inconsistency is tolerated. I have
heard some of my townsmen say, "I should like to have them order
me out to help put down an insurrection of the slaves, or to march
to Mexico;—see if I would go;" and yet these very men have each,
directly by their allegiance, and so indirectly, at least, by their
money, furnished a substitute. The soldier is applauded who refuses to serve in an unjust war by those who do not refuse to
sustain the unjust government which makes the war; is applauded
by those whose own act and authority he disregards and sets at
naught; as if the state were penitent to that degree that it hired
one to scourge it while it sinned, but not to that degree that it
left off sinning for a moment. Thus, under the name of Order and
Civil Government, we are all made at last to pay homage to and
support our own meanness. After the first blush of sin comes its
indifference; and from immoral it becomes, as it were, *un*moral,
and not quite unnecessary to that life which we have made.

14   The broadest and most prevalent error requires the most
disinterested virtue to sustain it. The slight reproach to which the

virtue of patriotism is commonly liable, the noble are most likely to incur. Those who, while they disapprove of the character and measures of a government, yield to it their allegiance and support are undoubtedly its most conscientious supporters, and so frequently the most serious obstacles to reform. Some are petitioning the state to dissolve the Union, to disregard the requisitions of the President. Why do they not dissolve it themselves,—the union between themselves and the state,—and refuse to pay their quota into its treasury? Do not they stand in the same relation to the state that the state does to the Union? And have not the same reasons prevented the state from resisting the Union which have prevented them from resisting the state?

15　　How can a man be satisfied to entertain an opinion merely, and enjoy *it*? Is there any enjoyment in it, if his opinion is that he is aggrieved? If you are cheated out of a single dollar by your neighbor, you do not rest satisfied with knowing that you are cheated, or with saying that you are cheated, or even with petitioning him to pay you your due; but you take effectual steps at once to obtain the full amount, and see that you are never cheated again. Action from principle, the perception and the performance of right, changes things and relations; it is essentially revolutionary, and does not consist wholly with anything which was. It not only divides states and churches, it divides families; ay, it divides the *individual*, separating the diabolical in him from the divine.

16　　Unjust laws exist: shall we be content to obey them, or shall we endeavor to amend them, and obey them until we have succeeded, or shall we transgress them at once? Men generally, under such a government as this, think that they ought to wait until they have persuaded the majority to alter them. They think that, if they should resist, the remedy would be worse than the evil. But it is the fault of the government itself that the remedy *is* worse than the evil. *It* makes it worse. Why is it not more apt to anticipate and provide for reform? Why does it not cherish its wise minority? Why does it cry and resist before it is hurt? Why does it not encourage its citizens to be on the alert to point out its faults, and *do* better than it would have them? Why does it always crucify Christ, and excommunicate Copernicus and Luther, and pronounce Washington and Franklin rebels?

17 One would think, that a deliberate and practical denial of its authority was the only offense never contemplated by government; else, why has it not assigned its definite, its suitable and proportionate penalty? If a man who has no property refuses but once to earn nine shillings for the state, he is put in prison for a period unlimited by any law that I know, and determined only by the discretion of those who placed him there; but if he should steal ninety times nine shillings from the state, he is soon permitted to go at large again.

18 If the injustice is part of the necessary friction of the machine of government, let it go, let it go: perchance it will wear smooth,—certainly the machine will wear out. If the injustice has a spring, or a pulley, or a rope, or a crank, exclusively for itself, then perhaps you may consider whether the remedy will not be worse than the evil; but if it is of such a nature that it requires you to be the agent of injustice to another, then, I say, break the law. Let your life be a counter friction to stop the machine. What I have to do is to see, at any rate, that I do not lend myself to the wrong which I condemn.

19 As for adopting the ways which the state has provided for remedying the evil, I know not of such ways. They take too much time, and a man's life will be gone. I have other affairs to attend to. I came into this world, not chiefly to make this a good place to live in, but to live in it, be it good or bad. A man has not everything to do, but something; and because he cannot do *everything*, it is not necessary that he should do *something* wrong. It is not my business to be petitioning the Governor or the Legislature any more than it is theirs to petition me; and if they should not hear my petition, what should I do then? But in this case the state has provided no way: its very Constitution is the evil. This may seem to be harsh and stubborn and unconciliatory; but it is to treat with the utmost kindness and consideration the only spirit that can appreciate or deserves it. So is all change for the better, like birth and death, which convulse the body.

20 I do not hesitate to say, that those who call themselves Abolitionists should at once effectually withdraw their support, both in person and property, from the government of Massachusetts and not wait till they constitute a majority of one, before they suffer the right to prevail through them. I think that it is enough if they have God on their side, without waiting for that other one.

Moreover, any man more right than his neighbors constitutes a majority of one already.

21 I meet this American government, or its representative, the state government, directly, and face to face, once a year—no more—in the person of its tax-gatherer; this is the only mode in which a man situated as I am necessarily meets it; and it then says distinctly, Recognize me; and the simplest, most effectual, and, in the present posture of affairs, the indispensablest mode of treating with it on this head, of expressing your little satisfaction with and love for it, is to deny it then. My civil neighbor, the tax-gatherer, is the very man I have to deal with,—for it is, after all, with men and not with parchment that I quarrel,—and he has voluntarily chosen to be an agent of the government. How shall he ever know well what he is and does as an officer of the government, or as a man, until he is obliged to consider whether he shall treat me, his neighbor, for whom he has respect, as a neighbor and well-disposed man, or as a maniac and disturber of the peace, and see if he can get over this obstruction to his neighborliness without a ruder and more impetuous thought or speech corresponding with his action. I know this well, that if one thousand, if one hundred, if ten men whom I could name,—if ten *honest* men only,—ay, if *one* HONEST man, in the State of Massachusetts, *ceasing to hold slaves,* were actually to withdraw from this copartnership, and be locked up in the county jail therefor, it would be the abolition of slavery in America. For it matters not how small the beginning may seem to be: what is once well done is done forever. But we love better to talk about it: that we say is our mission. Reform keeps many scores of newspapers in its service, but not one man. If my esteemed neighbor, the State's ambassador, who will devote his days to the settlement of the question of human rights in the Council Chamber, instead of being threatened with the prisons of Carolina, were to sit down the prisoner of Massachusetts, that State which is so anxious to foist the sin of slavery upon her sister,—though at present she can discover only an act of inhospitality to be the ground of a quarrel with her,—the Legislature would not wholly waive the subject the following winter.

22 Under a government which imprisons any unjustly, the true place for a just man is also a prison. The proper place to-day, the only place which Massachusetts has provided for her freer and less desponding spirits, is in her prisons, to be put out and locked out of the State by her own act, as they have already put themselves out by their principles. It is there that the fugitive slave, and the Mexican prisoner on parole, and the Indian come to plead the wrongs of his race should find them; on that separate, but more free and honorable ground, where the State places those who are not *with* her, but *against* her,—the only house in a slave State in which a free man can abide with honor. If any think that their influence would be lost there, and their voices no longer afflict the ear of the State, that they would not be as an enemy within its walls, they do not know by how much truth is stronger than error, nor how much more eloquently and effectively he can combat injustice who has experienced a little in his own person. Cast your whole vote, not a strip of paper merely, but your whole influence. A minority is powerless while it conforms to the majority; it is not even a minority then; but it is irresistible when it clogs by its whole weight. If the alternative is to keep all just men in prison, or give up war and slavery, the State will not hesitate to choose. If a thousand men were not to pay their tax-bills this year, that would not be a violent and bloody measure, as it would be to pay them, and enable the State to commit violence and shed innocent blood. This is, in fact, the definition of a peaceable revolution, if any such is possible. If the tax-gatherer, or any other public officer, asks me, as one has done, "But what shall I do?" my answer is, "If you really wish to do anything, resign your office." When the subject has refused allegiance, and the officer has resigned his office, then the revolution is accomplished. But even suppose blood should flow. Is there not a sort of blood shed when the conscience is wounded? Through this wound a man's real manhood and immortality flow out, and he bleeds to an everlasting death. I see this blood flowing now.

23   I have contemplated the imprisonment of the offender, rather than the seizure of his goods,—though both will serve the same purpose,—because they who assert the purest right, and consequently are most dangerous to a corrupt State, commonly have not spent much time in accumulating property. To such the State renders comparatively small service, and a slight tax is wont to appear exorbitant, particularly if they are obliged to earn it by special labor with their hands. If there were one who lived wholly without the use of money, the State itself would hesitate to demand it of him. But the rich man—not to make any invidious comparison

—is always sold to the institution which makes him rich. Absolutely speaking, the more money, the less virtue; for money comes between a man and his objects, and obtains them for him; and it was certainly no great virtue to obtain it. It puts to rest many questions which he would otherwise be taxed to answer; while the only new question which it puts is the hard but superfluous one, how to spend it. Thus his moral ground is taken from under his feet. The opportunities of living are diminished in proportion as what are called the "means" are increased. The best thing a man can do for his culture when he is rich is to endeavor to carry out those schemes which he entertained when he was poor. Christ answered the Herodians according to their condition. "Show me the tribute-money," said he;—and one took a penny out of his pocket;—if you use money which has the image of Caesar on it and which he has made current and valuable, that is, *if you are men of the State,* and gladly enjoy the advantages of Caesar's government, then pay him back some of his own when he demands it. "Render therefore to Caesar that which is Caesar's, and to God those things which are God's"—leaving them no wiser than before as to which was which; for they did not wish to know.

24   When I converse with the freest of my neighbors, I perceive that, whatever they may say about the magnitude and seriousness of the question, and their regard for the public tranquillity, the long and the short of the matter is, that they cannot spare the protection of the existing government, and they dread the consequences to their property and families of disobedience to it. For my own part, I should not like to think that I ever rely on the protection of the State. But, if I deny the authority of the State when it presents its tax-bill, it will soon take and waste all my property, and so harass me and my children without end. This is hard. This makes it impossible for a man to live honestly, and at the same time comfortably, in outward respects. It will not be worth the while to accumulate property; that would be sure to go again. You must hire or squat somewhere, and raise but a small crop, and eat that soon. You must live within yourself, and depend upon yourself always tucked up and ready for a start, and not have many affairs. A man may grow rich in Turkey even, if he will be in all respects a good subject of the Turkish government. Confucius said: "If a state is governed by the principles of reason, poverty and misery are subjects of shame; if a state is not gov-

erned by the principles of reason, riches and honors are the subjects of shame." No: until I want the protection of Massachusetts to be extended to me in some distant Southern port, where my liberty is endangered, or until I am bent solely on building up an estate at home by peaceful enterprise, I can afford to refuse allegiance to Massachusetts, and her right to my property and life. It costs me less in every sense to incur the penalty of disobedience to the State than it would to obey. I should feel as if I were worth less in that case.

25   Some years ago, the State met me in behalf of the Church, and commanded me to pay a certain sum toward the support of a clergyman whose preaching my father attended, but never I myself. "Pay," it said, "or be locked up in the jail." I declined to pay. But, unfortunately, another man saw fit to pay it. I did not see why the schoolmaster should be taxed to support the priest, and not the priest the schoolmaster; for I was not the State's schoolmaster, but I supported myself by voluntary subscription. I did not see why the lyceum should not present its tax-bill, and have the State to back its demand, as well as the Church. However, at the request of the selectmen, I condescended to make some such statement as this in writing:—"Know all men by these presents, that I, Henry Thoreau, do not wish to be regarded as a member of any incorporated society which I have not joined." This I gave to the town clerk; and he has it. The State, having thus learned that I did not wish to be regarded as a member of that church, has never made a like demand on me since; though it said that it must adhere to its original presumption that time. If I had known how to name them, I should then have signed off in detail from all the societies which I never signed on to; but I did not know where to find a complete list.

26   I have paid no poll-tax for six years. I was put into a jail once on this account, for one night; and, as I stood considering the walls of solid stone, two or three feet thick, the door of wood and iron, a foot thick, and the iron grating which strained the light, I could not help being struck with the foolishness of that institution which treated me as if I were mere flesh and blood and bones, to be locked up. I wondered that it should have concluded at length that this was the best use it could put me to, and had never thought to avail itself of my services in some way. I saw that, if there was a wall of stone between me and my townsmen, there

was a still more difficult one to climb or break through before they
could get to be as free as I was. I did not for a moment feel confined, and the walls seemed a great waste of stone and mortar. I felt
as if I alone of all my townsmen had paid my tax. They plainly
did not know how to treat me, but behaved like persons who are
underbred. In every threat and in every compliment there was
a blunder; for they thought that my chief desire was to stand the
other side of that stone wall. I could not but smile to see how in-
dustriously they locked the door on my meditations, which followed them out again without let or hinderance, and *they* were
really all that was dangerous. As they could not reach me, they
had resolved to punish my body; just as boys, if they cannot
come at some person against whom they have a spite, will abuse
his dog. I saw that the State was half-witted, that it was timid as
a lone woman with her silver spoons, and that it did not know
its friends from its foes, and I lost all my remaining respect for it,
and pitied it.

27   Thus the State never intentionally confronts a man's
sense, intellectual or moral, but only his body, his senses. It is not
armed with superior wit or honesty, but with superior physical
strength. I was not born to be forced. I will breathe after my own
fashion. Let us see who is the strongest. What force has a multitude? They only can force me who obey a higher law than I. They
force me to become like themselves. I do not hear of *men* being
forced to live this way or that by masses of men. What sort of life
were that to live? When I meet a government which says to me,
"Your money or your life," why should I be in haste to give it my
money? It may be in a great strait, and not know what to do: I
cannot help that. It must help itself; do as I do. It is not worth the
while to snivel about it. I am not responsible for the successful
working of the machinery of society. I am not the son of the
engineer. I perceive that, when an acorn and a chestnut fall side
by side, the one does not remain inert to make way for the other,
but both obey their own laws, and spring and grow and flourish
as best they can, till one, perchance, overshadows and destroys the
other. If a plant cannot live according to its nature, it dies; and so
a man.

28   The night in prison was novel and interesting enough.
The prisoners in their shirt-sleeves were enjoying a chat and the
evening air in the doorway, when I entered. But the jailer said,

"Come, boys, it is time to lock up;" and so they dispersed, and I heard the sound of their steps returning into the hollow apartments. My room-mate was introduced to me by the jailer as "a first-rate fellow and a clever man." When the door was locked, he showed me where to hang my hat, and how he managed matters there. The rooms were whitewashed once a month; and this one, at least, was the whitest, most simply furnished, and probably the neatest apartment in the town. He naturally wanted to know where I came from, and what brought me there; and, when I had told him, I asked him in my turn how he came there, presuming him to be an honest man, of course; and, as the world goes, I believe he was. "Why," said he, "they accuse me of burning a barn; but I never did it." As near as I could discover, he had probably gone to bed in a barn when drunk, and smoked his pipe there; and so a barn was burnt. He had the reputation of being a clever man, had been there some three months waiting for his trial to come on, and would have to wait as much longer; but he was quite domesticated and contented, since he got his board for nothing, and thought that he was well treated.

29   He occupied one window, and I the other; and I saw that if one stayed there long, his principal business would be to look out the window. I had soon read all the tracts that there were left there, and examined where former prisoners had broken out, and where a grate had been sawed off, and heard the history of the various occupants of that room; for I found that even here there was a history and a gossip which never circulated beyond the walls of the jail. Probably this is the only house in the town where verses are composed, which are afterward printed in a circular form, but not published. I was shown quite a long list of verses which were composed by some young men who had been detected in an attempt to escape, who avenged themselves by singing them.

30   I pumped my fellow-prisoner as dry as I could, for fear I should never see him again; but at length he showed me which was my bed, and left me to blow out the lamp.

31   It was like traveling into a far country, such as I had never expected to behold, to lie there for one night. It seemed to me that I never had heard the town-clock strike before, nor the evening sounds of the village; for we slept with the windows open, which were inside the grating. It was to see my native village in the light of the Middle Ages, and our Concord was turned into a

Rhine stream, and visions of knights and castles passed before me. They were the voices of old burghers that I heard in the streets. I was an involuntary spectator and auditor of whatever was done and said in the kitchen of the adjacent village-inn,—a wholly new and rare experience to me. It was a closer view of my native town. I was fairly inside of it. I never had seen its institutions before. This is one of its peculiar institutions; for it is a shire town. I began to comprehend what its inhabitants were about.

32   In the morning, our breakfasts were put through the hole in the door, in small oblong-square tin pans, made to fit, and holding a pint of chocolate, with brown bread, and an iron spoon. When they called for the vessels again, I was green enough to return what bread I had left; but my comrade seized it, and said that I should lay that up for lunch or dinner. Soon after he was let out to work at haying in a neighboring field, whither he went every day, and would not be back till noon; so he bade me good-day, saying that he doubted if he should see me again.

33   When I came out of prison,—for some one interfered, and paid that tax,—I did not perceive that great changes had taken place on the common, such as he observed who went in a youth and emerged a tottering and gray-headed man; and yet a change had to my eyes come over the scene,—the town, and State, and country,—greater than any that mere time could effect. I saw yet more distinctly the State in which I lived. I saw to what extent the people among whom I lived could be trusted as good neighbors and friends; that their friendship was for summer weather only; that they did not greatly propose to do right; that they were a distinct race from me by their prejudices and superstitions, as the Chinamen and Malays are; that in their sacrifices to humanity they ran no risks, not even to their property; that after all they were not so noble but they treated the thief as he had treated them, and hoped, by a certain outward observance and a few prayers, and by walking in a particular straight though useless path from time to time, to save their souls. This may be to judge my neighbors harshly; for I believe that many of them are not aware that they have such an institution as the jail in their village.

34   It was formerly the custom in our village, when a poor debtor came out of jail, for his acquaintances to salute him, looking through their fingers, which were crossed to represent the grating of a jail window, "How do ye do?" My neighbors did not thus salute me, but first looked at me, and then at one another, as if

I had returned from a long journey. I was put into jail as I was going to the shoemaker's to get a shoe which was mended. When I was let out the next morning, I proceeded to finish my errand, and, having put on my mended shoe, joined a huckleberry party, who were impatient to put themselves under my conduct; and in half an hour,—for the horse was soon tackled,—was in the midst of a huckleberry field, on one of our highest hills, two miles off, and then the State was nowhere to be seen.

35   This is the whole history of "My Prisons."

36   I have never declined paying the highway tax, because I am as desirous of being a good neighbor as I am of being a bad subject; and as for supporting schools, I am doing my part to educate my fellow-countrymen now. It is for no particular item in the tax-bill that I refuse to pay it. I simply wish to refuse allegiance to the State, to withdraw and stand aloof from it effectually. I do not care to trace the course of my dollar, if I could, till it buys a man or a musket to shoot with,—the dollar is innocent,—but I am concerned to trace the effects of my allegiance. In fact, I quietly declare war with the State, after my fashion, though I will still make what use and get what advantage of her I can, as is usual in such cases.

37   If others pay the tax which is demanded of me, from a sympathy with the State, they do but what they have already done in their own case, or rather they abet injustice to a greater extent than the State requires. If they pay the tax from a mistaken interest in the individual taxed, to save him property, or prevent his going to jail, it is because they have not considered wisely how far they let their private feelings interfere with the public good.

38   This, then, is my position at present. But one cannot be too much on his guard in such a case, lest his action be biased by obstinacy or an undue regard for the opinions of men. Let him see that he does only what belongs to himself and to the hour.

39   I think sometimes, Why, this people mean well, they are only ignorant; they would do better if they knew how: why give your neighbors this pain to treat you as they are not inclined to? But I think again, This is no reason why I should do as they do, or permit others to suffer much greater pain of a different kind. Again, I sometimes say to myself, When many millions of men, without heat, without ill will, without personal feeling of any kind, demand of you a few shillings only, without the possibility,

such is their constitution, of retracting or altering their present demand, and without the possibility, on your side, of appeal to any other millions, why expose yourself to this overwhelming brute force? You do not resist cold and hunger, the winds and the waves, thus obstinately; you quietly submit to a thousand similar necessities. You do not put your head into the fire. But just in proportion as I regard this as not wholly a brute force, but partly a human force, and consider that I have relations to those millions as to so many millions of men, and not of mere brute or inanimate things, I see that appeal is possible, first and instantaneously, from them to the Maker of them, and, secondly, from them to themselves. But if I put my head deliberately into the fire, there is no appeal to fire or to the Maker of fire, and I have only myself to blame. If I could convince myself that I have any right to be satisfied with men as they are, and to treat them accordingly, and not according, in some respects, to my requisitions and expectations of what they and I ought to be, then, like a good Mussulman and fatalist, I should endeavor to be satisfied with things as they are, and say it is the will of God. And, above all, there is this difference between resisting this and a purely brute or natural force, that I can resist this with some effect; but I cannot expect, like Orpheus, to change the nature of the rocks and trees and beasts.

40   I do not wish to quarrel with any man or nation. I do not wish to split hairs, to make fine distinctions, or set myself up as better than my neighbors. I seek rather, I may say, even an excuse for conforming to the laws of the land. I am but too ready to conform to them. Indeed, I have reason to suspect myself on this head; and each year, as the tax-gatherer comes round, I find myself disposed to review the acts and position of the general and State governments, and the spirit of the people, to discover a pretext for conformity.

> "We must affect our country as our parents,
> And if at any time we alienate
> Our love or industry from doing it honor,
> We must respect effects and teach the soul
> Matter of conscience and religion,
> And not desire of rule or benefit."

I believe that the State will soon be able to take all my work of this sort out of my hands, and then I shall be no better a patriot than my fellow-countrymen. Seen from a lower point of view, the

Constitution, with all its faults, is very good; the law and the courts are very respectable; even this State and this American government are, in many respects, very admirable, and rare things, to be thankful for, such as a great many have described them; but seen from a point of view a little higher, they are what I have described them; seen from a higher still, and the highest, who shall say what they are, or that they are worth looking at or thinking of at all?

41   However, the government does not concern me much, and I shall bestow the fewest possible thoughts on it. It is not many moments that I live under a government, even in this world. If a man is thought-free, fancy-free, imagination-free, that which *is not* never for a long time appearing *to be* to him, unwise rulers or reformers cannot fatally interrupt him.

42   I know that most men think differently from myself; but those whose lives are by profession devoted to the study of these or kindred subjects content me as little as any. Statesmen and legislators, standing so completely within the institution, never distinctly and nakedly behold it. They speak of moving society, but have no resting-place without it. They may be men of a certain experience and discrimination, and have no doubt invented ingenious and even useful systems, for which we sincerely thank them; but all their wit and usefulness lie within certain not very wide limits. They are wont to forget that the world is not governed by policy and expediency. Webster never goes behind government, and so cannot speak with authority about it. His words are wisdom to those legislators who contemplate no essential reform in the existing government; but for thinkers, and those who legislate for all time, he never once glances at the subject. I know of those whose serene and wise speculations on this theme would soon reveal the limits of his mind's range and hospitality. Yet, compared with the cheap professions of most reformers, and the still cheaper wisdom and eloquence of politicians in general, his are almost the only sensible and valuable words, and we thank Heaven for him. Comparatively, he is always strong, original, and, above all, practical. Still, his quality is not wisdom, but prudence. The lawyer's truth is not Truth, but consistency or a consistent expediency. Truth is always in harmony with herself, and is not concerned chiefly to reveal the justice that may consist with wrongdoing. He well deserves to be called, as he has been called, the Defender of the Constitution. There are really no blows to be

given by him but defensive ones. He is not a leader, but a follower.
His leaders are the men of '87. "I have never made an effort," he
says, "and never propose to make an effort; I have never counte-
nanced an effort, and never mean to countenance an effort, to
disturb the arrangement as originally made, by which the various
States came into the Union." Still thinking of the sanction which
the Constitution gives to slavery, he says, "Because it was a part of
the original compact,—let it stand." Notwithstanding his special
acuteness and ability, he is unable to take a fact out of its merely
political relations, and behold it as it lies absolutely to be disposed
of by the intellect,—what, for instance, it behooves a man to do
here in America to-day with regard to slavery,—but ventures, or
is driven, to make some such desperate answer as the following,
while professing to speak absolutely, and as a private man,—from
which what new and singular code of social duties might be inferred? "The manner," says he, "in which the governments of those
States where slavery exists are to regulate it is for their own consideration, under their responsibility to their constituents, to the
general laws of propriety, humanity, and justice, and to God.
Associations formed elsewhere, springing from a feeling of humanity, or other cause, have nothing whatever to do with it. They
have never received any encouragement from me, and they never
will."

43   They who know of no purer sources of truth, who have
traced up its stream no higher, stand, and wisely stand, by the
Bible and the Constitution, and drink at it there with reverence
and humility; but they who behold where it comes trickling into
this lake or that pool, gird up their loins once more, and continue
their pilgrimage toward its fountainhead.

44   No man with a genius for legislation has appeared in
America. They are rare in the history of the world. There are
orators, politicians, and eloquent men, by the thousand; but the
speaker has not yet opened his mouth to speak who is capable of
settling the much-vexed questions of the day. We love eloquence
for its own sake, and not for any truth which it may utter, or any
heroism it may inspire. Our legislators have not yet learned the
comparative value of free-trade and of freedom, of union, and of
rectitude, to a nation. They have no genius or talent for comparatively humble questions of taxation and finance, commerce
and manufactures and agriculture. If we were left solely to the

wordy wit of legislators in Congress for our guidance, uncorrected by the seasonable experience and the effectual complaints of the people, America would not long retain her rank among the nations. For eighteen hundred years, though perchance I have no right to say it, the New Testament has been written; yet where is the legislator who has wisdom and practical talent enough to avail himself of the light which it sheds on the science of legislation?

45   The authority of government, even such as I am willing to submit to,—for I will cheerfully obey those who know and can do better than I, and in many things even those who neither know nor can do so well,—is still an impure one: to be strictly just, it must have the sanction and consent of the governed. It can have no pure right over my person and property but what I concede to it. The progress from an absolute to a limited monarchy, from a limited monarchy to a democracy, is a progress toward a true respect for the individual. Even the Chinese philosopher was wise enough to regard the individual as the basis of the empire. Is a democracy, such as we know it, the last improvement possible in government? Is it not possible to take a step further towards recognizing and organizing the rights of man? There will never be a really free and enlightened State until the State comes to recognize the individual as a higher and independent power, from which all its own power and authority are derived, and treats him accordingly. I please myself with imagining a State at last which can afford to be just to all men, and to treat the individual with respect as a neighbor; which even would not think it inconsistent with its own repose if a few were to live aloof from it, not meddling with it, nor embraced by it, who fulfilled all the duties of neighbors and fellow-men. A State which bore this kind of fruit, and suffered it to drop off as fast as it ripened, would prepare the way for a still more perfect and glorious State, which also I have imagined, but not yet anywhere seen.

• **SUGGESTIONS** •

This essay demonstrates very well the ways in which confirmations and refutations are embedded in each other. Thoreau's essay obviously has paragraphs and passages devoted to denying the validity of opposing claims, but refutation is not his *primary* intention at any particular place. He ranges widely, meeting and briefly refuting issues arising from many areas; he does this, it seems, rather to confirm than to deny. The duty of civil disobedience is constantly before us. Examine the essay, state what seems to be its primary proposal, and show the accumulating evidence of reason and conviction that supports that position.

Refutation

A refutation is negative in the sense that it is devoted to preventing some action or actions or to denying the worth of some policy. Still, it is positive in the sense that any such prevention or denial is tantamount to a call for new doing or new thinking. And it has a positive function perhaps more direct than this. Offering no proposal and thus no proof, a refutation, by demonstrating failures resulting from action or by demonstrating weakness in policy and practice, is a way of getting to good proposals. Scrutiny of present practices and policies is presumably the *only* means for discovering where need for correction exists. And it is only this discovery of need that prompts the man of good will to go on in his thinking to practicable solutions and to the evaluation of those solutions to determine whether they are beneficial and whether they are superior to other possible solutions.

THE WASTED CLASSROOM*

Nathan Glazer

1   It is understandable that there should be so little fundamental criticism of our colleges and universities. Most original thinking still comes from them, but this is less because they are such good places for it than because there is hardly any place else with even the minor advantages they afford. Few students are unbiased or competent critics. Journalists too often today repro-

* From *Harper's Magazine*, October, 1961. By permission of Nathan Glazer.

duce others' views rather than develop their own—and the views they would reproduce on colleges and universities would be those naturally of the "experts"—presidents and admissions officers and professors. Perhaps most important, most people are too worried about getting their children into college to be concerned much about what goes on once they get there.

2 But there are extremely serious problems in the colleges. And despite the millions of dollars now being spent on research in higher education, we are not doing much to make college education more than a huge boondoggle—which is what most of it is today.

3 From where do I draw my evidence for this view? Aside from my own experience as a student (City College in New York, the University of Pennsylvania, Columbia University), I have been a college teacher: I taught sociology for a year at the University of California in Berkeley, a year at Bennington College in Vermont, a half-year at Smith College—a crude sampling of our better universities and colleges. I have lectured or engaged in research at a half-dozen more colleges and universities, and have friends with whom I have talked about teaching and its problems at almost every important university in the country. Of course I am aware of exceptions, but I am confident that my general conclusion about college holds.

4 And that conclusion, a sober and not extremist one, is that a very large part of what students and teachers do in the best colleges and universities is sheer waste. It is not particularly vicious waste, except insofar as it dulls minds and irritates and frustrates students and teachers. Nor does it prevent useful and necessary things from being done in the colleges. But it is worth speaking about the waste, not only because it is vast, but because, despite the common awareness that this is so, so little is done about it.

5 There are, I found, three main sources of waste in college teaching: the classroom system, the examination system, the departmental system.

6 No doubt certain college subjects do require both classroom teaching and as many classroom hours as are now given to them. But this is not the case with most college subjects. As to what goes on in the sciences, I cannot say—the fact that the radios work, the bridges stand, and the atom bombs explode, that this

complicated technical system works, suggests that teaching in the
sciences and technical subjects is not waste, and I will say nothing
about them (although I suspect a great deal could, and should, be
done to improve the teaching of fundamental scientific concepts
to nonspecialists). But I know how classes in literature, in history,
in political science and psychology and anthropology and sociology
are conducted. In these subjects a single classic mode of organization dominates our schools. Classes meet for three hours a week,
some for more, some for less. These classes are conducted by the
teacher in a lecture-discussion style—that is, informal lecturing (or
in large classes, more formal lecturing), which is often accompanied by some "discussion" initiated by students or teachers. In
fact, during most of the class time, the teacher talks to the
students.

7   There are, however, few college subjects in the humanities
and the social sciences in which forty-five hours of the teacher
lecturing and the students listening can be useful. Perhaps some
individual courses may require groups of fifteen to 125 students
to meet three hours a week for fifteen weeks with a teacher. But
when we realize that most students are expected to take four or
five such courses, and most teachers to give three of them, it is
perfectly clear what actually goes on. Teachers can perhaps (if
they are good) give one or two series of good lectures a year;
students, unless they are brilliant, may have something to contribute to an occasional discussion. As a matter of fact, however,
most teachers give lectures that are not as good as the average
texts in their fields—which are not very good—and most students
have not read enough or heard enough to make the kind of contribution that is worth making in a class of fifty students. But
both accept with amazingly little complaint the strait jacket of
the "course."

8   Now it is true that this strait jacket is broken at certain
times—particularly by seminars in which smaller groups meet only
once a week with teachers. The seminar system is an enormous
step forward: (a) the teacher generally lectures only once a week
(and can consequently lecture better), and (b) the students work
in small groups, on a single subject, and their personal confusion
about some matter—which is normally suppressed or, if raised, is
a waste of time in a large class—can be carefully dealt with in a
small group. More important, the students have a better chance

to discover that true education can only result from their own attempts to organize and clarify a problem, something which is seldom encouraged by lectures to large classes which read textbooks.

9 In other words, the seminar is the obvious and proper model for education in the humanities and social sciences. But it is rare. It is generally reserved for the graduate school and the graduate students (as if only they really have to learn anything); it is available only to seniors in most colleges, and even then is often reserved for honors students (again, as if only they need to learn).

10 But let us come back to the problem of the course meeting for forty-five hours a semester (and never forget—there are four or five of these for each student, two or three, in the best schools, for each teacher, and quite often four or even five). The advantage of talking or lecturing to someone is that he gets something in a form he cannot get from reading a book or listening to the radio or looking at television. If lecturing is to be worthwhile it should be personal, fresh, original. Perhaps at the beginning of European university education, students were willing to listen to the same lecture repeated year after year because books were in manuscript and rare, and one in effect had to record one's own book in the form of notes from the lips of the teacher. Perhaps too in an earlier epoch there was the feeling that knowledge was esoteric and should be communicated orally. Obviously such considerations no longer prevail, although thousands of students still scrawl endless pages of notes, often while sitting in a vacant daze.

11 This is not to say that there are no justifications at all for lecturing. There are teachers who are in effect writing their book as they lecture—if it is an important book (like the books Hegel was writing), then scholars will come to listen, rather than wait for the book itself. On the continent today a course of lectures, I understand, is often this book in process—it is the work that a man is doing, being presented to minds ready to understand and profit from it. And it can be argued that lecturing has its value as stimulation and entertainment—the art of lecturing is one that every academician appreciates, and that many students do too, and it certainly has a place in the university.

12 A teacher can indeed perform useful functions in his lectures: he may argue with what the students have been given

to read; he may supplement it or arrange it for them. But he does not need forty-five hours a semester to do this—the students would be better off reading more books, thinking more, working more, and taking fewer notes. I have heard a lot of lectures in my lifetime as a student, researcher, and teacher, and I would ask college teachers to honestly consider in how many courses a dozen good lectures would not do all that could be done—in the form of *lecturing*—for a class.

13   But the timetable traditionally called for forty-five hours, and now the students expect it, administrations demand it, and even teachers have become convinced there's no harm in it, although many are hard put to fill up the forty-five hours usefully. Hardly anyone thinks of beginning at the beginning, forgetting the system, and deciding when and where this form of course organization is best.

14   In the sciences, with their special laboratory periods, the courses are somewhat better arranged. And recently, one of the worst victims of the standard course arrangement, the teaching of languages, has also been freeing itself from the three-hours-a-week standard. But no such revolution in the arrangement of the course seems imminent in the social sciences and humanities, though the need is just as great.

▶ The Cold Hand of Catechism

15   Fortunately for the system this first skeleton is propped up by a second—the examination system. If there is no other way of making fruitful use of forty-five hours of class time, at least one can use this time to prepare the students for an equally fruitless practice required by the system—the examinations. Once again I remind the reader that I have limited myself to the humanities and social sciences. In technical subjects—sciences, mathematics, languages—subjects which develop specific skills and transmit (for the moment) a fixed body of laws, principles, and procedures, examinations are not only possible but necessary. One can arrange a language (I mean in learning it as a skill to use—not its literature) or a science or mathematical discipline into sections of hierarchal levels of complexity so that one must pass a test in step one before taking step two, and so on.

16   But in the humanities and the social sciences this kind of ordering often is literally not possible. I recall once being asked

by the college administration what were the "prerequisites" for two courses I was going to teach in sociology. Since the students had to take Math I before Math II, it was assumed that Sociology I—whatever that is—must come before Sociology II. But in fact I saw no reason why the students could not take the courses I was giving—one on American ethnic groups, another on cities and their problems—without having taken any other course in sociology. (Of course, it may be useful and illuminating to have studied one aspect of philosophy or history, or literature, or the social sciences, before another; but this is not a prerequisite in the way Math I is a prerequisite.)

17 The nature of examinations in the humanities and the social sciences must be different. For what are the examinations to contain? We do not transmit fixed bodies of law, principle, or skill in which students can be drilled and then examined by a simple and unambiguous test. Plenty of information is transmitted, but, in general, the mastery of pure facts or methods is not the essential skill in question. The aim in these disciplines is understanding, appreciation, discrimination, reasoning: and drill in them is only possible if they are taught badly, in catechistic fashion. When drill occurs in the social sciences and the humanities —as it often does—the teachers and students are likely to feel that they are still in high school, and they are right.

18 I have been told that if you ask a Soviet philosophy student what pragmatism is—or who Dewey or William James was—he can recite to you the definitions and brief one-sentence accounts from a Soviet philosophical dictionary. It is possible to drill the Soviet students in these subjects only because they are not learning them. And once again, we see the cold hand of the medieval university in the notion of examinations in the humanities and social sciences, for there too one could be drilled catechistically in received knowledge. But how silly to ask for the "right" answers to questions about poems or complicated movements in history or literature or complex social problems! However, one teaching skeleton props up the next. Since teachers are required to give courses and grades, they too often run their courses by feeding out neat interpretations which can be properly regurgitated at exam times, and marked "right."

19 Certainly not all courses are conducted like this. In some colleges, the requirements for grades are met by something far more adequate than the usual examinations—the student's own work. He is asked to apply what he learns from reading and discussion to the analysis of a piece of literature or the consideration of a problem, and in answering such an essay question the student may theoretically have an opportunity for a modulated presentation of a subject which catches up some of its complexity.

20   But the matter is not so simple. Many of the elementary courses in college are given in large lecture rooms, supplemented by discussion groups conducted by graduate students. How can the essay questions presented to large classes be graded so that equality and justice can prevail? What often happens is that factual questions are presented in essay form. The graduate students or assistants who administer and mark the tests get together and decide that in answering a particular question a student will have to refer to, say, four or five points, each to be given so much credit. This settled, they begin plowing through the stacks of papers.

21   But how can this bureaucratic system of marking take account of what is essentially important in any essay—understanding, a general grasp of the material, a capacity to see it freshly and originally? For teachers of the sciences, engineering, and languages, these qualities, of course, may not be essential. They want the students to get it right. But what good teacher in the humanities, merely wants it "right"—wants, in effect, a textbooky reproduction of his lecture which will be forgotten in a few weeks? Since the teacher is, in fact, forced to lecture, and forced to give examinations and grades, he will too often settle for this and could not in all justice give it a bad mark—but it is not what he is looking for. If it is, he is a bad teacher.

22   There is an obvious answer to this problem. For the examination, there could be substituted the demanding paper, the job of work, just as for the class there could be substituted the seminar. And yet, just as the seminar is something special and reserved for the graduate student, so too the paper is something special—the student may do one, but he still generally must take a meaningless examination, and somehow it must be graded. Since the system demands grades, no one questions them—and no one asks whether it really was worth it to have spent all that time deciding the marks for a hundred students. (Suppose this time

was spent in going over a student's research paper with him— something that is seldom done.)

23   Observing the examination system in operation, I have become more and more persuaded that it is fundamentally unjust to the student, for it assumes that the student is being graded for his work in the course. There is a certain rough truth to this when technical subjects, scientific skills, languages, and the like, are being studied. In the social sciences and humanities, this is simply not so. The student's grades reflect his general ability to use language, to organize, to think rapidly, at least as much as they show what he has gained from the course. Indeed, after working in schools where the atmosphere is dominated by the rituals of examinations and grades, I have often thought that it would be useful to give the examination the first day of the course and get that stupidity out of the way. This would at least turn the attention of the students to the substance of the course itself. For in fact, as the system now operates in most colleges, those who are gifted in the art of taking exams—who can write fluently, think quickly, regurgitate systematically—will generally do well in any case, and the relation of the amount of time and interest invested in the course to final grades is often accidental.

24   The entire concept of college examinations, in short, needs radical review. Even when students taking courses in the humanities and social sciences are asked challenging essay questions, and marked carefully, their performance must depend not simply on the specific matter that has been presented to them but on the entire world of reading and experience and perception they bring to the subject. In effect, they are being tested not on the specific course but on the sum of their work in the broad area of knowledge in question. Why bother then, with specific course examinations and grades—why not give the student a limited number of general tests toward the end of his college career, with a few over-all grades? If colleges emphasized intensive reading and seminars rather than sterile course exams—this kind of examination would seem natural—if examinations were required at all.

▶ *Shortchanging the Students*

25   Finally, we come to the third evil of college teaching to-day—the departments. If the classroom system needs grades to justify its existence, it also needs the departmental system to fill

up the class time and decide what to ask on the examinations.
Once again, let us divide what is necessary and useful from its
distortion. The departments of knowledge have a long and honorable history. To be a member of a department means that a
man owes his loyalty to his field of knowledge as well as to his
university. Indeed, the department, or rather the discipline (which
is expressed in the form of the department in each college or university), is more important to him generally than the school in
which he happens to teach. He may shift schools but scarcely
ever will he be able to shift departments. His advancement, within
his college or from a job in one college to another, will depend
not on his virtues as a teacher (who is to judge that?) but on his
standing in his discipline, and this standing is measured by (a)
his doctoral degree (granted by a group of people who have such
degrees in the same discipline); (b) his publications (in the
journals of his discipline); and (c) his research grants (given by
persons drawn from his discipline). And of course he has been
trained in that discipline, in a graduate school.

26   What this means is that it is much easier for a man to
think of himself as a psychologist, a historian, a sociologist, a
classicist, a specialist in Elizabethan drama than as someone who
is engaged in liberal education. And he is more concerned in
communicating his discipline to the students than in *educating*
them. Obviously this is a large and general charge and there are
exceptions. But since it is the discipline that has prestige, the professor is oriented generally to what is most characteristic of the
discipline. This means the newest thinking in his specialty, the
most abstract concepts, the things about which scholars do research and publish papers. In psychology, for example, he would
think he was engaged in the worst kind of sellout if he paid
attention to the psychological problems that concern the students
rather than to those that concern psychologists.

27   In effect, the making of scholars in the graduate schools,
while it does produce some good scholars, certainly makes many
poor teachers. But there are more pernicious effects of the system
of departments than the role of the discipline itself. There is first
of all the competition among the departments, for status, for
students, for prestige. This means that there is constant bickering
over how many courses a student must be required to take in this
or in that subject. And the central concern of such arguments,

unfortunately, is not what the student needs for a good education (though certainly such a motivation *does* play a role), but the interests of the department: Can we require fewer courses in our department than others require in their departments? Can we accept the fact that our discipline plays a less essential role in education than others? (The answer is usually no—departments fiercely insist on equal status.) Can we (and this is a most important consideration) accept the fact that if we allow this or that course to be dropped from the list of requirements, we will have to let a man go, or not be able to make a new appointment?

28   These questions are the very stuff of academic life. The question of building and teaching a curriculum relevant to the needs of the college-educated citizen is far less pressing.

29   Departmentalization thus means that liberal education is hurt in another and crucial way—educational programs that cannot be fitted into the departmental scheme are shortchanged. Everyone knows that sociology, anthropology, social psychology, political science, and history today deal in large part with a common subject matter. But joint courses in this general field must usually be conducted by people whose primary loyalty is to their discipline. Indeed, it is almost impossible to find distinguished people who are ready to devote themselves to interdepartmental courses in the social sciences. Professor Lewis Feuer, who conducts such a joint course in the social sciences at the University of California in Berkeley, is able to transcend these silly battles between disciplinary representatives, in part because he is a philosopher; Professor David Riesman, who gives a general course in the social sciences at Harvard, is also able to transcend them in part, because he has been formally trained in none of the competing disciplines. (He is a lawyer who trained himself in them.) But even when one finds such rare individuals to take over the so-called interdisciplinary courses, they are hampered in finding assistants and associates—for all advancement, as I have pointed out, is made through achievement in the disciplines. And if a graduate student or professor should devote himself to acquiring and teaching what everyone agrees is most important for a liberal education—the broad grounding that is common to a number of disciplines—how would he achieve advancement?

30   The predictable result of departmentalization—and I have not even begun to analyze the reasons for the strength of

the departments—has been that the great experiments in liberal education of the 'twenties and 'thirties have been grinding to a close.

31   Let us see what has happened. For many years the University of Chicago gave perhaps the best undergraduate education in the United States. Departments were entirely abolished in the College and all students were required to take broad courses in the Social Sciences (sociology, anthropology, political science, economics, etc.); the Humanities (drama, fiction, poetry, philosophy, etc.); the Natural Sciences (physics, biology, geology, astronomy, etc.); as well as Mathematics. Much of the instruction took place in seminars. It emphasized the intensive reading of original texts (not textbooks), and some of the most distinguished scholars in the University were willing to conduct small classes in the College. The admirable premise here was that the college-educated citizen should be exposed to important ideas and methods in the major fields of knowledge, whatever his ultimate choice of specialty, within the university or without. But now the College is succumbing to the power of research-oriented departments, and it is becoming more traditional in its approach.

32   Similarly, the Contemporary Civilization Course of Columbia College—another famous attempt at interdepartmental education—recently abandoned its second year. And, as Christopher Jencks' article in this magazine makes clear, Harvard's once ambitious General Education courses have failed to challenge the domination of its departments.

33   Indeed, as one looks over the American college scene, it becomes clear that American education has never been more conservative than it is today. Why is this so? It is not because the experiments in changing the undergraduate program have failed. It cannot be said that the students at Antioch, Bennington, and Sarah Lawrence are worse educated than those from traditional schools. Nor have general-education courses at Columbia, Harvard, and Chicago produced inferior students. Quite the contrary. What has happened is that the emphasis on achievement in the traditional departmental disciplines has become nearly irresistible. In recent years it has been reinforced by the enormous research funds which have been made available to the departments by government, industry, and foundations. As a result, the numbers and effectiveness of those men and women who might

be interested in new approaches to undergraduate education have been radically reduced. For a young scholar to devote time, thought, and energy to developing general-education programs may well involve risk to his career. Thus the general-education movement is being crushed, and the plague of departmentalization now grows even in the progressive colleges.

▶ *Straws in the Wind?*

34   No doubt, a good deal more is wrong with higher education. I speak from an intermediate level, higher than the students and lower than the administrators, and this is what I have seen, and I am not alone.

35   Recently, for example, a group of college teachers drawn from four colleges in the Connecticut Valley—Smith, Mt. Holyoke, Amherst, and the University of Massachusetts—spent some time thinking of how to set up a new college that would give an education as good as these colleges are reputed to give, at lower cost. They proposed a New College, one of whose main principles is the elimination of the usual classroom lecturing, in favor of seminars on the one hand and a few lectures on the other. The expectation is that in such a program students could do a better job educating themselves (with the serious help of their teachers) than in one where they were spending the best hours of the day going through the ritual of the classroom. Another major proposal for the New College was that it should not try to have a full roster of departments, with all the evil effects that this must entail in undergraduate education.

36   Perhaps it is another straw in the wind that the University of the Pacific in Stockton, California, has announced a radical reorganization in which students will take only three courses a semester, each course meeting five hours a week. Students' eligibility for graduation will be based on final examinations of proficiency and on the recommendations of tutors. Except for the fact that the new plan—apparently concerned that students and teachers will not put in enough time—assigns *five* hours to each course, it seems a hopeful one. One new experimental college, Monteith, recently founded at Wayne State University in Detroit, is carrying on the general-education approach that is declining at the University of Chicago. One of the most serious efforts to establish a strong general-education curriculum is being made by the new

York University in Toronto. And while it is true that general education is declining in the big universities, some of the small experimental colleges of the past—Antioch, Sarah Lawrence, Bennington
—with their individual and nontraditional approaches, still seem
strong. Their problem, however, is to find young teachers who
do not have a narrow disciplinary approach.

37   Unfortunately, no one has suggested any way of dealing
with this problem, which I believe is the crux of the matter. Educational reform must be the work of the administrators and the
professors who are truly concerned about the minds of undergraduates. A few have indicated what they implicitly think of
most American college education. But the rest . . . alas, the
pleasures of research are real, the disciplinary training is powerful,
and not many of them think that much is wrong with college
education. Nor does the general public seem worried. Higher education does after all train technicians, enough to keep things going;
it does hand out diplomas that qualify people for higher status and
better jobs. But the fact that it is largely a huge waste for our
young people who spent some of their best years there, and for
the thousands of teachers who spend most of their lives there,
does not seem to bother many people. It should.

• COMMENTARY •

What Glazer attacks is clear enough from his title; his procedure is also
clear. The first paragraph introduces the possibility of criticizing our
colleges and universities, and the second suggests the necessity for criticism in its complaint that "we are not doing much to make college
education more than a huge boondoggle—which is what most of it is
today." This done, Glazer offers in the third paragraph his authority
for saying what he has to say and in the fourth paragraph states (more
specifically than he had in paragraph two) the conviction upon which
his attack is based: "And that conclusion, a sober and not extremist
one, is that a very large part of what students and teachers do in the
best colleges and universities is sheer waste."

The short fifth paragraph is his *partitio* (see the section on organization), in which as he identifies the sources of waste he also forecasts the
parts of his essay. Paragraphs six through fourteen are devoted to the
first area of waste, the classroom system; fifteen through twenty-four to

the second, the examination system; and twenty-five to thirty-three to the third, the departmental system.

The last four paragraphs constitute the conclusion of the essay. Here, in paragraphs thirty-four through thirty-six, Glazer departs briefly from the attack to mention some "straws in the wind," some fleeting evidences of change. But this is not his purpose, and the evidence is fleeting; he returns in the last paragraph to the attack.

This essay may very well prompt refutations or full arguments. A writer disagreeing with Glazer's position and seeking to refute him might find it useful to examine his assumptions, such, for example, as the assumption that the seminar "is the obvious and proper model for education in the humanities and social sciences." Or a writer agreeing with Glazer might find it interesting to use his essay as a basis for new proposals and a complete argument.

WHAT HAPPENED TO COMMON SENSE?*

Calvin D. Linton

1   We live in the best-educated age in human history. It also may well be the most gullible. Gullibility is not a matter of *what* one believes, but of *why*. The modern educated man undoubtedly believes more true things than his predecessors. He has more to choose from. After all, our fund of knowledge doubled between 1900 and 1950, we are told; it doubled again between 1950 and 1960; and it is expected to redouble by 1963.

2   But it is just as gullible to believe the right thing for the wrong reason as to be convinced of a falsehood. And to believe nothing at all—as some highly educated people prefer to do—is the final, the ineffable gullibility.

3   It is the testimony of history that man has constantly exerted his efforts to know, to understand, to protect himself from deception. Our modern system of higher education, erected upon an ever-rising mountain of factual knowledge, is a monument to man's use of learning as a shield against credulity.

4   And to a certain extent it works. When a Communist tells us that it was largely due to the activities of the Red Army that

* From *The Saturday Evening Post*, April 28, 1962. By permission of Calvin D. Linton.

Japan was defeated in World War II, we know, through our learning in history, that he lies. When a quack tries to sell us a nostrum guaranteed simultaneously to cure cancer, dandruff and bunions, we know, through our learning in science, that he is trying to deceive us. When a politician tells us that all we need to do is to support a law that bread prices shall not rise above five cents a loaf, and all the hungry will be fed, our knowledge of economics shakes its wise head. When a philosopher tells us that chance is the ultimate cause of all order and meaning, our knowledge of logic rebels.

5   But factual knowledge does not work nearly so well as we like to think. Indeed—and here's the real rub—there is evidence that certain tendencies in modern education are more likely to *increase* than to decrease human gullibility.

6   Dark suspicions of this tendency have been uttered, but not listened to, for some time. In 1924 George Bernard Shaw declared twentieth-century credulity to be more gross than that of any previous period. Two decades later Alfred North Whitehead, kicking himself for having swallowed without question everything he was taught in his college years, including Newtonian physics, noted that "by 1900 Newtonian physics was demolished, done for! . . . I've been fooled once, and I'll be damned if I'll be fooled again." And in our own day, it is the conclusion of Martin Gardner's book, *Fads and Fallacies in the Name of Science,* that the national level of credulity is astonishingly high.

7   Gardner is particularly concerned with the tendency of the modern educated man to accept things on authority rather than on evidence. And I know what he means. In college classes I have seen students—and often professors—smile as they note instances, say, of the gullibility of the Middle Ages. How easily our ancestors believed the unreasonable, simply because the accepted authority of the day said so! How superior we are to them! I once even had a student who expressed the most generous admiration for William Shakespeare because, long before multiple college courses in psychology, he was able to depict characters with such astonishing psychological validity.

8   And yet ten minutes later these same sophisticates will buy a certain brand of cigarettes because it has "been proved to contain less" cancer-producing material—less than what is not stated; possibly a bonfire. Or they will swallow without a hiccup some incredi-

ble assertion about the nature of the atom—incredible and probably quite true. Or they will stand with well-simulated admiration and respect before some art exhibit which looks more like the scene of an accident, with heavy loss of life, than art. Or they will be convinced that the Kinsey report proves something. The catch-words trigger the automatic assent: "latest statistics show" or "science has proved" or "uniquely original vision" or "authorities now believe."

9   What characteristic of modern higher education fosters such credulity? There are several more or less obvious culprits. One is the development in many academic disciplines of an artifi-cially inflated vocabulary which only the initiated—and not all of them—can understand. Another is overspecialization and its consequence, fragmentation—ugly by-products of our explosion of knowledge.

10   But the key reason, to my mind, the one underlying all the rest, is the abdication of what used to be called "common sense" as the judge of what is or is not to be believed and trusted.

11   Common sense! That ultimate sovereign so praised by the Age of Reason, so ardently looked to in an earlier age as the unassailable arbiter, believed to be so inevitably right once arti-ficial pressures of prejudice and emotion are removed, so hopeful because it is "common" (universally distributed), so comforting in the very sound of the word "sense"—this sovereign has fled murmur-ing, and with it many rays of light. Psychologists have kicked it out, declaring—in Huck Finn's phrase—that "it's not a circum-stance" compared to the subconscious, where the real work goes on. Logicians have pointed out that common sense must be self-authenticating—it must, so to speak, take itself on faith. And that spoils all the fun at the outset. But most of all, worst of all, most ultimately annihilating of all, is the forced abandonment of com-mon sense by that pinnacle of our contemporary pride, science.

12   This is a controversial statement, so I run for cover to one qualified to speak. Huston Smith of the Massachusetts Institute of Technology said [ADVENTURES OF THE MIND: THE REVOLUTION IN WESTERN THOUGHT, *The Saturday Evening Post,* August 29, 1961]: "The problems the new physics poses for man's sense of order cannot be resolved by refinements in scale. Instead they appear to point to a radical disjunction between the way things behave and every possible way in which we might try to visualize them. How,

for example, are we to picture an electron traveling two or more different routes through space concurrently or passing from orbit to orbit without traversing the space between them at all? . . . It is such enigmas which are causing physicists like P. W. Bridgman of Harvard to suggest that 'the structure of nature may eventually be such that our processes of thought do not correspond to it sufficiently to permit us to think about it at all. . . . We have reached the limit of the vision of the great pioneers of science, the vision, namely, that we live in a sympathetic world in that it is comprehensible by our minds.' "

13   These are appalling words. Their implications are so vast that we cannot, at the moment of reading them, begin to grasp their significance.

14   But to some extent we all acknowledge their truth. Who among us would think for a moment of refuting some new discovery of science by arguing that it simply "does not make sense"? The day when we could, with Dr. Samuel Johnson, refute Berkeley's subjective idealism by kicking a stone is long past. Kick if we wish, but our sole reward is a sore toe.

15   For example, we have read recently of the discovery of yet another subatomic particle, the omega. And we read that some physicists believe that *protons* may contain as many subatomic particles as the ninety-odd chemical elements which, it was thought, compose all matter. The omega itself may turn out to have complicated structures of its own, and two of the discoverers of the omega, Dr. Luis W. Alvarez and Dr. M. L. Stevenson, declare that there may *never* be an end of this incredible process of peeling one layer from another.

16   Who among us would deny this on the grounds that it violates plain common sense? Or who would dare contradict the scientist who tells us that if all the space in each atom of the human body were squeezed out, the remaining matter would be invisibly small but would still register 170 pounds—or whatever—on the scales? Presumably the omega is true, the neutrino is true, the relative amount of space in the atom is true—but the layman can know neither the truth nor the possible falsity for himself. He must take such things—as people of the Middle Ages are alleged to have done—on the word of the acknowledged authority. Thus is the soil of gullibility plowed and ready for a rich seeding, either by truth or by falsehood.

17   Blind faith in authority in the realm of the arts is even easier to illustrate. Here is a single sentence from a piece of authoritative art criticism which appeared in *Art News* and was quoted in *The New Yorker:* "He (the artist) pictures the stultified intricacy of tension at the plasmic level; his prototypical zygotes and somnolent somatomes inhabit a primordial lagoon where impulse is an omnidirectional drift and isolation is the consequence of an inexplicable exogamy." For all its own desperate problems, ignorance permits a healthy disbelief in such semantic idiocy; excessive sophistication, on the other hand, compels acceptance—on faith. The author, after all, must be an authority or he could not write that way.

18   Indeed, it must be admitted that the pseudolearned mind is capable of a degree of confusion quite beyond the capacity of the unlettered. In such an atmosphere, fraud is easy to perpetrate. Several years ago two Australian soldiers with time on their hands decided to create a masterpiece of poetry. Taking words from a science textbook, an advertisement for sleeping pills, a tract on mosquito control and other sources, they strung them together and submitted the result to a poetry magazine. It was printed and hailed as "a work of genius," subtle in its balance of intension and extension, skillful in its maintenance of "aesthetic distance" and—somewhat understandably—magnificently broad in its vocabulary.

19   In early October, 1960, composer John Cage, assisted by pianist David Tudor, put on a concert at Venice's International Festival of Contemporary Music. The performance consisted chiefly of plucking a single string of the piano at twenty-second intervals and, later, of thumping the piano stool with a rock and attacking the insides of the piano itself with knives and pieces of tin. The result was solemnly written up by the critics.

20   Such bizarre performances cannot be compared to the magnificent hoax of the Piltdown man or the invention of those wholly mythical families, the Jukes and the Kallikaks, beloved of sociologists; but they are not inconsiderable efforts, and educated gullibility leaped to the bait.

21   And now, even at the risk of complicating my thesis, I must revert to an earlier statement: It is as gullible to believe too little as too much. Indeed, it is a rather common reaction against successive deceits for the victim to retreat into himself, like the Steig drawing of a man sitting in a box and saying, "I hate people."

Or perhaps it is the pose of the learned cynic whose elevated tastes permit him to like nothing at all. Such people are the professional nay-sayers.

22   Probably the most vivid recent advocacy of the universal "no" as a philosophy of life has come from the gifted pen of Leslie Fiedler in his book *No! In Thunder.* He has little praise for the "soft no." It is too easy to utter. One is simply against segregation or McCarthyism or the current best seller. The only worthy negative is the "hard no," the universal negative which infuriates Our Side as well as Theirs; which, indeed, reveals that all Sides are one. Insofar as anyone is a yea-sayer, he is a liar. This is mighty close to the philosophy of anarchy, of revolution for the sake of revolution, not for the sake of rebuilding.

23   In educational philosophy this mood is, in part, the product of supreme emphasis upon the material, the physical fact, at the expense of value. But we cannot "believe" in matter, we cannot say "yes" to it. An education focused chiefly on facts cannot reduce gullibility. Einstein declared that it produces the student "who is a kind of useful machine, a well-trained dog," whereas it is essential that "he acquire instead a vivid sense of the beautiful and the morally good." Only a communication of intellectual power can reduce gullibility, and this is not accomplished by saying no, in thunder, to everything.

24   So much for the lament. What's to do?

25   We might be able to rehabilitate common sense a bit, but we obviously cannot try to reenthrone it. In an era of geometrically expanding knowledge the most brilliant mind simply cannot, in a normal life span, join Francis Bacon in taking all knowledge for its province. Must we then reconcile ourselves to believing whatever we are told, to trusting the authority without question? If not, by what criterion can we avoid such a condition of complete credulity?

26   I can offer only a hint, a very ancient and a very modern one, and it is this: When our common sense staggers and when our reason sends us a note of regret, we must ultimately trust what we truly love. This may constitute a retreat from the outer walls to the inner fortress, but at least it is not a rout.

27   Before dismissing this as a sentimental platitude, consider, first, that so far as we are human we must trust our deepest human capacity, the most universally distributed, the one without which

man becomes less than man. If we do not, we commit a kind of hideous suicide without the honesty of a corpse. That capacity, that wellspring of humanness, is man's power to love—whether it be beauty, truth, his fellow creatures or God. Man is not mere matter. His search for that which satisfies the innermost yearning for order and meaning and purpose and beauty is motivated by his capacity for love. And any educational theory which does not deal with this factor is not reaching the deeps.

28   Consider, second, that trust based on love is the most broadly based of all trusts, the kind supported at the greatest number of points. Man's exercise of his capacity to love embraces his intellect, his emotions, his spirit, his body, all wielded by the mysterious power of the conscious will.

29   And consider, lastly, that only the trust based on love is immune to disaster. It carries its own antidote to deception. Not that we shall never trust that which proves unworthy, but that if our trust has been born of our deepest response to goodness, the deception is a disaster only to that which has failed us, not to us.

30   The man who trusts only in the material can find nothing but anguish when matter corrupts. The man who trusts his hates, as does the Communist, will eat death. But the man who trusts that which he loves, in the words of the poet, "and tho' he trip and fall, he shall not blind his soul with clay."

31   We must not become so highly educated that we forget such things.

• SUGGESTIONS •

Not all of this essay is meant as attack or refutation, but the two-sentence paragraph (number twenty-four) shows clearly that it is primarily opposition to accepted views. In his introductory paragraphs Linton speaks of our gullibility and insists that "there is evidence that certain tendencies in modern education are more likely to *increase* than to decrease human gullibility." With this as a beginning, he spends the bulk of his essay (paragraphs six through twenty-three) exploring and castigating our gullibility. Examine the essay to determine what he states is the major reason for this gullibility. Then show what kinds of evidence he uses in his attack.

TIME TO GET NEW SCHOOLBOOKS*

Jenkin Lloyd Jones

1   If we can ever cure the asininities of the "look-say" method of teaching reading, which has condemned many hundreds of thousands of young Americans to word-guessing, it will be time to start in on the content of grade-school textbooks.

2   These beautifully printed and illustrated books include texts so remarkable for their dullness that it is little wonder young America can hardly wait to get back to the TV. Most of them have been steam cleaned of every vestige of excitement, of inspiration and romance.

3   There is no reference to God or religion. This is regarded as controversial. There is no story of war. If we don't think about it, maybe it will go away. There is nothing that would give rise to patriotism. How old-fashioned!

4   I have before me a fifth-grade reader, "Days and Deeds," published last year by Scott, Foresman & Company and standard in many hundreds of American school systems.

5   With a puerile vocabulary, it discusses such things as Uncle Lem's new outboard motor, John's lawn-mowing business, and how Wally, the bloodhound, helped Jerry, the police dog, find his missing bone.

6   I have also before me a reprint of McGuffey's Fifth Eclectic Reader, published in 1879. Let's skip through the list of contents: "The Relief of Lucknow," London "Times"; "Battle of Blenheim" by Southey; "Sands of Dee" by Charles Kingsley; "An Old-Fashioned Girl" by Louisa May Alcott; an account of a riot in the Massachusetts State Prison; supposed speech of John Adams by Daniel Webster; excerpts from "The Virginian" by Thackeray and from Hamlet; "Dissertation on Roast Pig" by Charles Lamb; "A Frigate Chase in the English Channel" by James Fenimore Cooper; "The Boston Massacre" by Bancroft; "No Excellence Without Labor" by William Wirt; "Religion, the Only Basis of Society" by William Channing.

* From *The Changing World: An Editor's Outlook* by Jenkin Lloyd Jones. Copyright, 1964, by Fleet Publishing Corp. By permission of the publisher.

7   Blood and thunder? Plenty of it. Heroism? Of course. Moral homilies? In profusion. Religious preachments? Unashamed. Patriotism? With pride. And, in addition, tough words and involved sentences that would flabbergast the fifth-grader who has been brought up on the thin consommé of today's "Days and Deeds" series.

8   On June 20, 1961, Dr. Max Rafferty, school superintendent of La Canada, Calif., made a speech that caused a sensation and resulted in his election last fall as California superintendent of public instruction over the dead bodies of the progressive educators. He asked: "What happened to patriotism?" and I quote:

9   "We have been so busy educating for 'life adjustment' that we forgot to educate for survival. Words that America had treasured as a rich legacy, that had sounded like trumpet calls above the clash of arms and the fury of debate, we allowed to fade from the classrooms.

10   " 'Liberty and Union, now and forever, one and inseparable.'

11   " 'We have met the enemy and they are ours.'

12   " 'Millions for defense, but not one cent for tribute.' "

13   Search for these towering phrases in vain today in too many of our schools. The golden words are gone. Patriotism feeds on hero worship and we decided to abolish heroes.

14   The quest for the Golden Fleece has been crowded out by the visit of Tom and Susan to the zoo. The deeds of the heroes before Troy are now passé, and the peregrinations of the local milkman as he wends his way among the stodgy streets of Blah City have taken over. Bobby and Betty pursue this insipid goal of a ride in the district garbage truck while the deathless ride of Paul Revere goes unsung.

15   For Roland at Roncesvalles we have substituted Muk-Muk the Eskimo boy. It is, I think, significant that education during the past three decades has deliberately debunked the hero to make room for the jerk!

16   No wonder these heroless American kids often broke down before the Red brainwashers in the Korean prison camps. They had no points of reference. They had no understanding of the traditions of liberty. In many cases, the Communists were delighted that there was so little to erase. It was a cinch to unteach those who had never been taught.

17   In commenting on a modern sixth reader, "Bright Peaks," put out by Houghton Mifflin, Dr. Russell Kirk says: "With the exception of a poem by Sara Teasdale, another short poem by Robert Frost, and an autobiographical piece by John Muir, every selection is by a fourth or fifth-grade writer."

18   Why? Could it be that the fifth and sixth-graders can't read the classics as they did in the days of McGuffey? Could it be that the bankruptcy of the "look-say" method and the stubborn refusal of many school administrations to admit the error have required them to pretend that there is special virtue in extending kindergarten-style reading to the upper grades?

19   It's time America got a new set of textbooks. It's time we quit boring bright students to death with the banalities of John and Jane visiting the henhouse. It's time we put romance and courage and excitement and some frank moral indoctrination before our children in their most impressionable years.

20   We don't have to go back to McGuffey.

21   There's plenty of good writing. But let's give our children some literary taste, some ethical calories and patriotic vitamins.

22   To hell with these sawdust sandwiches!

• **SUGGESTIONS** •

While this is in effect a proposal that we must have new textbooks, it is made effective by its attack on present textbooks. Explain the reason for the typically short paragraphs.

A Sequence of Arguments

The three essays that follow are presented not necessarily because they present any new methods of argument, but because they all are addressed to the same controversial issue and should, therefore, enable you to follow more thoroughly the workings of argumentative discourse. It is an issue, incidentally, that may be of some immediate concern to your instructor, for all of these essays have a common interest in the relationship between teaching and publishing among English teachers. The first and the third share some views, though they do not coincide in all; both are opposed by the second, which argues that the professor is obligated first and last to the student and the lecture, publication being essentially an intrusion and a distraction.

PUBLISHING AND PROFESSIONALISM IN
ENGLISH DEPARTMENTS*

William Van O'Connor

1   Some of you will have read a strange piece by Jacques Barzun "The Cults of 'Research' and 'Creativity'" in a recent *Harper's*. Generally the article is an attack on "research." At one point in his article, Barzun asks, "Why does research bring so much prestige?" Let us assume with him that it does carry some prestige. (It also, as in this case, encourages ridicule from some quarters.) He says of the researcher: "Even if his subject is pure humanistic scholarship, he is 'in research' and can find admirers. Though only the little money of university advancement will reward his labors, this, coupled with the satisfaction or prestige, suffices to keep the system going and to multiply the products of research." In other words, Mr. Barzun asks why scholars pursue research, and he answers, because they love money (even in small amounts) and prestige. I prefer the more traditional and less cynical answers. Why does a scholar pursue learning? The traditional answer is that learning engages him at some deep level of his being, and, as we used to say, he wishes to contribute to the sum total of human knowledge. The poet or fiction writer—Mr. Barzun's creative types—also want to add to our understanding and to amuse or entertain us. If scholars and writers earn prestige, they deserve it. Presumably there are still many scholars or writers who would be uneasy or ashamed of prestige which they felt was factitious or unearned.

2   I want to make a plea for research, for the productive scholar, and for the writer. I am aware that we are confronted by

* From *College English*, October, 1961. Reprinted with permission of the National Council of Teachers of English and Professor William Van O'Connor.

students in greater and greater numbers and that they have to be taught. I don't think this can be made part of an equation that says Huge Numbers of Students Means Research Has to Stop.

3   We hear about deans who are indifferent to quality, and who measure publications by the yard or weigh them by the pound. There are fools in all professions. No administrator with any sense is going to ask a teacher to produce a quarter of a mile of copy or three and a half pounds of scholarship in a given period of time. All of us, I suspect, could point to scholars who over a lifetime wrote relatively little but who wrote well, and enlarged their fields. In history, a notable figure of this kind was Frederick Jackson Turner. In English literature, I think of Frederick Prescott who wrote a brilliant little book on psychology and poetry. And there is a posthumous volume entitled *The Meaning of Shakespeare* by Harold C. Goddard that is filled with sharp insights. So far as I know Goddard published very little.

4   Those among us who tell anecdotes about foolish requirements or who in one way or another rationalize nonproductivity are dodging the real issue—the inherent importance of scholarly writing. An experience that can happen to a middle-aged scholar like myself is to have a young wife say, "My husband hasn't published anything yet. The reason he hasn't is that he's devoted to his teaching and students." If I were ruthlessly honest—I'm not— I would say to the young wife, "My dear, if your husband is as unproductive as you say, he is (1) suffering from a writing block, (2) lazy, or (3) incompetent."

5   Sometimes, alas, the defense of he-doesn't-publish-but-he-is-devoted-to-his-teaching type comes in faculty meetings. The occasions are discussions of salary increases, tenure, or possible promotion. Usually the defense goes like this: It's true, John Jones doesn't do any research and never publishes, *but* he is a fine teacher. The conjunction *but* is usually intended to mean *therefore*—he doesn't do any research and never publishes, *therefore* he is a fine teacher.

6   This assumption that the nonproductive scholar is a better teacher, because somehow a more wholesome type in the classroom, is an old chestnut. It reminds me of the similar chestnut: "All fat men are happy." The truth probably is that relatively few fat men are happy, and the chestnut about nonproductive scholars being fine teachers is probably equally untrue. That there are

occasional good teachers who are unproductive should of course
be admitted. It should also be said that many of these are both lazy
and irresponsible.

7   In using the term productive scholar I have in mind three
kinds of writers, (1) the poet, dramatist or fiction writer, (2) the
critic, and (3) the research scholar. The critic and the scholar are
not always separable, and sometimes the creative writer takes a
turn at writing criticism—but for our present purposes we can
consider each to be separate. They are the three productive types
currently found in English departments. Each of them looks at
literature through truly professional eyes. They are initiates, or,
in Stephen Crane's term, they are *interpreters*. You will remember the ending of "The Open Boat":

> It seemed that instantly the beach was populated with men with
> blankets, clothes, and flasks, and women with coffeepots and all the
> remedies sacred to their minds. The welcome of the land to the men
> from the sea was warm and generous; but a still and dripping shape
> was carried slowly up the beach, and the land's welcome for it
> could only be the different and sinister hospitality of the grave.
>
> When it came night, the white waves paced to and fro in the
> moonlight, and the wind brought the sound of the great sea's voice
> to the men on the shore, and they felt that they could then be
> interpreters.

8   What, in general, has been the scholar's contribution? As
we all know, he filled us in on the historical background, Chaucer's
England, Shakespeare's England, Franklin's America, and Mark
Twain's Hannibal. Race-moment-milieu, Hippolyte Taine called
it. A few scholars studied literary conventions, or the nature of
the physical theatre, or, more recently, the audience. The scholars
have also edited texts, for example, Langland's A, B, or C versions,
or, more recently, Emily Dickinson's. The scholars were, by and
large, pretty good at digging up facts, but having dug out significant facts about major and minor figures, and having written up
the milieu of so-and-so or so-and-so, they began to scratch around,
looking for insignificant facts.

9   About this time, just prior to World War II, the New
Critics began lobbing some unpleasant smelling bombs inside the
scholarly compounds. I remember that Allen Tate, bless him,
chose Princeton to say this: "Scholars call English literature a

corpus because they are preparing it for burial." There was enough truth in the quip to make it sting. So an English department bought up Mr. Tate's option and made him a professor. If such things were going to be said they had best be said privately. Or, as we also say, "If you can't beat 'em, join 'em." The scholars, after the War, began to let the critic share the texts, and the jobs. (We have young critics now who are just as pedantic as any of their scholarly elders.) After a while the two groups began to get along, and even raided each other's territory. The critic found it might be useful to know something about books of rhetoric studied by seventeenth-century poets, and scholars found it useful (not to say exhilarating) to know or ask not merely what was Melville's source for *Billy Budd* but what was going on *in* the story itself. In other words, the shotgun marriage proved a satisfactory and possibly a happy union.

10   But life moves. Tempus flees. And there is a new group emerging on the scholarly-critical scene. They are the young writers, poets, dramatists, fiction writers. They can't make a living as writers. They can as teachers. Some are shrewd enough to take Ph.D.'s, to get the union card. Then they can write their novels or poems and tell their disapproving colleague who is a specialist in seventeenth-century church records to take a long running jump into the next churchyard. The older generations of scholars and the critics will be well advised not to fight this group. After all, it would be foolish to insist that the only valuable, good writers, like Indians, are the dead ones. Henry James taught a lot of English professors, scholars and critics alike, how to look at fiction, just as Coleridge had taught them how to examine a poem or a play. Why should we assume the young writer in 1960 has no place in an English department? Most likely he'll have a great many valuable things to say, not merely to his students but to his colleagues.

11   These groups—the scholars, the critics, and the imaginative writers—should not quarrel with each other. No single one of them knows, or is likely to know, everything about literature that he could with profit, know. And they may forget they have one important thing in common, *professionalism.*

12   Ernest Hemingway in *A Farewell to Arms* says that if you go to a good doctor and he decides you need an operation he will recommend a good surgeon. If you are unfortunate and go to a

messy doctor he will recommend a messy doctor to operate on you. It is a simple matter: a good professional, whether he is a doctor or a scholar, recognizes professional competence—and incompetence—when he sees it.

13   The English scholar's field, or supposed field, of competence is literature. If he never uncovers a new fact (of the sort that is publishable) or never perceives a theme in a poet or work of fiction hitherto undetected he can, at best, have only a hand-me-down set of responses to a work of literature. What would we think of a professor of physics who never made even a slight contribution to physics, or a professor of chemistry who made no contribution whatsoever to chemistry? What would we say to the wife of a professor of surgery who would say, "My husband has never written anything. The reason is he's devoted to his students." Pray God that the professor of surgery is in animal husbandry. But pity the poor cows!

14   Not very many years ago, instructors and professors in liberal arts were guffawing about the claims of Schools of Education that teachers teach children, not a subject matter. Yet here we are, deep in the P.S. (Post-Sputnik) era, tolerating this chatter about being so devoted to students that our subject will have to fend for itself. Encouraging the nonproductive staff member on the college level seems to me both unprofessional and dangerously irresponsible.

15   The study and teaching of literature enables a scholar and teacher to descend deeply into the wells of human experience—to live through his nights in Crane's open boat. He must understand the historical context of a work of literature, the literary conventions at work, and the quality of a writer's mind. He must be a disinterested, free, trained and mature intelligence. He must come at matters assured of his own professional competence or as assured as one can be in an uncertain world. He should take his job at least as seriously as the chemist who is trying to isolate certain antibodies. If he takes it any less seriously, he will soon find that there are plenty of "specialists" ready and eager not merely to single him out but to do-him-in because of his unprofessionalism.

16   Let me not seem to imply that all has been radiantly healthy in English departments for the past twenty-five or thirty years. All of us know the antediluvian types, the Andrew Dinosaurs and the Perry Pleistocenes of scholarship. They regret the

appearance of the twentieth century and bemoan everything that
happens in it. It is this type that has allowed—made inevitable—
the proliferation of humanities and general studies programs, of
the bologna sausage variety. Some of these programs are all right.
My point is that if English departments had done their job there
wouldn't have been a need for these programs. Committed to a
single discipline, a single type of scholarship, the antediluvian
types refused to admit the need for any development of the discipline. In short, these are the ones who fought criticism and who
currently throw up their hands when it is suggested that good
poets and good fiction writers are likely to know a great deal about
literature.

17   But let us not be side-tracked. These antediluvian types
have a discipline and have been devoted to it. This new type—
the man-who-loves-his-student-so-much-he-can't-find-time-to-think-
or-work-on-a-professional-level—is the current danger. In an increasingly and militantly professional world he is asking that the
English teacher and scholar retire from the fray.

18   And the intellectual life is a fray, a contest between a
changing world and intelligence. We can't go back to Gertrude
Stein's youth when *A fact was a fact, was a fact, was a fact.* A fact
never was a fact. It was a thing seen in its own *thingness,* but what
was seen also depended upon the atmosphere and the perspective
and the eyes of the viewer. That is the way it always has been, the
thing seen and the ways in which it is seen. A work of literature
is seen by the scholar, the linguist, the critic, steeped, say, in a
study of literary myths, and the novelist who from experience
knows how, say, to create Gothic effects. They know, as profes-
sionals, various significant things about a work of literature.

19   Having appeared in print, they presumably have also
been judged by their peers. Our colleagues, being what they are,
single out incompetence quickly, and single out competence too.
If the latter is not always lauded, it is at least silently accepted. All
of us, I believe, should appear in print if only so that our colleagues
may have an opportunity to judge our competence.

20   Some of you will say there are not enough magazines or
publishers to print all the junk that such a requirement would
call for. Admittedly, there would be a great deal of junk, and
more magazines. There is plenty of junk now, and there would be
more, much more. But the good work gets singled out, and the bad

is labelled for what it is. This knowledge is carried into the class-room.

21   We have a simple choice in these years of the Great Flood. Either we shall continue to be professional in the older and newer senses of *professional*, or we shall choose to be unprofessional, that is to say, amateurs, and that is to say, frequently incompetent. None of us can honestly say that we believe that the young men being granted Ph.D.'s in physics or chemistry or psychology or sociology are actively encouraged to be unproductive. They are, as we know, being encouraged to be productive, to do good work, excellent work, first-rate work, in research and in the classroom; for we all know in our heart of hearts that the latter, the classroom, depends on the former, the research. That it is otherwise is not even an arguable point.

PUBLISH AND PERISH *

Lester Hurt

1   The other day I happened to hear a senior professor of our faculty not too politely admonishing a younger member of the English department for his failure to publish. As a scholar himself, as a professor who exercises considerable power in the college hierarchy, and as a man who is concerned about the standards and reputation of the institution, the senior professor was perhaps within his rights to call his younger colleague to task. Indeed, as I listened, my own withers were not entirely unwrung; I ruefully had to confess to myself that I, too, had spent too much time with beer and Beethoven, too many hours with tennis and Toynbee, too many evenings with students and Schopenhauer, while neglecting to write up and send on the rounds my observations about water symbolism in the novels of William Faulkner—a subject well known to the students in my course in the modern novel but not yet decently embalmed in the pages of the scholarly journals, to the public credit of my chairman, the university which granted my doctorate, and the college which pays my salary.

* From *College English*, October, 1961. Reprinted with permission of the National Council of Teachers of English and Professor Lester Hurt.

2   But then as I defensively began to rationalize my short-comings in public scholarship I was suddenly seized by the idea that rather than excuse my conduct and that of my young colleague, I ought to proclaim it. By our graduate advisors, by our deans, and by our chairmen we have been made aware of our sacred duty to do research and to publish the results thereof. I think that we now ought to raise the question of our *duty not to publish*.

3   I am not talking about the fact, recognized by all but administration officials, that there simply are not enough professional publications to receive the outpouring erudition of all the faculty members of all the colleges whose administrations pant for the printed word. Assume, if you will, the happy land in which the scholarly journals proliferate and grow thick, where there is a place for every man's article, and where every article is but the prologue to promotion and fame. Then beware, my colleagues, beware! Such a land is a glittering academic Vanity Fair and there especially must Good Teacher gird up his loins and resolutely proclaim his *duty* not to publish.

4   Neither am I talking about those professors whose teaching duties consist of six to nine hours of graduate seminars. As specialists and graduate professors their duty to research and publication is clear and present.

5   I am talking about the majority of us who teach preponderantly undergraduate courses, who carry a load of twelve to fifteen hours, and who are, as often as not involved in one or more extracurricular activities on campus. It would be nice of course if we could get that article into print. But unless we are among those who believe that our profession would be perfect were it not for the students, perhaps we ought to ask seriously where our first duty lies. To my mind, our first clear duty is to the students whom we meet in classes three times a week and, one hopes, as individuals, not only across the conference desk but socially and informally as often as possible.

6   The best education still consists of Mark Hopkins on one end of the log and the student on the other; and the student deserves a full-face view of Mark—which he cannot have if Mark's left eye is on his file of index cards and his inner eye, here eschewing the bliss of solitude, is firmly fixed on the prestige of publication. For the log—both ends of it—floats precariously in time, and

no man, however stout of heart or, with adequate black coffee,
unwinking of eye, can do everything. Verily, no man can serve
two masters, for he will be tempted to serve the one who ushers
him on the way to promotion and pay and to neglect the other
who causes him to swear between his teeth and to write caustically
in margins.

7   Now if the undergraduate professor's first duty is to his
students, as I take it to be, we ought to inquire closely into the
nature of that duty. I believe that the teacher's first duty to his
students is to be a learned man, to be himself educated. And this
is the crux of the whole matter. It is especially important that the
teacher of literature be a learned man. If he is to teach his material at all he must, by the nature of the beast, have a wider education than, say, his friend the professor of physics. And by the
harsh limitations of time there is a conflict between writing and
publication on the one hand and a continuing education on the
other.

8   Let us look first at the teaching. The English teacher, if
he is to be successful in his teaching, simply has to know a great
deal more about a great many more things than he ever learned
in graduate school. In the first place, most teachers of undergraduates teach more than the narrow area of their Ph.D. specialty. And let us not kid ourselves about the level of our graduate
school training; if we are really to become competent in periods
and areas other than our specialty we must do so after the degree
has been completed. One reason so many undergraduates heartily
detest literature is that the survey courses are often so wretchedly
taught, and they are often so taught because the teacher simply
does not know enough about English, or American, literature—
outside his own special field. I know of one Ph.D. in English who,
in a survey course, glossed John Donne's "stiff twin compasses" as
instruments useful for finding directions in the woods and at sea!
Too many of us are equally at sea outside our special areas. The
world of literature is broad beyond all measure, and while we
certainly need the specialist for scholarship in depth we also very
badly need the general scholar, who, while he may never write,
can offer his students and his college community the considerable
benefits of a wide, comprehensive knowledge. The professor who
boasts that he never reads anything later than the fifteenth century may be valuable in the advanced seminars of the graduate

division of a large university, but he is a pious fraud in the classrooms of the average undergraduate college—even if he has
written twenty articles and a book on the great vowel movement!
Let us quietly and humbly spend our time filling in the blank
spots in our education in English and American literature, after
which, if we will, we may give ourselves up to that last infirmity
of noble minds.

9   But it is not enough that the teacher of English be thoroughly educated in literature; he ought to be generally learned.
Most of us are too ignorant; we do not know enough history to
teach *Caleb Williams* or *War and Peace;* we do not know enough
psychology to teach *Sons and Lovers;* we do not know enough philosophy to teach *The Magic Mountain.* I am constantly appalled
at the ignorance of myself and my colleagues in areas in which we
ought to have considerable knowledge if we are clearly and accurately to elucidate the works of literature which we offer our
students. I sometimes teach a course in the nineteenth-century
English novel, and the plain truth is that I do not presently know
enough about economic conditions and the trade union movement
in nineteenth-century England to do the kind of job that I ought to
do with, say Dickens' *Hard Times* or Kingsley's *Alton Locke.* I
claim pardon only in view of my good intentions: I now have four
or five books dealing with the period on my desk. And while they
will extend my education and make me a better teacher of literature, the time I spend in reading them will not be spent in writing
a paper on the water symbolism in William Faulkner's novels. No
solid object—not even an English professor's mind—can be in two
separate and distinct places at the same time.

10   The next time I teach a course in the modern novel I
should like to include Thomas Mann's *The Magic Mountain,* to
which I have already referred. To teach this novel will require
either that I spend at least a couple of weeks, probably more,
digging into the source and nature of the philosophical ideas there
dramatized or that I requisition the business office for an extra
coating of brass. And most of us have enough brass already; what
we need is more education. So I shall dig into the necessary volumes, in such time as I can rescue from conferences and term
papers, and let the symbolic water stand stagnant a little longer.

11   And there's a course I do occasionally in the American
novel of the twenties and thirties. Well, I've read some history

(and had some personal experience) in the period, and I've taken a couple of courses in political and economic theory, but I'd be a damned fraud to pretend to any real competence beyond the novels, *per se*—if there is any such thing as any kind of literature *per se*. It wouldn't be hard to find a half dozen or so books which would really help me in my exegesis of Dos Passos' novels. But by now tadpoles are wiggling in the water.

12   Like any other literate man, I have had hopes of extending my education beyond the limits of my native tongue. Unfortunately, like too many of us, my language study in college, while all very well for passing the qualifying examinations for the degree, was of little value in the actual use of French and German. Skipping for the moment the obvious duty of any educated man to be really competent in a couple of languages, it is enough to say that there are many modern novels in French and German that, by decent professional standards, I ought to read; and a few hours of study a week for a year would bring my German and French up to snuff. But the time spent in developing my linguistic ability cannot be devoted to writing that article on Faulkner's water symbolism.

13   But the teaching is not all of it and the teacher's business is not ended when he leaves the classroom or finishes reading the last theme of the week. By the nature of the material in which he traffics, dealing dramatically, as it does, with the very heart of human experience, from Lear and Oedipus to Archy the Cockroach, the teacher of literature is more likely than his colleagues to be drawn into a close and extra-academic relationship with his students. The calls which they will make upon his learning and his understanding will not be satisfied by his vertical scholarship in the variant verb forms in *Troilus and Cressida*. And their demands upon his time cannot really be met by the excuse of an article to prepare—not if the teacher cares more about people than about publication and promotion.

14   This is not an appeal to Come Back, Mr. Chips, but who can deny that the English teacher has a stronger responsibility for the whole cultural development of his students than do any of his colleagues? The professor of economics may be totally ignorant of painting and few eyebrows will be raised. But what English teacher would not be embarrassed for a colleague who could not distinguish between, say, Braque and Picasso, or who did not

understand the relationship between the Ash Can school of painters and the literary Naturalists—to use an easy example? Because
I unfortunately grew up musically illiterate, I am often embarrassed when my students want to talk music with me. I feel as
bound to the formation and correction of their taste in music as
in literature. I am not now as competent in this field as I ought to
be. But I am trying. An hour's listening a day, with the necessary
study, is helping to remedy my shortcomings, not to mention giving me considerable pleasure. But how can I listen to Mozart
while writing that article?

15   I ought to know more history than I do. I ought to know
more about economics. It wouldn't hurt me if I could manage to
educate myself in science. The other day I picked up a freshman
text in mathematics and I was fascinated at an attempt in the
introduction to define the nature of mathematics. What intrigued
me was that the statement could have been transposed, altering
hardly a word, to the introduction of a text in literature and used
as a definition of poetry. I do not have to tell my readers that there
is, deep down, a common principle which links literature, the visual
arts, music and mathematics into a single unity. I should like for
my students to have at least a glimmering of this concept. I need
only the time to continue my own study of literature, art, music
and mathematics until I understand the principle well enough to
try to explain it to the students. Who knows, a great work may be
possible here. If the poor, confused sophomore, bedeviled by
separate and distinct courses, could only be made to understand
that all the separate irritations forced upon him actually are parts
of a general pattern, a grand design in which his soul may find, if
not salvation, at least understanding and perhaps peace! Or is it
more important that a few of my colleagues be exposed to my
thoughts on Faulkner's water symbolism?

16   And did I mention earlier the matter of extracurricular
activities? A multitude of such activities is officially sponsored by
the college, and the teacher's participation in them is recognized,
if not rewarded. Teaching credit is given for some of the more
time-consuming chores—usually three hours credit for any job
which requires the equivalent of six hours of work and energy. But
I do not complain about this, nobody forces us to be advisors to
newspapers, magazines, and yearbooks. I do quarrel with the
idea that on top of all this we'd better knock off three or four articles a year and a book during the Sabbatical.

17   The official extracurricular activities are of course only part of the tale. A college ought to be a community of scholars, and, as T. V. Smith has said, the students are members of the community as junior scholars. If this is so, then by any definition of the word "community" we have not fulfilled our obligation when we walk out of the classroom. A couple of years ago several students asked me if I would guide them in an informal course of reading in philosophy and permit them to gather once a week in my home to discuss what they had read—they'd bring the beer. So rare a thirst for learning could not but excite the weariest and most disillusioned pedagogue. To respond to such an innocent outburst of intellectual curiosity with anything but enthusiastic acceptance and positive encouragement would be more than treason to the profession. It would be treason to the human race. And I knew that the weekly sessions could be exciting fun. The only catch was that I couldn't figure any way to find the time to do the minimum study necessary to prepare myself for the most elementary discussion of Plato and Aristotle, Kant and Hegel—not to mention the one evening in every seven which would be filled as long as their fire lasted, which would be as long as I could add fuel to it. That is, I couldn't find the time for this unexpected activity *and* for my paper on the Sacred Water as well. It is perhaps a pity you won't be reading my article next month, but we had a fine time. The students learned something, I learned a lot, and we are all better off. And some of these students are now teaching in New York public schools, and they tell me that they still read a little philosophy and even drop the name of Socrates occasionally in the classroom.

18   I would end this avowal of our *duty* not to publish by returning to my original point: the English teacher ought to be a learned man. The teacher of undergraduates must be more widely read than the graduate professor, the research specialist. We do not know enough. Many of our colleagues are so politically ignorant as to be absolute menaces in the midst of inquiring students. How many of us really know anything about anthropology? Or physics? Or biology? We make jokes about our inadequacies in mathematics (and how many good mathematicians know nothing about literature, or, too often, anything but math?). And how often are our cultivated sneers at professional education merely a reflection of our ignorance of education? One of the best things an English professor who has finally found the time to write that

article could do would be to forget it and read a good history of education. It wouldn't hurt him to read a couple of good books on educational theory—and there are some good ones.

19   We ought to know more about psychology than we do. Not only could we do a more competent job in teaching literature, but we might be better prepared to counsel intelligently the not insignificant number of students who seem to prefer to bring their troubles to English professors than to expose their naked frailties to the sharp eyes of the professional counselors.

20   We ought to know at least as much about history, sociology and economics as the student working for an M.A. degree in these areas. And there are fields beyond Academe that are not unworthy of our efforts. The teacher who knows nothing about sports, for example, is cut off from one of the important areas of American culture. The man who is ignorant of Hank Aaron and Floyd Patterson and Jimmy Brown and Ted Williams (that sterling perfectionist) is first cousin to the man who never heard of Shakespeare and Leonardo and William Faulkner.

21   The Ph.D. degree, save for the specialists, ought not to be the diving board from which the pundit can plummet into the depths of his specialty, never to be seen again except by a few of his fellows cavorting in the same depths. It ought rather to be a door opening into wider fields of knowledge. The undergraduate teacher, especially the English teacher, ought to devote his time more to the plain dame of continuing education and less to the Siren Publication.

22   The colleges are full of learned ignoramuses.

RESEARCH REVISITED: SCHOLARSHIP AND THE FINE ART OF TEACHING*

Donald H. Reiman

1   It encourages a young instructor in a highly competitive Department of English to read in journals speaking for the National

---

* From *College English*, October, 1961. Reprinted with permission of the National Council of Teachers of English and Professor Donald H. Reiman.

Council of Teachers of English and the Modern Language Association that the doctrine of "publish or perish" is coming under the fire of men higher up in the profession; it gratifies him even more to note that the provost of one of America's largest and most publication-minded universities has given of his time to preach among the intellectual laity the dangers of academic research. To one who studied at a liberal arts college where a heavy class load made scholarly publication by the faculty rather the exception than the rule, it is, moreover, pleasant to be assured that those who seek promotion by engaging in research are poorer teachers for it. But, after I have soothed my fears and salved my ego, I wonder if the problem is as simple as some have made it appear.

2   Although I would be unwise to engage in "research" on a topic like this (especially as to do so might endanger the welfare of my students), it occurs to me, as I think over the undergraduate and graduate teachers I have known, that there may be, after all, a direct correlation between productive research and effective teaching and that abuses of the publish-or-perish system may well be merely abuses, those inevitable serpents in any well-ordered garden, rather than tragic flaws in the system itself. Perhaps we can better serve the interests of higher education by rearticulating the purposes of scholarship than by rushing to the door with bathtub, water, and baby.

3   Unlike medical or industrial researchers, humanistic scholars cannot claim that immediate pragmatic benefits emanate from their studies; nor can they justify their research by pointing even to long-range advances in the standard of living: there are no "better *things* for better living—through explication." But teachers of the humanities, who must encounter great-souled works of art produced by intellectual and spiritual giants and who must somehow capture enough of this genius to plant in the minds of the young, seeds of intellectual maturity, may be excused for hunting in packs, for tying down the living masterpieces with threads of criticism as the Lilliputians secured Gulliver. Some teachers may indeed rise to the height of the great arguments unaided, but most of us require the discoveries and the insights of dozens of our colleagues before we can hope to do justice to the twenty-five or more achievements of genius with which we contend in the classroom each year—or each semester. This much would seem to be a clear-cut delineation of what constitutes useful scholarship and

criticism: how can an article justify space in the professional journals?

4   Literary *scholarship* should aid the teacher and student in understanding what a work of art did mean or should have meant to the sensitive reader at the time of its composition. To reconstruct this potential effect one must establish an accurate text of the work; define its words and terms; elucidate its allusions, literary or topical; explain the intellectual milieu in which the work of art grew (survey the world-view of the age together with the world-view of the author); and implicate any historical or bio-graphical information that contributes to the above ends. One can see that under these criteria a philologist's study in the mean-ings of Anglo-Saxon words, if related to particular contexts, is a legitimate literary as well as linguistic pursuit. Likewise, a com-parison of possible sources for an incident, character, or image may shed light on an author's meaning. Some scholarly endeavors, on the other hand, though they may have historical or human-interest value, are completely extra-literary. The discovery of a lock of Milton's hair, for instance, even the lock of Keats' lyric, possesses no relevance to the understanding of poems by Milton or Keats. And the unearthing of information about a poet's ancestry and family is useful only insofar as the poet's opinions or attitudes were affected by the heritage so made known.

5   *Criticism*, on the other hand, should aid the teacher and student in ascertaining what the work of art amounts to in the present tense. Criticism must always be in either the first-person, singular or the imperative. It is a normative act in which the critic witnesses to the value of a work of literature that he fully under-stands after a careful application of scholarship. Explication, which is simply the inevitable last step of scholarship, can never be divorced from less glamorous scholarly activities (such as textual and historical study) and forced to cohabit in isolation with criti-cism. Only bastard offspring can result from such a union, for no critic, new or old, can render normative judgments worth printing unless his evaluation is based upon a sound text of the work and upon a thorough knowledge of the language and ideas of the author and his times. T. S. Eliot, mistaking for an image of the moon what is obviously an image of the morning star, found Shelley's grasp on the actual to be weak; C. S. Lewis, while prais-ing Shelley's use of elegaic tradition in *Adonais,* cited as the poet's

one unclassical lapse in taste a passage in which Shelley closely paraphrases Bion's *Lament for Adonis;* F. O. Mattiessen acclaimed as one of Melville's most strikingly characteristic images a phrase in *White Jacket* that resulted from a typographical error. We remember these oversights in the great only because their criticism, in which such slips are infrequent, continues to stimulate us; how many "critical studies" have proven entirely useless or ephemeral because they contained little besides egregious blunders? Once the objective creation has been identified through careful analysis of its words, structure, and ideas, the critic must then determine the value of the experience captured in the work of art for the living man who re-experiences it. Landor was demanding this normative act when he wrote:

> In what volume of periodical criticism do you not find it stated that, the aim of an author being such or such, the only question is whether he has attained it? Now, instead of this being the only question to be solved, it is pretty nearly the one least worthy of attention. We are not to consider whether a foolish man has succeeded in a foolish undertaking: we are to consider whether his production is worth anything, and why it is, or why it is not?

6   Although criticism thus involves the so-called "affective fallacy" just as scholarship does the "intentional fallacy," neither violates the genuine autonomy of the work of art, which rests not on omission of such pertinent considerations as the author's aims and the effects upon a reading public, but on a comprehensive view of all stages of the author-to-reader communication that is a work of literature. Literature is a human product having relevance only to human beings: without the author and his imaginative soul, the work of art cannot exist at all, for although we can read *The Iliad* in complete ignorance of Homer as an individual man, we cannot remain ignorant of a human consciousness with particular ideals and aspirations that lies behind that magnificent achievement; without the reader, on the other hand, the poem is uncreated, becoming mere marks on paper or stone that await reanimation by a sensitive human soul.

7   Legitimate contributions to scholarship and criticism are irreplaceable tools of the conscientious classroom teacher. Asked to present, at least in his younger days, everything from *King Lear* to *Lucky Jim* and "The Wanderer" to "The Windhover," he must

rely on the specialized study of other teacher-scholars for an adequate understanding of these varied works. Only within a relatively narrow sphere can the average teacher hope for such mastery of an author's works that he can repay through original contributions to knowledge the bank of scholarship from which he borrows so freely.

8   Of even greater value than scholarship-in-general to the individual teacher, however, in his own research. Growth is the only sign of life in the world of the intellect, and intellectual curiosity is the lifeblood of the educated man. The teacher who remains *satisfied* with guesses, with half-answers, or even with the honest and necessary "I don't know" forfeits the respect of his students and colleagues alike. And the ultimate test of his quality of mind is whether or not he can contribute to teachers' or students' understanding of literature, in writing that will bear the scrutiny of his peers. Our love of knowledge, our enthusiasm for the mind's adventure, and our eagerness to grapple with life's great issues are the most valuable gifts we can bequeath to our society. A teacher who merely repeats what he has been told or what he has read can seldom generate the electric spark that will jump the gap between him and his students. The rigor of disciplined study does, however, generate that energy, and the excitement of personal discovery can transmit that enthusiasm.

9   Dedication to the ideals of the intellect and a willingness to sacrifice something of self for the promotion of knowledge have been hallmarks of the best teachers I have known, and although personal limitations interpose themselves, I am convinced that most productive scholars are better, not worse, teachers for their scholarly passion. Consider the alternative: a man of great intellect but somewhat introverted personality who concentrates on methods of teaching or superficial preparations for classes, rather than on deep knowledge of a field, is a teacher twice as self-conscious and half as effective because he is acutely aware that his mastery of the subject is inadequate. Buttressed, however, by the confidence that personal discovery brings, such men can become stimulating teachers as well as valuable contributors to the scholarly world.

10   What I have been saying is, of course, that although we should recognize effective teaching as the desired end, productive research is one of the best means to it. Now arises the question of

those abuses which have recently come under fire. How does one prevent a teacher from short-changing his students by overemphasizing his personal investigations to the detriment of preparation in other areas and interest in the students themselves? And how does one lessen the tendency of researchers to publish anything they can, whether or not it is stimulating, sound, or useful? Let me say first that these abuses do not seem to me any more widespread than abuses of another kind in schools where there is no emphasis upon publication. I have known graduate students who declared that they wanted to teach in college so that they would have more time free to play golf and travel. I have known teachers whose contempt for the intellectual adventures of scholarship was matched only by their disinterest in their students. Without responsible administration neither the pressurized publish-or-perish system nor the *laissez faire* approach will foster dedicated teaching.

11   The problem of undistinguished and useless publication can be met at two levels: first, editors of scholarly journals and university presses have a responsibility to maintain high standards, a duty which should prove easier under a system that encourages all teachers to compete for the available space. The quality of scholarly publication was not, on the whole, any higher in the days when there were fewer journals and only those teachers published who had an interest in such things; surely a great many keen minds occupied themselves in other ways—perhaps even went to sleep—when there was less incentive to engage in research. Second, administrators can curtail the proliferation of bad and useless scholarship if they will observe the end rather than the means and judge quality as well as quantity of publication. Difficult? Yes. Time-consuming? Undoubtedly. Unfair in some instances? Probably. But like all normative judgments, these evaluations create out of chaos a moral order.

12   The sacrifice of teaching-preparation time for one's own specialized investigations, like the desire to publish the same findings both early and late, arises in part from an emphasis on early blooming in scholarship. A man in his first years of teaching must spend considerable time preparing for his classes and grading student papers. As the years pass, he will draw upon his accumulated knowledge both for teaching and scholarship, but at this stage of his career when he finds the least free time to pursue his own in-

vestigations, he must do the most research to produce worthwhile results. Thus, to demand a certain quantity of publication from a novice within his first two or three years of teaching encourages him either to neglect his students or to "nickel and dime himself to death," in the words of one dean. The line of demarcation for those who are to be rewarded for dedicated teaching and useful scholarship ought, then, to fall between the ranks of assistant professor and associate professor rather than between instructor and assistant professor. If a man is not adequate as a teacher, he should be let out at the first convenient moment, but for a man who is intellectually alive, who shows evidence of improving in his teaching and devoting as much time as remains to research, there ought to be no arbitrary test by quantity of publication after so short a period of time. Young men should not be discouraged from undertaking important studies that require long, sustained effort.

13   We have been urged during recent years to establish a system of separate-but-equal rewards for two races, teachers and scholars. Those who have no interest in research would be given heavier class loads, while those who excel in scholarship would become full-time researchers at institutes for advanced study. What I have been arguing is that like so many dichotomies with which we are concerned—form and content, subject and object, life and art—the split between teaching and scholarship can be maintained only if we narrow our definitions of both and impoverish our understanding of their full potentialities. It has been my privilege to know two of America's most distinguished Renaissance scholars who since compulsory retirement from their own universities have taught each year at other institutions. When I asked one why he was not content to stay at home, working full time on his studies, he insisted that the stimulation of the classroom was necessary for his scholarship. Similarly, some of my best teachers have testified to the salutory effect of research upon their teaching. And from my limited personal experience I, too, can witness to the mutuality of these enterprises which, for the sake of analysis, we distinguish as teaching and scholarship.

14   If it seems paradoxical that one who may some day be the victim of the publish-or-perish system should defend its basic soundness, it is, perhaps, even more paradoxical to hear those who administer the system disavowing it. A far better course for those in authority would be, I think, to keep foremost the chief goal of

the system, which, for the humanities at least, is a dedicated teacher who learns from his colleagues to help his students and who studies deeply to help his colleagues, thus becoming an integral part of a true community of scholars.

Referring to the first pages of this section, to the brief introductory notes to each of the subsections, and to the selections themselves, establish a procedure for evaluating these essays—or any other argumentative discourses. One way to begin might be to state the position of each and to chart the steps in the development of each, observing any unproved assumptions and noting the kind of support each offers and the method of refutation each uses, if any. Establishment of a procedure such as this may serve two purposes: first, it will enable you to know these essays better; second, it may provide a method you can use at any time when you are called upon for such critical evaluation. Further suggestions for use of these essays are in the suggested Writing Program, which follows.

A Writing Program

1. Using a subject agreed upon by you and your instructor, write a short hortatory essay in the manner of either the Kennedy address, one of the selections from the Bible, or the Faulkner speech. Your imitation should use, for example, sentence structure identical with that of your model; the plans of development should also be similar.

2. Write a complete argument. Base your argument upon some expository essay you have already done, or upon a new expository essay which surveys some controversial subject. From that essay, formulate a proposal for action or for changed policy. Then collect the evidence you will need to support your view and to refute any opposing view. With the proposal and the collected materials before you, plan the

essay you are to write. Decide with your instructor whether the essay is to be informal argument in the manner, say, of the Linton, Glazer, or Jones selections, or a formal, documented argument. If you decide to do the latter, your task is in effect a research paper, and the evidence you might otherwise refer to more or less casually can now be quoted and given full credit in footnote documentation.

3. Using a subject agreed upon by you and your instructor, write a refutation in the manner of Glazer. Perhaps you will want to refute views expressed in articles in this section; the essays by O'Connor, Hurt, Reiman, Linton, and Glazer may offer a target for your refutation.

4. Write an expository essay, the purpose of which is analysis and evaluation of one of the arguments in this section.

Description

Purely descriptive writing occurs only occasionally. Variously charming, exciting, or otherwise effective in itself, descriptive writing frequently serves as a means to ends not descriptive. Vital as a method for giving a local habitation to narration, description also serves the purpose of argumentation and exposition. Stevenson's essay, "Pulvis et Umbra," which appears in this section, is not, for example, rendered entirely as description. Instead, the striking descriptive passages give color and vigor and concreteness to Stevenson's larger theme, to the evolutionary process. Similarly, the descriptive passages from *Look Homeward, Angel,* presented here in isolation from their context, were presumably not designed for their own sake, but rather for the purpose of giving solidity to the narrative of which they are a part.

A factual re-creation, even if it were possible, is not the sole nor even the first purpose of description. A writer uses description to reveal what a thing is like, to be sure, but he reveals it as it has already been shaped by his own sensory and sensitive reactions. By careful scrutiny of his subject and of his own responses, he seeks to record, through sharp images and impression, the uniqueness of a thing he has known, which he now wishes us to know.

Dominant Impression and Unity

For effective description, a writer works with sharp sensory images and impressions. But the haphazard collection of impressions and images serves only to dramatize illiteracy. Writers have always found it effective to arrange and manage details and images so that they coalesce to form one dominant impression. Doing so, they reap benefits similar to those gained through use of a thesis sentence, for to create and maintain a dominant impression requires the unification of all parts of an essay. Writers have found several ways to establish this key impression. They may, for example, completely eliminate all images and details that do not help to create the desired effect. Or they may by grammatical means subordinate impressions that are colorful but that do not contribute to their central purpose. Or they may seek to present *all* images, even those not apparently pertinent, in terms of the tone or mood or impression that is central to the essay.

CIRCUS AT DAWN*

Thomas Wolfe

1   There were times in early autumn—in September—when the greater circuses would come to town—the Ringling Brothers, Robinson's, and Barnum and Bailey shows, and when I was a route-boy on the morning paper, on those mornings when the circus would be coming in I would rush madly through my route in the cool and thrilling darkness that comes just before break of day, and then I would go back home and get my brother out of bed.

2   Talking in low excited voices we would walk rapidly back towards town under the rustle of September leaves, in cool streets just greyed now with that still, that unearthly and magical first light of day which seems suddenly to rediscover the great earth out of darkness, so that the earth emerges with an awful, a glorious sculptural stillness, and one looks out with a feeling of joy and disbelief, as the first men on this earth must have done, for to see this happen is one of the things that men will remember out of life forever and think of as they die.

3   At the sculptural still square where at one corner, just emerging into light, my father's shabby little marble shop stood with a ghostly strangeness and familiarity, my brother and I would

* Reprinted with the permission of Charles Scribner's Sons from *From Death to Morning* by Thomas Wolfe. Copyright, 1935, Charles Scribner's Sons; renewal copyright ©, 1963, Paul Gitlin.

"catch" the first streetcar of the day bound for the "depot" where the circus was—or sometimes we would meet someone we knew, who would give us a lift in his automobile.

4   Then, having reached the dingy, grimy, and rickety depot section, we would get out and walk rapidly across the tracks of the station yard, where we could see great flares and steamings from the engines, and hear the crash and bump of shifting engine, the tolling of bells, the sounds of great trains on the rails.

5   And to all these familiar sounds, filled with their exultant prophecies of flight, the voyage, morning, and the shining cities— to all the sharp and thrilling odors of the trains—the smell of cinders, acrid smoke, of musty, rusty freight cars, the clean pine board of crated produce, and the smells of fresh stored foods— oranges, coffee, tangerines, and bacon, ham and flour and beef— there would be added now, with an unforgettable magic and familiarity, all the strange sounds and smells of the coming circus.

6   The gay yellow sumptuous-looking cars in which the star performers lived and slept, still dark and silent, heavily and powerfully still, would be drawn up in long strings upon the tracks. And all around them the sounds of the unloading circus would go on furiously in the darkness. The receding gulf of lilac and depart- ing night would be filled with the savage roar of the lions, the murderously sudden snarling of great jungle cats, the trumpeting of the elephants, the stamp of the horses, and with the musty, pun- gent, unfamiliar odor of the jungle animals: the tawny camel smells, and the smells of panthers, zebras, tigers, elephants, and bears.

7   Then, along the tracks, beside the circus trains, there would be the sharp cries and oaths of the circus men, the magical swing- ing dance of lanterns in the darkness, the sudden heavy rumble of the loaded vans and wagons as they were pulled along the flats and gondolas, and down the runways to the ground. And everywhere, in the thrilling mystery of darkness and awakening light, there would be the tremendous conflict of a confused, hurried, and yet orderly movement.

8   The great iron-grey horses, four and six to a team, would be plodding along the road of thick white dust to a rattling of chains and traces and the harsh cries of their drivers. The men would drive the animals to the river which flowed by beyond the tracks, and water them; and as first light came one could see the

elephants wallowing the familiar river and the big horses going
slowly and carefully down to drink.

9   Then, on the circus grounds, the tents were going up already with the magic speed of dreams. All over the place (which
was near the tracks and the only space of flat land in the town that
was big enough to hold a circus) there would be this fierce, savagely
hurried, and yet orderly confusion. Great flares of gaseous circus
light would blaze down on the seared and battered faces of the
circus toughs as, with the rhythmic precision of a single animal
—a human riveting machine—they swung their sledges at the stakes,
driving a stake into the earth with the incredible instancy of
accelerated figures in a motion picture. And everywhere, as light
came, and the sun appeared, there would be a scene of magic,
order, and of violence. The drivers would curse and talk their
special language to their teams, there would be the loud, gasping,
and uneven labor of a gasoline engine, the shouts and curses of
the bosses, the wooden riveting of driven stakes, and the rattle of
heavy chains.

10   Already in an immense cleared space of dusty beaten
earth, the stakes were being driven for the main exhibition tent.
And an elephant would lurch ponderously to the field, slowly lower
his great swinging head at the command of a man who sat perched
upon his skull, flourish his grey wrinkled snout a time or two, and
then solemnly wrap it around a tent pole big as the mast of a
racing schooner. Then the elephant would back slowly away, dragging the great pole with him as if it were a stick of matchwood.

11   And when this happened, my brother would break into
his great *whah-whah* of exuberant laughter, and prod me in the
ribs with his clumsy fingers. And farther on, two town darkeys,
who had watched the elephant's performance with bulging eyes,
would turn to each other with apelike grins, bend double as they
slapped their knees and howled with swart rich nigger-laughter,
saying to each other in a kind of rhythmical chorus of question
and reply:

12   "He don't play with it, do he?"

"No, *suh!* He don't send no boy!"

"He don't say, 'Wait a minute,' do he?"

"No, suh! He say, 'Come with me!' That's what he say!"

"He go *boogety-boogety!*" said one, suiting the words with a
prowling movement of his black face towards the earth.

"He go rootin' faw it!" said the other, making a rooting movement with his head.

"He say, 'Ar-rumpf!' " said one.

"He say, 'Big boy, we is on ouah way!' " the other answered.

"Har! Har! Har! Har! Har!"—and they choked and screamed with their rich laughter, slapping their thighs with a solid smack as they described to each other the elephant's prowess.

13   Meanwhile, the circus food-tent—a huge canvas top without concealing sides—had already been put up, and now we could see the performers seated at long trestled tables underneath the tent, as they ate breakfast. And the savor of the food they ate—mixed as it was with our strong excitement, with the powerful but wholesome smells of the animals, and with all the joy, sweetness, mystery, jubilant magic, and glory of the morning and the coming of the circus—seemed to us to be of the most maddening and appetizing succulence of any food that we had ever known or eaten.

14   We could see the circus performers eating tremendous breakfasts, with all the savage relish of their power and strength; they ate big fried steaks, pork chops, rashers of bacon, a half-dozen eggs, great slabs of fried ham, and great stacks of wheat-cakes which a cook kept flipping in the air with the skill of a juggler, and which a husky-looking waitress kept rushing to their tables on loaded trays held high and balanced marvelously on the fingers of a brawny hand. And above all the maddening odors of the wholesome and succulent food, there brooded forever the sultry and delicious fragrance—that somehow seemed to add a zest and sharpness to all the powerful and thrilling life of morning—of strong boiling coffee, which we could see sending off clouds of steam from an enormous polished urn, and which the circus performers gulped down, cup after cup.

15   And the circus men and women themselves—these star performers—were such fine-looking people, strong and handsome, yet speaking and moving with an almost stern dignity and decorum, that their lives seemed to us to be as splendid and wonderful as any lives on earth could be. There was never anything loose, rowdy, or tough in their comportment . . .

16   Rather, these people in an astonishing way seemed to have created an established community which lived an ordered existence on wheels, and to observe with a stern fidelity unknown

in towns and cities the decencies of family life. There would be
a powerful young man, a handsome and magnificent young woman
with blonde hair and the figure of an Amazon, and a powerfully
built, thick-set man of middle age, who had a stern, lined, respon-
sible-looking face and a bald head. They were probably the members of a trapeze team—the young man and woman would leap
through space like projectiles, meeting the trip of the older man
and hurling back again upon their narrow perches, catching the
swing of their trapeze in midair, and whirling thrice before they
caught it, in a perilous and beautiful exhibition of human balance
and precision.

17   But when they came into the breakfast tent, they would
speak gravely yet courteously to other performers, and seat themselves in a family group at one of the long tables, eating their
tremendous breakfasts with an earnest concentration, seldom
speaking to one another, and then gravely, seriously, and briefly.

18   And my brother and I would look at them with fascinated
eyes: my brother would watch the man with the bald head for a
while and then turn towards me, whispering:

"D-d-do you see that f-f-fellow there with the bald head?
W-w-well he's the heavy man," he whispered knowingly. "He's the
one that c-c-catches them! You know what happens if he m-m-
misses, don't you?" said my brother.

"What?" I would say in a fascinated tone.

My brother snapped his fingers in the air.

19   "Over!" he said. "D-d-done for! W-w-why, they'd be
d-d-d-dead before they knew what happened. Sure!" he said,
nodding vigorously. "It's a f-f-f-fact! If he ever m-m-m-misses it's
all over! That boy has g-g-g-got to know his s-s-s-stuff!" my brother
said. "W-w-w-why," he went on in a low tone of solemn conviction, "it w-w-w-wouldn't surprise me at all if they p-p-p-pay him
s-s-seventy-five or a hundred dollars a week! It's a fact!" my
brother cried vigorously.

20   And we would turn our fascinated stares again upon these
splendid and romantic creatures, whose lives were so different from
our own, and whom we seemed to know with such familiar and
affectionate intimacy. And at length, reluctantly, with full light
come and the sun up, we would leave the circus grounds and start
for home.

21   And somehow the memory of all we had seen and heard
that glorious morning, and the memory of the food-tent with its

wonderful smells, would waken in us the pangs of such a ravenous hunger that we could not wait until we got home to eat. We would stop off in town at lunchrooms and, seated on tall stools before the counter, we would devour ham-and-egg sandwiches, hot hamburgers red and pungent at their cores with coarse spicy sanguinary beef, coffee, glasses of foaming milk and doughnuts, and then go home to eat up everything in sight upon the breakfast table.

• COMMENTARY •

Wolfe's essay is worthy of careful scrutiny of all its parts and of all the features of its style. In the simple, natural movements of the boys through the town and to the circus grounds there is established a point of view exactly appropriate to the scene and to the boys, a point of view that enables Wolfe to exploit the sense of wonder and magic aroused by the circus. And what they see and feel there is rendered in vivid, precise terms. But for the benefits that may accrue to your own writing through understanding of his methods, consider here just the one feature of his work, how he creates a central impression in this essay.

This central impression is the magic sense of wonder the boys experience. The sense stems from the setting and the way it makes ordinary things seem marvelous, from the chaos everywhere about them that suddenly becomes order, and from the mysterious incongruity of the strange and familiar. This impression is achieved by accumulation through several methods, including simple repetition, periodic constructions, paragraph arrangement, and keen imagery.

Wolfe accomplishes part of his purpose by simple repetition. The word "magic" and its variants, for example, occur nine times. Words such as "strangeness" that suggest the unfamiliar occur six times (a careful counter may find more), and words suggesting speed and chaos occur five times.

Periodic arrangements help to emphasize the sense of magic. The fifth paragraph of the essay is one long sentence, and that sentence is periodic, with its subject and verb reserved until the end of the sentence. More important, a part of the subject thus reserved for last is *magic*. Thus Wolfe calls attention to his dominant quality by withholding it until the last of a long periodic sentence. The same method is effectively used in the ninth paragraph. The second sentence is periodic, with the subject, *confusion*, which contributes to the boys' sense of wonder, withheld until last. Not structurally periodic, but nevertheless similarly effective are the first and fourth sentences, which stress *magic* at the end.

Just as the element withheld until the end of a sentence gets the sentence's primary stress, so does the sentence that occurs last in a paragraph get the paragraph's major stress. In paragraphs five, seven, and thirteen, Wolfe builds toward elements at the end that contribute to his dominant impression. Just secondary to this are those paragraphs in which he *begins* with images adding to his central impression (paragraphs two, three, and nine).

The well-known setting and its ordinary features are made marvelous by lighting in the first paragraphs of the essay. The darkness is "cool and thrilling," the first light of day is "unearthly and magical," and the square is "sculptural," the little shop ghostly by the morning light and by the proximity of the strange circus. Everywhere in the essay the familiar is made to seem strange and wonderful by its juxtaposition with the circus. Along the well-known tracks there stand the "gay yellow sumptuous-looking cars" of the circus, and with light the boys can see "elephants wallowing the familiar river." Adding to this wonder and mystery and magic is the surprise of watching chaos become order, particularly in paragraphs seven through nine, where the boys watch tents go up "with the magic speed of dreams" and see men drive stakes "with the incredible instancy of accelerated figures in a motion picture."

Finally, enchanted, the boys survey it all: "we would turn our fascinated stares again upon these splendid and romantic creatures, whose lives were so different from our own, and whom we seemed to know with such familiar and affectionate intimacy." And, enchanted, so do we all know them, caught remembering our own time by the power of the magic Wolfe creates in the essay.

From LETTER TO DOCTOR LEWIS *in*

HUMPHREY CLINKER [1771]

Tobias Smollett

Edinburgh, August 8
Though the villas of the Scotch nobility and gentry have generally an air of grandeur and state, I think their gardens and parks are not comparable to those of England; a circumstance the more remarkable, as I was told by the ingenious Mr. Philip Millar, of

Chelsea, that almost all the gardeners of South Britain were natives of Scotland. The verdure of this country is not equal to that of England. The pleasure-grounds are, in my opinion, not so well laid out, according to the *genius loci;* nor are the lawns, and walks, and hedges kept in such delicate order. The trees are planted in prudish rows, which have not such an agreeable natural effect as when they are thrown into irregular groups, with intervening glades; and the firs, which they generally raise around their houses, look dull and funereal in the summer season. I must confess, indeed, that they yield serviceable timber, and good shelter against the northern blasts; that they grow and thrive in the most barren soil, and continually perspire a fine balsam of turpentine, which must render the air very salutary and sanative to lungs of tender texture. . . .

• SUGGESTIONS •

Both the arrangement and the diction of this selection help to create a central impression. By its arrangement the paragraph calls attention to certain *features* of the landscape, and by its diction the paragraph calls attention to certain *qualities* of the landscape. In a short discussion show how we are led toward this dominant impression. Make your discussion specific by using exact references to the paragraph, quoting when necessary to illustrate your points.

From O PIONEERS! *

Willa Cather

One January day, thirty years ago, the little town of Hanover, anchored on a windy Nebraska tableland, was trying not to be blown away. A mist of fine snowflakes was curling and eddying about the cluster of low drab buildings huddled on the grey prairie, under a grey sky. The dwelling-houses were set about haphazard on the tough prairie sod; some of them looked as if

they had been moved in overnight, and others as if they were
straying off by themselves, headed straight for the open plain.
None of them had any appearance of permanence, and the howling wind blew under them as well as over them. The main street
was a deeply rutted road, now frozen hard, which ran from the
squat red railway station and the grain "elevator" at the north end
of the town to the lumber yard and the horse pond at the south
end. On either side of this road straggled two uneven rows of
wooden buildings; the general merchandise stores, the two banks,
the drugstore, the feed-store, the saloon, the post-office. The board
sidewalks were grey with trampled snow, but at two o'clock in the
afternoon the shopkeepers, having come back from dinner, were
keeping well behind their frosty windows. The children were all
in school, and there was nobody abroad in the streets but a few
rough-looking countrymen in coarse overcoats, with their long
caps pulled down to their noses. Some of them had brought their
wives to town, and now and then a red or a plaid shawl flashed out
of one store into the shelter of another. At the hitch-bars along
the street a few heavy work-horses, harnessed to farm wagons,
shivered under their blankets. About the station everything was
quiet, for there would not be another train in until night.

· SUGGESTIONS ·

Everything about this selection suggests silent, cold, depressing, and
yet impermanent simplicity. List the words, phrases, and sentences that
help to create this image. While such a list is little in itself, the accumulation of this kind of specific evidence is necessary to the kind of full
analysis that you may find it necessary to do at other times.

PULVIS ET UMBRA [1892]

Robert Louis Stevenson

1   We look for some reward of our endeavors and are disappointed; not success, not happiness, not even peace of conscience, crowns our ineffectual efforts to do well. Our frailties are

invincible, our virtues barren; the battle goes sore against us to the
going down of the sun. The canting moralist tells us of right and
wrong; and we look abroad, even on the face of our small earth,
and find them change with every climate, and no country where
some action is not honored for a virtue and none where it is not
branded for a vice; and we look in our experience, and find no
vital congruity in the wisest rules, but at the best a municipal fit-
ness. It is not strange if we are tempted to despair of good. We ask
too much. Our religions and moralities have been trimmed to
flatter us, till they are all emasculate and sentimentalized, and only
please and weaken. Truth is of a rougher strain. In the harsh face
of life, faith can read a bracing gospel. The human race is a thing
more ancient than the ten commandments; and the bones and revolutions of the Kosmos, in whose joints we are but moss and fungus,
more ancient still.

▶ *I*

2   Of the Kosmos in the last resort, science reports many
doubtful things and all of them appalling. There seems no substance on this solid globe on which we stamp: nothing but symbols
and ratios. Symbols and ratios carry us and bring us forth and beat
us down; gravity that swings the incommensurable suns and worlds
through space, is but a figment varying inversely as the squares
of distances; and the suns and worlds themselves, imponderable
figures of abstractions, NH_3 and H_2O. Consideration dares not
dwell upon this view; that way madness lies; science carries us
into zones of speculation, where there is no habitable city for the
mind of man.

3   But take the Kosmos with a grosser faith, as our senses
give it us. We behold space sown with rotatory islands, suns and
worlds and the shards and wrecks of systems: some, like the sun,
still blazing; some rotting, like the earth; others, like the moon,
stable in desolation. All of these we take to be made of something
we call matter: a thing no analysis can help us to conceive; to
whose incredible properties no familiarities can reconcile our
minds. This stuff, when not purified by the lustration of fire, rots
uncleanly into something we call life; seized through all its atoms
with a pediculous malady; swelling in tumors that become independent, sometimes even (by an abhorrent prodigy) locomotory;
one splitting into millions, millions cohering into one, as the malady

proceeds through varying stages. This vital putrescence of the dust, used as we are to it, yet strikes us with occasional disgust, and the profusion of worms in a piece of ancient turf, or the air of a marsh darkened with insects, will sometimes check our breathing so that we aspire for cleaner places. But none is clean: the moving sand is infected with lice; the pure spring, where it bursts out of the mountain, is a mere issue of worms; even in the hard rock the crystal is forming.

4   In two main shapes this eruption covers the countenance of the earth: the animal and the vegetable: one in some degree the inversion of the other: the second rooted to the spot, the first coming detached out of its natal mud, and scurrying abroad with the myriad feet of insects or towering into the heavens on the wings of birds: a thing so inconceivable that, if it be well considered, the heart stops. To what passes with the anchored vermin, we have little clue: doubtless they have their joys and sorrows, their delights and killing agonies: it appears not how. But of the locomotory, to which we ourselves belong, we can tell more. These share with us a thousand miracles: the miracles of sight, of hearing, of the projection of sound, things that bridge space; the miracles of memory and reason, by which the present is conceived, and when it is gone, its image kept living in the brains of man and brute; the miracle of reproduction, with its imperious desires and staggering consequences. And to put the last touch upon this mountain mass of the revolting and the inconceivable, all these prey upon each other, lives tearing other lives in pieces, cramming them inside themselves, and by that summary process, growing fat: the vegetarian, the whale, perhaps the tree, not less than the lion of the desert; for the vegetarian is only the eater of the dumb.

5   Meanwhile our rotatory island loaded with predatory life, and more drenched with blood, both animal and vegetable, than ever mutinied ship, scuds through space with unimaginable speed, and turns alternate cheeks to the reverberation of a blazing world, ninety million miles away.

▶ *II*

6   What a monstrous specter is this man, the disease of agglutinated dust, lifting alternate feet or lying drugged with slumber; killing, feeding, growing, bringing forth small copies of himself; grown upon with hair like grass, fitted with eyes that

move and glitter in his face; a thing to set children screaming; and yet looked at nearlier, known as his fellows know him, how surprising are his attributes! Poor soul, here for so little, cast among so many hardships, filled with desires so incommensurate and so inconsistent, savagely surrounded, savagely descended, irremediably condemned to prey upon his fellow lives: who should have blamed him had he been of a piece with his destiny and a being merely barbarous? And we look and behold him instead filled with imperfect virtues: infinitely childish, often admirably valiant, often touchingly kind; sitting down, amidst his momentary life, to debate of right and wrong and the attributes of the deity; rising up to do battle for an egg or die for an idea; singling out his friends and his mate with cordial affection; bringing forth in pain, rearing with long-suffering solicitude, his young. To touch the heart of his mystery, we find in him one thought, strange to the point of lunacy: the thought of duty; the thought of something owing to himself, to his neighbor, to his God: an ideal of decency, to which he would rise if it were possible; a limit of shame, below which, if it be possible, he will not stoop. The design in most men is one of conformity; here and there, in picked natures, it transcends itself and soars on the other side, arming martyrs with independence; but in all, in their degrees, it is a bosom thought:—Not in man alone, for we trace it in dogs and cats whom we know fairly well, and doubtless some similar point of honor sways the elephant, the oyster, and the louse, of whom we know so little:—But in man, at least, it sways with so complete an empire that merely selfish things come second, even with the selfish: that appetites are starved, fears are conquered, pains supported; that almost the dullest shrinks from the reproof of a glance, although it were a child's; and all but the most cowardly stand amid the risks of war; and the more noble, having strongly conceived an act as due to their ideal, affront and embrace death. Strange enough if, with their singular origin and perverted practice, they think they are to be rewarded in some future life: stranger still, if they are persuaded of the contrary, and think this blow, which they solicit, will strike them senseless for eternity. I shall be reminded what a tragedy of misconception and misconduct man at large presents: of organized injustice, cowardly violence, and treacherous crime; and of the damning imperfections of the best. They cannot be too darkly drawn. Man is indeed marked for failure in his efforts to do right. But where the best consistently miscarry, how tenfold more remarkable that all should continue to strive; and surely we should find it both touching and inspiriting, that in a field from which success is banished, our race should not cease to labor.

7   If the first view of this creature, stalking in his rotatory isle, be a thing to shake the courage of the stoutest, on this nearer sight, he startles us with an admiring wonder. It matters not where we look, under what climate we observe him, in what stage of society, in what depth of ignorance, burthened with what erroneous morality; by camp fires in Assiniboia, the snow powdering his shoulders, the wind plucking his blanket, as he sits passing ceremonial calumet and uttering his grave opinions like a Roman senator; in ships at sea, a man inured to hardship and vile pleasures, his brightest hope of a fiddle in a tavern and a bedizened trull who sells herself to rob him, and he for all that simple, innocent, cheerful, kindly like a child, constant to toil, brave to drown, for others; in the slums of cities, moving among indifferent millions to mechanical employments, without hope of change in the future, with scarce a pleasure in the present, and yet true to his virtues, honest up to his lights, kind to his neighbors, tempted perhaps in vain by the bright gin-palace, perhaps long-suffering with the drunken wife that ruins him; in India (a woman this time) kneeling with broken cries and streaming tears, as she drowns her child in the sacred river; in the brothel, the discard of society, living mainly on strong drink, fed with affronts, a fool, a thief, the comrade of thieves, and even here keeping the point of honor and the touch of pity, often repaying the world's scorn with service, often standing firm upon a scruple, and at a certain cost, rejecting riches:— everywhere some virtue cherished or affected, everywhere some decency of thought and carriage, everywhere the ensign of man's ineffectual goodness:—ah! if I could show you this! if I could show you these men and women, all the world over, in every stage of history, under every abuse of error, under every circumstance of failure, without hope, without help, without thanks, still obscurely fighting the lost fight of virtue, still clinging in the brothel or on the scaffold, to some rag of honor, the poor jewel of their souls! They may seek to escape, and yet they cannot; it is not alone their privilege and glory, but their doom; they are condemned to some nobility; all their lives long, the desire of good is at their heels, the implacable hunter.

8   Of all earth's meteors, here at least is the most strange and consoling: That this ennobled lemur, this hair-crowned bubble of the dust, this inheritor of a few years and sorrows, should yet deny himself his rare delights, and add to his frequent pains, and live for an ideal, however misconceived. Nor can we stop with man. A new doctrine, received with screams a little while ago by canting moralists, and still not properly worked into the body of our thoughts, lights us a step farther into the heart of this rough but noble universe. For nowadays the pride of man denies in vain his kinship with the original dust. He stands no longer like a thing apart. Close at his heels we see the dog, prince of another genus: and in him too, we see dumbly testified the same cultus of an un-attainable ideal, the same constancy in failure. Does it stop with the dog? We look at our feet where the ground is blackened with the swarming ant: a creature so small, so far from us in the hier-archy of brutes, that we can scarce trace and scarce comprehend his doings; and here also, in his ordered polities and rigorous jus-tice, we see confessed the law of duty and the fact of individual sin. Does it stop, then, with the ant? Rather this desire of well-doing and this doom of frailty run through all the grades of life: rather is this earth, from the frosty top of Everest to the next margin of the internal fire, one stage of ineffectual virtues and one temple of pious tears and perseverance. The whole creation groaneth and travaileth together. It is the common and the god-like law of life. The browsers, the biters, the barkers, the hairy coats of field and forest, the squirrel in the oak, the thousand-footed creeper in the dust, as they share with us the gift of life, share with us the love of an ideal: strive like us—like us are tempted to grow weary of the struggle—to do well; like us receive at times unmerited re-freshment, visitings of support, returns of courage; and are con-demned like us to be crucified between that double law of the members and the will. Are they like us, I wonder, in the timid hope of some reward, some sugar with the drug? do they, too, stand aghast at unrewarded virtues, and the prosperity of such as, in our blindness we call wicked? It may be, and yet God knows what they should look for. Even while they look, even while they repent, the foot of men treads them by thousands in the dust, the yelping hounds burst upon their trail, the bullet speeds, the knives are heating in the den of the vivisectionist; or the dew falls, and the generation of a day is blotted out. For these are creatures, com-

pared with whom our weakness is strength, our ignorance wisdom, our brief span eternity.

9   And as we dwell, we living things, in our isle of terror and under the imminent hand of death, God forbid it should be man the erected, the reasoner, the wise in his own eyes—God forbid it should be man that wearies in well-doing, that despairs of unrewarded effort, or utters the language of complaint. Let it be enough for faith, that the whole creation groans in mortal frailty, strives with unconquerable constancy: surely not all in vain.

· SUGGESTIONS ·

Obviously there is a great deal more here than description. This essay appeared in 1892 at a time when the Darwinian theory and other findings and discourses apparently inimical to traditional religious belief were still fresh enough to arouse anxiety, distrust, and even fear. Part of what Stevenson sets out to do here is to accomplish a reconciliation of the evolutionary views of some scientists and the traditional religious attitudes and beliefs of laymen. To do so, he deliberately accepts the scientists' description of the evolutionary life process, and then argues that through it all there is still that principle that exalts man. Thus his descriptions of man and of other physical phenomena are presented in terms of evolution, which makes the descriptions themselves seem ugly, distasteful, even repugnant, because he carefully avoids customary descriptions and focuses instead on human life simply as physical phenomena. Doing this, he is then able to make an effective contrast when in the latter part of the essay he reasserts the principle of faith and hope in this teeming process. Show (1) how Stevenson in his description abandons the customary description of man and substitutes for it description of physical facts, and (2) how, doing this, he achieves the dominant impression of dank, teeming life, which establishes the important contrast to his principle of faith.

Point of View and Consistency

While no one wants to be guilty of foolish and unbending consistency, a degree of stability is necessary for effective description. This is usually achieved when an author takes a position relative to the thing he is describing and describes his subject as it can be seen and known from the point of view that position affords. Accepting the angle of vision he has set for himself, the author can limit his work and describe his subject in terms and tones consistent with his viewpoint. Maintaining his point of view is one way the writer has of finding a community of vision and interest with his reader, for the reader is able to see that the writer is a person with a view, and he is enabled to know both person and view. A consistent point of view, incidentally, also provides the writer a means of natural transition, as all parts of his work cohere in the viewpoint from which they are seen.

The point of view a writer takes is subject to some restrictions. If physical, the point of view should be not only consistent but also natural. It is only in special circumstances where special effects are desired that a writer can expect good description to result from an unnatural physical viewpoint. If mental, the point of view should enable the author to exploit moods and associations and to subordinate physical impressions. Disregarding these restrictions results frequently in the failures common to beginning writers of description: adoption and misuse of an unnatural, stilted point of view; violation of the adopted point of view; or underestimation of the point of view, usually revealed in the writer's failure to exploit the possibilities given him by his viewpoint.

From HUCKLEBERRY FINN [1884]

Mark Twain

1   Two or three days and nights went by; I reckon I might say they swum by, they slid along so quiet and smooth and lovely. Here is the way we put in the time. It was a monstrous big river down there—sometimes a mile and a half wide; we run nights and laid up and hid daytimes; soon as night was gone we stopped navigating and tied up—nearly always in the dead water under a towhead; and then cut young cottonwoods and willows and hid the raft with them. Then we set out the lines. Next we slid into the river and had a swim, so as to freshen up and cool off; then we

set down on the sandy bottom where the water was about knee-
deep and watched the daylight come. Not a sound anywheres—
perfectly still—just like the whole world was asleep, only sometimes
the bullfrogs a-cluttering, maybe. The first thing to see, looking
away over the water, was a kind of dull line—that was the woods
on t'other side; you couldn't make nothing else out; then a pale
place in the sky; then more paleness spreading around; then the
river softened up away off, and warn't black any more, but gray;
you could see little dark spots drifting along ever so far away—
trading-scows, and such things; and long black streaks—rafts; sometimes you could hear a sweep screaking; or jumbled-up voices, it
was so still, and sounds come so far; and by and by you could see
a streak on the water which you know by the look of the streak
that there's a snag there in a swift current which breaks on it and
makes that streak look that way; and you see the mist curl up off of
the water, and the east reddens up, and the river, and you make
out a log cabin in the edge of the woods, away on the bank on
t'other side of the river, being a wood-yard, likely, and piled by
them cheats so you can throw a dog through it anywheres; then
the nice breeze springs up, and comes fanning you from over
there, so cool and fresh and sweet to smell on account of the woods
and the flowers; but sometimes not that way, because they've left
dead fish laying around, gars and such, and they do get pretty rank;
and next you've got the full day, and everything smiling in the sun,
and the song-birds just going it!

2   A little smoke couldn't be noticed now, so we would take
some fish off of the lines and cook up a hot breakfast. And afterwards we would watch the lonesomeness of the river, and kind of
lazy along and by and by lazy off to sleep. Wake up by and by, and
look to see what done it and maybe see a steamboat coughing
along up-stream, so far off towards the other side you couldn't tell
nothing about her only whether she was a stern-wheel or side-
wheel; then for about an hour there wouldn't be nothing to hear
nor nothing to see—just solid lonesomeness. Next you'd see a raft
sliding by, away off yonder, and maybe a galoot on it chopping, because they're most always doing it on a raft; you'd see the ax
flash and come down—you don't hear nothing; you see the ax go up
again, and by the time it's above the man's head then you hear the
k'chunk!—it had took all that time to come over the water. So we

would put in the day, lazying around, listening to the stillness.
Once there was a thick fog and the rafts and things that went by
was beating tin pans so the steamboats wouldn't run over them.
A scow or a raft went by so close we could hear them talking
and cussing and laughing—heard them plain; but we couldn't see
no sign of them; it made you feel crawly; it was like spirits carrying
on that way in the air. Jim said he believed it was spirits; but I
says:

3   "No; spirits wouldn't say, 'Dern the dern fog.'"

4   Soon as it was night out we shoved; when we got her out
to about the middle we let her alone and let her float wherever
the current wanted her to; then we lit the pipes and dangled our
legs in the water, and talked about all kind of things—we was
always naked, day and night, whenever the mosquitoes would let
us—the new clothes Buck's folks made for me was too good to be
comfortable and besides I didn't go much on clothes, nohow.

5   Sometimes we'd have that whole river all to ourselves for
the longest time. Yonder was the banks and the islands, across the
water; and maybe a spark—which was a candle in a cabin window;
and sometimes on the water you could see a spark or two—on a
raft or a scow, you know; and maybe you could hear a fiddle or a
song coming over from one of them crafts. It's lovely to live on a
raft. We had the sky up there, all speckled with stars, and we
used to lay on our backs and look up at them and discuss about
whether they was made or only just happened. Jim he allowed they
was made but I allowed they happened; I judged it would have
took too long to *make* so many. Jim said the moon could 'a' *laid*
them; well, that looked kind of reasonable, so I didn't say nothing
against it, because I've seen a frog lay most as many, so of course
it could be done. We used to watch the stars that fell, too, and see
them streak down. Jim allowed they'd got spoiled and was hove out
of the nest.

6   Once or twice of a night we would see a steamboat slipping
along in the dark, and now and then she would belch a whole world
of sparks up out of her chimbleys, and they would rain down in the
river and look awful pretty; then she would turn a corner and her
lights would wink out and her powwow shut off and leave the river
still again; and by and by her waves would get to us a long time
after she was gone, and joggle the raft a bit, and after that you

wouldn't hear nothing for you couldn't tell how long, except maybe frogs and something.

7 After midnight the people on shore went to bed, and then for two or three hours the shores was black—no more sparks in the cabin windows. These sparks was our clock—the first one that showed again meant morning was coming, so we hunted a place to hide and tie up right away.

• COMMENTARY •

Huck Finn's description of a typical day on the river, one of the finest pieces of description in our language, is effective partly because its author adopted a point of view appropriate to the context—that of the boy—and because the author accepted the limitations of that point of view.

The description is controlled by the boy's vision; we need not expect highly figurative or elaborate images: "It's lovely to live on a raft. We had the sky up there, all speckled with stars, and we used to lay on our backs and look up at them and discuss about whether they was made or only just happened." More obviously, the description is controlled by the physical position of the boy, the distances he sees, and the time that passes. It is a typical day, not one particular day, and time and space are all around from all their days. They would eat breakfast, he says "And afterwards we would watch the lonesomeness of the river, and kind of lazy along and by and by lazy off to sleep." Much of what he sees he sees at a distance; they would, he says, "maybe see a steamboat coughing along up-stream, so far off towards the other side you couldn't tell nothing about her only whether she was a stern-wheel or side-wheel." Distances on the river limit the detail he can note, but interestingly also provide Twain with details especially valuable because so often overlooked: "Next you'd see a raft sliding by, away off yonder, and maybe a galoot on it chopping, because they're most always doing it on a raft; you'd see the ax flash and come down—you don't hear nothing; you see that ax go up again, and by the time it's above the man's head then you hear the *k'chunk!*—it had took all that time to come over the water."

Twain's effective exploitation of the very limitations of the point of view can be seen best in the description of the sunrise. Huck's position and the distances involved limit what can be said. "The first thing to see," Huck says, "looking away over the water, was a kind of dull line— that was the woods on t'other side; you couldn't make nothing else out." Later, he speaks of the "little dark spots drifting along ever so far away," which he knows to be scows and such things. Not only his physical limitation, but his age and character control and limit the description, as the account of the actual dawn reveals. First, there is "a pale place in the sky; then more paleness spreading around; then the river softened up away off, and warn't black any more, but gray." A little later, the mist curls up off the water, and "the east reddens up," and, still later, "you've got the full day, and everything smiling in the sun, and the song-birds just going it!"

Twain's acceptance and exploitation of the very limitations of his point of view is part of what makes this good description. Given the experience entirely in terms of Huckleberry Finn, we know that it is a real experience, both shaping and shaped by the boy's perception. This description is ample evidence that descriptive writing need not be what freshmen sometimes call "flowery." What it must be is precise; and Huckleberry Finn tells precisely what he sees.

From THE CUSTOM HOUSE in THE SCARLET LETTER [1850]

Nathaniel Hawthorne

1 Here, with a view from its front windows adown this not very enlivening prospect, and thence across the harbor, stands a spacious edifice of brick. From the loftiest point of its roof, during precisely three and a half hours of each forenoon, floats or droops, in breeze or calm, the banner of the republic; but with the thirteen stripes turned vertically, instead of horizontally, and thus indicating that a civil, and not a military post of Uncle Sam's government is here established. Its front is ornamented with a portico of half a dozen wooden pillars, supporting a balcony, beneath which a flight of wide granite steps descends towards the street. Over the entrance hovers an enormous specimen of the American eagle, with outspread wings, a shield before her breast,

and if I recollect aright, a bunch of intermingled thunderbolts and barbed arrows in each claw. With the customary infirmity of temper that characterizes this unhappy fowl, she appears, by the fierceness of her beak and eye, and the general truculency of her attitude, to threaten mischief to the inoffensive community; and especially to warn all citizens, careful of their safety, against intruding on the premises which she overshadows with her wings. Nevertheless, vixenly as she looks, many people are seeking, at this very moment, to shelter themselves under the wing of the federal eagle; imagining, I presume, that her bosom has all the softness and snugness of an eider-down pillow. But she has no great tenderness, even in her best of moods, and sooner or later,—oftener soon than late,—is apt to fling off her nestlings, with a scratch of her claw, a dab of her beak, or a rankling wound from her barbed arrows.

2   The pavement round about the above-described edifice— which we may as well name at once the Custom House of the port —has grass enough growing in its chinks to show that it has not, of late days, been worn by any multitudinous resort of business. In some months of the year, however, there often chances a forenoon when affairs move onward with a livelier tread. Such occasions might remind the elderly citizen of that period before the last war with England, when Salem was a port by itself; not scorned, as she is now, by her own merchants and ship-owners, who permit her wharves to crumble to ruin, while their adventures go to swell, needlessly and imperceptibly, the mighty flood of commerce at New York or Boston.

• **SUGGESTIONS** •

The point of view adopted by Hawthorne here is a relatively simple physical point of view. The exterior of the Custom House is described first, apparently from a fixed position in front. Then the speaker moves inside to reveal what is there. The description is straightforward, the speaker appearing detached so that shifting moods do not appreciably effect what he describes. Compile a list of the words, phrases, and sentences that identify the point of view. Remember that compiling such a list may seem mechanical, but it is a sure way to be certain that you have understood the author's viewpoint, and it provides the kind of evidence you may need in analyses you will do later.

From THE COMPLEAT ANGLER [1653]

Sir Izaak Walton

1   Look, under that broad beech-tree I sat down, when I was last this way a-fishing, and the birds in the adjoining grove seemed to have a friendly contention with an echo, whose dead voice seemed to live in a hollow tree, near to the brow of that primrose hill; there I sat viewing the silver streams glide silently towards their centre, the tempestuous sea; yet sometimes opposed by rugged roots, and pebble-stones, which broke their waves, and turned them into foam: and sometimes I beguiled time by viewing the harmless lambs, some leaping securely in the cool shade, whilst others sported themselves in the cheerful sun; and saw others craving comfort from the swollen udders of their bleating dams. As I thus sat, these and other sights had so fully possessed my soul with content, that I thought, as the poet has happily expressed it,

> I was for that time lifted above earth,
> And possessed joys not promised in my birth.

2   As I left this place, and entered into the next field, a second pleasure entertained me; 'twas a handsome Milkmaid that had not yet attained so much age and wisdom as to load her mind with any fears of many things that will never be, as too many men too often do; but she cast away all care, and sung like a nightingale[. . . .]

• **SUGGESTIONS** •

The point of view in this brief passage is once again physical. But to the physical angle of vision has been added something else: Walton is not describing what he presently sees; he is describing what he *once* saw from that position. The passage of time then makes the physical point of view more complex, for added is the gentle mood of reminiscence. In a short discussion, show first what identifies the physical point of view; then explain how Walton adds to that viewpoint a layer of time and reminiscence.

Effective Observation and Diction

Dominant impressions and points of view notwithstanding, the *sine qua non* of descriptive writing is sharp, clear observation recorded in exact diction. None of us is guiltless; instead of precise images we offer handy labels, stereotyped pictures, vagaries, or precious purple prose. Readers will never respond to these methods, but invariably to the voice of a genuine individual using sure words to create clear images. The detail, the image taken for granted and so never seen, the sight seen and the sound heard but never considered consciously—of such things is good descriptive writing made.

From the AUTOBIOGRAPHY*

Mark Twain

1   As I have said, I spent some part of every year at the farm until I was twelve or thirteen years old. The life which I led there with my cousins was full of charm and so is the memory of it yet. I can call back the solemn twilight and mystery of the deep woods, the earthy smells, the faint odors of the wild flowers, the sheen of rain-washed foliage, the rattling clatter of drops when the wind shook the trees, the far-off hammering of woodpeckers and the muffled drumming of woodpheasants in the remoteness of the forest, the snapshot glimpses of disturbed wild creatures scurrying through the grass—I can call it all back and make it as real as it ever was, and as blessed. I can call back the prairie, and its loneliness and peace, and a vast hawk hanging motionless in the sky with his wings spread wide and the blue of the vault showing through the fringe of their end-feathers. I can see the woods in their autumn dress, the oaks purple, the hickories washed with gold, the maples and the sumachs luminous with crimson fires, and I can hear the rustle made by the fallen leaves as we plowed

* From *Mark Twain's Autobiography*, pp. 109–115. Copyright, 1924, by Clara Gabrilowitsch, renewed 1952 by Clara Clemens Samossoud. Reprinted with permission of Harper & Row, Publishers, Inc.

through them. I can see the blue clusters of wild grapes hanging amongst the foliage of the saplings, and I remember the taste of them and the smell. I know how the wild blackberries looked and how they tasted; and the same with the pawpaws, the hazelnuts, and the persimmons; and I can feel the thumping rain upon my head of hickory-nuts and walnuts when we were out in the frosty dawn to scramble for them with the pigs, and the gusts of wind loosed them and sent them down. I know the stain of walnut hulls and how little it minds soap and water, also what grudged experience it had of either of them. I know the taste of maple sap and when to gather it, and how to arrange the troughs and the delivery tubes, and how to boil down the juice, and how to hook the sugar after it is made; also how much better hooked sugar tastes than any that is honestly come by, let bigots say what they will.

2   I know how a prize watermelon looks when it is sunning its fat rotundity among pumpkin vines and "simblins"; I know how to tell when it is ripe without "plugging" it. I know how inviting it looks when it is cooling itself in a tub of water under the bed, waiting; I know how it looks when it lies on the table in the sheltered great floor-space between house and kitchen, and the children gathered for the sacrifice and their mouths watering. I know the crackling sound it makes when the carving knife enters its end and I can see the split fly along in front of the blade as the knife cleaves its way to the other end; I can see its halves fall apart and display the rich red meat and the black seeds, and the heart standing up, a luxury fit for the elect. I know how a boy looks behind a yard-long slice of that melon and I know how he feels, for I have been there. I know the taste of the watermelon which has been honestly come by and I know the taste of the watermelon which has been acquired by art. Both taste good but the experienced know which tastes best.

3   I know the look of green apples and peaches and pears on the trees, and I know how entertaining they are when they are inside of a person. I know how ripe ones look when they are piled in pyramids under the trees and how pretty they are and how vivid their colors. I know how a frozen apple looks in a barrel down cellar in the wintertime, and how hard it is to bite and how the frost makes the teeth ache, and yet how good it is notwithstanding. I know the disposition of elderly people to select the specked apples for the children and I once knew ways to beat the game.

I know the look of an apple that is roasting and sizzling on a hearth on a winter's evening, and I know the comfort that comes of eating it hot, along with some sugar and a drench of cream. I know the delicate art and mystery of so cracking hickory-nuts and walnuts on a flatiron with a hammer that the kernels will be delivered whole, and I know how the nuts, taken in conjunction with winter apples, cider, and doughnuts, make old people's tales and old jokes sound fresh and crisp and enchanting and juggle an evening away before you know what went with the time. I know the look of Uncle Dan'l's kitchen as it was on privileged nights when I was a child, and I can see the white and black children grouped on the hearth, with the firelight playing on their faces and the shadows flickering upon the walls clear back toward the cavernous gloom of the rear, and I can hear Uncle Dan'l telling the immortal tales which Uncle Remus Harris was to gather into his book and charm the world with by and by. And I can feel again the creepy joy which quivered through me when the time for the ghost story was reached—and the sense of regret too which came over me, for it was always the last story of the evening and there was nothing between it and the unwelcome bed.

4   I can remember the bare wooden stairway in my uncle's house and the turn to the left above the landing, and the rafters and the slanting roof over my bed, and the squares of moonlight on the floor and the white cold world of snow outside, seen through the curtainless window. I can remember the howling of the wind and the quaking of the house on stormy nights and how snug and cozy one felt under the blankets, listening; and how the powdery snow used to sift in around the sashes and lie in little ridges on the floor, and make the place look chilly in the morning and curb the wild desire to get up—in case there was any. I can remember how very dark that room was in the dark of the moon, and how packed it was with ghostly stillness when one woke up by accident away in the night, and forgotten sins came flocking out of the secret chambers of the memory and wanted a hearing; and how ill-chosen the time seemed for this kind of business and how dismal was the hoo-hooing of the owl and the wailing of the wolf, sent mourning by on the night wind.

5   I remember the raging of the rain on that roof, summer nights, and how pleasant it was to lie and listen to it and enjoy the white splendor of the lightning and the majestic booming and

crashing of the thunder. It was a very satisfactory room, and there was a lightning rod which was reachable from the window, an adorable and skittish thing to climb up and down, summer nights when there were duties on hand of a sort to make privacy desirable.

6   I remember the 'coon and 'possum hunts, nights, with the negroes, and the long marches through the black gloom of the woods and the excitement which fired everybody when the distant bay of an experienced dog announced that the game was treed; then the wild scramblings and stumblings through briers and bushes and over roots to get to the spot; then the lighting of a fire and the felling of the tree, the joyful frenzy of the dogs and the negroes, and the weird picture it all made in the red glare—I remember it all well, and the delight that everyone got out of it, except the 'coon.

7   I remember the pigeon seasons, when the birds would come in millions and cover the trees and by their weight break down the branches. They were clubbed to death with sticks; guns were not necessary and were not used. I remember the squirrel hunts and prairie-chicken hunts and wild-turkey hunts, and all that; and how we turned out, mornings, while it was still dark to go on these expeditions, and how chilly and dismal it was and how often I regretted that I was well enough to go. A toot on a tin horn brought twice as many dogs as were needed, and in their happiness they raced and scampered about and knocked small people down and made no end of unnecessary noise. At the word, they vanished away toward the woods and we drifted silently after them in the melancholy gloom. But presently the gray dawn stole over the world, the birds piped up, then the sun rose and poured light and comfort all around, everything was fresh and dewy and fragrant, and life was a boon again. After three hours of tramping we arrived back wholesomely tired, overladen with game, very hungry, and just in time for breakfast.

• COMMENTARY •

One reason that descriptive writing seems difficult is that all too often we don't know very much for sure. To write good description, a writer has to know his subject, and he has to know how to describe it.

Twain knows things for sure. He has seen things well enough to possess them, and he has seen things well enough to see in them the little identifying details that characterize them for us who so often take them for granted. The little refrain that runs through this selection, "I can call it all back," "I can remember," enables us to know that this is experience felt and seen and known familiarly. And the details make it all familiar to us. Twain reminds us, for example, how the blue of the sky can be seen through the fringe of the bird's wing end-feathers. He remembers for us how a watermelon was kept: "I know how inviting it looks when it is cooling itself in a tub of water under the bed, waiting." He records the isolated fact that exactly pictures the splitting of a watermelon: "I know how it looks when it lies on the table in the sheltered great floor-space between house and kitchen, and the children gathered for the sacrifice and their mouths watering. I know the crackling sound it makes when the carving knife enters its end and I can see the split fly along in front of the blade as the knife cleaves its way to the other end." Other sensory details pile up to picture the scenes of his experience. "I know how a frozen apple looks in a barrel down cellar in the wintertime," he says, "and how hard it is to bite and how the frost makes the teeth ache, and yet how good it is notwithstanding." Or later, "I can remember the howling of the wind and the quaking of the house on stormy nights, and how snug and cozy one felt under the blankets, listening; and how the powdery snow used to sift in around the sashes and lie in little ridges on the floor."

Knowing things well, Twain can describe them. The simple catalogues of names, the exactly identified flora and fauna of his experience, make his description vivid. "I can see the woods in their autumn dress," he says, "the oaks purple, the hickories washed with gold, the maples and the sumachs luminous with crimson fires." And again, "I know how the wild blackberries looked and how they tasted; and the same with the pawpaws, the hazelnuts, and the persimmons; and I can feel the thumping rain upon my head of hickory-nuts and walnuts when we were out in the frosty dawn to scramble for them with the pigs."

Twain's work here is very nearly all the evidence needed to demonstrate that sureness of observation and exactness of diction are the keys to effective description. A writer wants his audience to see what he has seen in the way he has seen it. Only by knowing it and naming it precisely can he accomplish this.

From LOOK HOMEWARD, ANGEL*

Thomas Wolfe

1   Spring was full of cool dewy mornings, spurting winds, and storms of intoxicating blossoms, and in this enchantment Eugene first felt the mixed lonely ache and promise of the seasons.

2   In the morning they rose in a house pungent with breakfast cookery, and they sat at a smoking table loaded with brains and eggs, ham, hot biscuit, fried apples seething in their gummed syrups, honey, golden butter, fried steak, scalding coffee. Or there were stacked batter-cakes, rum-colored molasses, fragrant brown sausages, a bowl of wet cherries, plums, fat juicy bacon, jam. At the mid-day meal, they ate heavily: a huge hot roast of beef, fat buttered lima-beans, tender corn smoking on the cob, thick red slabs of sliced tomatoes, rough savory spinach, hot yellow cornbread, flaky biscuits, a deep-dish peach and apple cobbler spiced with cinnamon, tender cabbage, deep glass dishes piled with preserved fruits—cherries, pears, peaches. At night they might eat fried steak, hot squares of grits fried in egg and butter, pork-chops, fish, young fried chicken.

3   For the Thanksgiving and Christmas feasts four heavy turkeys were bought and fattened for weeks: Eugene fed them with cans of shelled corn several times a day, but he could not bear to be present at their executions, because by that time their cheerful excited gobbles made echoes in his heart. Eliza baked for weeks in advance: the whole energy of the family focussed upon the great ritual of the feast. A day or two before, the auxiliary dainties arrived in piled grocer's boxes—the magic of strange foods and fruits was added to familiar fare: there were glossed sticky dates, cold rich figs, cramped belly to belly in small boxes, dusty raisins, mixed nuts—the almond, pecan, the meaty nigger-toe, the walnut, sacks of assorted candies, piles of yellow Florida oranges, tangerines, sharp, acrid, nostalgic odors.

* From *Look Homeward, Angel*, pp. 70, 71, 149, by Thomas Wolfe. Used by permission of Charles Scribner's Sons. Copyright, 1929, Charles Scribner's Sons; renewal copyright ©, 1957, Edward C. Ashwell and Fred W. Wolfe.

4   Seated before a roast or a fowl, Gant began a heavy clangor on his steel and carving knife, distributing thereafter Gargantuan portions to each plate. Eugene feasted from a high chair by his father's side, filled his distending belly until it was drumtight, and was permitted to stop eating by his watchful sire only when his stomach was impregnable to the heavy prod of Gant's big finger.

5   "There's a soft place there," he would roar, and he would cover the scoured plate of his infant son with another heavy slab of beef. That their machinery withstood this hammer-handed treatment was a tribute to their vitality and Eliza's cookery.

~~~~~~

6   Of mornings he stayed at Gant's with Helen, playing ball with Buster Isaacs, a cousin of Max, a plump jolly little boy who lived next door; summoned later by the rich incense of Helen's boiling fudge. She sent him to the little Jewish grocery down the street for the sour relishes she liked so well: tabled in mid-morning they ate sour pickles, heavy slabs of ripe tomatoes, coated with thick mayonnaise, amber percolated coffee, fig-newtons and lady-fingers, hot pungent fudge pebbled with walnuts and coated fragrantly with butter, sandwiches of tender bacon and cucumber, iced belchy soft-drinks.

• SUGGESTIONS •

In both of these selections, Wolfe relies on the naming of things for his descriptive effect. Remember that the best description is likely to rely on nouns and verbs for its effect, for these words best name and identify. Since men share many experiences, the writer can often by naming his experience precisely evoke in the mind of his reader the sensory catalogue-description.

From GOODBYE TO A RIVER*

John Graves

1   There was an island, long and slim, built up of the variegated Brazos chert gravel, which, when wet and shining, looks like
the jewels in a storybook treasure chest. Its top was padded with
white sand and bordered by big willows and small cottonwoods.
Toward the blunt upper end, where spring's drought-breaking
floods had worked to most effect, lay a bare-swept sandy plain,
and the few trees along the shoreline there were bent downstream
at steep angles. Against stubs and stumps down the length of the
island the same force had laid up tangled jams of driftwood—
ash and cedar, elm and oak, good fuel. Here and there where silt
had accumulated, Bermuda grass or weeds bristled in patches.

2   Because I liked the look of it, I stopped there in the
middle of a quiet bright afternoon and made a solid camp on flat
gravel under willows, eight feet above the water but only a few
nearly vertical steps from the canoe. I was tired and my gear
needed tending, and it looked like the kind of place I'd been
waiting for to spend a couple of nights and to loaf through a little
of what the abstractly alliterative military schedules used to call
"matériel maintenance." Islands are special, anyhow, as children
know with a leaping instinct, and when they lie in public domain
you can have a fine sense of temporary ownership about them
that's hard to get on shores, inside or outside of fences.

3   By the time I'd finished setting up and hauling my chattels
from the canoe—all of them, since they all needed cleaning or fixing—it was nearly evening. The stronger of the channels flanking
the island ran on the side where I was camped; I walked up the
narrow beach and put out a catfish line just below where the water

* Reprinted from *Goodbye to a River* by John Graves by permission of
Alfred A. Knopf, Inc. and Macmillan & Co., Ltd. Copyright ©, 1959, by
Curtis Publishing Co. Copyright ©, 1960, by John Graves.

dropped out of a rapids, tying a rock to the line's end and throwing it straight out so that when the line came taut the rock dropped
gurgling and anchored the line in a long bow across the head of
the deep run, back to a willow stub beside me. Trotlines from
shore to shore get you more fish and bigger ones, but they're also
more labor. After I'd finished with the line I worked along the
beach, spin-casting bootlessly for bass. Four Canada geese came
diagonally over the river, low, calling, and in a moment I heard
a clamor at the head of the island, shielded from me by the
island's duned fringe and by willows. I climbed up through them
to look. At least 200 more honkers took off screaming from the
sand bar at the upper end of the bare plain. The passenger ran
barking after them. Calling him back, I squatted beside a drift
pile, and in the rose half-light of dusk watched through the field
glass as they came wheeling in again, timid but liking the place
as I had liked it, and settled by tens and twenties at the bar and
in the shallows above it where the two channels split.

4   Nine skeptics, maybe the ones that had seen me at first and
raised the alarm, circled complaining for a time before they flew
on elsewhere. Black against water that held the west's reflected
red, the others stalked about till their alertness had softened, then
began to drink and cavort, lunging at one another, leaping into the
air with their wings spread and circling two by two in a kind of
dance.

5   Old John Magnificence was with me:

> *What call'st thou solitude, is not the Earth*
> *With various living creatures, and the Aire*
> *Replenisht, and all these at thy command*
> *To come and play before thee?* . . .

6   He was. I used to be suspicious of the kind of writing
where characters are smitten by correct quotations at appropriate
moments. I still am, but not as much. Things do pop out clearly
in your head, alone, when the upper layers of your mind are un-
misted by much talk with other men. Odd bits and scraps and
thoughts and phrases from all your life and all your reading keep
boiling up to view like grains of rice in a pot on the fire. Sometimes they even make sense . . .

7   I thought of the shotgun at my camp a hundred yards
below, but it would have been useless if I'd had it; they were a
long way from any cover. And for that matter there was about

them something of the feel that the bald eagle had had for me in the mountain country. I'd been a hunter most of my life, except for two or three years after the war. Young, I'd made two-hour crawls on my belly through standing swamp water for the mere hope of a shot at a goose, nearly always frustrated. Just now, though, it seemed to matter little that these were safe out of range. Watching the red-and-black shadow show of their awkward powerful play was enough, and listening to their occasional arrogant horn shouts. I squatted there watching until nearly dark, then backed down quietly to the beach and went to camp.

8   Supper was a young squirrel who had nevertheless achieved an elder's stringiness, roasted in foil on the embers, and a potato baked in the same way. I'd been going lazy on the cooking lately, mostly because I had little appetite, and that little most generally for things I'd have disliked in town—bouillon, or coffee thickly sweet with honey, or the stewed mixed fruit that made my breakfasts. From such sparse eating and from exercise I'd lost weight—maybe twelve or fifteen pounds since Possum Kingdom, to judge from the slack in my waistband. I ate the potato and chewed a little on the squirrel and gave the rest of it to the pup.

9   Hearing the geese honk still from time to time, I knew it would have been easy enough, on that moonless night, to ease up the defiladed beach near them and sneak across the sand on my stomach for a sniping shot. All it would take was patience. But I was years past being tempted by that kind of dirtiness; the contradictory set of rules that one works out for killing, if he keeps on killing past a certain age, usually makes an unreasonable distinction between ways that are honorable and ways that aren't, and for me night pot shots weren't . . . And I didn't think I needed anything as big as a goose.

10   Someone else's rules were less strict, or maybe his need was greater; when I'd put a couple of heavy chunks of elm on the fire and sat watching them, sniffing the faintly urinal sharpness of their burning, two rapid shots sounded far off down the river and a minute later geese were calling confusedly in the sky. Stacked alongside my own abstention it angered me a little, but on the other hand it was none of my right business.

11   From brief yards away, in a cottonwood, a barred owl cut loose with flourishes: *Who, who, whoo, whoo, whah, whah, hah,* HAH, HAH, WHO ALL!

12   Then, an afterthought, he said: YOU ALL!

13   Certain it meant specifically him, the passenger barked
back once almost under his breath, growled a little with an angry
ridge of short hair dark along his spine, and sought my lap.

~~~~~~~~~

14   Elm stinks, wherefore literal farmers give it a grosser
name, but it makes fine lasting coals. That morning I was up before dawn to blow away the ashes from the orange-velvet embers
underneath, and to build more fire on them with twigs and leaves
and brittle sticks of dead cottonwood. I huddled over it in the
cold, still, graying darkness and watched coffee water seethe at the
edges of a little charred pot licked by flame, and heard the horned
owl stop that deceptively gentle five-noted comment he casts on
the night. The geese at the island's head began to talk among
themselves, then to call as they rose to go to pastures and peanut
fields, and night-flushed bobwhites started whistling *where-you?*
where-you? to one another somewhere above the steep dirt river
bank. Drinking coffee with honey in it and canned milk, smoking
a pipe that had the sweetness pipes only have in cold quiet air, I
felt good if a little scratchy-eyed, having gone to sleep the night
before struck with the romance of stars and firelight, with the flaps
open and only the blanket over me, to wake at two thirty chilled
through.

15   On top of the food box alligator-skin corrugations of frost
had formed, and with the first touch of the sun the willows began
to whisper as frozen leaves loosed their hold and fell side-slipping
down through the others that were still green. Titmice called, and
flickers and a redbird, and for a moment, on a twig four feet from
my face, a chittering kinglet jumped around alternately hiding
and flashing the scarlet of its crown. . . . I sat and listened and
watched while the world woke up, and drank three cups of the
syrupy coffee, better I thought than any I'd ever tasted, and
smoked two pipes.

16   You run a risk of thinking yourself an ascetic when you
enjoy, with that intensity, the austere facts of fire and coffee and
tobacco and the sound and feel of country places. You aren't,
though. In a way you're more of a sensualist than a fat man
washing down sauerbraten and dumplings with heavy beer while
a German band plays and a plump blonde kneads his thigh. . . .
You've shucked off the gross delights, and those you have left are

few, sharp, and strong. But they're sensory. Even Thoreau, if I remember right a passage or so on his cornbread, was guilty, though mainly he was a real ascetic.

17   Real ones shouldn't care. They ought to be able to live on pâté and sweet peaches and roast suckling pig or alternatively on cheese and garlic in a windmill or the scraps that housewives have thrown in begging bowls. Groceries and shelter should matter only as fuel and frame for life, and life as energy for thought or beyond-communion or (Old Man Goodnight has to fit somewhere, and a fraught executive or two I've known, and maybe Davis Birdstong hurling his bulldozer against the tough cedar brush in a torn shirt and denim pants, coughing yellow flu sputum while the December rain pelts him, not caring) for action.

18   But I hadn't set up as an ascetic, anyhow. I sat for a long time savoring the privilege of being there, and didn't overlay the taste of the coffee with any other food. A big red-brown butterfly sat spread on the cottonwood log my ax was stuck in, warming itself in the sun. I watched until it flew stiffly away, then got up and followed, for no good reason except that the time seemed to have come to stir and I wanted a closer look at the island than I'd gotten the evening before.

19   It was shaped like an attenuated teardrop or the cross section of an airplane's wing, maybe three quarters of a mile long and 100 yards or so wide at its upper, thicker end. Its foundation everywhere appeared to be a heavy deposit of the multicolored gravel, and its flat top except for a few high dunes of the padding sand was eight or ten feet above the present level of the river. All around, it dropped off steeply, in spots directly to the water, in others to beaches, and toward the pointed tail the willows and weeds stood rank. I rooted about there and found nothing but coon tracks and a few birds still sleepy and cold on their roosts, but, emerging among cockleburs above a beach by the other channel, scared four ducks off a quiet eddy. I'd left the gun in the tent; shots from here and there under the wide sky's bowl reminded me that busier hunters than I were finding game.

20   Let them. I considered that maybe in the evening I'd crouch under a bush at the island's upper end and put out sheets of notepaper on the off chance that more geese would come, and the off-off chance that if they did they'd feel brotherly toward notepaper. You can interest them sometimes in newspapers.

21   And maybe I wouldn't.

22   The shores on either side of the river from the island were dirt and steep, twenty feet high, surmounted by pecans and oaks with the bare sky of fields or pastures beyond. They seemed separate from the island; it was big enough, with a strong enough channel on either side, to seem to have a kind of being of its own distinct from that of the banks—a sand and willow and cottonwood and driftwood biome—though in dry times doubtless there would be only one channel and no island, but just a great bar spreading out below the right bank.

23   Jays, killdeers, wrens, cardinals, woodpeckers . . . With minute and amateurish interest, I found atop a scoop in the base of a big, drifted, scorched tree trunk five little piles of fox dung, a big owl's puke ball full of hair and rat skulls, and three fresher piles of what had to be coon droppings, brown and small, shaped like a dog's or a human's.

24   Why, intrigued ignorance asked, did wild things so often choose to stool on rocks, stumps, and other elevations?

25   Commonsense replied: Maybe for the view.

26   On the flat beach at the head of the island the night's geese had laid down a texture of crisscrossed toe-prints. Elsewhere, in dry sand, I found little pointed diggings an inch in diameter and four to five inches deep, much like those an armadillo makes in grassland but with no tracks beside them. A bird? A land-foraging crawfish? Another puzzle for my ignorance, underlined now by the clear note of the unknown sad-whistling bird from a willow a few steps from me. He wouldn't show himself, and when I eased closer said irascibly: *Heap, heap!* and fluttered out the other side. . . .

27   The trouble was, I *was* ignorant. Even in that country where I belonged, my ken of natural things didn't include a little bird that went *heap-heap* and

————

———— ———— ————, ———— ———— ————,

————

and a few moronic holes in the sand. Or a million other matters worth the kenning.

28   I grew up in a city near there—more or less a city, any-how, a kind of spreading imposition on the prairies—that was waked from a dozing cow-town background by a standard boom

after the First World War and is still, civic-souled friends tell me, bowling right along. It was a good enough place, not too big then, and a mile or so away from where I lived, along a few side streets and across a boulevard and a golf course, lay woods and pastures and a blessed river valley, where the stagnant Trinity writhed beneath big oaks. In retrospect, it seems we spent more time there than we did on pavements, though maybe it's merely that remembrance of that part is sharper. There were rabbits and squirrels to hunt, and doves and quail and armadillos and foxes and skunks. A few deer ran the woods, and one year, during a drouth to the west, big wolves. Now it's mostly subdivisions, and even then it lay fallow because it was someone's real-estate investment. The fact that caretakers were likely to converge on us blaspheming at the sound of a shot or a shout, scattering us to brush, only made the hunting and the fishing a bit saltier. I knew one fellow who kept a permanent camp there in a sumac thicket, with a log squat-down hut and a fireplace and all kinds of food and utensils hidden in tin-lined holes in the ground, and none of the caretakers ever found it. Probably they worried less than we thought; there weren't many of us.

29   I had the Brazos, too, and South Texas, where relatives lived, and my adults for the most part were good people who took me along on country expeditions when they could. In terms of the outdoors, I and the others like me weren't badly cheated as such cheatings go nowadays, but we were cheated nevertheless. We learned quite a lot, but not enough. Instead of learning to move into country, as I think underneath we wanted, we learned mostly how to move onto it in the old crass Anglo-Saxon way, in search of edible or sometimes just mortal quarry. We did a lot of killing, as kids will, and without ever being told that it was our flat duty, if duty exists, to know all there was to know about the creatures we killed.

30   Hunting and fishing are the old old entry points into nature for men, and not bad ones either, but as standardly practiced these days, for the climactic ejaculation of city tensions, they don't go very deep. They aren't thoughtful; they hold themselves too straitly to their purpose. Even for my quail-hunting uncles in South Texas, good men, good friends to me, all smaller birds of hedge and grass were "cheechees," vermin, confusers of dogs' noses. . . . And if, with kids' instinctive thrustingness, we picked

up a store of knowledge about small things that lived under logs
and how the oriole builds its nest, there was no one around to
consolidate it for us. Our knowledge, if considerable, remained
random.

31   This age, of course, is unlikely to start breeding people
who have the organic kinship to nature that the Comanches had,
or even someone like Mr. Charlie Goodnight. For them every
bush, every bird's cheep, every cloud bank had not only utilitarian
but mystical meaning; it was all an extension of their sensory systems, an antenna as rawly receptive as a snail's. Even if their natural
world still existed, which it doesn't, you'd have to snub the whole
world of present men to get into it that way.

32   Nor does it help to be born in the country. As often as
not these days, countrymen know as little as we others do about
those things. They come principally of the old hardheaded tradition that moved onto the country instead of into it. For every
Charles Goodnight there were several dozen Ezra Shermans, a
disproportion that has bred itself down through the generations.
Your standard country lore about animals—about the nasal love
life of the possum, or the fabled hoop snake—is picturesque rather
than accurate, anthropocentric rather than understanding.

33 But Charlie Goodnight and the Ezra Shermans and their
children and grandchildren all combined have burned out and
chopped out and plowed out and grazed out and killed out a
good part of that natural world they knew, or didn't know, and
we occupy ourselves mainly, it sometimes seems, in finishing the
job. The rosy preindustrial time is past when the humanism of a
man like Thoreau (*was* it humanism?) could still theorize in terms
of natural harmony. Humanism has to speak in the terms of extant
human beings. The terms of today's human beings are air condi-
tioners and suburbs and water impoundments overlaying whole
countrysides, and the hell with nature except maybe in a cross-
sectional park here and there. In our time quietness and sun and
leaves and bird song and all the multitudinous lore of the natural
world have to come second or third, because whether we wanted
to be born there or not, we were all born into the prickly machine-
humming place that man has hung for himself above that natural
world.

34   Where, tell me, is the terror and wonder of an elephant,
now that they can be studied placid in every zoo, and any office-

dwelling sport with a recent lucky break on the market can buy himself one to shoot through telescopic sights with a cartridge whose ballistics hold a good fileful of recorded science's findings? With a box gushing refrigerated air (or warmed, seasonally depending) into a sealed house and another box flashing loud bright images into jaded heads, who gives a rat's damn for things that go bump in the night? With possible death by blast or radiation staring at us like a buzzard, why should we sweat ourselves over where the Eskimo curlew went?

35   The wonder is that a few people do still sweat themselves, that the tracks of short varmints on a beach still have an audience. A few among the audience still know something, too. If they didn't, one wouldn't have to feel so cheated, not knowing as much. . . . Really knowing, I mean—from childhood up and continuously, with all of it a flavor in you . . . Not just being able to make a little seem a lot; there is enough of that around. I can give you as much book data about the home life of the yellow-breasted chat as the next man can. Nor do I mean vague mystic feelings of unity with Comanche and Neanderthal as one wanders the depleted land, gun at the ready, a part of the long flow of man's hunting compulsion. I mean *knowing*.

36   So that what one does in time, arriving a bit late at an awareness of the swindling he got—from no one, from the times— is to make up the shortage as best he may, to try to tie it all together for himself by reading and adult poking. But adult poking is never worth a quarter as much as kid poking, not in those real terms. There's never the time for that whole interest later, or ever quite the pure and subcutaneous receptiveness, either.

37   I mean, too—obviously—if you care. I know that the whicker of a plover in the September sky doesn't touch all other men in their bowels as it touches me, and that men whom it doesn't touch at all can be good men. But it touches me. And I care about knowing what it is, and—if I can—why.

38   Disgruntled from caring, I went to run my throwline. Coons' fresh tracks along the beach overlaid my own of the evening before; one had played with the end of the line and had rolled the jar of blood bait around on the sand trying to get inside it. The passenger followed some of the tracks into a drift tangle but lost interest, not knowing what he was trailing, robbed by long generations of show-breeding of the push that would have

made him care. . . . In my fingers the line tugged with more than the pulse of the current, but when I started softly hand-over-handing it in, it gave a couple of stiff jerks and went slacker, and I knew that something on it in a final frenzy had finished the job of twisting loose. They roll and roll and roll, and despite swivels at last work the staging into a tight snarl against whose solidity they can tear themselves free. Whatever it had been, channel or yellow or blue, it had left a chunk of its lip on the second hook, and two hooks beyond that was a one-pounder which I removed, respectful toward the sharp septic fin spines.

39   In the old days we'd taken the better ones before they rolled loose by running the lines every hour or so during the night, a sleepless process and in summer a mosquito-chewed one. Once in Hood County, Hale and I and black Bill Briggs had gotten a twenty-five-pounder, and after an argument with Bill, who wanted to try to eat it, we sold it to a bridge-side café for a dime a pound. Another time on the Guadalupe to the south—but this is supposed to be about the Brazos . . .

40   Tethering the little catfish to the chain stringer by the canoe, I got a rod and went down to the sharp tail of the island to cast a plug into green deep eddies I'd seen there while exploring. Without wind, the sun was almost hot now. From a willow a jay resented me with a two-note muted rasp like a boy blowing in and out on a harmonica with stuck reeds, and in an almost bare tree on the high river bank a flock of bobolinks fed and bubbled and called, resting on their way south.

41   Cast and retrieve, shallow and deep, across current and down and up, and no sign of bass. . . . The sun's laziness got into me and I wandered up the lesser channel, casting only occasionally into holes without the expectation of fish. Then, on a long flow-dimpled bar, something came down over my consciousness like black pain, and I dropped the rod and squatted, shaking my head to drive the blackness back. It receded a little. I waddled without rising to the bar's edge and scooped cold water over my head. After four or five big throbs it went away, and I sat down half in the water and thought about it. It didn't take much study. My stomach was giving a lecture about it, loud. What it amounted to was that I was about half starved.

42   I picked up the rod, went back to camp, stirred the fire, and put on a pot of water into which I dumped enough dried lima

beans for four men, salt, an onion, and a big chunk of bacon. Considering, I went down to the stringer and skinned and gutted the little catfish and carried him up and threw him in the pot, too. While it boiled, I bathed in the river, frigid in contrast to the air, sloshed out the canoe and sponged it down, and washed underclothes and socks. In shorts, feeling fine now but so hungry it hurt, I sat by the fire and sharpened knives and the ax for the additional hour the beans needed to cook soft in the middle. Fishing out the skeleton of the disintegrated catfish, and using the biggest spoon I had, I ate the whole mess from the pot almost without stopping, and mopped up its juices with cold biscuit bread.

43   Then I wiped my chin and lay back against the cottonwood log with my elbows hanging over it behind and my toes digging into the sand, and considered that asceticism, most certainly, was for those who were built for it. Some were. Some weren't. I hadn't seen God in the black headache on the sand bar and I didn't want to try to any more, that way. . . . Starving myself hadn't had much to do with spirituality, anyhow, but only with the absence of company.

44   Philosophically equilibrated, I rolled down into the sand and went to sleep for two or three hours, waking into a perfect blue-and-yellow afternoon loud with the full-throat chant of the redbird.

45   Wood . . . I went roaming with the honed ax among the piles of drift, searching out solid timber. Bleached and unbarked as much of it is, you have a hard time seeing what it may be, but a two-lick notch with the ax usually bares its grain enough to name it. Cottonwood and willow slice soft and white before the first blow, and unless you're hard up you move on to try your luck on another piece; they're not serious fuel:

> The fire devoureth both the ends of it, and the midst of it is burnt. Is it meet for any work?

But the river is prodigal of its trees, and better stuff is usually near.

46   If food is to sit in the fire's smoke as it cooks, any of the elms will give it a bad taste, though they last and give good heat. Cedar's oil eats up its wood in no time, and stinks food, too, but the tinge of it on the air after supper is worth smelling if you want to cut a stick or so of it just for that. Rock-hard bodark—Osage orange if you want; bois d'arc if you're etymological—sears

a savory crust on meat and burns a long time, if you don't mind losing a flake out of your ax's edge when you hit it wrong. For that matter, not much of it grows close enough to the river to become drift. Nor does much mesquite—a pasture tree and the only thing a conscientious Mexican cook will barbecue kid over. Ash is all right but, as dry drift anyhow, burns fast. The white oaks are prime, the red oaks less so, and one of the finest of aromatic fuels is a twisted, wave-grained branch of live oak, common in the limestone country farther down the river.

47   Maybe, though, the nutwoods are best and sweetest, kind to food and long in their burning. In the third tangle I nicked a huge branch of walnut, purple-brown an inch inside its sapwood's whitened skin. It rots slowly; this piece was sound enough for furniture making—straight-grained enough, too, for that matter. I chopped it into long pieces. The swing and the chocking bite of the ax were pleasant; the pup chased chips as they flew, and I kept cutting until I had twice as many billets as I would need. Then I stacked them for later hauling and went to camp to use up the afternoon puttering with broken tent loops and ripped tarps and sprung hinges on boxes, throwing sticks for the passenger, looking in a book for the differences among small streaked finches, airing my bed, sweeping with a willow branch the sandy gravel all through a camp I'd leave the next day. . . .

48   I lack much zeal for camping, these years. I can still read old Kephart with pleasure: nearly half a century later hardly anyone else has come anywhere near him for information and good sense. But there's detachment in my pleasure now. I no longer see myself choosing a shingle tree and felling it and splitting out the shakes for my own roof, though if I did want to he would tell me how. . . . Nor have I passion for canoeing, as such; both it and the camping are just ways to get somewhere I want to be, and to stay there for a time. I can't describe the cross-bow rudder stroke or stay serene in crashing rapids. I carry unconcentrated food in uncompact boxes. I forget to grease my boots and suffer from clammy feet. I slight hygiene, and will finger a boiled minnow from the coffee with equanimity, and sleep with my dog. My tent in comparison to the aluminum-framed, tight-snapping ones available is a ragged parallelogrammatic disaster.

49   Nevertheless, when camping for a time is the way of one's life, one tries to improve his style. One resolves on changes for

future trips—a tiny and exactly fitted cook box; a contour-cut tarp over the canoe hooking to catches beneath the gunwales; no peaches in the mixed dried fruit. . . . One experiments and invents, and ends up, for instance, with a perfect aluminum-foil reflector for baking that agreeable, lumpy, biscuit-mixed bread that the Mexicans call "*pan ranchero*" and the northwoods writers "bannock" and other people undoubtedly other names.

50   One way or the other, it all generally turns out to be work. Late that afternoon, carrying abrasive armloads of the walnut from where I'd chopped it to camp, I got as though from the air the answer to a question that used to come into mind in libraries, reading about the old ones and the Indians. I used to wonder why, knowing Indians were around, the old ones would let themselves be surprised so often and so easily. Nearly all the ancient massacres resulted from such surprise.

51   The answer, simple on the island, was that the old ones were laboring their tails off at the manifold tasks of the primitive life, hewing and hauling and planting and plowing and breaking and fixing. They didn't have time to be wary. Piped water and steam heat and tractors might have let them be alert, just as I'd been among the stacked tomes of the Southwest Collection.

52   It was a good day, work and all. At evening I sat astraddle the bow of the canoe on the beach, putting new line on the spinning reel, when three big honkers came flying up the river slowly, low searchers like the first ones of the evening before. The gun was at hand. Even though they veered, separating, as I reached for it, they still passed close, and it needed only a three-foot lead on the front one's head to bring him splashing solidly, relaxed, dead, into the channel. I trotted downstream abreast of him as he drifted and finally teased him ashore with a long crooked piece of cottonwood.

53   Till then I'd had the visceral bite of the old excitement in me, the gladness of clean shooting, the fulfillment of quarry sought and taken. But when I got him ashore and hefted the warm, handsome eight or nine pounds of him, and ran my fingers against the grain up through the hot thick down of his neck, the just-as-old balancing regret came into it. A goose is a lot of bird to kill. Maybe size shouldn't matter, but it seems to. With something that big and that trimly perfect and, somehow, that meaningful, you wonder about the right of the thing. . . .

54   For a while after the war I did no shooting at all, and thought I probably wouldn't do any more. I even chiseled out a little niche for that idea, half Hindu and tangled with the kind of reverence for life that Schweitzer preaches. But then one day in fall beside a stock tank in a mesquite pasture a friend wanted me to try the heft of a little engraved L. C. Smith, and when I'd finished trying it I'd dropped ten doves with sixteen shots and the niche didn't exist any longer.

55   Reverence for life in that sense seems to me to be like asceticism or celibacy: you need to be built for it. I no longer kill anything inedible that doesn't threaten me or mine, and I never cared anything about big-game hunting. Possibly I'll give up shooting again and for good one of these years, but I believe the killing itself can be reverent. To see and kill and pluck and gut and cook and eat a wild creature, all with some knowledge and the pleasure that knowledge gives, implies a closeness to the creature that is to me more honorable than the candle-lit consumption of rare prime steaks from a steer bludgeoned to death in a packing-house chute while tranquilizers course his veins. And if there's a difference in nobility between a Canada goose and a fat white-faced ox (there is), how does one work out the quantities?

56   Though I threw the skin and head and guts into the river to keep them away from the pup, an eddy drifted them into shore and he found them and ate a good bit before I caught him at it. The two big slabs of breast hissed beautifully in foil on the fire after dark. When they were done I hung them up for a time uncovered in the sweet walnut smoke and then ate nearly all of one of them. The other would make sandwiches at noon for two or three days, tucked inside chunks of biscuit bread. Despite his harsh appetizers, the passenger gobbled the drumsticks and organs I'd half roasted for him, and when I unrolled the sleeping bag inside the tent he fought to be first into it.

57   Later, in half-sleep, I heard a rattle of dirty metal dishes beside the fire. I shot the flashlight's beam out there and a sage, masked face stared at me, indignant. Foreseeing sport, I hauled the pup up for a look. He blinked, warm and full, and dug in his toes against ejection into the cold air, and when I let him go he burrowed all the way down beside my feet, not a practical dog and not ashamed of it, either. The coon went away.

58 Later still, the goosefeathers began their emetic work and I woke to the rhythmic *wump, wump, wump* that in dogs precedes a heave. Though the account of it may lack wide interest, later it seemed to me that there had been heroic co-ordination in the way I came out of sleep and grabbed him, holding his jaws shut with one hand while I fought to find the bag's zipper with the other, then fought to find and loose the zipper of the tent, too, and hurled him out into the night by his nose. He stayed there for a while, and when I was sure he'd finished I let him back in, low-eared and shivering, but I preferred his unhappiness to what might have been.

59 It came to me then who it was that had slept with a dog for his health. Leopold Bloom's father. The dog's name had been . . . Athos! Old man Bloom had slept with Athos to cure his aches and pains.

60 One can get pretty literary on islands.

• SUGGESTIONS •

This selection is taken from a book that records a three-week solitary journey by canoe down the Brazos River in Texas. It is clearly far more than just descriptive writing. Yet it just as clearly rewards consideration for its descriptive effects.

Write an analysis of this piece as descriptive writing. Before beginning, you will probably find it necessary first to accumulate evidence in ways suggested earlier indicating the central impression, if any, the manner of handling point of view, and the preciseness of observation and diction. Once your evidence is gathered, one way to plan the essay would be to use the three features just suggested as three basic parts of your essay. Any other striking features of the work should also be included. You may also find it useful to arrange the three basic parts along with other major parts of your discussion in some order, ascending, descending, or otherwise.

A Writing Program

---

1. Write several descriptive paragraphs, setting out in each deliberately to create a predetermined mood. Try using the same subject in several paragraphs, varying the mood by focusing everything on different central impressions.

2. Write several short descriptive pieces using different points of view. Try, for example, a fixed, physical point of view; a moving physical point of view complicated by a given mood; and some unusual point of view.

3. After conference with your instructor and discussion of possible subjects, write one or two extended pieces of description. If you find it better, design these pieces for use with some longer work in exposition or narration.

Narration

Narrative writing, at its best, presents life directly, dramatizing the words and deeds of men. Exposition and argumentation are usually preoccupied with meaning (explanations, conclusions) abstracted from life, while description reports our impressions of life's circumstances. But it is the narrative account that is the most direct rendition of life, even though the narrative writer selects and arranges. Perhaps the oldest form of discourse, narration is a means of preserving human experience and a means men have for knowing other men and being known.

Other purposes may also be served through narration. It often uses techniques typical of other kinds of writing, employing descriptive, expository, and argumentative methods to invest the people and the events of narrative with all the color and shape and sound and being that make them real. And as it uses other techniques for its own purposes, so narration can be used for expository, descriptive, and argumentative purposes.

This kinship with other forms may provide some insight into the character of narrative writing. As we saw earlier, narrative writing and exposition of sequences (see Exposition) are clearly related. Both are determined by a time scheme of some kind since both record a progression through time. Despite this similarity, there is a sharp distinction between the exposition of sequences and narrative writing, a distinction that helps to clarify just what narration is. The writer of this special kind of exposition is engaged in explaining a process, a series of related events. His sequence of events is therefore usually calculated to culminate in some major point or to develop a thesis. The purpose, in other words, is clearly expository. In narrative writings, the sequence of events *is* the point; there is usually no thesis developed, no conclusion drawn—the story is all. To be sure, we can find meaning in narrative writing, but it is meaning to be found in the whole chronicle, not meaning previously established and illustrated by a chronological record of events.

The sections that follow contain illustrations of several kinds of factual narrative. As usual, introductory notes offer further suggestions for the management of the method in question.

Autobiographical and Biographical Writing and the Problem of Particularity

The uses of exposition in autobiographical and biographical writing have already been mentioned. These traditional forms are, however, by their very definitions narrative in character, for they are the writing of a life or portion thereof. This means, among other things, that narrative writing cannot succeed if the writer trades only in ideas and ghosts. His business is with actual men, with specific, identifiable human beings, and with their specific actions. Nor can narrative writing succeed if the writer only summarizes the actions of his people. Life matters. Every single, solitary moment of every single, solitary life matters, but the only way we can know it matters, except in our vague and benevolent altruism, is to know the life and all its solitary moments in their very *particular* forms.

If the writer is to let us know as thoroughly as we must, he will employ descriptive methods in the midst of his narrative. For we must *see* men and their actions, and we must *see* their environs. And he will employ some of the methods of exposition as well, for we must be able to understand the actions of the people involved in the narrative. But over and above all else, the narrative writer will seek to focus our attention on individual characters and specific actions in specific places, giving us a direct impression of what transpires. He is obliged, in order to do this, to re-create reality faithfully, selecting those details of appearance, action, and conversation that give the events their peculiar quality.

From THE DIARY

Samuel Pepys

1661

April 23rd. About four I rose and got to the Abbey, where I followed Sir J. Denham, the Surveyor, with some company that he was leading in. And with much ado, by the favour of Mr. Cooper, his man, did get up into a great scaffold across the north end of the Abbey, where with a great deal of patience I sat from past four till eleven before the King came in. And a great pleasure it was to see the Abbey raised in the middle, all covered with red, and a throne (that is a chair) and footstool on the top of it; and all the officers of all kinds, so much as the very fiddlers, in red vests. At last comes in the Dean and Prebends of Westminster, with the Bishops (many of them in cloth of gold copes), and after them the Nobility, all in their Parliament robes, which was a most magnificent sight. Then the Duke, and the King with a scepter (carried by my Lord Sandwich) and sword and mond before him, and the crown too. The King in his robes, bare-headed, which was very fine. And after all had placed themselves, there was a sermon and the service; and then in the choir at the high altar, the King passed through all the ceremonies of the Coronation, which to my great grief I and most in the Abbey could not see. The crown being put upon his head, a great shout begun, and he came forth to the throne, and there passed more ceremonies: as taking the oath, and having things read to him by the Bishop; and his lords (who put on their caps as soon as the King put on his crown) and bishops come, and kneeled before him. And three times the King-at-Arms went to the three open places on the scaffold, and proclaimed, that if any one could show any reason why Charles Stuart should not be King of England, that now he should come and speak. And a General Pardon also was read by the Lord Chancellor, and medals flung up and down by my Lord Cornwallis, of silver, but I could not come by any. But so great a noise that I could make but little of the music; and indeed it was lost to everybody. I went out a little while before the King had done all his ceremonies, and went round the Abbey to Westminster Hall, all the way within rails, and 10,000 people with the ground covered with blue cloth; and scaffolds all the way. Into the Hall I got, where it was very fine with hangings and scaffolds one upon another full of brave ladies; and my wife in one little one, on the right hand. Here I staid walking up and down, and at last upon one of the side stalls I stood and saw the King come in with all the persons (but the soldiers) that were yesterday in the cavalcade; and a most pleasant sight it was to see them in their several robes. And the King come in with his crown on, and his scepter in his hand, under a canopy borne up by six silver staves, carried by Barons of the Cinque Ports, and little bells at every end. And after a long time, he got up to the farther end, and all set themselves down at their several tables; and that was also a brave sight: and the King's first course carried up by the Knights of the Bath. And many fine ceremonies there was of the Heralds leading up people before him, and bowing; and my Lord of Albemarle's going to the kitchen and eating a bit of the first dish that was to go to the King's table. But, above all, was these three lords, Northumberland, and Suffolk, and the Duke of Ormond, coming before the courses on horseback, and staying so all dinner-time, and at last bringing up the King's Champion, all in armor on horseback, with his spear and target carried before him. And a Herald proclaims "That if any dare deny Charles Stuart to be lawful King of England, here was a Champion that would fight with him;" and with these words, the Champion flings down his gauntlet, and all this he do three times in his going up towards the King's Table. At last, when he is come, the King drinks to him, and then sends him the cup, which is of gold, and he drinks it off, and then rides back again with the cup in his hand. I went from table to table to see the Bishops and all others at their dinner, and was infinitely pleased with it. And at the Lords' table, I met with William Howe, and he spoke to my Lord for me, and he did give him four rabbits and a pullet, and so Mr. Creed and I got Mr. Minshell to give us some bread, and so we at a stall ate it, as everybody else did what they could get. I took a great deal of pleasure to go up and down, and look upon the ladies, and to hear the music of all sorts, but above all, the 24 violins. About six at night they had dined, and I went up to my wife. And strange it is to think that these two days have held up fair till now that all is done, and the King gone out of the Hall; and then it fell a-raining and thundering and lightening as I have not seen it do for some years: which people did take great notice of; God's blessing of the work of these two days, which is a foolery to take too much notice of such things. I observed little disorder in all this, only the King's footmen had got hold of the canopy, and would keep it from the Barons of the Cinque Ports, which they endeavored to force from them again, but could not do it till my Lord Duke of Albemarle caused it to be put into Sir R. Pye's hand till to-morrow to be decided. At Mr. Bowyer's; a great deal of company, some I knew, others I did not. Here we staid upon the leads and below till it was late, expecting to see the fire-works, but they were not performed to-night: only the City had a light like a glory round about it, with bonfires. At last, I went to King Street, and there sent Crockford to my father's and my house, to tell them I could not come home to-night, because of the dirt, and a coach could not be had. And so I took my wife and Mrs. Frankleyn (who I proffered the civility of lying with my wife at Mrs. Hunt's to-night) to Axe Yard, in which, at the further end, there were three great bonfires, and a great many gallants, men and women; and they laid hold of us, and would have us drink the King's health upon our knees, kneeling upon a faggot, which we all did, they drinking to us one after another, which we thought a strange frolic; but these gallants continued there a great while, and I wondered to see how the ladies did tipple. At last, I sent my wife and her bed-fellow to bed, and Mr. Hunt and I went in with Mr. Thornbury (who did give the company all their wine, he being yeoman of the wine-cellar to the King); and there, with his wife and two of his sisters, and some gallant sparks that were there, we drank the King's health, and nothing else, till one of the gentlemen fell down stark drunk, and there lay; and I went to my Lord's pretty well. But no sooner a-bed with Mr. Shepley but my head began to turn, and I to vomit, and if ever I was foxed, it was now, which I cannot say yet, because I fell asleep, and slept till morn-ing. Thus did the day end with joy everywhere; and blessed be God, I have not heard of any mischance to anybody through it all, but only to Serjeant Glynne, whose horse fell upon him yesterday, and is like to kill him, which people do please them-selves to see how just God is to punish the rogue at such a time as this, he being now one of the King's serjeants, and rode in the cavalcade with Maynard, to whom people wish the same fortune. There was also this night, in King Street, a woman had her eye put out by a boy's flinging a firebrand into the coach. Now, after all this, I can say that, besides the pleasure of the sight of these glorious things, I may now shut my eyes against any other objects, nor for the future trouble myself to see things of state and show, as being sure never to see the like again in this world.

September 7th. Having appointed the young ladies at the Wardrobe to go with them to the play to-day, my wife and I took them to the theater, where we seated ourselves close by the King, and Duke of York, and Madame Palmer, which was great content; and, indeed, I can never enough admire her beauty. And here was *Bartholomew Fair*, with the puppet-show, acted to-day, which had not been these forty years, it being so satirical against Puritanism, they durst not till now, which is strange they should already dare to do it, and the King countenance it, but I do never a whit like it the better for the puppets, but rather the worse. Thence home with the ladies, it being by reason of our staying a great while for the King's coming, and the length of the play, near nine o'clock before it was done.

* COMMENTARY *

This selection is from a most unusual work. Pepys' diary was apparently not intended for publication, in his lifetime or later; done in a kind of shorthand of his own devising and probably never revised or changed once set down, the papers comprising the diary were left in manuscript form to Magdalene College, Cambridge, and were not deciphered until 1825. Its curious history in a way contributes to its effectiveness as narration, for Pepys quite frankly records the events of his life, even some that another man might not have written privately.

This selection records the activities of an eventful day, the coronation of Charles II. The record is chronological, but Pepys does not treat all time in the same way. Portions of the day not notable in any way he moves over rather quickly. Early in the selection he speaks of waiting from "past four till eleven before the King came in." This time is recorded, not in detail, for it is a time needing no record, but in two words, "At last," which are sufficient to indicate that a long time in which nothing much happened has passed. Similarly after the coronation itself, Pepys speaks of the long wait in Westminster Hall: "here I staid walking up and down, and at last upon one of the side stalls I stood and saw the King come in. . . ." The King's progress through the hall to his place is given no special detail; Pepys indicates only that "after a long time, he got up to the farther end."

But the most striking feature of Pepys' work illustrated here is the careful, almost loving attention to detail. And it is this quality that has made his work endure, for it is the detail of his portraits and records that enables us to see and to know him and his time. Consider, for example, his care in naming people, even such as Mr. Cooper, who otherwise presumably do not play a very important role. And notice how frequently a relatively trivial detail brings history to life. Lord Cornwallis flings medals of silver up and down, Pepys tells us, well enough, but what makes the act matter is that Pepys scrambled for them with the rest, but "could not come by any." Or the King comes by, borne under a canopy of six silver staves, but what catches the scene to life is "little bells at every end," of that splendid canopy. Everywhere in the selection, it is not the pomp of the coronation and procession that makes the moments glitter to Pepys and to us, but the moments he sees clearly for himself, moments which though not of the coronation do embody the grandeur of the occasion. The account of the Champion's appearance is such a moment, as is that late quiet time when Pepys and friends lean from a window expecting fireworks and see instead that "the City had a light like a glory round about it, with bonfires." And to cap it all, to make the day a day of human beings in all their finiteness, there is the honestly rendered, if somewhat drunken, distress of Mr. Pepys himself as he retires.

THE EXECUTION OF LADY JANE GREY [1563]

John Foxe

1   When she first mounted the scaffold, she spake to the spectators in this manner: "Good people, I am come hither to die, and by a law I am condemned to the same. The fact against the queen's highness was unlawful, and the consenting thereunto by me: but, touching the procurement and desire thereof by me, or on my behalf, I do wash my hands thereof in innocency before God, and the face of you, good christian people, this day:" and therewith she wrung her hands, wherein she had her book. Then

she said, "I pray you all, good christian people, to bear me witness that I die a good christian woman, and that I do look to be saved by no other means, but only by the mercy of God in the blood of his only Son Jesus Christ: and I confess, that when I did know the word of God, I neglected the same, loved myself and the world, and therefore this plague and punishment is happily and worthily happened unto me for my sins: and yet I thank God, that of his goodness he hath thus given me a time and a respite to repent: and now, good people, while I am alive, I pray you assist me with your prayers." And then, kneeling down, she turned to Feckenham, saying, "Shall I say this Psalm?" and he said, "Yea." Then she said the Psalm of Miserere mei Deus, in English, in a most devout manner throughout to the end; and then she stood up, and gave to her maid, Mrs. Ellen, her gloves and handkerchief, and her book to Mr. Bruges; and then she untied her gown, and the executioner pressed upon her to help her off with it: but she, desiring him to let her alone, turned toward her two gentlewomen, who helped her off therewith, and also with her frowes, paste, and neckerchief, giving her a fair handkerchief to put about her eyes.

2   Then the executioner kneeled down, and asked her forgiveness, whom she forgave most willingly. Then he desired her to stand upon the straw; which doing, she saw the block. Then she said, "I pray you despatch me quickly." Then she kneeled down, saying, "Will you take it off before I lay me down?" And the executioner said, "No, madam." Then she tied the handkerchief about her eyes, and feeling for the block, she said, "What shall I do? Where is it? Where is it?" One of the standers-by guiding her thereunto, she laid her head down upon the block, and then stretched forth her body, and said, "Lord, into thy hands I commend my spirit:" and so finished her life, in the year of our Lord 1554, the 12th day of February, about the seventeenth year of her age.

3   Thus died the Lady Jane: and on the same day the Lord Guildford, her husband, one of the Duke of Northumberland's sons, was likewise beheaded, two innocents in comparison of them that sat upon them. For they were both very young, and ignorantly accepted that which others had contrived, and by open proclamation consented to take from others, and give to them.

4   Touching the condemnation of this pious lady, it is to be noted, that Judge Morgan who gave sentence against her, soon

after he had condemned her, fell mad, and in his raving cried out
continually, to have the Lady Jane taken away from him, and so he
ended his life. . . .

• SUGGESTIONS •

Here again it is not the major action or the long speech that makes
this action genuine, but rather the carefully observed and faithfully
recorded details that would otherwise seem unimportant. Catalogue the
sentences, clauses, or phrases that record Lady Jane or others *doing*
something specific. This should give you sufficient evidence to write a
short analysis of this selection as narrative writing. Perhaps you could
call your analysis "Handkerchiefs and History."

THE EXECUTION OF MARY QUEEN OF
SCOTS [1870]

James Anthony Froude

1   Briefly, solemnly, and sternly they (Lords Kent and Shrewsbury) delivered their awful message. They informed her (Mary
Queen of Scots) that they had received a commission under the
great seal to see her executed, and she was told that she must
prepare to suffer on the following morning.

2   She was dreadfully agitated. For a moment she refused to
believe them. Then, as the truth forced itself upon her, tossing
her head in disdain and struggling to control herself, she called
her physician and began to speak to him of money that was owed
to her in France. At last it seems that she broke down altogether,
and they left her with a fear either that she would destroy herself
in the night, or that she would refuse to come to the scaffold, and
that it might be necessary to drag her there by violence.

3   The end had come. She had long professed to expect it,
but the clearest expectation is not certainty. The scene for which
she had affected to prepare she was to encounter in its dread
reality, and all her busy schemes, her dreams of vengeance, her

visions of a revolution, with herself ascending out of the convulsion and seating herself on her rival's throne—all were gone. She had played deep, and the dice had gone against her.

4   Yet in death, if she encountered it bravely, victory was still possible. Could she but sustain to the last the character of a calumniated suppliant accepting heroically for God's sake and her creed's the concluding stroke of a long series of wrongs, she might stir a tempest of indignation which, if it could not save herself, might at least overwhelm her enemy. Persisting, as she persisted to the last, in denying all knowledge of Babington, it would be affectation to credit her with a genuine feeling of religion; but the imperfection of her motive exalts the greatness of her fortitude. To an impassioned believer death is comparatively easy.

5   Her chaplain was lodged in a separate part of the castle. The commissioners, who were as anxious that her execution should wear its real character as she was herself determined to convert it into a martyrdom, refused, perhaps unwisely, to allow him access to her, and offered her again the assistance of an Anglican dean. They gave her an advantage over them which she did not fail to use. She would not let the dean come near her. She sent a note to the chaplain telling him that she had meant to receive the sacrament, but as it might not be she must content herself with a general confession. She bade him watch through the night and pray for her. In the morning when she was brought out she might perhaps see him, and receive his blessing on her knees. She supped cheerfully, giving her last meal with her attendants a character of sacred parting; afterwards she drew aside her apothecary M. Gorion, and asked him if she might depend upon his fidelity. When he satisfied her that she might trust him, she said she had a letter and two diamonds which she wished to send to Mendoza. He undertook to melt some drug and conceal them in it where they would never be looked for, and promised to deliver them faithfully. One of the jewels was for Mendoza himself; the other and the largest was for Philip. It was to be a sign that she was dying for the truth, and was meant also to bespeak his care for her friends and servants. Every one of them so far as she was able, without forgetting a name, she commended to his liberality. Arundel, Paget, Morgan, the Archbishop of Glasgow, Westmoreland, Throgmorton, the Bishop of Ross, her two secretaries, the ladies who had shared the trials of her imprisonment, she remem-

bered them all, and specified the sums which she desired Philip to bestow on them. And as Mary Stuart then and throughout her life never lacked gratitude to those who had been true to her, so then as always she remembered her enemies. There was no cant about her, no unreal talk of forgiveness of injuries. She bade Gorion tell Philip it was her last prayer that he should persevere, notwithstanding her death, in the invasion of England. It was God's quarrel, she said, and worthy of his greatness; and as soon as he had conquered it, she desired not to forget how she had been treated by Cecil, and Leicester, and Walsingham; by Lord Huntingdon, who had ill-used her fifteen years before at Tutbury; by Sir Amyas Paulet, and Secretary Wade.

6   Her last night was a busy one. As she said herself, there was much to be done and the time was short. A few lines to the King of France were dated two hours after midnight. They were to insist for the last time that she was innocent of the conspiracy, that she was dying for religion, and for having asserted her right to the crown; and to beg that out of the sum which he owed her, her servants' wages might be paid and masses provided for her soul. After this she slept for three or four hours, and then rose and with the most elaborate care prepared to encounter the end.

7   At eight in the morning the provost-marshal knocked at the outer door which communicated with her suite of apartments. It was locked and no one answered, and he went back in some trepidation lest the fears might prove true which had been entertained the preceding evening. On his returning with the sheriff, however, a few minutes later, the door was open, and they were confronted with the tall majestic figure of Mary Stuart standing before them in splendor. The plain gray dress had been exchanged for a robe of black satin; her jacket was of black satin also, looped and slashed and trimmed with velvet. Her false hair was arranged studiously with a coif, and over her head and falling down over her back was a white veil of delicate lawn. A crucifix of gold hung from her neck. In her hand she held a crucifix of ivory, and a number of jeweled paternosters was attached to her girdle. Led by two of Paulet's gentlemen, the sheriff walking before her, she passed to the chamber of presence in which she had been tried, where Shrewsbury, Kent, Paulet, Druary, and others were waiting to receive her. Andrew Melville, Sir Robert's brother, who had been master of her household, was kneeling in tears. "Melville,"

she said, "you should rather rejoice than weep that the end of my troubles is come. Tell my friends I die a true Catholic. Commend me to my son. Tell him I have done nothing to prejudice his kingdom of Scotland, and so, good Melville, farewell." She kissed him, and turning asked for her chaplain Du Preau. He was not present. There had been a fear of some religious melodrama which it was thought well to avoid. Her ladies, who had attempted to follow her, had been kept back also. She could not afford to leave the account of her death to be reported by enemies and Puritans, and she required assistance for the scene which she meditated. Missing them she asked the reason of their absence, and said she wished them to see her die. Kent said he feared they might scream or faint, or attempt perhaps to dip their handkerchiefs in her blood. She undertook that they should be quiet and obedient. "The queen," she said, "would never deny her so slight a request"; and when Kent still hesitated, she added with tears, "You know I am cousin to your queen, of the blood of Henry VII, a married Queen of France, and anointed Queen of Scotland."

8   It was impossible to refuse. She was allowed to take six of her own people with her, and select them herself. She chose her physician Burgoyne, Andrew Melville, the apothecary Gorion, and her surgeon, with two ladies, Elizabeth Kennedy and Curle's young wife Barbara Mowbray, whose child she had baptized.

9   *Allons donc,* she then said—"Let us go," and passing out attended by the earls, and leaning on the arm of an officer of the guard, she descended the great staircase to the hall. The news had spread far through the country. Thousands of people were collected outside the walls. About three hundred knights and gentlemen of the county had been admitted to witness the execution. The tables and forms had been removed, and a great wood fire was blazing in the chimney. At the upper end of the hall, above the fireplace, but near it, stood the scaffold, twelve feet square and two feet and a half high. It was covered with black cloth; a low rail ran round it covered with black cloth also, and the sheriff's guard of halberdiers was ranged on the floor below on the four sides to keep off the crowd. On the scaffold was the block, black like the rest; a square black cushion was placed behind it, and behind the cushion a black chair; on the right were two other chairs for the earls. The ax leaned against the rail, and two masked figures stood like mutes on either side at the back. The Queen of

Scots as she swept in seemed as if coming to take a part in some solemn pageant. Not a muscle of her face could be seen to quiver; she ascended the scaffold with absolute composure, looked round her smiling, and sat down. Shrewsbury and Kent followed and took their places, the sheriff stood at her left hand, and Beale then mounted a platform and read the warrant aloud.

10   In all the assembly Mary Stuart appeared the person least interested in the words which were consigning her to death.

11   "Madam," said Lord Shrewsbury to her, when the reading was ended, "you hear what we are commanded to do."

12   "You will do your duty," she answered, and rose as if to kneel and pray.

13   The Dean of Peterborough, Dr. Fletcher, approached the rail. "Madam," he began, with a low obeisance, "the queen's most excellent majesty"; "madam, the queen's most excellent majesty"—thrice he commenced his sentence, wanting words to pursue it. When he repeated the words a fourth time, she cut him short.

14   "Mr. Dean," she said, "I am a Catholic, and must die a Catholic. It is useless to attempt to move me, and your prayers will avail me but little."

15   "Change your opinion, madam," he cried, his tongue being loosed at last; "repent of your sins, settle your faith in Christ, by him to be saved."

16   "Trouble not yourself further, Mr. Dean," she answered; "I am settled in my own faith, for which I mean to shed my blood."

17   "I am sorry, madam," said Shrewsbury, "to see you so addicted to popery."

18   "That image of Christ you hold there," said Kent, "will not profit you if he be not engraved in your heart."

19   She did not reply, and turning her back on Fletcher, knelt for her own devotions.

20   He had been evidently instructed to impair the Catholic complexion of the scene, and the Queen of Scots was determined that he should not succeed. When she knelt he commenced an extempore prayer in which the assembly joined. As his voice sounded out in the hall she raised her own, reciting with powerful deep-chested tones the penitential psalms in Latin, introducing English sentences at intervals that the audience might know what she was saying, and praying with especial distinctness for her Holy Father the Pope.

21   From time to time, with conspicuous vehemence, she struck the crucifix against her bosom, and then, as the dean gave up the struggle, leaving her Latin, she prayed in English wholly, still clear and loud. She prayed for the Church which she had been ready to betray, for her son whom she had disinherited, for the queen whom she had endeavored to murder. She prayed God to avert his wrath from England, that England which she had sent a last message to Philip to beseech him to invade. She forgave her enemies, whom she had invited Philip not to forget, and then, praying to the saints to intercede for her with Christ, and kissing the crucifix and crossing her own breast, "Even as thy arms, O Jesus," she cried, "were spread upon the cross, so receive me into thy mercy and forgive my sins."

22   With these words she rose; the black mutes stepped forward, and in the usual form begged her forgiveness.

23   "I forgive you," she said, "for now I hope you shall end all my troubles." They offered their help in arranging her dress. "Truly, my lords," she said with a smile to the earls, "I never had such grooms waiting on me before." Her ladies were allowed to come up upon the scaffold to assist her; for the work to be done was considerable, and had been prepared with no common thought.

24   She laid her crucifix on her chair. The chief executioner took it as a perquisite, but was ordered instantly to lay it down. The lawn veil was lifted carefully off, not to disturb the hair, and was hung upon the rail. The black robe was next removed. Below it was a petticoat of crimson velvet. The black jacket followed, and under the jacket was a body of crimson satin. One of her ladies handed her a pair of crimson sleeves, with which she hastily covered her arms; and thus she stood on the black scaffold with the black figures all around her, blood-red from head to foot.

25   Her reasons for adopting so extraordinary a costume must be left to conjecture. It is only certain that it must have been carefully studied, and that the pictorial effect must have been appalling.

26   The women, whose firmness had hitherto borne the trial, began now to give way, spasmodic sobs bursting from them which they could not check. *Ne crienz vous*, she said, *j'ay promis pour vous*. Struggling bravely, they crossed their breasts again and again, she crossing them in turn and bidding them to pray for her.

Then she knelt on the cushion. Barbara Mowbray bound her eyes with a handkerchief. *Adieu,* she said, smiling for the last time and waving her hand to them, *Adieu, au revoir.* They stepped back from off the scaffold and left her alone. On her knees she repeated the psalm, *In te, Domine, confido,* "In Thee, O Lord, have I put my trust." Her shoulders being exposed, two scars became visible, one on either side, and the earls being now a little behind her, Kent pointed to them with his white wand and looked inquiringly at his companion. Shrewsbury whispered that they were the remains of two abscesses from which she had suffered while living with him at Sheffield.

27   When the psalm was finished she felt for the block, and laying down her head muttered; *In manus, Domine tuas, commendo animam meam.* The hard wood seemed to hurt her, for she placed her hands under her neck. The executioners gently removed them, lest they should deaden the blow, and then one of them holding her slightly, the other raised the ax and struck. The scene had been too trying even for the practiced headsman of the Tower. His arm wandered. The blow fell on the knot of the handkerchief, and scarcely broke the skin. She neither spoke nor moved. He struck again, this time effectively. The head hung by a shred of skin, which he divided without withdrawing the ax; and at once a metamorphosis was witnessed, strange as was ever wrought by wand of fabled enchanter. The coif fell off and the false plaits. The labored illusion vanished. The lady who had knelt before the block was in the maturity of grace and loveliness. The executioner, when he raised the head, as usual, to show it to the crowd, exposed the withered features of a grizzled, wrinkled old woman.

28   "So perish all enemies of the queen," said the Dean of Peterborough. A loud Amen rose over the hall. "Such end," said the Earl of Kent, rising and standing over the body, "to the queen's and the Gospel's enemies."

29   Orders had been given that everything which she had worn should be immediately destroyed, that no relics should be carried off to work imaginary miracles. Sentinels stood at the doors who allowed no one to pass out without permission; and after the first pause, the earls still keeping their places, the body was stripped. It then appeared that a favorite lapdog had followed its mistress unperceived, and was concealed under her clothes; when

discovered it gave a short cry, and seated itself between the head and the neck, from which the blood was still flowing. It was carried away and carefully washed, and then beads, paternosters, handkerchief—each particle of dress which the blood had touched, with the cloth on the block and on the scaffold, was burned in the hall fire in the presence of the crowd. The scaffold itself was next removed: a brief account of the execution was drawn up, with which Henry Talbot, Lord Shrewsbury's son, was sent to London, and then everyone was dismissed. Silence settled down on Fotheringay, and the last scene of the life of Mary Stuart, in which tragedy and melodrama were so strangely intermingled, was over. . . .

• SUGGESTIONS •

Discuss the uses of exposition and description in this selection. Examine the selection especially for the telling glimpse, the vivid detail that makes action real—for example the little moment when Mary places her hands under her neck against the hardness of the block. This we can comprehend, and comprehending this, we can know something of the hideousness and irrationality of the death itself.

Other Forms of Factual Narration and Some Special Problems

Nonfiction narrative occurs most frequently as historical writing of some kind. Autobiography and biography are history, perhaps the most immediate and vivid kind of history, but certainly there are other narratives whose intent is in some way to preserve the past, to get down the very things and doings of our time before they go forever. And surely no kind of writing can have greater worth than that seeking to preserve the past in all its texture; especially can we value no form higher than at a time when we daily condemn the past to extinction as surely as we tear down a building and plow up a million green acres.

That such writing devotes itself to *actual* occurrences does not prevent your exercising some of the functions of art and craft upon your record. Frequently, for example, narrative writing can be ruined by slavish devotion to chronology. The good narrative writer knows that not all our moments are filled, that not all our moments tell what we are. Knowing this, he will search in any train of events for those revealing moments that capture men and actions, and he will frequently pace his chronology so as to dwell on the revealing moment, giving it its due while moving past those moments when all is static—unless, indeed, he wishes to tell of that very stasis. The pacing of a narrative work can then be crucial to its effectiveness. Useful here is an understanding of some special strategies of narration: foreshortening, foreshadowing, and flashback.

The term *foreshortening* is used to label any device that represents the passage of time, often long periods of time, in a short space. Needless to say, it may be accomplished in an almost infinite number of ways. Pepys, in the selection in the preceding group, accomplished this foreshortening at one point with "here I staid walking up and down, and at last upon one of the side stalls I stood and saw the King come in." We know from this that he was *engaged* during that time; Pepys does not merely summarize the passing of time but in effect dramatizes it by telling us of the characteristic activity of the period. And we know from the words "at last" that the time was considerable.

A degree of suspense is beneficial even to nonfiction narrative. One method authors have found useful in creating suspense is called *foreshadowing*. In much narrative writing the audience does not know what is to happen, and some suspense is natural. In much factual narrative, including historical narratives, the audience does know what is to happen later. In the first case, the author may vary what would otherwise be monotonous chronology and propel his reader forward by forecasting events to come, or perhaps only by hinting at things to come. He will not reveal everything, but seek to maintain interest in his chronology by arousing his reader to knowledge that events do have consequence. In the second case, where the audience already knows the outcome of the action, this method may be used to enliven and give meaning to the early stages of action—it is, indeed, a way the author has of demonstrating meaning in actions that may otherwise seem inconsequential.

The *flashback* is also a useful device to the narrative writer.

Unless the occasion gives you the leisure of a whole book to record your narrative, it is usually effective to begin at a point in the action near its climactic moments. Doing so frequently necessitates omitting important background material along with any antecedent actions, and you can effectively involve this preliminary matter in the immediate action by halting your narrative—perhaps at a point where action is slow or where some foreshortening is required—to move back momentarily to an earlier time.

The point of view from which narrative is given requires considerable care. A writer, depending upon the kind of action he relates, may employ an omniscient viewpoint, or he may develop his narrative from an eyewitness viewpoint, or he may use several points of view, shifting from one to another. The first may be useful in achieving a kind of panoramic view of the action, but the other two probably lend greater authority and realism to a narrative account. The physical point of view is not, however, always the controlling factor, for the passage of time, the increase of nostalgia, the burden of mood may pack a physical viewpoint with more meaning, or even with more limitations, than the physical viewpoint alone would indicate.

From GOODBYE TO A RIVER*

John Graves

1   When you see Rock Creek after a rain, you know what is happening to that country, and has been for a century. Above it, even in wet times, the river is likely to run fairly clear, since most of the tributary streams up to Possum Kingdom drain sandstone country without much rich dirt. But Rock Creek carried the runoff from the steeply up-and-down western part of Parker County which used to be an oak forest with grassed glades, and since the whites moved in with axes and moldboard plows and too many chattel ruminants, the western part of Parker County has been flowing down Rock Creek to the Brazos, and down the Brazos to

* Reprinted from *Goodbye to a River* by John Graves by permission of Alfred A. Knopf, Inc. and Macmillan & Co., Ltd. Copyright ©, 1959, by Curtis Publishing Co. Copyright ©, 1960, by John Graves.

the Gulf. After rain, the creek and the river below its mouth run thick as black-bean soup; it was the old men from up that way who could brag the loudest later, in front of the feed stores, about the farms they'd worn out. Now the S. C. S. tells them how to terrace, and a lot of them do, but that barn's door gaped wide for a long long time.

2   Rock Creek was a main avenue for Indian depredations into the richer low country. Dozens of people died up its valley, most of them interestingly, if your interests run so. But maybe Mrs. Sherman's story will suffice to give the tone of that warfare. . . .

3   They rode up to the cabin while the Shermans were at dinner on November 27, 1860—dinner in rural Texas then and up into my young years being the noontime meal. There were half a hundred of them, painted, devil-ugly in look and mood. It was the year after the humiliating march up across the Red under good, dead Neighbors; the frontier country was not yet strange to The People, nor were they yet convinced they had lost it. They wanted rent-pay for it in horses, and trophies, and blood, and boasting-fuel for around the prairie campfires in the years to come. Horses they had taken in plenty—300 or so of them by the time they reached the Shermans'—and they had just lanced John Brown to death among his ponies to the east, and the day before had raped and slaughtered and played catch-ball with babies' bodies at the Landmans' and the Gages' to the north.

4   Though the Shermans did not know about any of that, their visitors lacked the aspect that a man would want to see in his luncheon guests—even a sharper frontiersman than Ezra Sherman, who, in that particular time and place, with a wife and four kids for a responsibility, had failed to furnish himself with firearms.

5   The oldest boy, Mrs. Sherman's by an earlier husband who had died, said: "Papa. . ."

6   But by the time Ezra Sherman turned around, they were inside the one-room cabin, a half-dozen of them, filling it with hard tarnished-copper bodies and the flash of flat eyes and a smell of woodsmoke and horse sweat and leather and wild armpits and crotches. Behind them, through the door, were the urgent jostle and gabble and snickering of the rest.

7   "God's Heaven!" Sherman said, gripping the table's edge.

8   Martha Sherman said: "Don't show nothin'. Don't scare."

9   She had come to the frontier young with a brother and his family, but even if she'd only come the year before she'd have known more about it than her husband. There was sense in her, and force. Her youngest started bawling at the Indians; she took his arm and squeezed it hard until he shushed, looking up the while into the broad face, slash-painted diagonally in scarlet and black, of the big one who moved grinning toward the table. He wore two feathers slanting up from where a braid fanned into the hair of his head, and held a short lance.

10   "Hey," he said.

11   "Hey," Ezra Sherman answered.

12   The Indian said something.

13   "No got whisky," Ezra Sherman said. "No got horse. Want 'lasses? *Good* 'lasses."

14   "You're fixin' to have us kilt," his wife said, and stood up. "Git!" she told the big Indian.

15   He grinned still, and gabbled at her. She shook her head and pointed to the door, and behind her heard the youngest begin again to cry. The Indian's gabble changed timbre; it was Spanish now, she knew, but she didn't understand that either.

16   "Git out!" she repeated.

17   "*Hambre*," he said, rubbing his bare belly and pointing to the bacon and greens and cornbread and buttermilk on the table.

18   "No, you ain't," she said, and snatched up a willow broom that was leaned against the wall. But her eye caught motion to the left and she spun, swinging the broom up and down and whack against the ear of the lean, tall, bowlegged one who had hold of her bolt of calico. She swung again and again, driving him back with his hands raised, and then one of the hands was at a knife in his belt, and Two-feather's lance came down like a fence between them. Her broom hit it and bounced up. The three of them stood there. . . .

19   Two-feathers was laughing. The lean Indian wasn't. The calico lay on the floor, trampled; she bent and picked it up, and her nervous fingers plucked away its wrinkles and rolled it again into a bolt.

20   "Martha, you're gonna rile 'em," her husband said.

21   "Be quiet," she told him without looking away from Two-feather's laughing eyes.

22   "Good," the big Indian's mouth said in English from out of the black-and-red smear. With his hand he touched the long chestnut hair at her ear; she tossed her head away from the touch, and he laughed again. "*Mucha mujer*," he said.

23   The lean one jabbered at him spittingly.

24   Martha Sherman's oldest said calmly: "That's red hair."

25   It was. In the cabin's windowless gloom she had not noticed, but now she saw that the lean one's dirty braids glinted auburn, and that his eyes, flicking from her to the authoritative big one, were green like her own. Finally he nodded sulkily to something that Two-feathers said. Two-feathers waved the other warriors back and turned to where Ezra Sherman stood beside the dinner table.

26   "No hurt," he said, and jerked his head toward the door. "Vamoose."

27   "Yes," Ezra Sherman said, and stuck out his hand. "Friend. Good fellow."

28   The big Indian glanced ironically at the hand and touched it with his own. "Vamoose," he repeated.

29   Ezra Sherman said: "You see? He don't mean no trouble. I bet if I dip up some molasses they'll just . . ."

30   "He means go," Martha Sherman said levelly. "You bring Alfie."

31   "Go where?"

32   "*Come on!*" she said, and the force of her utterance bent him down and put his callus-crusted farmer's hands beneath his baby's arms and straightened him and pulled him along behind her as she walked, holding the hands of the middle children, out the door into the stir and murmur of the big war party. It was misting lightly, grayly. . . . The solemn oldest boy came last, and as he left the cabin he was still looking back at the green-eyed, lean, redheaded Comanche.

33   Two-feathers shouted from the door and the gabble died, and staring straight ahead Martha Sherman led her family across the bare wet dirt of the yard and through the gate, past ponies' tossing hackamored heads and the bristle of bows and muskets and lances and the flat dark eyes of fifty Comanches. She took the road toward the creek. In a minute they were in brush, out of

sight of the house, and they heard the voices begin loud again behind them. Martha Sherman began to trot, dragging the children.

34 "Where we goin' to?" Ezra Sherman said.

35 "Pottses'."

36 He said: "I don't see how you could git so ugly about a little old hank of cloth and then leave the whole house with—"

37 "Don't talk, Ezra," she said. "Move. Please, please move."

38 But then there was the thudding rattle of unshod hooves on the road behind them, and a hard-clutching hand in her chestnut hair, and a ring of ponies dancing around them, with brown riders whose bodies gave and flexed with the dancing like joined excrescences of the ponies' spines.

39 Before she managed to twist her head and see him, she knew it was the redheaded one who had her; he gabbled contemptuously at Ezra Sherman, and with the musket in his other hand pointed down the road toward the creek. The pony shied at the motion, yanking her off balance. She did not fight now, knowing it pointless or worse.

40 "Durn you, let her be!" Ezra Sherman yelled, moving, but a sharp lancepoint pricked his chest two inches from the baby's nose and he stopped, looking up.

41 "Go on, Ezra," his wife said. "They'll let you go."

42 "Ain't right," he said. The lancepoint jabbed; he backed away a half-foot.

43 "Go on."

44 He went, trailing stumbling children, and the last she saw of them was the back-turned face of her oldest, but one of the horsemen made a plunging run at him, and he turned and followed the family. . . . The redhead's pony spun and started dancing back up the road. The hand jerked her hair, and she went half down, and a hoof caught her ankle; then she was running to keep from dragging. Snow was drifting horizontally against the chinaberries she had planted around her dooryard, though it was not cold; she saw finally that it was feathers from her bed, which one of them had ripped open and was shaking in the doorway while others laughed. In a shed some of them had found the molasses barrel and had axed its top and were drinking from tin cups and from their hands, throwing the ropy liquid over each other with yells. The old milk cow came loping and bawling grotesquely from

behind the house, a Comanche astride her neck, three arrows
through her flopping bag. . . .

45   Deftly, without loosening his grip, the redhead swung
his leg across his pony's neck and slid to the ground and in one
long strong motion, like laying out a rope or a blanket, threw her
flat. Two of the others took her legs, pulling them apart. She
kicked. The flame-pain of a lance knifed into her ribs and through
her chest and out the back and into the ground and was with-
drawn; she felt each inch of its thrust and retreat, and in a
contraction of shock there relaxed elsewhere, and her legs were
clamped out wide, and the lean redhead had let go of her hair and
stood above her, working at his waistband.

46   Spread-eagled, she twisted her head and saw Two-
feathers a few yards away, her big Bible in his hands, watching.
Her eyes spoke, and maybe her mouth; he shrugged and turned
toward the shed where the molasses barrel stood, past a group that
was trying to light fire against the wet cabin wall. . . .

47   The world was a wild yell, and the redhead was first, and
the third one, grunting, had molasses smeared over his chest and
bed feathers stuck in it, and after that she didn't count; though
trying hard she could not slip over into the blackness that lay just
beyond an uncrossable line. Still conscious, and that part over, she
knew when one on horseback held her arms up and another
worked a steel-pointed arrow manually, slowly, into her body
under her shoulderblade, and left it there. Knew, too, when the
knife made its hot circumcision against the bone of her skull, and
when a horseman meshed his fingers into her long hair again and
she was dragging beside his panicked, snorting pony. But the hair
was good and held, and finally a stocky warrior had to stand with
a foot on each of her shoulders as she lay in the plowed field
before the house, and peel off her scalp by main force.

48   For a time after that they galloped back and forth across
her body, yelling—one thing she recalled with a crystallinity that
the rest of it lost, or never had, was that no hoof touched her—
and shot two or three more arrows into her, and went away. She
lived for four days (another writer says three, and another still says
one, adding the detail that she gave birth to a dead child; take
your pick), tended by neighbor women, and if those days were
anything but a continuing fierce dream for her, no record of it has
come down.

49   In delirium, she kept saying she wouldn't have minded half so much if it hadn't been for that red hair. . . .

50   The oldest boy had quit his stepfather and had circled back through the brush and had watched it all from hiding. No record, either, states how he felt about Comanches afterward, or the act of love, or anything.

51   It seems clear that The People were good haters. So were the whites, though, and that was a year before a war unconnected with Indians was to draw away many of the tough young ones. The Brazos frontier stewed; citizens and Rangers and soldiers joined into a pursuit to follow the party and its big herd of horses (500 or 600 by the time they left the settlements) to the Comanche winter villages in the northwest. Charles Goodnight was along, and Sul Ross, and Captain Jack Cureton, and nearly everybody else, and most of them left accounts of it which flatly conflict. What is sure is that they found Comanches on the Pease, and smote them hip and thigh, man and woman and child, and took back Mrs. Sherman's Bible and a blue-eyed, sullen squaw who turned out to be Cynthia Ann Parker, kidnapped twenty-four years previously on the Navasota. Her Uncle Isaac (Parker County is named for him, and he died there) journeyed up to Camp Cooper to identify her when the expedition returned. She lived for four captive years among relatives, scarcely ever breaking silence except to beg brokenly that they let her go back to her husband and her children and the free, dirty, shifting life of the plains. Since of course they wouldn't, she died in the damp windless forests of East Texas. But Peta Nocona had sired a son on her, Quanah, who was to be one of the great chiefs in the last years of the fighting, and who survived to wear black suits on visits to Fort Worth and to be friends with Theodore Roosevelt.

52   (That story trails on: Theodore Roosevelt gave Quanah land in perpetuity in Oklahoma, pretty land along Cache Creek, and just last year—perpetuity, as is its wont with Indians, having expired—his children and grandchildren and the last of his wives came protestingly into the news again when the Field Artillery had the place condemned and grabbed it.)

53   Maybe the redheaded Comanche had been another one like Cynthia Ann, or maybe like Quanah the half-white son of another woman captured long before. The bag of fragmentary, jumbled, contradictory tales left over from the frontier is lumpy

with mysteries like that, and no one will ever solve them now. The reason Cynthia Ann's story is famous, besides her relation to Quanah, is that it came to the surface again, and had an end, whereas most of the others didn't. Captive children, renegades white and black, Mexicans by the hundreds—The People weren't exclusive in terms of race. They'd been winners for too long to be a pure blood, anyhow; women go to winners. They were a spirit, another on the roster of the world's proud savages who had to win totally or lose totally, like Zulus and Araucanians and Moros and Pathans and Fuzzy-Wuzzies. All colonial and imperial histories are smoky with their fighting. There's more pathos in the defeat of gentle and reasonable peoples, but the fall of pride strikes more sparks.

54   If the river has meaning for you, you can see all of that from the sandstone bluffs where the mountains drop away. You don't have to strain to impose the tales on the landscape; they're there. . . . Margaret Barton at Brannon's Crossing with an arrow next to her heart which they were afraid to pull out, throbbing in the air with her blood beat, all night long . . . Bill Youngblood, whose cohorts gave chase and killed the Indian who had his scalp, and galloped to the graveyard just in time to put it back on his head—their literal, Calvinistic application of the doctrine of corporeal resurrection agreeing with the Comanches that it was bad to go to your earthly resting place in more than one piece, or for that matter less. . . . Dignified Mr. Couts, later the big man at Weatherford, who ranched in the early days opposite Palo Pinto mouth and refused to take guff from the four hairiest white bully-boys in the neighborhood; they waited for him with snotguns between the spring and the church door at Soda Springs one Sunday morning, and knowing them there, he walked on into them with a bucket of cool water in his hand and a Colt's Navy in his waistband. When they opened fire, he got the first one through the heart, the second one through the trigger hand and then the shoulder, and the third in the hip. ("The reason I didn't kill him as he went in at the door," he told Mr. Holland analytically later, "was that he jumped up about two feet getting in and I hit him that much below where I aimed.") The fourth, comprehensibly spooked, piled his horse into a ditch and smashed up his face and shoulder. Mr. Couts counted the bullet holes in his hat and his black silk vest, and the neighborhood was reasonably lawful for

a time after that. . . . In '66 he drove 1,000 longhorns to California, rode back alone across the plains and down the Platte to
the Missouri with $50,000 in gold in his saddlebags, caught a
boat south, and opened a bank.

55   Most of those stories are recorded, though only a few
are recorded well. In what scholars call "primary sources"—pioneers' memoirs and little county histories with a genealogical slant
—they're likely to be a bit prejudiced and fragmentary, with the
choicest details left out either from delicacy or because cowards
and scoundrels have descendants. In the Texas brag-books and
their ilk, a teeming species, they're most often contorted beyond
recognition. Only in the work of a few people who for the past
score or so of years have been trying, literately and otherwise, to
see shape in the too turbulent century behind us, do they come out
straight—or fairly straight, since the old folks those historians
talked to had written nothing down when things were popping,
and only spoke of them later when memory was playing its dirty
tricks.

56   There is consequently a mistiness. . . . Take Andrew
Berry. The People caught him down the river a way from the
Point with a wagonload of pumpkins, and after killing him scalped
him and broke the pumpkins over his bloody skull. But one
version of the story has him killed just below Lazy Bend, and
another far down by Spring Creek, and a third, more dramatic
but just as likely to be true, has two little red-headed sons along
with him who were scalped and crowned with pumpkins, too.

57   The fact is, the stories have been retreating into fog for
a long time, as maybe they should. Boosters in compulsory beards
stage centennials in the little towns and resurrect the old blood-
shed in pamphlets and festivals, and have high times dunking one
another in reconstructed horse troughs. Some towns maintain
annual pageants, and museums. But the significances are trans-
muted there, more often than not, by what Hollywood and television and the *Post* and who-not have said the general West was
like, and by the Texas paranoia (petroleum and carved belts and
bourbon and country clubs and nickeled six-guns and aircraft
factories and the excessive regional glee of the newly arrived:
mingle them with the old leathery thing if you can), so that the
rough-edged realities of the past have faded dimmer each year.

58   Probably a man from that bump of the country who has

soaked the tales in runs a danger of overappraising their worth. In
kind, they don't differ sharply from the lore most regions west of
the Mississippi can muster. In weight—in, say, the number of
people killed or the human glory or shame manifested in their
slaughter—they're dustmote-sized when you compare them to the
violences two wars in two generations have wrought among our
race. I once saw 4,000 Japanese stacked like cordwood, the harvest
of two days' fighting, on one single islet of one single atoll awaiting
bulldozer burial, more dead than the Brazos country could show
for its whole two or three decades of travail, and just as brave.
Almost daily for years, Belsen or Dachau could have matched the
flavor of Mrs. Sherman's agony. . . .

59   What it amounts to is that a short segment of the American frontier, distinctive in its way but not as distinctive as a local
might be tempted to think, paused in the Brazos country, crackled
and smoked for a few years like fire in underbrush while the
Indians were being fought out of existence and the cattle were
being harried north, and then moved on, carrying most of the
vigorous frontiersmen with it.

60   Nothing that happened in this segment, then or later,
made any notable dent in human history. From one very possible
point of view, the stories tell of a partly unnecessary, drawn-out
squabble between savages and half-illiterate louts constituting the
fringes of a culture which, two and a half centuries before, had
spawned Shakespeare, and which even then was reading Dickens
and Trollope and Thoreau and considering the thoughts of Charles
Darwin. They tell too—the stories—of the subsequent squabbles
among the louts themselves: of cattle thievery, corn whisky, Reconstruction, blood feuds, lynchings, splinter sectarianism, and
further illiteracy.

61   Can they then have any bearing on mankind's adventure?

62   Maybe, a little. They don't all tell of louts. There was
something of a showing-through; meanings floated near the surface
which have relevance to the murkier thing Americans have become. It didn't happen just on the Brazos, certainly, but all along
the line of that moving brush fire. There's nothing new in the idea
that the frontier had continuing impact on our character, or that
one slice of that frontier, examined, may to some degree explain
the whole. . . .

63   But in truth such gravities were not what salted the tales

I could read, looking off over the low country from the point atop the bluffs. Mankind is one thing; a man's self is another. What that self is tangles itself knottily with what his people were, and what they came out of. Mine came out of Texas, as did I. If those were louts, they were my own louts.

• COMMENTARY •

This gripping, vivid, brutal narrative is given force and value beyond its own inherent meaning, which is considerable, by its thick context.

Consider first what makes it a strikingly vivid narrative in its own right: we can attribute its forcefulness in large part to the particularity of the rendition and to its pacing. The people and the place are realized not just in their primary actions and obvious features, but in the incidental detail that makes recorded life real. We are told of the "flat eyes" of the Comanche raiders, and we know almost unbearably the overpowering stench of their bodies. The monstrous attack upon Mrs. Sherman is made all the more monstrous and irrational to us when we know that one of the raiders "had molasses smeared over his chest and bed feathers stuck in it." Forcing the brutality in upon us is our constant knowledge of the sane background, a setting warped and frenzied by the events told here: "Snow was drifting horizontally against the chinaberries she had planted around her dooryard, though it was not cold; she saw finally that it was feathers from her bed, which one of them had ripped open and was shaking in the doorway while others laughed." The scalping itself culminates in what may be after all the most inhuman act of all: "But the hair was good and held, and finally a stocky warrior had to stand with a foot on each of her shoulders as she lay in the plowed field before the house, and peel off her scalp by main force." No wailing or gnashing of teeth could have given more truthfully the nightmarish quality of the scene than this objectively presented last brutal detail.

The pacing also contributes to the effectiveness of the narrative. From the beginning the very rush of events impels us forward, and the narrative slows only when it must slow, when it comes to the time of the attack itself, which no man can tell. The weapon wounds, to be sure, can be described and their inflicting related, but the attack itself is foreshortened in one devastating clause, "The world was a wild yell." Similarly the delirium of Mrs. Sherman's final days is packed into

a last brief passage: ". . . if those days were anything but a continuing fierce dream for her, no record of it has come down."

The viewpoint controlling the narrative gives the story its ultimate
value. The author uses (with some elaboration) multiple eyewitness
viewpoints, and he tells us himself how he could do so. There remains
to us, he says, a tradition of such stories: "The bag of fragmentary,
jumbled, contradictory tales left over from the frontier is lumpy with
mysteries. . . ." The stories "have been retreating into fog for a long
time." But to offset that we know that he has the records, however fragmentary, of Mrs. Sherman's own words, and of what her surviving family
saw and heard. But the unique and at last beautiful quality of even such
a hellish story is found in that mood, that wish that also controls the
point of view. The telling of such a tale is in addition to the worth found
in the telling, a way of keeping the fog away, of saving the time of man
from being only history, of making the time of a people present. Graves
concludes his tale, after some account of other depredations, with "If
the river has meaning for you, you can see all of that from the sandstone bluffs where the mountains drop away. You don't have to strain to
impose the tales on the landscape; they're there. . . ." That they are
there is important, for what the self is "tangles knottily with what his
people were, and what they came out of."

THE CHASE [1849]

Francis Parkman

1   The country before us was now thronged with buffalo, and
a sketch of the manner of hunting them will not be out of place.
There are two methods commonly practised, "running" and "approaching." The chase on horseback, which goes by the name of
"running," is the more violent and dashing mode of the two, that
is to say, when the buffalo are in one of their wild moods; for
otherwise it is tame enough. A practised and skilful hunter, well
mounted, will sometimes kill five or six cows in a single chase,
loading his gun again and again as his horse rushes through the
tumult. In attacking a small band of buffalo, or in separating a
single animal from the herd and assailing it apart from the rest,
these is less excitement and less danger. In fact, the animals are
at times so stupid and lethargic that there is little sport in killing

them. With a bold and well-trained horse the hunter may ride so close to the buffalo that as they gallop side by side he may touch him with his hand; nor is there much danger in this as long as the buffalo's strength and breath continue unabated; but when he becomes tired and can no longer run with ease, when his tongue lolls out and the foam flies from his jaws, then the hunter had better keep a more respectful distance; the distressed brute may turn upon him at any instant; and especially at the moment when he fires his gun. The horse then leaps aside, and the hunter has need of a tenacious seat in the saddle, for if he is thrown to the ground there is no hope for him. When he sees his attack defeated, the buffalo resumes his flight, but if the shot is well directed he soon stops; for a few moments he stands still, then totters and falls heavily upon the prairie.

2   The chief difficulty in running buffalo, as it seems to me, is that of loading the gun or pistol at full gallop. Many hunters for convenience's sake carry three or four bullets in the mouth; the powder is poured down the muzzle of the piece, the bullet dropped in after it, the stock struck hard upon the pommel of the saddle, and the work is done. The danger is obvious. Should the blow on the pommel fail to send the bullet home, or should the bullet, in the act of aiming, start from its place and roll towards the muzzle, the gun would probably burst in discharging. Many a shattered hand and worse casualties besides have been the result of such an accident. To obviate it, some hunters make use of a ramrod, usually hung by a string from the neck, but this materially increases the difficulty of loading. The bows and arrows which the Indians use in running buffalo have many advantages over firearms, and even white men occasionally employ them.

3   The danger of the chase arises not so much from the onset of the wounded animal as from the nature of the ground which the hunter must ride over. The prairie does not always present a smooth, level, and uniform surface; very often it is broken with hills and hollows, intersected by ravines, and in the remoter parts studded by the stiff wild-sage bushes. The most formidable obstructions, however, are the burrows of wild animals, wolves, badgers, and particularly prairie-dogs, with whose holes the ground for a very great extent is frequently honey-combed. In the blindness of the chase the hunter rushes over it unconscious of danger; his horse, at full career, thrusts his leg deep into one of

the burrows; the bone snaps, the rider is hurled forward to the
ground and probably killed. Yet accidents in buffalo running
happen less frequently than one would suppose; in the recklessness
of the chase, the hunter enjoys all the impunity of a drunken man,
and may ride in safety over gullies and declivities, where, should
he attempt to pass in his sober senses, he would infallibly break
his neck.

4   The method of "approaching," being practised on foot,
has many advantages over that of "running"; in the former, one
neither breaks down his horse nor endangers his own life; he must
be cool, collected, and watchful; must understand the buffalo,
observe the features of the country and the course of the wind,
and be well skilled in using the rifle. The buffalo are strange
animals; sometimes they are so stupid and infatuated that a man
may walk up to them in full sight on the open prairie, and even
shoot several of their number before the rest will think it necessary
to retreat. At another moment they will be so shy and wary that in
order to approach them the utmost skill, experience, and judgment
are necessary. Kit Carson, I believe, stands pre-eminent in running
buffalo; in approaching, no man living can bear away the palm
from Henry Chatillon.

5   After Tête Rouge had alarmed the camp, no further disturbance occurred during the night. The Arapahoes did not attempt mischief, or if they did the wakefulness of the party deterred
them from effecting their purpose. The next day was one of
activity and excitement, for about ten o'clock the man in advance
shouted the gladdening cry of *buffalo, buffalo!* and in the hollow
of the prairie just below us, a band of bulls was grazing. The
temptation was irresistible, and Shaw and I rode down upon
them. We were badly mounted on our travelling horses, but by
hard lashing we overtook them, and Shaw, running alongside a
bull, shot into him both balls of his double-barrelled gun. Looking
round as I galloped by, I saw the bull in his mortal fury rushing
again and again upon his antagonist, whose horse constantly
leaped aside, and avoided the onset. My chase was more protracted, but at length I ran close to the bull and killed him with
my pistols. Cutting off the tails of our victims by way of trophy,
we rejoined the party in about a quarter of an hour after we had
left it. Again and again that morning rang out the same welcome
cry of *buffalo, buffalo!* Every few moments, in the broad meadows

along the river, we saw bands of bulls, who, raising their shaggy heads, would gaze in stupid amazement at the approaching horsemen, and then breaking into a clumsy gallop, file off in a long line across the trail in front, towards the rising prairie on the left. At noon, the plain before us was alive with thousands of buffalo,— bulls, cows, and calves,—all moving rapidly as we drew near; and far off beyond the river the swelling prairie was darkened with them to the very horizon. The party was in gayer spirits than ever. We stopped for a nooning near a grove of trees by the river.

6   "Tongues and hump-ribs tomorrow," said Shaw, looking with contempt at the venison steaks which Deslauriers placed before us. Our meal finished, we lay down to sleep. A shout from Henry Chatillon aroused us, and we saw him standing on the cartwheel, stretching his tall figure to its full height, while he looked towards the prairie beyond the river. Following the direction of his eyes, we could clearly distinguish a large, dark object, like the black shadow of a cloud, passing rapidly over swell after swell of the distant plain; behind it followed another of similar appearance, though smaller, moving more rapidly, and drawing closer and closer to the first. It was the hunters of the Arapahoe camp chasing a band of buffalo. Shaw and I caught and saddled our best horses, and went plunging through sand and water to the farther bank. We were too late. The hunters had already mingled with the herd, and the work of slaughter was nearly over. When we reached the ground we found it strewn far and near with numberless carcasses, while the remnants of the herd, scattered in all directions, were flying away in terror, and the Indians still rushing in pursuit. Many of the hunters, however, remained upon the spot, and among the rest was our yesterday's acquaintance, the chief of the village. He had alighted by the side of a cow, into which he had shot five or six arrows, and his squaw, who had followed him on horseback to the hunt, was giving him a draught of water from a canteen, purchased or plundered from some volunteer soldier. Recrossing the river, we overtook the party, who were already on their way.

7   We had gone scarcely a mile when we saw an imposing spectacle. From the river-bank on the right, away over the swelling prairie on the left, and in front as far as the eye could reach, was one vast host of buffalo. The outskirts of the herd were within a quarter of a mile. In many parts they were crowded so densely

together that in the distance their rounded backs presented a
surface of uniform blackness; but elsewhere they were more
scattered, and from amid the multitude rose little columns of dust
where some of them were rolling on the ground. Here and there
a battle was going forward among the bulls. We could distinctly
see them rushing against each other, and hear the clattering of
their horns and their hoarse bellowing. Shaw was riding at some
distance in advance, with Henry Chatillon; I saw him stop and
draw the leather covering from his gun. With such a sight before
us, but one thing could be thought of. That morning I had used
pistols in the chase. I had now a mind to try the virtue of a gun.
Deslauriers had one, and I rode up to the side of the cart; there he
sat under the white covering, biting his pipe between his teeth and
grinning with excitement.

8   "Lend me your gun, Deslauriers."

9   "*Oui, Monsieur, oui,*" said Deslauriers, tugging with might
and main to stop the mule, which seemed obstinately bent on
going forward. Then everything but his mocassins disappeared as
he crawled into the cart and pulled at the gun to extricate it.

10   "Is it loaded?" I asked.

11   "*Oui, bien chargé;* you'll kill, *mon bourgeois;* yes, you'll
kill—*c'est un bon fusil.*"

12   I handed him my rifle and rode forward to Shaw.

13   "Are you ready?" he asked.

14   "Come on," said I.

15   "Keep down that hollow," said Henry, "and then they
won't see you till you get close to them."

16   The hollow was a kind of wide ravine; it ran obliquely
towards the buffalo, and we rode at a canter along the bottom
until it became too shallow; then we bent close to our horses' necks,
and, at last, finding that it could no longer conceal us, came out of
it and rode directly towards the herd. It was within gunshot; before
its outskirts, numerous grizzly old bulls were scattered, holding
guard over their females. They glared at us in anger and astonishment, walked towards us a few yards, and then turning slowly
round, retreated at a trot which afterwards broke into a clumsy
gallop. In an instant the main body caught the alarm. The buffalo
began to crowd away from the point towards which we were approaching, and a gap was opened in the side of the herd. We
entered it, still restraining our excited horses. Every instant the

tumult was thickening. The buffalo, pressing together in large bodies, crowded away from us on every hand. In front and on either side we could see dark columns and masses, half hidden by clouds of dust, rushing along in terror and confusion, and hear the tramp and clattering of ten thousand hoofs. That countless multitude of powerful brutes, ignorant of their own strength, were flying in a panic from the approach of two feeble horsemen. To remain quiet longer was impossible.

17   "Take that band on the left," said Shaw, "I'll take these in front."

18   He sprang off, and I saw no more of him. A heavy Indian whip was fastened by a band to my wrist; I swung it into the air and lashed my horse's flank with all the strength of my arm. Away she darted, stretching close to the ground. I could see nothing but a cloud of dust before me, but I knew that it concealed a band of many hundreds of buffalo. In a moment I was in the midst of the cloud, half suffocated by the dust and stunned by the trampling of the flying herd; but I was drunk with the chase and cared for nothing but the buffalo. Very soon a long dark mass became visible, looming through the dust; then I could distinguish each bulky carcass, the hoofs flying out beneath, the short tails held rigidly erect. In a moment I was so close that I could have touched them with my gun. Suddenly, to my amazement, the hoofs were jerked upwards, the tails flourished in the air, and amid a cloud of dust the buffalo seemed to sink into the earth before me. One vivid impression of that instant remains upon my mind. I remember looking down upon the backs of several buffalo dimly visible through the dust. We had run unawares upon a ravine. At that moment I was not the most accurate judge of depth and width, but when I passed it on my return, I found it about twelve feet deep and not quite twice as wide at the bottom. It was impossible to stop; I would have done so gladly if I could; so, half sliding, half plunging, down went the little mare. She came down on her knees in the loose sand at the bottom; I was pitched forward against her neck and nearly thrown over her head among the buffalo, who amid dust and confusion came tumbling in all around. The mare was on her feet in an instant and scrambling like a cat up the opposite side. I thought for a moment that she would have fallen back and crushed me, but with a violent effort she clambered out and gained the hard prairie above. Glancing back, I saw

the huge head of a bull clinging as it were by the forefeet at the edge of the dusty gulf. At length I was fairly among the buffalo. They were less densely crowded than before, and I could see nothing but bulls, who always run at the rear of a herd to protect their females. As I passed among them they would lower their heads, and turning as they ran, try to gore my horse; but as they were already at full speed there was no force in their onset, and as Pauline ran faster than they, they were always thrown behind her in the effort. I soon began to distinguish cows amid the throng. One just in front of me seemed to my liking, and I pushed close to her side. Dropping the reins, I fired, holding the muzzle of the gun within a foot of her shoulder. Quick as lightning she sprang at Pauline; the little mare dodged the attack, and I lost sight of the wounded animal amid the tumult. Immediately after, I selected another, and urging forward Pauline, shot into her both pistols in succession. For a while I kept her in view, but in attempting to load my gun, lost sight of her also in the confusion. Believing her to be mortally wounded and unable to keep up with the herd, I checked my horse. The crowd rushed onwards. The dust and tumult passed away, and on the prairie, far behind the rest, I saw a solitary buffalo galloping heavily. In a moment I and my victim were running side by side. My firearms were all empty, and I had in my pouch nothing but rifle bullets, too large for the pistols and too small for the gun. I loaded the gun, however, but as often as I levelled it to fire, the bullets would roll out of the muzzle and the gun returned only a report like a squib, as the powder harmlessly exploded. I rode in front of the buffalo and tried to turn her back; but her eyes glared, her mane bristled, and lowering her head, she rushed at me with the utmost fierceness and activity. Again and again I rode before her, and again and again she repeated her furious charge. But little Pauline was in her element. She dodged her enemy at every rush, until at length the buffalo stood still, exhausted with her own efforts, her tongue lolling from her jaws.

19   Riding to a little distance, I dismounted, thinking to father a handful of dry grass to serve the purpose of wadding, and load the gun at my leisure. No sooner were my feet on the ground than the buffalo came bounding in such a rage towards me that I jumped back again into the saddle and with all possible despatch. After waiting a few minutes more, I made an attempt

to ride up and stab her with my knife; but Pauline was near being gored in the attempt. At length, bethinking me of the fringes at the seams of my buckskin trousers, I jerked off a few of them, and, reloading the gun, forced them down the barrel to keep the bullet in its place; then approaching, I shot the wounded buffalo through the heart. Sinking to her knees, she rolled over lifeless on the prairie. To my astonishment, I found that, instead of a cow, I had been slaughtering a stout yearling bull. No longer wondering at his fierceness, I opened his throat, and cutting out his tongue, tied it at the back of my saddle. My mistake was one which a more experienced eye than mine might easily make in the dust and confusion of such a chase.

20   Then for the first time I had leisure to look at the scene around me. The prairie in front was darkened with the retreating multitude, and on either hand the buffalo came filing up in endless columns from the low plains upon the river. The Arkansas was three or four miles distant. I turned and moved slowly towards it. A long time passed before, far in the distance, I distinguished the white covering of the cart and the little black specks of horse-men before and behind it. Drawing near, I recognized Shaw's elegant tunic, the red flannel shirt, conspicuous far off. I overtook the party, and asked him what success he had had. He had assailed a fat cow, shot her with two bullets, and mortally wounded her. But neither of us was prepared for the chase that afternoon, and Shaw, like myself, had no spare bullets in his pouch; so he aban-doned the disabled animal to Henry Chatillon, who followed, despatched her with his rifle, and loaded his horse with the meat.

21   We encamped close to the river. The night was dark, and as we lay down we could hear, mingled with the howling of wolves, the hoarse bellowing of the buffalo, like the ocean beating upon a distant coast.

• SUGGESTIONS •

What is the purpose of the expository account that takes up the first four paragraphs? Does it diminish the effect of the narrative? The first-person point of view lends authenticity to this account. Explain the limitations of this viewpoint and show how they are used in the course of the narrative.

A Writing Program

1. After the manner of Pepys, write an account of a single day in your life, preferably one in which an event of some importance took place. If you truly adopt his manner, you will not be able to do this in 250 words.

2. Compose an "artistic" autobiographical essay, that is, one unlike Pepys' work, which has no developing conflict and is not intended to arrive at a given point. Compose your essay, using perhaps some pivotal point in your life, so as to show a conflict developing and so as to show, if possible, the resolution of that conflict.

3. Using primary source material for your information, write a short narrative of some crucial time in the life of a historical figure. The selections by Foxe and Froude should be helpful as models.

4. Compose a narrative essay using some story or group of stories handed down in your family. The Graves' selection may be useful as a model.

Recommended Readings

Some traditional labels have been used throughout this book to designate four basic kinds of discourse—exposition, argumentation, description, and narration. These terms help us to understand differences in point of view, method, and purpose found in different kinds of writing, and while they are traditional and conventional terms, they remain useful and valid. Most specialized, practical writing tasks that an educated person may wish or need to do stem from commercial, academic, social, or other necessities requiring explanation, persuasion, description, or narration.

You may wish to consult further readings in order to observe methods used in some practical types of EXPOSITORY writing. For public letters, consult any of several textbooks on business and technical writing; you should also consult newspaper and magazine "Letters to Editors" columns and various collections of public letters such as those of our presidents. For encomia and other public speeches, consult anthologies of great speeches by various authors and collected speeches by such orators as Winston Churchill, Daniel Webster, and Adlai Stevenson. To learn more about technical writing, you should consult—and habitually read—such magazines as *Scientific American* and *National Geographic*. Most technical and scientific professions, furthermore, have specialized journals; you should soon acquaint yourself with those in your field. For critical writing, including book reports, book reviews, and critical essays, you should frequently read newspaper and magazine book review sections, journals such as *College English,* *American Literature,* and *American Scholar,* and the journals in your own field. For expository research and historical writing, magazines such as *America West* and *National Geographic* will be useful, as well as the journals in your own field.

Many types of writing in daily use are fundamentally DESCRIPTIVE. For help with laboratory reports and other descriptive technical writing, observe methods used in *Scientific American.* Many companies involved in technical and scientific work publish their own style sheets with recommended procedures.

ARGUMENT is common in daily amateur and professional writing. Public letters of refutation and confirmation are common in "Letters to Editors" sections of newspapers and magazines. Much research writing is argumentative; consult *College English, American Scholar,* and other journals listed above, and the journals in your own field. Your minister's sermons are presumably persuasive; you should observe his methods. In addition, you should make it a habit to examine popular magazines such as *Time* and *Newsweek* to see how they use resources for either expository or argumentative purposes.

Many types of NARRATION are also used regularly. Frequent reading of biography and autobiography will be useful to you. Especially useful here are essays and technical papers in journals given to the study of sociology, psychology, and history.

Finally, for various examples of explanation, description, argumentation, and narration, and for your own education, you should read regularly such magazines as *Harper's Magazine, The Atlantic Monthly, The New Republic, Saturday Review, The New Yorker, Holiday,* and *Horizon, A Magazine of the Arts,* and such newspapers as the *Christian Science Monitor* and the *Manchester Guardian.*

Index

About the Author

JIM W. CORDER is Associate Professor of English at Texas Christian University. He received his B.A. and M.A. (both in 1954) from Texas Christian University and his Ph.D. (1958) from the University of Oklahoma. He is co-author, with Lyle H. Kendall, Jr., of *A College Rhetoric* (1962) and has frequently contributed to scholarly journals.

A NOTE ON THE TYPE

The text of this book is set in Caledonia, a typeface designed by W(illiam) A(ddison) Dwiggins for the Mergenthaler Linotype Company in 1939. Dwiggins chose to call his new typeface Caledonia, the Roman name for Scotland, because it was inspired by the Scotch types cast about 1833 by Alexander Wilson & Son, Glasgow type founders. However, there is a calligraphic quality about this face that is totally lacking in the Wilson types. Dwiggins referred to an even earlier typeface for this "liveliness of action"—one cut around 1790 by William Martin for the printer William Bulmer. Caledonia has more weight than the Martin letters, and the bottom finishing strokes (serifs) of the letters are cut straight across, without brackets, to make sharp angles with the upright stems, thus giving a "modern face" appearance.

W. A. Dwiggins (1880–1956) was born in Martinsville, Ohio, and studied art in Chicago. In 1904 he moved to Hingham, Massachusetts, where he built a solid reputation as a designer of advertisements and as a calligrapher. He began an association with the Mergenthaler Linotype Company in 1929, and over the next twenty-seven years designed a number of book types for that firm. Of especial interest are the Metro series, Electra, Caledonia, Eldorado, and Falcon. In 1930, Dwiggins first became interested in marionettes, and through the years made many important contributions to the art of puppetry and the design of marionettes.